MAR CARIBE

OCÉANO ATLÁNTICO

Barranquilla
Maracaibo
Caracas
PANAMÁ
GUYANA
VENEZUELA
Georgetown
Medellín
Paramaribo
Panamá
Río Orinoco
Cayena
Bogotá
SURINAME
GUYANA FRANCESA
Cali
COLOMBIA
Quito
Ecuador
ECUADOR
Río Amazonas
Belém
Guayaquil
Manaus
PERÚ
BRASIL
Recife
Cuzco
Lima
La Paz
Brasília
Arequipa
BOLIVIA
Sucre
PARAGUAY
Antofagasta
Río de Janeiro
CHILE
Trópico de Capricornio
San Miguel
Asunción
OCÉANO
de Tucumán
São Paulo
PACÍFICO
La Serena
OCÉANO
ATLÁNTICO
Córdoba
Rosario
Valparaíso
URUGUAY
Santiago
ARGENTINA
Montevideo
Concepción
Buenos Aires
Río de la Plata
Bahía Blanca
Puerto Montt
Bariloche
Chiloé

N

Islas Malvinas
Estrecho de Magallanes
Punta Arenas
Tierra del Fuego
Cabo de Hornos

AMÉRICA DEL SUR

0	1500 kilómetros

0	1000 millas

CORDILLERA DE LOS ANDES

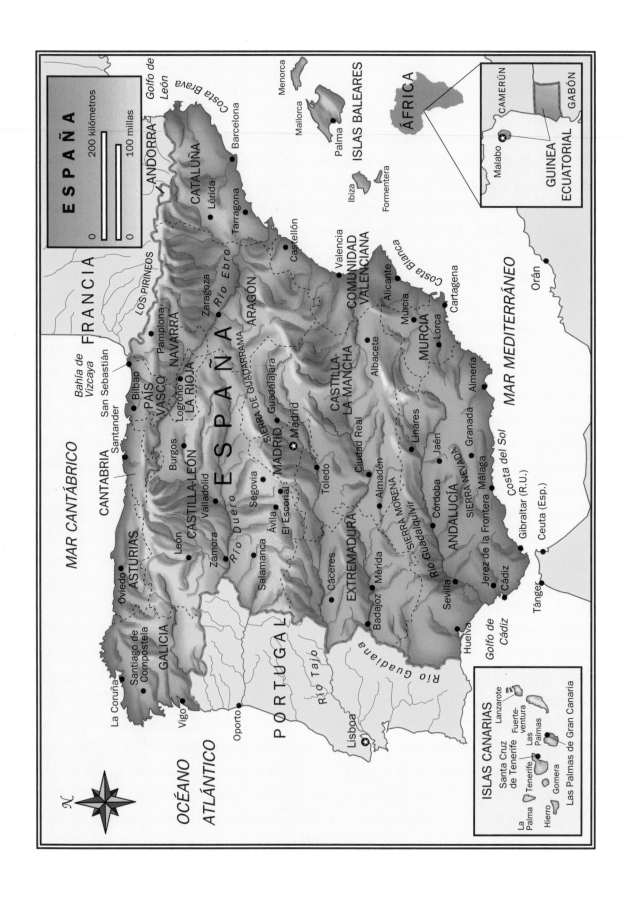

IMPORTANT

HERE IS YOUR REGISTRATION CODE TO ACCESS MCGRAW-HILL PREMIUM CONTENT AND MCGRAW-HILL ONLINE RESOURCES

For key premium online resources you need THIS CODE to gain access. Once the code is entered, you will be able to use the web resources for the length of your course.

Access is provided only if you have purchased a new book.

If the registration code is missing from this book, the registration screen on our website, and within your WebCT or Blackboard course will tell you how to obtain your new code. Your registration code can be used only once to establish access. It is not transferable.

To gain access to these online resources

1. **USE** your web browser to go to: **http://www.mhhe.com/quetal7**

2. **CLICK** on "First Time User"

3. **ENTER** the Registration Code printed on the tear-off bookmark on the right

4. After you have entered your registration code, click on "Register"

5. **FOLLOW** the instructions to setup your personal UserID and Password

6. **WRITE** your UserID and Password down for future reference. Keep it in a safe place.

If your course is using WebCT or Blackboard, you'll be able to use this code to access the McGraw-Hill content within your instructor's online course.

To gain access to the McGraw-Hill content in your instructor's WebCT or Blackboard course simply log into the course with the user ID and Password provided by your instructor. Enter the registration code exactly as it appears to the right when prompted by the system. You will only need to use this code the first time you click on McGraw-Hill content.

These instructions are specifically for student access. Instructors are not required to register via the above instructions.

Thank you, and welcome to your McGraw-Hill Online Resources.

10 Digit 0-07-320806-X
t/a Dorwick, Que Tal? Se, 7/e

W9TX–NVPA–8DHM–88CH–PYHB

REGISTRATION CODE

¿Qué tal?

An Introductory Course

Valerie Y. Job,
*South Plains College,
Levelland*
Hilda M. Kachmar,
*Southern Methodist
University*
Paula A. Kellar,
*Pennsylvania State
University, Altoona*
Marilyn Kiss,
Wagner College
Sara Smith Laird,
*Texas Lutheran
University*
Paul Larson,
Baylor University
Leticia P. López,
San Diego Mesa College
María López Morgan,
*Okaloosa-Walton
Community College*
Monica Malamud,
Cañada College
Jude Thomas Manzo,
San Antonio College
Patricia A. Marshall,
Wesleyan University

Lisa M. McCallum,
Auburn University
Bette J. McLaud,
*Onondaga Community
College*
María-Teresa Moinette,
*University of Central
Oklahoma*
Kathryn A. Mussett,
*Pennsylvania State
University, Altoona*
Eunice D. Myers,
Wichita State University
Duane C. Nelson,
*Cloud County
Community College*
Michelle Renee Orecchio,
University of Michigan
Jorge Pérez,
*University of California,
Santa Barbara*
Oralia Preble-Niemi,
*University of Tennessee,
Chattanooga*
Jessica J. Ramírez,
*Grand Valley State
University*

Tracy Rasmussen,
*Lake Tahoe Community
College*
Kathleen Regan,
University of Portland
Duane Rhoades,
University of Wyoming
Zaira Rivera Casellas,
*University of the
Sacred Heart, San
Juan*
Claudia Sahagún,
*Broward Community
College*
Maritza Salgueiro-
Carlisle,
Bakersfield College
Jaime Sánchez,
*Volunteer State
Community College*
Carmen Schlig,
*Georgia State
University*
Charles C. Schroeder,
*North Iowa Area
Community College–
Mason City*

Georgia Seminet,
*Texas A&M University,
Commerce*
Philippe P. Seminet,
*Texas A&M University,
Commerce*
Mary-Lee Sullivan,
Binghamton University
Fausto Vergara,
*Houston Community
College*
Deborah Walker,
*Muscatine Community
College*
Alex Whitman,
Lower Columbia College
Gloria Williams,
Lincoln University
Joy S. Woolf,
Westminster College
Jiyoung Yoon,
University of North Texas
Francisco Zabaleta,
San Diego State University
Patricia Zuker,
*University of California,
San Diego*

Many other individuals deserve our thanks and appreciation for their help and support. Among them are the people who, in addition to the authors, read the seventh edition at various stages of development to ensure its linguistic and cultural authenticity and pedagogical accuracy: Alice A. Arana (United States), Oswaldo Arana (Peru), Laura Chastain (El Salvador), and María Sabló-Yates (Panama).

Special thanks are also due to Margaret Metz who arranged and conducted the instructor focus groups and coordinated the contributions of our Special Consultants. Margaret's participation made it possible for us to incorporate such a vast amount of feedback from instructors, and we are very grateful for her help.

Within the McGraw-Hill family, we would like to acknowledge the contributions of the following individuals: Linda Toy and the McGraw-Hill production group, especially Violeta Díaz for her inspired work on the design of the seventh edition, Mel Valentín for his invaluable assistance as Production Editor, and Randy Hurst and Louis Swaim for their work on various aspects of production. We would also like to thank Amanda Peabody for her helpful editorial assistance. Special thanks are due to Eirik Børve, who originally brought some of us together, and to Nick Agnew and the McGraw-Hill marketing and sales staff for their constant support and efforts. We especially thank Christa Harris, our Sponsoring Editor, who helped us keep our sights and efforts focused on the main goals of this edition. We are especially appreciative of the work of Pennie Nichols, who adroitly wove together the feedback and contributions from many sources into a coherent whole.

The only reasons for publishing a new textbook or to revise an existing one are to help the profession evolve in meaningful ways and to make the task of daily classroom instruction easier and more enjoyable for experienced instructors and teaching assistants alike. Language teaching has changed in important ways since the publication of the first edition of *¿Qué tal?*. We are delighted to have been—and to continue to be—agents of that evolution. And we are grateful to McGraw-Hill for its continuing support of our ideas.

Special Consultants

We are especially indebted to the many instructors who completed intense "how does this work in the classroom?" reviews of the text. Their comments and the comments of their students were truly the informing voice of this edition, helping us fine-tune every aspect of the text to ensure that everything "works." These consultants also provided the **Bright Idea** annotations for the *Instructor's Edition*.

Yvette Aparicio,
Grinnell College
Ellen Brennan,
*Indiana University–
Purdue University
Indianapolis*
Obdulia Castro,
*University of Colorado,
Boulder*
Arleen Chiclana,
University of North Florida
Stephen Clark,
*Northern Arizona
University*
Elisabeth Combier,
*North Georgia College
and State University*

Kathy Dwyer Navajas,
*University of Florida at
Gainesville*
Delia Escalante,
Phoenix College
Celia Esplugas,
*West Chester University
of Pennsylvania*
Charles Grove,
*West Chester University
of Pennsylvania*
Marilen Loyola,
*University of Wisconsin,
Madison*
April Marshall,
New York University

Delia Montesinos,
University of Texas, Austin
Sherrie Nunn,
*University of Florida at
Gainesville*
Lynne Overesch-Maister,
*Johnson County
Community College*
Tina Peña,
Tulsa Community College
Marcia Picallo,
County College of Morris
Stacy Powell,
Auburn University
Silvia Ramírez,
University of Texas, Austin

Jeffrey T. Reeder,
Sonoma State University
Jaime Sánchez,
*Volunteer State
University*
Emily Scida,
*University of Virginia,
Charlottesville*
Louis Silvers,
*Monroe Community
College*
Bretton White,
*University of Wisconsin,
Madison*
María José Zubieta,
New York University

Reviewers

We are grateful to the following reviewers, whose insight and suggestions have helped shape the seventh edition.

Esther Aguilar,
*San Diego State
University*
Serge Ainsa,
*Yavapai College,
Prescott*
Enrica J. Ardemagni,
*Indiana University–
Purdue University
Indianapolis*
Bobbie L. Arndt,
*Pennsylvania State
University, Altoona*
Haydee Ayala-Richards,
*Shippensburg University
of Pennysylvania*
Angela Bagués,
*Shippensburg University
of Pennsylvania*
Nancy J. Barclay,
*Lake Tahoe Community
College*

Brenda Calderon,
*Oral Roberts
University*
Stephen Clark,
*Northern Arizona
University*
Daria Cohen,
Princeton University
Linda H. Colville,
Citrus College
Brian Cope,
*University of California,
Irvine*
Roselyn Costantino,
*Pennsylvania State
University, Altoona*
Kit Decker,
*Piedmont Virginia
Community College*
Danion L. Doman,
*Truman State
University*

Hector F. Espitia,
*Grand Valley State
University*
Rafael Falcón,
Goshen College
Alla N. Fil,
New York University
Laura A. Fox,
*Grand Valley State
University*
Khédija Gadhoum,
*Grand Valley State
University*
Martha Goldberg,
*California Polytechnic
State University*
Andrew Steven
Gordon,
Mesa State College
Antonio Gragera,
*Southwest Texas State
University*

Betty Gudz,
Sierra College
Ellen Haynes,
*University of Colorado,
Boulder*
Candy Henry,
*Westmoreland
Community College,
Youngwood*
Carmen M. Hernández,
Grossmont College
Todd Anthony
Hernández,
University of Kansas
María Cecilia Herrera,
*University of Wisconsin,
Oshkosh*
Ann M. Hilberry,
University of Michigan
Danielle Holden,
*Oakton Community
College*

- Dr. Manuel Cortés-Castañeda (Eastern Kentucky University), whose engaging and creative **A conversar** activities provide wonderful chapter-culminating communicative tasks and projects.

- Dr. Gail Fenderson (Brock University), whose work on the revised **En los Estados Unidos y el Canadá** sections has expanded our knowledge of the Hispanic community in Canada.

- Dr. Lynne Lemley (University of Texas, Austin), who created the engaging new cultural cloze passages that appear in the **Un poco de todo** sections.

- Dr. Jane Johnson (University of Texas, Austin), who created the activities that accompany the new **Entrevista cultural** video segments.

- Becky S. Jaimes and Talía Loaiza (both of Austin Community College), whose **Notas culturales** offer students a series of outstanding cultural readings on a wide range of high-interest topics.

- Dr. A. Raymond Elliott (University of Texas, Arlington) whose contributions to the Instructor's Edition and Instructor's Manual and Resource Kit have served to make those supplements even more invaluable teaching resources.

- Laura Chastain (El Salvador), whose invaluable contributions to the text range from language usage to suggestions for realia.

- Ruth Ordás and Dr. Theodore V. Higgs, whose contributions to previous editions are still evident in the seventh edition.

In addition, the publishers wish to acknowledge the suggestions received from the following instructors and professional friends across the country. The appearance of their names in this list does not necessarily constitute their endorsement of the text or its methodology.

Instructor Focus Group Participants

We thank our instructor focus group participants, who graciously gave us their detailed feedback and suggestions. Their honesty and constructive criticism have greatly enhanced the seventh edition.

Juan Bernal,
San Diego City College
Ezequiel Cárdenas,
Cuyamaca College
Margaret Eomurian,
Houston Community College
Raquel N. González,
University of Michigan, Ann Arbor
María Grana,
Houston Community College
Yolanda Guerrero,
Grossmont College

Carmen M. Hernández,
Grossmont College
Judy Hittle,
Indiana University Northwest
Casilde Isabelli,
University of Nevada, Reno
Joseph P. Kelliher,
Cuyamaca College
Ruth Fátima Konopka,
Grossmont College
José Manuel Lacorte,
University of Maryland

Eva Mendieta,
Indiana University Northwest
Judith Minarick,
Grossmont College
Lizette Moon,
Houston Community College
Nora Olmos,
Houston Community College
Nancy Pinnick,
Indiana University Northwest

Janet Sandarg,
Augusta State University
Jacquelyn Sandone,
University of Missouri–Columbia
Edda Temoche-Weldele,
Grossmont College
Omaida Westlake,
Grossmont College
Carlos H. Villacis,
Houston Community College

and grammar practice activities, vocabulary games, review activities, interactive grammar tutorials, video-based activities, speaking activities that simulate conversations with native speakers, cultural activities, reading and writing activities, a "talking" dictionary, and much more. This highly popular interactive supplement has been revised and upgraded for the seventh edition and includes new activities and features not available on earlier versions.

- The *Video on CD* provides students with access to the entire *¿Qué tal? Video Program*. Available for purchase, this set of two CD-ROMs includes every video segment from the *Video Program*, as well as follow-up activities for every segment. Instructors who find they do not have the time to show the *Video Program* in class will be pleased to know that it is available to students in this format, providing students with a wealth of authentic and natural linguistic and cultural input.

The *Instructor's Manual and Resource Kit* offers an extensive introduction to teaching techniques, general guidelines for instructors, suggestions for lesson planning in semester and quarter schedules, and additional pre- and post-viewing activities for the video. Also included are a wide variety of interactive and communicative games for practicing vocabulary and grammar. We are very grateful to Linda H. Colville of Citrus College for creating these games.

The *Testing Program* reflects the revisions in the student text for the seventh edition. It also includes sections for testing reading and listening comprehension, as well as tests for oral proficiency and sections designed to test cultural material presented in the program.

- A new *Video Program* accompanies the seventh edition of *¿Qué tal?*. It includes two new video segments for every chapter: The **Entrevista cultural** segment and the **Entre amigos** segment. In addition, the highly popular **Minidramas** vignettes, the **En contexto** functional segments, and the **Conozca...** cultural footage have been retained from the previous edition, resulting in a *Video Program* of approximately five hours in length. This rich resource offers instructors a wide variety of video material of differing types that correspond directly to every chapter of the textbook.

- The *Adopter's Audio CD Program*, provided free to adopting institutions, contains all of the audio CDs from the *Laboratory Audio Program* as well as the *Textbook Listening CD*. It also contains an *Audioscript*. Adopting institutions may use this *Adopter's Audio CD Program* in their Language Laboratory. In addition, institutions may make copies of these materials for students, provided that students are only charged for the cost of blank tapes or CDs.

A set of *Overhead Transparencies*, most in full color, contains drawings from the text and supplementary drawings for use with vocabulary and grammar presentation. An electronic online version of the Transparencies is available to instructors on the *¿Qué tal?* Online Learning Center Website.

- The *Institutional CD-ROM* package consists of twenty copies of the *Interactive CD-ROM*. This package is made available for purchase by departments and laboratories.

ACKNOWLEDGMENTS

The suggestions, advice, and work of the following friends and colleagues are gratefully acknowledged by the authors of the seventh edition.

- Dr. Bill VanPatten (University of Illinois, Chicago), whose creativity has been an inspiration to us and from whom we have learned so very much about language teaching and how students learn.

- María Sabló-Yates, whose extensive research provides the basis for many of the **Enfoque cultural** sections.

As with all previous editions of *¿Qué tal?*, the seventh edition is based on the highly successful *Puntos de partida* first-year Spanish text. Responding to the wishes of many instructors across the country, *¿Qué tal?* retains the methodology and functionality of the *Puntos* program but in a shorter version, which can be ideal for classes meeting three or fewer times per week.

In order to create *¿Qué tal?* from *Puntos,* the coauthors reduced the amount of activities and exercises in the *Puntos* main text and supplements as well as the actual number of grammar points presented in *Puntos.* Additional points are subsumed within related structures or within other parts of the text (Instructor's Edition annotations, **Nota comunicativa** features, and so on).

The *Puntos* grammar points that were modified or removed for the sixth edition of *¿Qué tal?* are:

- Asking Yes/No Questions
- Relative Pronouns
- **Hace... que** + *present* and *preterite*
- Summary of the Subjunctive
- Stressed Possessives
- Hypothetical Situations

With one to three grammar points per chapter, we feel *¿Qué tal?* to be a very manageable book for you and your students. Above all, we believe *¿Qué tal?* to be a *flexible* program, one that can be adapted to suit different teaching and learning styles.

SUPPLEMENTARY MATERIALS FOR THE SEVENTH EDITION

The supplements listed here may accompany the seventh edition of *¿Qué tal?*. Please contact your local McGraw-Hill Higher Education representative for details concerning policies, prices, and availability, as some restrictions may apply.

Workbook / Laboratory Manual and ***Audio Program,*** by Alice A. Arana (formerly of Fullerton College), Oswaldo Arana (formerly of California State University, Fullerton), and María Sabló-Yates (Delta College). The two volumes of the Workbook / Laboratory Manual provide a wealth of activities, both aural and written, that reinforce chapter content. Audio Program CDs are free to adopting institutions and are also available for student purchase upon request. An Audioscript is also available for instructors.

- The *Online Workbook/Laboratory Manual,* developed in collaboration with Quia™, offers an online version of this printed supplement. Increasingly popular, this online version of the printed material offers such benefits for the student as an integrated *Laboratory Audio Program,* self-scoring activities, and instant feedback. Benefits for the instructor include a gradebook that automatically scores, tracks, and records student

grades and provides the opportunity to review individual and class performance. Other benefits include customizable activities and features and instant access to grades and performance.

- The *Online Learning Center* Website provides students with a wealth of exercises and activities specially created for use with *¿Qué tal?*. The *Online Learning Center* consists of two general areas: the free content and the premium content. *Free content* includes additional vocabulary and grammar practice quizzes, cultural activities, chapter overviews, and more. All students have access to free content through the *¿Qué tal?* Website (www.mhhe.com/quetal7). *Premium content* includes the *Laboratory Audio Program,* the **Enfoque cultural** video footage, and the **Flash Grammar Tutorials.** Students have access to the premium content through the *Online Learning Center* passcode that is packaged free with every new student text. Students that purchase a used text may purchase a passcode separately at a nominal price if they wish to access this premium content.

- The *Interactive CD-ROM* is an exciting, multimedia supplement that offers additional vocabulary

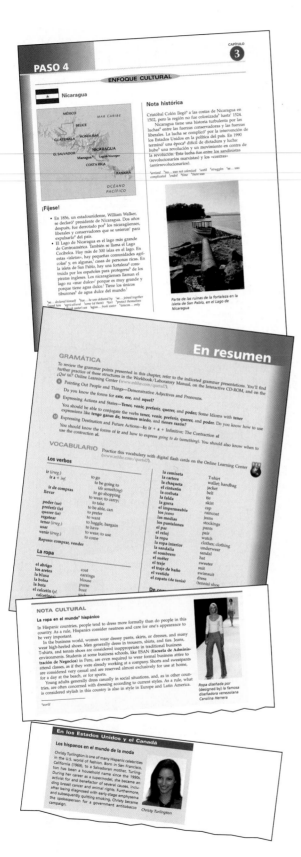

and discussion questions); **Enfoque cultural** (brief readings, photos, and a map that present historical and cultural information about the chapter's country or countries of focus); **A leer** (readings and pre-reading strategies); **A escribir** (brief writing assignments based on the chapter theme); and **A conversar** (chapter-culminating communicative activities). The **A leer** and **A escribir** sections are found in odd-numbered chapters; **A conversar** activities are found in even-numbered chapters.

En resumen

This end-of-chapter grammar and vocabulary summary consists of two sections: **Gramática** and **Vocabulario.** The **Gramática** section provides students with a quick overview of the major grammar points within the chapter as well as a reminder of what they should know for assessment purposes. The **Vocabulario** section includes all important words and expressions from the chapter that are considered active.

Additional features

- **Un poco de todo: Lengua y cultura** activities, found in **Paso 3: Gramática,** combine and review grammar presented in the chapter as well as important grammar from previous chapters. Major topics that are continuously spiraled in this section include **ser** and **estar**, preterite and imperfect, gender and gender agreement, and indicative and subjunctive.

- **Nota cultural** features highlight an aspect of Hispanic cultures throughout the world.

- **En los Estados Unidos y el Canadá** are brief sections that focus on U.S. and Canadian Hispanics and institutions. Key words and phrases are highlighted in these sections in order to facilitate comprehension.

- **Nota comunicativa** sections provide additional information about communication in Spanish.

- **Vocabulario útil** boxes give additional vocabulary that may be necessary to work through a chapter's activities.

- **Autoprueba** boxes that follow grammar presentations provide students with the opportunity to quickly check their understanding of a specific grammar point.

For more information on these and other features of *¿Qué tal?*, please visit the text-specific website at **www.mhhe.com/quetal7**.

The seventh edition of *¿Qué tal?* features a uniquely clear and user-friendly **paso** organization. Each of its eighteen regular chapters is divided into four **pasos,** highlighted with color tabs for easy reference, with the **Voces de...** cultural feature in the middle. Thus, each regular chapter has the following structure.

> Paso 1: **Vocabulario**
> Paso 2: **Gramática**
> **Voces de...**
> Paso 3: **Gramática**
> Paso 4: **Un paso más**

Paso 1: Vocabulario

This section presents and practices the chapter's thematic vocabulary. The lexical lists in these sections are read on the Listening Comprehension Audio CD and are signaled by a headphone icon. Each new lexical list is followed by a **Conversación** section that practices the new vocabulary in context.

Pasos 2 and 3: Gramática

These sections present one to two grammar points each. Each grammar point is introduced by a minidialogue, a cartoon or drawing, realia, or a brief reading that presents the grammar topic in context. Grammar explanations, in English, appear in the left-hand column of the two-column design; paradigms and sample sentences appear in the right-hand column. Each grammar presentation is followed by a series of contextualized exercises and activities that progress from more controlled (**Práctica**) to more open-ended (**Conversación**).

Voces de...

The cultures of the Spanish-speaking world are an integral part of every section of *¿Qué tal?,* but literature and music take central stage in the **Voces de...** section of each chapter. Located between **Pasos 2** and **3, Voces de...** has two parts: **Literatura** and **Música. Literatura** introduces an important writer from the featured country with a brief biography of him or her and a fragment of an important work. **Música** highlights one or more of the musical traditions of the chapter's country of focus.

Paso 4: Un paso más

This section integrates the vocabulary and grammar from the first three **pasos** in a rich and stimulating selection of skill-building activities: **Videoteca** (video comprehension

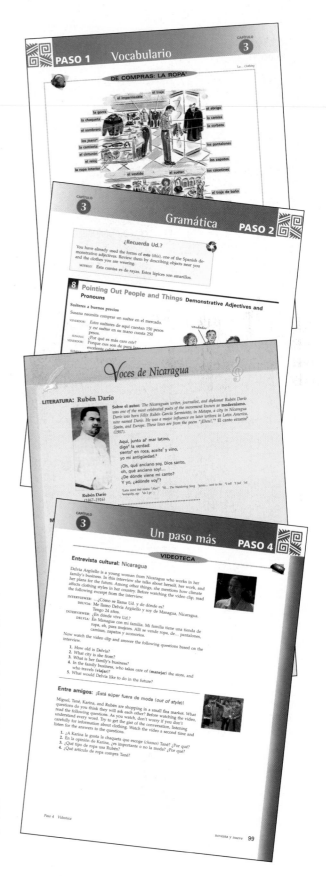

features musical traditions of the featured country or countries. Magazine-style short reading passages provide information on traditional instruments, musical styles and genres, famous musicians, traditional dances, and so on. These brief reading passages are accompanied by photos or drawings.

Videoteca

The **Videoteca** page found in every chapter is completely new. It has two sections.

- **Entrevista cultural,** a video-based interview with a native speaker from the country of focus. Each interview, directly related to the chapter theme, reflects the native speakers' interests, professions, studies, or background. Student viewers of the interview benefit from the country-specific cultural information in it and also from the link to the chapter's vocabulary and, at times, grammar. When two countries are covered, there is a corresponding interview with a native speaker from each country.

- **Entre amigos,** a video-based feature that follows the entertaining discussions of a group of four college students. These students reflect the geographic and cultural diversity of the Spanish-speaking world.

Rubén is from Spain, Miguel from Mexico, Karina from Venezuela, and Tané from Cuba. In these segments, the four students informally discuss chapter-related topics that affect their daily lives. The language is natural and nonscripted, resulting in spontaneous discussions that reflect the interests and concerns of today's Spanish-speaking young adults, in an environment that encourages cross-cultural comparison.

Un poco de todo

The **Un poco de todo** review sections are again part of the **Paso 3** of each chapter, the final step in the presentation and practice of the new grammar structures. This edition features twelve new engaging cloze paragraphs that present cultural information as they review the grammatical and lexical material from both the corresponding chapter and previous chapters. Each **Un poco de todo** cloze paragraph is identified as a **Lengua y cultura** activity to underscore the recycling of vocabulary and structures and highlight the activity's cultural focus. This cultural focus is directly related to the theme of the chapter or the chapter's country of focus. Thus, culture and language are naturally integrated in the **Un poco de todo** sections of every chapter.

New Art

Instructors will immediately notice the new art in this edition of *¿Qué tal?* While the art of previous editions has always been well received, we felt it was time for a change. The artists were carefully guided so that the art would be both pedagogically sound and visually beautiful. The result of the art is a visually enhanced seventh edition that satisfies the needs of today's sophisticated students and instructors, both pedagogically and visually.

Chapter Themes

The positive response from instructors using earlier editions confirmed that the chapter themes found in *¿Qué tal?* provide engaging and relevant content for exploration and discussion. Theme vocabulary for all chapters has, of course, been updated to reflect changes in the areas of technology, recreational activities, and so forth. The vocabulary lists in **Capítulos 7** and **16** have been reorganized for easier practice and study. The vocabulary of **Capítulo 14** has been modified to focus more on the natural world, and the vocabulary of **Capítulo 18** now reflects travel vocabulary students are likely to use in today's traveling environment.

New Chapter Opening Page

We have redesigned the chapter opening page. The result is an introduction to the chapter that is more engaging and more purposeful to the instructor and the student. Spending class time on the chapter opener will provide a useful introduction to the chapter for the student and set the stage for a more successful experience with the chapter content. (A visual presentation of the new Chapter Opener is provided in the Guided Tour presented in this Preface.)

Capítulo preliminar: Primeros pasos

Responding to reviewer feedback, the authors have carefully recrafted and shortened the **Capítulo preliminar.** Its purpose remains the same: to introduce students to the sounds of Spanish and to a variety of high-frequency language that will ease their transition into the course. In addition, this special chapter continues to introduce students to the geographic and cultural diversity of the Spanish-speaking world. However, the amount of material has been considerably reduced, resulting in two **pasos** rather than three. The material that has been eliminated from the preliminary chapter has been integrated into other chapters of *¿Qué tal?*

User-Friendly Activities

In addition to being carefully ordered from form-focused to more open-ended, communicative tasks, the activities are now also carefully placed on the pages so that students and instructors will not need to flip pages as they complete an activity. Additional models provide more support and materials, and elicit more student interaction. Many activities focus even more on reviewing and recycling vocabulary and structure from previous chapters.

Notas culturales

Many of the **Notas culturales** have been replaced with new **Notas** or revised. Instructors will find that the **Notas culturales** consistently reflect some aspect of the chapter theme and focus on high-interest topics. In addition, the *Instructor's Edition* now features a series of follow-up questions for each **Nota,** providing instructors with ready-made activities to use in class.

Voces de... (country)

Instructors familiar with the previous editions of *¿Qué tal?* will notice a new feature: the new **Voces de...** page. Found between **Pasos 2** and **3, Voces de...** highlights two cultural aspects of the country or countries of focus: literature and music.

- **Literatura de...** This section, developed in response to instructor's requests for more country-specific literature and culture, features an important author from the chapter's country of focus and includes an excerpt from one of that author's works. A short biographical note provides information on the author's life. The intent of this section is to raise students' awareness of the amazingly rich literary tradition of the Spanish-speaking world, as well as give them a "taste" of some **obras maestras.**

  While these brief readings will be challenging for most students, some at least will profit from and be motivated by reading them . . . and perhaps a few will become Spanish majors in part because they were "touched" by one or more selections. While choosing these excerpts was not an easy task for the *¿Qué tal?* author team, all of us—whether we are linguists or literary specialists—remembered and reconnected with our early enthusiasm for Spanish literature as we tried to read the excerpts through the eyes of today's students.

- The purpose of the **Música** section of the **Voces de...** page is to introduce students to the rich diversity of music in the Spanish-speaking world. The section

when their Spanish language skills are better developed. The **Música** section presents the rich diversity of musical traditions and styles from the featured country or countries.

An All-New Video Program That Brings Language and Hispanic Cultures to Life

- The **Entrevista cultural** segments introduce students to a Spanish-speaker from a different country in each chapter, providing a unique glimpse into their lives and their culture. Accompanying activities in the new **Videoteca** section of each chapter both prepare students for viewing and assess comprehension.

- The **Entre amigos** episodes present four students from different countries (Spain, Mexico, Venezuela, and Cuba) who tell entertaining stories as they meet and talk at a university in Mexico. These entertaining vignettes also review vocabulary themes and grammatical structures in each chapter, bringing the language to life. Taken together, both video segments provide an opportunity for students to hear authentic Spanish spoken by real Spanish speakers who interact with each other, rather than actors speaking for the camera.

- The popular video episodes from the previous edition of ¿Qué tal? continue to be available on the *Video Program*, and can still be used, chapter-by-chapter, with the seventh edition.

Diverse Cultural Content

- Each chapter focuses on one area of the Spanish-speaking world. A large photo on the chapter opening pages introduces students to the chapter's themes as well as to the country of focus, and provides an engaging starting point for conversation.

- Special cultural features, including the **Nota cultural** and the **En los Estados Unidos y el Canadá** boxes, give quick and interesting glimpses into Hispanic cultures.

- The new **Voces de...** and **Videoteca** section in each chapter, as well as the **Enfoque cultural** section, highlight the country of focus through video segments, texts, and photos.

While much is new to this edition of ¿Qué tal?, you will continue to find the many hallmarks that make it the book of choice for hundreds of instructors across the country. These hallmark features include:

- the user-friendly **Paso** structure that facilitates lesson planning and helps students stay focused

- an abundance of classroom-tested practice material, ranging from form-focused activities to communicative activities that promote real conversation

- vocabulary, grammar, and culture that work together as interactive units, unifying this important aspect of language learning

- an emphasis on the meaningful use of Spanish

- a positive portrayal of contemporary Hispanic cultures

- print and media supplementary materials that are carefully coordinated with the core text

The pages that follow provide a more detailed overview of changes to this edition in a section called "What's New in the Seventh Edition?" The next section, "A Guided Tour," explains and shows the organization and features of ¿Qué tal? (useful to both instructors and students!), followed by a comprehensive discussion of supplementary materials. The Preface closes with the acknowledgment of the many instructors and students who helped shape this new edition.

" . . . to help students develop proficiency in the four language skills essential to truly communicative language learning . . . "

from the preface to *¿Qué tal?*, first edition, 1983

Welcome to the seventh edition of *¿Qué tal? An Introductory Course.* It has been more than twenty years since the publication of the first edition, and the coauthors are grateful to the instructors and students who have responded so positively to the goals and approach of *¿Qué tal?*

In those years, much has changed and much has remained constant in *¿Qué tal? ¿Qué tal?* has remained true to the goals of the first edition, as cited above. The approach, however, has evolved and kept pace with technological advances and our increasing knowledge of how languages are learned. The ancillary package for the first edition of *¿Qué tal?* was excellent for its time but seems small in comparison to the plethora of materials available to instructors and students today. Particularly noteworthy are the wide variety of new technologies that enhance language learning in ways not yet dreamed of twenty years ago.

In addition to these new technologies, instructors will find in the seventh edition those features that they have come to know and trust over the years as well as many new features. These features include:

A Design that Promotes Learning and Teaching

- More than 500 new color illustrations and photographs bring an exciting new visual appeal to the program and enhance the pedagogy of the text. Beautiful drawings illustrate vocabulary words in each chapter, allowing students to make important connections between the Spanish word and the conceptual meaning. Many activities are also enlivened through lively illustrations that review vocabulary and grammar and promote real communication.

- The flow of presentations and activities within the chapter has been carefully crafted to keep students on task and focused. Activities do not break over the front and back of pages, thus eliminating the need for students and instructors to "flip" pages while completing activities.

- Sentence-formation and cloze passage activities are now pedagogically improved through the use of special shading and color that highlight key elements of the activity and keep students focused on the tasks they are performing.

Student-Friendly Grammar Features

- Paradigms and charts within grammar presentations have been enhanced by the use of a colored font that directs students' attention to key aspects of the grammar point, such as spelling changes in stem-changing verbs and agreement of adjectives.

- New timelines place major grammar tenses on a continuum from Past ←→ Present ←→ Future and help students understand the "big picture" as they move through the sequence of tenses presented throughout the text.

- **Autoprueba** quizzes allow students to do quick self-assessments of their understanding of key grammar points in every chapter, before they begin the exercises and activities.

- New drawings illustrate many new verb infinitives, encouraging students to learn meaning through visual association.

- Interactive **Flash Grammar** tutorials on the CD-ROM and the *Online Learning Center* Website allow students to "see" core grammar structures. The tutorials are enriched by interactive paradigms and sample sentences.

An Introduction to Literary Masterpieces and Musical Traditions

- New to this edition, the **Voces de...** (country) page features literature and music from the country or countries of focus in the chapter. The **Literatura** section profiles renowned authors from these countries, accompanied by a brief extract from one of their works. These brief extracts—just a "taste" of some **obras maestras**—will enrich students' appreciation of the literary heritage of the Spanish-speaking world and hopefully motivate some students to continue reading

The McGraw·Hill Companies

Mc Graw Hill **Higher Education**

This is an book.

¿Qué tal?
An Introductory Course

Published by McGraw-Hill, an imprint of The McGraw-Hill Companies, Inc., 1221
Avenue of the Americas, New York, NY 10020. Copyright © 2007 by The McGraw-Hill
Companies, Inc. All rights reserved. No part of this publication may be reproduced or
distributed in any form or by any means, or stored in a database or retrieval system,
without the prior written consent of The McGraw-Hill Companies, Inc., including, but
not limited to, in any network or other electronic storage or transmission, or broadcast
for distance learning.

This book is printed on acid-free paper.

1 2 3 4 5 6 7 8 9 0 DOW DOW 0 9 8 7 6

ISBN-13: 978-007-304850-5 (Student Edition)
ISBN-10: 0-07-304850-X

ISBN-13: 978-007-320799-5 (Instructor's Edition)
ISBN-10: 0-07-320799-3

Vice president and Editor-in-chief: *Emily G. Barrosse*
Publisher: *William R. Glass*
Senior sponsoring editor: *Christa Harris*
Director of development: *Scott Tinetti*
Development editor: *Pennie Nichols*
Executive marketing manager: *Nick Agnew*
Production editor: *Mel Valentín*
Lead production supervisor: *Randy Hurst*
Senior supplements producer: *Louis Swaim*
Design manager/cover designer: *Violeta Diaz*
Interior designer: *Linda Robertson*
Photo editor: *Alexandra Ambrose*
Photo researcher: *Susan Friedman*
Art editor: *Robin Mouat*
Compositor: *TechBooks/GTS Companies, York, PA*
Typeface: *10/12 Palatino*
Printer and binder: *Donnelley—Willard*

Cover image: Carlos Planck, *La Danza*, 1969. Collection of Annie Orban. Courtesy of
Mosto & Rojas Arte, Buenos Aires, Argentina.

Because this page cannot accommodate all the copyright notices, credits are listed after
the index and constitute an extension of the copyright page.

LIBRARY OF CONGRESS CATALOGING-IN-PUBLICATION DATA

Que tal? : an introductory course / Thalia Dorwick . . . [et al.].—7th ed.
   p. cm.
  Includes index.
  ISBN 0-07-304850-X (alk. paper : instructor's ed.)
  1. Spanish language—Textbooks for foreign speakers—English. I. Dorwick, Thalia,
1944–

PC4129.E5Q4 2006
468.2'421—dc22

2005058008

http://www.mhhe.com

¿Qué tal?
An Introductory Course

SEVENTH EDITION

Thalia Dorwick

Ana María Pérez-Gironés
Wesleyan University

Marty Knorre

William R. Glass

Hildebrando Villarreal
California State University, Los Angeles

CONTRIBUTING WRITERS:

Manuel Cortés-Castañeda
Eastern Kentucky University

Becky S. Jaimes
Austin Community College

Talía Loaiza
Austin Community College

Jane Johnson
University of Texas, Austin

Boston   Burr Ridge, IL   Dubuque, IA   Madison, WI   New York   San Francisco   St. Louis
Bangkok   Bogotá   Caracas   Kuala Lumpur   Lisbon   London   Madrid   Mexico City
Milan   Montreal   New Delhi   Santiago   Seoul   Singapore   Sydney   Taipei   Toronto

Primeros pasos°

Primeros... *First steps*

Santiago, Chile

San Juan, Puerto Rico

PRIMER PASO
- Saludos y expresiones de cortesía
- El alfabeto español
- ¿Cómo es usted?

SEGUNDO PASO
- Los números 0–30; *hay*
- Gustos y preferencias
- ¿Qué hora es?

PRONUNCIACIÓN
- Las vocales: *a, e, i, o, u*

CULTURA
- **Nota cultural:** Spanish in the United States and in the World
- **A leer:** La geografía del mundo hispánico
- **Videoteca**
    Entre amigos: ¡Encantada!

As you study Spanish in *¿Qué tal?*, you will also learn about the ethnic, racial, and cultural diversity of the Spanish-speaking world.

¿Qué tal? means *Hi, how are you doing?* in Spanish. This textbook, called *¿Qué tal?*, will help you begin to learn Spanish and get ready to communicate with Spanish speakers in this country and elsewhere in the Spanish-speaking world.

To speak a language involves much more than just learning its grammar and vocabulary; to know a language is to know the people who speak it. For this reason *¿Qué tal?* will provide you with cultural information to help you understand and appreciate the traditions and values of Spanish-speaking people all over the world.

Are you ready for the adventure of learning Spanish? **Pues, ¡adelante!** (*Well, let's go!*)

Primer paso

Saludos° y expresiones de cortesía   *Greetings*

Here are some words, phrases, and expressions that will enable you to meet and greet others appropriately in Spanish.

1.   MANOLO: ¡Hola, Maricarmen!
MARICARMEN: ¿Qué tal, Manolo? ¿Cómo estás?
MANOLO: Muy bien. ¿Y tú?
MARICARMEN: Regular. Nos vemos, ¿eh?
MANOLO: Hasta mañana.

1.   Sevilla, España

2.   ELISA VELASCO: Buenas tardes, señor Gómez.
MARTÍN GÓMEZ: Muy buenas, señora Velasco. ¿Cómo está?
ELISA VELASCO: Bien, gracias. ¿Y usted?
MARTÍN GÓMEZ: Muy bien, gracias. Hasta luego.
ELISA VELASCO: Adiós.

2.   Quito, Ecuador

¿Qué tal?, **¿Cómo estás?**, and **¿Y tú?** are expressions used in informal situations with people you know well, on a first-name basis.

¿Cómo está? and **¿Y usted?** are used to address someone with whom you have a formal relationship.

3.   LUPE: Buenos días, profesor.
PROFESOR: Buenos días. ¿Cómo te llamas?
LUPE: Me llamo Lupe Carrasco.
PROFESOR: Mucho gusto, Lupe.
LUPE: Igualmente.

3.   La Ciudad de México, México

---

1. MANOLO: Hi, Maricarmen! MARICARMEN: How's it going, Manolo? How are you? MANOLO: Very well. And you? MARICARMEN: OK. See you around, OK? MANOLO: See you tomorrow.
2. ELISA VELASCO: Good afternoon, Mr. Gómez. MARTÍN GÓMEZ: Afternoon, Mrs. Velasco. How are you? ELISA VELASCO: Fine, thank you. And you? MARTÍN GÓMEZ: Very well, thanks. See you later. ELISA VELASCO: Bye.
3. LUPE: Good morning, professor. PROFESSOR: Good morning. What's your name? LUPE: My name is Lupe Carrasco. PROFESSOR: Nice to meet you, Lupe. LUPE: Likewise.

¿Cómo se llama usted? is used in formal situations. ¿Cómo te llamas? is used in informal situations—for example, with other students. The phrases **mucho gusto** and **igualmente** are used by both men and women when meeting for the first time. In response to **mucho gusto,** a woman can also say **encantada;** a man can say **encantado.**

4.	MIGUEL:	Hola, me llamo Miguel René. ¿Y tú? ¿Cómo te llamas?
	KARINA:	Me llamo Karina. Mucho gusto.
	MIGUEL:	Mucho gusto, Karina. Y, ¿de dónde eres?
	KARINA:	Yo soy de Venezuela. ¿Y tú?
	MIGUEL:	Yo soy de México.

4. La Ciudad de México, México

¿De dónde eres? is used in informal situations to ask where someone is from. In formal situations the expression used is ¿De dónde es usted? To reply to either question, the phrase (**Yo**) **Soy de** _____ is used.

NOTA COMUNICATIVA

Otros saludos y expresiones de cortesía

buenos días	good morning (_used until the midday meal_)
buenas tardes	good afternoon (_used until the evening meal_)
buenas noches	good evening; good night (_used after the evening meal_)
señor (Sr.)	Mr., sir
señora (Sra.)	Mrs., ma'am
señorita (Srta.)	Miss
gracias	thanks, thank you
muchas gracias	thank you very much
de nada, no	you're welcome
hay de qué	
por favor	please (_also used to get someone's attention_)
perdón	pardon me; excuse me (_to ask forgiveness or to get someone's attention_)
con permiso	pardon me; excuse me (_to request permission to pass by or through a group of people_)

OJO * There is no Spanish equivalent for _Ms._ Use **Sra.** or **Srta.,** as appropriate.

---

*Watch out, Careful. ¡**OJO**! (sometimes just **OJO**) will be used throughout ¿Qué tal? to alert you to pay special attention to the information that follows._

4. MIGUEL: _Hello, my name is Miguel René. And you? What's your name?_ KARINA: _My name is Karina. Nice to meet you._ MIGUEL: _Nice to meet you, Karina. And where are you from?_ KARINA: _I'm from Venezuela. And you?_ MIGUEL: _I'm from Mexico._

■ Conversación

A. Cortesía. How many different ways can you respond to the following greetings and phrases?

1. Buenas tardes.
2. Adiós.
3. ¿Qué tal?
4. Hola.
5. ¿Cómo está?
6. Buenas noches.
7. Muchas gracias.
8. Hasta mañana.
9. ¿Cómo se llama usted?
10. Mucho gusto.
11. ¿De dónde eres?

B. Situaciones. If the following people met or passed each other at the times given, what might they say to each other? Role-play the situations with a classmate.

1. Mr. Santana and Miss Pérez, at 5:00 P.M.
2. Mrs. Ortega and Pablo, at 10:00 A.M.
3. Ms. Hernández and Olivia, at 11:00 P.M.
4. you and a classmate, just before your Spanish class
5. you and your Spanish professor, at 11 A.M.
6. you and your cousin, at 10 P.M.
7. you and the president of your university, at 4 P.M.

C. Más (*More*) **situaciones.** Are the people in these drawings saying **por favor, con permiso,** or **perdón? ¡OJO!** More than one response is possible for some items.

D. Entrevista (*Interview*)

PASO (*Step*) 1 Turn to a person sitting next to you and do the following.

- Greet him or her appropriately, that is, with informal forms.
- Ask where he or she is from.
- Find out his or her name.
- Ask how he or she is.
- Conclude the exchange.

PASO 2 Now have a similar conversation with your instructor, using the appropriate forms (formal or informal, according to your instructor's preference).

El alfabeto español

There are twenty-nine letters in the Spanish alphabet (**el alfabeto** or **el abecedario**)—three more than in the English alphabet. The three additional letters are the **ch,** the **ll,** and the **ñ.** The letters **k** and **w** appear only in words borrowed from other languages.

In 1994, the **Real Academia Española** (*Royal Spanish Academy*), which establishes many of the guidelines for the use of Spanish throughout the world, decided to adopt the universal Latin order when alphabetizing. In that order, **ch** and **ll** are not considered separate letters. Thus, in dictionaries and other alphabetized materials published since 1994, you will not find separate listings for the letters **ch** and **ll.** They are, however, still considered separate letters by the **Real Academia** and are part of the Spanish alphabet.*

LETTERS	NAMES OF LETTERS	EXAMPLES		
a	a	Antonio	Ana	(la) Argentina
b	be	Benito	Blanca	Bolivia
c	ce	Carlos	Cecilia	Cáceres
ch	che	Pancho	Chabela	La Mancha
d	de	Domingo	Dolores	Durango
e	e	Eduardo	Elena	(el) Ecuador
f	efe	Felipe	Francisca	Florida
g	ge	Gerardo	Gloria	Guatemala
h	hache	Héctor	Hortensia	Honduras
i	i	Ignacio	Inés	Ibiza
j	jota	José	Juana	Jalisco
k	ca (ka)	(Karl)	(Kati)	(Kansas)
l	ele	Luis	Lola	Lima
ll	elle	Guillermo	Estrella	Sevilla
m	eme	Manuel	María	México
n	ene	Nicolás	Nati	Nicaragua
ñ	eñe	Íñigo	Begoña	España
o	o	Octavio	Olivia	Oviedo
p	pe	Pablo	Pilar	Panamá
q	cu	Enrique	Raquel	Quito
r	ere	Álvaro	Rosa	(el) Perú
s	ese	Salvador	Sara	San Juan
t	te	Tomás	Teresa	Toledo
u	u	Agustín	Lucía	(el) Uruguay
v	ve *or* uve	Víctor	Victoria	Venezuela
w	doble ve, ve doble, *or* uve doble	Oswaldo	(Wilma)	(Washington)
x	equis	Xavier	Ximena	Extremadura
y	i griega	Pelayo	Yolanda	(el) Paraguay
z	ceta (zeta)	Gonzalo	Esperanza	Zaragoza

*The **ch** is pronounced with the same sound as in English cherry or chair, as in Spanish **nachos** or **muchacho.** The **ll** is pronounced as a type of y sound. Spanish examples of this sound that you may already know are **tortilla** and **Sevilla.** The grouping **rr** is not considered a separate letter by the **Real Academia.**

■ Práctica

A. ¡Pronuncie!   The letters and combinations of letters listed below represent the Spanish sounds that are the most different from English. Pay particular attention to their pronunciation. Can you match the Spanish letters with their equivalent pronunciation?

EXAMPLES/SPELLING

1. mucho: **ch**
2. Geraldo: **ge** (also: **gi**)
   Jiménez: **j**
3. hola: **h**
4. gusto: **gu** (also: **ga, go**)
5. me llamo: **ll**
6. señor: **ñ**
7. profesora: **r**
8. Ramón: **r** (to start a word)
   Monterrey: **rr**
9. nos vemos: **v**

PRONUNCIATION

a. like the *g* in English *garden*
b. similar to *tt* of *butter* when pronounced very quickly
c. like *ch* in English *cheese*
d. like Spanish **b**
e. similar to a "strong" English *h*
f. like *y* in English *yes* or like the *li* sound in *million*
g. a trilled sound, several Spanish *r*'s in a row
h. similar to the *ny* sound in *canyon*
i. never pronounced

B. ¿Cómo se deletrea... ? (*How do you spell . . . ?*)

PASO 1   Pronounce these U.S. place names in Spanish. Then spell the names aloud in Spanish. All of them are of Hispanic origin: **Toledo, Los Ángeles, Texas, Montana, Colorado, El Paso, Florida, Las Vegas, Amarillo, San Francisco.**

PASO 2   Spell your own name aloud in Spanish, and listen as your classmates spell their names. Try to remember as many of their names as you can.

MODELO: Me llamo María: **M** (eme) **a** (a) **r** (ere) **í** (i acentuada) **a** (a).

NOTA COMUNICATIVA

Los cognados

As you begin your study of Spanish, you will probably notice that many Spanish and English words are similar or identical in form and meaning. These related words are called *cognates* (**los cognados**). You will see them used in **Primeros pasos** and throughout *¿Qué tal?* At this early stage of language learning, it's useful to begin recognizing cognates and how they are pronounced in Spanish. Here are some examples of Spanish words that are cognates of English words. These cognates and others will help you enrich your Spanish vocabulary and develop your language proficiency!

SOME ADJECTIVES				SOME NOUNS	
cruel	inteligente	pesimista	banco	estudiante	oficina
elegante	interesante	responsable	bar	examen	parque
flexible	optimista	sentimental	café	hotel	teléfono
importante	paciente	terrible	diccionario	museo	televisión

¿Cómo es usted?°

¿Cómo… What are you like?

You can use these forms of the verb **ser** (*to be*) to describe yourself and others.

(yo)	**soy**	I am
(tú)	**eres**	you (*familiar*) are
(usted)	**es**	you (*formal*) are
(él, ella)	**es**	he/she is

—¿Cómo es usted?
—Bueno…° Yo soy moderna, independiente, sofisticada…

Well…

■ Conversación

Descripciones

PASO 1 Form complete sentences with the cognates given. Use **no** when necessary.

1. Yo (no) soy…
   estudiante.
   cruel.
   responsable.
   optimista.
   paciente.

2. El presidente (no) es…
   importante.
   inteligente.
   pesimista.
   flexible.
   extrovertido.

3. Jennifer López (no) es…
   elegante.
   introvertida.
   romántica.
   sentimental.
   egoísta.

PASO 2 Now think of people you might describe with the following additional cognates. Use **es** to express *is*.

MODELO: eficiente → La profesora es eficiente.

1. arrogante
2. egoísta
3. emocional
4. idealista
5. impaciente
6. independiente
7. liberal
8. materialista
9. realista
10. rebelde

PRONUNCIACIÓN

You have probably already noted that there is a very close relationship between the way Spanish is written and the way it is pronounced. This makes it relatively easy to learn the basics of Spanish spelling and pronunciation.

Many Spanish sounds, however, do not have an exact equivalent in English, so you should not trust English to be your guide to Spanish pronunciation. Even words that are spelled the same in both languages are usually pronounced quite differently. It is important to become so familiar with Spanish sounds that you can pronounce them automatically, right from the beginning of your study of the language.

Las vocales (Vowels): *a, e, i, o, u*

Unlike English vowels, which can have many different pronunciations or may be silent, Spanish vowels are always pronounced, and they are almost always pronounced in the same way. Spanish vowels are always short and tense. They are never drawn out with a *u* or *i* glide as in English: **lo** ≠ *low*; **de** ≠ *day*.

a: pronounced like the *a* in *father*, but short and tense
e: pronounced like the *e* in *they*, but without the *i* glide
i: pronounced like the *i* in *machine*, but short and tense*
o: pronounced like the *o* in *home*, but without the *u* glide
u: pronounced like the *u* in *rule*, but short and tense

OJO The *uh* sound or schwa (which is how most unstressed vowels are pronounced in English: *canal, waited, atom*) does not exist in Spanish.

A. Sílabas. Pronounce the following Spanish syllables, being careful to pronounce each vowel with a short, tense sound.

1. ma fa la ta pa
2. me fe le te pe
3. mi fi li ti pi
4. mo fo lo to po
5. mu fu lu tu pu
6. mi fe la tu do
7. su mi te so la
8. se tu no ya li

B. Palabras (*Words*). Repeat the following words after your instructor.

1. hasta tal nada mañana natural normal fascinante
2. me qué Pérez Elena rebelde excelente elegante
3. sí señorita permiso terrible imposible tímido Ibiza
4. yo con como noches profesor señor generoso
5. uno usted tú mucho Perú Lupe Úrsula

C. Naciones

PASO 1 Here is part of a rental car ad in Spanish. Say aloud the names of the countries where you can find this company's offices. Can you recognize all of the countries?

PASO 2 Find the following information in the ad.

1. How many cars does the agency have available?
2. How many offices does the agency have?
3. What Spanish word expresses the English word *immediately*?

*The word **y** (and) is also pronounced like the letter **i**.

Capítulo preliminar • Primeros pasos

NOTA CULTURAL

Spanish in the United States and in the World

Although no one knows exactly how many languages are spoken around the world, linguists estimate that there are between 3,000 and 6,000. Spanish, with 425 million native speakers, is among the top five languages. It is the official language spoken in Spain, in Mexico, in all of South America (except Brazil and the Guianas), in most of Central America, in Cuba, in Puerto Rico, in the Dominican Republic, and in Ecuatorial Guinea (in Africa)—in approximately twenty-one countries in all. It is also spoken by a great number of people in the United States and Canada.

Like all languages spoken by large numbers of people, modern Spanish varies from region to region. The Spanish of Madrid is different from that spoken in Mexico City, Buenos Aires, or Los Angeles. Although these differences are most noticeable in pronunciation ("accent"), they are also found in vocabulary and special expressions used in different geographical areas. Despite these differences, misunderstandings among native speakers are rare, since the majority of structures and vocabulary are common to the many varieties of each language.

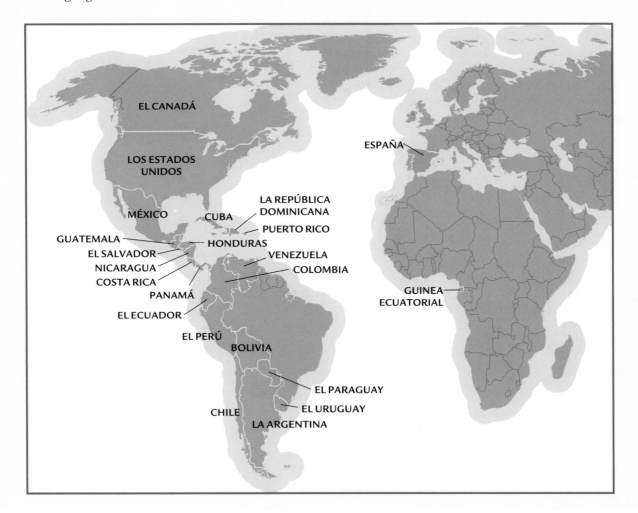

You don't need to go abroad to encounter people who speak Spanish on a daily basis. The Spanish language and people of Hispanic descent have been an integral part of U.S. and Canadian life for centuries. In fact, the United States has the fifth largest Spanish-speaking population in the world!

There is also great regional diversity among U.S. Hispanics. Many people of Mexican descent inhabit the southwestern part of the United States, including populations as far north as Colorado. Large groups of Puerto Ricans can be found in New York, while Florida is host to a large Cuban and Central American population. More recent immigrants include Nicaraguans and Salvadorans, who have established large communities in many U.S. cities, among them San Francisco and Los Angeles.

As you will discover in subsequent chapters of *¿Qué tal?*, the Spanish language and people of Hispanic descent have been and will continue to be an integral part of the fabric of this country. Take special note of **En los Estados Unidos y el Canadá,** a routinely occurring section of *¿Qué tal?* that profiles Hispanics in these two countries.

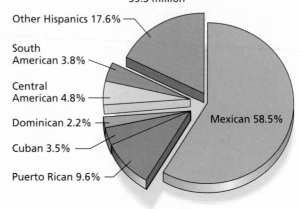

Comparing origins of U.S. Hispanic population
Total population based on U.S. census,
2000 estimate*
35.3 million

- Other Hispanics 17.6%
- South American 3.8%
- Central American 4.8%
- Dominican 2.2%
- Cuban 3.5%
- Puerto Rican 9.6%
- Mexican 58.5%

*Source: Census Bureau. The Hispanic Population: Information from the 2000 Census.

Mural en la Pequeña Habana, el barrio cubano de (of) Miami

Need more practice?

- Workbook/Laboratory Manual
- Interactive CD-ROM
- Online Learning Center
  (www.mhhe.com/quetal7)

Los números 0–30; *hay*

Canción infantil

Dos y dos son cuatro,
cuatro y dos son seis,
seis y dos son ocho,
y ocho dieciséis.

Los números 0–30

0	cero				
1	uno	11	once	21	veintiuno
2	dos	12	doce	22	veintidós
3	tres	13	trece	23	veintitrés
4	cuatro	14	catorce	24	veinticuatro
5	cinco	15	quince	25	veinticinco
6	seis	16	dieciséis*	26	veintiséis
7	siete	17	diecisiete	27	veintisiete
8	ocho	18	dieciocho	28	veintiocho
9	nueve	19	diecinueve	29	veintinueve
10	diez	20	veint**e**	30	treint**a**

The number *one* has several forms in Spanish. **Uno** is the form used in counting. The forms **un** and **una** are used before nouns. How will you know which one to use? It depends on the gender of the noun.

In **Capítulo 1,** you will learn that all Spanish nouns are either masculine or feminine in gender. For example, the noun **señor** is masculine (*m.*) in gender, and the noun **señora** is feminine (*f.*) in gender. (As you will learn, Spanish nouns that are not sex-linked also have gender.) Here is how the word *one* is expressed with these nouns: **un señor, una señora.** Also note that the number **veintiuno** becomes **veintiún** before masculine nouns and **veintiuna** before feminine nouns: **veintiún señores, veintiuna señoras.** Do learn how to use **un** and **uno** with nouns now, but don't worry about the concept of gender for the moment.

> **noun** = a word that denotes a person, place, thing, or idea

uno, dos, tres,... veint**iuno,** veintidós,... *but*
un señor, veinti**ún** señores
una señora, veinti**una** señoras

A children's song   Two and two are four, four and two are six, six and two are eight, and eight (makes) sixteen.

*The numbers 16 to 19 and 21 to 29 can be written as one word (**dieciséis... veintiuno...**) or as three (**diez y seis... veinte y uno...**).*

Hay

Use the word **hay** to express both *there is* and *there are* in Spanish. **No hay** means *there is not* and *there are not.* **¿Hay. . . ?** asks *Is there. . . ?* or *Are there. . . ?*

hay = there is / there are

—¿Cuántos estudiantes **hay** en la clase? *How many students are there in the class?*
—(**Hay**) Treinta. *(There are) Thirty.*

—¿**Hay** pandas en el zoo? *Are there any pandas at the zoo?*
—**Hay** veinte osos, pero **no** hay pandas. *There are twenty bears, but there aren't any pandas.*

■ Práctica

A. Los números. Practique los números según (*according to*) el modelo.

MODELO: 1 señor → Hay un señor.

1. 4 señoras
2. 12 pianos
3. 1 café (*m.*)
4. 21 cafés (*m.*)
5. 14 días
6. 1 clase (*f.*)
7. 21 ideas (*f.*)
8. 11 personas
9. 15 estudiantes
10. 13 teléfonos
11. 28 naciones
12. 5 guitarras
13. 1 león (*m.*)
14. 30 señores
15. 20 oficinas

B. Problemas de matemáticas. Do the following simple mathematical equations in Spanish. *Note:* + (**y**), − (**menos**), = (**son**).

MODELOS: $2 + 2 = 4$ → Dos y dos son cuatro.
$4 - 2 = 2$ → Cuatro menos dos son dos.

1. $2 + 4 = ?$
2. $8 + 17 = ?$
3. $11 + 1 = ?$
4. $3 + 18 = ?$
5. $9 + 6 = ?$
6. $5 + 4 = ?$
7. $1 + 13 = ?$
8. $15 - 2 = ?$
9. $9 - 9 = ?$
10. $13 - 8 = ?$
11. $14 + 12 = ?$
12. $23 - 13 = ?$
13. $1 + 4 = ?$
14. $1 - 1 + 3 = ?$
15. $8 - 7 = ?$
16. $13 - 9 = ?$
17. $2 + 3 + 10 = ?$
18. $28 - 6 = ?$
19. $30 - 17 = ?$
20. $28 - 5 = ?$
21. $19 - 7 = ?$

■ Conversación

Preguntas (*Questions*)

1. ¿Cuántos (*How many*) estudiantes hay en la clase de español? ¿Cuántos estudiantes hay en clase hoy (*today*)? ¿Hay tres profesores o un profesor / una profesora?
2. ¿Cuántos días hay en una semana (*week*)? ¿Hay seis? (No, no hay...) ¿Cuántos días hay en un fin de semana (*weekend*)? ¿Cuántos días hay en el mes de febrero? ¿en el mes de junio? ¿Cuántos meses hay en un año?
3. Hay muchos edificios (*many buildings*) en una universidad. En esta (*this*) universidad, ¿hay una cafetería? (Sí, hay... / No, no hay...) ¿un teatro? ¿un laboratorio de lenguas (*languages*)? ¿un bar? ¿una clínica? ¿un hospital? ¿un museo? ¿muchos estudiantes? ¿muchos profesores?

Gustos° y preferencias

Likes

¿Te gusta el fútbol? → • Sí, me gusta mucho el fútbol.
• No, no me gusta el fútbol.

To indicate you like something:	**Me gusta** _____.
To indicate you don't like something:	**No me gusta** _____.
To ask a classmate if he or she likes something:	**¿Te gusta** _____?
To ask your instructor the same question:	**¿Le gusta** _____?

In the following conversations, you will use the word **el** to mean *the* with masculine nouns and the word **la** with feminine nouns. Don't try to memorize which nouns are masculine and which are feminine. Just get used to using the words **el** and **la** before nouns.

You will also be using a number of Spanish verbs in the infinitive form, which always ends in **-r**. Here are some examples: **estudiar** = *to study;* **comer** = *to eat.* Try to guess the meaning of the infinitives used in these activities from context. If someone asks you, for instance, **¿Te gusta *beber* Coca-Cola?,** it is a safe guess that **beber** means *to drink.*

En español, **fútbol** = soccer y **fútbol americano** = football

verb = a word that describes an action or a state of being

Do you like soccer? → • *Yes, I like soccer very much.* • *No, I don't like soccer.*

Vocabulario útil*

el café, el té, la limonada, la cerveza (beer)

la música moderna, la música clásica, el rap, la música *country*

la pizza, la pasta, la comida (*food*) **mexicana, la comida de la cafetería**

el actor _____, **la actriz** _____

el/la cantante (singer) _____
(**¡OJO!** The word **cantante** is used for both men *and* women.)

el cine (movies), **el teatro, la ópera, el arte abstracto, el fútbol**

■ Conversación

A. Gustos y preferencias

PASO 1 Make a list of six things you like and six things you don't like, following the model. If you wish, you may choose items from the **Vocabulario útil** box. All words are provided with the appropriate definite article, **el** or **la**, the Spanish equivalent of *the*, depending on the gender of the noun.

> MODELO: Me gusta *la clase de español*. No me gusta *la clase de matemáticas*.

> 1. Me gusta _____. No me gusta _____. 3. _____ 5. _____
> 2. Me gusta _____. No me gusta _____. 4. _____ 6. _____

PASO 2 Now ask a classmate if he or she shares your likes and dislikes.

> MODELO: ¿Te gusta la clase de español? ¿y la clase de matemáticas?

B. Más gustos y preferencias

PASO 1 Here are some useful verbs and nouns for talking about what you like. For each item, combine a verb (shaded) with a noun to form a sentence that is true for you. Can you use context to guess the meaning of verbs you don't know?

> MODELO: Me gusta _____. → Me gusta *estudiar inglés*.

> 1. beber   café   té   limonada   chocolate
> 2. comer   pizza   enchiladas   hamburguesas   pasta   ensalada
> 3. estudiar español   matemáticas   historia   computación (*computer science*)
> 4. hablar   español   con mis amigos (*with my friends*)   por teléfono (*on the phone*)
> 5. jugar   al tenis   al fútbol   al fútbol americano   al béisbol al basquetbol
> 6. tocar   la guitarra   el piano   el violín

PASO 2 Ask a classmate about his or her likes using your own preferences as a guide.

> MODELO: ¿Te gusta *comer enchiladas*?

PASO 3 Now ask your professor if he or she likes certain things.
¡OJO! Remember to address your professor in a formal manner if that is his or her preference.

> MODELO: ¿Le gusta *jugar al tenis*?

---

*The material in **Vocabulario útil** lists is not active; that is, it is not part of what you need to focus on learning at this point. You may use these words and phrases to complete exercises or to help you converse in Spanish, if you need them.*

¿Qué hora es?

Es la una.   **Son** las dos.   **Son** las cinco.

¿Qué hora es? is used to ask *What time is it?* In telling time, one says *Es* **la una** but *Son* **las dos** (**las tres, las cuatro,** and so on).

Es la una y {**cuarto.** / **quince.**}   Son las dos y {**media.** / **treinta.**}   Son las cinco **y diez.**   Son las ocho **y veinticinco.**

Note that from the hour to the half-hour, Spanish, like English, expresses time by adding minutes or a portion of an hour to the hour.

Son las dos **menos** {**cuarto.** / **quince.**}   Son las ocho **menos diez.**   Son las once **menos veinte.**

From the half-hour to the hour, Spanish usually expresses time by subtracting minutes or a part of an hour from the *next* hour.

NOTA COMUNICATIVA

Para expresar° la hora   Para... *To express*

de la mañana	A.M., in the morning
de la tarde	P.M., in the afternoon (and early evening)
de la noche	P.M., in the evening
en punto	exactly, on the dot, sharp
¿a qué hora...?	(at) what time . . . ?
a la una (**las dos,** . . .)	at 1:00 (2:00, . . .)

OJO Don't confuse **Es la... / Son las...** with **A la(s)...** The first two are used for telling time, the third for telling *at* what time something happens (at what time class starts, at what time one arrives, and so on).

Son las cuatro de la tarde **en punto.**   *It's exactly 4:00 P.M.*
¿A qué hora es la clase de español?   *(At) What time is Spanish class?*
Hay una recepción **a las once** de la mañana.   *There is a reception at 11:00 A.M.*

■ Práctica

A. ¡Atención! Listen as your instructor says a time of day. Find the clock or watch face that corresponds to the time you heard and say its number in Spanish. (Note the sun or the moon that accompanies each clock; these indicate whether the time shown is day or night.)

1.   **2.**   **3.**   **4.**   **5.**   **6.**   **7.**   **8.**

B. ¿Qué hora es? Express the time in full sentences in Spanish.

1. 1:00 P.M.   **4.** 1:30   **7.** 4:15   **9.** 9:10 on the dot
2. 6:00 P.M.   **5.** 3:15   **8.** 11:45 exactly **10.** 9:50 sharp
3. 11:00 A.M.   **6.** 6:45

■ Conversación

A. Entrevista

PASO 1 Ask a classmate at what time the following events or activities take place. He or she will answer according to the cue.

MODELO: la clase de español (10:00 A.M.) →
          ESTUDIANTE 1: ¿A qué hora es la clase de español?
          ESTUDIANTE 2: A las diez de la mañana… ¡en punto!

1. la clase de francés (1:45 P.M.)   **3.** la excursión (8:45 A.M.)
2. la sesión de laboratorio (3:10 P.M.) **4.** el concierto (7:30 P.M.)

PASO 2 Now ask at what time your partner likes to perform these activities. He or she should provide the necessary information.

MODELO: cenar (*to have dinner*) →
          ESTUDIANTE 1: ¿A qué hora te gusta cenar?
          ESTUDIANTE 2: Me gusta cenar a las ocho de la noche.

1. almorzar (*to have lunch*)   **3.** ir (*to go*) al (*to the*) laboratorio
2. mirar (*to watch*)   de lenguas
    la televisión   **4.** ir al cine

B. Situaciones. How might the following people greet each other if they met at the indicated time? With a classmate, create brief dialogues.

MODELO: Jorge y María, a las once de la noche →
        JORGE: Buenas noches, María.
        MARÍA: Hola, Jorge. ¿Cómo estás?
        JORGE: Bien, gracias. ¿Y tú?
        MARÍA: ¡Muy bien!

1. el profesor Martínez y Gloria, a las diez de la mañana
2. la Sra. López y la Srta. Luna, a las cuatro y media de la tarde
3. usted y su (*your*) profesor(a) de español, en la clase de español

Need more practice?

■ Workbook/Laboratory Manual
■ Interactive CD-ROM
■ Online Learning Center
  (www.mhhe.com/quetal7)

A LEER

ESTRATEGIA: Guessing Meaning from Context

You will recognize the meaning of a number of cognates in the following reading about the geography of the Hispanic world. In addition, you should be able to guess the meaning of the underlined words from the context (the words that surround them); they are the names of geographical features. The photo captions will also be helpful.

Note also that a series of headings divides the reading into brief parts. It is always a good idea to scan such headings before starting to read, in order to get a sense of a reading's overall content.

La geografía del mundo[a] hispánico

Introducción

La geografía del mundo hispánico es impresionante y muy variada. En algunas[b] regiones hay de todo.[c]

En las Américas

En la Argentina hay <u>pampas</u> extensas en el sur[d] y la <u>cordillera</u> de los Andes en el oeste. En partes de Venezuela, Colombia y el Ecuador, hay regiones tropicales de densa <u>selva</u>. En el Brasil está[e] el famoso <u>Río</u> Amazonas. En el centro de México y también[f] en El Salvador, Nicaragua y Colombia, hay <u>volcanes</u> activos. A veces[g] producen erupciones catastróficas. El Perú y Bolivia comparten[h] el enorme <u>Lago</u> Titicaca, situado en una <u>meseta</u> entre los dos países.[i]

La <u>cordillera</u> de los Andes, Chile

La <u>isla</u> de Caja de Muertos, Puerto Rico

En las naciones del Caribe

Cuba, Puerto Rico y la República Dominicana son tres <u>islas</u> situadas en el <u>Mar</u> Caribe. Las bellas playas[j] del Mar Caribe y de la <u>península</u> de Yucatán son populares entre[k] los turistas de todo el mundo.

[a]*world* [b]*some* [c]*de… a bit of everything* [d]*south* [e]*is* [f]*also* [g]*A… Sometimes* [h]*share* [i]*naciones* [j]*bellas… beautiful beaches* [k]*among*

En la Península Ibérica

España comparte[l] la Península Ibérica con Portugal. También tiene[m] una geografía variada. En el norte están los Pirineos, la <u>cordillera</u> que separa a España del[n] resto de Europa. Madrid, la capital del país, está situada en la <u>meseta</u> central. En las <u>costas</u> del sur y del este hay playas tan bonitas como las de[o] Latinoamérica y del Caribe.

Una <u>meseta</u> de La Mancha, España

Una <u>selva</u> tropical en Colombia

¿Y las <u>ciudades</u>?

Es importante mencionar también la gran[p] diversidad de las ciudades del mundo hispánico. En la Argentina está la gran ciudad de Buenos Aires. Muchos consideran a Buenos Aires «el París» o «la Nueva York» de Sudamérica. En Venezuela está Caracas, y en el Perú está Lima, la capital, y Cuzco, una ciudad antigua de origen indio.

Conclusión

En fin,[q] el mundo hispánico es diverso respecto a la geografía. ¿Y Norteamérica? ∎

La <u>ciudad</u> de Montevideo, Uruguay

[l]*shares* [m]*it has* [n]*from the* [o]*tan… as pretty as those of* [p]*great* [q]*En… In short*

Comprensión

A. Ejemplos (*Examples*).   Demonstrate your understanding of the words underlined in the reading and other words from the reading by giving an example of a similar geographical feature found in this country or close to it. Then give an example from the Spanish-speaking world.

MODELO: un río → *the Mississippi*, el Río Orinoco

1. un lago
2. una cordillera
3. un río
4. una isla
5. una playa
6. una costa
7. un mar
8. un volcán
9. una península

B. Descripciones.   Write short sentences with the following words, based on the information provided in **A leer** or on your own knowledge of world geography.

MODELOS: una ciudad → Buenos Aires es una ciudad de la Argentina.
           un lago → En el Canadá hay lagos.

1. una ciudad
2. una capital
3. un lago
4. un volcán
5. una playa
6. una isla
7. una nación
8. una península
9. un río
10. un mar

VIDEOTECA

Entre amigos: ¡Encantada!

You will watch a video clip of four college students who meet each other for the first time. What questions do you think they will ask each other? Before watching the video, read the following questions. As you watch, don't worry if you don't understand every word. Try to get the gist of the conversation, listening carefully for names and where people are from. Watch the video a second time and listen for the answers to the questions.

1. ¿De dónde es Miguel?
2. ¿Cuántos años tiene (*How old is*) Tané, la señorita de Cuba?
3. ¿De dónde es Rubén?
4. ¿Cómo se llama la señorita de Venezuela?
5. ¿Cuántos años tiene Rubén?

En resumen

VOCABULARIO

Practice this vocabulary with digital flash cards on the Online Learning Center (www.mhhe.com/quetal7).

Although you have used and heard many words in this preliminary chapter of *¿Qué tal?*, the following words are the ones considered to be active vocabulary. Be sure that you know all of them, including the meaning of all of the words in group titles, before beginning **Capítulo 1.**

Saludos y expresiones de cortesía

Buenos días. Buenas tardes. Buenas noches.
  Muy buenas.
Hola. ¿Qué tal? ¿Cómo está(s)?
Regular. (Muy) Bien.
¿Y tú? ¿Y usted?
Adiós. Hasta mañana. Hasta luego. Nos vemos.

¿Cómo te llamas? ¿Cómo se llama usted?
  Me llamo _____.

¿De dónde eres? ¿De dónde es usted?
  (Yo) Soy de _____.

señor (Sr.), señora (Sra.), señorita (Srta.)

(Muchas) Gracias.
De nada. No hay de qué.
Por favor. Perdón. Con permiso.
Mucho gusto. Igualmente. Encantado/a.

¿Cómo es usted?

soy, eres, es

Los números 0–30

cero	
uno	once
dos	doce
tres	trece
cuatro	catorce
cinco	quince
seis	dieciséis
siete	diecisiete
ocho	dieciocho
nueve	diecinueve
diez	veinte
	treinta

Gustos y preferencias

¿Te gusta _____? ¿Le gusta _____?

(Sí,) Me gusta _____. (No,) No me gusta _____.

¿Qué hora es?

es la… , son las…
y/menos cuarto (quince)
y media (treinta)
en punto
de la mañana (tarde, noche)
¿a qué hora… ?, a la(s)…

Palabras interrogativas

¿cómo?	how?; what?
¿dónde?	where?
¿qué?	what?

Palabras adicionales

sí	yes
no	no
hay	there is/are
no hay	there is not / are not
hoy	today
mañana	tomorrow
y	and
o	or
a	to; at (*with time*)
de	of; from
en	in; on; at
pero	but
también	also

En la universidad

Unos estudiantes universitarios que hablan de (who are talking about) las clases

EN LA CLASE

la pizarra

la profesora

el profesor

la ventana

la puerta

Rosa

la estudiante

el estudiante

Javier

el diccionario

el libro de texto

la calculadora

el bolígrafo

el dinero

la silla

la mesa

el cuaderno

la mochila

el papel

el libro

el escritorio

el lápiz

¿Dónde? Lugares en la universidad

la biblioteca	the library
la cafetería	the cafeteria
la clase	the class(room)
el edificio	the building
la librería	the bookstore
la oficina	the office
la residencia	the dormitory

¿Quién? Personas

el bibliotecario	the (male) librarian
la bibliotecaria	the (female) librarian

el compañero de clase	the (male) classmate
la compañera de clase	the (female) classmate
el compañero de cuarto	the (male) roommate
la compañera de cuarto	the (female) roommate
el consejero	the (male) advisor
la consejera	the (female) advisor
el hombre	the man
la mujer	the woman
el secretario	the (male) secretary
la secretaria	the (female) secretary

■ **Conversación**

A. ¿Dónde están ahora (*are they now*)**?** First, tell where these people are. Then identify the numbered people and things: 1 = **la consejera,** 2 = **la estudiante,** and so on. Refer to the drawing and lists on page 22 as much as you need to.

1. Están en _____.

2. Están en _____.

MATRÍCULA I TRIMESTRE

3. Están en _____.

4. Están en _____.

B. Identificaciones. ¿Es hombre o mujer?

MODELO: ¿La consejera? → Es mujer.

1. ¿El profesor?
2. ¿La estudiante?
3. ¿El secretario?
4. ¿El estudiante?
5. ¿La bibliotecaria?
6. ¿El compañero de cuarto?

PASO 1

NOTA CULTURAL

Las universidades del mundoᵃ hispánico

Universities have a long history in the Spanish-speaking world. The very first university in the western hemisphere was **la Universidad de Santo Domingo,** founded in 1538 in what is now the Dominican Republic. Other early universities in this hemisphere include **la Real y Pontificia Universidad de América** (Mexico City, 1553) and **la Universidad de San Marcos** (Lima, Peru, 1551). Early Spanish colonial cities were meticulously designed and planned, and it is no accident that these universities were established in three of the most important cities. The Spaniards already had almost 300 years of experience with university-level education. **La Universidad de Salamanca,** one of the oldest universities in the world, was founded in 1220 in Salamanca, Spain.

_____

ᵃ*world*

Esta estatua de Fray Luis de León está en la Universidad de Salamanca. La Universidad, que (which) *data del año 1220 (*mil doscientos veinte*), es una de las más antiguas (*oldest*) del mundo.*

LAS MATERIAS°

Las… (*School*) *Subjects*

The names for most of these subject areas are cognates. See if you can recognize their meaning without looking at the English equivalent. You should learn in particular the names of subject areas that are of interest to you.

la administración de empresas	business
las comunicaciones	communications
la economía	economics
el español	Spanish
la filosofía	philosophy
la literatura	literature
las matemáticas	mathematics
la sociología	sociology
las ciencias	sciences
las humanidades	humanities
las lenguas (extranjeras)	(foreign) languages

■ Conversación

A. Asociaciones. ¿Con qué materia(s) asocia usted las siguientes (*following*) cosas (*things*) y las siguientes personas?

1. el nitrógeno, el hidrógeno
2. la doctora Joyce Brothers, el doctor Sigmund Freud
3. NBC, CBS
4. Sócrates, Nietzsche
5. Mark Twain, Toni Morrison, J. K. Rowling
6. Frida Kahlo, Pablo Picasso
7. Microsoft, IBM
8. la civilización azteca, una guerra (*war*) civil

B. ¿Qué estudia usted? (*What are you studying?*) The right-hand column lists a number of university subjects. Tell about your academic interests by creating sentences using one word or phrase from each column. You can tell what you *are* studying (**Estudio…**), *want* to study (**Deseo estudiar…**), *need* to study (**Necesito estudiar…**), and *like* to study (**Me gusta estudiar…**). Using the word **no** makes the sentence negative.

(No) Estudio _____.
(No) Deseo estudiar _____.
(No) Necesito estudiar _____.
(No) Me gusta estudiar _____.

+

español, francés, inglés
arte, filosofía, literatura, música
ciencias políticas, historia
antropología, sicología, sociología
biología, física, química
matemáticas, computación
¿ ?

NOTA COMUNICATIVA

Palabras interrogativas

You have already used a number of interrogative words and phrases to get information. Those and some other useful ones are listed here. You will learn more in later chapters.

¿a qué hora?	¿A qué hora es la clase?	**¿cuántos?,**	¿Cuántos días hay en una semana?
¿cómo?	¿Cómo estás? ¿Cómo es Gloria Estefan?	**¿cuántas?**	¿Cuántas naciones hay en Sudamérica?
	¿Cómo te llamas?	**¿dónde?**	¿Dónde está España?
¿cuál?*	¿Cuál es la capital de Colombia?	**¿qué?***	¿Qué es un hospital? ¿Qué es esto (*this*)?
¿cuándo?	¿Cuándo es la fiesta?		¿Qué hora es?
¿cuánto?	¿Cuánto (*How much*) es?	**¿quién?**	¿Quién es el presidente?

Note that in Spanish the voice falls at the end of questions that begin with interrogative words.

¿Qué es un tren?   ¿Cómo estás?

> **interrogative** = a word, phrase, or sentence used to ask a question

---

*Use **¿qué?** to mean* what? *when you are asking for a definition or an explanation. Use **¿cuál?** to mean* what? *in all other circumstances. See also* **Gramática 28** *in* **Capítulo 9.**

C. Preguntas (*Questions*).   What questions are being asked by the indicated people? More than one answer is possible for some items. Select questions from the following list or create your own questions.

PREGUNTAS

¿A qué hora es el programa sobre (*about*) México?

¿Cómo estás?

¿Cuál es la capital de Colombia?

¿Cuándo es la fiesta?

¿Cuántas personas hay en la fiesta?

¿Dónde está Buenos Aires?

¿Dónde está el diccionario?

¿Qué es esto (*this*)?

¿Qué hay en la televisión hoy?

¿Quién es?

D. Entrevista.   Work with a classmate and use the following questions to interview each other. Find out as much as possible about each other's classes and schedules. Follow up your answers by returning the question or asking for more information.

MODELO: ESTUDIANTE 1: ¿Qué estudias este semestre/trimestre (*this term*)?

ESTUDIANTE 2: Estudio matemáticas, historia, literatura y español. Y tú, ¿qué estudias?

1. ¿Qué estudias este semestre/trimestre?
2. ¿Cuántas horas estudias por semana (*per week*)?
3. ¿Cuándo estudias, por (*in*) la mañana, por la tarde o por la noche?
4. ¿Dónde te gusta estudiar?
5. ¿Quién es tu profesor favorito (profesora favorita)? (Mi profesor...)
6. ¿Cuál es tu clase favorita? (Mi clase...)

Need more practice?

■ Workbook/Laboratory Manual
■ Interactive CD-ROM
■ Online Learning Center
  (www.mhhe.com/quetal7)

PRONUNCIACIÓN: DIPHTHONGS AND LINKING

Two successive weak vowels (**i, u**) or a combination of a strong vowel (**a, e,** or **o**) and a weak vowel (**i** or **u**) are pronounced as a single syllable in Spanish, forming a *diphthong* (**un diptongo**): **L**u**is, si**e**te, c**u**aderno.**

When words are combined to form phrases, clauses, and sentences, they are linked together in pronunciation. In spoken Spanish, it is usually impossible to hear the word boundaries—that is, where one word ends and another begins.

> **diphthong** = a combination of two vowel sounds in one syllable

A. Vocales. Más práctica con las vocales.

1. hablar   regular   reservar   compañera
2. trece   clase   papel   general
3. pizarra   oficina   bolígrafo   libro
4. hombre   profesor   dólares   los
5. universidad   gusto   lugar   mujer

B. Diptongos. Practique las siguientes palabras.

1. historia   secretaria   gracias   estudiante   materia
2. bien   Oviedo   siete   ciencias   diez
3. secretario   biblioteca   adiós   diccionario   Antonio
4. cuaderno   Eduardo   el Ecuador   Guatemala   Managua
5. bueno   nueve   luego   pueblo   Venezuela

C. Frases y oraciones (*sentences*). Practice saying each phrase or sentence as if it were one long word, pronounced without a pause.

1. el papel y el lápiz
2. la profesora y la estudiante
3. las ciencias y las matemáticas
4. la historia y la sicología
5. la secretaria y el profesor
6. el inglés y el español
7. la clase en la biblioteca
8. el libro en la librería
9. Es la una y media.
10. Hay siete estudiantes en la oficina.
11. No estoy muy bien.
12. No hay un consejero en la clase.
13. Hay siete edificios en la universidad.
14. Estudio historia y comercio.
15. Deseo estudiar computación y matemáticas.
16. Necesito un diccionario y una mochila.

1 Identifying People, Places, Things, and Ideas
Singular Nouns: Gender and Articles*

En *la clase* del *profesor* Durán: *El primer día*

PROFESOR DURÁN: Aquí está *el programa* del *curso*. Son necesarios *el libro* de *texto* y *un diccionario*. También hay *una lista* de *novelas* y *libros* de *poesía*.

ESTUDIANTE 1:   ¡Es *una lista* infinita!

ESTUDIANTE 2:   Sí, y *los libros* cuestan demasiado.

ESTUDIANTE 1:   No, *el problema* no es *el precio* de *los libros*. ¡Es *el tiempo* para leer *los libros*!

Comprensión

Elija (*Choose*) las palabras o frases correctas según (*according to*) el diálogo.

1. La clase del profesor Durán es de (literatura / filosofía).
2. En el curso del profesor Durán (es necesario / no es necesario) leer (*to read*) mucho.
3. En un curso de literatura (es lógico / no es lógico) usar un diccionario.

To name people, places, things, or ideas, you need to be able to use nouns. In Spanish, all *nouns* (**los sustantivos**) have either masculine or feminine *gender* (**el género**). This is a purely grammatical feature of nouns; it does not mean that Spanish speakers perceive things or ideas as having male or female attributes.

Since the gender of all nouns must be memorized, it is best to learn the definite article along with the noun; that is, learn **el lápiz** rather than just **lápiz.** The definite article will be given with nouns in vocabulary lists in this book.

> **article** = a determiner that sets off a noun
>
> **definite article** = an article that indicates a specific noun
>
> **indefinite article** = an article that indicates an unspecified noun

	Masculine Nouns		Feminine Nouns	
Definite Articles	**el** hombre	*the man*	**la** mujer	*the woman*
	el libro	*the book*	**la** mesa	*the table*
Indefinite Articles	**un** hombre	*a (one) man*	**una** mujer	*a (one) woman*
	un libro	*a (one) book*	**una** mesa	*a (one) table*

*The grammar sections of ¿Qué tal? are numbered consecutively throughout the book. If you need to review a particular grammar point, the index will refer you to its page number.

In Professor Durán's class: The first day PROFESSOR DURÁN: *Here's the course syllabus. The textbook and a dictionary are required. There is also a list of novels and poetry books.* STUDENT 1: *It's a really long list!* STUDENT 2: *Yes, and the books cost too much.* STUDENT 1: *No, the problem isn't the price of the books. It's the time to read the books!*

Gender

A. Nouns that refer to male beings and most other nouns that end in **-o** are *masculine* (**masculino**) in gender.	**sustantivos masculinos:** hombre, libro
B. Nouns that refer to female beings and most other nouns that end in **-a, -ción, -tad,** and **-dad** are *feminine* (**femenino**) in gender.	**sustantivos femeninos:** mujer, mesa, nación, libertad, universidad
C. Nouns that have other endings and that do not refer to either male or female beings may be masculine or feminine. The gender of these words must be memorized.	el lápiz, la clase, la tarde, la noche

D. Many nouns that refer to people indicate gender . . .

1. by changing the last vowel.

OR

| | el compañero → la compañer**a** |
| | el bibliotecario → la bibliotecari**a** |

2. by adding **-a** to the last consonant of the masculine form to make it feminine.

| | un profesor → una profesor**a** |

E. Many other nouns that refer to people have a single form for both masculine and feminine genders. Gender is indicated by an article.	**el** estudiante → **la** estudiante
	(*the male student*) (*the female student*)
	el cliente → **la** cliente
	(*the male client*) (*the female client*)
However, a few nouns that end in **-e** also have a feminine form that ends in **-a.**	el presidente → la president**a**
	(*the male president*) (*the female president*)
	el dependiente → la dependient**a**
	(*the male clerk*) (*the female clerk*)

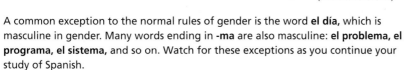

OJO A common exception to the normal rules of gender is the word **el día,** which is masculine in gender. Many words ending in **-ma** are also masculine: **el problema, el programa, el sistema,** and so on. Watch for these exceptions as you continue your study of Spanish.

Articles

A. In English, there is only one *definite article* (**el artículo definido**): *the*. In Spanish, the definite article for masculine singular nouns is **el;** for feminine singular nouns it is **la.**	definite article: *the*
	m. sing. → **el**
	f. sing. → **la**
B. In English, the singular *indefinite article* (**el artículo indefinido**) is *a* or *an*. In Spanish, the indefinite article, like the definite article, must agree with the gender of the noun: **un** for masculine nouns, **una** for feminine nouns. **Un** and **una** can mean *one* as well as *a* or *an*. Context determines meaning.	indefinite article: *a, an*
	m. sing. → **un**
	f. sing. → **una**

PASO 2

Need more practice?

- Workbook/Laboratory Manual
- Interactive CD-ROM
- Online Learning Center
  (www.mhhe.com/quetal7)

Categorías

cosa
edificio
materia
persona

■ Práctica

A. Artículos

PASO 1   Dé (*Give*) el artículo definido apropiado (**el, la**).

1. escritorio	5. hombre	9. mujer
2. biblioteca	6. diccionario	10. nación
3. bolígrafo	7. universidad	11. bibliotecario
4. mochila	8. dinero	12. calculadora

PASO 2   Ahora (*Now*) dé el artículo indefinido apropiado (**un, una**).

1. día	4. lápiz	7. papel
2. mañana	5. clase	8. condición
3. problema	6. noche	9. programa

B. Escenas de la universidad

PASO 1   Haga una oración (*Form a sentence*) con las palabras indicadas.

MODELO: estudiante / librería → Hay un estudiante en la librería.

1. consejero / oficina	6. bolígrafo / silla
2. profesora / clase	7. palabra / papel
3. lápiz / mesa	8. oficina / residencia
4. cuaderno / escritorio	9. compañero / biblioteca
5. libro / mochila	

PASO 2   Now create new sentences by changing one of the words in each item in **Paso 1**. If you do this with a partner, try to come up with as many variations as possible.

MODELO: Hay un estudiante en *la residencia*. (Hay *una profesora* en la librería.)

■ Conversación

A. Definiciones.   Con un compañero / una compañera, defina estas palabras en español según el modelo.

MODELO: biblioteca / edificio → ESTUDIANTE 1: ¿La biblioteca?
                                              ESTUDIANTE 2: Es un edificio.

1. cliente / persona	4. dependiente / ¿ ?	7. computación / ¿ ?
2. bolígrafo / cosa	5. hotel (*m.*) / ¿ ?	8. inglés / ¿ ?
3. residencia / edificio	6. calculadora / ¿ ?	9. ¿ ?

B. Asociaciones.   Identifique una cosa y una persona que usted asocia con los siguientes lugares.

MODELO: la clase → una silla, un profesor

1. la biblioteca   2. la librería   3. una oficina   4. la residencia

---

Autoprueba means Self-quiz. *These self-quizzes appear at the end of* **Gramática** *explanations and will help you determine if you understand the basics of the grammar point.*

2 Identifying People, Places, Things, and Ideas
Nouns and Articles: Plural Forms

- You can find many nouns in this ad. Can you guess the meaning of most of them?
- Some of the nouns in this ad are plural. Can you tell how to make nouns plural in Spanish, based on these nouns?
- Look for the Spanish equivalent of the following words.

    adult   preparation   program   course

- **Idioma** is another word for *language*, and it is a false cognate. It never means *idiom*.
- Using the vocabulary in the ad, guess what **en el extranjero** means.

Cursos de Idiomas en el Extranjero

Financiación
SIN INTERESES
en 3, 6 ó 12 meses

- Cursos para jóvenes de 7 a 17 años
- Cursos para adultos a partir de 18 años
- Cursos en Universidades: Idioma general y/o técnico
- Minimasters en Universidades USA, Inglaterra e Irlanda
- Programa residencial en Sevilla y/o Madrid con inglés
- Preparación para TOEFL, GMAT, SAT, GRE, USMLE
- Cursos de idiomas en Madrid

Instituto ProLengua ofrece pagar su curso aplazado en 3, 6 ó 12 meses

INSTITUTO PROLENGUA

Infórmate
902-253 797

	Singular	Plural	
Nouns Ending in a Vowel	**el** libro	**los** libros	*the books*
	la mesa	**las** mesas	*the tables*
	un libro	**unos** libros	*some books*
	una mesa	**unas** mesas	*some tables*
Nouns Ending in a Consonant	**la** universidad	**las** universidad**es**	*the universities*
	un papel	**unos** papel**es**	*some papers*

A. Spanish nouns that end in a vowel form plurals by adding **-s.** Nouns that end in a consonant add **-es.** Nouns that end in the consonant **-z** change the **-z** to **-c** before adding **-es: lápiz → lápices.**

Plurals in Spanish:

vowel + **–s**
consonant + **–es**
–z → –ces

B. The definite and indefinite articles also have plural forms: **el → los, la → las, un → unos, una → unas. Unos** and **unas** mean *some, several,* or *a few.*

el → los
la → las
un → unos
una → unas

C. In Spanish, the masculine plural form of a noun is used to refer to a group that includes both males and females.

los amig**os**
the friends (both male and female)

unos extranjer**os**
some foreigners (both male and female)

PASO 2

Palabras útiles

la computadora
el experimento
la planta
el teléfono

Need more practice?

- Workbook/Laboratory Manual
- Interactive CD-ROM
- Online Learning Center
  (www.mhhe.com/quetal7)

■ Práctica

A. Singular → plural. Dé la forma plural.

1. la mesa
2. el papel
3. el amigo
4. la oficina
5. un cuaderno
6. un lápiz
7. una universidad
8. un bolígrafo

B. Plural → singular. Dé la forma singular.

1. los profesores
2. las calculadoras
3. las bibliotecarias
4. los estudiantes
5. unos hombres
6. unas tardes
7. unas residencias
8. unas sillas
9. unos escritorios

■ Conversación

A. Identificaciones. Identifique las personas, las cosas y los lugares.

MODELO: Hay _____ en _____. → Hay *unos estudiantes* en *la clase*.

1.

2.

Palabras útiles

la **alfombra** (rug)
la **almohada** (pillow)
la **cama** (bed)
el **cuadro** (picture)
el **espejo** (mirror)
la **lámpara** (lamp)
el **monitor**

B. ¡Ojo alerta! (*Eagle eye!*)* ¿Cuáles son las semejanzas (*similarities*) y las diferencias entre los dos cuartos? Hay por lo menos (*at least*) seis diferencias. Después de identificar (*After identifying*) las diferencias, indique qué hay en su propio (*your own*) cuarto.

MODELOS: En el dibujo A, hay _____. En el dibujo B, hay sólo (*only*) _____.
En el escritorio del dibujo A, hay _____.
En mi cuarto hay _____. En mi escritorio hay _____.

Ⓐ

Ⓑ

---

*In Spanish, activities like this one are often called **¡Ojo alerta!**

Voces de los Estados Unidos

LITERATURA: Sandra Cisneros

Sobre (About) **la autora:** *Sandra Cisneros was born in Chicago. She is one of the most prominent Hispanic female writers in the United States. She writes in English, but her prose and poetry are infused with the Hispanic-American experience. She now lives and writes in San Antonio, Texas. The following is from the novel* Caramelo *(2002).*

Outside, roaring like the ocean, Chicago traffic from the Northwest and Congress Expressways. Inside, another roar; in Spanish from the kitchen radio, in English from TV cartoons, and in a mix of the two from her boys begging for, —*Un nikle* for Italian lemonade. But Aunty Licha doesn't hear anything. Under her breath Aunty is bargaining,

—*Virgen Purísima,* if we even make it to Laredo, even that, I'll say three rosaries . . .

Sandra Cisneros
(1954–)

MÚSICA: El tejano

El tejano, un género[a] musical mexico-americano, tradicionalmente se toca[b] con el acordeón y el bajo sexto.[c] Esta[d] música tradicional es especialmente popular en el suroeste[e] de los Estados Unidos.

[a]*genre, type*   [b]*se... is played*   [c]*bajo... type of guitar*   [d]*This*
[e]*southwest*

La joven estrella[f] Selena (1971–1995 [mil novecientos setenta y uno a mil novecientos noventa y cinco]), que cantaba[g] en inglés y español, popularizó[h] el tejano fuera de[i] la comunidad mexicoamericana.

[f]*joven... young star*   [g]*que... who sang*   [h]*popularized*   [i]*fuera... outside of*

Los Lonely Boys, un conjunto[j] popular que canta principalmente en inglés, representa la nueva onda[k] del tejano. Su[l] música, rock «texicano», es una fusión de diferentes estilos.[m]

[j]*band*   [k]*nueva... new wave*   [l]*Their*   [m]*styles*

3 Expressing Actions Subject Pronouns; Present Tense of *-ar* Verbs; Negation

Diego *habla* de su vida con su amiga Lupe

Imagine que usted es Lupe y conteste las preguntas de Diego. Use **no** si es necesario.

DIEGO: *Yo hablo* con mi familia con frecuencia. Por eso *pago* mucho en cuentas de teléfono. ¿Y *tú*?

LUPE: [...]

DIEGO: *Necesito* dinero para *comprar* libros. Por eso *enseño* inglés a un estudiante de matemáticas. ¿Y *tú*?

LUPE: [...]

DIEGO: En mi tiempo libre *escucho* música. También *toco* la guitarra. En las fiestas *bailo* mucho y *tomo* cerveza con mis amigos. Los fines de semana, *busco* libros de antropología en las librerías. ¿Y *tú*?

LUPE: [...]

Comprensión: ¿Cierto o falso?

1. Diego no habla mucho con su familia.
2. Es estudiante de ciencias.
3. No le gusta la música.
4. Es una persona introvertida y solitaria.
5. Enseña francés.

Subject Pronouns

subject = the person or thing that performs the action

pronoun = a word that takes the place of a noun or represents a person

Subject Pronouns			
Singular		**Plural**	
yo	I	**nosotros / nosotras**	we
tú	you (*fam.*)	**vosotros / vosotras**	you (*fam. Sp.*)
usted (Ud.)*	you (*form.*)	**ustedes (Uds.)***	you (*form.*)
él	he	**ellos**	they (*m, m. + f.*)
ella	she	**ellas**	they (*f.*)

Diego talks about his life with his friend Lupe Imagine that you are Lupe and answer Diego's questions. Use no if necessary.
DIEGO: *I speak often with my family. That's why I pay a lot in telephone bills. And you?* LUPE: [...]
DIEGO: *I need money to buy books. That's why I teach English to a math student. And you?* LUPE: [...]
DIEGO: *In my spare time I listen to music. I also play the guitar. At parties I dance a lot and drink beer with my friends. On weekends, I look for anthropology books in bookstores. And you?* LUPE: [...]

***Usted** and **ustedes** are frequently abbreviated in writing as **Ud.** or **Vd.**, and **Uds.** or **Vds.**, respectively.*

A. *Subject pronouns* (**Los pronombres personales**) can represent the person that performs the action in a sentence.

In Spanish, several subject pronouns have masculine and feminine forms. The masculine plural form is used to refer to a group of males as well as to a group of males and females.

Mark → *he*   Marcos → **él**
Martha → *she*   Marta → **ella**
Mark and Paul →   Marcos y Pablo →
   they   **ellos** (*all male*)
Mark and Martha →   Marcos y Marta →
   they   **ellos** (*male and female*)
Martha and Emily →   Marta y Emilia →
   they   **ellas** (*all female*)

B. Spanish has different words for *you*. In general, **tú** is used to refer to a close friend or a member of your family, while **usted** is used with people with whom the speaker has a more formal or distant relationship. The situations in which **tú** and **usted** are used also vary among different countries and regions.

tú → close friend, family member

usted (Ud.) → formal or distant relationship

C. In Latin America and in the United States and Canada, the plural for both **usted** and **tú** is **ustedes**. In Spain, however, **vosotros/vosotras** is the plural of **tú**, while **ustedes** is used as the plural of **usted** exclusively.

Latin America, North America

tú
usted (Ud.) } ustedes (Uds.)

Spain

tú → vosotros/vosotras
usted (Ud.) → ustedes (Uds.)

D. Subject pronouns are not used as frequently in Spanish as they are in English and may usually be omitted. You will learn more about the uses of Spanish subject pronouns in **Capítulo 2.**

Present Tense of -*ar* Verbs

Past ----------------- **PRESENT** ---------------- Future
present

A. The *infinitive* (**el infinitivo**) of a verb indicates the action or state of being, with no reference to who or what performs the action or when it is done (present, past, or future). In Spanish all infinitives end in **-ar, -er,** or **-ir.** Infinitives in English are indicated by *to: to* speak, *to* eat, *to* live.

-ar: habl**ar**   *to speak*
-er: com**er**   *to eat*
-ir: viv**ir**   *to live*

infinitive = a verb form expressing action or condition without reference to person, tense, or number

tense = the form of a verb indicating time: present, past, or future

B. To *conjugate* (**conjugar**) a verb means to give the various forms of the verb with their corresponding subjects: *I speak, you speak, she speaks,* and so on. All regular Spanish verbs are conjugated by adding *personal endings* (**las terminaciones personales**) that reflect the subject doing the action. These are added to the *stem* (**la raíz** or **el radical**), which is the infinitive minus the infinitive ending.

Infinitive		Stem
hablar	→	habl-
comer	→	com-
vivir	→	viv-

C. The right-hand column shows the personal endings that are added to the stem of all regular **-ar** verbs to form the *present tense* (**el presente**).

Regular **-ar** verb endings in the present tense:
o, -as, -a, -amos, -áis, -an

hablar (*to speak; to talk*): habl-					
Singular			**Plural**		
(yo)	habl**o**	*I speak*	(nosotros) (nosotras)	habl**amos**	*we speak*
(tú)	habl**as**	*you speak*	(vosotros) (vosotras)	habl**áis**	*you speak*
(Ud.) (él) (ella)	habl**a**	*you speak* *he speaks* *she speaks*	(Uds.) (ellos) (ellas)	habl**an**	*you speak* *they (m.) speak* *they (f.) speak*

D. Some important **-ar** verbs in this chapter include those in the drawings and list on the right.

bailar
cantar
tocar
escuchar

buscar	*to look for*
comprar	*to buy*
desear	*to want*
enseñar	*to teach*
estudiar	*to study*
hablar	*to speak; to talk*
necesitar	*to need*
pagar	*to pay (for)*
practicar	*to practice*
regresar	*to return* (to a place)
tomar	*to take; to drink*
trabajar	*to work*

OJO Note that in Spanish the meaning of the English word *for* is included in the verbs **buscar** (*to look for*) and **pagar** (*to pay for*); *to* is included in **escuchar** (*to listen to*).

E. As in English, when two Spanish verbs are used in sequence and there is no change of subject, the second verb is usually in the infinitive form.

Necesito llamar a mi familia.
I need to call my family.

Me gusta bailar.
I like to dance.

F. In both English and Spanish, conjugated verb forms also indicate the *time* or *tense* (**el tiempo**) of the action: *I speak* (present), *I spoke* (past).

Some English equivalents of the present tense forms of Spanish verbs are shown at the right.

hablo {

I speak	Simple present tense
I am speaking	Present progressive (indicates an action in progress)
I will speak	Near future action

Negation

In Spanish the word **no** is placed before the conjugated verb to make a negative sentence.

El estudiante **no** habla español.
The student doesn't speak Spanish.

No, **no** necesito dinero.
No, I don't need money.

■ Práctica

A. Mis compañeros y yo

PASO 1 **¡Anticipemos!*** Read the following statements and tell whether they are true for you and your classmates and for your classroom environment. If any statement is not true for you or your class, make it negative or change it in another way to make it correct.

MODELO: Toco el piano → Sí, toco el piano.
(No, no toco el piano. Toco la guitarra.)

1. Necesito más (*more*) dinero.
2. Trabajo en la biblioteca.
3. Tomo ocho clases este semestre/trimestre.
4. En clase, cantamos en francés.
5. Deseamos practicar español.
6. Tomamos café en clase.
7. El profesor / La profesora enseña italiano.
8. El profesor / La profesora habla muy bien el alemán (*German*).

PASO 2 Now turn to the person next to you and restate each sentence as a question, using **tú** forms of the verbs in all cases. Your partner will indicate whether the sentences are true for him or her.

MODELO: ¿Tocas el piano? → Sí, toco el piano. (No, no toco el piano.)

AUTOPRUEBA

Give the present tense endings for **pagar**.

1. yo pag____
2. tú pag____
3. ella pag____
4. nosotros pag____
5. ellos pag____

Answers: 1. pago 2. pagas 3. paga 4. pagamos 5. pagan

*****¡Anticipemos!** (*Lets look ahead!*) *identifies activities or* **pasos** *that allow you to see words and structures in context before you begin to use them actively.*

B. En una fiesta. The following paragraphs describe a party. First scan the paragraphs to get a general sense of their meaning. Then complete the paragraphs with the correct form of the numbered infinitives.

Esta noche[a] hay una fiesta en el apartamento de Marcos y Julio. Todos[b] los estudiantes (cantar[1]) y (bailar[2]). Una persona (tocar[3]) la guitarra y otras personas (escuchar[4]) la música.

Jaime (buscar[5]) una Coca-Cola. Marta (hablar[6]) con un amigo. María José (desear[7]) enseñarles a todos[c] un baile[d] de Colombia. Todas las estudiantes desean (bailar[8]) con el estudiante mexicano—¡él (bailar[9]) muy bien!

La fiesta es estupenda, pero todos (necesitar[10]) regresar a casa[e] o a su[f] cuarto temprano.[g] ¡Hay clases mañana!

[a]Esta... *Tonight* [b]*All* [c]enseñarles... *to teach everyone* [d]*dance* [e]a... *home* [f]*their* [g]*early*

Comprensión: ¿Cierto o falso?

1. Marcos es profesor de español.
2. A Jaime le gusta el café.
3. María José es de Colombia.
4. Los estudiantes desean bailar.

■ Conversación

NOTA COMUNICATIVA

The Verb *estar*

Estar is another Spanish **-ar** verb. It means *to be*, and you have already used forms of it to ask how others are feeling or to tell where things are located. Here is the complete present tense conjugation of **estar.** Note that the **yo** form is irregular. The other forms take regular **-ar** endings, and some have a shift in the stress pattern (indicated by the accented **á**).

yo	**estoy**	nosotros/as	**estamos**
tú	**estás**	vosotros/as	**estáis**
Ud., él, ella	**está**	Uds., ellos, ellas	**están**

You will learn the uses of the verb **estar,** along with those of **ser** (the other Spanish verb that means *to be*) gradually, over the next several chapters. In the following questions, **estar** is used to inquire about location or feelings.

1. ¿Cómo está Ud. en este momento (*right now*)?
2. ¿Cómo están sus (*your*) compañeros? (Mis compañeros...)
3. ¿Dónde está Ud. en este momento?

A. ¿Qué hacen? (*What are they doing?*)
Tell where these people are and
what they are doing. Note that the
definite article is used with titles
when you are talking about a
person: **el señor, la señora, la
señorita, el profesor, la profesora.**

> **Frases útiles**
>
> **hablar por teléfono**
> **preparar la lección**
> **pronunciar las palabras**
> **tomar apuntes** (to take notes)
> **trabajar en la caja** (at the register)
> **usar una computadora**

MODELO: La Sra. Martínez _____. →
La Sra. Martínez está en la
oficina. Busca un
documento, trabaja…

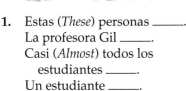

1. Estas (*These*) personas _____.
   La profesora Gil _____.
   Casi (*Almost*) todos los
   estudiantes _____.
   Un estudiante _____.

2. Estas personas están _____.
   El Sr. Miranda _____.
   La bibliotecaria _____.
   El estudiante _____.

3. Estas personas _____.
   El cliente _____.
   La dependienta _____.

B. Entrevista. Use the following questions as a guide to interview a
classmate, and take notes on what he or she says. (Write down what
your partner says using the **él/ella** form of the verbs.) Your instructor
may want you to hand in your notes so that he or she can get to know
the students in the class better.

> **Frases útiles**
>
> **por** (in) **la mañana**
> **por la tarde**
> **por la noche**

MODELO: ESTUDIANTE 1: Karen, ¿estudias filosofía?
ESTUDIANTE 2: No, no estudio filosofía. Estudio música.
ESTUDIANTE 1: (escribe [*writes*]): Karen no estudia filosofía.
Estudia música.

1. ¿Estudias mucho o poco (*a little*)? ¿Dónde estudias, en casa, en la
   residencia o en la biblioteca? ¿Cuándo estudias, por la mañana, por
   la tarde o por la noche?
2. ¿Cantas bien o mal (*poorly*)? ¿Tocas un instrumento musical? ¿Cuál
   es? (el piano, la guitarra, el violín…)
3. ¿Trabajas? ¿Dónde? ¿Cuántas horas a la semana (*per week*) trabajas?
   ¿Trabajas todos los días de la semana? ¿hasta muy tarde (*late*)?
4. ¿Quiénes pagan los libros de texto, tú o los profesores? ¿Qué más necesitas pagar? ¿Diccionarios? ¿el alquiler (*rent*)? ¿la matrícula (*tuition*)? ¿ ?

C. **¿Qué pasa** (*What's happening*) **en la fiesta?**

PASO 1 With a classmate, describe what's going on in the following scene.

MODELO: Pilar y Ana bailan en la fiesta.

Vocabulario útil

descansar (to rest)
escuchar
fumar (to smoke)
mirar (to watch)
  una película (a movie)
  la tele (TV)
tocar
  la batería (drums)
  la guitarra
  el piano
tomar
  cerveza
  refrescos (soft drinks)
  vino

PASO 2 Now compare the scene above with parties *you* go to. Use the **nosotros** form of verbs to describe what you and your friends do at these parties.

MODELO: Mis amigos y yo bailamos en las fiestas.

En los Estados Unidos y el Canadá

Jaime Escalante: Profesor de matemáticas

Jaime Escalante was born in La Paz, Bolivia, where he was a math and physics teacher for fourteen years. He emigrated to California in 1964 when he was 33. Since he did not speak English, he took menial jobs while he learned the language and went to college to become an accredited teacher. He started teaching in 1974 at Garfield High School, in East Los Angeles, where the students were mostly low-income Hispanics. In 1982, with Escalante's help, his students did so well on an advanced placement calculus test that the Educational Testing Service thought they had cheated and asked them to retake the test. The 1988 film *Stand and Deliver* portrays Escalante and his students' efforts. He was later awarded the United States Presidential Medal and the Andrés Bello award by the Organization of American States.

Jaime Escalante

UN POCO DE TODO

Lengua y cultura: La universidad perfecta.   Complete Ángela's letter to her cousin about her search for the perfect college. Give the correct form of the verbs in parentheses, as suggested by context. When two possibilities are given in parentheses, select the correct word.

Mi querida Carmen:

Mi amiga Luisa y yo buscamos la universidad perfecta para nosotras. Deseamos ser (compañeras / consejeras[1]) de cuarto.

Mañana (*nosotras:* visitar[2]) la Universidad de Texas en Austin. ¡(Ser[3]) muy grande[a]! Hay veinticuatro grupos sociales para estudiantes hispanos y (un/una[4]) biblioteca especial. (El/La[5]) colección latinoamericana es muy grande. (Los/Las[6]) materias más populares son (el/la[7]) administración de empresas, (el/la[8]) ingeniería, (los/las[9]) humanidades y (los/las[10]) comunicaciones. Muchos estudiantes (estudiar[11]) en (el/la[12]) Instituto de Estudios[b] Latinoamericanos y en (el/la[13]) Centro para Estudios Mexicoamericanos. La matrícula no es cara,[c] pero el problema es que no me gusta (el/la[14]) idea de estudiar en (un/una[15]) universidad muy grande.

(*Yo:* Desear[16]) estudiar en (un/una[17]) universidad menos grande, como Stanford. Tiene[d] nueve grupos sociales para estudiantes hispanos y (un/una[18]) casa especial para estudiantes de español. Se llama la Casa Zapata y es (un/una[19]) residencia. (Los/Las[20]) estudiantes (practicar[21]) español y participan en celebraciones hispanas. Las (mochilas/materias[22]) más populares de Stanford son la biología, (el/la[23]) economía, la sicología, (el/la[24]) inglés y (los/las[25]) ciencias políticas. Luisa y yo (visitar[26]) Stanford en dos semanas.[e] Pero la matrícula... ¡Los estudiantes (pagar[27]) mucho (dinero/papel[28]) para estudiar en Stanford!

Te hablo[f] por teléfono pronto.[g]
Con cariño,
Ángela

[a]*big* [b]*Studies* [c]*expensive* [d]*It has* [e]*weeks* [f]*Te... I'll speak to you* [g]*soon*

La Benson Latin American Collection (*en la Universidad de Texas en Austin*) *es una colección comprensiva de libros, documentos, revistas* (magazines) *y periódicos* (newspapers) *relacionados con* (related to) *Latinoamérica.*

Comprensión.   Which of these statements do you agree with after reading Ángela's letter? Change incorrect statements to make them true.

1. Luisa y Ángela son amigas.
2. Ángela desea estudiar en una universidad muy grande.
3. En el Instituto de Estudios Latinoamericanos hay pocos (*few*) estudiantes.
4. La Casa Zapata es una biblioteca importante.

Resources for Review and Testing Preparation

- Workbook/Laboratory Manual
- Interactive CD-ROM
- Online Learning Center (www.mhhe.com/quetal7)

VIDEOTECA

Entrevista cultural: Los Estados Unidos

Carlos Rivera is a university professor from San Antonio, Texas. In this interview, Professor Rivera talks about where he lives now and his experiences as a professor. Before watching the video clip, read the following excerpt from the interview.

INTERVIEWER: ¿Cuántas clases enseña Ud.?

PROF. RIVERA: Este semestre, enseño tres clases. Una clase de literatura contemporánea de los Estados Unidos, una clase de literatura chicana y una clase de composición.

Now watch the video clip and answer the following questions based on the interview.

1. Where does Professor Rivera live now?
2. What subject does Professor Rivera teach?
3. How many classes is Professor Rivera teaching this semester?
4. Does he have a favorite class? If so, what is it?
5. Why does Professor Rivera like his job?

Entre amigos: ¿Qué clases tomas?

Miguel, Tané, Rubén, and Karina are getting to know each other. What questions do you think they will ask each other? Before watching the video, read the following questions. As you watch, don't worry if you don't understand every word. Try to get the gist of the conversation, listening carefully for information about classes. Watch the video a second time and listen for the answers to the questions.

1. ¿De dónde es Rubén?
2. ¿Qué clases toma Rubén? (¡OJO! Rubén usa un sinónimo para «la computación».)
3. ¿Qué hace Miguel (*What does Miguel do*) los fines de semana?

───────────────── ENFOQUE CULTURAL ─────────────────

 Los hispanos en los Estados Unidos

¡Fíjese![a]

- En 2001 (dos mil uno) había[b] veintiún hispanos en el Congreso de los Estados Unidos. ¿Cuántos hay ahora? (www.house.gov)
- De los más de[c] 35 millones de hispanos en los Estados Unidos, la mayoría[d] habla español (mucho o poco).
- Las palabras **hispano** e[e] **hispánico** se refieren al[f] idioma y a la cultura, no a la raza[g] o grupo étnico.

[a]*Check it out!* [b]*there were* [c]*De… Of the more than* [d]*majority* [e]*y* [f]*se… refer to the* [g]*race*

Personas famosas: César Chávez

La contribución de César Chávez (1927–1993 [mil novecientos veintisiete a mil novecientos noventa y tres]) al movimiento de los trabajadores agrícolas[a] es enorme. La educación de Chávez, hijo de campesinos migrantes,[b] sólo llega al séptimo grado.[c]

En 1962 (mil novecientos sesenta y dos), Chávez organiza a los campesinos que cosechan uvas.[d] Como resultado de las huelgas[e] y el boicoteo de las uvas de mesa,[f] los campesinos reciben contratos más favorables para ellos; el United Farm Workers se establece[g] como sindicato[h] oficial.

En 2003 (dos mil tres), el servicio postal de los Estados Unidos honra a Chávez con un sello[i] especial.

Hoy en día,[j] la vida,[k] los sacrificios y los ideales de Chávez sirven de[l] inspiración a muchas personas.

[a]*trabajadores… agricultural workers* [b]*hijo… son of migrant farm workers* [c]*llega… reaches the seventh grade* [d]*que… who harvest grapes* [e]*strikes* [f]*uvas… table grapes* [g]*se… is established* [h]*union* [i]*stamp* [j]*Hoy… Nowadays* [k]*life* [l]*sirven… serve as an*

El sello estadounidense (U.S.) con la imagen de César Chávez

Learn more about Hispanics in the United States with the Video, Interactive CD-ROM, and the Online Learning Center (www.mhhe.com/quetal7).

PASO FINAL

A LEER

ESTRATEGIA: More on Guessing Meaning from Context

As you learned in **La geografía del mundo hispánico (Primeros pasos),** you can often guess the meaning of unfamiliar words from the context (the words that surround them) and by using your knowledge about the topic in general. Making "educated guesses" about words in this way will be an important part of your reading skills in Spanish.

What is the meaning of the underlined words in these sentences?

1. En una lista alfabetizada, la palabra **grande** aparece <u>antes de</u> **grotesco.**
2. El edificio no es moderno; es <u>viejo</u>.
3. Me gusta estudiar español, pero detesto la biología. En general, <u>odio</u> las ciencias como materia.

Some words are underlined in the following reading (and in the readings in subsequent chapters). Try to guess their meaning from context.

Like the passages in **Primeros pasos** and some others in subsequent chapters, this reading contains section subheadings. Scanning these subheadings in advance will help you make predictions about the reading's content, which will also help to facilitate your overall comprehension. Another useful way to manage longer passages is to read section by section. At this point, don't try to understand every word. Your main objective should be to understand the general content of the passage.

> **Sobre** (About) **la lectura...**
> This reading was written by the authors of *¿Qué tal?* for students of Spanish like you. Later on in this text, you will have the chance to read more "authentic" selections.

Las universidades hispánicas

Introducción

En el mundo hispánico —y en los Estados Unidos y el Canadá— hay universidades grandes[a] y <u>pequeñas</u>; públicas, religiosas y privadas; modernas y antiguas. Pero el concepto de «vida[b] universitaria» es diferente.

El *campus*

Por ejemplo, en los países[c] hispánicos la universidad no es un centro de actividad social. No hay muchas residencias estudiantiles. En general, los estudiantes <u>viven</u> en pensiones[d] o en casas particulares[e] y <u>llegan</u> a la universidad en coche o en autobús. En algunas[f] universidades hay un *campus* similar a los de[g] las universidades de los Estados Unidos y el Canadá. En estos casos se habla[h] de la «ciudad[i] universitaria». Otras universidades ocupan sólo un edificio grande, o posiblemente varios edificios, pero no hay zonas verdes.[j]

Estudiantes de medicina en Caracas, Venezuela

[a]*large* [b]*life* [c]*naciones* [d]*boardinghouses* [e]*private* [f]*some* [g]*los... those of* [h]*se... one speaks* [i]*city* [j]*green*

Los <u>deportes</u>

Otra diferencia es que en la mayoría de las universidades hispánicas los deportes no son muy importantes. Si los estudiantes desean practicar un deporte —el tenis, el fútbol o el béisbol— hay clubes deportivos, pero estos[k] no forman parte de la universidad.

Las diversiones[l]

Como se puede ver,[m] la forma y la organización de la universidad son diferentes en las dos culturas. Pero los estudiantes estudian y se divierten[n] en todas partes.[o] A los estudiantes hispanos, así como[p] a los estadounidenses* y canadienses,[q] les gusta mucho toda clase de música: la música clásica, la música con raíces[r] tradicionales y la música moderna —la nacional[s] y la <u>importada</u>. Y hay para todos: Usher, Alicia Keys, Green Day... Otras diversiones preferidas por los estudiantes son las discotecas y los cafés. Hay cafés ideales para hablar con los amigos. También hay exposiciones de arte, <u>obras</u> de teatro y películas[t] interesantes.

Conclusión

Los días favoritos de muchos jóvenes[u] hispánicos son los fines de semana. ¿Realmente son muy distintos los estudiantes hispanos? ∎

[k]*they* (lit. *these*) [l]*Las... Entertainment* [m]*Como... As you can see* [n]*se... have a good time* [o]*en... everywhere* [p]*así... like* [q]*estadounidenses... people from the United States and Canada* [r]*roots* [s]*la... (music) from their own country* [t]*movies* [u]*young people*

Comprensión

A. ¿Cierto o falso?   Indique si las siguientes oraciones son ciertas o falsas.

1. En los países hispánicos, la mayoría de los estudiantes vive en residencias.
2. En las universidades hispánicas, los deportes ocupan un lugar esencial en el programa de estudios del estudiante.
3. En una universidad hispánica, no hay mucho tiempo para asistir a (*time for attending*) conciertos y exposiciones de arte.
4. No hay mucha diferencia entre (*between*) una universidad hispánica y una universidad norteamericana con respecto al *campus.*
5. La música es una diversión para los estudiantes en todas partes.
6. Hay grandes jardines (*gardens*) y zonas verdes en las universidades hispánicas.

B. ¿Qué universidad?   Indique si las siguientes oraciones son de un estudiante de la Universidad de Sevilla o de un estudiante de la Universidad de Michigan... ¡o de los dos!

	SEVILLA	MICHIGAN	LOS DOS
1. «Me gusta jugar al Frisbee en el *campus.*»	☐	☐	☐
2. «La casa es muy cómoda (*comfortable*) y tengo derecho a usar la cocina (*I have kitchen privileges*).»	☐	☐	☐
3. «Después de (*After*) mi clase, ¿qué tal si tomamos un café?»	☐	☐	☐
4. «El sábado (*Saturday*) hay un partido de basquetbol. ¿Deseas ir (*to go*)?»	☐	☐	☐
5. «Me gusta hablar con mis amigos entre clases en los jardines de la universidad.»	☐	☐	☐

*Although, technically, **norteamericano** refers to all North Americans (people from Canada, the United States, and Mexico), the term is sometimes used to refer solely to people from the United States of America. In this book, **estadounidenses** will refer to people from the United States and **norteamericanos** to North Americans.*

A ESCRIBIR

A. Una comparación. Compare su propia (*your own*) universidad con una universidad hispánica, completando (*by completing*) la siguiente tabla con información de la lectura.

	La universidad hispánica	Mi universidad
Alojamiento (*Housing*)	pensiones, casas particulares	
El *campus*		
Deportes		
Diversiones	música, discotecas, cafés, películas, exposiciones de arte	

B. Mi universidad

PASO 1 In light of what you now know about some differences and similarities between universities in this country and in Hispanic countries, what information do you think would be important to share with a Hispanic student planning on studying at *your* university?

First, use the following questions to organize your ideas.

1. ¿Es grande o pequeña la universidad? (Mi universidad...)
2. ¿Es pública o privada?
3. ¿Cuántas residencias hay en el *campus*?
4. ¿Cuántas cafeterías hay? ¿En qué edificios están las cafeterías?
5. En general, ¿viven los estudiantes en residencias, en apartamentos o con su (*their*) familia?
6. ¿Cuántas bibliotecas hay? ¿Hay bibliotecas especializadas? ¿Hay computadoras para los estudiantes en las bibliotecas?
7. ¿Dónde vive Ud.? (Yo vivo...)
8. ¿Cómo llega Ud. al *campus*? ¿En coche o en autobús? ¿O camina Ud.? (*Or do you walk?*)
9. ¿En que edificios del *campus* estudia Ud.?
10. ¿Qué materia le gusta más?

PASO 2 Now use your answers to form two paragraphs: 1–6 for the first paragraph and 7–10 for the second paragraph. Remember that you are describing your university and your university life to a student from a Spanish-speaking country.

Mi universidad...

GRAMÁTICA

To review the grammar points presented in this chapter, refer to the indicated grammar presentations. You'll find further practice of these structures in the Workbook/Laboratory Manual, on the Interactive CD-ROM, and on the *¿Qué tal?* Online Learning Center (www.mhhe.com/quetal7).

1 Identifying People, Places, Things, and Ideas—Singular Nouns: Gender and Articles

Do you understand the gender of nouns and how to use the articles **el, la, un,** and **una?**

2 Identifying People, Places, Things, and Ideas—Nouns and Articles: Plural Forms

Do you know how to make nouns plural and use the articles **los, las, unos,** and **unas?**

3 Expressing Actions—Subject Pronouns: Present Tense of **-ar** Verbs; Negation

You should be able to use subject pronouns, conjugate regular **-ar** verbs in the present tense, and form negative sentences.

VOCABULARIO

Practice this vocabulary with digital flash cards on the Online Learning Center (www.mhhe.com/quetal7).

Los verbos

bailar	to dance
buscar	to look for
cantar	to sing
comprar	to buy
desear	to want
enseñar	to teach
escuchar	to listen (to)
estar *(irreg.)*	to be
estudiar	to study
hablar	to speak; to talk
hablar por teléfono	to talk on the phone
necesitar	to need
pagar	to pay (for)
practicar	to practice
regresar	to return (*to a place*)
regresar a casa	to go home
tocar	to play (*a musical instrument*)
tomar	to take; to drink
trabajar	to work

Los lugares

el apartamento	apartment
la biblioteca	library
la cafetería	cafeteria
la clase	class(room)
el cuarto	room
el edificio	building
la fiesta	party
la librería	bookstore
la oficina	office
la residencia	dormitory
la universidad	university

Las personas

el/la amigo/a	friend
el/la bibliotecario/a	librarian
el/la cliente	client
el/la compañero/a (de clase)	classmate
el/la compañero/a de cuarto	roommate
el/la consejero/a	advisor
el/la dependiente/a	clerk
el/la estudiante	student
el/la extranjero/a	foreigner
el hombre	man
la mujer	woman
el/la profesor(a)	professor
el/la secretario/a	secretary

Las cosas

el bolígrafo	pen
la calculadora	calculator
el cuaderno	notebook
el diccionario	dictionary
el dinero	money
el escritorio	desk
el lápiz (*pl.* lápices)	pencil
el libro (de texto)	(text)book
la mesa	table
la mochila	backpack
el papel	paper
la pizarra	chalkboard
la puerta	door
la silla	chair
la ventana	window

Las materias

la administración de empresas	business administration
las ciencias	science
la computación	computer science
la física	physics
las lenguas extranjeras	foreign languages
la química	chemistry
la sicología	psychology

Cognados: el arte, las comunicaciones, la economía, la filosofía, la historia, las humanidades, la literatura, las matemáticas, la sociología

Las lenguas (extranjeras)

el alemán	German
el español	Spanish
el francés	French
el inglés	English
el italiano	Italian

Otros sustantivos

el café	coffee
la cerveza	beer
la cosa	thing

el día	day
el lugar	place
la materia	(school) subject
la matrícula	tuition

Palabras interrogativas

¿cuál?	what?; which?
¿cuándo?	when?
¿cuánto?	how much?
¿cuántos/as?	how many?
¿quién?	who?; whom?

Repaso (*Review*): ¿a qué hora?, ¿cómo?, ¿dónde?, ¿qué?

¿Cuándo?

ahora	now
con frecuencia	frequently
el fin de semana	weekend
por la mañana (tarde, noche)	in the morning (afternoon, evening)
tarde/temprano	late/early
todos los días	every day

Pronombres personales

yo, tú, usted (Ud.), él/ella, nosotros/nosotras, vosotros/vosotras, ustedes (Uds.), ellos/ellas

Palabras adicionales

aquí	here
con	with
en casa	at home
mal	poorly
más	more
mucho	much; a lot
muy	very
poco	little
por eso	therefore
sólo	only

La familia

Una familia mexicana en el Parque Ecológico de Xochimilco, en la Ciudad de México

LA FAMILIA Y LOS PARIENTES°

relatives

La familia de Patricia*

los abuelos (maternos) de Patricia

el abuelo   **la abuela**

Pedro Vargas Núñez —   — Eliana Gómez Vargas

los padres de Patricia

la madre   **el padre**

— Felipe Castro Ruiz

Gloria Vargas Castro

los tíos de Patricia

el tío   **la tía**

Luis Vargas Gómez —

Isabel López de Vargas

los primos de Patricia

el primo   **la prima**

Carlos Vargas López —

los hermanos de Patricia

la hermana   **el hermano**

— José Castro Vargas

Ana Vargas López

Rita Castro Vargas

Pícaro,
el perro de
Carlos

*Patricia Castro Vargas

la madre (mamá)	mother (mom)	**la sobrina**	niece
el padre (papá)	father (dad)	**el sobrino**	nephew
la hija	daughter		
el hijo	son	**Las mascotas°**	Las… *Pets*
los hijos	children		
la esposa	wife	**el gato**	cat
el esposo	husband	**el pájaro**	bird
la nieta	granddaughter	**el perro**	dog
el nieto	grandson		

Vocabulario útil

el padrastro / la madrastra	stepfather / stepmother
el hijastro / la hijastra	stepson / stepdaughter
el hermanastro / la hermanastra	stepbrother / stepsister
el medio hermano / la media hermana	half-brother / half-sister
el suegro / la suegra	father-in-law / mother-in-law
el yerno / la nuera	son-in-law / daughter-in-law
el cuñado / la cuñada	brother-in-law / sister-in-law
...(ya) murió	. . . has (already) died

▓ Conversación

A. ¿Cierto o falso? Look at the drawings of the family that appear on page 50. Decide whether each of the following statements is true (**cierto**) or false (**falso**) according to the drawings. Correct the false statements.

1. José es el hermano de Ana.
2. Eliana es la abuela de Patricia.
3. Ana es la sobrina de Felipe y Gloria.
4. Patricia y José son primos.
5. Gloria es la tía de José.
6. Carlos es el sobrino de Isabel.
7. Pedro es el padre de Luis y Gloria.
8. Isabel y Gloria son las esposas de Luis y Felipe, respectivamente.

B. ¿Quién es?

PASO 1   Complete las oraciones lógicamente.

1. La madre de mi (*my*) padre es mi _____.
2. El hijo de mi tío es mi _____.
3. La hermana de mi padre es mi _____.
4. El esposo de mi abuela es mi _____.

PASO 2   Ahora defina estas (*these*) personas, según (*according to*) el mismo (*same*) modelo.

1. prima   **2.** sobrino   **3.** tío   **4.** abuelo

C. Entrevista. Find out as much as you can about the family of a classmate using the following dialogue as a guide. Use **tengo** (*I have*) and **tienes** (*you have*), as indicated. Use **¿cuántos?** with male relations and **¿cuántas?** with females.

MODELO: E1:*¿Cuántos hermanos tienes?
       E2: Bueno (*Well*), tengo seis hermanos y una hermana.
       E1: ¿Y cuántos primos?
       E2: ¡Uf! Tengo un montón (*bunch*). Más de (*More than*) veinte.

---

*From this point on in the text, ESTUDIANTE 1 *and* ESTUDIANTE 2 *will be abbreviated as* E1 *and* E2, *respectively.*

LOS NÚMEROS 31–100

Continúe la secuencia:

treinta y uno, treinta y dos…
ochenta y cuatro, ochenta y cinco…

31 treinta y uno		**40** cuarenta
32 treinta y dos		**50** cincuenta
33 treinta y tres		**60** sesenta
34 treinta y cuatro		**70** setenta
35 treinta y cinco		**80** ochenta
36 treinta y seis		**90** noventa
37 treinta y siete		**100** cien, ciento
38 treinta y ocho		
39 treinta y nueve		

Beginning with 31, Spanish numbers are *not* written in a combined form; **treinta y uno,** * **cuarenta y dos, sesenta y tres,** and so on, must be three separate words.

Cien is used before nouns and in counting.

cien casas	*a (one) hundred houses*
noventa y ocho, noventa y nueve, **cien**	*ninety-eight, ninety-nine, one hundred*

■ Conversación

A. Problemas de matemáticas. Recuerde: + **y,** − **menos,** = **son.**

1. 30 + 50 = ?   **2.** 45 + 45 = ?   **3.** 32 + 58 = ?   **4.** 77 + 23 = ?

NOTA CULTURAL

Los apellidos hispánicos

In most Hispanic countries, people are given two last names (**apellidos**). The custom is demonstrated in this wedding invitation. The names of the bride's parents are in the top left corner: Ramón Ochoa Benítez and Ana Márquez Blanco de Ochoa. Their daughter's name, before her marriage, is Ana Luisa Ochoa Márquez. Her first last name (Ochoa) is her father's first last name, and her second last name (Márquez) is her mother's first last name. The groom's parents are in the top right corner. What do you think his full name (with both last names) is? If you said Antonio Lázaro Pérez, you are correct. Some Spanish-speaking women take their husband's first last name as their new second last name, dropping the second last name they had before marriage. Ana Luisa Ochoa Márquez's name will change to Ana Luisa Ochoa de Lázaro.

Ramón Ochoa Benítez
Ana Márquez Blanco de Ochoa

Antonio Lázaro Aguirre
Susana Pérez de Lázaro

tienen el gusto de anunciar la boda de sus hijos

Ana Luisa y Antonio

*La ceremonia tendrá lugar
el 2 de julio, a las 12 del mediodía
en la Iglesia de la Candelaria*

*Almuerzo en Restaurante Don Paco
Avda. de la Constitución, 7*

Lista de bodas: El Corte Inglés

---

*Remember that when **uno** is part of a compound number (**treinta y uno,** and so on), it becomes **un** before a masculine noun and **una** before a feminine noun: **setenta y un coches; cincuenta y una mesas.**

B. Los números de teléfono

PASO 1 Here is part of a page from an Hispanic telephone book. What can you tell about the names? (See the **Nota cultural** on page 52.)

PASO 2 With a classmate, practice giving telephone numbers at random from the list. Your partner will listen and identify the person. **¡OJO!** In many Hispanic countries phone numbers are said differently than in this country. Follow the model.

MODELO: 4–15–00–46 →

     E1: Es el *cuatro-quince-cero cero-cuarenta y seis.*

     E2: Es el número de *A. Lázaro Aguirre.*

PASO 3 Now give your classmate your phone number and get his or hers.

MODELO: Mi número es el…

LAZARO AGUIRRE, A. –Schez Pacheco, 17	415 0046
LAZCANO DEL MORAL, A. –E. Larreta, 14	215 8194
LAZCANO DEL MORAL, A. –Ibiza, 8	274 6868
LEAL ANTON, J. –Pozo, 8	222 3894
LIEBANA RODRIGUEZ, A.	
Guadarrama, 10	463 2593
LOPEZ BARTOLOME, J. –Palma, 69	232 2027
LOPEZ CABRA, J. –E. Solana, 118	407 5086
LOPEZ CABRA, J. –L. Van, 5	776 4602
LOPEZ GONZALEZ, J. A. –Ibiza, 27	409 2552
LOPEZ GUTIERREZ, G. –S. Cameros, 7	478 8494
LOPEZ LOPEZ, J. –Alamedilla, 21	227 3570
LOPEZ MARIN, V. –Illescas, 53	218 6630
LOPEZ MARIN, V. –N. Rey, 7	463 6873
LOPEZ MARIN, V. –Valmojado, 289	717 2823
LOPEZ NUÑEZ, J. –Pl. Pinazo, s/n	796 0035
LOPEZ NUÑEZ, J. –Rocafort, Bl. 321	796 5387
LOPEZ RODRIGUEZ, C. –Pl. Jesús, 7	429 3278
LOPEZ RODRIGUEZ, J. –Pl. Angel, 15	239 4323
LOPEZ RODRIGUEZ, M. E.	
B. Murillo, 104	233 4239
LOPEZ TRAPERO, A. –Cam. Ingenieros, 1	462 5392
LOPEZ VAZQUEZ, J. –A. Torrejón, 17	433 4646
LOPEZ VEGA, J. –M. Santa Ana, 5	231 2131
LORENTE VILLARREAL, G. –Gandia, 7	252 2758
LORENZO MARTINEZ, A. –Moscareta, 5	479 6282
LORENZO MARTINEZ, A. –P. Laborde, 21	778 2800
LORENZO MARTINEZ, A.	
Av. S. Diego, 116	477 1040
LOSADA MIRON, M. –Padilla, 31	276 9373
LOSADA MIRON, M. –Padilla, 31	431 7461
LOZANO GUILLEN, E.	
Juan H. Mendoza, 5	250 3884
LOZANO PIERA, F. J. –Pinguino, 8	466 3205
LUDEÑA FLORES, G. –Lope Rueda, 56	273 3735
LUENGO CHAMORRO, J.	
Gral Ricardos, 99	471 4906
LUQUE CASTILLO, J. –Pto Arlaban, 121	478 5253
LUQUE CASTILLO, L. –Cardeñosa, 15	477 6644

NOTA COMUNICATIVA

Expressing Age

NORA: ¿Cuántos años tienes, abuela?

ABUELA: Setenta y tres, Nora.

NORA: ¿Y cuántos años tiene el abuelo?

ABUELA: Setenta y cinco, mi amor (*love*). Y ahora, dime (*tell me*), ¿cuántos años tienes tú?

NORA: Tengo cuatro.

In Spanish, age is expressed with the phrase **tener _____ años** (literally, *to have . . . years*). You have now seen all the singular forms of **tener** (*to have*): **tengo, tienes, tiene.**

C. ¡Seamos (*Let's be*) lógicos! Complete las oraciones lógicamente.

1. Un hombre que (*who*) tiene _____ años es muy viejo (*old*).
2. Un niño (*small child*) que tiene sólo _____ año es muy joven (*young*).
3. La persona más vieja (*oldest*) de mi familia es mi _____. Tiene _____ años.
4. La persona más joven (*youngest*) de mi familia es mi _____. Tiene _____ años.
5. En mi opinión, es ideal tener_____ años.
6. Si (*If*) una persona tiene _____ años, ya (*already*) es adulta.
7. Para (*In order to*) tomar cerveza en este estado (*this state*) o en esta provincia es necesario tener _____ años.
8. Para mí (*For me*), ¡la idea de tener _____ años es inconcebible (*inconceivable*)!

ADJETIVOS

guapo	handsome; good-looking
bonito	pretty
feo	ugly
grande	large, big
pequeño	small
casado	married
soltero	single
simpático	nice, likeable
antipático	unpleasant
corto	short (*in length*)
largo	long
bueno	good
malo	bad
listo	smart; clever
tonto	silly, foolish
trabajador	hardworking
perezoso	lazy
rico	rich
pobre	poor
delgado	thin, slender
gordo	fat

Pepe   Juan

Luisito   Esteban

don Paco   Jaime

To describe a masculine singular noun, use **alt*o*, baj*o*,** and so on; use **alt*a*, baj*a*,** and so on for feminine singular nouns.

■ Conversación

A. Preguntas (*Questions*). Conteste según los dibujos (*drawings*).

1. Einstein es listo. ¿Y el chimpancé, en comparación con Einstein?

José   Roberto

2. Roberto es trabajador. ¿Y José?

Pablo
Pepe

3. Pepe es bajo. ¿Y Pablo?

Jaime
Memo

4. Jaime es bueno y simpático. También es guapo. ¿Y Memo?

Paco   Ramón

5. Ramón Ramírez es casado. ¿Y Paco Pereda?

6. El libro es viejo. ¿Y el lápiz?

B. ¿Cómo es?   Describe a famous personality, using as many adjectives as possible so that your classmates can guess who the person is. Don't forget to use cognate adjectives that you have seen in **Primeros pasos** and **Capítulo 1.**

MODELO: Es un hombre importante; controla una gran compañía de *software*. Es muy trabajador y muy rico. (*Bill Gates*)

Need more practice?

- Workbook/Laboratory Manual
- Interactive CD-ROM
- Online Learning Center
  (www.mhhe.com/quetal7)

PRONUNCIACIÓN: Stress and Written Accent Marks (Part 1)

Some Spanish words have *written accent marks* over one of the vowels. That mark is called **el acento (ortográfico).** It means that the syllable containing the accented vowel is stressed when the word is pronounced, as in the word **bolígrafo (bo-LÍ-gra-fo),** for example.

Although all Spanish words of more than one syllable have a stressed vowel, most words do not have a written accent mark. Most words have the spoken stress exactly where native speakers of Spanish would predict it. These two simple rules tell you which syllable is accented when a word does not have a written accent.

> In this chapter you will learn predictable patterns of stress. In the next chapter, you will learn when the written accent mark is needed.

- Words that end in a vowel, or **-n,** or **-s** are stressed on the next-to-last syllable.

  co-sa   **gra**-cias   e-**xa**-men   **e**-res   i-ta-**lia**-no   **len**-guas

- Words that end in any other consonant are stressed on the last syllable.

  us-**ted**   na-tu-**ral**   es-pa-**ñol**   pro-fe-**sor**   doc-**tor**   es-**tar**

A. Sílabas.   The following words have been separated into syllables for you. Read them aloud, paying careful attention to where the spoken stress should fall.

1. Stress on the next-to-last syllable

chi-no	si-lla	li-te-ra-tu-ra
ar-te	Car-men	cien-cias
cla-se	li-bro	o-ri-gen
me-sa	con-se-je-ra	com-pu-ta-do-ra

2. Stress on the last syllable

se-ñor	co-lor	sen-ti-men-tal
mu-jer	po-pu-lar	lu-gar
fa-vor	li-ber-tad	u-ni-ver-si-dad
ac-tor	ge-ne-ral	con-trol

B. Vocales.   Indicate the stressed vowel in each of the following words.

1. mo-chi-la
2. me-nos
3. re-gu-lar
4. i-gual-men-te
5. E-cua-dor
6. e-le-gan-te
7. li-be-ral
8. hu-ma-ni-dad

4   Describing Adjectives: Gender, Number, and Position

Un poema sencillo

Amigo	Amiga
Fiel	Fiel
Amable	Amable
Simpático	Simpática
¡Lo admiro!	¡La admiro!

According to their form, which of the adjectives below can be used to describe each person? Which can refer to you?

Marta: ⎰
Mario: ⎱   fiel   amable   simpática   simpático

Adjectives (**Los adjetivos**) are words used to talk about nouns or pronouns. Adjectives may describe or tell how many there are.

You have been using adjectives to describe people since **Primeros pasos.** In this section, you will learn more about describing the people and things around you.

> **adjective** = a word used to describe a noun or pronoun

large desk	*few* desks
tall woman	*several* women

Adjectives with *ser*

In Spanish, forms of **ser** are used with adjectives that describe basic, inherent qualities or characteristics of the nouns or pronouns they modify. **Ser** establishes the "norm," that is, what is considered basic reality: *snow is cold, water is wet.*

Tú eres amable.
You're nice. (You're a nice person.)

El diccionario es barato.
The dictionary is inexpensive.

A simple poem   Friend Loyal Kind Nice I admire him/her!

Forms of Adjectives

Spanish adjectives agree in gender and number with the noun or pronoun they modify. Each adjective has more than one form.

A. Adjectives that end in **-o (alto)** have four forms, showing gender and number.*

	Masculine	Feminine
Singular	amigo alto	amiga alta
Plural	amigos altos	amigas altas

B. Adjectives that end in **-e (amable)** or in most consonants (**fiel**) have only two forms, a singular and a plural form. The plural of adjectives is formed in the same way as that of nouns.

[Práctica A–B]

> Notes in brackets, like [**Práctica A–B**] here, let you know that you are now ready to do all of the indicated activities, in this case, **Práctica A–B** (page 59). Then, after you read grammar point C (the next one in this section), you will be prepared to do **Práctica C** on page 59, as the bracketed reference in C indicates.

	Masculine	Feminine
Singular	amigo amable	amiga amable
	amigo fiel	amiga fiel
Plural	amigos amables	amigas amables
	amigos fieles	amigas fieles

C. Most adjectives of nationality have four forms.

The names of many languages—which are masculine in gender—are the same as the masculine singular form of the corresponding adjective of nationality: **el español, el inglés, el alemán, el francés,** and so on.

[Práctica C]

> **OJO** Note that in Spanish the names of languages and adjectives of nationality are not capitalized, but the names of countries are: **español, española,** but **España.**

	Masculine	Feminine
Singular	el doctor	la doctora
	mexicano	mexicana
	español	española
	alemán	alemana
	inglés	inglesa
Plural	los doctores	las doctoras
	mexicanos	mexicanas
	españoles	españolas
	alemanes	alemanas
	ingleses	inglesas

Placement of Adjectives

As you have probably noticed, adjectives do not always precede the noun in Spanish as they do in English. Note the following rules for adjective placement.

A. Adjectives of quantity, like numbers, *precede* the noun, as do the interrogatives **¿cuánto/a?** and **¿cuántos/as?**

Hay **muchas** sillas y **dos** escritorios.
There are many chairs and two desks.

¿Cuánto dinero necesitas?
How much money do you need?

---

*Adjectives that end in **-dor, -ón, -án,** and **-ín** also have four forms: **trabajador, trabajadora, trabajadores, trabajadoras.**

PASO 2

OJO **Otro/a** by itself means *another* or *other.* The indefinite article is never used with **otro/a.**

Busco **otro** coche.
I'm looking for another car.

B. Adjectives that describe the qualities of a noun and distinguish it from others generally *follow* the noun. Adjectives of nationality are included in this category.

un perro **bueno**
un dependiente **trabajador**
una mujer **delgada** y **morena**
un hombre **español**

C. The adjectives **bueno** and **malo** may *precede or follow* the noun they modify. When they precede a masculine singular noun, they shorten to **buen** and **mal,** respectively.

[Conversación]

un **buen** perro / un perro **bueno**
una **buena** perra / una perra **buena**
un **mal** día / un día **malo**
una **mala** noche / una noche **mala**

D. The adjective **grande** may also *precede or follow* the noun. When it precedes a singular noun—masculine or feminine—it shortens to **gran** and means *great* or *impressive.* When it follows the noun, it means *large* or *big.*

[Conversación]

Nueva York es una ciudad **grande.**
New York is a large city.

Nueva York es una **gran** ciudad.
New York is a great (impressive) city.

Forms of *this/these*

A. The demonstrative adjective *this/these* has four forms in Spanish.* Learn to recognize them when you see them.

este	hijo	*this son*
esta	hija	*this daughter*
estos	hijos	*these sons*
estas	hijas	*these daughters*

B. You have already seen the neuter demonstrative **esto.** It refers to something that is as yet unidentified.

¿Qué es esto?
What is this?

AUTOPRUEBA

Give the correct adjective endings.

1. una casa viej_____
2. los tíos español_____
3. un primo alt_____
4. un sobrino guap_____
5. las hermanas rubi_____
6. buen_____ amigos

Answers: 1. vieja 2. españoles 3. alto 4. guapo 5. rubias 6. buenos

---

*You will learn all forms of the Spanish demonstrative adjectives (this, that, these, those) in **Gramática 8.**

■ Práctica

A. La familia de José Miguel. The following incomplete sentences describe some members of the family of José Miguel Martín Velasco, a student from Quito, Ecuador. Scan the adjectives to see which ones can complete the statement. Pay close attention to the form of each adjective.

1. El tío Miguel es _____. (trabajador / alto / nueva / grande / fea / amable)
2. Los abuelos son _____. (rubio / antipático / inteligentes / viejos / religiosos / sinceras)
3. La madre de José Miguel es _____. (rubio / elegante / sentimental / buenas / casadas / simpática)
4. Las primas son _____. (solteras / morenas / lógica / bajos / mala)

B. ¡Dolores es igual! Cambie (*Change*) Diego → Dolores.

Diego es un buen estudiante. Es listo y trabajador y estudia mucho. Es estadounidense de origen mexicano, y por eso habla español. Desea ser profesor de antropología. Diego es moreno, guapo y atlético. Le gustan las fiestas grandes y tiene buenos amigos en la universidad. Tiene parientes estadounidenses y mexicanos. Diego tiene 20 años.

NOTA COMUNICATIVA

Más nacionalidades de Latinoamérica

CENTROAMÉRICA		SUDAMÉRICA	
costarricense	nicaragüense	argentino/a	ecuatoriano/a
guatemalteco/a	panameño/a	boliviano/a	paraguayo/a
hondureño/a	salvadoreño/a	brasileño/a	peruano/a
		chileno/a	uruguayo/a
		colombiano/a	venezolano/a

C. Nacionalidades. Tell what nationality the following persons could be and in which country from the box they might live. For number 2, select an adjective (**Nota comunicativa**) and supply a country.

1. Monique habla francés; es _____ y vive (*she lives*) en _____.
2. José habla español; es _____ y vive en _____.
3. Greta y Hans hablan alemán; son _____ y viven en _____.
4. Gilberto habla portugués; es _____ y vive en _____.
5. Gina y Sofía hablan italiano; son _____ y viven en _____.
6. Winston habla inglés; es _____ y vive en _____.
7. Hai (*m.*) y Han (*m.*) hablan chino; son _____ y viven en _____.

Naciones

Alemania (Germany)
el Brasil
China
Francia
Inglaterra (England)
Italia

Need more practice?

- Workbook/Laboratory Manual
- Interactive CD-ROM
- Online Learning Center
  (www.mhhe.com/quetal7)

■ Conversación

A. Descripciones. Describa a su familia, haciendo oraciones completas con estas palabras o las palabras de **Vocabulario útil.**

MODELO: Mi familia no es grande. Es pequeña. Mi padre tiene 50 años.

| Mi familia
Mi padre/madre
Mi ¿ ? (otro pariente)
Mi perro/gato | **+** | (no) es | **+** | interesante
amable
grande
intelectual
nuevo | bueno
famoso
importante
(im)paciente
pequeño | fiel
viejo
malo
¿ ? |

Vocabulario útil

Here are some additional adjectives. You should be able to guess the meaning of some of them.

agresivo/a	¿ ?	**difícil**	difficult
amistoso/a	friendly	**encantador(a)**	delightful
animado/a	lively	**fácil**	easy
atrevido/a	daring	**sensible**	sensitive
cariñoso/a	affectionate	**sentimental**	¿ ?
chistoso/a	amusing	**tolerante**	¿ ?
comprensivo/a	understanding	**travieso/a**	mischievous

B. Asociaciones. With several classmates, talk about people or things you associate with the following phrases. Use the model as a guide. To express agreement or disagreement, use **(No) Estoy de acuerdo.**

MODELO: un gran hombre →
    E1: Creo que (*I believe that*) el presidente es un gran hombre.
    E2: No estoy de acuerdo.

1. un mal restaurante
2. un buen programa de televisión
3. una gran mujer, un gran hombre
4. un buen libro (¿una novela?), un libro horrible
5. un buen coche

¿Recuerda Ud.?

Before beginning **Gramática 5,** review the forms and uses of **ser** that you have already learned by answering these questions.

1. ¿Es Ud. estudiante o profesor(a)?
2. ¿Cómo es Ud.? ¿Es una persona sentimental? ¿inteligente? ¿paciente? ¿elegante?
3. ¿Qué hora es? ¿A qué hora es la clase de español?
4. ¿Qué es un hospital? ¿Es una persona? ¿una cosa? ¿un edificio?

5 Expressing *to be* Present Tense of *ser;* Summary of Uses

Presentaciones

Manolo Durán y Lola Benítez *son* esposos. Manolo habla de quiénes *son*.

—Hola. Me llamo Manolo Durán.

- *Soy* profesor en la universidad.
- *Soy* alto y moreno.
- *Soy* de Sevilla, España.

—¿Y Lola Benítez, mi esposa? Complete la descripción de ella.

Es _____ (profesión).	Málaga, España
Es _____ y _____ (descripción).	bonita
Es de _____ (origen).	profesora
	delgada

ser (*to be*)			
yo	soy	nosotros/as	somos
tú	eres	vosotros/as	sois
Ud. ⎱ él ⎰ ella	es	Uds. ⎱ ellos ⎰ ellas	son

There are two Spanish verbs that mean *to be:* **ser** and **estar.** They are not interchangeable; the meaning that the speaker wishes to convey determines their use. In this chapter, you will review the uses of **ser** that you already know and learn some new ones. Remember to use **estar** to express location and to ask how someone is feeling. You will learn more about the uses of **estar** in **Capítulo 5.**

Some basic language functions of **ser** are presented here. You have used or seen all of them already in this and previous chapters.

To Identify

To *identify* people and things

[Práctica A]

> Remember that the notes in brackets refer you to activities that practice the grammar point.

Yo soy estudiante.
Alicia y yo somos amigas.
La doctora Ramos es profesora.
Esto es un libro.

To Describe

To *describe* people and things*	**Soy sentimental.** *I'm sentimental (a sentimental person).*
	El coche es muy viejo. *The car is very old.*

Origin

With **de,** to express *origin* [Práctica B–C]		**Somos de los Estados Unidos,** pero nuestros padres son **de la Argentina. ¿De dónde** es Ud.? *We're from the United States, but our parents are from Argentina. Where are you from?*

Generalization

To express *generalizations* (only **es**) [Conversación B]		**Es importante** estudiar, pero no es **necesario** estudiar todos los días. *It's important to study, but it's not necessary to study every day.*

Here are two basic language functions of **ser** that you have not yet practiced.

Possession

With **de,** to express *possession* [Práctica D]	**Es el perro de Carla.** *It's Carla's dog.*
Note that there is no **'s** in Spanish.	**Son las gatas de Jorge.** *They're Jorge's (female) cats.*
OJO The masculine singular article **el** contracts with the preposition **de** to form **del.** No other article contracts with **de.**	**de + el → del**
	Es la casa del profesor. *It's the (male) professor's house.*
	Es la casa de la profesora. *It's the (female) professor's house.*

Destination

With **para,** to tell for whom or what something *is intended* [Conversación A]	*¿Romeo y Julieta?* Es **para** la clase de inglés. *Romeo and Juliet? It's for English class.*
	—¿**Para** quién son los regalos? —(Son) **Para** mi nieto. *Who are the presents for?* *(They're) For my grandson.*

*You practiced this language function of **ser** in **Gramática 4** in this chapter.

■ Práctica

A. ¡Anticipemos! Los parientes de Gloria. Look back at the family drawings on page 50. Then tell whether the following statements are true (**cierto**) or false (**falso**) from Gloria's standpoint. Correct the false statements.

1. Felipe y yo somos hermanos.
2. Pedro es mi esposo.
3. Pedro y Eliana son mis (*my*) padres.
4. Carlos es mi sobrino.
5. Mi hermano es el esposo de Isabel.
6. El padre de Felipe no es abuelo todavía (*yet*).
7. Mi familia no es muy grande.

B. Nacionalidades

PASO 1 ¿De dónde son, según los nombres, apellidos y ciudades?

MODELO: João Gonçalves, Lisboa →
João Gonçalves es de Portugal.

1. John Doe, Nueva York
2. Karl Lotze, Berlín
3. Graziana Lazzarino, Roma
4. María Gómez, Ciudad Juárez
5. Claudette Moreau, París
6. Timothy Windsor, Londres

PASO 2 Ahora, ¿de dónde es Ud.? ¿De este estado / esta provincia? ¿de una metrópoli? ¿de un área rural? ¿Es Ud. de una ciudad que tiene un nombre hispano? ¿Es de otro país (*country*)?

Naciones

**Alemania
los Estados Unidos
Francia
Inglaterra
Italia
México
Portugal**

C. Personas extranjeras

PASO 1 ¿Quiénes son, de dónde son y dónde trabajan ahora?

MODELO: Teresa: actriz / de Madrid / en Cleveland →
Teresa es actriz. Es de Madrid. Ahora trabaja en Cleveland.

1. Carlos Miguel: médico (*doctor*) / de Cuba / en Milwaukee
2. Maripili: profesora / de Burgos / en Miami
3. Mariela: dependienta / de Buenos Aires / en Nueva York
4. Juan: dentista* / de Lima / en Los Ángeles

PASO 2 Ahora hable sobre un amigo o pariente según el **Paso 1.**

D. ¡Seamos lógicos! ¿De quién son estas cosas? Con un compañero/una compañera, haga y conteste preguntas (*ask and answer questions*) según el modelo. Las respuestas pueden variar (*can vary*).

MODELO: E1: ¿De quién es el perro?
E2: Es de…

¿De quién es/son… ?

1. la casa en Beverly Hills
2. la casa en Viena
3. la camioneta (*station wagon*)
4. el perro
5. las fotos de la Argentina
6. las mochilas con todos los libros

Personas

**la actriz
el estudiante extranjero
las estudiantes
la familia con diez hijos
el niño
los Sres. Schmidt**

Need more practice?

■ Workbook/Laboratory Manual
■ Interactive CD-ROM
■ Online Learning Center (www.mhhe.com/quetal7)

---

*A number of professions end in **-ista** in both masculine and feminine forms. The article indicates gender:* **el/la dentista, el/la artista,** *and so on.*

PASO 2

■ Conversación

A. El regalo (*gift*) **ideal.** Look at Diego's list of gifts and what his family members like. With a partner, decide who receives each gift and why. The first one is done for you.

MODELO: **1.** una novela de Stephen King →
E1: ¿Para quién es la novela de Stephen King?
E2: Es para la prima.
E1: ¿Por qué?
E2: Porque le gustan las novelas de horror.

REGALOS

2. la calculadora
3. los libros de literatura clásica
4. los discos compactos de Andrés Segovia
5. el televisor
6. el radio
7. el dinero

MIEMBROS DE LA FAMILIA

a. el padre: Le gusta escuchar las noticias (*news*).
b. los abuelos: Les gusta mucho la música de guitarra clásica.
c. la madre: Le gusta mirar programas cómicos.
d. el hermano: Le gustan mucho las historias viejas.
e. la hermana: Desea estudiar en otro estado.
f. el primo: Le gustan las matemáticas.
g. la prima: Le gustan las novelas de horror.

B. ¿Qué opina Ud.? Exprese opiniones originales, afirmativas o negativas, con estas palabras.

MODELO: Es importante hablar español en la clase de español.

(No) Es importante (No) Es muy práctico (No) Es necesario (No) Es tonto (*foolish*) (No) Es fascinante (No) Es una lata (*pain, drag*) (No) Es posible	**+** mirar la televisión todos los días hablar español en la clase tener muchas mascotas llegar (*to arrive*) a clase puntualmente tomar cerveza en clase hablar con los animales / las plantas tomar mucho café y fumar cigarrillos trabajar dieciocho horas al día tener muchos hermanos estar en las fiestas familiares

Voces de México

LITERATURA: Rosario Castellanos

Sobre la autora: *Rosario Castellanos was born in Mexico City in 1925 but spent much of her childhood in Chiapas, a region in the south of Mexico with a large indigenous population. She returned to the province of Chiapas as an adult to work with Indian theater groups and the Indigenous Institute of San Cristóbal. Castellanos wrote in many forms, from poetry to journalism. The following lines are from "Economía doméstica," a poem in her most famous collection of poetry,* Poesía no eres tú *(1972).*

Rosario Castellanos
(1925–1974)

He aquí la regla de oro,ª el secreto del orden:

tener un sitioᵇ para cadaᶜ cosa
y tener
cada cosa en suᵈ sitio. Así arregléᵉ mi casa.

ªHe… *Here is the golden rule* ᵇ*place* ᶜ*each* ᵈ*its* ᵉAsí… *That's how I organized*

MÚSICA: El corrido

El corrido es una canciónª que narraᵇ eventos importantes o históricos, seanᶜ heroicos o escandalosos, de valentíaᵈ o crueldad. Las canciones, acompañadas de guitarra y acordeón, son cortas para que el cantante,ᵉ tradicionalmente del sexo masculino, pueda cantarlas a todo pulmón.ᶠ El grupo mexicano Los Tigres del Norte canta muchos corridos tradicionales.

ª*song* ᵇ*narrates* ᶜ*whether they be* ᵈ*bravery* ᵉpara… *so that the singer* ᶠpueda… *can sing them at the top of his lungs*

Estos versos son del corrido «Romanceᵍ de Román Castillo».

¿Dónde vas,ʰ Román Castillo?
¿Dónde vas? ¡Pobre de tiⁱ!
Ya no busques más querellas,ʲ
Por nuestrasᵏ damas de aquí….

[…]

Tú eres noble, eres bravo,
Hombre de gran corazón;ˡ
Pero que tu amor no manche
Nunca mi reputación.ᵐ

ᵍ*Song* ʰ¿Dónde… *Where are you going* ⁱde… *you* ʲYa… *Don't look for any more fights*
ᵏPor… *Because of our* ˡ*heart* ᵐque… *may your love never stain my reputation*

6   Expressing Possession   Possessive Adjectives (Unstressed)

La familia de Carlos IV (cuarto)

Aquí está la familia de Carlos IV, un rey español del siglo XVIII. En el cuadro están *su* esposa, *sus* hijos… ¿Y *sus* padres y *sus* abuelos? ¿Quiénes son las personas a la izquierda del rey?

¿Y Ud.?

¿Tiene Ud. una foto reciente de su familia? ¿Quiénes están en la foto?

La familia de Carlos IV, por el pintor español Francisco Goya y Lucientes

Possessive adjectives are words that tell to whom or to what something belongs: *my* (book), *his* (sweater). You have already seen and used several possessive adjectives in Spanish. Here is the complete set.

> **possessive adjective** = adjective that shows who owns or has something

Possessive Adjectives

my	**mi** hijo/hija **mis** hijos/hijas	*our*	nuestro hijo nuestros hijos	nuestra hija nuestras hijas
your (fam.)	**tu** hijo/hija **tus** hijos/hijas	*your (fam.)*	vuestro hijo vuestros hijos	vuestra hija vuestras hijas
your (form.), *his, her, its*	**su** hijo/hija **sus** hijos/hijas	*your (form.),* *their*	**su** hijo/hija **sus** hijos/hijas	

In Spanish, the ending of a possessive adjective agrees in form with the person or thing possessed, not with the owner or possessor. Note that these possessive adjectives are placed before the noun.

$$\text{Son} \left\{ \begin{array}{l} \text{mis} \\ \text{tus} \\ \text{sus} \end{array} \right\} \text{hermanos.}$$

The possessive adjectives **mi(s), tu(s),** and **su(s)** show agreement in number only. **Nuestro/a/ os/as** and **vuestro/a/os/as,** like all adjectives that end in **-o,** show agreement in both number and gender.

$$\text{Es} \left\{ \begin{array}{l} \text{nuestra} \\ \text{vuestra} \\ \text{su} \end{array} \right\} \text{familia.}$$

---

*Another set of possessives are called the *stressed possessive adjectives*. They can be used as nouns. For information on them, see Appendix 2, Using Adjectives as Nouns.

Carlos IV's family   *Here is the family of Carlos IV, an 18th-century Spanish king. In the painting are his wife, his children . . . And his parents and grandparents? Who are the people to the left of the king?*

The forms **vuestro/a/os/as** are used extensively in Spain, but are not common in Latin America.

 Su(s) can have several different equivalents in English: *your* (*sing.*), *his, her, its, your* [*pl.*], and *their*. Usually its meaning will be clear in context. When the meaning of **su[s]** is not clear, **de** and a pronoun are used instead to indicate the possessor.

el padre
la madre   } de él (de ella, de Ud., de
los abuelos   ellos, de ellas, de Uds.)
las tías

¿Son jóvenes los hijos **de él**?
Are his children young?

¿Dónde vive el abuelo **de ellas**?
Where does their grandfather live?

■ Práctica

A. Posesiones. Which nouns can these possessive adjectives modify without changing form?

1. su: problema primos dinero tías escritorios familia
2. tus: perro idea hijos profesoras abuelo examen
3. mi: ventana médicos cuarto coche abuela gatos
4. sus: animales oficina nietas padre hermana abuelo
5. nuestras: guitarra libro materias lápiz sobrinas tía
6. nuestros: gustos consejeros parientes puerta clase residencia

B. ¿Cómo es la familia de David?

PASO 1   Mire (*Look at*) la familia de David en el dibujo. Complete las oraciones según el modelo.

MODELO: familia / pequeño →
         Su familia es pequeña.

1. hijo pequeño / guapo
2. perro / feo
3. hija / rubio
4. padre / viejo
5. esposa / bonito

PASO 2   Imagine que Ud. es David y cambie las respuestas (*answers*).

MODELO: familia / pequeño →
         Mi familia es pequeña.

PASO 3   Imagine que Ud. es la esposa de David y hable por (*speak for*) Ud. y por su esposo. Cambie sólo las respuestas del 1 al 3.

MODELO: familia / pequeño →
         Nuestra familia es pequeña.

David

Need more practice?

- Workbook/Laboratory Manual
- Interactive CD-ROM
- Online Learning Center
  (www.mhhe.com/quetal7)

■ Conversación

A. Entrevista. Take turns asking and answering questions about your families. Talk about what family members are like, their ages, some things they do, and so on. Use the model as a guide. Take notes on what your partner says. Then report the information to the class.

MODELO: tu abuela →
E1: Mi abuela es alta. ¿Y tu abuela? ¿Es alta?
E2: Bueno, no. Mi abuela es baja.
E1: ¿Cuántos años tiene?...

1. tu familia en general
2. tus padres
3. tus abuelos
4. tus hermanos / hijos
5. tu esposo/a / compañero/a de cuarto

B. Asociaciones. Working with several classmates, see how many words you can associate with the following phrases. Everyone in the group must agree with the associations decided on. Remember to use the words and phrases you know to agree or disagree with the suggestions of others.

MODELO: nuestro país →
Nuestro país es _____. (En nuestro país hay _____. En nuestro país uno puede [*can*] _____.)

1. nuestro país
2. nuestra clase de español
3. nuestra universidad (librería)
4. nuestra ciudad (nuestro estado / nuestra provincia)
5. el centro de nuestra ciudad

¿Recuerda Ud.?

The personal endings used with **-ar** verbs share some characteristics of those used with **-er** and **-ir** verbs, which you will learn in the next section. Review the present tense endings of **-ar** verbs by telling which subject pronoun(s) you associate with each of these endings.

1. -amos   2. -as   3. -áis   4. -an   5. -o   6. -a

---

7 | Expressing Actions Present Tense of *-er* and *-ir* Verbs; More About Subject Pronouns

Diego se presenta

Hola. Me llamo Diego González. Soy estudiante de UCLA, pero este año *asisto* a la Universidad Nacional Autónoma de México. *Vivo* con mi tía Matilde en la Ciudad de México. *Como* pizza con frecuencia y *bebo* cerveza en las fiestas. Me gusta la ropa de moda; por eso *recibo* varios catálogos. *Leo* muchos libros de antropología para mi especialización. También *escribo* muchas cartas a mi familia. *Creo* que una educación universitaria es muy importante. Por eso estudio y *aprendo* mucho. ¡Pero *comprendo* también que es muy importante estar con los amigos y con la familia!

¿Y Ud.?

¿Es Diego un estudiante típico? ¿Cómo es Ud.? Adapte las oraciones de Diego a su conveniencia.

Past -------------------- **PRESENT** -------------------- Future
present

Verbs That End in *-er* and *-ir*

A. The present tense of **-er** and **-ir** verbs is formed by adding personal endings to the stem of the verb (the infinitive minus its **-er/-ir** ending). The personal endings for **-er** and **-ir** verbs are the same except for the first and second person plural.

comer (*to eat*)		vivir (*to live*)	
como	comemos	vivo	vivimos
comes	coméis	vives	vivís
come	comen	vive	viven

B. These are the frequently used **-er** and **-ir** verbs you will find in this chapter.

	-er verbs		*-ir* verbs	
aprender	*to learn*	**abrir**	*to open*
comprender	*to understand*	**asistir (a)**	*to attend,*
creer (en)	*to think; to*		*go to*
	believe (in)		*(a class,*
deber (+ *inf.*)	*should, must,*		*function)*
	ought to (do	**recibir**	*to receive*
	something)	**vivir**	*to live*
vender	*to sell*		

Diego introduces himself   *Hello. My name is Diego González. I'm a student at UCLA, but this year I attend the* **Universidad Nacional Autónoma de México.** *I live with my aunt Matilde in Mexico City. I eat pizza frequently and I drink beer at parties. I like fashionable clothes; that's why I receive various catalogues. I read lots of anthropology books for my major. I also write a lot of letters to my family. I think that a university education is very important. That's why I study and learn a lot. But I also understand that it's very important to be with friends and family!*

PASO 3

Remember that the Spanish present tense has a number of present tense equivalents in English. It can also be used to express future meaning.

como = *I eat, I am eating, I will eat*

Use and Omission of Subject Pronouns

In English, a verb must have an expressed subject (a noun or pronoun): ***she*** *says,* ***the train*** *arrives*. In Spanish, however, as you have probably noticed, an expressed subject is not required. Verbs are accompanied by a subject pronoun only for clarification, emphasis, or contrast.

- *Clarification:* When the context does not make the subject clear, the subject pronoun is expressed. This happens most frequently with third person singular and plural verb forms.
- *Emphasis:* Subject pronouns are used in Spanish to emphasize the subject when in English you would stress it with your voice.
- *Contrast:* Contrast is a special case of emphasis. Subject pronouns are used to contrast the actions of two individuals or groups.

Ud. / él / ella vende
Uds. / ellos / ellas venden

—¿Quién debe pagar?   *Who should pay?*
—¡**Tú** debes pagar!   *You should pay!*

Ellos leen mucho; **nosotros** leemos poco.
They read a lot; we read little.

AUTOPRUEBA

Give the correct verb forms.

1. Elena (comer) _____
2. yo (beber) _____
3. nosotros (leer) _____
4. José (escribir) _____
5. Uds. (vivir) _____
6. tú (abrir) _____

Answers: 1. come 2. bebo 3. leemos 4. escribe 5. viven 6. abres

■ Práctica

A. En la clase de español

PASO 1 **¡Anticipemos!** Read the following statements and tell whether they are true for your classroom environment. If any statement is not true for you or your class, make it negative or change it in another way to make it correct.

MODELO: Bebo café en clase. →
    Sí, bebo café en clase.
    (No, no bebo café en clase. Bebo café en casa.)

1. Debo estudiar más para esta clase.
2. Leo todas (*all*) las partes de las lecciones.
3. Comprendo bien cuando mi profesor(a) habla español.
4. Asisto al laboratorio con frecuencia.
5. Debemos abrir más los libros en clase.
6. Escribimos mucho en esta clase.
7. Aprendemos a hablar español en esta clase.*
8. Vendemos nuestros libros al final del año.

PASO 2   Now turn to the person next to you and rephrase each sentence, using **tú** forms of the verbs. Your partner will indicate whether the sentences are true for him or her.

MODELO: Debes estudiar más para esta clase, ¿verdad (*right*)? →
    Sí, debo estudiar más.
    (No, no debo estudiar más.)
    (No. Debo estudiar más para la clase de matemáticas.)

*Note: **aprender** + **a** + *infinitive* = *to learn how to* (do something)

B. Diego habla de su padre. Complete este párrafo con la forma correcta de los verbos entre paréntesis.

Mi padre (vender[1]) coches y trabaja mucho. Mis hermanos y yo (aprender[2]) mucho de papá. Según mi padre, los jóvenes (deber[3]) (asistir[4]) a clase todos los días, porque es su obligación. Papá también (creer[5]) que no es necesario mirar la televisión por la noche. Es más interesante (leer[6]) el periódico,[a] una revista[b] o un buen libro. Por eso nosotros (leer[7]) o (escribir[8]) por la noche y no miramos la televisión mucho. Yo admiro mucho a* mi papá y (creer[9]) que él (comprender[10]) la importancia de la educación.

[a]*newspaper* [b]*magazine*

Comprensión: ¿Cierto o falso?

1. Diego y sus hermanos venden coches.
2. Diego mira mucho la televisión.
3. El padre de Diego probablemente lee mucho.

C. Un sábado (*Saturday*) **en Sevilla.** In this activity you will take the part of Manolo, who lives with his family in Sevilla. Using all the cues given, form complete sentences about a Saturday at home with your family. Make any changes and add words when necessary. When the subject pronoun is in parentheses, do not use it in the sentence.

MODELO: (nosotros) beber / café / por / mañana →
Bebemos café por la mañana.

1. yo / leer / periódico
2. mi hija, Marta / mirar / televisión
3. también / (ella) escribir / composición / en inglés
4. no / (ella) comprender / todo / instrucciones
5. (ella) deber / usar / diccionario
6. mi esposa, Lola / abrir / y / leer / cartas
7. ¡hoy / (nosotros) recibir / carta / de / tío Ricardo!
8. (él) ser de / España / pero / ahora / vivir / en México
9. ¡ay! / ser / dos / de / tarde
10. ¡(nosotros) deber / comer / ahora!
11. (nosotros) comer / a / dos / todo / días
12. hoy / un / amigos / comer / con / nosotros / y / llegar (*to arrive*) / diez minutos

Need more practice?

■ Workbook/Laboratory Manual
■ Interactive CD-ROM
■ Online Learning Center
(www.mhhe.com/quetal7)

---

*Note the use of **a** here. In this context, the word **a** has no equivalent in English. It is used in Spanish before a direct object that is a specific person. You will learn more about this use of **a** in **Capítulo 6.** Until then, the exercises and activities in ¿Qué tal? will indicate when to use it.*

■ **Conversación**

NOTA COMUNICATIVA

Telling How Frequently You Do Things

Use the following words and phrases to tell how often you perform an activity. Some of them will already be familiar to you.

todos los días, siempre	every day, always	**una vez a la semana**	once a week
con frecuencia	frequently	**casi nunca**	almost never
a veces	at times	**nunca**	never

Hablo con mis amigos **todos los días.** Hablo con mis padres **una vez a la semana. Casi nunca** hablo con mis abuelos. Y **nunca** hablo con mis tíos que viven en Italia.

For now, use the expressions **casi nunca** and **nunca** only at the beginning of a sentence. You will learn more about how to use them in **Gramática 18.**

¿Con qué frecuencia?

PASO 1 How frequently do you do the following things?

	CON FRECUENCIA	A VECES	CASI NUNCA	NUNCA
1. Asisto al laboratorio de lenguas (o uso los discos compactos).	☐	☐	☐	☐
2. Recibo cartas.	☐	☐	☐	☐
3. Escribo poemas.	☐	☐	☐	☐
4. Leo novelas románticas.	☐	☐	☐	☐
5. Como en una pizzería.	☐	☐	☐	☐
6. Recibo y leo catálogos.	☐	☐	☐	☐
7. Aprendo palabras nuevas en español.	☐	☐	☐	☐
8. Asisto a todas las clases.	☐	☐	☐	☐
9. Compro regalos para los amigos.	☐	☐	☐	☐
10. Vendo los libros al final del semestre/trimestre.	☐	☐	☐	☐

PASO 2 Now compare your answers with those of a classmate. Then answer the following questions. (*Note:* **los/las dos** = *both* [*of us*]; **ninguno/a** = *neither*)

	YO	MI COMPAÑERO/A	LOS/LAS DOS	NINGUNO/A
1. ¿Quién es muy estudioso/a?	☐	☐	☐	☐
2. ¿Quién necesita mucho dinero?	☐	☐	☐	☐
3. ¿Quién lee mucho?	☐	☐	☐	☐
4. ¿Quién come mucha pizza?	☐	☐	☐	☐
5. ¿Quién compra muchas cosas?	☐	☐	☐	☐
6. ¿Quién es muy romántico/a?	☐	☐	☐	☐
7. ¿Quién recibe mucho por correo (*by mail*)?	☐	☐	☐	☐

En los Estados Unidos y el Canadá

Los Sheen: Una familia de actores

Two generations of Sheens have made names for themselves in film and television. Martin Sheen, the father, was born Ramón Estévez in Dayton, Ohio (1940–), to a Spanish father and an Irish mother. Martin explains that he felt he needed to change his Hispanic name in order to successfully pursue an acting career in the 1950s. In his heart, however, he says he is still Ramón. Martin's acting career spans several decades and includes important movies such

Charlie Sheen, Martin Sheen y Emilio Estévez

as *Apocalypse Now.* Most recently, he stars in the television series "The West Wing," winner of more than fifty Emmys, including four for Outstanding Drama Series.

Martin and his wife of more than 40 years, Janet Sheen, have four children—Emilio (1962–), Ramón (1963–), Carlos (1965–), and Renée (1967–)—all of whom have pursued acting careers. Emilio, who uses his father's original last name, Estévez, and Carlos, who is known as Charlie Sheen, are the most famous actors of the Sheen children.

UN POCO DE TODO

Lengua y cultura: ¿Existe la familia hispánica típica? Complete the following paragraphs about families. Give the correct form of the words in parentheses, as suggested by the context.

Muchas personas (creer[1]) que (todo[2]) las familias (hispánico[3]) son (grande[4]). Pero el concepto de la familia (ser[5]) diferente ahora, sobre todo[a] en las ciudades (grande[6]).

(Ser[7]) cierto que la familia rural (típico[8]) es grande, pero es así[b] en casi (todo[9]) las sociedades rurales del mundo.[c] Muchos hijos (trabajar[10]) la tierra[d] con sus padres. Por eso es bueno y (necesario[11]) tener muchos niños.

Pero en los grandes centros (urbano[12]) las familias con sólo dos o tres hijos (ser[13]) más comunes. Es difícil[e] tener (mucho[14]) hijos en una sociedad (industrializado[15]). Y cuando los padres (trabajar[16]) fuera de[f] casa, ellos (pagar[17]) mucho para cuidar a[g] los niños. Esto pasa especialmente en las familias de la clase media.[h]

Pero es realmente difícil (hablar[18]) de una familia (hispánico[19]) típica. ¿Hay una familia (norteamericano[20]) típica?

[a]sobre... *especially* [b]es... *that's the way it is* [c]*world* [d]*land* [e]*difficult* [f]fuera... *outside of the* [g]cuidar... *care for* [h]*middle*

La familia, *por Fernando Botero, de Colombia*

Comprensión: ¿Cierto o falso? Corrija (*Correct*) las oraciones falsas.

1. Todas las familias hispánicas son iguales.
2. Las familias rurales son grandes en casi todas partes del mundo.
3. Las familias rurales necesitan muchos niños.
4. Por lo general (*Generally*), las familias urbanas son más pequeñas.
5. Las madres urbanas típicamente cuidan a los hijos durante el día.

Resources for Review and Testing Preparation

- Workbook/Laboratory Manual
- Interactive CD-ROM
- Online Learning Center (www.mhhe.com/quetal7)

VIDEOTECA

Entrevista cultural: México

Dolores Suárez is from Mexico. In this interview, she talks about her family. Like many grandparents, she is proud of her grandchildren. Before watching the video clip, read the following excerpt from the interview.

INTERVIEWER: ¿Cómo se llama Ud. y de dónde es?
  DOLORES: Me llamo Dolores Suárez. Soy de aquí, del Distrito Federal.[a]
INTERVIEWER: ¿Cómo es su familia, Sra. Dolores?
  DOLORES: Pues es una familia muy bonita porque es una familia muy numerosa. Tengo seis hijos y tengo ocho nietos. Entonces eh,[b] somos muy unidos y por eso es muy bonito.

[a]Distrito… *what Mexicans call Mexico City* [b]Entonces… *Well then*

Now watch the video clip and answer the following questions based on the interview.

1. What city is Dolores from?
2. How does she describe her family?
3. How many grandchildren does Dolores have?
4. How does she describe her grandchildren in general?
5. What are some of the specific interests of her grandchildren?

Entre amigos: ¿Cuántos hermanos tienes?

Miguel, Tané, Karina, and Rubén are talking about their families. What questions do you think they will ask each other? Before watching the video, read the following questions. As you watch, don't worry if you don't understand every word. Try to get the gist of the conversation, listening carefully for information about their family members. Watch the video a second time and listen for the answers to the questions.

1. ¿Cuántas hermanas tiene Karina?
2. ¿Cuántos hermanos tiene Rubén?
3. ¿Cómo son los hermanos de Rubén?
4. ¿Vive Karina con sus padres o vive sola (*alone*)?

ENFOQUE CULTURAL

 México

¡Fíjese!

- México tiene 31 estados y el Distrito Federal.
- La población de México es aproximadamente: 30% (por ciento) indígena, 9% blanca,[a] 60% mestiza (que se refiere a las personas de padres de razas indígena y blanca) y 1% de otros orígenes.
- Los indígenas mexicanos pertenecen a[b] grupos diversos: aztecas, mayas, zapotecas, mixtecas, olmecas y otros. La influencia de estas culturas indígenas contribuye a la diversidad y la riqueza de la cultura mexicana actual.[c]
- La ciudad de México ocupa el lugar del antiguo[d] Lago Texcoco. En el centro del lago estaba[e] Tenochtitlán, la capital del imperio azteca. Tenochtitlán era[f] una de las ciudades más grandes del mundo en el siglo XVI.[g]
- La Universidad Nacional Autónoma de México es una de las universidades más antiguas[h] de las Américas: es del año[i] 1551 (mil quinientos cincuenta y uno).

[a]*white* [b]*pertenecen... belong to* [c]*current* [d]*old, ancient* [e]*was* [f]*was*
[g]*siglo... 16th century* [h]*más... oldest* [i]*es... it dates from the year*

Personas famosas: Los grandes muralistas mexicanos

El muralismo es el estilo de pintura[a] que decora las paredes[b] de edificios públicos. Con su obra,[c] los muralistas desean enseñar la historia y la cultura de su país, y con frecuencia sus murales representan sus ideales políticos también.

Los tres grandes muralistas mexicanos son Diego Rivera (1886–1957 [mil ochocientos ochenta y seis a mil novecientos cincuenta y siete]), José Clemente Orozco (1883–1949 [mil ochocientos ochenta y tres a mil novecientos cuarenta y nueve]) y David Alfaro Siqueiros (1898–1974 [mil ochocientos noventa y ocho a mil novecientos setenta y cuatro]). Hay muchos murales de estos tres grandes muralistas por todo México.

[a]*painting* [b]*walls* [c]*work*

El mural The Epic of American Civilization *por Orozco, en Dartmouth College*

Learn more about Mexico with the Video, Interactive CD-ROM, and the Online Learning Center (www.mhhe.com/quetal7).

PASO FINAL

A CONVERSAR

La familia y los amigos

PASO 1 Using the verbs and adjectives you have learned, write five sentences describing what your family members and friends do or what they are like.

> **MODELO:** Mi padre trabaja mucho. Mi amigo John es perezoso.

PASO 2 Work with a partner to find out which of your family members and friends do the same thing or fit the same description. Use **¿Quién de tu familia... ?** (*Who in your family . . . ?*) and **¿Cuál de tus amigos... ?** (*Which of your friends . . . ?*) to get the information. If your answer to a question is *no one* or *none*, use **Nadie en mi familia es...** (*No one in my family is . . .*) or **Ninguno de mis amigos es...** (*Not one of my friends is . . .*).

> **MODELOS:** E1: Mi padre trabaja mucho. ¿Quién de tu familia trabaja mucho?
>
> E2: Mi tía Anita trabaja mucho. (o: Nadie en mi familia trabaja mucho.) Pero mi amigo John es perezoso. ¿Cuál de tus amigos es perezoso?
>
> E1: Mi amiga Raquel es perezosa. (o: Ninguno de mis amigos es perezoso.)

PASO 3 Ask follow-up questions about information you learned.

> **MODELO:** E1: ¿Dónde trabaja tu tía Anita?
>
> E2: Trabaja en un hospital.

PASO 4 Compare notes with the rest of the class. Talk about your family and friends and what you learned about your partner's family and friends.

> **MODELO:** La tía de Jorge, Anita, trabaja en un hospital. Ella trabaja mucho...

Tamalada (*Making Tamales*), *por Carmen Lomas Garza (estadounidense)*

GRAMÁTICA

To review the grammar points presented in this chapter, refer to the indicated grammar presentations. You'll find further practice of these structures in the Workbook/Laboratory Manual, on the Interactive CD-ROM, and on the *¿Qué tal?* Online Learning Center (www.mhhe.com/quetal7).

4 Describing—Adjectives: Gender, Number, and Position

You should know how to place adjectives as well as how to make adjectives like **alto, inteligente, español,** and **inglés** agree with the nouns they describe.

5 Expressing *to be*—Present Tense of **ser;** Summary of Uses

Can you conjugate and use the irregular verb **ser** in the present tense?

6 Expressing Possession—Possessive Adjectives (Unstressed)

You should be able to recognize and use the possessive adjectives **mi, tu, su, nuestro,** and **vuestro.**

7 Expressing Actions—Present Tense of **-er** and **-ir** Verbs; More About Subject Pronouns

Can you conjugate verbs like **comer** and **escribir** in the present tense? Do you know how to use subject pronouns and when to omit them?

VOCABULARIO

Practice this vocabulary with digital flash cards on the Online Learning Center (www.mhhe.com/quetal7).

Los verbos

abrir	to open
aprender	to learn
asistir (a)	to attend, go to (*a class, function*)
beber	to drink
comer	to eat
comprender	to understand
creer (en)	to think; to believe (in)
deber (+ *inf.*)	should, must, ought to (*do something*)
escribir	to write
leer	to read
mirar	to look at, watch
mirar la televisión	to watch television
recibir	to receive
ser (*irreg.*)	to be
vender	to sell
vivir	to live

La familia y los parientes

el/la abuelo/a	grandfather/grandmother
los abuelos	grandparents
el/la esposo/a	husband/wife
el/la hermano/a	brother/sister
el/la hijo/a	son/daughter
los hijos	children
la madre (mamá)	mother (mom)
el/la nieto/a	grandson/granddaughter
el/la niño/a	small child; boy/girl
el padre (papá)	father (dad)
los padres	parents
el/la pariente	relative
el/la primo/a	cousin
el/la sobrino/a	nephew/niece
el/la tío/a	uncle/aunt

Las mascotas

el gato	cat
la mascota	pet
el pájaro	bird
el perro	dog

Otros sustantivos

la carta	letter
la casa	house, home
la ciudad	city
el coche	car
el estado	state
el/la médico/a	(medical) doctor
el país	country
el periódico	newspaper
el regalo	present, gift
la revista	magazine

Los adjetivos

alto/a	tall
amable	kind; nice
antipático/a	unpleasant
bajo/a	short (in height)
bonito/a	pretty
buen, bueno/a	good
casado/a	married
corto/a	short (in length)
delgado/a	thin, slender
este/a	this
estos/as	these
feo/a	ugly
fiel	faithful
gordo/a	fat
gran, grande	large, big; great
guapo/a	handsome; good-looking
inteligente	intelligent
joven	young
largo/a	long
listo/a	smart; clever
mal, malo/a	bad
moreno/a	brunet(te)
mucho/a	a lot (of)
muchos/as	many
necesario/a	necessary
nuevo/a	new
otro/a	other, another
pequeño/a	small
perezoso/a	lazy
pobre	poor
posible	possible
rico/a	rich
rubio/a	blond(e)
simpático/a	nice, likeable
soltero/a	single (not married)
todo/a	all; every
tonto/a	silly, foolish
trabajador(a)	hardworking
viejo/a	old

Los adjetivos de nacionalidad

alemán/alemana	German
español(a)	Spanish
estadounidense	U.S. (adj.)
francés/francesa	French
inglés/inglesa	English

Cognado: mexicano/a

Los adjetivos posesivos

mi(s)	my
tu(s)	your (fam. sing.)
nuestro/a(s)	our
vuestro/a(s)	your (fam. pl. Sp.)
su(s)	his, hers, its, your (form. sing.); their, your (form. pl.)

Los números 31–100

treinta, cuarenta, cincuenta, sesenta, setenta, ochenta, noventa, cien (ciento)

¿Con qué frecuencia... ?

a veces	sometimes, at times
casi nunca	almost never
nunca	never
siempre	always
una vez a la semana	once a week

Repaso: con frecuencia, todos los días

Palabras adicionales

bueno...	well . . .
casi	almost
¿de quién?	whose?
del	of the, from the
esto	this
(no) estoy de acuerdo	I (don't) agree
para	(intended) for; in order to
¿por qué?	why?
porque	because
que	that; who
según	according to
si	if
tener (irreg.)... años	to be . . . years old

Repaso: ¿de dónde es Ud.?

De compras°

°De... *Shopping*

De compras en Plaza Inter, un centro comercial en Managua, Nicaragua

La... Clothing

DE COMPRAS: LA ROPA°

el impermeable
el traje
la gorra
la chaqueta
el sombrero
los *jeans**
la camiseta
el cinturón
el reloj
la ropa interior
el abrigo
la camisa
la corbata
los pantalones
los zapatos
el vestido
el suéter
los calcetines
la blusa
el traje de baño
las botas
la falda
un par de sandalias
los zapatos de tenis
la bolsa
las medias

Los verbos

comprar	to buy
llevar	to wear; to carry; to take
regatear	to haggle, bargain
usar	to wear; to use
vender	to sell
venden de todo	they sell (have) everything

Los lugares

el almacén	department store
el centro	downtown
el centro comercial	shopping mall
el mercado	market(place)
la tienda	shop, store

*The influx of U.S. goods to Latin America and Spain has affected common language. Jeans *is one example of an English word that is commonly used in Spanish-speaking countries.*

¿Cuánto cuesta?

la ganga	bargain	
el precio	price	
el precio fijo	fixed (set) price	
las rebajas	sales, reductions	
barato/a	inexpensive	
caro/a	expensive	

Otras palabras y expresiones útiles

la cartera	wallet; handbag*
es de (algodón, lana, seda)†	it is made of (cotton, wool, silk)
¡Es de última moda!	It's the latest style!

■ Conversación

A. La ropa

PASO 1   ¿Qué ropa llevan estas personas?

1. El Sr. Rivera lleva _____.

2. La Srta. Alonso lleva _____. El perro lleva _____.

3. Sara lleva _____.

4. Alfredo lleva _____. Necesita comprar _____.

PASO 2   De estas personas, ¿quién trabaja hoy? ¿Quién va a (*is going to*) una fiesta? ¿Quién no trabaja en este momento?

B. Asociaciones.   Complete las oraciones lógicamente con palabras de **De compras: La ropa.**

1. Un _____ es una tienda grande.
2. No es posible _____ cuando hay precios fijos.
3. En la librería, _____ de todo: textos y otros libros, cuadernos, lápices, discos compactos. Hay grandes _____ al final del semestre/trimestre, en los cuales (*in which*) todo es muy barato.
4. Siempre hay *boutiques* en los _____.
5. El _____ de una ciudad es la parte céntrica.
6. Estos artículos de ropa no son para hombres: _____.
7. Estos artículos de ropa son para hombres y mujeres: _____.
8. La ropa de _____ (material) es muy elegante.
9. La ropa de _____ es muy práctica.

---

*In some South American Spanish-speaking countries, speakers use la cartera to refer to a purse.

†Note another use of **ser** + **de:** to tell what material something is made of.

PASO 1

The preposition **para** can be used to express *in order to*, followed by an infinitive.

Para ir al centro, me gusta llevar pantalones, una camiseta y sandalias.
(*In order*) *To go downtown, I like to wear pants, a T-shirt, and sandals.*

Tag phrases can turn statements into questions. They are the equivalent of English *right?*, *don't they?*, *do I?*, *do you?*, and so on, at the end of a sentence.

Venden de todo aquí, **¿no?**
(**¿verdad?**)
No necesito impermeable hoy, **¿verdad?**

C. ¿Qué lleva Ud.?   Para hablar de Ud. y de la ropa, complete estas oraciones lógicamente.

1. Para ir a la universidad, me gusta llevar _____.
2. Para ir a las fiestas con los amigos, me gusta usar _____.
3. Para pasar un día en la playa (*beach*), me gusta llevar _____.
4. Cuando estoy en casa todo el día, llevo _____.
5. Nunca uso _____.
6. _____ es un artículo / son artículos de ropa absolutamente necesario(s) para mí.

D. Entrevista.   Using **¿no?** and **¿verdad?** (*right?*), ask a classmate questions based on the following statements. He or she will answer based on general information—or as truthfully as possible—if the question is about aspects of his or her life.

MODELO: E1: Estudias en la biblioteca por la noche, ¿verdad? (¿no?)
           E2: No. Estudio en la biblioteca por la mañana. (No, no estudio en la biblioteca. Me gusta estudiar en casa.)

1. En un almacén hay precios fijos.
2. Regateamos mucho en este país.
3. No hay muchos mercados en esta ciudad.
4. Los *jeans* Gap son muy baratos.
5. Es necesario llevar traje y corbata a clase.
6. Eres una persona muy independiente.
7. Tienes una familia muy grande.
8. No hay examen (*test*) mañana.

NOTA CULTURAL

La ropa en el mundo[a] hispánico

In Hispanic countries, people tend to dress more formally than do people in this country. As a rule, Hispanics consider neatness and care for one's appearance to be very important.

In the business world, women wear dressy pants, skirts, or dresses, and many wear high-heeled shoes. Men generally dress in trousers, shirts, and ties. Jeans, T-shirts, and tennis shoes are considered inappropriate in traditional business environments. Students at some business schools, like ESAN (**Escuela de Administración de Negocios**) in Peru, are even required to wear formal business attire to attend classes, as if they were already working at a company. Shorts and sweatpants are considered very casual and are reserved almost exclusively for use at home, for a day at the beach, or for sports.

Young adults generally dress casually in social situations, and, as in other countries, are often concerned with dressing according to current styles. As a rule, what is considered stylish in this country is also in style in Europe and Latin America.

[a]*world*

Ropa diseñada por (designed by) la famosa diseñadora venezolana Carolina Herrera

¿DE QUÉ COLOR ES?

Here are colors you can use to describe clothing and other objects.

rosado
blanco
negro
rojo
gris
anaranjado
amarillo
verde
morado   azul   (de) color café*

OJO Remember that colors, like all adjectives, must agree in gender and number with the nouns they modify. Note, however, that some colors only have one form for masculine and feminine nouns.

el traje **azul,** la camisa **azul**

■ Conversación

A. **Muchos colores.** ¿Cuántos colores hay en este cuadro (*painting*) de Gonzalo Endara Crow? ¿Cuáles son?

B. **Asociaciones.** ¿Qué colores asocia Ud. con… ?

1. el dinero
2. la una de la mañana
3. una mañana bonita
4. una mañana fea
5. el demonio
6. los Estados Unidos / el Canadá
7. una jirafa
8. un pingüino
9. un limón
10. una naranja
11. un elefante
12. las flores (*flowers*)

Después de (After) *la noche,* por el pintor ecuatoriano Gonzalo Endara Crow

*The expression **(de) color café** is invariable: **el sombrero (de) color café, la falda (de) color café, los pantalones (de) color café.**

Palabras útiles

de rayas (striped) **multicolor**

C. **¡Ojo alerta! ¿Escaparates (*Window displays*) idénticos?**   These window displays are almost alike . . . but not quite! Work with a partner to find at least eight differences between them.

MODELO: En el dibujo A hay _____, pero en el dibujo B hay _____.

A.   **B.**

Más... *Beyond the*

MÁS ALLÁ DEL° NÚMERO 100

Continúe la secuencia:

noventa y nueve, cien, ciento uno...
mil, dos mil...
un millón, dos millones...

100	cien, ciento	700	setecientos/as
101	ciento uno/una	800	ochocientos/as
200	doscientos/as	900	novecientos/as
300	trescientos/as	1.000*	mil
400	cuatrocientos/as	2.000	dos mil
500	quinientos/as	1.000.000	un millón
600	seiscientos/as	2.000.000	dos millones

- **Ciento** is used in combination with numbers from 1 to 99 to express the numbers 101 through 199: **ciento uno, ciento dos, ciento setenta y nueve,** and so on. **Cien** is used in counting and before numbers greater than 100: **cien mil, cien millones.**
- When the numbers 200 through 900 modify a noun, they must agree in gender: **cuatrocientas niñas, doscientas dos casas.**
- **Mil** means *one thousand* or *a thousand*. It does not have a plural form in counting, but **millón** does. When directly followed by a noun, **millón** (**dos millones,** and so on) must be followed by **de.**

  3.000 habitantes   tres mil habitantes
  14.000.000 **de** habitantes   catorce millones **de** habitantes

- Note how years are expressed in Spanish.

  1899   mil ochocientos noventa y nueve   2005   dos mil cinco

*In many parts of the Spanish-speaking world, a period in numerals is used where English uses a comma, and a comma is used to indicate the decimal where English uses a period: **$1.500; $1.000.000; $10,45; 65,9%.**

■ Conversación

A. ¿Cuánto pesan? (*How much do they weigh?*)

PASO 1   Estos son los animales terrestres más grandes. ¿Cuánto pesan en kilos? ¡OJO! Use el artículo masculino, menos para (*except for*) **jirafa.**

MODELO: El elefante pesa cinco mil kilos.

PASO 2   Pregúntele (*Ask*) a un compañero / una compañera aproximadamente cuánto pesan en libras las siguientes cosas.

1. su perro/gato
2. su mochila con los libros para hoy
3. su coche
4. su libro de español
5. el animal más grande del mundo (*world*)

B. ¿Cuánto es?   Diga (*Say*) los precios.

1. 7.345 euros
2. $100
3. 5.710 quetzales
4. 670 bolívares
5. $1.000.000
6. 528 nuevos pesos
7. 836 bolívares
8. 101 euros
9. $4.000.000,00
10. 6.000.000 quetzales

---

el dólar (los Estados Unidos, el Canadá, Puerto Rico)
el nuevo peso (México)
el bolívar (Venezuela)
el euro (España)
el quetzal (Guatemala)

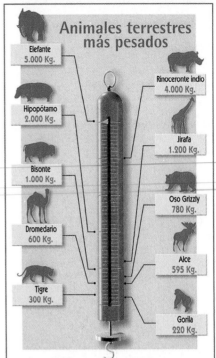

Animales terrestres más pesados

Elefante 5.000 Kg.
Rinoceronte indio 4.000 Kg.
Hipopótamo 2.000 Kg.
Jirafa 1.200 Kg.
Bisonte 1.000 Kg.
Oso Grizzly 780 Kg.
Dromedario 600 Kg.
Alce 595 Kg.
Tigre 300 Kg.
Gorila 220 Kg.

De los animales terrestres, el elefante, con sus 5.000 kilos de peso medio entre todas sus especies, es sin duda el mamífero más pesado. El hipopótamo y el rinoceronte son los siguientes en la lista, y el hombre, ni aparece.

Need more practice?

- Workbook/Laboratory Manual
- Interactive CD-ROM
- Online Learning Center (www.mhhe.com/quetal7)

PRONUNCIACIÓN: Stress and Written Accent Marks (Part 2)

¿Recuerda Ud.?

Most Spanish words do not need a written accent mark because their pronunciation is completely predictable by native speakers. Here are the two basic rules.

- A word that ends in a vowel, **-n,** or **-s** is stressed on the next-to-last syllable.
- A word that ends in any other consonant is stressed on the last syllable.

The written accent mark is used in the following situations.

- A written accent mark is needed when a word does not follow the two basic rules presented. Look at the words in this group.

  ta-bú   ca-fé   a-le-mán   na-ción   in-glés   es-tás

The preceding words end in a vowel, **-n,** or **-s,** so one would predict that they would be stressed on the next-to-last syllable. But the written accent mark shows that they are in fact accented on the last syllable.

- Now look at the words in this group.

lá-piz	dó-lar	ál-bum	á-gil	dó-cil

These words end in a consonant (other than **-n** or **-s**), so one would predict that they would be stressed on the last syllable. But the written accent mark shows that they are in fact accented on the next-to-last syllable.

- All words that are stressed on the third-to-last syllable must have a written accent mark.

bo-lí-gra-fo	ma-trí-cu-la	ma-te-má-ti-cas

- When a stressed weak vowel (**i** or **u**) is directly preceded or followed by a strong vowel (**a, e,** or **o**), it will have a written accent mark. This pattern is very frequent in words that end in **-ía.**

Ma-rí-a	po-li-cí-a	as-tro-no-mí-a
dí-a	bio-lo-gí-a	

- Contrast the pronunciation of those words with the following words in which the vowels **i** and **a** *do* form a diphthong.

Patricia	Francia	infancia	distancia

- Some one-syllable words have accents to distinguish them from other words that sound like them. For example:

él (*he*)/el (*the*)	tú (*you*)/tu (*your*)
sí (*yes*)/si (*if*)	mí (*me*)/mi (*my*)

- Interrogative and exclamatory words have a written accent on the stressed vowel. For example:

¿quién?	¡Qué ganga! (*What a bargain!*)
¿dónde?	

A. Sílabas. The following words have been separated into syllables for you. Read them aloud, paying careful attention to where the spoken stress should fall. Don't worry about the meaning of words you haven't heard before. The rules you have learned will help you pronounce them correctly.

1. a-quí	pa-pá	a-diós	bus-qué
2. prác-ti-co	mur-cié-la-go	te-lé-fo-no	ar-chi-pié-la-go
3. Ji-mé-nez	Ro-drí-guez	Pé-rez	Gó-mez
4. si-co-lo-gí-a	so-cio-lo-gí-a	sa-bi-du-rí-a	e-ner-gí-a
5. his-to-ria	te-ra-pia	Pre-to-ria	me-mo-ria

B. Reglas (*Rules*). Indicate the stressed vowel of each word in the following list. Give the rule that determines the stress of each word.

1. exámenes	**5.** actitud	**9.** están	**13.** plástico
2. lápiz	**6.** acciones	**10.** hombre	**14.** María
3. necesitar	**7.** dólares	**11.** peso	**15.** Rodríguez
4. perezoso	**8.** francés	**12.** mujer	**16.** Patricia

¿Recuerda Ud.?

You have already used the forms of **este** (*this*), one of the Spanish demonstrative adjectives. Review them by describing objects near you and the clothes you are wearing.

MODELO: Esta camisa es de rayas. Estos lápices son amarillos.

8 Pointing Out People and Things Demonstrative Adjectives and Pronouns

Suéteres a buenos precios

Susana necesita comprar un suéter en el mercado.

vendedor

Jorge

Susana

VENDEDOR: *Estos* suéteres de aquí cuestan 150 pesos y *ese* suéter en su mano cuesta 250 pesos.

SUSANA: ¿Por qué es más caro *este*?

VENDEDOR: Porque *esos* son de pura lana virgen, de excelente calidad.

SUSANA: ¿Y *aquellos* suéteres de rayas?

VENDEDOR: *Aquellos* cuestan cien pesos solamente; son acrílicos.

Comprensión: ¿Quién habla, Susana, Jorge o el vendedor?

1. Me gustan estos suéteres de rayas, y sólo cuestan cien pesos.
2. Señores, miren (*look at*) estos suéteres en mi mesa. Cuestan 150 pesos.
3. Voy a (*I am going to*) comprar este suéter. Me gusta la ropa de lana.
4. Este suéter acrílico es más barato que aquel suéter de lana.

Demonstrative Adjectives

Demonstrative Adjectives

	Singular			Plural	
this	este abrigo	esta gorra	*these*	estos abrigos	estas gorras
that	ese abrigo aquel abrigo (allí)	esa gorra aquella gorra (allí)	*those*	esos abrigos aquellos abrigos (allí)	esas gorras aquellas gorras (allí)

Sweaters at good prices Susana needs to buy a sweater in the market. SALESMAN: *These sweaters here cost 150 pesos and that sweater in your hand costs 250 pesos.* SUSANA: *Why is this one more expensive?* SALESMAN: *Because those are of pure virgin wool, of excellent quality.* SUSANA: *What about those striped sweaters over there?* SALESMAN: *Those cost only one hundred pesos; they are acrylic.*

PASO 2

OJO Note that the final **-e** in the singular forms **este** and **ese** becomes an **-o** in the plural forms: **estos, esos.**

Demonstrative adjectives (**Los adjetivos demostrativos**) are used to indicate a specific noun or nouns. In Spanish, demonstrative adjectives precede the nouns they modify. They also agree in number and gender with the nouns.

In the chart on page 87, **allí** ([*over*] *there*) is provided as a clue that **aquel, aquella, aquellos,** and **aquellas** refer to a more remote location. However, it is not obligatory to use the word **allí** when using forms of **aquel.**

> **demonstrative adjective** = adjective used in place of a definite article to indicate a particular person, place, thing, or idea

There are two ways to say *that/those* in Spanish. Forms of **ese** refer to nouns that are not close to the speaker in space or in time. Forms of **aquel** refer to nouns that are even farther away.

Este niño es mi hijo. **Ese** joven es mi hijo también. Y **aquel** señor allí es mi esposo.
This boy is my son. That young man is also my son. And that man over there is my husband.

Demonstrative Pronouns*

- *Demonstrative pronouns* (**Los pronombres demostrativos**) are used to point out or indicate people, places, or things when omitting the noun they refer to (remember that pronouns replace nouns). *Demonstrative pronouns* are the same as *demonstrative adjectives,* except that the noun is not used. In English, the demonstrative pronouns are *this* (*one*), *that* (*one*), *these,* and *those.*

- In Spanish, demonstrative pronouns agree in gender and number with the noun they are replacing, as in the preceding example.

—¿Te gusta aquella casa?
Do you like that house?

—¿Cuál?
Which one?

—**Aquella,** con las ventanas grandes.
***That one,** with the big windows.*

—¡Ah, **aquella** me gusta mucho!
*Oh, I like **that one** a lot!*

- Use the neuter demonstratives **esto, eso,** and **aquello** to refer to as yet unidentified objects or to a whole idea, concept, or situation.

¿Qué es **esto?** **Eso** es todo. ¡**Aquello** es terrible!
What is this? *That's it. That's all.* *That's terrible!*

AUTOPRUEBA

Match each word with the corresponding meaning in English.

1. _____ estas   a. that
2. _____ aquellos   b. those (over there)
3. _____ ese   c. these
4. _____ esas   d. this
5. _____ este   e. those

Answers: 1. c 2. b 3. a 4. e 5. d

*Some Spanish speakers prefer to use accents on these forms: **este coche y ése, aquella casa y ésta.** However, it is acceptable in modern Spanish, per the **Real Academia Española** in Madrid, to omit the accent on these forms when context makes the meaning clear and no ambiguity is possible. To learn more about these forms, consult Appendix 2, Using Adjectives As Nouns.

■ Práctica

A. Comparaciones. Restate the sentences, changing forms of **este** to **ese** and adding **también,** following the model. Then restate a second time changing the forms of **este** to **aquel.**

MODELO: Este abrigo es muy grande. →
Ese abrigo también es muy grande.
Aquel abrigo también es muy grande.

1. Esta falda es muy pequeña.
2. Estos pantalones son muy largos.
3. Este libro es muy bueno.
4. Estas corbatas son muy feas.

B. Situaciones. Find an appropriate response for each situation.

1. Aquí hay un regalo para Ud.
2. Ocurre un accidente en la cafetería: Ud. tiene tomate en su camisa favorita.
3. No hay clases mañana.
4. La matrícula cuesta más este semestre/ trimestre.
5. Ud. tiene una A en su examen de español.

Posibilidades

¡Eso es un desastre!
¿Qué es esto?
¡Eso es magnífico!
¡Eso es terrible!

Need more practice?
■ Workbook/Laboratory Manual
■ Interactive CD-ROM
■ Online Learning Center (www.mhhe.com/quetal7)

■ Conversación

Una tarde en un patio mexicano

PASO 1 Write brief descriptions of the following people and pets without identifying their location in the drawing.

MODELO: Lleva una falda y zapatos azules…

 PASO 2 Now take turns with a partner reading a description. Your partner will guess who you're talking about. You should use demonstratives (**este/ese/aquel**) to identify the person.

MODELO: E1: Lleva una falda y zapatos azules…
E2: Es esta mujer.

PASO 3 Now work with your partner to invent information about the people. Include names, where they're from, and their relationship to others in the drawing.

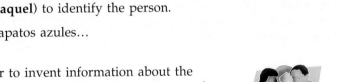

MODELO: Esta mujer se llama María. Es de Cuernavaca. Es la hermana de aquel hombre…

PASO 2

9 Expressing Actions and States *Tener, venir, preferir, querer,* and *poder;* Some Idioms with *tener*

Una gorra para José Miguel

Elisa acompaña a* su hijo José Miguel para buscar una gorra.

ELISA: ¿Qué gorra *prefieres,* José Miguel?

JOSÉ MIGUEL: *Prefiero* la gris.

ELISA: ¡Pero ya *tienes* una gris, y es casi idéntica!

JOSÉ MIGUEL: Pues, no *quiero* esas otras gorras. ¿*Podemos* mirar en la tienda anterior otra vez?

ELISA: ¿Otra vez? Bueno, si realmente insistes…

Comprensión: ¿Sí o no?

1. José Miguel quiere comprar una corbata.
2. Él prefiere la gorra azul.

3. No puede decidir entre las gorras.
4. Elisa tiene mucha paciencia.

Tener, venir, preferir, querer, **and** *poder*

tener (*to have*)

tengo	tenemos
tienes	tenéis
tiene	tienen

venir (*to come*)

vengo	venimos
vienes	venís
viene	vienen

preferir (*to prefer*)

prefiero	preferimos
prefieres	preferís
prefiere	prefieren

querer (*to want*)

quiero	queremos
quieres	queréis
quiere	quieren

poder (*to be able, can*)

puedo	podemos
puedes	podéis
puede	pueden

- The **yo** forms of **tener** and **venir** are irregular.

- In other forms of **tener** and **venir,** and in **preferir** and **querer,** the stressed stem vowel **e** becomes **ie.**

- Similarly, the stem vowel **o** in **poder** becomes **ue** when stressed.

- In vocabulary lists these changes are shown in parentheses after the infinitive: **poder (ue).** Verbs of this type are called *stem-changing verbs.* You will learn more verbs of this type in **Gramática 10.**

Irregularities:

tener: yo tengo, tú tienes (e → ie)…
venir: yo vengo, tú vienes (e → ie)…
preferir, querer: (e → ie)

poder: (o → ue)

 The **nosotros** and **vosotros** forms of these verbs do not have changes in the stem vowel because it is not stressed.

A cap for José Miguel *Elisa accompanies her son José Miguel to look for a cap.* ELISA: *Which cap do you prefer, José Miguel?* JOSÉ MIGUEL: *I prefer the gray one.* ELISA: *But you already have a gray one, and it's almost identical!* JOSÉ MIGUEL: *Well, I don't want those other caps. Can we look in the previous store again?* ELISA: *Again? Well, if you really insist . . .*

*Remember that the word **a** is necessary before a direct object that is a specific person. You will learn more about this use of **a** in **Capítulo 6.**

Some Idioms with *tener*

A. Many ideas expressed in English with the verb *to be* are expressed in Spanish with *idioms* (**los modismos**) using **tener.** You have already used one **tener** idiom: **tener… años.** At the right are some additional ones. Note that they describe a condition or state that a person can experience.

> **idiom** = an expression whose meaning cannot be inferred from the meanings of the words that make it up

Idiomatic expressions are often different from one language to another. For example, in English, *to pull Mary's leg* usually means *to tease her,* not *to grab her leg and pull it.* In Spanish, *to pull Mary's leg* is **tomarle el pelo a Mary** (literally, *to take hold of Mary's hair*).

tener miedo (de)

tener prisa

tener razón

no tener razón

tener sueño

B. Other **tener** idioms include **tener ganas de** (*to feel like*) and **tener que** (*to have to*). The infinitive is always used after these two idiomatic expressions.

> Note that the English translation of one of these examples results in a verb ending in *-ing,* not the infinitive.

Tengo ganas de **comer.**
I feel like eating.

¿No tiene Ud. que **leer** este capítulo?
Don't you have to read this chapter?

AUTOPRUEBA

Give the missing letters in each verb.

1. p____des
2. pr____fiere
3. ve____o
4. t____nemos
5. qu____ro
6. t____nen

Answers: 1. puedes 2. prefiere 3. vengo 4. tenemos 5. quiero 6. tienen

---

Paso 2 Gramática

■ Práctica

A. ¡Sara tiene mucha tarea (*homework*)!

PASO 1 Haga (*Form*) oraciones con las palabras indicadas. Añada (*Add*) palabras si es necesario.

MODELO: Sara / tener / que / estudiar / mucho / hoy → Sara tiene que estudiar mucho hoy.

1. Sara / tener / muchos exámenes
2. (ella) venir / a / universidad / todos los días
3. hoy / trabajar / hasta / nueve / de / noche
4. preferir / estudiar / en / biblioteca
5. querer / leer / más / pero / no poder
6. por eso / regresar / a / casa
7. tener / ganas de / leer / más
8. pero / unos amigos / venir a mirar / televisión
9. Sara / decidir / mirar / televisión / con ellos

PASO 2 Now retell the same sequence of events, first as if they had happened to you, using **yo** as the subject of all but sentence number 8, then as if they had happened to you and your roommate, using **nosotros/as**.

B. Situaciones. Expand the situations in these sentences by using an appropriate idiom with **tener.** There is often more than one possible answer.

MODELO: Tengo un examen mañana. Por eso… →
Por eso tengo que estudiar mucho.

1. ¿Cuántos años? ¿Cuarenta? No, yo…
2. Un perro grande y feo vive en esa casa. Por eso yo…
3. ¿Ya son las tres de la mañana? Ah, por eso yo…
4. No, dos y dos no son cinco. Son cuatro. Tú…
5. Son las tres menos cuarto y tengo que estar en el centro a las tres. Yo…
6. Cuando hay un terremoto (*earthquake*), todos…
7. ¿Los exámenes de esa clase? ¡Esos son siempre muy fáciles (*easy*)! Yo no…
8. Sí, la capital de la Argentina es Buenos Aires. Tú…

■ Conversación

Need more practice?

- Workbook/Laboratory Manual
- Interactive CD-ROM
- Online Learning Center (www.mhhe.com/quetal7)

NOTA COMUNICATIVA

Using *mucho* and *poco*

In the first chapters of *¿Qué tal?*, you have used the words **mucho** and **poco** as both adjectives and adverbs. *Adverbs* (**Los adverbios**) are words that modify verbs, adjectives, or other adverbs: *quickly, very* smart, *very quickly*. In Spanish and in English, adverbs are invariable in form. However, in Spanish adjectives agree in number and gender with the word they modify.

> **adverb** = a word that modifies a verb, adjective, or another adverb

ADVERB

Rosario estudia **mucho** hoy.
Julio come **poco.**

Rosario is studying a lot today.
Julio doesn't eat much.

ADJECTIVE

Rosario tiene **mucha** ropa. Sobre todo tiene **muchos** zapatos.
Julio come **poca** carne. Come **pocos** postres.

Rosario has a lot of clothes. She especially has a lot of shoes.
Julio doesn't eat much meat. He eats few desserts.

A. Preferencias

PASO 1 Working with a classmate, try to predict the choices your instructor will make in each of the following cases.

MODELO: El profesor / La profesora tiene… muchos / pocos libros →
muchos libros

1. El profesor / La profesora tiene…
   mucha ropa / poca ropa   sólo un coche / varios coches
2. Prefiere…
   los gatos / los perros   la ropa elegante / la ropa informal
3. Quiere comprar…
   un coche deportivo (*sports car*), por ejemplo, un Porsche / una
   camioneta (*station wagon*)
   un abrigo / un impermeable
4. Viene a la universidad…
   todos los días / sólo tres veces a la semana
   en coche / en autobús / en bicicleta / a pie (*on foot*)
5. Esta noche tiene muchas ganas de…
   mirar la televisión / leer   comer en un restaurante / comer en casa
6. Su color favorito es… verde / rojo / amarillo
7. Prefiere usar… botas / zapatos / sandalias

PASO 2 Now, using tag questions, ask your instructor questions to find out if you are correct.

MODELO: muchos libros →
Ud. tiene muchos libros, ¿verdad?

B. Estereotipos.
Draw some conclusions about Isabel based on this scene. Think about things that she has, needs to or has to do or buy, likes, and so on. When you have finished, compare your predictions with a classmate's. Did you both reach the same conclusions?

MODELO: Isabel tiene cuatro gatos. Tiene que…

Palabras útiles
los aretes (earrings) **el juguete** (toy) **los muebles** (furniture) **el sofá**
hablar por teléfono **tener** (*irreg.*) **alergia a** (to be allergic to)

LITERATURA: Rubén Darío

Rubén Darío
(1867–1916)

Sobre el autor: *The Nicaraguan writer, journalist, and diplomat Rubén Darío was one of the most celebrated poets of the movement known as* **modernismo.** *Darío was born Félix Rubén García Sarmiento, in Metapa, a city in Nicaragua now named Darío. He was a major influence on later writers in Latin America, Spain, and Europe. These lines are from the poem "¡Eheu!,"[a] El canto errante[b] (1907).*

> Aquí, junto al[c] mar latino,
> digo[d] la verdad:
> siento[e] en roca, aceite[f] y vino,
> yo mi antigüedad.[g]
>
> ¡Oh, qué anciano soy, Dios santo,
> oh, qué anciano soy!...
> ¿De dónde viene mi canto?
> Y yo, ¿adónde voy[h]?

[a]*Latin word that means "Alas!"* [b]*El… The Wandering Song* [c]*junto… next to the* [d]*I tell* [e]*I feel* [f]*oil* [g]*antiquity, age* [h]*do I go*

MÚSICA: Los garífuna

La punta es la música tradicional de los garífuna, un grupo afro-indígena de las costas de Nicaragua, Honduras y Belice. Su música es esencial en sus ritos[a] y tradiciones. Los instrumentos tradicionales son el garawón[b] y otros instrumentos de percusión. Típicamente hay competencias[c] entre parejas[d] que bailan. Como muchos otros géneros[e] de música caribeña, se basa[f] en la llamada y respuesta.[g]

[a]*rituals* [b]*traditional drum of Central America* [c]*competitions* [d]*entre… between couples* [e]*Como… Like many other genres, types* [f]*se… it is based* [g]*llamada… call and response (in music, a succession of phrases in which the second phrase is a response to the first, and so on; the "communication" is between two different musicians, between a musician and a singer or dancer, or between two or more singers)*

Todos los años[h] en mayo[i] en Bluefields en la costa atlántica de Nicaragua, se celebra[j] el festival Palo de Mayo.[k] El festival es una tradición que refleja[l] la confluencia[m] de tradiciones europeas y africanas. De Europa vienen las fiestas del *maypole*, y de África, las celebraciones en honor a Mayaya, diosa[n] de la fertilidad. Antes bailaban las damas y caballeros[o] alrededor del[p] palo de mayo a la música del vals,[q] la polka y la mazurca. Ahora comparsas[r] del pueblo[s] garífuna bailan al ritmo[t] de sus garawones.

[h]*Todos… Every year* [i]*May* [j]*se… is celebrated* [k]*Palo… Maypole* [l]*reflects* [m]*coming together* [n]*goddess* [o]*Antes… Before ladies and noblemen used to dance* [p]*alrededor… around the* [q]*waltz* [r]*dance troupes* [s]*people* [t]*rhythm*

10 Expressing Destination and Future Actions Ir; ir + a + Infinitive; The Contraction *al*

¿Adónde *vas*?

Rosa y Casandra son compañeras de cuarto.

CASANDRA:	¿Adónde *vas*?
ROSA:	*Voy al* centro.
CASANDRA:	¿Qué *vas a* hacer en el centro?
ROSA:	*Voy a* comprar un vestido para la fiesta de Javier. ¿No *vas a ir* a su fiesta este fin de semana?
CASANDRA:	¡Claro que *voy*!

Comprensión: ¿Sí o no?

1. Rosa va a estudiar.
2. Rosa va a hacer (*give*) una fiesta.
3. Casandra va a asistir a la fiesta.

Ir is the irregular Spanish verb used to express *to go*.

ir (*to go*)	
voy	**vamos**
vas	**vais**
va	**van**

The first person plural of **ir, vamos** (*we go, are going, do go*), is also used to express *let's go*.

Vamos a clase ahora mismo.
Let's go to class right now.

Ir + a + Infinitive

Ir + a + infinitive is used to describe actions or events in the near future.

Van a venir a la fiesta esta noche.
They're going to come to the party tonight.

Where are you going? Rosa and Casandra are roommates. CASANDRA: *Where are you going?* ROSA: *I'm going downtown.* CASANDRA: *What are you going to do downtown?* ROSA: *I'm going to buy a dress for Javier's party. Aren't you going to go to his party this weekend?* CASANDRA: *Of course I'm going!*

The Contraction *al*

In **Capítulo 2** you learned about the contraction **del (de + el → del).** The only other contraction in Spanish is **al (a + el → al). ¡OJO!** Both **del** and **al** are obligatory contractions.

a + el → al

Voy **al** centro comercial.
I'm going to the mall.

Vamos **a la** tienda.
We're going to the store.

■ Práctica

A. ¿Adónde van de compras? Haga oraciones completas usando **ir.** Recuerde: **a + el → al.**

MODELO: Marta / el centro → Marta *va al* centro.

1. nosotros / una *boutique*
2. Francisco / el almacén Goya
3. Juan y Raúl / el centro comercial
4. tú / un mercado
5. Ud. / una tienda pequeña
6. yo / ¿ ?

B. ¡Vamos de compras! Describa el día, desde el punto de vista (*from the point of view*) de Lola, la esposa de Manolo. Use **ir + a +** el infinitivo, según el modelo.

MODELO: Manolo compra un regalo para su madre. →
        Manolo *va a comprar* un regalo para su madre.

1. Llegamos al centro a las diez de la mañana.
2. Mi hija Marta quiere comer algo (*something*).
3. Compro unos chocolates para Marta.
4. Manolo busca una blusa de seda.
5. No compras esta blusa azul, ¿verdad?
6. Buscamos algo más barato.
7. ¿Vas de compras mañana también?

Need more practice?

■ Workbook/Laboratory Manual
■ Interactive CD-ROM
■ Online Learning Center
  (www.mhhe.com/quetal7)

■ Conversación

A. ¿Adónde va Ud. si... ? ¿Cuántas oraciones puede hacer?

MODELO: Me gusta leer novelas. Por eso voy a una librería.

Me gusta	+	leer novelas. ir de compras —¡y no regateo! buscar gangas y regatear. hablar con mis amigos. comer en restaurantes elegantes. mirar programas de detectives.	+	Por eso voy a _____.

B. Entrevista: El fin de semana

PASO 1   Interview a classmate about his or her plans for the weekend. "Personalize" the interview with additional questions. For example, if your partner is going to read a novel, ask **¿Qué novela?** or **¿Quién es el autor?**

¿Vas a... ?

1. ir de compras
2. leer una novela
3. asistir a un concierto
4. estudiar para un examen
5. ir a una fiesta
6. escribir una carta
7. ir a bailar
8. escribir los ejercicios para la clase de español
9. practicar un deporte (*sport*)
10. mirar mucho la televisión
11. comprar ropa en un centro comercial
12. escuchar cintas (*tapes*) o CDs en español

PASO 2   En el **Paso 1,** los números pares (2, 4, 6,...) son actividades pasivas o tranquilas. Los números impares (1, 3, 5,...) son más activas. ¿Cómo es su compañero/a? ¿Es activo/a? ¿O prefiere la tranquilidad?

En los Estados Unidos y el Canadá

Los hispanos en el mundo de la moda

Christy Turlington is one of many Hispanic celebrities in the U.S. world of fashion. Born in San Francisco, California (1969), to a Salvadoran mother, Turlington has been a household name since the 1990s. During her career as a supermodel, she became an activist for and benefactor of several causes, including breast cancer and animal rights. Furthermore, after being diagnosed with early-stage emphysema and subsequently quitting smoking, Christy became the spokesperson for a government antitobacco campaign.

Christy Turlington

UN POCO DE TODO

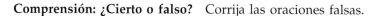

Lengua y cultura: Pero, ¿no se puede *(can't one)* **regatear?** Complete the following paragraph with the correct form of the words in parentheses, as suggested by the context. When two possibilities are given in parentheses, select the correct word.

¿A Ud. le gusta ir de compras? ¿Le gusta regatear? En (los/las[1]) ciudades hispánicas, hay una (grande[2]) variedad de tiendas para (ir[3]) de compras. Hay almacenes, centros comerciales y *boutiques* (elegante[4]), como en (los/las[5]) Estados Unidos y el Canadá, donde los precios son siempre (fijo[6]).

También hay tiendas (pequeño[7]) que venden un solo[a] producto. Por ejemplo,[b] en una zapatería sólo hay zapatos. En español el sufijo **-ería** se usa[c] para (formar[8]) el nombre de la tienda. ¿Dónde (creer[9]) Ud. que venden papel y (otro[10]) artículos de escritorio? ¿A qué tienda (ir[11]) a ir Ud. a comprar fruta?

Si Ud. (poder[12]) pagar el precio que piden,[d] (deber[13]) comprar los recuerdos[e] en (los/las[14]) almacenes o *boutiques*. Pero si (tener[15]) ganas o necesidad de regatear, tiene (de/que[16]) ir a un mercado: un conjunto[f] de tiendas o locales[g] donde el ambiente[h] es más (informal[17]) que[i] en los (grande[18]) almacenes. Ud. no (deber[19]) pagar el primer[j] precio que menciona el vendedor.[k] ¡Casi siempre va (a/de[20]) ser muy alto!

[a]*single* [b]*Por... For example* [c]*se... is used* [d]*they ask* [e]*souvenirs* [f]*group* [g]*stalls* [h]*atmosphere* [i]*than* [j]*first* [k]*seller*

Comprensión: ¿Cierto o falso? Corrija las oraciones falsas.

1. En el mundo hispánico, todas las tiendas son similares.
2. Uno puede regatear en un almacén hispánico.
3. Es posible comprar limones en una papelería.
4. En un mercado, el vendedor siempre ofrece un precio bajo al principio *(beginning)*.

Un mercado en Chincheros, Perú

Resources for Review and Testing Preparation

- Workbook/Laboratory Manual
- Interactive CD-ROM
- Online Learning Center (www.mhhe.com/quetal7)

Un paso más   PASO 4

VIDEOTECA

Entrevista cultural: Nicaragua

Delvia Argüello is a young woman from Nicaragua who works in her family's business. In this interview she talks about herself, her work, and her plans for the future. Among other things, she mentions how climate affects clothing styles in her country. Before watching the video clip, read the following excerpt from the interview.

INTERVIEWER: …¿Cómo se llama Ud. y de dónde es?
DELVIA: Me llamo Delvia Argüello y soy de Managua, Nicaragua. Tengo 24 años.
INTERVIEWER: ¿En dónde vive Ud.?
DELVIA: En Managua con mi familia. Mi familia tiene una tienda de ropa, eh, para mujeres. Allí se vende ropa, de… pantalones, camisas, zapatos y accesorios.

Now watch the video clip and answer the following questions based on the interview.

1. How old is Delvia?
2. What city is she from?
3. What is her family's business?
4. In the family business, who takes care of (**manejar**) the store, and who travels (**viajar**)?
5. What would Delvia like to do in the future?

Entre amigos: ¡Está súper fuera de moda (*out of style*)!

Miguel, Tané, Karina, and Rubén are shopping in a small flea market. What questions do you think they will ask each other? Before watching the video, read the following questions. As you watch, don't worry if you don't understand every word. Try to get the gist of the conversation, listening carefully for information about clothing. Watch the video a second time and listen for the answers to the questions.

1. ¿A Karina le gusta la chaqueta que escoge (*chooses*) Tané? ¿Por qué?
2. En la opinión de Karina, ¿es importante o no la moda? ¿Por qué?
3. ¿Qué tipo de ropa usa Rubén?
4. ¿Qué artículo de ropa compra Tané?

ENFOQUE CULTURAL

Nicaragua

¡Fíjese!

- En 1856, un estadounidense, William Walker, se declaró[a] presidente de Nicaragua. Dos años después, fue derrotado por[b] los nicaragüenses, liberales y conservadores que se unieron[c] para expulsarlo[d] del país.
- El Lago de Nicaragua es el lago más grande de Centroamérica. También se llama el Lago Cocibolca. Hay más de 300 islas en el lago. En estas «isletas», hay pequeñas comunidades agrícolas[e] y, en algunas,[f] casas de personas ricas. En la isleta de San Pablo, hay una fortaleza[g] construida por los españoles para protegerse[h] de los piratas ingleses. Los nicaragüenses llaman el lago su «mar dulce»[i] porque es muy grande y porque tiene agua dulce.[j] Tiene los únicos tiburones[k] de agua dulce del mundo.[l]

[a]se… declared himself [b]fue… he was defeated by [c]se… joined together [d]expel him [e]agricultural [f]some (of them) [g]fort [h]protect themselves [i]mar… sweet (fresh water) sea [j]agua… fresh water [k]únicos… only sharks [l]world

Learn more about Nicaragua with the Video, Interactive CD-ROM, and the Online Learning Center (www.mhhe.com/quetal7).

Nota histórica

Cristóbal Colón llegó[a] a las costas de Nicaragua en 1502, pero la región no fue colonizada[b] hasta[c] 1524.

Nicaragua tiene una historia turbulenta por las luchas[d] entre las fuerzas conservadoras y las fuerzas liberales. La lucha se complicó[e] por la intervención de los Estados Unidos en la política del país. En 1990 terminó[f] una época[g] difícil de dictadura y lucha: hubo[h] una revolución y un movimiento en contra de la revolución. Esta lucha fue entre los sandinistas (revolucionarios marxistas) y los «contras» (antirrevolucionarios).

[a]arrived [b]no… was not colonized [c]until [d]struggles [e]se… was complicated [f]ended [g]time [h]there was

Parte de las ruinas de la fortaleza en la isleta de San Pablo, en el Lago de Nicaragua

Sobre la lectura… This reading is adapted from an article that appeared in *Quo*, a magazine published in Spain that is comparable to *Vanity Fair*, *Details*, and other glossy general interest magazines. *Quo* publishes articles about topics ranging from diet and health to fashion to politics.

PASO FINAL

 A LEER

ESTRATEGIA: Using Visual Clues to Predict Content

In **Capítulo 1** you learned that you can use section subheadings to help you better understand a passage. Another useful strategy is to use photographs and other visual clues (charts, drawings, graphic images, and so on) that accompany the reading as tools to help you predict the content of the passage. A successful reader is able to make predictions about content in advance, and then confirms or rejects these predictions while reading.

Before reading the article that follows, look at the titles above each paragraph. What predictions can you make based on the visual presentation of these paragraph titles?

La psicología de los colores

«Está demostrado[a] que los colores percibidos[b] por la vista[c] <u>provocan</u> una reacción psicológica sobre nuestro estado de ánimo[d]», asegura Carlos Obelleiro, <u>experto</u> en la utilización de color. Y de un buen estado de ánimo depende mucho la salud física. Según expertos en psicología de los colores, cada uno indica una actitud en quien lo lleva puesto.[e]

Rojo
Es el color que produce mayor impacto visual. Actúa como un estimulante psíquico, pero activa la <u>agresividad</u> y si alguien lo lleva puede incomodar a los demás.[f]

Amarillo
Está íntimamente relacionado con la autoestima[g] y <u>estimula</u> la creatividad, pero puede resultar agresivo para gente emocionalmente <u>frágil</u>.

Azul
Favorece la calma y la concentración en trabajos que exigen[h] esfuerzo[i] mental. Tranquiliza, pero puede dar imagen de frialdad.[j] Cuanto más oscuro es,[k] más idea da[l] de eficiencia y autoridad.

Verde
Es el color más relajante y suele[m] provocar una sensación de <u>equilibrio</u> y de tranquilidad personal.

Blanco
Aunque[n] es muy higiénico, puede resultar muy severo y dar la impresión de que la persona que lo lleva quiere crear una barrera.[o]

Rosado
Es la más pura expresión de la <u>feminidad</u>. Utilizado en decoración actúa como relajante, pero en exceso causa debilitamiento.[p]

Negro
Es elegante, pero puede resultar amenazador[q] y, como el blanco, crear barreras entre la persona que lo lleva y el resto de la gente.

Violeta
Es el color de la introversión. Puede transmitir la sensación de que quien lo viste[r] quiere estar solo, sin intromisiones.[s]

Gris
Se trata del único color totalmente <u>neutro</u>, con lo que no tiene apenas[t] propiedades psicológicas. A veces puede indicar falta[u] de confianza en uno mismo. ◼

[a]*Está… It has been shown* [b]*perceived* [c]*sight* [d]*estado… state of mind* [e]*quien… the person who wears it* [f]*incomodar… make others uncomfortable* [g]*self-esteem* [h]*demand* [i]*effort* [j]*coldness* [k]*Cuanto… The darker it is* [l]*it gives* [m]*it tends to* [n]*Although* [o]*crear… to create a barrier* [p]*debilitation, weakness* [q]*threatening* [r]*quien… the person who wears it* [s]*sin… without intrusions* [t]*hardly any* [u]*a lack*

PASO 4

Comprensión

A. ¿Qué color?   Identify the color (or colors!) that corresponds to each psychological trait below, according to the reading.

1. Este color no se asocia con la extroversión, sino lo contrario (*but rather the opposite*).
2. A veces este color se asocia con la frigidez.
3. Estos dos colores dan la impresión de crear obstáculos.
4. Este color provoca reacciones muy agresivas.
5. Este color provoca la creatividad.
6. Este color es un estimulante psíquico.
7. Este color tiene muy poco estímulo psíquico.
8. Estos colores son relajantes.
9. Este color puede expresar eficiencia.

B. ¿Qué color recomienda Ud. (*do you recommend*)**?**   Which color do you recommend a person use in order to make the following impressions or provoke the following reactions?

1. Una persona desea crear una impresión de control y poder (*power*).
2. Una persona quiere expresar su confianza en sí misma (*confidence in him- or herself*).
3. Una persona no quiere producir ningún (*any*) impacto.
4. Una persona quiere tener un lugar muy tranquilo y relajante en su casa.

 A ESCRIBIR

A. Mi ropa favorita.   In a brief paragraph, write a description of your favorite article of clothing. Use the questions that follow to organize your thoughts. Your instructor can help you with words or constructions that are unfamiliar to you.

¿De qué material es?
¿Por qué le gusta?
¿De qué color es?
¿Cómo se siente (*do you feel*) cuando lleva este artículo de ropa? (Me siento… tranquilo/a, enérgico/a, etcétera.)
¿Provoca el color algunas (*any*) reacciones como las reacciones descritas (*described*) en la lectura? ¿Cuáles?

B. El inventario.   Take an inventory of the clothing you have and express it in Spanish.

- What items do you have? How many of each? What colors?
- Do you have clothes that you wear almost every week? What items are they? Why do you wear them often?
- How many things do you have in your closet and drawers that you no longer wear or do not need? What are they?

You can describe your clothing inventory in paragraph form or create a table or list to show the things you have.

GRAMÁTICA

To review the grammar points presented in this chapter, refer to the indicated grammar presentations. You'll find further practice of these structures in the Workbook/Laboratory Manual, on the Interactive CD-ROM, and on the *¿Qué tal?* Online Learning Center (www.mhhe.com/quetal7).

8 Pointing Out People and Things—Demonstrative Adjectives and Pronouns.

Do you know the forms for **este, ese,** and **aquel?**

9 Expressing Actions and States—**Tener, venir, preferir, querer,** and **poder;** Some Idioms with **tener**

You should be able to conjugate the verbs **tener, venir, preferir, querer,** and **poder.** Do you know how to use expressions like **tengo ganas de, tenemos miedo,** and **tienes razón?**

10 Expressing Destination and Future Actions—**Ir; ir + a +** Infinitive; The Contraction **al**

You should know the forms of **ir** and how to express *going to do* (*something*). You should also know when to use the contraction **al.**

VOCABULARIO
Practice this vocabulary with digital flash cards on the Online Learning Center (www.mhhe.com/quetal7).

Los verbos

ir (*irreg.*)	to go
ir a + *inf.*	to be going to (*do something*)
ir de compras	to go shopping
llevar	to wear; to carry; to take
poder (ue)	to be able, can
preferir (ie)	to prefer
querer (ie)	to want
regatear	to haggle, bargain
tener (*irreg.*)	to have
usar	to wear; to use
venir (*irreg.*)	to come

Repaso: comprar, vender

La ropa

el abrigo	coat
los aretes	earrings
la blusa	blouse
la bolsa	purse
la bota	boot
el calcetín (*pl.* calcetines)	sock socks
la camisa	shirt

la camiseta	T-shirt
la cartera	wallet; handbag
la chaqueta	jacket
el cinturón	belt
la corbata	tie
la falda	skirt
la gorra	cap
el impermeable	raincoat
los *jeans*	jeans
las medias	stockings
los pantalones	pants
el par	pair
el reloj	watch
la ropa	clothes; clothing
la ropa interior	underwear
la sandalia	sandal
el sombrero	hat
el suéter	sweater
el traje	suit
el traje de baño	swimsuit
el vestido	dress
el zapato (de tenis)	(tennis) shoe

De compras

la ganga	bargain
el precio (fijo)	(fixed, set) price
las rebajas	sales, reductions

de todo	everything
de última moda	the latest style
¿cuánto cuesta?	how much does it cost?
¿cuánto es?	how much is it?

Los materiales

es de...	it is made of . . .
algodón (*m.*)	cotton
lana	wool
seda	silk

Los lugares

el almacén	department store
el centro	downtown
el centro comercial	shopping mall
el mercado	market(place)
la tienda	shop, store

Los colores

amarillo/a	yellow
anaranjado/a	orange
azul	blue
blanco/a	white
(de) color café	brown
gris	gray
morado/a	purple
negro/a	black
rojo/a	red
rosado/a	pink
verde	green

Otros sustantivos

la cinta	tape
el ejercicio	exercise
el examen	exam, test

Los adjetivos

barato/a	inexpensive
caro/a	expensive
poco/a	little

Repaso: mucho/a

Más allá del número 100

doscientos/as
trescientos/as
cuatrocientos/as
quinientos/as
seiscientos/as
setecientos/as
ochocientos/as
novecientos/as
mil
un millón (de)

Repaso: cien(to)

Formas demostrativas

aquel, aquella, aquellos/as	that, those (over there)
ese/a, esos/as	that, those
eso, aquello	that, that (over there)

Repaso: este/a, esto, estos/as

Palabras adicionales

¿adónde?	where (to)?
al	to the
algo	something
allí	(over) there

tener (*irreg.*)...	
ganas de + *inf.*	to feel like (*doing something*)
miedo (de)	to be afraid (of)
prisa	to be in a hurry
que + *inf.*	to have to (*do something*)
razón	to be right
sueño	to be sleepy
no tener (*irreg.*) razón	to be wrong

¿no?, ¿verdad?	right?, don't they (you, . . . ?)

Repaso: mucho (*adv.*), poco (*adv.*)

En casa°

°En... *At home*

Una casa en San José, Costa Rica

CULTURA

- **Nota cultural:** Las casas en el mundo hispánico
- **En los Estados Unidos y el Canadá:** Las misiones de California
- **Voces** de Costa Rica
    - **Literatura:** Carmen Naranjo
    - **Música:** La marimba y el punto guanacaste
- **Videoteca**
    - **Entrevista cultural:** Costa Rica
    - **Entre amigos:** Quiero cambiar los muebles.
- **Enfoque cultural:** Costa Rica

VOCABULARIO

- ¿Qué día es hoy?
- Los muebles, los cuartos y otras partes de la casa
- ¿Cuándo? Las preposiciones

GRAMÁTICA

11 **Hacer, oír, poner, salir, traer,** and **ver**

12 Present Tense of Stem-Changing Verbs

13 Reflexive Pronouns

¿QUÉ DÍA ES HOY?

lunes

Javier asiste a clase
a las ocho el lunes.

los lunes, los martes…	on Mondays, on Tuesdays . . .
Hoy (Mañana) es viernes.	Today (Tomorrow) is Friday.
Ayer fue (miércoles).	Yesterday was (Wednesday).
el fin de semana	(on) the weekend
pasado mañana	the day after tomorrow
el próximo (martes, miércoles,…)	next (Tuesday, Wednesday, . . .)
la semana que viene	next week

- In Spanish-speaking countries, the week usually starts with **lunes.**
- The days of the week are not capitalized in Spanish.
- Except for **el sábado / los sábados** and **el domingo / los domingos,** all the days of the week use the same form for the plural as they do for the singular.
- The definite articles are used to express *on* with the days of the week. Use **el** before a day of the week to refer to a specific day (**el lunes** = *on Monday*), and **los** to refer to that day of the week in general (**los lunes** = *on Mondays*).

martes

Javier mira la televisión
el martes.

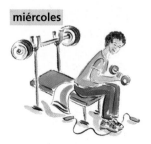

miércoles

Javier va al gimnasio
el miércoles.

jueves

Javier trabaja cuatro
horas el jueves.

viernes

El viernes va al mercado
con unos amigos.

sábado

El sábado Javier va a un
restaurante con Elena.

domingo

El domingo va a jugar al
basquetbol con sus amigos.

■ Conversación

A. Entrevista. Con un compañero / una compañera, haga y conteste las siguientes (*following*) preguntas.

1. ¿Qué día es hoy? ¿Qué día es mañana? Si hoy es sábado, ¿qué día es mañana? Si hoy es jueves, ¿qué día es mañana? ¿Qué día fue ayer?
2. ¿Qué días de la semana tenemos clase? ¿Qué días no?
3. ¿Estudias mucho durante (*during*) el fin de semana? ¿y los domingos por la noche?
4. ¿Qué te gusta hacer (*to do*) los viernes por la tarde? ¿Te gusta salir (*to go out*) con los amigos los sábados por la noche?

B. Mi semana. Indique una cosa que Ud. quiere, puede o tiene que hacer cada (*each*) día de esta semana.

MODELO: El lunes tengo que (puedo, quiero) ir al laboratorio de lenguas.

Palabras útiles

descansar (to rest)
dormir (to sleep) **hasta muy tarde**
ir (*irreg.*) **al bar (al parque, al museo, a…)**
ir (*irreg.*) **al cine** (movies)
jugar (to play) **al tenis (al golf, al vólibol, al…)**

LOS MUEBLES,° LOS CUARTOS Y OTRAS PARTES DE LA CASA

Los… *Furniture*

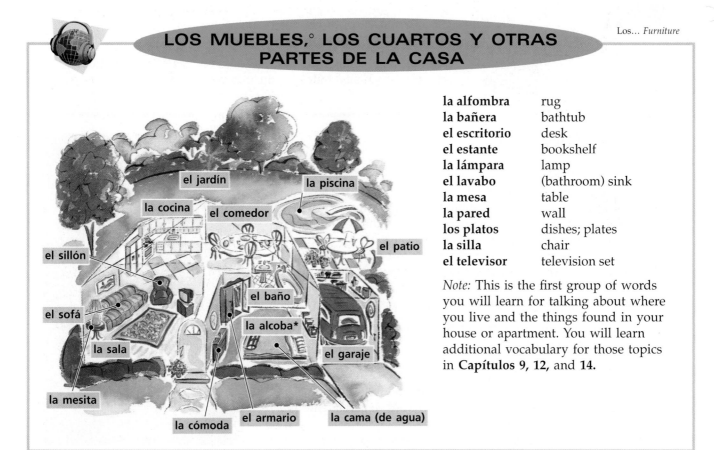

el jardín · la piscina · la cocina · el comedor · el patio · el sillón · el baño · la alcoba* · el garaje · el sofá · la sala · la mesita · la cómoda · el armario · la cama (de agua)

la alfombra	rug
la bañera	bathtub
el escritorio	desk
el estante	bookshelf
la lámpara	lamp
el lavabo	(bathroom) sink
la mesa	table
la pared	wall
los platos	dishes; plates
la silla	chair
el televisor	television set

Note: This is the first group of words you will learn for talking about where you live and the things found in your house or apartment. You will learn additional vocabulary for those topics in **Capítulos 9, 12,** and **14.**

---

*Other frequently used words for bedroom include **el dormitorio** and **la habitación.**

■ Conversación

A. ¿Qué hay en esta casa? Con un compañero / una compañera, identifique las partes de esta casa y diga lo que (*what*) hay en cada cuarto.

MODELO: 7 →

E1: El número 7 es el patio de la casa.
E2: ¿Qué hay en el patio? ¿Hay una piscina?
E3: No, sólo hay plantas.

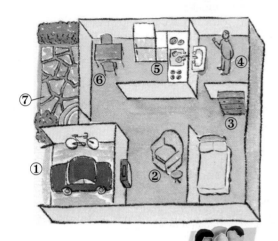

B. Asociaciones

PASO 1 ¿Qué muebles o partes de la casa asocia Ud. con las siguientes actividades?

1. estudiar para un examen
2. dormir la siesta (*taking a nap*) por la tarde
3. pasar una noche en casa con la familia
4. celebrar con una comida (*meal*) especial
5. tomar el sol (*sunbathing*)
6. hablar de temas (*topics*) serios con los amigos (padres, hijos)

PASO 2 Ahora compare sus asociaciones con las (*those*) de otros estudiantes. ¿Tienen todos las mismas costumbres (*same customs*)?

NOTA CULTURAL

Las casas del mundo hispánico

There is no such thing as a typical Hispanic house. Often, the style of housing depends on geographic location. For example, in hot regions such as southern Spain, many houses are built around a central interior patio. These patios are filled with plants, and some even have a fountain.

The population in Hispanic countries tends to be centered in urban areas. Due to population density in cities, many people live in apartments, like people in larger cities in this country.

Here are some more details about Hispanic houses.

- While the Spanish word **hogar** literally means *home,* the word **casa** is often used to mean *home.*

  Voy a casa.   *I'm going home.*   Estoy en casa.   *I'm at home.*

- In Spain, people use the word **piso** or **apartamento** to refer to an apartment; in some Hispanic countries, the word **departamento** is used.
- In big Latin American cities and especially with reference to more modern homes, a small front yard with ornamental plants and/or small trees is called **un jardín.** Large backyards are uncommon (except in rural areas and small towns) because the lots where houses are built are rather small. If a house has a back area, it is generally referred to as **el patio.** This area, usually paved, adjoins the house and is commonly enclosed by the walls of neighboring buildings.

El patio interior de una casa, en Sevilla, España

¿CUÁNDO? • LAS PREPOSICIONES

Antes de la fiesta, Rosa prepara la comida.

Durante la fiesta, Rosa baila.

Después de la fiesta, Rosa limpia la sala.

Prepositions (**Las preposiciones**) express relationships in time and space.

The book is *on* the table.　　The homework is *for* tomorrow.

Some common prepositions you have already used include **a, con, de, en, para,** and **por.** Here are some prepositions that express time relationships.

> **preposition** = a word or phrase that specifies the relationship, usually spatial or temporal, of one word to another

| **antes de** | *before* | **después de** | *after* | **durante** | *during* | **hasta** | *until* |

The infinitive is the only verb form that can follow a preposition.

¿Adónde vas **después de estudiar**?　　*Where are you going after studying (after you study)?*

■ Conversación

A. ¿Antes o después?　Complete las oraciones con **antes de** o **después de.**

1. Voy a la clase de español _____ preparar la lección.
2. Los viernes siempre descanso _____ salir para una fiesta.
3. Me gusta investigar un tema _____ escribir una composición.
4. Prefiero comer fuera (*to eat out*) _____ ir al cine.
5. Tengo que estudiar mucho _____ tomar un examen

B. Entrevista.　Con un compañero / una compañera, haga y conteste las siguientes preguntas.

1. ¿Estudias durante tu programa favorito de televisión? ¿Qué más haces (*do you do*) cuando estudias?
2. ¿Hablas por teléfono antes o después de estudiar? ¿Dónde hablas por teléfono, en la sala o en tu cuarto?
3. ¿Hasta qué hora estudias, generalmente? ¿Estudias después de medianoche (*midnight*)?
4. ¿Trabajas durante las vacaciones? ¿Cuántas horas? ¿Trabajas por la noche hasta muy tarde?

Need more practice?
- Workbook/Laboratory Manual
- Interactive CD-ROM
- Online Learning Center
(www.mhhe.com/quetal7)

11 Expressing Actions *Hacer, oír, poner, salir, traer,* and *ver*

Los jóvenes de hoy

«¡Estos muchachos sólo quieren *salir*! No *ponen* sus cosas en orden en sus cuartos… Los jóvenes de hoy día no *hacen* nada bien; no son responsables… ¡Hasta quieren *traer* muchachas a sus cuartos!»

¿Y Ud.?

¿Son estos comentarios típicos de las personas mayores (*older adults*) de su país? ¿Cree Ud. que tienen razón?

¿Tienen los jóvenes algunos (*any*) estereotipos sobre (*about*) las personas mayores?

hacer (*to do; to make*)		oír (*to hear*)		poner (*to put; to place*)		salir (*to leave; to go out*)		traer (*to bring*)		ver (*to see*)	
hago	hacemos	oigo	oímos	pongo	ponemos	salgo	salimos	traigo	traemos	veo	vemos
haces	hacéis	oyes	oís	pones	ponéis	sales	salís	traes	traéis	ves	veis
hace	hacen	oye	oyen	pone	ponen	sale	salen	trae	traen	ve	ven

• **hacer**

Some common idioms with **hacer:**

   hacer ejercicio (*to exercise*)
   hacer un viaje (*to take a trip*)
   hacer una pregunta (*to ask a question*)

¿Por qué no **haces** la tarea?
Why aren't you doing the homework?

Quieren **hacer un viaje** al Perú.
They want to take a trip to Peru.

Los niños siempre **hacen muchas preguntas.**
Children always ask a lot of questions.

• **oír**

The command forms of **oír** are used to attract someone's attention in the same way that English uses *Listen!* or *Hey!*

oye (tú)   **oiga** (Ud.)   **oigan** (Uds.)

Oye, Juan, ¿vas a la fiesta?
Hey, Juan, are you going to the party?

¡**Oigan!** ¡Silencio, por favor!
Listen! Silence, please!

No **oigo** bien por el ruido.

Today's young people These boys only want to go out! They don't put things in order in their rooms . . . Today's young people don't do anything right; they are not responsible people . . . They even want to bring girls to their rooms!

• **poner**

Many Spanish speakers use **poner** with appliances to express *to turn on*.

Voy a **poner** el televisor.
I'm going to turn on the TV.

Siempre **pongo** leche y mucho azúcar en el café.

• **salir**

Note that **salir** is always followed by **de** to express leaving a place.

Salir con can mean *to go out with, to date.*

Use **salir para** to indicate destination.

Salgo con el hermano de Cecilia.
I'm going out with Cecilia's brother.

Salimos para la sierra pasado mañana.
We're leaving for the mountains the day after tomorrow.

Salen de la clase ahora.

• **traer**

¿Por qué no **traes** el radio a la cocina?
Why don't you bring the radio to the kitchen?

• **ver**

No **veo** bien sin mis lentes de contacto.
I can't see well without my contact lenses.

■ Práctica

Cosas rutinarias

PASO 1   **¡Anticipemos!** ¿Cierto o falso?

1. Hago ejercicio en el gimnasio con frecuencia.
2. Veo a mis amigos los viernes por la tarde.
3. Nunca salgo con mis primos por la noche.
4. Siempre hago los ejercicios para la clase de español.
5. Salgo para la universidad a las ocho de la mañana.
6. Nunca pongo la ropa en la cómoda o en el armario.
7. Siempre traigo todos los libros necesarios a clase.
8. Siempre oigo todo lo que (*what*) dice (*says*) el profesor / la profesora de español.

PASO 2   Now rephrase each sentence in **Paso 1** as a question and interview a classmate. Use the **tú** forms of the verbs.

MODELO: Hago ejercicio en el gimnasio con frecuencia. →
¿Haces ejercicio en el gimnasio con frecuencia?

AUTOPRUEBA

Give the correct present tense **yo** forms for these verbs.

1. hacer   4. oír
2. ver   5. traer
3. poner   6. salir

Answers: 1. hago 2. veo 3. pongo 4. oigo 5. traigo 6. salgo

Need more practice?

■ Workbook/Laboratory Manual
■ Interactive CD-ROM
■ Online Learning Center
  (www.mhhe.com/quetal7)

■ Conversación

A. Consecuencias lógicas. Con un compañero / una compañera, indique una acción lógica para cada situación, usando (*using*) las **Frases útiles**.

MODELO: No tengo tarea. Por eso… → pongo el televisor.

1. Me gusta esquiar en las montañas. Por eso…
2. En la clase de español usamos este libro todos los días. Por eso…
3. Mis compañeros de cuarto hacen mucho ruido en la sala. Por eso…
4. El televisor no funciona. Por eso…
5. Hay mucho ruido en la clase. Por eso…
6. Estoy en la biblioteca y ¡no puedo estudiar más! Por eso…
7. Queremos bailar y necesitamos música. Por eso…
8. No comprendo la lección. Por eso…

B. Entrevista. Con un compañero / una compañera, haga y conteste las siguientes preguntas.

1. ¿Qué pones en el armario? ¿en la cómoda? ¿en el cajón (*drawer*) del escritorio?
2. Generalmente, ¿qué traes a clase todos los días? ¿Crees que traes más cosas que tus compañeros o menos? ¿Sales a veces para la clase sin tu libro de texto? ¿Qué traen tus profesores a clase?
3. ¿Qué haces los jueves por la noche? ¿Cuándo sales con los amigos? ¿Adónde van cuando salen juntos (*together*)?
4. ¿Pones el televisor con frecuencia cuando estás en casa? ¿Qué programa(s) ves todos los días? ¿Pones el radio con frecuencia? ¿Prefieres oír las noticias por radio o verlas (*to see them*) en la televisión? ¿Cuál es la estación de radio que más escuchas? ¿el canal de televisión que más miras? ¿Por qué te gusta tanto (*so much*)?
5. ¿Te gusta hacer ejercicio? ¿Haces ejercicios aeróbicos? ¿Dónde haces ejercicio? ¿En casa? ¿en el gimnasio? ¿en la piscina?

Frases útiles

hacer (*irreg.*) **un viaje / una pregunta**
oír (*irreg.*) **al profesor / a la profesora***
poner (*irreg.*) **el televisor / el estéreo**
salir (*irreg.*) **con / de / para…**
traer (*irreg.*) **el libro a clase**
ver (*irreg.*) **mi programa favorito**

¿Recuerda Ud.?

The change in the stem vowels of **querer** and **poder** (e and o, respectively) follows the same pattern as that of the verbs presented in the next section. Review the forms of **querer** and **poder** before beginning that section.

querer: **e** → ¿ ?

qu__ro	queremos
qu__res	queréis
qu__re	qu__ren

poder: **o** → ¿ ?

p__do	podemos
p__des	podéis
p__de	p__den

Remember that the word **a is necessary in front of a human direct object. You will study this usage of **a** in* **Capítulo 6.** *For now, you can answer following the pattern of the* **Frases útiles.**

12 Expressing Actions Present Tense of Stem-Changing Verbs

Una fiesta para Marisa

Hoy es el cumpleaños de Marisa. Gracia y Catalina preparan una pequeña sorpresa para su compañera de cuarto.

GRACIA: ¿A qué hora *vuelve* Marisa?

CATALINA: No estoy segura pero *pienso* que *vuelve* a las cinco.

GRACIA: ¡No *podemos* estar listas a las cinco!

CATALINA: ¡Con calma! La sala está arreglada ahora y la comida casi está lista. A las cinco, *empieza* a llegar la gente y cuando Marisa abra la puerta, gritamos: «¡Sorpresa!» Entonces *sirvo* el champán y traigo la comida. Ya verás. Una sorpresa pequeña pero perfecta.

Comprensión: ¿Cierto o falso?

1. Gracia y Catalina empiezan a preparar una fiesta muy grande para Marisa.
2. Marisa vuelve a casa por la noche.
3. Marisa sirve la comida.
4. Catalina piensa que necesitan más tiempo (*time*).

| Past ------------------- PRESENT ------------------- Future |
| present |

e → ie **pensar (ie)** (*to think*)		o (u) → ue **volver (ue)** (*to return*)		e → i **pedir (i)** (*to ask for; to order*)	
pienso	pensamos	vuelvo	volvemos	pido	pedimos
piensas	pensáis	vuelves	volvéis	pides	pedís
piensa	piensa	vuelve	vuelve	pide	piden

A party for Marisa *Today is Marisa's birthday. Gracia and Catalina are preparing a small surprise for their roommate.* GRACIA: *When is Marisa getting back?* CATALINA: *I'm not sure but I think she returns at five.* GRACIA: *We can't be ready by five!* CATALINA: *Calm down! The living room is straightened up now and the food is almost ready. At five, people will begin to arrive, and when Marisa opens the door, we'll shout "Surprise!" Then I'll serve champagne and bring the food. You'll see. A small surprise, but perfect.*

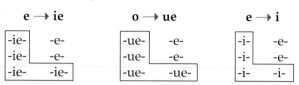
A. You have already learned five *stem-changing verbs* (**los verbos que cambian el radical**).

querer   preferir   tener   venir   poder

In these verbs the stem vowels **e** and **o** become **ie** and **ue**, respectively, in stressed syllables. There is also another group of stem-changing verbs in which the stem vowel **e** becomes **i** in stressed syllables. The stem vowels are stressed in all present tense forms of these verbs except **nosotros** and **vosotros**. All three classes of stem-changing verbs follow this regular "boot" pattern in the present tense.

Stem vowel changes:

e → ie		o → ue		e → i	
-ie-	-e-	-ue-	-e-	-i-	-e-
-ie-	-e-	-ue-	-e-	-i-	-e-
-ie-	-ie-	-ue-	-ue-	-i-	-i-

Nosotros and **vosotros** forms do not have a stem vowel change.

> In vocabulary lists, the stem change will always be shown in parentheses after the infinitive: **volver (ue)**.

B. Some stem-changing verbs practiced in this chapter include the following.

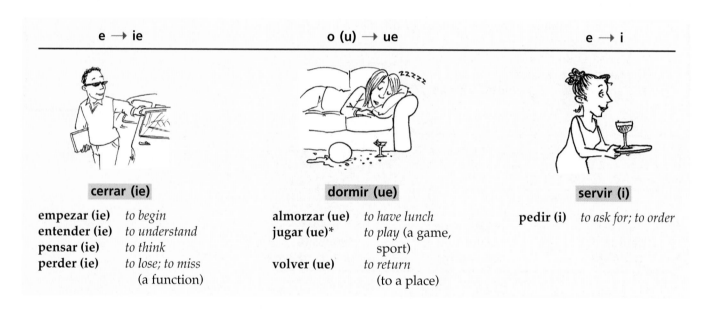

e → ie	o (u) → ue	e → i
cerrar (ie)	**dormir (ue)**	**servir (i)**

e → ie		o (u) → ue		e → i	
empezar (ie)	*to begin*	**almorzar (ue)**	*to have lunch*	**pedir (i)**	*to ask for; to order*
entender (ie)	*to understand*	**jugar (ue)***	*to play (a game, sport)*		
pensar (ie)	*to think*				
perder (ie)	*to lose; to miss (a function)*	**volver (ue)**	*to return (to a place)*		

• When used with an infinitive, **empezar** is followed by **a**.

Uds. **empiezan a hablar** muy bien el español.
You're beginning to speak Spanish very well.

• When used with an infinitive, **volver** is also followed by **a**. The phrase then means *to do (something) again*.

¿Cuándo **vuelves a jugar** al tenis?
When are you going to play tennis again?

• When followed directly by an infinitive, **pensar** means *to intend, plan to*.

The phrase **pensar en** can be used to express *to think about*.

¿Cuándo **piensas** almorzar?
When do you plan to eat lunch?

—¿**En** qué **piensas**?
What are you thinking about?

—**Pienso en** las cosas que tengo que hacer el domingo.
I'm thinking about the things I have to do on Sunday.

---

*Jugar is the only **u** → **ue** stem-changing verb in Spanish. **Jugar** is usually followed by **al** when used with the name of a sport: **Juego al tenis.** Some Spanish speakers, however, omit the **al**.

■ Práctica

A. ¿Dónde están Jacobo y Margarita? Tell in what part of Jacobo and Margarita's house the following things are happening. More than one answer is possible in some cases.

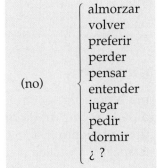
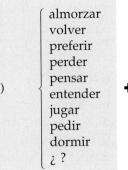

MODELO: Jacobo y Margarita empiezan a preparar el desayuno (*breakfast*). → Están en la cocina.

1. Jacobo sirve el desayuno.
2. Margarita cierra la revista y pone el televisor.
3. Los dos almuerzan con un amigo del barrio (*neighborhood*).
4. Los dos juegan al ajedrez (*chess*), y Jacobo pierde. No entiende bien el juego.
5. Margarita piensa en las cosas que tiene que hacer hoy.
6. Jacobo vuelve a casa después de ir al supermercado.
7. Margarita duerme la siesta.
8. Jacobo pide una pizza por teléfono.

B. Una tarde típica en casa. ¿Cuáles son las actividades de todos? Haga oraciones completas con una palabra o frase de cada grupo. Use sólo los sujetos que son apropiados para Ud.

| yo
mi padre/madre
mi esposo/a
los niños
mi amigo/a (*nombre*) y yo
el perro/gato
mi compañero/a | **+** | (no) | almorzar
volver
preferir
perder
pensar
entender
jugar
pedir
dormir
¿ ? | **+** | descansar, dormir
en un sillón / en la cocina
toda la tarde / la siesta
su pelota (*ball*) / sus llaves (*keys*) / su mochila
tarde / temprano a casa
en el patio / en la piscina / afuera (*outside*)
al golf / tenis / vólibol / ¿ ?
las películas (*movies*) viejas / recientes
el ajedrez / la lección
¿ ? |

Need more practice?

- Workbook/Laboratory Manual
- Interactive CD-ROM
- Online Learning Center (www.mhhe.com/quetal7)

■ Conversación

¿Qué piensas hacer esta semana?

PASO 1 Organice la semana que viene. Indique lo que Ud. va a hacer **por la mañana, por la tarde** y **por la noche** cada día (de lunes a domingo). Puede usar las **Frases útiles,** pero invente por lo menos tres actividades que no están en la lista.

PASO 2 **Entrevista.** Ahora, hable con un compañero / una compañera de sus horarios (*schedules*) esta semana, basándose (*based*) en el **Paso 1.**

MODELO: E1: ¿Qué piensas hacer el domingo por la tarde?
E2: Pienso ver un poco la televisión y dormir una siesta. Y tú, ¿qué haces el domingo?
E1: El domingo juego al tenis con mi amigo Alex.

Frases útiles

almorzar (ue) en un restaurante con _____
dormir (ue) una siesta
empezar (ie) un proyecto para _____
hacer (*irreg.*) **ejercicio**
hacer (*irreg.*) **la tarea de** _____
jugar (ue) al tenis/golf/ basquetbol con _____
servir (i) una comida (meal) para mis amigos
ver (*irreg.*) **la televisión**
volver (ue) a ver a _____

Voces de Costa Rica

LITERATURA: Carmen Naranjo

Carmen Naranjo
(1929–)

Sobre la autora: *Carmen Naranjo was born in Cartago, Costa Rica. She was a student of philology, and she has done graduate studies at the* **Universidad Nacional Autónoma de México** *as well as at the University of Iowa, Iowa City. She is a prolific writer of novels, stories, essays, and poetry. The following poem is from* En esta tierra redonda[a] y plana[b] *(XLVII) (2001).*

Ayer te busqué[c]
en ese asiento vacío[d]
del avión
en ese asiento vacío
del parque
en ese asiento vacío
del vestíbulo
en ese asiento vacío
del taxi
en ese asiento vacío
del comedor
en ese asiento vacío
de mi cuarto.
Hoy te seguiré buscando.[e]

[a]*round* [b]*flat* [c]*te... I looked for you* [d]*asiento... empty seat* [e]*te... I will continue to look for you*

MÚSICA: La marimba y el punto guanacaste

En Costa Rica, como en muchos países latinoamericanos, la marimba es un instrumento de la música tradicional y folklórica. Hay muchas variaciones de este instrumento: doble o sencilla,[a] de materiales naturales, como calabazas[b] y madera,[c] o de metales o plástico. La marimba costarricense es sencilla, de materiales naturales y a veces pintada[d] de colores vivos.[e] La música de marimba costarricense se distingue[f] por ser suave[g] y serena.[h]

[a]*single (row of keys)* [b]*gourds* [c]*wood* [d]*painted* [e]*lively* [f]*se... is unique* [g]*por... for being soft* [h]*restrained*

De la región de Guanacaste viene el baile nacional, punto guanacaste. La música del punto guanacaste se toca con marimbas de calabaza y guitarra.

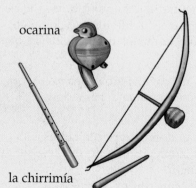

ocarina

el quijongo

la chirrimía

La música indígena de Costa Rica se toca con instrumentos tradicionales como el quijongo,[i] la ocarina[j] y la chirimía.[k]

[i]*single-string bow with gourd resonator* [j]*potato-shaped wind instrument* [k]*clarinet-type wind instrument*

13 Expressing *-self/-selves* Reflexive Pronouns

La rutina diaria de Andrés

La rutina de Andrés empieza a las siete y media.

1.

2.   **3.**

4.

(1) *Me despierto* a las siete y media y *me levanto* en seguida. Primero, (2) *me ducho* y luego (3) *me cepillo* los dientes. (4) *Me peino*, (5) *me pongo* la bata y (6) voy al cuarto a *vestirme*. Por fin, (7) salgo para mis clases. No tomo nada antes de salir para la universidad porque, por lo general, ¡tengo prisa!

5.

6.   **7.**

¿Y Ud.? ¿Cómo es la rutina diaria de Ud.?

1. Yo me levanto a las _____.
2. Me ducho por la (mañana/noche).
3. Me visto en (el baño/mi cuarto).

4. Me peino (antes de/después de) vestirme.
5. Antes de salir para las clases, (tomo/no tomo) el desayuno.

Uses of Reflexive Pronouns

bañarse *(to take a bath)*

(yo)	**me** baño	*I take a bath*	(nosotros)	**nos** bañamos	*we take baths*
(tú)	**te** bañas	*you take a bath*	(vosotros)	**os** bañáis	*you take baths*
(Ud.)		*you take a bath*	(Uds.)		*you take baths*
(él)	**se** baña	*he takes a bath*	(ellos)	**se** bañan	*they take baths*
(ella)		*she takes a bath*	(ellas)		*they take baths*

Andrés's daily routine   Andrés's routine begins at seven-thirty. (1) I wake up at seven-thirty and I get up right away. First, (2) I take a shower and then (3) I brush my teeth. (4) I comb my hair, (5) I put on my robe, and (6) I go to my room to get dressed. Finally, (7) I leave for my classes. I don't eat or drink anything before leaving for the university because I'm generally in a hurry!

A. The pronoun **se** at the end of an infinitive indicates that the verb is used reflexively. The reflexive pronoun in Spanish reflects the subject doing something to or for himself, herself, or itself. When the verb is conjugated, the reflexive pronoun that corresponds to the subject must be used.

> **bañarse** = to take a bath (to bathe oneself)
> **me baño** = I take a bath (bathe myself)
>
> Many English verbs that describe parts of one's daily routine—to get up, to take a bath, and so on—are expressed in Spanish with a reflexive construction.

Reflexive Pronouns

me	myself		**nos**	ourselves
te	yourself (*fam. sing.*)		**os**	yourselves (*fam. pl. Sp.*)
se	himself, herself, itself; yourself (*form. sing.*)		**se**	themselves; yourselves (*form. pl.*)

B. Here are some reflexive verbs you will find useful as you talk about daily routines. Note that some of these verbs are also stem-changing.

despertarse (ie)

ducharse

afeitarse

vestirse (i)

sentarse (ie)

acostarse (ue)	*to go to bed*	**levantarse**	*to get up; to stand up*
bañarse	*to take a bath*	**peinarse**	*to comb one's hair*
cepillarse los dientes	*to brush one's teeth*	**ponerse**	*to put on (clothing)*
divertirse (ie)	*to have a good time, enjoy oneself*	**quitarse**	*to take off (clothing)*
dormirse (ue)	*to fall asleep*		

Note also the verb **llamarse** (*to be called*), which you have been using since **Primeros pasos: Me llamo _____.**
¿Cómo se llama Ud.?

All of these verbs can also be used nonreflexively, often with a different meaning. Some examples of this appear at the right:

dormir = to sleep   **dormirse** = to fall asleep
poner = to put, place   **ponerse** = to put on

OJO

After **ponerse** and **quitarse**, the definite article, not the possessive as in English, is used with articles of clothing.

[Práctica A–B, Paso 1]

Se pone **el** abrigo.   Se quitan **el** sombrero.
He's putting on his coat.   *They're taking off their hats.*

Placement of Reflexive Pronouns

Reflexive pronouns are placed before a conjugated verb. In a negative sentence, they are placed in between the word **no** and the conjugated verb: **No *se* bañan.** When a conjugated verb is followed by an infinitive, the pronouns may either precede the conjugated verb or be attached to the infinitive.

[Práctica B, Paso 2]

Me tengo que levantar temprano.
Tengo que levantar**me** temprano.
I have to get up early.

> ### AUTOPRUEBA
>
> Match each reflexive pronoun with the correct verb form.
>
> **1.** se _____ **3.** te _____ **a.** bañas **c.** acuesto
> **2.** nos _____ **4.** me _____ **b.** afeitamos **d.** levanta
>
> *Answers: 1. d 2. b 3. a 4. c*

■ Práctica

A. ¡Anticipemos! Su rutina diaria ¿Hace Ud. lo mismo (*the same thing*) todos los días? Indique si hace las siguientes cosas los lunes o los sábados. ¿Tiene Ud. una rutina diferente los sábados? ¿Prefiere el sábado o el lunes? ¿Por qué?

1. Me levanto antes de las ocho.
2. Siempre me baño o me ducho.
3. Siempre me afeito.
4. Me pongo un traje / un vestido / una falda.
5. Me quito los zapatos después de llegar a casa.
6. Me acuesto antes de las once de la noche.

B. Mi rutina diaria

PASO 1 ¿Qué acostumbra Ud. a hacer en un día típico? Use las siguientes frases para describir su rutina diaria. Añada (*Add*) otras ideas si quiere. Use las palabras de la **Nota comunicativa** en sus oraciones.

MODELO: despertarse / a (hora) → Me despierto a las siete (de la mañana). Luego,…

1. despertarse / a (hora)
2. levantarse / a (hora)
3. (no) ducharse o bañarse / por la mañana
4. vestirse / antes o después de tomar algo
5. ir / a / universidad / y / asistir / a (número) clases
6. sentarse / en (lugar) / para estudiar
7. volver / a / casa o apartamento o residencia / a (hora)
8. comer / con (persona[s]) o solo/a (*alone*)
9. acostarse / tarde o temprano
10. dormirse / a (hora)

PASO 2 Use las oraciones del **Paso 1** para indicar lo que Ud. va a hacer mañana. Añada información si puede.

MODELO: despertarse / a (hora) → Primero, voy a despertarme (me voy a despertar) a las diez. ¡Es sábado! Luego…

> ### NOTA COMUNICATIVA
>
> **Sequence Expressions**
>
> These phrases will help you indicate the sequence of events.
>
> **primero** first **luego** then, afterward
> **después** later **finalmente** finally
> **entonces** then, next **por fin** finally
>
> **Primero,** me ducho y me visto. **Entonces,** tomo un café y leo el periódico. **Luego,** salgo para el trabajo.

Need more practice?

■ Workbook/Laboratory Manual
■ Interactive CD-ROM
■ Online Learning Center (www.mhhe.com/quetal7)

■ Conversación

Entrevista: ¿Cómo es tu rutina diaria?

PASO 1   Con un compañero / una compañera, haga y conteste preguntas sobre su rutina diaria. Anote (*Jot down*) las respuestas de su compañero/a.

1. Los días de la semana (*weekdays*), ¿te levantas temprano? ¿antes de las siete de la mañana? ¿A qué hora te levantas los sábados?
2. ¿Te bañas o te duchas? ¿Cuándo lo haces (*do you do it*), por la mañana o por la noche?
3. ¿Te afeitas todos los días? ¿Usas una afeitadora eléctrica? ¿Prefieres no afeitarte los fines de semana?
4. Por lo general, ¿te vistes con elegancia o informalmente? ¿Qué ropa te pones cuando quieres estar elegante? ¿cuando quieres estar muy cómodo/a (*comfortable*)? ¿Qué te pones para ir a la universidad?
5. ¿A qué hora vuelves a casa, generalmente? ¿Qué haces cuando regresas? ¿Te quitas los zapatos? ¿Te pones ropa más cómoda? ¿Estudias? ¿Miras la televisión? ¿Preparas la cena (*dinner*)?
6. ¿A qué hora te acuestas? ¿Cuál es la última (*last*) cosa que haces antes de acostarte? ¿Cuál es la última cosa o persona en que piensas antes de dormirte?

PASO 2   Ahora, describa la rutina de su compañero/a a la clase, usando las respuestas del **Paso 1.** ¿Cuántos estudiantes de la clase tienen rutinas parecidas (*similar*)?

En los Estados Unidos y el Canadá

Las misiones de California

The twenty-one **misiones** in California along what was called **el Camino Real** (*the Royal Highway*) were founded between 1769 and 1817 as outposts for bringing the Catholic religion to new lands. The indigenous people of California whose territories were colonized by these first Spanish settlements were deeply impacted. Some groups eventually became known by the name of a nearby **misión**—for example, the **diegueños** (**Misión de San Diego**), the **luiseños** (**Misión de San Luis Obispo**), and the **gabrielinos** (**Misión de San Gabriel**). Many of these missions later became important cities, including San Diego, San Francisco, and Santa Barbara.

La Misión San Juan Capistrano en San Juan Capistrano, California

UN POCO DE TODO

Lengua y cultura: Una visita a una familia «tica».   Complete the following letter with the correct forms of the words in parentheses, as suggested by the context. When two possibilities are given in parentheses, select the correct word. In addition to reviewing vocabulary from previous chapters, you will decide when to use **ser** or **estar** in situations that you have already learned. You will learn more about **ser** and **estar** in **Capítulo 5.**

Melissa, una estudiante de los Estados Unidos, está en Costa Rica por seis semanas con una familia «tica», es decir, costarricense. Este es uno de los primero mensajes electrónicos[a] que les manda[b] a sus amigos estadounidenses.

El Parque Nacional Cahuita, en Costa Rica

¡Hola a todos!

Por fin (*yo:* ir[1]) a contestar[c] todos (su/sus[2]) mensajes. Perdón por no escribir antes. Siempre (*yo:* estar[3]) ocupada con muchas actividades con mi familia de acá[d] y con mis clases.

En casa de los Arriaga, mi familia tica (las personas de Costa Rica [llamarse[4]] ticos y costarricenses), (*yo:* divertirse[5]) mucho porque todos son superamables. En general, todos los ticos (ser[6]) muy simpáticos con las personas (extranjero[7]). Siempre (*ellos:* venir[8]) a hablar conmigo[e] cuando (*yo:* estar/ser[9]) con mi familia y me[f] (hacer[10]) muchas preguntas sobre[g] los Estados Unidos. Muchos estadounidenses que visitan (este[11]) país no (tener[12]) ganas (de/en[13]) volver a casa.

La casa de mi familia (costarricense[14]), como[h] muchas otras casas de San José, es más pequeña que[i] (nuestro[15]) casas en Chicago. Está pintada de un azul claro[j] muy bonito; por aquí hay muchas otras casas pintadas de (unas/unos[16]) colores pastel que yo no (ver[17]) mucho en Illinois. Los ticos (tener[18]) las casas abiertas al aire libre[k] todo el día, porque la temperatura casi nunca (llegar[19])[l] a los 80° (grados). Por (eso/ese[20]), los ticos casi no tienen aire acondicionado. ¡Es (muy/mucho[21]) agradable!

Costa Rica es famosa por (su/sus[22]) parques nacionales y por la ecología. Los parques incluyen un 25 por ciento del país y (un/una[23]) variedad de volcanes, selvas[m] (tropical[24]) y playas. (*Yo:* Ir[25]) a visitar varios parques durante mi visita. También la familia Arriaga me quiere llevar a Sarchí, (un/una[26]) pueblo cerca de[n] San José. En Sarchí, uno (poder[27]) comprar muchas artesanías de Costa Rica. El pueblo también es famoso por (su/sus[28]) carretas[o] de brillantes colores.

Bueno, con esto, voy a despedirme[p] porque tengo (a/que[29]) (ducharse[30]). Si yo no (vestirse[31]) pronto, voy a (salir[32]) tarde para las clases.

Un abrazo muy fuerte,
Melissa.

[a]mensajes… *e-mails* [b]les… *she sends* [c]*answer* [d]*aquí* [e]*with me* [f]*of me* [g]*about* [h]*like* [i]*than* [j]*light* [k]abiertas… *open to fresh air* [l]*to get up to* [m]*jungles* [n]cerca… *close to* [o]*wooden carts* [p]*say good-bye*

Comprensión: ¿Hay evidencia o no? Decide whether there is evidence in Melissa's letter to support the following statements. For each statement, say **Sí, hay evidencia de esto** or **No, no hay evidencia de esto.** Change statements for which there is no evidence in the letter so that they will contain information that is included in the letter.

Resources for Review and Testing Preparation

- Workbook/Laboratory Manual
- Interactive CD-ROM
- Online Learning Center (www.mhhe.com/quetal7)

1. Melissa les escribe muchos mensajes a sus amigas estadounidenses.
2. Melissa toma clases en la universidad.
3. A Melissa le gusta mucho estar en Costa Rica.
4. Los ticos tienen cierta curiosidad acerca de (*about*) los estadounidenses.
5. Melissa prefiere las casas de los Estados Unidos.
6. Los ticos no tienen mucha necesidad del aire acondicionado.

VIDEOTECA

Entrevista cultural: Costa Rica

Alexander Burbón is a Costa Rican who works in real estate. In this interview he talks about his country and his work. One topic he discusses is the "typical" Costa Rican home. Before watching the video clip, read the following excerpt from the interview.

INTERVIEWER: ¿Cómo te llamas tú y en dónde trabajas?

ALEXANDER: Mi nombre es Alexander Burbón y trabajo en Costa Rica en una compañía de bienes raíces[a] que queda[b] en San José, en la capital. Eh, los bienes raíces, básicamente lo que yo hago es ir y mostrarles casas a personas que las quieren comprar o alquilar.[c] Y entonces, luego, los ayudo con los trámites[d] para comprar o para alquilar.

[a]bienes... *real estate* [b]está [c]*rent* [d]*details*

Now watch the video clip and answer the following questions based on the interview.

1. In what city does Alexander work?
2. What does he do for his clients?
3. What differences are there between a "typical" home in the city and outside the city?
4. How does he describe the difference between a furnished and unfurnished apartment? What items does he mention?
5. Does Alexander own his home?

Entre amigos: Quiero cambiar los muebles.

Rubén is waiting for Karina when Tané arrives. Tané is going shopping for furniture. What questions do you think they will ask each other? Before watching the video, read the following questions. As you watch, don't worry if you don't understand every word. Try to get the gist of the conversation, listening carefully for information about their plans for the day. Watch the video a second time and listen for the answers to the questions.

1. ¿Por qué espera Rubén a Karina?
2. ¿Trabaja Rubén mucho o poco? ¿Cuándo estudia?
3. ¿Por qué está cansada (*tired*) Karina?
4. ¿Adónde va Rubén?

ENFOQUE CULTURAL

Costa Rica

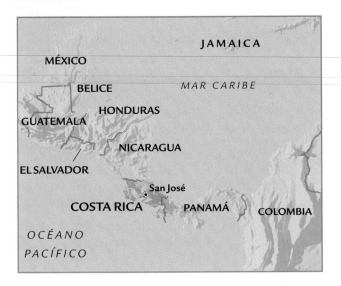

¡Fíjese!

- El ecoturismo es importante para la economía de Costa Rica y para la preservación de la biodiversidad y la belleza[a] natural que existe en el país. El ecoturismo tiene como propósito[b] controlar la entrada[c] de turistas en regiones protegidas[d] y, a la vez,[e] obtener fondos[f] para continuar con la protección de las regiones naturales. Aproximadamente un treinta por ciento (%) del territorio costarricense está cubierto de selvas o bosques.[g] En total, más de un cuarto[h] del territorio del país ha sido destinado[i] para la preservación.

- Costa Rica es una de las primeras democracias de las Américas. En 1821, convocaron[j] las primeras elecciones. Costa Rica tiene tres ramas[k] gubernamentales: ejecutiva (un presidente y dos vicepresidentes), legislativa y judicial. Es notable que Costa Rica no tiene un esfuerzo militar[l] permanente. Muchos consideran que Costa Rica es «la Suiza[m] de las Américas» porque es un país «amistoso»[n] que se mantiene neutro durante conflictos entre naciones. A menudo[o] los líderes de Costa Rica intervienen para negociar la paz[p] durante un conflicto internacional.

[a]beauty [b]purpose [c]entrance [d]protected [e]a... at the same time [f]funds
[g]está... is covered with jungles or forests [h]fourth [i]ha... has been set aside
[j]they held [k]branches [l]esfuerzo... military force [m]Switzerland
[n]friendly [o]A... Often [p]peace

Personas famosas: Óscar Arias Sánchez

Óscar Arias Sánchez (1941–), presidente de Costa Rica de 1986 a 1990, asistió a[a] la Universidad de Costa Rica, a Boston University y a otras universidades en Inglaterra.[b] En 1987, Arias recibió[c] el Premio Nóbel de la Paz[d] por sus esfuerzos[e] por aliviar las tensiones entre el gobierno sandinista de Nicaragua y los Estados Unidos. El acuerdo de paz[f] de Arias se firmó[g] en 1986. Desde 1990, se encarga de[h] la Fundación Arias para la paz y el progreso humano.

[a]asistió... attended [b]England [c]received [d]Premio... Nobel Peace Prize
[e]efforts [f]acuerdo... peace agreement [g]se... was signed [h]se... he has
been running

Óscar Arias Sánchez

Learn more about Costa Rica with the Video, the Interactive CD-ROM, and the Online Learning Center (www.mhhe.com/quetal7).

PASO 4

PASO FINAL

 A CONVERSAR

Compartiendo° casa

Sharing

Imagine that you and two classmates live in the same house. There's only one bedroom, one living room, and one kitchen. While you all get along, you don't always want to do the same things together. Try to come up with a plan for sharing the house.

PASO 1   Working individually, write three sentences for each room, describing what you do in that room and at what time.

> MODELO: la sala → Leo el periódico por la mañana antes de ir a clase (a eso de [*around*] las siete y media). Miro la televisión por la noche, después de hacer la tarea (a eso de las nueve). Me gusta leer una novela antes de dormir (a eso de las once).

PASO 2   Take turns telling what you do and when in the three rooms. If there is a conflict of time or activity, try to reach a compromise.

> MODELO: E1: Me ducho por la mañana antes de desayunar, a eso de las seis y media.
> E2: Yo también me ducho a eso de las seis y media.
> E1: Está bien. Yo puedo ducharme primero, a las seis.

PASO 3   As a group, create schedules for the three rooms. Use a separate sheet of paper to create a schedule for each room similar to the one below for Juan, María, and Esteban.

> MODELO:

Hora	El baño	La sala	La cocina
6:00	Juan: ducharse	María: leer el periódico	
6:30	María: ducharse		Esteban y Juan: desayunar
7:00			María: desayunar

GRAMÁTICA

To review the grammar points presented in this chapter, refer to the indicated grammar presentations. You'll find further practice of these structures in the Workbook/Laboratory Manual, on the Interactive CD-ROM, and on the *¿Qué tal?* Online Learning Center (www.mhhe.com/quetal7).

11 Expressing Actions—**Hacer, oír, poner, salir, traer,** and **ver**

Do you know the forms of **hacer, oír, poner, salir, traer,** and **ver** and how to use them?

12 Expressing Actions—Present Tense of Stem-Changing Verbs

Do you know the forms of verbs like **pensar (ie), volver (ue),** and **pedir (i)?**

13 Expressing *-self/-selves*—Reflexive Pronouns

You should be able to talk about your daily routine using reflexive verbs like **levantarse, bañarse,** and **afeitarse.**

VOCABULARIO

Practice this vocabulary with digital flash cards on the Online Learning Center (www.mhhe.com/quetal7).

Los verbos

almorzar (ue)	to have lunch
cerrar (ie)	to close
contestar	to answer
descansar	to rest
dormir (ue)	to sleep
dormir la siesta	to take a nap
empezar (ie)	to begin
empezar a + *inf.*	to begin to (*do something*)
entender (ie)	to understand
hacer (*irreg.*)	to do; to make
hacer ejercicio	to exercise
hacer un viaje	to take a trip
hacer una pregunta	to ask a question
jugar (ue) (al)	to play (*a game, sport*)
oír (*irreg.*)	to hear
pedir (i)	to ask for; to order
pensar (ie) (en)	to think (about); to intend, plan to
perder (ie)	to lose; to miss (*a function*)
poner (*irreg.*)	to put; to place; to turn on (*appliances*)
salir (*irreg.*) (de)/ (para)/(con)	to leave (*a place*); to leave (for/to) (*a place*); to go out (with)
servir (i)	to serve
traer (*irreg.*)	to bring
ver (*irreg.*)	to see
volver (ue)	to return (*to a place*)
volver a + *inf.*	to (*do something*) again

Los verbos reflexivos

acostarse (ue)	to go to bed
afeitarse	to shave
bañarse	to take a bath
cepillarse los dientes	to brush one's teeth
despertarse (ie)	to wake up
divertirse (ie)	to have a good time, enjoy oneself
dormirse (ue)	to fall asleep
ducharse	to take a shower
levantarse	to get up; to stand up
llamarse	to be called
peinarse	to comb one's hair
ponerse (*irreg.*)	to put on (*clothing*)
quitarse	to take off (*clothing*)
sentarse (ie)	to sit down
vestirse (i)	to get dressed

Los cuartos y otras partes de una casa

la alcoba	bedroom
el baño	bathroom
la cocina	kitchen
el comedor	dining room
el jardín	yard

la pared	wall
el patio	patio; yard
la piscina	swimming pool
la sala	living room

Cognado: el garaje

Los muebles y otras cosas de una casa

la alfombra	rug
el armario	closet
la bañera	bathtub
la cama (de agua)	(water) bed
la cómoda	bureau; dresser
el estante	bookshelf
la lámpara	lamp
el lavabo	(bathroom) sink
la mesita	end table
los muebles	furniture
los platos	dishes; plates
el sillón	armchair
el sofá	sofa
el televisor	television set

Repaso: el escritorio, la mesa, la silla

Otros sustantivos

el ajedrez	chess
el cine	movies; movie theater
el desayuno	breakfast
el/la muchacho/a	boy/girl
la película	movie
el ruido	noise
la rutina diaria	daily routine
la tarea	homework

Los adjetivos

cada (inv.)*	each, every
cómodo/a	comfortable
siguiente	following

Las preposiciones

antes de	before
después de	after
durante	during
hasta	until
por	during; for
sin	without

Repaso: a, con, de, en, para, por (in)

¿Cuándo?

Los días de la semana
lunes
martes
miércoles
jueves
viernes
sábado
domingo

ayer fue (miércoles)	yesterday was (Wednesday)
pasado mañana	the day after tomorrow
el próximo (martes)	next (Tuesday)
la semana que viene	next week

Repaso: el fin de semana, hoy, mañana

Palabras adicionales

lo que	what
luego	then; afterwards
por fin	finally
por lo general	generally
primero	first

---

*The abbreviation inv. means invariable in form. The adjective **cada** is used with masculine and feminine nouns (**cada libro, cada mesa**), and it is never used in the plural.

Las estaciones y el tiempo°

°**Las...** *The seasons and the weather*

Unos catamaranes en el lago Atitlán, en Guatemala

¿Qué... *What's the weather like today?*

¿QUÉ TIEMPO HACE HOY?°

Hace fresco.

Hace (mucho) sol.

Hace (mucho) calor.

Llueve.

Está (muy) nublado.

Hace (mucho) viento.

Hay mucha contaminación.

Hace (mucho) frío.

Nieva.

In Spanish, many weather conditions are expressed with **hace**. The adjective **mucho** is used with the nouns **frío, calor, viento,** and **sol** to express *very.*

Hace (muy) buen/mal tiempo.   It's (very) good/bad weather. The weather is (very) good/bad.

Pronunciation hint: Remember that, in most parts of the Spanish-speaking world, **ll** is pronounced exactly like **y: llueve.**

■ Conversación

A. **El tiempo y la ropa.**   Diga qué tiempo hace, según la ropa de cada persona.

MODELO: Miami: Todos llevan traje de baño y sandalias. →
Hace calor. (Hace buen tiempo.)

1. San Diego: María lleva pantalones cortos y una camiseta.
2. Madison: Juan lleva suéter, pero no lleva chaqueta.
3. Toronto: Roberto lleva suéter y chaqueta.
4. San Miguel de Allende, México: Ramón lleva impermeable y botas y también tiene paraguas (*umbrella*).
5. Buenos Aires, Argentina: Todos llevan abrigo, botas y sombrero.

B. Consejos (*Advice*) para Joaquín. Joaquín es de Valencia, España. El clima (*climate*) allí es mediterráneo: hace mucho sol y las temperaturas son moderadas. No hay mucha contaminación.

PASO 1 Joaquín tiene una lista de lugares que desea visitar en los Estados Unidos. Con un compañero / una compañera, ayúdelo (*help him*) con información sobre el clima. Como Joaquín no sabe (*As Joaquín doesn't know*) en qué estación va a viajar (*travel*), es bueno ofrecerle información sobre el clima de todo el año (*year*).

1. Seattle, Washington
2. Los Ángeles, California
3. Phoenix, Arizona
4. Buffalo, Nueva York
5. las islas hawaianas
6. Chicago, Illinois

PASO 2 Es obvio que la lista de Joaquín no está completa. ¿Qué otros tres lugares cree Ud. que debe visitar? ¿Qué clima hace allí?

C. El tiempo y las actividades. Haga oraciones completas, indicando una actividad apropiada para cada situación.

cuando llueve
cuando hace buen/mal tiempo
cuando hace calor
cuando hace frío
cuando nieva
cuando hay mucha contaminación

+

me quedo (*I stay*) en cama/casa
juego al basquetbol/vólibol con mis amigos
almuerzo afuera (*outside*) / en el parque
me divierto en el parque / en la playa (*beach*) con mis amigos
no salgo de casa
vuelvo a casa y trabajo o estudio

NOTA COMUNICATIVA

More *tener* Idioms

More conditions expressed in Spanish with **tener** idioms—not with *to be*, as in English—include the following.

tener (mucho) calor   to be (very) warm, hot
tener (mucho) frío   to be (very) cold

These expressions are used to describe people or animals only. To be comfortable—neither hot nor cold—is expressed with **estar bien.**

D. ¿Tienen frío o calor? ¿Están bien? Describe the following weather conditions, and tell how the people depicted are feeling.

1. 2. 3. 4. 5. 6. 7.

LOS MESES Y LAS ESTACIONES DEL AÑO

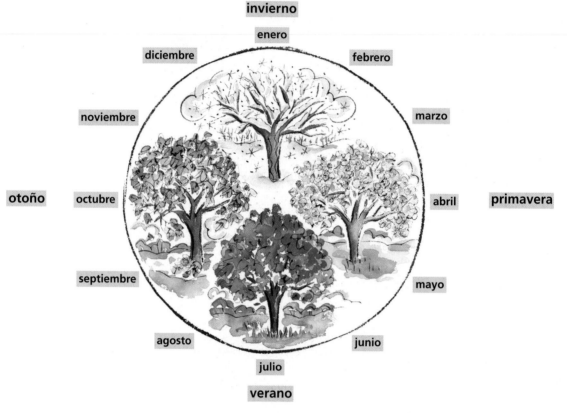

invierno

enero

diciembre | febrero

noviembre | marzo

otoño | octubre | abril | **primavera**

septiembre | mayo

agosto | junio

julio

verano

¿Cuál es la fecha de hoy?	What is today's date?
(Hoy es) El primero de abril.	(Today is) The first of April.
(Hoy es) El cinco de febrero.	(Today is) The fifth of February.

- The ordinal number **primero** is used to express the first day of the month. Cardinal numbers (**dos, tres,** and so on) are used for other days.
- The definite article **el** is used before the date. However, when the day of the week is expressed, **el** is omitted: **Hoy es jueves, tres de octubre.**
- As you know, **mil** is used to express the year after 999.

  1950   mil novecientos cincuenta   2004   dos mil cuatro

■ Conversación

A. **El mes de noviembre.**   Mire este calendario para el mes de noviembre. ¿Qué día de la semana es el 12 (1, 20, 16, 11, 4, 29) de noviembre?

MODELO: ¿Qué día de la semana es el 5 de noviembre? → El 5 es lunes.

B. Fechas

PASO 1 Exprese estas fechas en español. ¿En qué estación caen (*do they fall*)?

1. March 7
2. August 24
3. December 1
4. June 5
5. September 19, 1997
6. May 30, 1842
7. January 31, 1660
8. July 4, 1776

PASO 2 ¿Cuándo se celebran? ¿Y en qué día de la semana caen (*do they fall*) este año?

1. el Día de la Raza (*Columbus Day*)
2. el Día del Año Nuevo
3. el Día de los Enamorados (de San Valentín)
4. el Día de la Independencia de los Estados Unidos
5. el Día de los Inocentes (*Fools*), en los Estados Unidos
6. la Navidad (*Christmas*)
7. su cumpleaños (*birthday*)
8. el cumpleaños de su novio/a (*boy/girlfriend*), esposo/a, mejor (*best*) amigo/a…

OJO Note that the word **se** before a verb changes the verb's meaning slightly. **¿Cuándo se celebran?** = *When are they celebrated?* You will see this construction throughout *¿Qué tal?* Learn to recognize it, for it is frequently used in Spanish.

NOTA CULTURAL

El Niño

Most people have heard of El Niño, a weather phenomenon that is often associated with devastating climatic events. But why is it called El Niño?

The name El Niño dates from the end of the nineteenth century, when Peruvian fishermen noticed the periodic appearance of an abnormally warm ocean current off the coast of Peru. This warm current made its appearance around Christmas time. The name *El Niño* is a reference to the Christ Child, or El Niño Jesús, whose birth is celebrated by Christians at Christmas. At the time the name only referred to the current. Nowadays, it is used to refer to the meteorological phenomenon as a whole. Torrential rains, flooding, and landslides can occur from the southwestern United States to Peru, whereas in Australia, Indonesia, and southeast Africa, the opposite may happen: severe droughts and the potential for destructive fires.

Destrucción causada (caused) *en California por* (by) *El Niño*

C. Entrevista: ¡Feliz (*Happy*) cumpleaños!

Entreviste a un compañero / una compañera de clase acerca de (*about*) su cumpleaños. Use las siguientes preguntas.

1. ¿Cuál es la fecha de tu cumpleaños? ¿Cuál es tu signo del horóscopo?
2. ¿En qué estación es tu cumpleaños?
3. Generalmente, ¿qué tiempo hace en tu ciudad el día de tu cumpleaños?
4. ¿Cómo celebras tu cumpleaños? (por lo menos tres actividades)
5. ¿Con quién(es) prefieres celebrar tu cumpleaños?

Los signos del horóscopo	
Aries	Libra
Tauro	Escorpión
Géminis	Sagitario
Cáncer	Capricornio
Leo	Acuario
Virgo	Piscis

¿DÓNDE ESTÁ? • LAS PREPOSICIONES

La silla está **a la derecha de** la puerta.

Teresa está **entre** Carmen y Pablito.

El libro está **encima de** la mesa.

La mochila está **debajo de** la mesa.

cerca de	close to
lejos de	far from
encima de	on top of
debajo de	below
al lado de	alongside of
entre	between, among
delante de	in front of
detrás de	behind
a la izquierda de	to the left of
a la derecha de	to the right of
al este/oeste/	to the east/west/
norte/sur de	north/south of

Nueva York está al norte de Miami. México está al sur de los Estados Unidos.

NORTEAMÉRICA

el Canadá
los Estados Unidos
San Francisco
Los Ángeles
México
Nueva York
Miami

Pablito
Luis
Teresa
Carmen

■ Conversación

OJO

Note that **mí** has a written accent, but **ti** does not. This is to distinguish the object of a preposition (**mí**) from the possessive adjective (**mi**).

NOTA COMUNICATIVA

Los pronombres preposicionales

In Spanish, the pronouns that serve as objects of prepositions are identical in form to the subject pronouns, except for **mí** and **ti.**

Julio está delante de **mí.**	*Julio is in front of me.*
María está detrás de **ti.**	*María is behind you.*
Me siento a la izquierda de **ella.**	*I sit on her left.*

Mí and **ti** combine with the preposition **con** to form **conmigo** (*with me*) and **contigo** (*with you*), respectively.

¿Vienes **conmigo?**	*Are you coming with me?*
Sí, voy **contigo.**	*Yes, I'll go with you.*

A. ¿Quién?/¿Qué es? Describa a una persona o una cosa en la sala de clase, sin nombrarla (*without naming him/her/it*), usando (*using*) las preposiciones y los pronombres preposicionales. Su compañero/a debe adivinar (*guess*) quién o qué es la persona o cosa descrita.

MODELO: E1: Está a la derecha de nosotros ahora, pero a veces se sienta detrás de mí. Siempre llega a clase contigo.
E2: Es Antonio.

B. Entrevista: ¿De dónde eres? Find out as much information as you can about the location of each others' hometown or state, or about the country you are from. You should also tell what the weather is like, and ask if the other person would like to go there with you.

MODELO: E1: ¿De dónde eres?
E2: Soy de Tylertown.
E1: ¿Dónde está Tylertown?
E2: Está cerca de…

C. ¿De qué país se habla?

PASO 1 Escuche la descripción que da (*gives*) su profesor(a) de un país de Sudamérica. ¿Puede Ud. identificar el país?

PASO 2 Ahora describa un país de Sudamérica. Sus compañeros de clase van a identificarlo. Siga (*Follow*) el modelo, usando (*using*) todas las frases que sean (*are*) apropiadas.

MODELO: Este país está al norte/sur/este/oeste de _____.
También está cerca de _____.
Pero está lejos de _____. Está entre _____ y _____. ¿Cómo se llama?

PASO 3 A la derecha hay una lista de los nombres de las capitales de varios países de Sudamérica. Sin mirar el mapa, empareje (*match*) los nombres con el país correspondiente.

MODELO: _____ es la capital de _____.

Capitales	
Asunción	**La Paz**
Bogotá	**Lima**
Brasilia	**Montevideo**
Buenos Aires	**Quito**
Caracas	**Santiago**

Need more practice?

■ Workbook/Laboratory Manual
■ Interactive CD-ROM
■ Online Learning Center
  (www.mhhe.com/quetal7)

14   ¿Qué están haciendo?   Present Progressive: *estar* + *-ndo*

¿Qué *están haciendo* en Quito, Ecuador?

Hoy es sábado y José Miguel y su madre Elisa no están en la universidad o en el trabajo. ¿Qué *están haciendo*?

José Miguel juega al tenis y levanta pesas con frecuencia. Ahora no *está jugando* al tenis. Tampoco *está levantando* pesas. ¿Qué *está haciendo*?
Está _____.

Elisa es periodista. Por eso escribe mucho y habla mucho por teléfono. Pero ahora, no *está escribiendo*. Tampoco *está hablando* por teléfono. ¿Qué *está haciendo*?
Está _____.

¿Y Ud.?

¿Qué está haciendo Ud. en este momento?

1. ¿Está estudiando en casa? ¿en clase? ¿en la cafetería?
2. ¿Está leyendo? ¿Está mirando la tele al mismo tiempo (*at the same time*)?
3. ¿Está escuchando al profesor / a la profesora?

```
Past -------------------- PRESENT -------------------- Future
                          present
                     present progressive
```

Uses of the Progressive

In Spanish, you can use special verb forms to describe an action in progress— that is, something actually happening at the time it is being described. These Spanish forms, called **el progresivo,** correspond in form to the English *progressive: I am walking, we are driving, she is studying.* But their use is not identical. Compare the Spanish and English verb forms in the sentences on the next page.

> **progressive** = a verb form that expresses continuing action

What are they doing in Quito, Ecuador?   Today is Saturday, and José Miguel and his mother Elisa aren't at the university or at work. What are they doing? José Miguel often plays tennis and lifts weights. Now he isn't playing tennis. He isn't lifting weights either. What's he doing? He's _____. Elisa is a journalist. That's why she writes a great deal and talks on the phone a lot. But now she isn't writing. She isn't talking on the phone either. What's she doing? She's _____.

In Spanish, the present progressive is used primarily to describe an action that is actually *in progress*, as in the first example. The simple Spanish present is used in other cases where English would use the present progressive: to tell what is going to happen (the second sentence), and to tell what someone is doing over a period of time but not necessarily at this very moment (the third sentence).

1. Ramón **está comiendo** ahora mismo.
   Ramón is eating right now.

2. **Compramos** la casa mañana.
   We're buying the house tomorrow.

3. Adelaida **estudia** química este semestre.
   Adelaida is studying chemistry this semester.

Formation of the Present Progressive

A. The Spanish present progressive is formed with **estar** plus the *present participle* (**el gerundio**).

The present participle is formed by adding **-ando** to the stem of **-ar** verbs and **-iendo** to the stem of **-er** and **-ir** verbs.*

The present participle never varies; it always ends in **-o**.

estar + present participle

tomar →	**tomando**	*taking; drinking*
comprender →	**comprendiendo**	*understanding*
abrir →	**abriendo**	*opening*

OJO Unaccented **i** represents the sound [y] in the participle ending **-iendo: comiendo, viviendo.** Unaccented **i** between two vowels becomes the letter **y**:

leer: le + iendo → le**y**endo
oír: o + iendo → o**y**endo

B. The stem vowel in the present participle of **-ir** stem-changing verbs also shows a change. From this point on in *¿Qué tal?*, both stem changes for **-ir** verbs will be given with infinitives in vocabulary lists.

preferir (ie, i) →	pre**fi**riendo	*preferring*
pedir (i, i) →	p**i**diendo	*asking*
dormir (ue, u) →	d**u**rmiendo	*sleeping*

Using Pronouns with the Present Progressive

Reflexive pronouns may be attached to a present participle or precede the conjugated form of **estar**. Note the use of a written accent mark when pronouns are attached to the present participle.

Pablo **se** está bañando.
Pablo está bañándo**se**. } *Pablo is taking a bath.*

AUTOPRUEBA

Form the correct present participle.

a. -ando   **b.** -iendo   **c.** -yendo

1. pid_____   **4.** le_____
2. bañ_____   **5.** durm_____
3. hac_____   **6.** estudi_____

Answers: 1. b 2. a 3. b 4. c 5. b 6. a

*****Ir, poder,** and **venir** *have irregular present participles:* **yendo, pudiendo, viniendo.** *These three verbs, however, are seldom used in the progressive.*

PASO 2

■ Práctica

A. En casa con la familia Duarte

PASO 1 The Duarte family leads a busy life. Each set of drawings shows what the parents, the teen-age daughter, and the twins (**los gemelos**) are doing at a particular time of their day. Read the following sentences and tell to which set each statement refers.

MODELO: Se está duchando. → por la mañana

1. Está levantándose.
2. Está haciendo la tarea.
3. Se está vistiendo.
4. Está preparando la cena (*dinner*).
5. Está leyendo el periódico.

6. Están durmiendo.
7. Está trabajando.
8. Están jugando con el perro.
9. Están comiendo.
10. Está quitándose la blusa.

Por la mañana

Más tarde

Por la tarde

PASO 2 Now tell what is happening at each time of day.

MODELO: Son las seis de la mañana. Los niños están…

Capítulo 5 • Las estaciones y el tiempo

B. ¿Qué están haciendo? Diga qué están haciendo las siguientes personas, usando una palabra o frase de cada columna y la forma progresiva. Si Ud. no sabe (*know*) qué están haciendo esas personas, ¡use su imaginación!

MODELO: (Yo) Estoy escribiendo la tarea.

yo
mi mejor amigo/a
mis padres
los Bills de Buffalo / los Bulls de Chicago
el rector / la rectora (*president*) de la universidad
el presidente de los Estados Unidos
el profesor / la profesora de español
_____ (un compañero / una compañera de la clase de español que está ausente hoy)
mi consejero/a

+

jugar (al)
dormir(se)
leer
descansar
viajar (*to travel*)
escuchar
trabajar
practicar
hacer
escribir
¿ ?

+

fútbol/basquetbol
un libro / una novela
la radio
a los estudiantes / a sus consejeros
la tarea
un informe
ejercicio físico
¿ ?

Need more practice?

- Workbook/Laboratory Manual
- Interactive CD-ROM
- Online Learning Center (www.mhhe.com/quetal7)

■ Conversación

Entrevista

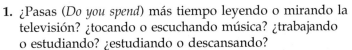

1. ¿Pasas (*Do you spend*) más tiempo leyendo o mirando la televisión? ¿tocando o escuchando música? ¿trabajando o estudiando? ¿estudiando o descansando?
2. ¿Cómo te diviertes más, mirando la tele o bailando en una fiesta? ¿practicando un deporte o leyendo una buena novela? ¿haciendo un *picnic* o preparando una cena (*dinner*) elegante en casa? ¿mirando una película en casa o en el cine?

¿Recuerda Ud.?

You have been using forms of **ser** and **estar** since **Primeros pasos,** the preliminary chapter of *¿Qué tal?* The following section will help you consolidate everything you know so far about these two verbs, both of which express *to be* in Spanish. You will learn a bit more about them as well.

Before you begin, think in particular about the following questions: **¿Cómo está Ud? ¿Cómo es Ud.?** What do these questions tell you about the difference between **ser** and **estar?**

PASO 2

15 ¿Ser o estar? Summary of the Uses of *ser* and *estar*

Una conversación por larga distancia

Aquí hay un lado de la conversación entre una esposa que *está* en un viaje de negocios y su esposo, que *está* en casa. Habla el esposo. ¿Qué contesta la esposa?

Aló. [...1] ¿Cómo *estás*, mi amor? [...2] ¿Dónde *estás* ahora? [...3] ¿Qué hora *es* allí? [...4] ¡Huy!, *es* muy tarde. Y el hotel, ¿cómo *es*? [...5] Oye, ¿qué *estás* haciendo ahora? [...6] Ay, pobrita, lo siento. *Estás* muy ocupada. ¿Con quién *estás* citada mañana? [...7] ¿Quién *es* el dueño de la compañía? [...8] Ah, él *es* de Cuba, ¿verdad? [...9] Bueno, ¿qué tiempo hace allí? [...10] Muy bien, mi vida. Hasta luego, ¿eh? [...11] Adiós.

Comprensión

Aquí está el otro lado de la conversación... pero las respuestas no están en orden. Ponga las respuestas en el orden apropiado.

a. _____ Es muy moderno. Me gusta mucho.
b. _____ Sí, pero vive en Nueva York ahora.
c. _____ Son las once y media.
d. _____ Hola, querido (*dear*). ¿Qué tal?
e. _____ Es el Sr. Cortina.
f. _____ Pues, todavía (*still*) tengo que trabajar.
g. _____ Sí, hasta pronto.
h. _____ Estoy en Nueva York.
i. _____ Un poco cansada (*tired*), pero estoy bien.
j. _____ Pues, hace buen tiempo, pero está un poco nublado.
k. _____ Con un señor de Computec, una nueva compañía de computadoras.

A long-distance conversation Here is one side of a conversation between a wife who is on a business trip and her husband, who is at home. The husband is speaking. What does the wife answer? Hello . . . How are you, dear? . . . Where are you now? . . . What time is it there? . . . Boy, it's very late. And how's the hotel? . . . Hey, what are you doing now? . . . You poor thing, I'm sorry. You're very busy. Who are you meeting with tomorrow? . . . Who's the owner of the company? . . . Ah, he's from Cuba, isn't he? . . . Well, what's the weather like? . . . Very well, sweetheart. See you later, OK? . . . Good-bye.

Summary of the Uses of *ser*

• To *identify* people and things	Ella **es doctora.** Tikal **es una ciudad maya.**
• To express *nationality;* with **de** to express *origin*	**Son cubanos.** **Son de La Habana.**
• With **de** to tell of what *material* something is made.	Este bolígrafo **es de plástico.**
• With **de** to express *possession*	**Es de Carlota.**
• With **para** to tell *for whom something is intended*	El regalo **es para Sara.**
• To tell *time*	**Son las once.** **Es la una y media.**
• With *adjectives* that describe *basic, inherent characteristics*	Ramona **es inteligente.**
• To form many *generalizations*	**Es necesario** llegar temprano. **Es importante** estudiar.

Summary of the Uses of *estar*

• To tell *location*	El libro **está en la mesa.**
• To describe *health*	**Estoy** muy **bien,** gracias.
• With *adjectives* that describe *conditions*	**Estoy** muy **ocupada.**
• In a number of *fixed expressions*	**(No) Estoy de acuerdo. Está bien.**
• With *present participles* to form the *progressive tense*	**Estoy estudiando** ahora mismo.

Ser and *estar* with Adjectives

A. Ser is used with adjectives that describe the fundamental qualities of a person, place, or thing.

Esa mujer es muy **baja.**
That woman is very short.

Sus calcetines son **morados.**
His socks are purple.

Este sillón es **cómodo.**
This armchair is comfortable.

Sus padres son **cariñosos.**
Their parents are affectionate people.

PASO 2

B. **Estar** is used with adjectives to express conditions or observations that are true at a given moment but that do not describe inherent qualities of the noun. The following adjectives are generally used with **estar.**

abierto/a	open	**limpio/a**	clean
aburrido/a	bored	**loco/a**	crazy
alegre	happy	**nervioso/a**	nervous
cansado/a	tired	**ocupado/a**	busy
cerrado/a	closed	**ordenado/a**	neat
congelado/a	frozen; very cold	**preocupado/a**	worried
contento/a	content, happy	**seguro/a**	sure, certain
desordenado/a	messy	**sucio/a**	dirty
enfermo/a	sick	**triste**	sad
furioso/a	furious, angry		

C. Many adjectives can be used with either **ser** or **estar,** depending on what the speaker intends to communicate. In general, when *to be* implies *looks, feels,* or *appears,* **estar** is used. Compare the following pairs of sentences.

Daniel **es** guapo.
Daniel is handsome. (He is a handsome person.)

Daniel **está** muy guapo esta noche.
Daniel looks very nice (handsome) tonight.

—¿Cómo **es** Amalia?
What is Amalia like (as a person)?
—**Es** simpática.
She's nice.

—¿Cómo **está** Amalia?
How is Amalia (feeling)?
—**Está** enferma todavía.
She's still sick.

AUTOPRUEBA

¿**Ser** o **estar**?

	SER	ESTAR
1. to describe a health condition	☐	☐
2. to tell time	☐	☐
3. to describe inherent qualities	☐	☐
4. to tell where a thing or person is located	☐	☐

Answers: 1. estar 2. ser 3. ser 4. estar

■ Práctica

A. Un regalo especial. Hay algo nuevo en el comedor. Es una computadora. ¿Qué puede Ud. decir de ella (*say about it*)? Haga oraciones completas con **es** o **está.**

La computadora es/está…

1. en la mesa del comedor.
2. un regalo de cumpleaños.
3. para mi compañero de cuarto.
4. de la tienda Computec.
5. en una caja (*box*) verde.
6. de los padres de mi compañero.
7. un regalo muy caro pero estupendo.
8. de metal y plástico gris.
9. una Dell, el último (*latest*) modelo.
10. muy fácil (*easy*) de usar.

B. Una tarde terrible

PASO 1   Describa lo que pasa hoy por la tarde en esta casa, cambiando por antónimos las palabras indicadas.

1. No hace *buen* tiempo; hace _____.
2. El bebé no está *bien;* está _____.
3. El gato no está *limpio;* está _____.
4. El esposo no está *tranquilo;* está _____ por el bebé.
5. El garaje no está *cerrado;* está _____.
6. Los niños no están *ocupados;* están _____.
7. La esposa no está *contenta;* está _____ por (*about*) el tiempo.
8. El baño no está *ordenado;* está _____.

PASO 2   Ahora imagine que son las seis y media de la tarde. Exprese lo que están haciendo los miembros de la familia en este momento. Use su imaginación y diga también lo que generalmente hacen estas personas a esa hora.

MODELO: Hoy, a las seis y media, la madre está conduciendo su coche a casa. Generalmente prepara la comida a esa hora.

> **Palabras útiles**
>
> **cenar** (to have dinner)
> **conducir (conduzco)** (to drive)
> **ladrar** (to bark)
> **llorar** (to cry)

Need more practice?

- Workbook/Laboratory Manual
- Interactive CD-ROM
- Online Learning Center (www.mhhe.com/quetal7)

■ Conversación

A. Ana y Estela.   Describa este dibujo de un cuarto típico de la residencia. Conteste las preguntas e invente los detalles necesarios.

1. ¿Quiénes son las dos compañeras de cuarto?
2. ¿De dónde son? ¿Cómo son?
3. ¿Dónde están en este momento?
4. ¿Qué hay en el cuarto?
5. ¿En qué condición está el cuarto?
6. ¿Son ordenadas o desordenadas las dos?

> **Palabras útiles**
>
> **el cajón** (drawer)
> **el cartel** (poster)
> **la foto**

Ana

Estela

B. Sentimientos. Complete the following sentences by telling how you feel in the situations described. Then ask questions of other students in the class to find at least one person who completed a given sentence the way you did.

MODELO: Cuando saco (*I get*) una «A» en un examen, estoy *alegre.* →
¿Cómo te sientes (*do you feel*) cuando sacas una «A» en un examen?

1. Cuando el profesor / la profesora da (*assigns*) una tarea difícil (fácil), estoy ____.
2. Cuando tengo mucho trabajo, estoy ____.
3. En otoño generalmente estoy ____ porque ____.
4. En verano estoy ____ porque ____.
5. Cuando llueve (nieva), estoy ____ porque ____.
6. Los lunes por la mañana estoy ____.
7. Los viernes por la noche estoy ____.
8. Cuando me acuesto muy tarde, estoy ____ al día siguiente (*the next day*).
9. Cuando otra persona habla y habla y habla, estoy ____.
10. Cuando estoy con mi familia, estoy ____.
11. Cuando estoy de vacaciones, estoy ____.
12. Cuando tengo problemas con mi coche, estoy ____.
13. Cuando voy al dentista, estoy ____.

En los Estados Unidos y el Canadá

Alfredo Jaar: América y su expresión artística

Upon arriving in the United States, Chilean artist Alfredo Jaar was surprised to learn that English speakers generally don't think of Canadians, Mexicans, Colombians, and so forth as "Americans." It bothered him that he was perceived as "Hispanic" or "Latin" but not as "American." "This country has co-opted the word *America*," he claimed.

So, Jaar used his artistic talents in an effort to enlighten people in the United States about the true meaning of the word *America.* He created a computerized animation that appeared on a sign board above New York City's Times Square in April 1987. The computer animation depicted a lighted map of the United States with the statement "This is not America" written across it. Slowly the word *America* grew larger and larger until it filled

El arte electrónico de Alfredo Jaar

the entire sign. At the same time, the letter *R* transformed itself into a map of North and South America. This use of *America* is the meaning used in Spanish, the meaning that Jaar had known.

The message that Jaar was trying to send was that *America* does not belong only to the United States. Another thirty-three nations say that they are a part of America and that their approximately 500 million inhabitants are also Americans.

Jaar was also trying to combat the stereotype that all Hispanics are alike and that all the inhabitants of South America are Hispanics. For one thing, many inhabitants of South America are Brazilians, and thus of Portuguese rather than of Spanish heritage. In addition, there are many indigenous peoples throughout the Americas that have traditions, cultures, and languages that precede Columbus's arrival in this hemisphere.

LITERATURA: Miguel Ángel Asturias

Sobre el autor: *Miguel Ángel Asturias was born near Guatemala City. One of the more important themes in his creative works is the indigenous peoples of Guatemala. In 1967, he was awarded the Nobel Prize for Literature. He spent many of his adult years in France, where he was buried in 1974. The following excerpt is from the poem "Letanías del desterrado[a]," published in* Páginas de lumbre de Miguel Ángel Asturias *(1999).*

**Miguel Ángel
Asturias**
(1899–1974)

Y, tú, desterrado:

Estar de paso,[b] siempre de paso,
tener la tierra como posada,[c]
contemplar cielos que no son nuestros,
vivir con gente[d] que no es la nuestra,
cantar canciones que no son nuestras,
reír con risa[e] que no es la nuestra,
estrechar manos[f] que no son nuestras,
llorar con llanto[g] que no es el nuestro,
tener amores que no son nuestros,
probar[h] comida que no es la nuestra,
rezar a dioses[i] que no son nuestros,
oír un nombre que no es el nuestro,
pensar en cosas que no son nuestras,
usar moneda[j] que no es la nuestra,
sentir caminos[k] que no son nuestros...

[a]*exile* [b]*de... passing through* [c]*boardinghouse* [d]*people* [e]*reír... to laugh with laughter* [f]*estrechar... to shake hands* [g]*llorar... to cry with tears* [h]*to taste/try* [i]*rezar... to pray to gods* [j]*currency* [k]*roads*

MÚSICA: La marimba y la banda cívica

La marimba, el instrumento musical nacional de Guatemala, es de origen africano, y originalmente se hacía[a] con calabazas.[b] Es un instrumento importante en casi todas las ocasiones sociales en Guatemala, desde[c] las fiestas populares hasta las celebraciones formales.

[a]*se... it was made* [b]*gourds* [c]*from*

Muchas ciudades tienen una banda, estilo militar, en que predominan los tambores[d] y los cobres.[e] Los músicos tocan en procesiones y otras festividades religiosas solemnes, como, por ejemplo, la Semana Santa,[f] y también en los funerales.

[d]*drums* [e]*brass instruments* [f]*Semana... Holy Week*

16 Describing Comparisons

Dos ciudades

México, D.F. (Distrito Federal)

El barrio de Santa Cruz, Sevilla, España

Ricardo, el tío de Lola Benítez, hace comparaciones entre la Ciudad de México, o el D.F. (Distrito Federal), y Sevilla.

«De verdad, me gustan las dos ciudades.

- La Ciudad de México es *más* grande *que* Sevilla.
- Tiene *más* edificios altos *que* Sevilla.
- En el D.F. no hace *tanto* calor *como* en Sevilla.

Pero…

- Sevilla es *tan* bonita *como* la Ciudad de México.
- No tiene *tantos* habitantes *como* el D.F.
- Sin embargo, los sevillanos son *tan* simpáticos *como* los mexicanos.

En total, ¡me gusta Sevilla *tanto como* la Ciudad de México!»

¿Y Ud.?

Describa su ciudad o pueblo.

Mi ciudad/pueblo…

- (no) es tan grande como Chicago
- es más/menos cosmopolita que Quebec

Me gusta _____ (nombre de mi ciudad/pueblo)…

- más que _____ (nombre de otra ciudad)
- menos que _____ (nombre de otra ciudad)
- tanto como _____ (nombre de otra ciudad)

Equal Comparisons		Unequal Comparisons
tan _____ como	**With Adjectives or Adverbs**	más/menos _____ que
tanto/a/os/as _____ como	**With Nouns**	
_____ tanto como	**With Verbs**	_____ más/menos que

Two cities   *Ricardo, Lola Benítez's uncle, makes comparisons between Mexico City, or* **el D.F.** (*Federal District*), *and Seville. Really, I like both cities.* • *Mexico City is bigger than Seville.* • *It has more tall buildings than Seville.* • *It is not as hot in Mexico City as it is in Seville. But . . .* • *Seville is as beautiful as Mexico City.* • *It doesn't have as many inhabitants as Mexico City.* • *Nevertheless, the people from Seville are as nice as those from Mexico City. All told, I like Seville as much as Mexico City!*

In English the *comparative* (**el comparativo**) is formed in a variety of ways. Equal comparisons are expressed with the word *as*. Unequal comparisons are expressed with the adverbs *more* or *less*, or by adding *-er* to the end of the adjective.

as cold *as*
as many *as*

more intelligent,
less important
taller, smarter

comparative = form of or structure with adjectives and adverbs used to compare nouns or actions

Comparison of Adjectives

EQUAL COMPARISONS	**tan** + *adjective* + **como**	Enrique es **tan** trabajador **como** Amalia. *Enrique is as hardworking as Amalia.*
UNEQUAL COMPARISONS (REGULAR)	**más** + *adjective* + **que** **menos** + *adjective* + **que**	Alicia es **más** perezosa **que** Marta. *Alicia is lazier than Marta.* Julio es **menos** listo **que** Jaime. *Julio is not as bright as Jaime.*
UNEQUAL COMPARATIVES WITH IRREGULAR FORMS	bueno/a → mejor malo/a → peor mayor (*older*) menor (*younger*)	Estos coches son **buenos,** pero esos son **mejores.** *These cars are good, but those are better.* Mi lámpara es **peor que** esta. *My lamp is worse than this one.* Mi hermana es **mayor que** yo. *My sister is older than I (am).* Mis primos son **menores que** yo. *My cousins are younger than I (am).*

Comparison of Nouns

EQUAL COMPARISONS **Tanto** must agree in gender and number with the noun it modifies.	**tanto/a/os/as** + *noun* + **como**	Alicia tiene **tantas** bolsas **como** Pati. *Alicia has as many purses as Pati (does).* Pablo tiene **tanto** dinero **como** Sergio. *Pablo has as much money as Sergio (does).*
UNEQUAL COMPARISONS	**más/menos** + *noun* + **que**	Alicia tiene **más/menos** bolsas **que** Susana. *Alicia has more/fewer purses than Susana (does).*
The preposition **de** is used when the comparison is followed by a number.	**más/menos de** + *noun*	Alicia tiene **más de** cinco bolsas. *Alicia has more than five purses.*

[Práctica A–C]

Comparison of Verbs

EQUAL COMPARISONS	**tanto como**	Yo estudio **tanto como** mi hermano mayor. *I study as much as my older brother (does).*

Note that **tanto** is invariable in this usage.

UNEQUAL COMPARISONS	**más/menos que**	Yo duermo **más que** mi hermano menor. *I sleep more than my younger brother (does).*

Comparison of Adverbs

EQUAL COMPARISONS	**tan** + *adverb* + **como**	Yo juego al tenis **tan** bien **como** mi hermano. *I play tennis as well as my brother (does).*

UNEQUAL COMPARISONS	**más/menos** + *adverb* + **que**	Yo como **más** rápido **que** mi padre. *I eat faster than my father (does).*
	mejor/peor que	Yo juego al tenis **peor que** mi hermana. *I play tennis worse than my sister (does).*

[Práctica D]

AUTOPRUEBA

Match each word with the corresponding conjunction.

a. como   **b.** que

1. más + _____
2. tantos + _____
3. peor + _____
4. tan + _____
5. menos + _____
6. tanta + _____

Answers: 1. b 2. a 3. b 4. a 5. b 6. a

■ Práctica

A. ¿Es Ud. sincero/a?   Conteste las preguntas lógicamente.

¿Es Ud.... ?   **1.** tan guapo/a como Antonio Banderas / Jennifer López
2. tan rico como Bill Gates
3. tan fiel como su mejor amigo/a
4. tan inteligente como Einstein
5. tan honesto/a como su padre/madre (novio/a...)

¿Tiene Ud.... ?   **1.** tantos tíos como tías
2. tantos amigos como amigas
3. tanto talento como Carlos Santana
4. tanta sabiduría (*knowledge*) como su profesor(a)

B. Alfredo y Gloria.   Compare la casa y las posesiones de Alfredo y Gloria.

MODELOS: La casa de Alfredo tiene tantas alcobas como la casa de Gloria. Sin embargo, Gloria tiene más camas que Alfredo.

	cuartos en total	baños	alcobas	camas	coches	bicicletas	dinero en el banco
Alfredo	8	2	3	3	3	2	$500.000
Gloria	6	1	3	5	1	2	$5.000

C. Opiniones. Cambie las siguientes oraciones para expresar su opinión personal. Si está de acuerdo con la oración, diga **Estoy de acuerdo.**

MODELO: El invierno es *tan divertido* como el verano. →
El invierno es *más/menos divertido* que el verano.
Estoy de acuerdo.

1. Mi casa (apartamento/residencia) es *tan grande* como la casa de Bill Gates.
2. El fútbol (*soccer*) es *tan popular* como el fútbol americano.
3. Las artes son *tan importantes* como las ciencias.
4. Los estudios son *menos importantes* que los deportes.
5. La comida (*food*) de la cafetería es *tan buena* como la de mi mamá/papá (esposo/a, compañero/a…).

D. Más opiniones. Cambie, indicando su opinión personal: **tanto como** → **más/menos que,** o vice versa. O, si es apropiado, diga **Estoy de acuerdo.**

1. Los profesores trabajan más que los estudiantes.
2. Me divierto tanto con mis amigos como con mis parientes.
3. Los niños duermen tanto como los adultos.
4. Aquí llueve más en primavera que en invierno.
5. Necesito más el dinero que la amistad (*friendship*).

Need more practice?
- Workbook/Laboratory Manual
- Interactive CD-ROM
- Online Learning Center
  (www.mhhe.com/quetal7)

■ Conversación

A. La familia de Lucía y Miguel

PASO 1 Mire el dibujo e identifique a los miembros de esta familia. Luego compárelos (*compare them*) con otro pariente. **¡OJO!** Lucía y Miguel tienen tres hijos: Amalia, Ramón y Sancho. Laura y Javier son los padres de Miguel.

MODELO: Amalia es la hermana de Sancho. Ella es menor que Sancho, pero es más alta que él.

Amalia (19)   Ramón (24)
Sancho (20)

Laura (75) Javier (80)

Lucía (43) Miguel (45)
Sarita (25)
Ramoncito (1)

PASO 2 **Su familia.** Now compare the members of your own family, making ten comparative statements.

MODELOS: Mi hermana Mary es mayor que yo, pero yo soy más alto/a que ella.

Mi abuela es mayor que mi abuelo; sin embargo ella es más activa que él.

PASO 3 Now read your sentences from **Paso 2** to a classmate. Then ask him or her questions about your comparisons and see if he or she remembers the details of your family.

MODELO: ¿Qué miembro de mi familia es mayor que yo?

PASO 3

B. La rutina diaria... en invierno y en verano

PASO 1   ¿Es diferente nuestra rutina diaria en las diferentes estaciones? Complete las siguientes oraciones sobre su rutina.

EN INVIERNO...

1. me levanto a _____ (hora)
2. almuerzo en _____
3. me divierto con mis amigos / mi familia en _____
4. estudio _____ horas todos los días
5. estoy / me quedo en _____ (lugar) por la noche
6. me acuesto a _____

EN VERANO...

me levanto a _____
almuerzo en _____
me divierto con mis amigos / mi familia en _____
(no) estudio _____ horas todos los días
estoy / me quedo en _____ por la noche
me acuesto a _____

PASO 2   Compare sus actividades en invierno y en verano, según los modelos.

MODELO: En invierno me levanto más temprano/tarde que en verano.
(En invierno me levanto a la misma hora que en verano.)
(En invierno me levanto tan temprano como en verano.)

Palabras útiles

el gimnasio
el parque

afuera

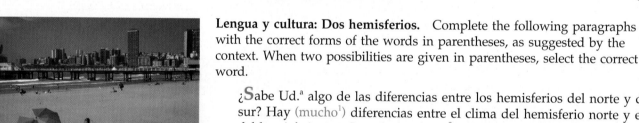

UN POCO DE TODO

En la playa Mar del Plata, en el mes de diciembre, en la Argentina

Resources for Review and Testing Preparation

- Workbook/Laboratory Manual
- Interactive CD-ROM
- Online Learning Center (www.mhhe.com/quetal7)

Lengua y cultura: Dos hemisferios.   Complete the following paragraphs with the correct forms of the words in parentheses, as suggested by the context. When two possibilities are given in parentheses, select the correct word.

¿Sabe Ud.[a] algo de las diferencias entre los hemisferios del norte y del sur? Hay (mucho[1]) diferencias entre el clima del hemisferio norte y el del hemisferio sur. Cuando (ser/estar[2]) invierno en este país, por ejemplo, (ser/estar[3]) verano en la Argentina, en Bolivia, en Chile... Cuando yo (salir[4]) para la universidad en febrero, con frecuencia tengo que (llevar[5]) abrigo y botas. En (los/las[6]) países del hemisferio sur, una persona (poder[7]) asistir (a/de[8]) un concierto en febrero llevando sólo pantalones (corto[9]), camiseta y sandalias. En muchas partes de este país, (antes de / durante[10]) las vacaciones en diciembre, casi siempre (hacer[11]) frío y a veces (nevar[12]). En (grande[13]) parte de Sudamérica, al otro lado del ecuador, hace calor y (muy/mucho[14]) sol durante (ese[15]) mes. A veces en enero hay fotos, en los periódicos, de personas que (tomar[16]) el sol y nadan[b] en las playas sudamericanas.

Tengo un amigo que (ir[17]) a (hacer/tomar[18]) un viaje a Buenos Aires. Él me dice[c] que allí la Navidad[d] (ser/estar[19]) una fiesta de verano y que todos (llevar[20]) ropa como la que[e] llevamos nosotros en julio. Parece[f] increíble, ¿verdad?

[a]¿Sabe... *Do you know*   [b]*are swimming*   [c]*Él... He tells me*   [d]*Christmas*   [e]*la... that which*   [f]*It seems*

Comprensión: ¿Probable o improbable?

1. Los estudiantes argentinos van a la playa en julio.
2. Muchas personas sudamericanas hacen viajes de vacaciones en enero.
3. Hace frío en Santiago (Chile) en diciembre.

VIDEOTECA

Entrevista cultural: Guatemala

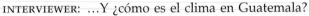

Débora David is a meteorologist from Guatemala. In this interview she describes the climate in her country. Before watching the interview, read the following excerpt.

INTERVIEWER: …Y ¿cómo es el clima en Guatemala?

DÉBORA: Bueno, este…ª Guatemala está en la América Central y… y tiene un clima templado, moderado, ni tanto frío ni tanto calor. Yo creo que por eso se le llama «el país de la eterna primavera».

INTERVIEWER: Y ¿hay temporadasᵇ de mal tiempo en Guatemala?

DÉBORA: Sí sí sí, tenemos temporadas de mal tiempo, este…, cuando vienen las lluvias, eh, también a raíz de esoᶜ los huracanes ¿no? que han pegadoᵈ lo que es las costas de Guatemala, eh, pero normalmente el clima en Guatemala es superagradable así como también toda América Central.

ªEste *is a filler word, like the English* uh *or* um.   ᵇestaciones   ᶜa… por eso   ᵈhan… *have hit*

Now watch the video and answer the following questions based on the interview.

1. Where does Débora work?
2. Basically, what is the climate like in Guatemala?
3. What is the most severe weather problem in Guatemala?
4. What is considered bad weather?
5. When does the bad weather come?

Entre amigos: ¡A mí me encanta (*I love*) el verano!

Tané, Karina, Miguel, and Rubén are talking about birthdays, seasons, and different times of the year. What questions do you think they will ask each other? Before watching the video, read the following questions. As you watch, don't worry if you don't understand every word. Try to get the gist of the conversation, listening carefully for information about seasons and times of the year. Watch the video a second time and listen for the answers to the questions.

1. ¿Cuándo es el cumpleaños de Karina?
2. ¿Adónde va Tané este verano, y qué va a hacer allí?
3. ¿Qué planes tiene Rubén para el verano?
4. ¿Qué estación del año prefiere Miguel, y por qué?
5. ¿Por qué le gusta el verano a Karina?

PASO 4

ENFOQUE CULTURAL

 Guatemala

¡Fíjese!

Más del cincuenta por ciento de los habitantes de Guatemala son descendientes de los antiguos[a] mayas. Esta civilización antigua tenía[b] un sistema de escritura jeroglífica que usaban[c] para documentar su historia, sus costumbres[d] religiosas y su mitología. El calendario maya, base del famoso calendario azteca, era[e] el calendario más exacto de su época. Los mayas también tenían un sistema político y social muy desarrollado.[f] Tikal, en Guatemala, fue[g] una de las ciudades mayas más importantes y también una de las más grandes. Las ruinas de Tikal son muestra[h] de la grandeza de la civilización maya. Hoy día,[i] son un lugar turístico muy visitado.

[a]ancient [b]had [c]they used [d]customs [e]was [f]developed [g]was [h]an example [i]Hoy… Nowadays

Learn more about Guatemala with the Video, Interactive CD-ROM, and the Online Learning Center (www.mhhe.com/quetal7).

Personas famosas: Rigoberta Menchú

Al período entre los años 1978 y 1985 en Guatemala se le llama[a] con frecuencia «La violencia». Durante este tiempo el ejército guatemalteco[b] empieza una campaña[c] violenta contra la población indígena[d] del oeste del país.

Rigoberta Menchú, mujer de la región indígena y de lengua[e] quiché (un grupo étnico de la familia de los mayas) pierde a sus padres y dos hermanos, todos asesinados por el ejército. Menchú describe esta tragedia durante «La violencia» en su famosa autobiografía *Yo, Rigoberta Menchú*.

El trabajo de Menchú a favor de los derechos humanos[f] y del pluralismo étnico de Guatemala le otorgó[g] el Premio Nóbel de la Paz en 1992, exactamente quinientos años después de la llegada[h] de Cristóbal Colón a América.

[a]Al… *The period between 1978 and 1985 in Guatemala is called* [b]ejército… *Guatemalan army* [c]*campaign* [d]población… *indigenous population* [e]*language* [f]a… *on behalf of human rights* [g]le… *won her* [h]*arrival*

Tikal, Guatemala

A LEER

ESTRATEGIA: Forming a General Idea About Content

Before starting a reading, it is a good idea to try to form a general sense of the content. The more you know about the reading before you begin to read, the easier it will seem to you. Here are some things you can do to prepare yourself for reading. You have already applied some of these strategies to the readings thus far in *¿Qué tal?*

1. Make sure you understand the title. Think about what it suggests to you and what you already know about the topic. Do the same with any subtitles in the reading.
2. Look at the drawings, photos, or other visual clues that accompany the reading. What do they indicate about the content?
3. Read the comprehension questions before starting to read the selection. They will direct you to the kind of information you should be looking for.

You should be able to determine the general message of the reading if you apply the preceding strategies.

- **The title.** The reading, **"Todos juntos en los trópicos,"** contains a key word in the title: **trópicos.** It is a cognate. Can you guess what it means?
- **The art.** The reading is accompanied by a photograph and caption. What additional information do these tell you about the reading?
- **The comprehension questions.** Scan the questions in **Comprensión.** What additional clues do they give you about the content of the passage?

> **Sobre la lectura…** This reading is taken from the magazine *Muy interesante*, which generally contains articles about popular science and related topics. Knowing the source of a passage can also help you formulate hypotheses about the reading before you begin to read.

Todos juntos en los trópicos

Los trópicos son las regiones biológicamente más diversas del planeta y cuentan con[a] el triple de <u>especies</u> que en cualquier otra zona. Pero, ¿por qué? Los biólogos no han sido capaces[b] de dar una respuesta unívoca.[c] Es más, las diferentes teorías que se han propuesto[d] tienen todos sus puntos débiles.[e]

En resumen, existen tres <u>razones</u> expuestas para esta riqueza.[f] La primera teoría fue diseñada[g] hace 20 años[h] por Michael Rosenzweigh, de Arizona. Según él, en los trópicos hay más especies, sencillamente[i] porque se cuenta con más espacio geográfico <u>habitable</u>.

No hay una teoría única para explicar la exuberancia natural que se produce en los trópicos.

[a]cuentan… *tienen* [b]no… *have not been able* [c]respuesta… *unambiguous answer*
[d]que… *that have been proposed* [e]puntos… *weak points* [f]expuestas… *given for this wealth* [g]fue… *was outlined* [h]hace… *20 years ago* [i]simply

La <u>segunda</u> es de los últimos años 80 y fue diseñada por George Stevens, de Nuevo México: las especies tropicales son esclavas[j] de sus condiciones térmicas;[k] por eso no pueden <u>colonizar</u> nuevos territorios menos cálidos[l] y se concentran como un gueto[m] en el trópico.

La <u>tercera</u> es una teoría histórica y explica que los trópicos fueron[n] las áreas de la Tierra que escaparon al efecto destructor del aumento[o] de las regiones heladas[p] durante las <u>glaciaciones</u>.

Ninguna de las tres ha sido confirmada.[q] ■

[j]*slaves* [k]*thermal* [l]*hot* [m]*ghetto* [n]*were* [o]*increase* [p]*frozen* [q]*ha... has been confirmed*

Comprensión

A. ¿Se menciona o no? ¿Cuáles de los siguientes temas se mencionan en la lectura?

	SÍ	NO
1. Información sobre la gente (*people*) indígena de los trópicos.	☐	☐
2. Teorías que explican (*explain*) la biodiversidad de los trópicos.	☐	☐
3. Información sobre la deforestación de los trópicos.	☐	☐
4. Teorías que explican la climatología de los trópicos.	☐	☐
5. La contaminación de algunas regiones de los trópicos.	☐	☐

B. Resumen. En inglés, escriba un breve resumen de las tres teorías presentadas en la lectura. Compare su resumen con el de otro estudiante. ¿Cuál de las teorías parece más factible (*feasible*)?

La biodiversidad de los trópicos se demuestra (is demonstrated) en la gran variedad de especies que viven en estas regiones. Las ranas (frogs) son parte de esta biodiversidad.

A ESCRIBIR

A. La biodiversidad local. La lectura comenta la gran biodiversidad de los trópicos, y propone teorías que explican este fenómeno. Escriba un breve ensayo (*essay*) que comente cómo es el clima donde Ud. vive y qué animales y plantas habitan la zona. Use las siguientes preguntas para empezar y consulte un diccionario bilingüe si es necesario.

¿Cómo es la biodiversidad en la región donde Ud. vive?
¿Hay muchos animales y plantas indígenas?
¿Cuál es la relación entre el clima de la región y la flora y la fauna?

B. Las selvas latinoamericanas. Busque información sobre las selvas en Latinoamérica. Use las siguientes preguntas como guía para empezar una introducción. Luego dé más detalles sobre la selva de un país específico.

¿Qué países tienen selvas tropicales?
¿Cómo se llaman las selvas?
¿Qué grupos indígenas viven en las selvas?
¿Qué tiempo hace en las selvas y cuáles son las estaciones?

En resumen

GRAMÁTICA

To review the grammar points presented in this chapter, refer to the indicated grammar presentations. You'll find further practice of these structures in the Workbook/Laboratory Manual, on the Interactive CD-ROM, and on the *¿Qué tal?* Online Learning Center (www.mhhe.com/quetal7).

14 ¿Qué están haciendo?— Present Progressive: **estar** + **-ndo**

Do you know how to form and when to use the present progressive in Spanish?

15 ¿**Ser** o **estar**?— Summary of the Uses of **ser** and **estar**

Should you use **ser** or **estar** to describe inherent qualities, to describe health and physical conditions, to express time, to form the present progressive?

16 Describing—Comparisons

Do you know how to compare things and people?

VOCABULARIO
Practice this vocabulary with digital flash cards on the Online Learning Center (www.mhhe.com/quetal7).

Los verbos

celebrar	to celebrate
pasar	to spend (*time*); to happen
quedarse	to stay, remain (*in a place*)

¿Qué tiempo hace?

está (muy) nublado	it's (very) cloudy, overcast
hace...	it's . . .
(muy) buen/mal tiempo	(very) good/bad weather
(mucho) calor	(very) hot
fresco	cool
(mucho) frío	(very) cold
(mucho) sol	(very) sunny
(mucho) viento	(very) windy
hay (mucha) contaminación	there's (lots of) pollution
llover (ue)	to rain
llueve	it's raining
nevar (ie)	to snow
nieva	it's snowing

Los meses del año

¿Cuál es la fecha de hoy?	What's today's date?
el primero de	the first of (*month*)

enero	julio
febrero	agosto
marzo	septiembre
abril	octubre
mayo	noviembre
junio	diciembre

Las estaciones del año

la primavera	spring
el verano	summer
el otoño	fall, autumn
el invierno	winter

Los lugares

la capital	capital city
la isla	island
el parque	park
la playa	beach

ciento cincuenta y tres **153**

Otros sustantivos

el año	year
el clima	climate
el cumpleaños	birthday
la estación	season
el mes	month
el/la novio/a	boyfriend/girlfriend
la respuesta	answer
el tiempo	weather

Los adjetivos

abierto/a	open
aburrido/a	bored
alegre	happy
cansado/a	tired
cariñoso/a	affectionate
cerrado/a	closed
congelado/a	frozen; very cold
contento/a	content, happy
desordenado/a	messy
difícil	hard, difficult
enfermo/a	sick
fácil	easy
furioso/a	furious, angry
limpio/a	clean
loco/a	crazy
nervioso/a	nervous
ocupado/a	busy
ordenado/a	neat
preocupado/a	worried
querido/a	dear
seguro/a	sure, certain
sucio/a	dirty
triste	sad

Las comparaciones

más/menos... que	more/less . . . than
tan... como	as . . . as
tanto como	as much as
tanto/a(s)... como	as much/many . . . as
mayor	older
mejor	better; best
menor	younger
peor	worse

Las preposiciones

a la derecha de	to the right of
a la izquierda de	to the left of
al lado de	alongside of
cerca de	close to
debajo de	below
delante de	in front of
detrás de	behind
encima de	on top of
entre	between, among
lejos de	far from

Los puntos cardinales

el norte, el sur, el este, el oeste

Palabras adicionales

afuera	outdoors
conmigo	with me
contigo	with you (*fam.*)
esta noche	tonight
estar (*irreg.*) bien	to be comfortable (*temperature*)
mí (*obj. of prep.*)	me
sin embargo	however
tener (*irreg.*) (mucho) calor	to be (very) warm, hot
tener (*irreg.*) (mucho) frío	to be (very) cold
ti (*obj. of prep.*)	you
todavía	still

¿Qué le gusta comer?

6

CULTURA

- **Nota cultural:** La comida del mundo hispánico
- **En los Estados Unidos y el Canadá:** Goya Foods, Inc.
- **Voces** de Panamá
    Literatura: Carlos Guillermo Wilson
    Música: El calipso
- **Videoteca**
    Entrevista cultural: Panamá
    Entre amigos: ¿Quién cocina en tu casa?
- **Enfoque cultural:** Panamá

VOCABULARIO

- La comida
- ¿Qué sabe Ud. y a quién conoce?

GRAMÁTICA

17 Direct Object Pronouns

18 Indefinite and Negative Words

19 Formal Commands

Un mercado en la Ciudad de Panamá

La... *Food*

LA COMIDA°

Las comidas (*Meals*)

el desayuno
(*breakfast*)

el jugo (de fruta) · el cereal · la leche · la mantequilla · el pan tostado · el té · el huevo · el café

el almuerzo
(*lunch*)

el sándwich · la manzana · el queso · la cerveza · el agua mineral* · el tomate · la lechuga · la hamburguesa · la ensalada · la sopa

la cena
(*dinner, supper*)

el pastel · el vino blanco · el vino tinto · las zanahorias · las arvejas · el bistec · el pescado · el pan · la patata / la papa† · el pollo (asado)

---

*The noun **agua** (water) *is feminine, but the masculine articles are used with it in the singular:* **el agua.** *This occurs with all feminine nouns that begin with a stressed* **a** *sound, for example,* **el (un) ama de casa** (homemaker).

†*In Latin America, many Spanish speakers use* **la papa,** *not* **la patata,** *to refer to potatoes.*

Otra bebida		Otros pescados y mariscos	
el refresco	soft drink	el atún	tuna
		los camarones	shrimp
Otras frutas		la langosta	lobster
la banana	banana	el salmón	salmon
la naranja	orange		
		Otros postres	
Otras verduras		el flan	(baked) custard
		la galleta	cookie
el champiñón	mushroom	el helado	ice cream
los espárragos	asparagus		
los frijoles	beans	**Otras comidas**	
		el arroz	rice
Otras carnes		el yogur	yogurt
la chuleta (de cerdo)	(pork) chop		
el jamón	ham	**Otras expresiones**	
el pavo	turkey	desayunar	to have (eat) breakfast
la salchicha	sausage; hot dog	almorzar (ue)	to have (eat) lunch
		cenar	to have (eat) dinner, supper

■ Conversación

A. ¿Qué quiere tomar? Match the following descriptions of meals with a category.

1. _____una sopa fría, langosta, espárragos, una ensalada de lechuga y tomate, todo con vino blanco y, para terminar, un pastel
2. _____jugo de fruta, huevos con jamón, pan tostado y café
3. _____pollo asado, arroz, arvejas, agua mineral y, para terminar, una manzana
4. _____una hamburguesa con patatas fritas, un refresco y un helado

a. un menú ligero (*light*) para una dieta
b. una comida rápida
c. una cena elegante
d. un desayuno estilo norteamericano

B. Definiciones. ¿Qué es?

1. un plato (*dish*) de lechuga y tomate
2. una bebida alcohólica blanca o roja
3. un líquido caliente (*hot*) que se toma* con cuchara (*spoon*)
4. una verdura anaranjada
5. la carne típica para la barbacoa en este país
6. una comida muy común en la China y en el Japón
7. la comida favorita de los ratones (*mice*)
8. una verdura frita que se come con las hamburguesas
9. una fruta roja o verde
10. una fruta amarilla de las zonas tropicales

---

*Remember that placing **se** before a verb form can change its English equivalent slightly: **usa** (he/she/it uses) → **se usa** (is used).

NOTA COMUNICATIVA

More *tener* Idioms

Use these **tener** idioms to talk about foods and eating.

tener (mucha) hambre	to be (very) hungry
tener (mucha) sed	to be (very) thirsty

C. Entrevista. Consejos (*Advice*) **a la hora de comer.** ¿Qué debe comer o beber su compañero/a en las siguientes situaciones? Déle consejos según el modelo.

MODELO: E1: Tengo mucha hambre.
E2: Debes comer un bistec con patatas fritas.

1. Quiero comer algo ligero porque no tengo hambre.
2. Quiero comer algo fuerte (*heavy*) porque tengo mucha hambre.
3. Tengo un poco de sed y quiero tomar algo antes de la comida.
4. Quiero comer algo antes del plato principal (*main course*).
5. Quiero comer algo después del plato principal.
6. Estoy a dieta (*on a diet*).
7. Estoy de vacaciones en Maine (o Boston).
8. Después de levantarme, no estoy completamente despierto/a (*awake*).

NOTA CULTURAL

La comida del mundo hispánico

Often when we think of dishes from the Spanish-speaking world, what comes to mind are rice, beans, spicy **chiles,** corn or flour **tortillas,** and **burritos.** That, however, is a misconception. Corn and flour tortillas and burritos are unknown in many Spanish-speaking countries. Many Hispanic cuisines are not spicy at all, and if you are in Spain and order **una tortilla,** you will be served a wedge of potato omelette!

The cuisines of Spanish-speaking countries are as diverse as their inhabitants. With the arrival of the Spaniards in the Americas, indigenous cuisines were influenced by European foods that did not exist there before, such as beef and chicken. Likewise, European cuisines were influenced by the introduction of foods from the Americas, such as the tomato, the potato, and chocolate. Later, immigration from countries such as Ireland, Germany, Italy, China, and Japan further influenced American cuisines.*

Una tortilla española

Unas tortillas mexicanas

Remember that, in this context, American refers to all the countries in North, Central, and South America.

¿QUÉ SABE UD. Y A QUIÉN CONOCE?

¡*Gran apertura!*[a]
Restaurante panameño

Nuestro chef, Felipe Prado, los invita a disfrutar de nuestros platos típicos panameños.

El Restaurante Chiriquí está en la calle Remedios, esquina con la avenida Vizcaya.

—¿**Conoces** el restaurante Chiriquí?
—Sí, es muy bueno. Sirven platos panameños.
—¿**Sabes** la dirección?[b]
—No exactamente, pero **sé** que está en la calle Remedios. ¡Y también **conozco al** chef! ¡Felipe **sabe preparar** mis platos panameños favoritos!
—¿Ah, sí? Pues… ¡quiero **conocer a** Felipe!

[a]¡*Gran… Grand opening!*   [b]*address*

Saber **and** *conocer*

Two Spanish verbs express *to know:* **saber** and **conocer.**

saber (to know)		conocer (to know)	
sé	sabemos	conozco	conocemos
sabes	sabéis	conoces	conocéis
sabe	saben	conoce	conocen

Saber expresses *to know* facts or pieces of information. Followed by an infinitive, it means *to know how* (*to do something*).

¿**Sabes** la dirección?	*Do you know the address?*
¡Felipe **sabe** preparar mis platos panameños favoritos!	*Felipe knows how to prepare my favorite Panamanian dishes.*

Conocer is used to express *to know* or *be acquainted* (*familiar*) *with* a person, place, thing, or idea. It can also mean *to meet.*

¿**Conoces** el restaurante Chiriquí?	*Do you know (Are you familiar with) the restaurant Chiriquí?*
Sí… ¡Y también **conozco** al chef!	*Yes . . . And I also know the chef!*
¡Quiero **conocer** a Felipe!	*I want to meet Felipe!*

The Personal *a*

Note (on page 159) the use of the word **a** before the nouns **chef** and **Felipe** in the brief dialogue and in the last two examples. In Spanish, the word **a** immediately precedes the direct object* of a sentence when the direct object refers to a specific person or persons. This **a,** called the **a personal,** has no equivalent in English.† Remember that **a** contracts with the article **el: a + el = al.**

 The personal a is used before the interrogative words **¿quién?** and **¿quiénes?** when they function as direct objects.

¿**A quién** llamas?
Who(m) are you calling?

 The verbs **buscar** (*to look for*), **escuchar** (*to listen to*), **esperar** (*to wait for; to expect*), and **mirar** (*to look at*) include the sense of the English prepositions *for, to,* and *at.* These verbs take direct objects in Spanish (not prepositional phrases, as in English).

Busco **mi abrigo.**
I'm looking for my overcoat.

Espero **a mi hijo.**
I'm waiting for my son.

■ Conversación

A. ¿Dónde cenamos? Lola y Manolo quieren cenar fuera. Pero, ¿dónde? Complete el diálogo con la forma correcta de **saber** o **conocer.**

LOLA: ¿(Sabes/Conoces¹) adónde quieres ir a cenar?

MANOLO: No (sé/conozco²). ¿Y tú?

LOLA: No. Pero hay un restaurante nuevo en la calle Betis. Creo que se llama Guadalquivir. ¿(Sabes/Conoces³) el restaurante?

MANOLO: No, pero (sé/conozco⁴) que tiene mucha fama. Es el restaurante favorito de Virginia. Ella (sabe/conoce⁵) al dueño.ᵃ

LOLA: ¿(Sabes/Conoces⁶) qué tipo de comida tienen?

MANOLO: No (sé/conozco⁷). Pero podemos llamar a Virginia. ¿(Sabes/Conoces⁸) su teléfono?

LOLA: Está en mi guía telefónica. Y pregúntaleᵇ a Virginia si ella (sabe/conoce⁹) si aceptan reservas con anticipaciónᶜ o no.

ᵃ*owner* ᵇ*ask* ᶜ*con... in advance*

B. Entrevista

1. ¿Qué restaurantes conoces en esta ciudad? ¿Cuál es tu restaurante favorito? ¿Por qué? ¿Es buena la comida allí? ¿Qué tipo de comida sirven? ¿Te gusta el ambiente (*atmosphere*)? ¿Comes allí con frecuencia?
2. ¿Conoces a alguna persona famosa? ¿Quién es? ¿Cómo es? ¿Qué detalles sabes de la vida de esta persona?
3. ¿Qué platos sabes preparar? ¿Tacos? ¿enchiladas? ¿pollo frito? ¿Te gusta cocinar (*to cook*)? ¿Siempre usas ingredientes frescos?
4. ¿Esperas a tus amigos para ir a la universidad / después de la clase? ¿A quién buscas cuando necesitas ayuda (*help*) con el español? ¿Dónde buscas a tus amigos por la noche / cuando es hora de comer?

Need more practice?

■ Workbook/Laboratory Manual
■ Interactive CD-ROM
■ Online Learning Center
  (www.mhhe.com/quetal7)

The direct object (el complemento directo**) is the part of the sentence that indicates to whom or to what the action of the verb is directed or upon whom or upon what it acts. In the sentence I saw John, the direct object is John. The direct object is explained in more detail in **Gramática 17** of this chapter.*

*†The personal **a** is not generally used with **tener**: Tengo cuatro hijos.*

17 **Expressing** *what* **or** *whom* **Direct Object Pronouns**

De compras en el supermercado

LA MODERNA MARKET

930-932 State Street • New Haven, CT • (203) 776-2333

AHORA ABIERTO EN NEW HAVEN

• **TODA CLASE DE CARNES FRESCAS**

• **VEGETALES FRESCOS**
• **GROCERY**

• **LÍNEA COMPLETA DE PRODUCTOS MEXICANOS**
La Moderna • La Morena
• La Costeña • Nestle

Solicite Nuestra Propia Longaniza y Cesina

ATENDEMOS PEDIDOS PARA NEGOCIOS

Indique cuáles de estas afirmaciones son verdaderas para Ud.

1. la carne
   ☐ *La* como todos los días. Por eso tengo que comprar*la* con frecuencia.
   ☐ *La* como de vez en cuando (*once in a while*). Por eso no *la* compro a menudo (*often*).
   ☐ Nunca *la* como. No necesito comprar*la*.

2. el café
   ☐ *Lo* bebo todos los días. Por eso tengo que comprar*lo* con frecuencia.
   ☐ *Lo* bebo de vez en cuando. Por eso no *lo* compro a menudo.
   ☐ Nunca *lo* bebo. No necesito comprar*lo*.

3. los huevos
   ☐ *Los* como todos los días. Por eso tengo que comprar*los* con frecuencia.
   ☐ *Los* como de vez en cuando. Por eso no *los* compro a menudo.
   ☐ Nunca *los* como. No necesito comprar*los*.

4. las bananas
   ☐ *Las* como todos los días. Por eso tengo que comprar*las* con frecuencia.
   ☐ *Las* como de vez en cuando. Por eso no *las* compro a menudo.
   ☐ Nunca *las* como. No necesito comprar*las*.

5. el agua
   ☐ *La* tomo todos los días. Por eso tengo que comprar*la* con frecuencia.
   ☐ *La* tomo de vez en cuando. Por eso no *la* compro a menudo.
   ☐ Nunca *la* tomo. No necesito comprar*la*.

Direct Object Pronouns

me	me		nos	us
te	you (*fam. sing.*)		os	you (*fam. pl.*)
lo*	you (*form. sing.*), him, it (*m.*)		los	you (*form. pl.*), them (*m., m. + f.*)
la	you (*form. sing.*), her, it (*f.*)		las	you (*form. pl.*), them (*f.*)

A. Like direct object nouns, *direct object pronouns* (**los pronombres del complemento directo**) are the first recipient of the action of the verb. Direct object pronouns are placed before a conjugated verb and after the word **no** when it appears. Third person direct object pronouns are used only when the direct object noun has already been mentioned.

[Práctica A]

¿El menú? Diego no **lo** necesita.
The menu? Diego doesn't need it.

¿Dónde están el pastel y el helado? **Los** necesito ahora.
Where are the cake and the ice cream? I need them now.

Ellos **me** ayudan.
They're helping me.

> **direct object** = the noun or pronoun that receives the action of a verb

B. The direct object pronouns may be attached to an infinitive or a present participle.

[Práctica B–C]

Las tengo que leer.
Tengo que leer**las**. } *I have to read them.*

Lo estoy comiendo.
Estoy comiéndo**lo**. } *I am eating it.*

C. Note that the direct object pronoun **lo** can refer to actions, situations, or ideas in general. When used in this way, **lo** expresses English *it* or *that*.

Lo comprende muy bien.
He understands it (that) very well.

No **lo** creo.
I don't believe it (that).

Lo sé.
I know (it).

AUTOPRUEBA

Match the direct object pronouns with the nouns and subject pronouns.

1. ____ los	**a.** Ana		
2. ____ la	**b.** tú		
3. ____ te	**c.** Pedro y Carolina		
4. ____ lo	**d.** María y yo		
5. ____ las	**e.** Jorge		
6. ____ nos	**f.** Elena y Rosa		

Answers: 1. c 2. a 3. b 4. e 5. f 6. d

---

*In Spain and in some other parts of the Spanish-speaking world, **le** is frequently used instead of **lo** for the direct object pronoun* him. *This usage, called **el leísmo**, will not be followed in* ¿Qué tal?

■ Práctica

A. ¿Qué comen los vegetarianos?

PASO 1   Aquí hay una lista de diferentes comidas. ¿Van a formar parte de la dieta de un vegetariano? Conteste según los modelos.

MODELOS: el bistec → No *lo* va a comer.
  la banana → *La* va a comer.

1. las patatas	**7.** los camarones
2. el arroz	**8.** el pan
3. las chuletas de cerdo	**9.** los champiñones
4. el pollo	**10.** los frijoles
5. las zanahorias	**11.** la ensalada
6. las manzanas	

PASO 2   Si hay un estudiante vegetariano / una estudiante vegetariana en la clase, pídale que verifique (*ask him or her to verify*) las respuestas de Ud.

B. La cena de Lola y Manolo.

La siguiente descripción de la cena de Lola y Manolo es muy repetitiva. Combine las oraciones, cambiando los nombres de complemento directo por pronombres cuando sea (*whenever it is*) necesario.

MODELO: El camarero (*waiter*) trae un menú. Lola lee *el menú*. →
  El camarero trae un menú y Lola *lo* lee.

1. El camarero trae una botella de vino tinto. Pone *la botella* en la mesa.
2. El camarero trae las copas (*glasses*) de vino. Pone *las copas* delante de Lola y Manolo.
3. Lola quiere la especialidad de la casa. Va a pedir *la especialidad de la casa*.
4. Manolo prefiere el pescado fresco (*fresh*). Pide *el pescado fresco*.
5. Lola quiere una ensalada también. Por eso pide *una ensalada*.
6. El camerero trae la comida. Sirve *la comida*.
7. Manolo necesita otra servilleta (*napkin*). Pide *otra servilleta*.
8. «¿La cuenta (*bill*)? El dueño está preparando *la cuenta* para Uds.»
9. Manolo quiere pagar con tarjeta (*card*) de crédito. Pero no trae *su tarjeta*.
10. Por fin, Lola toma la cuenta. Paga *la cuenta*.

NOTA COMUNICATIVA

Talking About What You Have Just Done

To talk about what you have *just* done, use the phrase **acabar** + **de** with an infinitive.

Acabo de llegar con Beto.	*I just arrived with Beto.*
Acabas de celebrar tu cumpleaños, ¿verdad?	*You just celebrated your birthday, didn't you?*

Note that the infinitive follows **de.** Remember that the infinitive is the only verb form that can follow a preposition in Spanish.

PASO 2

Need more practice?

- Workbook/Laboratory Manual
- Interactive CD-ROM
- Online Learning Center
  (www.mhhe.com/quetal7)

C. ¡Acabo de hacerlo! Imagine that a friend is pressuring you to do the following things. With a classmate, tell him or her that you just did each one, using either of the forms in the model.

MODELO: E1: ¿Por qué no estudias la lección? →
E2: Acabo de estudiar*la*. (*La* acabo de estudiar.)

1. ¿Por qué no escribes las composiciones para tus clases?
2. ¿Vas a comprar el periódico hoy?
3. ¿Por qué no pagas los cafés?
4. ¿Vas a preparar la comida para la fiesta?
5. ¿Puedes pedir la cuenta?
6. ¿Quieres ayudarme con la lección?

■ Conversación

A. ¿Quién ayuda? Todos necesitamos ayuda en diferentes circunstancias. ¿Quién los ayuda a Uds. con lo siguiente? Use **nos** en sus respuestas.

MODELO: con las cuentas → Nuestros padres *nos* ayudan con las cuentas.

1. con las cuentas
2. con la tarea
3. con la matrícula
4. con el horario de clases
5. con los problemas personales

Palabras útiles

nuestros padres (compañeros, consejeros, amigos...)

Palabras y frases útiles

la cafeína
las calorías
el colesterol
la grasa (fat)

estar (*irreg.*) **a dieta**
ser (*irreg.*) **alérgico/a a**
ser (*irreg.*) **bueno/a para la salud**
  (health)

lo/la/los/las detesto
me da asco (it makes me sick) /
  me dan asco (they make me sick)
me pone (it makes me)
  nervioso/a

B. Una encuesta sobre la comida. Hágales (*Ask*) preguntas a sus compañeros de clase para saber si toman las comidas o bebidas indicadas y con qué frecuencia. Deben explicar por qué toman o *no* toman cierta cosa.

MODELO: la carne → E1: ¿Comes carne?
E2: No, no *la* como casi nunca porque tiene mucho colesterol.

1. la carne
2. los mariscos
3. el yogur
4. la pizza
5. las hamburguesas
6. el pollo
7. el café
8. los dulces (*sweets; candy*)
9. el alcohol
10. el atún
11. los espárragos
12. el hígado (*liver*)

18 Expressing Negation Indefinite and Negative Words

En la cocina de Diego y Antonio

Diego llega a casa y tiene hambre.

DIEGO: Quiero comer *algo*, pero *no* hay *nada* de comer en esta casa. Y *no* tengo ganas de ir de compras. Y además, ¡*no* tengo *ni* un centavo!

ANTONIO: ¡Ay! *Siempre* eres así. Tú *nunca* tienes ganas de ir de compras. Y lo del dinero… ¡esa ya es otra historia!

Comprensión: ¿Quién… ?

1. tiene hambre
2. nunca tiene dinero
3. critica a su amigo
4. no quiere ir de compras

Here is a list of the most common indefinite and negative words in Spanish. You have been using many of them since the first chapters of *¿Qué tal?*

algo	something, anything	**nada**	nothing, not anything
alguien	someone, anyone	**nadie**	no one, nobody, not anybody
algún (alguno/a/os/as)	some, any	**ningún (ninguno/a)**	no, none, not any
siempre	always	**nunca, jamás**	never
también	also	**tampoco**	neither, not either

Pronunciation hint: Remember to pronounce the **d** in **nada** and **nadie** as a fricative, that is, like a *th* sound: **na đa, na đie.**

The Double Negative

When a negative word comes after the main verb, Spanish requires that another negative word—usually **no**—be placed before the verb. When a negative word precedes the verb, **no** is not used.

¿No estudia **nadie?**
¿Nadie estudia? } *Isn't anyone studying?*

No estás en clase **nunca.**
Nunca estás en clase. } *You're never in class.*

No quieren cenar aquí **tampoco.**
Tampoco quieren cenar aquí. } *They don't want to have dinner here, either.*

In Diego and Antonio's kitchen *Diego arrives home and he's hungry.* DIEGO: *I want to eat something, but there's nothing to eat in this house. And I don't feel like going shopping. And furthermore, I don't have a cent!* ANTONIO: *Ah! You're always like that. You never feel like going shopping. And that bit about the money . . . , that's another story!*

Alguno and *ninguno*

Alguno and **ninguno** are adjectives. Unlike **nadie** and **nada** (nouns) or **nunca, jamás,** and **tampoco** (adverbs), **alguno** and **ninguno** must agree with the noun they modify.

Alguno and **ninguno** shorten to **algún** and **ningún,** respectively, before a masculine singular noun—just as **uno** shortens to **un, bueno** to **buen,** and **malo** to **mal.**

The plural forms **ningunos** and **ningunas** are rarely used.

—¿Hay **algunos** recados para mí hoy?
Are there any messages for me today?
—Lo siento, pero hoy no hay **ningún** recado para Ud.
I'm sorry, but there are no messages for you today.
(There is not a single message for you today.)

AUTOPRUEBA

Give the corresponding negative word.

1. siempre
2. también
3. alguien

4. alguna
5. algo

Answers: 1. nunca 2. tampoco 3. nadie 4. ninguna 5. nada

■ **Práctica**

A. ¡Anticipemos! ¿Qué pasa esta noche en casa? Tell whether the following statements about what is happening at this house are true (**cierto**) or false (**falso**). Then create as many additional sentences as you can about what is happening, following the model of the sentences.

1. No hay nadie en el baño.
2. En la cocina, alguien está preparando la cena.
3. No hay ninguna persona en el patio.
4. Hay algo en la mesa del comedor.

5. Algunos amigos se están divirtiendo en la sala.
6. Hay algunos platos en la mesa del comedor.
7. No hay ningún niño en la casa.

B. ¡Por eso no come nadie allí! Exprese negativamente, usando la negativa doble.

MODELO: Hay alguien en el restaurante. → *No* hay *nadie* en el restaurante.

1. Hay algo interesante en el menú.
2. Tienen algunos platos típicos.
3. El profesor cena allí también.
4. Mis amigos siempre almuerzan allí.
5. Preparan algo especial para grupos grandes.
6. Siempre hacen platos nuevos.
7. Y también sirven paella, mi plato favorito.

Need more practice?

■ Workbook/Laboratory Manual
■ Interactive CD-ROM
■ Online Learning Center
  (www.mhhe.com/quetal7)

■ Conversación

Preguntas

1. ¿Vamos a vivir en la luna (*moon*) algún día? ¿Vamos a viajar (*travel*) a otros planetas? ¿Vamos a vivir allí algún día? ¿Vamos a establecer contacto con seres (*beings*) de otros planetas algún día?

2. ¿Algunos de los estudiantes de esta universidad son de países extranjeros? ¿De dónde son? ¿Algunos de sus amigos son de habla española (*Spanish-speaking*)? ¿De dónde son?

3. En esta clase, ¿quién…

siempre tiene algunas buenas ideas?	nunca contesta ninguna pregunta?
nunca les pregunta nada a sus compañeros?	va a ser muy rico algún día?
tiene algunos amigos españoles?	nunca tiene tiempo para divertirse?
siempre lo entiende todo?	nunca mira la televisión?
	no practica ningún deporte?
	siempre invita a los otros a comer?

En los Estados Unidos y el Canadá*

Goya Foods, Inc.

En Norteamérica muchos conocen **la marca Goya:** hay frijoles, arroz, condimentos, bebidas, café, productos de coco,[a] jugos de frutas tropicales y muchos **productos** más que son **fundamentales para las cocinas caribeña, mexicana, centroamericana y sudamericana.**

En los años 30 Prudencio Unanue, **un emigrante vasco** del norte de España, **funda**[b] **la compañía Goya.** Unanue y su esposa puertorriqueña llegan a Nueva York en 1916 y fundan Unanue Inc. en Manhattan en 1935, una compañía **especializada en importaciones de productos españoles** como olivas, aceite de oliva[c] y sardinas enlatadas.[d] En 1936 la compañía adopta el nombre de Goya. Desde 1974

la oficina principal está en Nueva Jersey. Hoy tiene **centros de procesamiento y distribución** en diversos estados, además de Puerto Rico, la República Dominicana y España.

La compañía Goya **está todavía en manos de**[e] **la familia Unanue:** los hijos de Prudencio y seis miembros de la tercera[f] generación. Goya es la primera compañía propiedad de hispanos representada en el Museo Nacional de Historia Americana del Instituto Smithsonian, en Washington, D.C., donde hay una colección de sus anuncios y envases.[g]

[a]*coconut* [b]*founds, starts* [c]*aceite… olive oil* [d]*canned* [e]*está… still belongs to* [f]*third* [g]*anuncios… ads and containers*

---

*From this point on in ¿Qué tal?, the **En los Estados Unidos y el Canadá** sections will be written in Spanish. Important words will be in boldface type. Scanning those words before you begin to read will help you get the gist of the passage.

Voces de Panamá

LITERATURA: Carlos Guillermo Wilson

Carlos Guillermo Wilson (1941–)

Sobre el autor: *Carlos Guillermo Wilson es originario de Panamá. Actualmente enseña literatura en San Diego State University en California. Su poesía y sus cuentos tratan con frecuencia los temas de la raza y el prejuicio racial. El siguiente poema es del cuento «Los mosquitos de orixá Changó[a]»**

Desarraigado[b]

Abuelita africana,
¿no me reconoces?

Mi lengua es cervantina
Mi letanía[c] es cristiana
Mi danza es flamenca
Mi raza es mulata

Abuelita africana,
¿por qué no me reconoces?

[a]orixá… *the ancient deity Changó, a god representing man's virility* [b]*Uprooted* [c]*litany (religious rite)*

MÚSICA: El calipso

El calipso es una de las formas musicales más populares de Panamá. El calipso tuvo su origen[a] en Trinidad entre los esclavos[b] africanos. Llegó[c] a Panamá con los muchos obreros[d] contratados[e] para la construcción del Canal de Panamá. Desde[f] los tiempos de la esclavitud[g] en Trinidad, los duelos de improvisación[h] entre los cantantes[i] del calipso han sido[j] populares. Estos duelos se parecen a[k] los duelos del estilo musical *rap* de este país.

[a]tuvo… *originated* [b]*slaves* [c]*It came* [d]*workers* [e]*contracted* [f]*Since* [g]*slavery* [h]duelos… *extemporization, improvisation duels* [i]*singers* [j]han… *have been* [k]se… *resemble*

Para tocar el calipso, se puede usar casi cualquier[l] instrumento. Con frecuencia se usan instrumentos hechos[m] en casa, de bambú o de bidones.[n] La música del calipso es menos importante que su letra,[o] que con frecuencia es improvisada y satírica. Ofrece una crítica de la política y la vida social.

[l]*any* [m]*made* [n]*(oil) drums* [o]*lyrics*

Julio Mou, descendiente de padres chinos y arquitecto de profesión, es ahora uno de los compositores de música del calipso más conocidos[p] en Panamá. Aquí está Julio (a la izquierda) con el acordeonista Juancín Henríquez.

[p]*well-known*

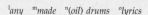

Publication of the Afro-Latin/American Research Association (PALARA), #1, 1997: 138–142.

¿Recuerda Ud.?

In **Gramática 19,** you will learn to form one type of command. In Spanish, the formal commands are based on the first person singular of the present tense. To review what you already know about irregular first person present tense forms, give the **yo** form of the following infinitives.

1. salir   **2.** tener   **3.** conocer   **4.** pedir   **5.** hacer   **6.** dormir   **7.** perder   **8.** traer

---

19 Influencing Others Formal Commands

Receta para guacamole

En español, los mandatos se usan con frecuencia en las recetas. Estos verbos se usan en forma de mandato en esta receta. ¿Puede encontrarlos?

añadir	to add
cortar	to cut
mezclar	to mix
servir (i, i)	to serve

^a*avocado*   ^b*diente… clove of garlic*   ^c*crushed*   ^d*fresh*   ^e*pieces*   ^f*corn*

El guacamole

Ingredientes:
1 aguacate^a
1 diente de ajo,^b
  prensado^c
1 tomate
jugo de un limón
sal
un poco de cilantro
  fresco^d

Cómo se prepara
Corte el aguacate y el tomate en trozos^e pequeños. *Añada* el jugo del limón, el ajo, el cilantro y la sal a su gusto. *Mezcle* bien todos los ingredientes y *sírvalo* con tortillas fritas de maíz.^f

---

Past - **PRESENT** - - - - - - - - - - - - - - - - - - - Future
present
present progressive
formal commands

Formal Command Forms

In *¿Qué tal?* you have seen formal commands in the direction lines of activities since the beginning of the text: **haga, complete, conteste,** and so on.

Commands (imperatives) are verb forms used to tell someone to do something. In Spanish, *formal commands* (**los mandatos formales**) are used with people whom you address as **Ud.** or **Uds.** Here are some of the basic forms.

	hablar	comer	escribir	volver	poner
Ud.	hable	coma	escriba	vuelva	ponga
Uds.	hablen	coman	escriban	vuelvan	pongan
English	*speak*	*eat*	*write*	*come back*	*put, place*

> **command or imperative** = a verb form used to tell someone to do something

A. Most formal command forms can be derived from the **yo** form of the present tense.

    -ar: -o → **-e**   **-er/-ir: -o** → **-a**
             -en   **-an**

hablo → hable
como → coma
escribo → escriba

B. Formal commands of stem-changing verbs will show the stem change.

piense Ud.
vuelva Ud.
pida Ud.

C. Verbs ending in **-car, -gar,** and **-zar** have a spelling change to preserve the **-c-, -g-,** and **-z-** sounds.

c → qu   buscar: busque Ud.
g → gu   pagar: pague Ud.
z → c   empezar: empiece Ud.

D. Verbs that have irregular **yo** forms in the present tense will reflect the irregularity in the **Ud./Uds.** commands.

conocer: conozco	→ conozca Ud.
decir* (*to say, tell*): digo	→ diga Ud.
hacer: hago	→ haga Ud.
oír: oigo	→ oiga Ud.
poner: pongo	→ ponga Ud.
salir: salgo	→ salga Ud.
tener: tengo	→ tenga Ud.
traer: traigo	→ traiga Ud.
venir: vengo	→ venga Ud.
ver: veo	→ vea Ud.

E. A few verbs have irregular **Ud./Uds.** command forms.

dar* (*to give*)	→ **dé** Ud.
estar	→ **esté** Ud.
ir	→ **vaya** Ud.
saber	→ **sepa** Ud.
ser	→ **sea** Ud.

Position of Pronouns with Formal Commands

• Direct object pronouns and reflexive pronouns must follow affirmative commands and be attached to them. In order to maintain the original stress of the verb form, an accent mark is added to the stressed vowel if the original command has two or more syllables.

Pídalo Ud.   *Order it.*
Siéntese, por favor.   *Sit down, please.*

• Direct object and reflexive pronouns must precede negative commands.

No lo pida Ud.   *Don't order it.*
No se siente.   *Don't sit down.*

Decir and **dar** *are used primarily with indirect objects. Both of these verbs and indirect object pronouns will be formally introduced in* **Capítulo 7.**

■ Práctica

A. Profesor(a) por un día. Imagine que Ud. es el profesor / la profesora hoy. ¿Qué mandatos debe dar a la clase?

MODELOS: hablar español → Hablen Uds. español.
hablar inglés → No hablen Uds. inglés.

1. llegar a tiempo
2. leer la lección
3. escribir una composición
4. abrir los libros
5. estar en clase mañana
6. traer los libros a clase
7. estudiar los verbos nuevos
8. ¿ ?

B. ¡Pobre Sr. Casiano!

PASO 1   El Sr. Casiano no se siente (*feel*) bien. Lea la descripción que él da de algunas de sus actividades.

«Trabajo[1] muchísimo[a] —¡me gusta trabajar! En la oficina, soy[2] impaciente y critico[3b] bastante[c] a los otros. En mi vida personal, a veces soy[4] un poco impulsivo. Fumo[5d] bastante y también bebo[6] cerveza y otras bebidas alcohólicas, a veces sin moderación… Almuerzo[7] y ceno[8] fuerte, y casi nunca desayuno.[9] Por la noche, con frecuencia salgo[10] con los amigos —me gusta ir a las discotecas— y vuelvo[11] tarde a casa.»

[a]*a great deal*   [b]critico → criticar   [c]*a good deal*   [d]Fumo → fumar

PASO 2   ¿Qué *no* debe hacer el Sr. Casiano para estar mejor? Aconséjele (*Advise him*) sobre lo que no debe hacer. Use los verbos indicados en azul o cualquier (*any*) otro, según los modelos.

MODELOS: Trabajo → Sr. Casiano, no trabaje tanto.
soy → Sr. Casiano, no sea tan impaciente.

C. Situaciones.   El Sr. Casiano quiere adelgazar (*to lose weight*). ¿Debe o no debe comer o beber las siguientes cosas? Con otro/a estudiante, haga y conteste preguntas según los modelos:

MODELOS: ensalada → E1: ¿Ensalada?   postres → E1: ¿Postres?
E2: Cóma*la*.   E2: No *los* coma.

1. alcohol (*m.*)
2. verduras
3. pan
4. dulces
5. leche
6. hamburguesas con queso
7. frutas frescas
8. refrescos dietéticos
9. pollo
10. carne
11. pizza
12. jugo de fruta

PASO 3

D. ¡Estoy harto de Uds. dos! (*I'm fed up with you two!*)   Imagine que Ud. acaba de volver de clase y la casa es un desastre. Está enojado/a (*angry*) y empieza a gritarles (*yell*) mandatos a sus compañeros de casa sobre su apariencia física y sus hábitos.

MODELO: afeitarse → ¡Aféitense!

1. despertarse más temprano
2. levantarse más temprano
3. bañarse más
4. quitarse esa ropa sucia
5. ponerse ropa limpia
6. vestirse mejor
7. estudiar más
8. no divertirse todas las noches con los amigos
9. ir más a la biblioteca
10. no acostarse tan tarde
11. ayudar con los quehaceres
12. ¿ ?

NOTA COMUNICATIVA

El subjuntivo

Except for the command form, all verb forms that you have learned thus far in *¿Qué tal?* have been part of the *indicative mood* (**el modo indicativo**). In both English and Spanish, the indicative is used to state facts and to ask questions. It objectively expresses most real-world actions or states of being.

Both English and Spanish have another verb system called the *subjunctive mood* (**el modo subjuntivo**), which will be introduced in **Capítulo 12.** The **Ud./Uds.** command forms that you have just learned are part of the subjunctive system. From this point on in *¿Qué tal?* you will see the subjunctive used where it is natural to use it. What follows is a brief introduction to the subjunctive that will make it easy for you to recognize it when you see it.

Here are some examples of the forms of the subjunctive. The **Ud./Uds.** forms (identical to the **Ud./Uds.** command forms) are highlighted.

HABLAR		COMER		SERVIR		SALIR	
hable	hablemos	coma	comamos	sirva	sirvamos	salga	salgamos
hables	habléis	comas	comáis	sirvas	sirváis	salgas	salgáis
hable	hablen	coma	coman	sirva	sirvan	salga	salgan

The subjunctive is used to express more subjective or conceptualized states, in contrast to the indicative, which reports facts, information that is objectively true. Here are just a few of the situations in which the subjunctive is used in Spanish.

- to express what the speaker wants others to do (I want you to . . .)
- to express emotional reactions (I'm glad that . . .)
- to express probability or uncertainty (It's likely that . . .)

E. El cumpleaños de María. Fíjese en (*Notice*) los verbos subrayados (*underlined*) en los siguientes diálogos. Diga en inglés por qué razón están subrayados. (Use la lista de la **Nota comunicativa.**)

En el parque

RAÚL: Como hoy es tu cumpleaños, quiero invitarte a cenar. ¿En qué restaurante quieres que <u>cenemos</u>?

MARÍA: Prefiero que tú me[a] <u>prepares</u> una de tus espléndidas cenas.

RAÚL: ¡Con mucho gusto!

En casa de María

MADRE: (*Hablando por teléfono.*) No, lo siento,[b] pero María no está en casa.

LUISA: ¿Es posible que <u>esté</u> en la biblioteca?

MADRE: No. Sé que ella y Raúl están cenando en casa de él.

LUISA: Ah, sí. Bueno, ¿puede pedirle a ella que <u>llame</u> a Luisa cuando regrese?

MADRE: Sí, cómo no,[c] Luisa. Adiós.

LUISA: Hasta luego.

[a]*for me* [b]lo... *I'm sorry* [c]*cómo... of course*

Need more practice?

- Workbook/Laboratory Manual
- Interactive CD-ROM
- Online Learning Center (www.mhhe.com/quetal7)

■ Conversación

En la oficina del consejero. Imagine that you are a guidance counselor. Students consult you with all kinds of questions, some trivial and some important. Offer advice to them in the form of affirmative or negative commands. Working with a partner, how many different commands can you invent for each situation?

MODELO: Primero, hábleme de su horario.
Y, por favor, incluya las comidas y...

1. EVELIA: No me gusta tomar clases por la mañana. Siempre estoy muy cansada durante esas clases y además (*besides*) a esa hora tengo hambre. Pienso constantemente en el almuerzo... y no puedo concentrarme en las explicaciones.

2. FABIÁN: En mi clase de cálculo, ¡no entiendo nada! No puedo hacer los ejercicios y durante la clase tengo miedo de hacer preguntas, porque no quiero parecer (*seem*) tonto.

3. FAUSTO: Fui (*I went*) a México el verano pasado y me gustó (*I liked it*) mucho. Quiero volver a México este verano. Ahora que lo conozco mejor, quiero ir en mi coche y no en autobús como el verano pasado. Desgraciadamente (*Unfortunately*) no tengo dinero para hacer el viaje.

4. RAMÓN: Siempre llego tarde a las clases. Como tengo tanta prisa, no traigo los libros ni los papeles que necesito. Hoy no desayuné pero, ¡ni eso (*not even that*) me ayudó (*helped*)!

UN POCO DE TODO

Lengua y cultura: La cocina (*cooking*) **panameña.**   Complete the following passages with the correct forms of the words in parentheses, as suggested by the context. When two possibilities are given in parentheses, select the correct word. **¡OJO!** As you conjugate verbs in this activity, note that you will make formal commands with some infinitives.

¿**C**reen Uds. que la comida panameña es similar a la[a] de México? ¿(*Uds.*: Creer[1]) que los tacos y las tortillas (ser / estar[2]) parte de la comida de los panameños? Si creen que sí,[b] entonces[c] no (*Uds.*: saber / conocer[3]) (algo / nada[4]) de la comida de (esto[5]) nación. (*Uds.*: Empezar[6]) (a / de[7]) leer esta lectura, porque van a aprender mucho.

Hoy en dia, Panamá tiene muy (bueno[8]) relaciones con los Estados Unidos y el Canadá, especialmente por[d] la (grande[9]) importancia para Norteamérica que tiene su canal. En Panamá, observamos mucho la influencia de los Estados Unidos. Muchos panameños (saber / conocer[10]) inglés perfectamente y (lo/la[11]) hablan con frecuencia.

La influencia (extranjero[12]) en la comida de la cosmopolita ciudad de Panamá es muy visible. Hay (mucho[13]) restaurantes que (servir[14]) comida italiana, china, (francés[15]), estadounidense y otras de otros países también.

Los panameños no (perder[16]) su identidad nacional, y frecuentemente (preferir[17]) servir la comida tradicional. En la comida tradicional panameña hay muchos platos de mariscos y pescados, especialmente el ceviche. Las personas vegetarianas no (tener[18]) problema con la comida tradicional porque hay una variedad de platos (preparado[19]) con verduras y arroz. El arroz es un ingrediente importante en la comida de Panamá. Generalmente cuando los turistas (preguntar[20]) «¿Cuál es el plato nacional de Panamá?», los panameños (contestar[21]): «Es el arroz con pollo. (*Uds.*: Pedirlo[22]). Les va a gustar».

[a]la... *that*   [b]Si... *If you think so*   [c]*then*   [d]*because of*

Comprensión: La cocina panameña.   Conteste las siguientes preguntas.

1. ¿Por qué tiene Panamá muy buenas relaciones con los Estados Unidos y el Canadá?
2. ¿Cómo se sabe que la ciudad de Panamá es cosmopolita?
3. ¿Cuál es el plato que representa mejor la cocina panameña?
4. ¿Qué ingredientes son muy comunes en la comida de Panamá? ¿Cómo se puede explicar esto?

El arroz con pollo, un plato panameño típico

Resources for Review and Testing Preparation

- Workbook/Laboratory Manual
- Interactive CD-ROM
- Online Learning Center (www.mhhe.com/quetal7)

Entrevista cultural: Panamá

Maír Citón Moreno es dueño de un restaurante en su país, Panamá. En esta entrevista habla de los platos que se sirven en su restaurante. También habla de los ingredientes más comunes y de su plato favorito. Antes de ver el vídeo, lea el siguiente fragmento de la entrevista.

ENTREVISTADORA: ¿Qué tipo de restaurante es, y qué tipo de comida se sirve?

MAÍR: Es un restaurante exclusivamente de comida típica panameña y en base al maíz[a] y el arroz.

ENTREVISTADORA: ¿Cuáles son los platillos más típicos de Panamá?

MAÍR: Los platillos más típicos de Panamá serían[b] el arroz de frijoles de palo,[c] el sancocho de gallina,[d] los tamales, las tortillas asadas, entre otros.

[a]en... *corn-based*   [b]*would be*   [c]frijoles... *palo beans*   [d]sancocho... *dish with chicken, yucca, plantain, and other ingredients*

Ahora vea el vídeo y conteste las siguientes preguntas basándose en la entrevista.

1. ¿Dónde vive y trabaja Maír?
2. ¿Qué tipo de comida se sirve en el restaurante de Maír?
3. ¿Cuáles son los ingredientes básicos de la cocina panameña?
4. ¿Cuáles son unos ingredientes tropicales y unos tipos de carne que se mencionan en la entrevista?
5. ¿Cuál es el plato favorito de Maír?

Entre amigos: ¿Quién cocina en tu casa?

Tané prepara la comida para una fiesta. Karina, Rubén y Miguel van a ayudarla a cocinar. En su opinión, ¿qué preguntas van a hacerse (*ask each other*)? Antes de mirar el vídeo, lea las preguntas a continuación (*that follow*). Mientras mire el vídeo, trate de entender la conversación en general y fíjese en la información sobre la comida. Luego mire el vídeo una segunda (*second*) vez, fijándose en la información que necesita para contestar las preguntas.

1. ¿Qué prepara Tané?
2. ¿Quién cocina en casa de Tané?
3. ¿Sabe cocinar Rubén? ¿Por qué sí o por qué no?
4. Según Miguel, ¿cómo se prepara el pozole, un plato mexicano muy conocido (*well-known*)?

PASO 4

Panamá

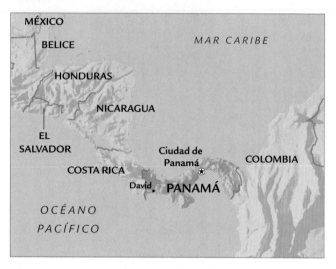

MÉXICO

BELICE

MAR CARIBE

HONDURAS

NICARAGUA

EL SALVADOR

COSTA RICA

Ciudad de Panamá

COLOMBIA

David · PANAMÁ

OCÉANO PACÍFICO

¡Fíjese!

- Panamá es una palabra indígena que significa «tierra de muchos peces[a]».
- La Carretera[b] Panamericana, el sistema de carreteras que va de Alaska a la Argentina, se interrumpe[c] en la densa e[d] impenetrable selva[e] panameña de Darién. Para llegar a Sudamérica es necesario tomar un barco[f] hasta Colombia, donde continúa la carretera.
- La Sra. Mireya Moscoso ganó[g] las elecciones presidenciales de 1998. La viuda[h] de otro presidente, doña Mireya es la primera mujer panameña en asumir el cargo.[i]

[a]fish [b]Highway [c]se… breaks off, is interrupted [d]y [e]jungle [f]boat [g]won [h]widow [i]post

Learn more about Panama with the Video, the Interactive CD-ROM, and the Online Learning Center (www.mhhe.com/quetal7).

Lugares famosos: el Canal de Panamá

El Canal de Panamá, construido a través del[a] istmo entre los dos continentes americanos, comunica los océanos Atlántico y Pacífico. Mide[b] aproximadamente 80 kilómetros (50 millas) de largo, 12,5 metros (41 pies[c]) de ancho[d] y 200 metros (más de 63 pies) de profundidad. Su construcción facilita la comunicación marítima entre las costas este y oeste de los continentes. Antes de la existencia del canal, los barcos tenían que darle la vuelta a[e] América del Sur para ir de una costa a otra. Hoy, el viaje por el Canal de Panamá toma aproximadamente ocho horas, pues[f] es necesario pasar por un número de esclusas.[g]

La idea de construir un canal a través del istmo data de 1534, cuando el emperador español Carlos V (Quinto) la propone. Más tarde, en 1881, el ingeniero francés Fernando de Lesseps también sugiere un proyecto similar. Pero el canal no se construye hasta el siglo XX, por los Estados Unidos. Esto ocasiona[h] la presencia de los Estados Unidos en la vida de Panamá. Como resultado, hay un uso extendido del inglés en el país, se usa el dólar y ha habido[i] una gran intervención en la política del país.

El canal se inaugura en 1914 y es administrado por los Estados Unidos hasta 1999. Desde el primero de enero del año 2000, la República de Panamá está a cargo de[j] su gran canal.

[a]construido… built across the [b]It measures [c]feet [d]de… in width [e]tenían… had to go around [f]because [g]canal locks [h]brings about [i]ha… there has been [j]a… in control of

Una esclusa del Canal de Panamá

PASO FINAL

 A CONVERSAR

El menú del día

PASO 1　En grupos de tres o cuatro estudiantes, lean el siguiente menú del restaurante 'El toro bravo'. Basándose en el menú, ¿qué tipo de restaurante es? ¿Creen que es un restaurante con un ambiente elegante y caro o un restaurante con un ambiente relajado y precios módicos (*moderate*)? El menú que Uds. leen es el menú del día, es decir (*that is*), las especialidades del día. En su opinión, ¿qué otras cosas sirven en este restaurante?

Restaurante 'El toro bravo'
Menú del día: €12,60

De entrada:

Ensalada mixta
(lechuga, tomate, zanahoria, cebolla[a] y
aceitunas[b] verdes con salsa vinagreta)

Sopa de cebolla con queso fundido[c]

Espárragos con jamón serrano[d]

De plato principal:

Paella de mariscos
(arroz, camarones, almejas,[e] pescado, salchicha[f])

Pollo asado con patatas al horno

Verduras asadas con cous-cous
(pimiento verde, cebolla, berenjena,[g]
broculí, champiñones)

De postre:

Ensalada de frutas
(fresas,[h] melón, manzana, naranja)

Flan

Varios helados

[a]*onion*　[b]*olives*　[c]*melted*　[d]jamón... *type of cured Spanish ham*　[e]*clams*　[f]*sausage*　[g]*eggplant*　[h]*strawberries*

PASO 2 Ahora, imaginen que Uds. están en el restaurante. Uno/a de Uds. es camarero/a y los demás (*the rest*) son clientes que desean cenar. Antes de improvisar una escena, revisen (*look over*) las expresiones a continuación y piensen en el tipo de personaje que van a representar (un camarero difícil o un camarero simpático, una clienta exigente [*demanding*] o una clienta paciente, etcétera).

Clientes	Camarero/a
¿Qué recomienda (de plato principal / de postre)?	¿Qué le(s)* traigo (hoy / de beber)?
¿Qué hay en (la sopa de cebolla)?	¿Ya saben lo que desean tomar?
Quiero (la paella de mariscos), por favor.	¿Y qué quiere de (entrada [*first course*] / plato principal / postre)?
Para mí, (los espárragos), por favor.	¿Y para Ud.?
¿Hay (tomates) en (la ensalada mixta)?	Lo siento mucho (*I'm very sorry*). No hay más (flan) hoy.
Por favor, preparen (los espárragos) sin (jamón).	Le(s)* recomiendo (la sopa de cebolla).
	La especialidad de la casa es (la paella).
	Lo siento; no podemos preparar (los espárragos) sin (jamón).
	Muy bien. Le* preparamos (los espárragos) sin (jamón).

PASO 3 Improvisen una escena entre los clientes y el camarero / la camarera. La escena debe incluir saludos, pregunatas y respuestas sobre los platos, recomendaciones y sugerencias, el orden. Después de practicar la escena, represéntenla para la clase.

---

*Le and les are *indirect object pronouns.* Their equivalents in English are (*to / for*) *you* (*sing.*) and *you* (*pl.*), respectively. You will learn more about indirect object pronouns in **Capítulo 7.** For now, you can just use them in the phrases indicated.

GRAMÁTICA

To review the grammar points presented in this chapter, refer to the indicated grammar presentations. You'll find further practice of these structures in the Workbook/Laboratory Manual, on the Interactive CD-ROM, and on the *¿Qué tal?* Online Learning Center (www.mhhe.com/quetal7).

17 Expressing *what* or *whom*—Direct Object Pronouns

Do you know how to avoid repetition by using direct object pronouns?

18 Expressing Negation—Indefinite and Negative Words

Do you know how to use the double negative in Spanish?

19 Influencing Others—Formal Commands

You should know how to use commands to order in restaurants and to have someone do something for you.

VOCABULARIO   Practice this vocabulary with digital flash cards on the Online Learning Center (www.mhhe.com/quetal7).

Los verbos

acabar de + *inf.*	to have just (*done something*)
ayudar	to help
cenar	to have (eat) dinner, supper
cocinar	to cook
conocer (zc)*	to know, be acquainted with
desayunar	to have (eat) breakfast
esperar	to wait (for); to expect
invitar	to invite
llamar	to call
preguntar	to ask (a question)
preparar	to prepare
saber (*irreg.*)	to know
saber + *inf.*	to know how to (*do something*)

Repaso: almorzar (ue) (c)*

La comida

el arroz	rice
las arvejas	peas
el atún	tuna
el bistec	steak
los camarones	shrimp
la carne	meat
el champiñón	mushroom
la chuleta (de cerdo)	(pork) chop
los dulces	sweets; candy
los espárragos	asparagus
el flan	(baked) custard
los frijoles	beans
la galleta	cookie
el helado	ice cream
el huevo	egg
el jamón	ham
la langosta	lobster
la lechuga	lettuce
la mantequilla	butter
la manzana	apple
los mariscos	shellfish
la naranja	orange
el pan	bread
el pan tostado	toast
la papa	potato
el pastel	cake; pie
la patata (frita)	(French fried) potato
el pavo	turkey
el pescado	fish
el pollo (asado)	(roast) chicken
el postre	dessert
el queso	cheese
la salchicha	sausage; hot dog

*From this chapter on, the spelling changes for verbs in the subjunctive and formal commands such as
-c- → -qu-, -g- → -gu-, -z- → -c-, as well as verbs with -zc- and -g- changes in the present tense **yo**
form, will be indicated in parentheses in the vocabulary lists.*

la sopa	soup	el consejo	(piece of) advice
las verduras	vegetables	el detalle	detail
la zanahoria	carrot	el/la dueño/a	owner
		la tarjeta de crédito	credit card

Cognados: la banana, el cereal, la ensalada, la fruta, la hamburguesa, el salmón, el sándwich, el tomate, el yogur

Las bebidas

el agua (mineral)	(mineral) water
el jugo (de fruta)	(fruit) juice
la leche	milk
el refresco	soft drink
el vino (blanco, tinto)	(white, red) wine

Cognado: el té
Repaso: el café, la cerveza

Las comidas

el almuerzo	lunch
la cena	dinner, supper

Repaso: el desayuno

En un restaurante

el/la camarero/a	waiter/waitress
la cuenta	check, bill
el plato	dish; course

Cognado: el menú

Otros sustantivos

la bebida	drink, beverage
la comida	food; meal

Los adjetivos

fresco/a	fresh
frito/a	fried
fuerte	heavy (*meal, food*); strong
ligero/a	light, not heavy
rápido/a	fast

Palabras indefinidas y negativas

alguien	someone, anyone
algún (alguno/a/os/as)	some, any
jamás	never
nada	nothing, not anything
nadie	no one, nobody, not anybody
ningún (ninguno/a)	no, none, not any
tampoco	neither, not either

Repaso: algo, nunca, siempre, también

Palabras adicionales

estar (*irreg.*) a dieta	to be on a diet
tener (*irreg.*) (mucha) hambre	to be (very) hungry
tener (*irreg.*) (mucha) sed	to be (very) thirsty

Capítulo 6 • ¿Qué le gusta comer?

De vacaciones

CULTURA

- **Nota cultural:** Los nuevos tipos de turismo en el mundo hispánico
- **En los Estados Unidos y el Canadá:** Ellen Ochoa: Una viajera espacial
- **Voces** de Honduras y El Salvador
    Literatura: Clementina Suárez
    Música: Yolocamba I Ta y el folklore
- **Videoteca**
    Entrevista cultural: Honduras y El Salvador
    Entre amigos: El verano pasado, me fui al Canadá
- **Enfoque cultural:** Honduras y El Salvador
- **A leer:** El Salvador: Un tesoro al alcance de la mano

VOCABULARIO

- De viaje
- De vacaciones

GRAMÁTICA

20 Indirect Object Pronouns; **dar** and **decir**

21 **Gustar**

22 Preterite of Regular Verbs and of **dar, hacer, ir,** and **ser**

Una playa de Roatán, una isla en la Bahía (Bay) de Honduras

DE VIAJE

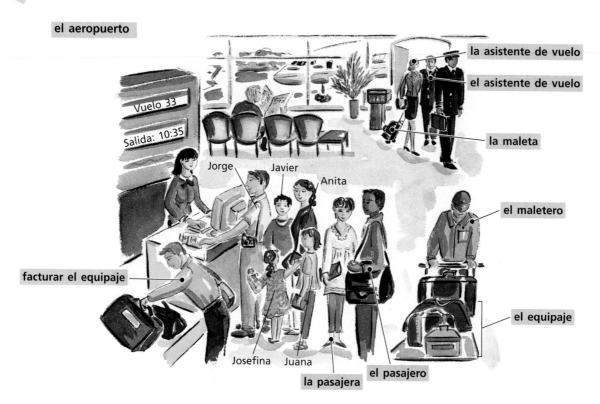

el aeropuerto

Vuelo 33

Salida: 10:35

la asistente de vuelo

el asistente de vuelo

la maleta

Jorge   Javier

Anita

el maletero

facturar el equipaje

el equipaje

Josefina   Juana

la pasajera   el pasajero

Modos de transporte

el barco	boat, ship
la cabina	cabin (*on a ship*)
la estación	station
de autobuses	bus
del tren	train
el puerto	port
la sala de espera	waiting room
la sección de (no)	(non)smoking
fumar	section
el vuelo	flight
ir (*irreg.*) **en...**	to go / travel by . . .
autobús	bus
avión	plane
barco	boat, ship
tren	train

El viaje

la agencia de viajes	travel agency
el/la agente de viajes	travel agent
el asiento	seat
el billete/el boleto/ el pasaje*	ticket
de ida	one-way
de ida y vuelta	round-trip
la demora	delay
la llegada	arrival
la salida	departure
bajar (de)	to get down (from); to get off (of) (*a vehicle*)
estar (*irreg.*) **atrasado/a**	to be late
guardar (un puesto)	to save (a place [*in line*])
hacer (*irreg.*) **cola**	to stand in line

---

*Throughout Spanish America, **el boleto** is the word used for a ticket for travel. **El billete** is commonly used in Spain. **El pasaje** is used throughout the Spanish-speaking world. The words **la entrada** and **la localidad** are used to refer to tickets for movies, plays, or similar functions.

hacer (*irreg.*) **escalas/paradas**	to make stops	**pasar por el control de la seguridad**	to go/pass through security (check)
hacer (*irreg.*) **la(s) maleta(s)**	to pack one's suitcase(s)	**subir (a)**	to go up; to get on (*a vehicle*)
hacer (*irreg.*) **un viaje**	to take a trip	**viajar**	to travel

▪ Conversación

A. Un viaje en avión. Imagine que Ud. va a hacer un viaje en avión. El vuelo sale a las siete de la mañana. Usando los números del 1 al 9, indique en qué orden van a pasar las siguientes cosas.

a. _____ Subo al avión.

b. _____ Voy a la sala de espera.

c. _____ Hago cola para comprar el boleto y facturar el equipaje.

d. _____ Llego al aeropuerto a tiempo (*on time*) y bajo del taxi.

e. _____ Por fin se anuncia la salida del vuelo.

f. _____ Estoy atrasado/a. Salgo para el aeropuerto en taxi.

g. _____ La asistente me indica el asiento en clase turística.

h. _____ Pido un asiento de ventanilla (*window seat*).

i. _____ Hay demora. Por eso todos tenemos que esperar el vuelo.

B. ¡Seamos (*Let's be*) **lógicos!** ¿Qué va a hacer Ud. en estas situaciones?

1. Ud. no tiene mucho dinero. ¿Qué clase de pasaje va a comprar?
a. clase turística   **b.** primera clase   **c.** clase de negocios (*business*)

2. Ud. es una persona muy nerviosa y tiene miedo de viajar en avión. Necesita ir desde Nueva York a Madrid. ¿Qué pide Ud.?
a. una cabina en un barco   **b.** un vuelo sin escalas

3. Ud. viaja en tren y tiene muchas maletas. Pesan (*They weigh*) mucho y no puede cargarlas (*carry them*). ¿Qué hace Ud.?
a. Compro boletos.   **b.** Guardo un asiento.   **c.** Facturo el equipaje.

C. En el aeropuerto. ¿Cuántas cosas y acciones puede Ud. identificar o describir en este dibujo? Trabaje con un compañero / una compañera.

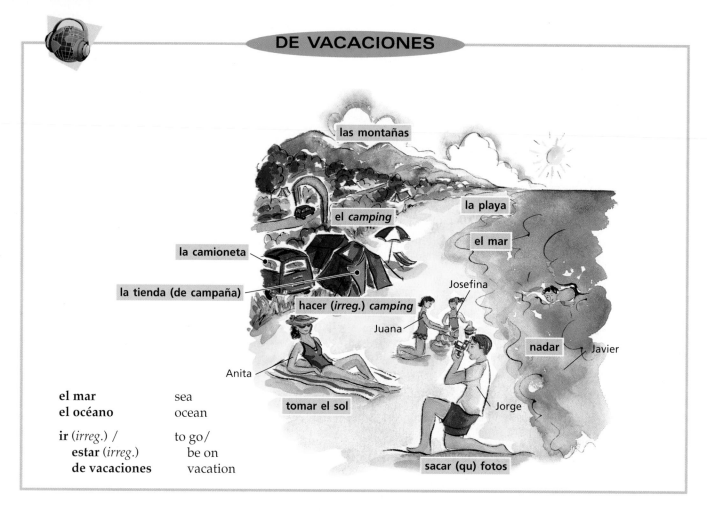

DE VACACIONES

las montañas

el *camping*

la playa

el mar

la camioneta

la tienda (de campaña)

hacer (*irreg.*) *camping*

Josefina

Juana

nadar   Javier

Anita

el mar	sea
el océano	ocean
ir (*irreg.*) / **estar** (*irreg.*) **de vacaciones**	to go/ be on vacation

tomar el sol

Jorge

sacar (qu) fotos

■ Conversación

A. ¿Qué hace Ud.? ¿Cierto o falso? Lea las siguientes oraciones e indique si son ciertas o falsas para Ud.

1. Cuando estoy de vacaciones, tomo el sol.
2. Prefiero ir de vacaciones a las montañas.
3. Duermo muy bien en una tienda de campaña.
4. Saco muchas fotos cuando estoy de vacaciones.
5. Es fácil viajar a playas bonitas desde (*from*) aquí.

B. Entrevista

1. Por lo general, ¿cuándo tomas tus vacaciones? ¿En invierno? ¿en verano? En las vacaciones, ¿te gusta viajar o prefieres no salir de tu ciudad? ¿Te gusta ir de vacaciones con tu familia? ¿Prefieres ir solo/a (*alone*), con un amigo / una amiga o con un grupo de personas? ¿Prefieres viajar sólo a lugares en este país o te gustaría (*would you like*) viajar por otros países del mundo (*world*)?

2. De los medios de transporte mencionados en **De viaje** (página 182), ¿cuáles conoces por experiencia? ¿Cuál es el más rápido? ¿el más económico? ¿Cuáles hacen más escalas o hacen paradas con más frecuencia? ¿Cómo prefieres viajar? ¿Prefieres un asiento de ventanilla o un asiento de pasillo? ¿la clase turística o primera clase?

NOTA COMUNICATIVA

Other Uses of *se* (For Recognition)

It is likely that you have often seen and heard the phrase shown in the photo that accompanies this box: **Se habla español.** (*Spanish is spoken* [*here*]). Here are some additional examples of this use of **se** with Spanish verbs. Note how the meaning of the verb changes slightly.

Se venden billetes aquí.   *Tickets are sold here.*

Aquí no **se fuma.**   *You don't (One doesn't) smoke here. Smoking is forbidden here.*

Be alert to this use of **se** when you see it because it will occur with some frequency in readings and in direction lines in *¿Qué tal?* The activities in this text will not require you to use this grammar point on your own, however.

Nueva York

C. ¿Dónde se hace esto?   Indique el lugar (o los lugares) donde se hacen las siguientes actividades.

1. Se factura el equipaje.
2. Se hacen las maletas.
3. Se compran los pasajes y se anuncian los vuelos.
4. Se hace una reservación.
5. Se espera en la sala de espera.
6. Se pide una bebida.
7. Se mira una película.
8. Se nada y se toma el sol.

Lugares

en casa
en el aeropuerto
en el avión
en la agencia de viajes
en la playa

NOTA CULTURAL

Los nuevos tipos de turismo en el mundo hispánico

El turista de hoy ya no es el turista tradicional y fácil de complacer.[a] Por eso hay nuevas industrias para satisfacer su interés en **la ecología, la agricultura** o **la aventura: el ecoturismo, el agroturismo y el aventurismo.** Los países hispánicos ofrecen ricas oportunidades para disfrutar de[b] estas nuevas formas de hacer turismo.

El ecoturismo consiste en **viajar a lugares no explotados por el ser humano.**[c] El ecoturista puede visitar **las selvas tropicales** de Centroamérica y la Amazonia. También puede explorar la Patagonia (en el sur de la Argentina y Chile) y las Islas Galápagos (el Ecuador).

El agroturismo implica **viajes a lugares rurales** donde el turista se queda en casas rurales renovadas. Algunas excursiones son informativas o educativas, con visitas a **granjas y campos de cultivo.**[d] Otras son simplemente parte de un programa para renovar casas y pueblos rurales. España ofrece varias oportunidades al agroturista por todo el país, especialmente en el País Vasco y en las Islas Baleares. La isla Chiloé de Chile también tiene una organización agroturística.

El aventurista, o sea[e] el turista que busca **viajes emocionantes, a veces peligrosos,**[f] también tiene amplias oportunidades en los países hispánicos. En los Andes, la Patagonia y las montañas de España, puede practicar **el alpinismo, el ciclismo de montaña, la navegación en rápidos, el esquí, el** *snowboard* y otros deportes **extremos.**

Ecoturistas en la Amazonia, en Perú

[a]*please* [b]*disfrutar... enjoying* [c]*por... by humans* [d]*granjas... farms and croplands* [e]*o... or in other words* [f]*dangerous*

20   Expressing *to whom* or *for whom*   Indirect Object Pronouns; *dar* and *decir*

Las vacaciones de primavera

Javier habla con sus padres de sus planes para las vacaciones de primavera. *Les* pide un poco de dinero para su pasaje de avión.

JAVIER: …así que mis amigos y yo ya tenemos todas las reservaciones. Pero tengo muy poco dinero para el viaje. Yo nunca *les* pido dinero a Uds. durante el semestre y trabajo mucho. Por esta vez, ¿*me* pueden *dar* un poco de dinero para el pasaje de avión?

MADRE: Siempre *le digo* a tu padre que eres muy trabajador y sé que nunca *nos* pides dinero.

PADRE: Es verdad. *Te* podemos *dar* un cheque para el pasaje y para la comida durante el viaje.

Comprensión

1. ¿Qué les pide Javier a sus padres?
2. ¿Qué le dice la madre al padre de Javier?
3. ¿Qué le dan los padres a Javier?

Spring vacation (break)   *Javier talks to his parents about his plans for spring break. He asks them for a little money for his airplane ticket.* JAVIER: *. . . so, my friends and I already have all of the reservations. But I don't have much money for the trip. I never ask you for money during the semester and I work very hard. Just this once, can you give me a little money for the airplane ticket?* MOTHER: *I always tell your father that you are very hardworking and I know you never ask us for money.* FATHER: *It's true. We can give you a check for the airplane ticket and for food during the trip.*

Indirect Object Pronouns

me	to/for me	nos	to/for us
te	to/for you (*fam. sing.*)	os	to/for you (*fam. pl.*)
le	to/for you (*form. sing.*), him, her, it	les	to/for you (*form. pl.*), them

Note that indirect object pronouns have the same form as direct object pronouns, except in the third person: **le, les.**

indirect object = noun or pronoun that indicates for whom an action is performed

---

A. Indirect object nouns and pronouns are the second recipient of the action of the verb. They usually answer the questions *to whom?* or *for whom?* in relation to the verb. The word *to* is frequently omitted in English.

Indicate the direct and indirect objects in the following sentences.

1. I'm giving her the present tomorrow.
2. Could you tell me the answer now?
3. El profesor nos va a hacer algunas preguntas.
4. ¿No me compras una revista ahora?

B. Like direct object pronouns, *indirect object pronouns* (**los pronombres del complemento indirecto**) are placed immediately before a conjugated verb. They may also be attached to an infinitive or a present participle.

No, no **te** presto el coche.
No, I won't lend you the car.

Voy a guardar**te** el asiento.
Te voy a guardar el asiento.
I'll save your seat for you.

Le estoy escribiendo una carta **a Marisol.**
Estoy escribiéndo**le** una carta **a Marisol.**
I'm writing Marisol a letter.

C. Since **le** and **les** have several different equivalents, their meaning is often clarified or emphasized with the preposition **a** followed by a pronoun (object of a preposition).

Voy a mandar**le** un telegrama **a Ud. (a él, a ella).**
I'm going to send you (him, her) a telegram.

Les hago una comida **a Uds. (a ellos, a ellas).**
I'm making you (them) a meal.

D. It is common for a Spanish sentence to contain both the indirect object noun and the indirect object pronoun, especially with third person forms.

Vamos a decir**le** la verdad **a Juan.**
Let's tell Juan the truth.

¿Les guardo los asientos **a Jorge y Marta?**
Shall I save the seats for Jorge and Marta?

E. As with direct object pronouns, indirect object pronouns are attached to the affirmative command form and precede the negative command form.

Sírva**nos** un café, por favor.
Serve us some coffee, please.

No **me** dé su número de teléfono ahora.
Don't give me your phone number now.

F. Here are some verbs frequently used with indirect objects.

escribir	*to write*	**preguntar**	*to ask* (a question)
explicar (qu)	*to explain*	**prestar**	*to lend*
hablar	*to speak*	**prometer**	*to promise*
mandar	*to send*	**recomendar (ie)**	*to recommend*
mostrar (ue)	*to show*	**regalar**	*to give* (as a gift)
ofrecer (zc)	*to offer*	**servir (i, i)**	*to serve*
pedir (i, i)	*to ask for*		

Dar and *decir*

	dar (to give)		**decir** (to say; to tell)	
	doy	damos	digo	decimos
	das	dais	dices	decís
	da	dan	dice	dicen

Javier les **dice** a sus padres que necesita dinero.

Su padre le **da** un cheque.

- **Dar** and **decir** are almost always used with indirect object pronouns in Spanish.

 In Spanish there are two verbs for *to give*: **dar** (*to give* [in general]) and **regalar** (*to give as a gift*). Also, do not confuse **decir** (*to say* or *to tell*) with **hablar** (*to speak*).

¿Cuándo **me das** el dinero?
When will you give me the money?

¿Por qué no **le dice** Ud. la verdad, señor?
Why don't you tell him/her the truth, sir?

- **Dar** and **decir** also have irregular formal command forms. There is a written accent on **dé** to distinguish it from the preposition **de.**

Formal commands of **dar** and **decir:**

dar → **dé, den**
decir → **diga, digan**

AUTOPRUEBA

Give the correct Spanish equivalent for the indirect object pronoun.

a. me   **b.** te   **c.** le   **d.** nos   **e.** les

1. _____ John gave it to *you,* Carol.
2. _____ Mr. Hopkins, Mrs. Simmons sent *you* this message, sir.
3. _____ Bring *them* some cookies.
4. _____ Don't tell *me* anything more.
5. _____ He didn't give *us* much time.

Answers: 1. b 2. c 3. e 4. a 5. d

■ Práctica

A. De vuelta a Honduras. Your friends the Padillas, from Honduras, need help arranging for and getting on their flight back home. Explain how you will help them, using the cues as a guide.

MODELO: confirmar el vuelo → *Les* confirmo el vuelo.

1. llamar un taxi
2. bajar (*to carry down*) las maletas
3. guardar el equipaje
4. facturar el equipaje
5. guardar el puesto en la cola
6. guardar el asiento en la sala de espera
7. comprar una revista
8. por fin decir adiós

B. ¿Qué hacen estas personas? Complete las siguientes oraciones con un verbo lógico y un pronombre de complemento indirecto.

MODELO: El vicepresidente _le ofrece_ consejos al presidente.

Verbos útiles
dar (*irreg.*) **decir** (*irreg.*) **ofrecer (zc)** **prestar** **servir (i, i)**

1. Romeo _____ flores (*flowers*) a Julieta.
2. Snoopy _____ besos (*kisses*) a Lucy… ¡Y a ella no le gusta!
3. Eva _____ una manzana a Adán.
4. Los bancos _____ dinero a las personas que quieren comprar una casa.
5. Los asistentes de vuelo _____ bebidas a los pasajeros.
6. Yo siempre _____ la verdad a todos.

C. En un restaurante. Imagine that your four-year-old cousin Benjamín has never eaten in a restaurant before. Explain to him what will happen, filling in the blanks with the appropriate indirect object pronoun.

Need more practice?

- Workbook/Laboratory Manual
- Interactive CD-ROM
- Online Learning Center (www.mhhe.com/quetal7).

Primero el camarero _____¹ indica una mesa desocupada.ª Luego tú _____² pides el menú al camarero. También _____³ haces preguntas sobre los platos y las especialidades de la casa y _____⁴ dices tus preferencias. El camarero _____⁵ trae la comida. Por fin tu papá _____⁶ pide la cuenta al camarero. Si tú quieres pagar, _____⁷ pides dinero a tu papá y _____⁸ das el dinero al camarero.

ª*vacant*

■ Conversación

Entrevista: ¿Quién… ? Read through the following items and think about people whom you associate with the indicated action. Then, working with a partner, ask and answer questions to find out information about each topic.

MODELO: darle consejos →
    E1: ¿A quién le das consejos?
    E2: Con frecuencia le doy consejos a mi compañero de cuarto. ¡Él los necesita!
    E1: ¿Quién te da consejos a ti?
    E2: Mis abuelos me dan muchos consejos.

1. darle consejos
2. pedirle ayuda con los estudios
3. prestarle la ropa
4. mandarle flores
5. decirle secretos
6. hacerle favores
7. escribirle tarjetas postales (*postcards*)
8. ofrecerle bebidas
9. mostrarle fotos de las vacaciones
10. servirle la comida

¿Recuerda Ud.?

In **Primeros pasos** you started to use forms of **gustar** to express your likes and dislikes. Review what you know by answering the following questions. Then, changing their form as needed, use the forms of **gustar** to interview your instructor.

1. ¿Te gusta el café (el vino, el té...)?
2. ¿Te gusta jugar al béisbol (al golf, al vólibol, al...)?
3. ¿Te gusta viajar en avión (fumar, viajar en tren...)?
4. ¿Qué te gusta más, estudiar o ir a fiestas (trabajar o descansar, cocinar o comer)?

21 Expressing Likes and Dislikes *Gustar*

Los chilenos viajeros

Según el anuncio, a muchos chilenos *les gusta* viajar a otros países. Lea el anuncio y luego indique si las oraciones son ciertas o falsas.

1. A los chilenos *les gusta* viajar sólo en este hemisferio.
2. A los chilenos *les gustan* mucho las playas.
3. Sólo *les gusta* viajar en países de habla española.
4. No *les gustaría* el precio del viaje.

¿Y Ud.?

¿A Ud. le gusta viajar? ¿Le gustan los viajes en avión? ¿Cuál de estos lugares le gustaría visitar?

MEDIO MILLON DE CHILENOS
DE VACACIONES 2003 AL EXTRANJERO
Y USTED... NO SE QUEDE SIN VIAJAR
¡RESERVE AHORA MISMO!

El próximo verano '06, con el bajo valor del dólar, muchas personas desearán viajar, los cupos disponibles se agotarán rapidamente. ¡Asegure sus vacaciones! Elija ahora cualquiera de nuestros fantásticos programas.

MIAMI - ORLANDO - BAHAMAS - MÉXICO - CANCÚN
ACAPULCO - IXTAPA - COSTA RICA - RIO - SALVADOR
PLAYA TAMBOR - PUNTA CANA - LA HABANA
VARADERO - GUATEMALA - SUDÁFRICA

Infórmese sobre nuestro SUPER CRÉDITO PREFERENCIAL

Economy Tour

Santa Magdalena 94, Providencia
☎2334429 · 2331774 · 2314252
2328294 · 2318608 · 2334862
Fax: 2334428

Constructions with *gustar*

Spanish	Literal Equivalent	English Phrasing
Me gusta la playa.	The beach is pleasing to me.	*I like the beach.*
No le gustan sus cursos.	His courses are not pleasing to him.	*He doesn't like his courses.*
Nos gusta leer.	Reading is pleasing to us.	*We like to read.*

You have been using the verb **gustar** since the beginning of *¿Qué tal?* to express likes and dislikes. However, **gustar** does not literally mean *to like,* but rather *to be pleasing.*

Me gusta viajar.
Traveling is pleasing to me. (I like traveling.)

Note that an infinitive is viewed as a singular subject in Spanish.

A. **Gustar** is always used with an indirect object pronoun: Someone or something is pleasing *to* someone else. The verb must agree with the subject of the sentence—that is, the person or thing that is pleasing.

Me **gusta** la comida mexicana.
Mexican food is pleasing to me. (I like Mexican food.)

Me **gustan** los viajes aventureros.
Adventurous trips are pleasing to me. (I like adventurous trips.)

B. When the person pleased is a noun, a phrase with **a** + a *noun* must be used in addition to the indirect object pronoun. The prepositional phrase usually appears before the indirect object pronoun, but it can also appear after the verb.

A David no **le** gustan los aviones.
No le gustan los aviones a **David.**
David doesn't like airplanes.

C. A phrase with **a** + a *pronoun* is often used for clarification or emphasis. The prepositional phrase can appear before the indirect object pronoun or after the verb.

CLARIFICATION

¿Le gusta **a Ud.** viajar?
Do you like to travel?

EMPHASIS

A **mí** me gusta viajar en avión, pero **a mi esposo** le gusta viajar en coche. **Y a ti,** ¿cómo te gusta viajar?

*I like to travel by plane, but my husband likes to travel by car. And how do **you** like to travel?*

> Remember that **mí** (with an accent) and **ti** (no accent) are used as the object of a preposition in Spanish. Subject pronouns are used for all other persons.

OJO Remember that the indirect object pronoun *must* be used with **gustar** even when the prepositional phrase **a** + *noun* or *pronoun* is used.

[Práctica A]

Would Like / Wouldn't Like

What one *would* or *would not* like to do is expressed with the form **gustaría***+*infinitive* and the appropriate indirect objects.

[Práctica B]

A **mí** me **gustaría** viajar a Colombia.
I would like to travel to Colombia.

Nos gustaría hacer *camping* este verano.
We would like to go camping this summer.

———————

*This is one of the forms of the conditional of **gustar.** You will study all of the forms of the conditional in **Gramática 45.**

PASO 2

■ Práctica

A. Gustos y preferencias

PASO 1 Use the models as a guide to tell whether or not you like the following.

MODELOS: ¿el café? → (No) Me gusta el café.

¿los pasteles? → (No) Me gustan los pasteles.

1. ¿el vino?
2. ¿los niños pequeños?
3. ¿la música clásica?
4. ¿Ricky Martin?
5. ¿el invierno?
6. ¿hacer cola?
7. ¿el chocolate?
8. ¿las películas de terror?
9. ¿las clases que empiezan a las ocho de la mañana?
10. ¿cocinar?
11. ¿la gramática?
12. ¿las clases de este semestre/trimestre?
13. ¿los vuelos con muchas escalas?
14. ¿bailar en las discotecas?
15. ¿el béisbol?
16. ¿el fútbol?

> **Reacciones**
>
> **A mí también.** (So do I.)
> **A mí tampoco.** (I don't either. [Neither do I.])
> **Pues a mí, sí.** (Well, I do.)
> **Pues a mí, no.** (Well, I don't.)

 PASO 2 Share your reactions with a classmate. He or she will respond with one of the reactions. How do your likes and dislikes compare?

B. ¿Adónde vamos este verano?

PASO 1 The members of the Soto family all prefer different vacation activities and, of course, would like to go to different places this summer. Imagine that you are one of the Sotos and describe the family's various preferences, following the model.

MODELO: padre / nadar: ir a la playa →
A mi padre *le gusta* nadar. *Le gustaría* ir a la playa.

1. padre / el océano: ir a la playa
2. hermanos pequeños / nadar: también ir a la playa
3. hermano Ernesto / hacer *camping*: ir a las montañas
4. abuelos / descansar: quedarse en casa
5. madre / la tranquilidad: visitar un pueblecito (*small town*) en la costa
6. hermana Elena / discotecas: pasar las vacaciones en una ciudad grande
7. ti / los sitios que prefiere la familia Soto: visitar a la familia
8. el perro / no / quedarse en casa: ir con la familia
9. la tía Ramona / las visitas de la familia: recibirlos en su casa
10. mí/¿ ?

PASO 2 Now, remembering what you have learned about the vacation preferences of your imaginary family, answer the following questions.

1. ¿A quién le gustaría ir a Nueva York?
2. ¿A quién le gustaría viajar a Acapulco?
3. ¿Quién no quiere salir de casa?
4. ¿A quién le gustaría ir a Cabo San Lucas, un pueblo de Baja California, en México?
5. ¿Quién quiere ir a Colorado?
6. ¿Quién quiere recibir a la familia en su casa?

Need more practice?

■ Workbook/Laboratory Manual
■ Interactive CD-ROM
■ Online Learning Center (www.mhhe.com/quetal7)

■ Conversación

A. ¿Conoce bien a sus compañeros de clase? Piense en una persona de la clase que Ud. conoce. En su opinión, ¿a esa persona le gustan o no las siguientes cosas? Apunte: **Sí, le gusta(n)** o **No, no le gusta(n).** Luego, entreviste a su compañero/a para verificar sus respuestas.

1. la música clásica
2. el color negro
3. viajar en coche
4. la comida mexicana
5. tener clases por la mañana
6. estudiar otras lenguas
7. las películas trágicas
8. las casas viejas

NOTA COMUNICATIVA

More About Expressing Likes and Dislikes

Here are some ways to express intense likes and dislikes.

- Use the phrases **mucho/muchísimo** or **(para) nada.**

Me gusta mucho/muchísimo.	*I like it a lot / a whole lot.*
No me gusta (para) nada.	*I don't like it at all.*

- To express *love* and *hate* in reference to likes and dislikes, you can use **encantar** and **odiar.**

Encantar is used just like **gustar.**

Me encanta el chocolate.	*I love chocolate.*
Les encanta viajar, ¿verdad?	*They love traveling, right?*

Odiar, on the other hand, functions like a transitive verb (one that can take a direct object).

Odio el apio.	*I hate celery.*
Mi madre **odia** viajar sola.	*My mother hates traveling alone.*

- To express interest in something, use **interesar.** This verb is also used like **gustar** and **encantar.**

Me interesa la comida salvadoreña.	*I'm interested in Salvadoran food.*

B. ¿Qué te gusta? ¿Qué odias? Almost every situation has aspects that one likes or dislikes, even hates. Pick at least two of the following situations and tell what you like or don't like about them. Add as many details as you can, using **me gustaría** when possible.

MODELO: en la playa →
Me gusta mucho el agua, pero no me gusta el sol. Por eso no me gusta pasar todo el día en la playa. Me encanta nadar pero odio la arena (*sand*). Por eso me gustaría más ir a nadar en una piscina.

Situaciones	
en un almacén grande	en clase
en un autobús	en el coche
en un avión	en una discoteca
en la biblioteca	en una fiesta
en una cafetería	en un parque
en casa con mis amigos	en la playa
en casa con mis padres/hijos	en un tren

Voces de Honduras y El Salvador

LITERATURA: Clementina Suárez

Clementina Suárez
(1902–1991)

Sobre la autora: *Clementina Suárez nació[a] en Olancho, Honduras. Desde joven, rechazó[b] los privilegios y la posición social de su familia. Viajó[c] sola por todo el mundo y vivió sola durante una época en que no se aceptaba[d] la independencia femenina.*

Canto a la encontrada[e] patria y su héroe

No puedo llegar...
Porque jamás me he ido.[f]
Eres una Patria construida
en lo interior.
Caminas[g] dentro de mí
como un abierto[h] río.
Vienes desde muy atrás[i]
rebelde y vegetal,
todo en ti es nuevo y viejo
tierra para la infancia
y para inmortalizar el tiempo.

[a]*was born* [b]*she rejected* [c]*She traveled* [d]*no... people didn't accept* [e]*found* [f]*jamás... I have never left* [g]*You walk* [h]*free-flowing* [i]*desde... from long ago*

MÚSICA: Yolocamba I Ta y el folklore

El nombre indígena del grupo Yolocamba I Ta significa «la rebelión de la siembra[a]». Por unos treinta años, el grupo ha interpretado[b] ritmos nativos de El Salvador que enfocan en la realidad[c] histórico-social de su país y promueven[d] la paz[e] y la justicia. En 1975, los hermanos Franklin y Roberto Quezada, junto con[f] otros estudiantes, fundaron[g] este grupo para difundir[h] la música popular salvadoreña. Por[i] sus canciones de protesta, sufrieron[j] persecución política, y por muchos años vivieron[k] en México.

[a]*harvest* [b]*ha... has been performing* [c]*reality* [d]*promote* [e]*peace* [f]*junto... along with* [g]*formed* [h]*spread* [i]*Because of* [j]*they suffered* [k]*they lived*

La suaca, música y danza folklóricas típicas de El Salvador, representa las bodas[l] de los años 30 del siglo pasado,[m] en las que[n] varias parejas[o] de indígenas se casaban[p] en una boda colectiva.

[l]*weddings* [m]*siglo... last century* [n]*las... which* [o]*varias... several couples* [p]*se... would get married*

22 Talking About the Past (1) Preterite of Regular Verbs and of *dar, hacer, ir,* and *ser*

Elisa habla de su viaje a Puerto Rico

Elisa es reportera. Recientemente *fue* a Puerto Rico para escribir un artículo.

«Recientemente *fui* a Puerto Rico para escribir un artículo sobre esa isla. *Hice* el viaje en avión. El vuelo *fue* largo, pues el avión *hizo* escala en Miami. *Pasé* una semana entera en la Isla. *Hablé* con muchas personas de la industria turística y *visité* los lugares más interesantes de Puerto Rico. También *comí* mucha comida típica de la Isla. Además, *tomé* el sol en las preciosas playas puertorriqueñas y *nadé* en el mar Caribe. Me *divertí* mucho. ¡Mi viaje *fue* casi como unas vacaciones!»

Comprensión: ¿Cierto o falso?

1. Elisa fue a Puerto Rico para pasar sus vacaciones.
2. El avión hizo escala en los Estados Unidos.
3. Elisa no visitó ningún lugar importante de Puerto Rico.
4. Elisa también pasó tiempo cerca del océano.

In previous chapters of *¿Qué tal?*, you have talked about a number of your activities, but always in the present tense. In this section, you will begin to work with the forms of the preterite, one of the tenses that will allow you to talk about the past. To talk about all aspects of the past in Spanish, you need to know how to use two *simple tenses* (tenses formed without an auxiliary or "helping" verb): the preterite and the imperfect. In this chapter, you will learn the regular forms of the preterite and those of four irregular verbs: **dar, hacer, ir,** and **ser.** In this chapter and in **Capítulos 8, 9, 10,** and **11,** you will learn more about preterite forms and their uses as well as about the imperfect and the ways in which it is used alone and with the preterite.

The *preterite* (**el pretérito**) has several equivalents in English. For example, **hablé** can mean *I spoke* or *I did speak.* The preterite is used to report finished, completed actions or states of being in the past. If the action or state of being is viewed as completed—no matter how long it lasted or took to complete—it will be expressed with the preterite.

PAST	Present	Future
preterite	**present**	
	present progressive	
	formal commands	

Elisa talks about her trip to Puerto Rico Elisa is a reporter. She recently went to Puerto Rico to write an article. "Recently I went to Puerto Rico to write an article about that island. I made the trip by plane. The flight was long because the plane made a stop in Miami. I spent a whole week on the Island. I spoke with many people in the tourist industry and I visited the most interesting places in Puerto Rico. I also ate lots of typical food from the Island. Furthermore, I sunbathed on beautiful Puerto Rican beaches and swam in the Caribbean Sea. I had lots of fun. My trip was almost like a vacation!"

Preterite of Regular Verbs

hablar		comer		vivir	
hablé	*I spoke (did speak)*	comí	*I ate (did eat)*	viví	*I lived (did live)*
hablaste	*you spoke*	comiste	*you ate*	viviste	*you lived*
habló	*you/he/she spoke*	comió	*you/he/she ate*	vivió	*you/he/she lived*
hablamos	*we spoke*	comimos	*we ate*	vivimos	*we lived*
hablasteis	*you spoke*	comisteis	*you ate*	vivisteis	*you lived*
hablaron	*you/they spoke*	comieron	*you/they ate*	vivieron	*you/they lived*

- Note that, in the preterite, the **nosotros** forms of regular -**ar** and -**ir** verbs are the same as the present tense forms. Context usually helps determine meaning.

Hoy **hablamos** con la profesora Benítez.
Today we're speaking with Professor Benítez.

Ayer **hablamos** con el director de la facultad.
Yesterday we spoke with the head of the department.

- Note the accent marks on the first and third person singular of the preterite tense. These accent marks are dropped in the conjugation of **ver: vi, vio.**

ver:	vi	vimos
	viste	visteis
	vio	vieron

- Verbs that end in -**car**, -**gar**, and -**zar** show a spelling change in the first person singular (**yo**) of the preterite. (This is the same change you have already learned to make in formal commands.)

-car → **qu**	**buscar**	
	busqué	buscamos
	buscaste	buscasteis
	buscó	buscaron
-gar → **gu**	**pagar**	
	pagué	pagamos
	pagaste	pagasteis
	pagó	pagaron
-zar → **c**	**empezar**	
	empecé	empezaron
	empezaste	empezasteis
	empezó	empezaron

- -**Ar** and -**er** stem-changing verbs show no stem change in the preterite.
  -**Ir** stem-changing verbs do show a change.*

despertar (ie): **desperté, despertaste,**…
volver (ue): **volví, volviste,**…

- An unstressed -**i**- between two vowels becomes -**y**-. Also, note the accent on the **í** in the **tú, nosotros,** and **vosotros** forms.

creer		leer	
creí	creímos	leí	leímos
creíste	creísteis	leíste	leísteis
creyó	creyeron	leyó	leyeron

---

*You will learn more about and practice the preterite of stem-changing verbs in **Capítulo 8.**

Irregular Preterite Forms

dar		hacer		ir/ser	
di	dimos	hice	hicimos	fui	fuimos
diste	disteis	hiciste	hicisteis	fuiste	fuisteis
dio	dieron	hizo	hicieron	fue	fueron

- The preterite endings for **dar** are the same as those used for regular **-er/-ir** verbs in the preterite, except that the accent marks are dropped.

- **Hizo** is spelled with a **z** to keep the [s] sound of the infinitive.

  hic- + **-o** → **hizo**

- **Ir** and **ser** have identical forms in the preterite. Context will make the meaning clear.

  Fui a la playa el verano pasado.
  I went to the beach last summer.

  Fui agente de viajes.
  I was a travel agent.

AUTOPRUEBA

Give the correct preterite forms.

1. (nosotros) buscar
2. (mi papá) volver
3. (yo) despertarme
4. (Ud.) ver
5. (ellas) leer
6. (tú) ser

Answers: 1. buscamos 2. volvió 3. me desperté 4. vio 5. leyeron 6. fuiste

Práctica

A. ¡Anticipemos! ¿Qué hizo Ud. el verano pasado? Indique las oraciones que son ciertas para Ud., contestando con **sí** o **no.**

El verano pasado...

1. tomé una clase en la universidad.
2. asistí a un concierto.
3. trabajé mucho.
4. hice *camping* con algunos amigos / mi familia.
5. viví con mis padres / mis hijos.
6. me quedé en este pueblo / esta ciudad.
7. fui a una playa.
8. hice una excursión a otro país.
9. fui a muchas fiestas.
10. no hice nada especial.

B. El día de tres compañeras

PASO 1 Teresa, Evangelina y Liliana comparten (*share*) un apartamento. Ayer Teresa y Evangelina fueron a la universidad mientras Liliana se quedó en casa. Describa lo que hicieron, según la perspectiva de cada una.

MODELO: (nosotras) levantarse / a / siete y media →
Nos levantamos a las siete y media.

TERESA Y EVANGELINA

1. (nosotras) salir / de / apartamento / a / nueve
2. llegar / biblioteca / a / diez
3. estudiar / toda la mañana / para / examen
4. escribir / muchos ejercicios
5. almorzar / con / amigos / en / cafetería
6. ir / a / laboratorio / a / una
7. hacer / todos los experimentos / de / manual (*m.*)
8. tomar / examen / a / cuatro
9. ¡examen / ser / horrible!
10. regresar / a casa / después de / examen
11. ayudar / Liliana / a / preparar / cena
12. cenar / todas juntas / a / siete

LILIANA

1. (yo) quedarse / en casa / todo el día
2. ver / televisión / por / mañana
3. llamar / mi / padres / a / once
4. tomar / café / con / vecinos (*neighbors*)
5. estudiar / para / examen / de / historia / y / escribir / composición / para / clase / sociología
6. ir / a / garaje / para / dejar / muebles / viejo / allí
7. ir / a / supermercado / y / comprar / comida
8. empezar / a / preparar / cena / a / cinco

PASO 2 ¿Quién lo dijo (*said*), Evangelina o Liliana?

1. Mis compañeras no pasaron mucho tiempo en casa hoy.
2. ¡El examen fue desastroso!
3. Estudié mucho hoy.
4. Me gustó mucho el programa de «Oprah» hoy.
5. ¿Saben? Hablé con mis padres hoy y…

PASO 3 Ahora vuelva a contar (*tell*) cómo fue el día de Liliana, pero desde el punto de vista de sus compañeras de cuarto. Luego diga cómo fue el día de Teresa y Evangelina según Liliana.

■ Conversación

Need more practice?

■ Workbook/Laboratory Manual
■ Interactive CD-ROM
■ Online Learning Center
  (www.mhhe.com/quetal7)

A. Entrevista

1. ¿Qué le(s) diste a tu mejor amigo/a (tu esposo/a, tu novio/a, tus hijos) para su cumpleaños el año pasado? ¿Qué te regaló a ti esa persona para tu cumpleaños? ¿Alguien te mandó flores el año pasado? ¿Le mandaste flores a alguien? ¿Te gusta que te traigan chocolates? ¿otras cosas?

2. ¿Dónde y a qué hora comiste ayer? ¿Con quién(es) comiste? ¿Te gustaron todos los platos que comiste? Si comiste fuera, ¿quién pagó?
3. ¿Cuándo decidiste estudiar español? ¿Cuándo lo empezaste a estudiar? ¿Vas a seguir (*continue*) con el español el semestre/trimestre que viene?
4. ¿Qué hiciste ayer? ¿Adónde fuiste? ¿Con quién(es)? ¿Ayudaste a alguien a hacer algo? ¿Te llamó alguien? ¿Llamaste a alguien? ¿Te invitaron a hacer algo especial algunos amigos?

B. El viernes por la tarde... The following drawings depict what Julián did last Friday night. Match the phrases with the individual drawings in the sequence. Then narrate what Julián did using verbs in the preterite. Use words and phrases like **primero, luego, después,** and **finalmente** to indicate sequence.

1.

2.

3.

4.

5.

6.

7.

8.

9.

10.

11.

12.

a. _____ hacer cola para comprar las entradas (*tickets*)
b. _____ regresar tarde a casa
c. _____ volver a casa después de trabajar
d. _____ ir a un café a tomar algo
e. _____ llegar al cine al mismo tiempo
f. _____ llamar a un amigo
g. _____ no gustarles la película
h. _____ comer rápidamente
i. _____ ducharse y afeitarse
j. _____ entrar en el cine
k. _____ ir al cine en autobús
l. _____ decidir encontrarse (*to meet up*) en el cine

En los Estados Unidos y el Canadá

Ellen Ochoa: Una viajera[a] espacial

La Dra. Ellen L. Ochoa, de California (1958–), es **la primera mujer hispana astronauta** de los Estados Unidos; trabaja en la NASA desde 1990. Se graduó con **un doctorado[b]** en **ingeniería eléctrica** de la Universidad de Stanford. Pasó **más de 975 horas viajando en el espacio,** la misión más reciente en el año 2002. Entre sus muchos honores está el de ser[c] miembro de la Comisión Presidencial para la Celebración de Mujeres en la Historia Americana.

    La Dra. Ochoa no es la única persona hispana en la NASA. Hay **otros cinco astronautas hispanos** en misiones espaciales: el argentino Frank Caldeiro, el costarricense[d] Franklin Chang-Díaz, los españoles Pedro Duque y Michael López-Alegría y el peruano Carlos Noriega.

Ellen Ochoa

[a]*traveler*   [b]*Ph.D.*   [c]*el… that of being*   [d]*Costa Rican*

Las ruinas incaicas de Machu Picchu

Resources for Review and Testing Preparation

- Workbook/Laboratory Manual
- Interactive CD-ROM
- Online Learning Center (www.mhhe.com/quetal7)

UN POCO DE TODO

Lengua y cultura: Machu Picchu, la ciudad perdida (*lost*) **de los incas.** Complete the following vacation suggestion with the correct form of the words in parentheses, as suggested by the context. When two possibilities are given in parentheses, select the correct word.

Los países de Centro y Sudamérica ofrecen una gran variedad de posibilidades para el viajero. Si a Uds. les interesa un viaje menos típico, deben planear una aventura en el mundo hispánico.

    (Les/Los[1]) quiero decir (algo/nada[2]) sobre (el/la[3]) ciudad de Machu Picchu. ¿Ya (lo/la[4]) (saber/conocer[5]) Uds.? (Ser/Estar[6]) situada en los Andes, a unos ochenta kilómetros[a] de la ciudad de Cuzco, Perú. Machu Picchu (ser/estar[7]) conocida[b] como la ciudad escondida[c] de los incas. Se dice que (ser/estar[8]) una de las manifestaciones (más/tan[9]) importantes de la arquitectura incaica. Era[d] refugio y a la vez[e] ciudad de vacaciones de los reyes[f] (incaico[10]).

    Uds. deben (visitarlo/visitarla[11]). (Le/Les[12]) gustaría porque (ser/estar[13]) un sitio inolvidable.[g] Es mejor (ir/van[14]) a Machu Picchu en primavera o verano —son las (mejor[15]) estaciones para visitar este lugar. Pero es necesario (comprar/compran[16]) los boletos con anticipación,[h] porque (mucho[17]) turistas de todos los (país[18]) del mundo visitan este sitio extraordinario. ¡(*Yo:* Saber/Conocer[19]) que a Uds. (los/les[20]) va a gustar el viaje!

[a]*ochenta… 50 millas*   [b]*known*   [c]*hidden*   [d]*It was*   [e]*a… at the same time*   [f]*kings*   [g]*unforgettable*   [h]*con… ahead of time*

Comprensión: ¿Cierto o falso?   Corrija las oraciones falsas.

1. Machu Picchu está en Chile.
2. Fue un lugar importante en el pasado.
3. Todavía es una atracción turística de gran interés.
4. Sólo los turistas latinoamericanos conocen Machu Picchu.

VIDEOTECA

Entrevista cultural: Honduras

Heidi Luna es una agente de viajes hondureña. Aquí habla de los destinos favoritos de sus clientes y también menciona sus propios planes para viajar. Antes de ver el vídeo, lea el siguiente fragmento de la entrevista.

HEIDI: …La mayoría de nuestros clientes nos busca para que los ayudemos en viajes especiales o en vacaciones especiales. Es muy divertido poder ayudarlos.

Ahora vea el vídeo y conteste las siguientes preguntas basándose en la entrevista.

1. ¿Qué destinos latinoamericanos menciona Heidi como los preferidos de sus clientes? ¿Qué destinos norteamericanos menciona?
2. ¿Adónde piensa viajar Heidi? ¿Por qué?

Entrevista cultural: El Salvador

Rubén Guillén es de El Salvador. En la entrevista, explica por qué le encanta ser guía turístico. Antes de ver el vídeo, lea el siguiente fragmento de la entrevista.

RUBÉN: Bueno, yo soy guía turístico y trabajo precisamente en un hotel de la capital y me encargo de[a] organizar excursiones y viajes hacia las diferentes playas y lugares turísticos de nuestro país. Eso, exactamente.

[a]me… I'm in charge of

Ahora vea el vídeo y conteste las siguientes preguntas basándose en la entrevista.

1. ¿Dónde trabaja Rubén?
2. Según Rubén, ¿cuáles son algunas de las ventajas de su trabajo?

Entre amigos: El verano pasado, me fui al Canadá

Rubén, Tané, Miguel y Karina pasan una tarde en el Parque Ecológico de Xochimilco. Hablan de las vacaciones. En su opinión, ¿qué preguntas van a hacerse? Antes de mirar el vídeo, lea las preguntas a continuación. Mientras mire el vídeo, trate de entender la conversación en general y fíjese en la información sobre las vacaciones. Luego mire el vídeo una segunda vez, fijándose en la información que necesita para contestar las preguntas.

1. A Karina, ¿qué le gusta hacer durante las vacaciones? ¿Y a Tané?
2. ¿Adónde fue Tané el verano pasado? ¿Y Miguel?
3. ¿Qué hizo Rubén el verano pasado?

Honduras y El Salvador

¡Fíjese!

- El centro ceremonial maya de Copán, en Honduras, es hoy un parque nacional que contiene una colección de ruinas mayas superadas[a] sólo por las ruinas de Tikal en Guatemala.
- La moneda de Honduras, el lempira, lleva el nombre de un cacique[b] indígena que luchó contra[c] los españoles.
- El nombre indígena de la capital de Honduras, Tegucigalpa, significa «cerros de plata».[d] Honduras recibió su nombre español por la profundidad[e] de sus aguas costeras.[f] El nombre indígena de El Salvador era[g] Cuzcatlán, que significa «tierra de joyas[h] y cosas preciosas».
- Las erupciones del Volcán de Izalco en El Salvador fueron constantes entre los años 1770 y 1966, por casi dos siglos.[i] Este volcán se conoce con el nombre de «el faro[j] del Pacífico», porque estuvo encendido[k] por muchos años y sirvió de[l] guía a los navegantes.

[a]*exceeded (in quality)* [b]*chief* [c]*luchó… fought against* [d]*cerros… silver hills* [e]*depth* [f]*coastal* [g]*was* [h]*jewels* [i]*centuries* [j]*lighthouse* [k]*estuvo… it was lit up* [l]*sirvió… served as a*

Personas famosas: El Arzobispo[a] Óscar Arnulfo Romero

El 24 de marzo de 1980 un héroe de El Salvador fue asesinado mientras oficiaba una misa.[b] En vida,[c] el arzobispo Óscar Arnulfo Romero (1917–1980) fue la conciencia de su país. Criticó a los líderes políticos por su violencia e injusticia, y trabajó para mejorar[d] las condiciones económicas y sociales del país. Por eso, fue nominado para el premio Nóbel de la Paz[e] en 1979.

[a]*Archbishop* [b]*oficiaba… he was celebrating a Mass* [c]*life* [d]*improve* [e]*premio… Nobel Peace Prize*

El Volcán de Izalco, El Salvador

Learn more about Honduras and El Salvador with the Video, the Interactive CD-ROM, and the Online Learning Center (www.mhhe.com/quetal7).

A LEER

ESTRATEGIA: Identifying the Source of a Passage

If you pick up a copy of the *New England Journal of Medicine*, what sort of articles do you expect to find? For whom are they written and for what purpose? Would you anticipate finding similar articles in *People* magazine? You can often make useful predictions about an article—the article's content, its narrative style, the target audience, the author's purpose, and so on—if you know something about the magazine or journal from which it comes. The article you are about to read was first published in *Nexos*, a Spanish-language in-flight magazine published by American Airlines for its Spanish-speaking customers. Knowing this, which of the following topics do you think might be treated in a given issue of this magazine?

> **Sobre la lectura…** *Nexos* is for the reader who is interested in all aspects of travel, different cultures and customs, and similar issues. The following article was taken from a section called **"Destinos"** (*Destinations*). This particular article deals with El Salvador.

1. the Incas and Machu Picchu
2. how to install a ceiling fan
3. a walking tour of Boston
4. Miami by night

All but number 2 might logically appear in *Nexos*. Keeping in mind the source of a reading will often help you to predict its content.

El Salvador: Un tesoro[a] al alcance de la mano[b]

En sus 20.742 kilómetros cuadrados, el territorio salvadoreño ofrece al visitante una rica mezcla de cultura y <u>entretenimiento</u> bajo la premisa de la inmediatez.[c] En la ciudad se encuentra una amplia oferta <u>hotelera</u>. Por su seguridad y facilidad de desplazamiento,[d] hospédese[e] cerca de centros comerciales, como Metrocentro, Galerías y la Zona Rosa. En esta última,[f] visite el Museo de Antropología David J. Guzmán y el <u>recién inaugurado</u> Museo de Arte (MARTE), que ofrece un itinerario por[g] los momentos clave[h] del arte salvadoreño. Al sur de la ciudad, a un costado del Parque Cuscatlán, hallará[i] el Museo Tin Marín y su <u>santuario</u> de mariposas.[j]

El Salvador, antiguamente llamado en náhuatl[k] «Cuzcatlán» o «Tierra de Riquezas o Preseas[l]», fue conquistado[m] en 1524 por el capitán español Pedro de Alvarado. La influencia colonial se aprecia en la arquitectura del Palacio y el Teatro Nacional, en el centro histórico de San Salvador.

Visite el Mercado de Artesanías de la Avenida Manuel Enrique Araujo, en donde venden bellas artesanías.

Las playas salvadoreñas son un imán,[n] especialmente las[o] del Puerto de La Libertad y la Costa del Sol.

Fresco gracias a su exuberante vegetación, Los Planes de Renderos es el sitio ideal afuera[p] de la ciudad para degustar[q] el platillo nacional: las pupusas, que son tortillas de maíz rellenas de frijoles molidos,[r] queso derretido[s] y chicharrón.[t]

El Palacio Nacional, en San Salvador

[a]*treasure* [b]*al… within easy reach* [c]*bajo… all within reach; easily accessible* [d]*facilidad… moving around easily (in the city)* [e]*(you should) stay* [f]*esta… the latter* [g]*through* [h]*key* [i]*you will find* [j]*butterflies* [k]*Nahuatl, indigenous language of the Aztecs* [l]*Treasures* [m]*fue… was conquered* [n]*magnet* [o]*those* [p]*outside* [q]*trying, sampling* [r]*tortillas… corn tortillas filled with refried beans* [s]*melted* [t]*pork flavorings*

PASO 4

La vida nocturna capitalina caracteriza a los restaurantes y bares de la calle San Antonio Abad. Si desea bailar, escoja una discoteca de la Zona Rosa.

Su visita no debe concluir sin un vistazo[u] a Joya de Cerén, en San Juan Opico, La Libertad, 35 kilómetros al occidente de San Salvador. Este poblado maya, enterrado[v] bajo las cenizas volcánicas hace 1.400 años[w] y declarado Patrimonio de la Humanidad por la UNESCO en 1993, da cuenta de[x] cómo transcurría[y] la vida cotidiana[z] en una aldea[aa] indígena.

Tampoco se vaya sin recorrer[bb] los pueblos de La Ruta de la Paz[cc]: Perquín, Arambala, Villa Rosario, Joateca, Cacaopera, Corinto y Guatajiagua en Morazán, 170 kilómetros al noreste de San Salvador. Ahí podrá deleitarse[dd] en las aguas del río Sapo y la cascada[ee] de Olomina, además de explorar las cuevas del cerro El Pericón.[ff]

[u]*glimpse* [v]*buried* [w]*hace… 1400 years ago* [x]*da… shows* [y]*used to be* [z]*daily* [aa]*pueblo pequeño* [bb]*Tampoco… You shouldn't go without visiting* [cc]*pueblos… towns of The Road of Peace* [dd]*Ahí… There you can have fun* [ee]*waterfall* [ff]*cuevas… caves of El Pericón hill*

Comprensión

A. ¿Adónde les gustaría ir? A base del (*Based on the*) artículo, identifique un lugar de interés para los siguientes turistas norteamericanos.

1. la profesora Martínez, arqueóloga dedicada al estudio de las culturas indígenas
2. el Sr. Nelson, propietario de una tienda de artefactos importados
3. María Rosa, pintora y artista

B. El título. Lea otra vez el título del artículo. ¿Por qué se titula así esta lectura? Es decir, ¿cuál es el mensaje (el tema principal) del artículo?

1. Hay pocas atracciones turísticas en El Salvador.
2. El Salvador es tan grande que es difícil visitar y ver todos los sitios de interés.
3. El Salvador tiene mucho que ofrecer al turista y todo está accesible.

A ESCRIBIR

De vacaciones en El Salvador. Prepare un breve informe sobre dos de los lugares mencionados en el artículo. Consulte recursos (*resources*) en la biblioteca o en el Internet para hacer su investigación. Use los siguientes pasos como guía.

PASO 1 Escoja los lugares que van a ser el enfoque (*focus*) de su investigación.

PASO 2 Piense en el tipo de información que quiere incluir.

PASO 3 Vaya a la biblioteca o consulte sitios del Internet para hacer su informe.

PASO 4 Escriba una breve composición para presentar a la clase.

GRAMÁTICA

To review the grammar points presented in this chapter, refer to the indicated grammar presentations. You'll find further practice of these structures in the Workbook/Laboratory Manual, on the Interactive CD-ROM, and on the *¿Qué tal?* Online Learning Center (www.mhhe.com/quetal7).

20 Expressing *to whom* or *for whom*—Indirect Object Pronouns; **dar** and **decir**

Do you know how to use indirect object pronouns to express *to whom* or *for whom*?

21 Expressing Likes and Dislikes—**Gustar**

Do you know how to talk about things you and others like and like to do?

22 Talking About the Past (1)—Preterite of Regular Verbs and of **dar, hacer, ir,** and **ser**

You should know how to conjugate regular preterite verbs. Can you use the irregular verbs **dar, hacer, ir,** and **ser** in the preterite as well?

VOCABULARIO

Practice this vocabulary with digital flash cards on the Online Learning Center (www.mhhe.com/quetal7).

Los verbos

anunciar	to announce
contar (ue)	to tell
dar (*irreg.*)	to give
decir (*irreg.*)	to say; to tell
encantar	to like very much, love
explicar (qu)	to explain
fumar	to smoke
gustar	to be pleasing
interesar	to be interesting
mandar	to send
mostrar (ue)	to show
odiar	to hate
ofrecer (zc)	to offer
prestar	to lend
prometer	to promise
recomendar (ie)	to recommend
regalar	to give (*as a gift*)

De viaje

el aeropuerto	airport
la agencia de viajes	travel agency
el/la agente de viajes	travel agent
el asiento	seat
el/la asistente de vuelo	flight attendant
el autobús	bus
el avión	airplane
el barco	boat, ship
el billete	ticket
de ida	one-way
de ida y vuelta	round-trip
el boleto	ticket
de ida	one-way
de ida y vuelta	round-trip
la cabina	cabin (*on a ship*)
la clase turística	tourist class
la demora	delay
el equipaje	baggage, luggage
la estación	station
de autobuses	bus
del tren	train
la llegada	arrival
la maleta	suitcase
el maletero	porter
el modo (de transporte)	means (of transportation)
el pasaje	passage; ticket
el/la pasajero/a	passenger
la primera clase	first class
el puerto	port
la sala de espera	waiting room
la salida	departure
la sección de (no) fumar	(non)smoking section
la tarjeta (postal)	(post)card
el tren	train

el viaje	trip
el vuelo	flight
bajar (de)	to get down (from); to get off (of) (*a vehicle*)
facturar	to check (*baggage*)
guardar (un puesto)	to save (a place) (*in line*)
hacer (*irreg.*) cola	to stand in line
hacer (*irreg.*) escalas	to make stops
hacer (*irreg.*) la(s) maleta(s)	to pack one's suitcase(s)
hacer (*irreg.*) paradas	to make stops
ir (*irreg.*) en...	to go/travel by . . .
autobús	bus
avión	plane
barco	boat, ship
tren	train
pasar por el control de la seguridad	to go/pass through security (check)
subir (a)	to go up; to get on (*a vehicle*)
viajar	to travel

Repaso: hacer (*irreg.*) **un viaje**

De vacaciones

la camioneta	station wagon
el *camping*	campground
la foto(grafía)	photo(graph)
el mar	sea
la montaña	mountain
el océano	ocean

la tienda (de campaña)	tent

Repaso: la playa

estar (*irreg.*) de vacaciones	to be on vacation
hacer (*irreg.*) camping	to go camping
ir (*irreg.*) de vacaciones	to go on vacation
nadar	to swim
sacar (qu)	to take (*photos*)
tomar el sol	to sunbathe

Otros sustantivos

la flor	flower
el mundo	world

Los adjetivos

atrasado/a (*with* estar)	late
solo/a	alone

Palabras adicionales

a tiempo	on time
de viaje	on a trip
desde	from
me gustaría...	I would (really) like . . .
muchísimo	an awful lot

Los días festivos°

°**Los…** *Holidays*

CULTURA

- **Nota cultural:** Días festivos importantes del mundo hispánico
- **En los Estados Unidos y el Canadá:** El Día de César Chávez
- **Voces** de Cuba
  - **Literatura:** José Martí
  - **Música:** El son
- **Videoteca**
  - **Entrevista cultural:** Cuba
  - **Entre amigos:** ¡Comemos «las uvas de la suerte»!
- **Enfoque cultural:** Cuba

VOCABULARIO

- La fiesta de Javier
- Emociones y condiciones

GRAMÁTICA

Una muchacha cubana reza (prays) en una iglesia (church) en Santiago, Cuba, durante las Navidades

LA FIESTA DE JAVIER

Fiesta de sorpresa para Javier
¡Se gradúa y cumple 21 años!
¿Dónde es la fiesta?
¡La fiesta es en casa de Javier!

cumplir años

la sorpresa   ¡Qué sorpresa!

pasarlo mal

¡Es para ti!

divertirse (ie, i) / pasarlo bien

regalar

los entremeses   los refrescos

celebrar	to celebrate	**reunirse (me reúno) (con)**	to get together (with)
cumplir años	to have a birthday		
dar (*irreg.*)/**hacer** (*irreg.*) **una fiesta**	to give/have a party	**ser** (*irreg.*) + **en** + *place*	to take place at/in (*place*)
faltar (a)	to be absent (from), not attend	—¿**Dónde es** la fiesta?	Where is the party?
gastar (dinero)	to spend (money)	—(**Es**) **En** casa de Javier.	(It's) At Javier's house.
		gracias por	thanks for

Vocabulario útil*

el Día de Año Nuevo	New Year's Day
el Día de los Reyes Magos	Day of the Magi (Three Kings) (January 6)
el Día de San Patricio	Saint Patrick's Day (March 17)
la Pascua (judía)	Passover
la Pascua (Florida)	Easter
las vacaciones de primavera	spring break
el Cinco de Mayo	Cinco de Mayo (*Mexican awareness celebration in some parts of the United States*)
el Día del Canadá	Canada Day (July 1)
el Cuatro de Julio (el Día de la Independencia [estadounidense])	Fourth of July ([*U.S.*] Independence Day)
el Día de la Raza	Columbus Day (*Hispanic awareness day in some parts of the United States*) (October 12)
el Día de todos los Santos	All Saints' Day (November 1)
el Día de los Muertos	Day of the Dead (November 2)
el Día de Acción de Gracias	Thanksgiving
la Nochebuena	Christmas Eve
la Noche Vieja	New Year's Eve
el cumpleaños	birthday
el día del santo	saint's day (*the saint for whom one is named*)
la quinceañera	young woman's fifteenth birthday party

la Navidad

el Día de San Valentín
(de los Enamorados)

la Fiesta de las Luces

■ Conversación

A. Definiciones. ¿Qué palabra o frase corresponde a estas definiciones?

1. el día en que se celebra el nacimiento (*birth*) de Jesús
2. algo que alguien no sabe o no espera
3. algo de comer y algo de beber que se sirven en las fiestas (dos respuestas)
4. el día en que algunos hispanos visitan el cementerio para honrar la memoria de los difuntos (*deceased*)
5. la fiesta en que se celebra el hecho (*fact*) de que una muchacha cumple quince años
6. el día en que todo el mundo (*everybody*) debe llevar ropa verde
7. la noche en que se celebra el final del año
8. palabra que se dice para mostrar una reacción muy favorable, por ejemplo, cuando un amigo cumple años
9. una fiesta de ocho días, muy importante para los judíos (*Jewish people*)

All of the items on this list are not considered active vocabulary for this chapter. Just learn the holidays and celebrations that are relevant to you.

NOTA CULTURAL

Días festivos importantes del mundo hispánico

Algunas fiestas se celebran **en casi todos los países hispánicos.**

La Nochebuena   En esta fiesta los hispanos cristianos siguen princi-palmente sus **tradiciones católicas.** Celebran la víspera[a] de la Navidad con **una gran cena.** Esta **celebración familiar** puede incluir también a amigos y vecinos.[b] Muchas familias van a la Misa del Gallo,[c] un **servi-cio religioso** que se celebra a medianoche. Es posible que la fiesta de Nochebuena termine muy tarde con música y baile. A veces, los niños reciben **la visita de Papá Noel,** otro nombre para Santa Claus, quien les deja regalos.

Una quinceañera mexicana

La Noche Vieja   Como en este país, la Noche Vieja es una ocasión para **grandes celebraciones,** tanto entre familia como en lugares públicos. En España y otros países algunos practican la tradición de comer una uva[d] por cada una de las doce campanadas[e] de medianoche.

El Día de los Reyes Magos   En España y otros países, muchas personas (especialmente los católicos) cele-bran **el 6 de enero,** el día de los Reyes Magos, también conocido como la Epifanía. Los tres Reyes son los en-cargados[f] de traer regalos. Muchos niños ponen sus zapatos en la ventana o balcón antes de acostarse la noche del 5 de enero. Los Reyes llegan en camellos durante la noche y llenan los zapatos con regalos y dulces.

El Día de la Independencia   Todos los países latinoamericanos celebran el día de **la declaración de su independencia de España.** Por ejemplo, México celebra su independencia el 16 de septiembre, Bolivia el 6 de agosto, el Paraguay el 15 de mayo y El Salvador el 15 de septiembre.

La quinceañera   Las **muchachas que cumplen quince años** celebran ese día especial que marca su paso de niña a mujer con **una gran fiesta entre la familia y los amigos.** La muchacha se viste de largo[g] y, con sus invitados, asiste a una misa especial para ella. Luego hay una cena y una fiesta con música para bailar.

[a]*eve*   [b]*neighbors*   [c]*Misa… Midnight Mass*   [d]*grape*   [e]*strokes*   [f]*los… in charge*   [g]*se… dresses up (in a gown)*

Vocabulario útil

el árbol (tree)
el corazón (heart)
la corona (wreath)
el desfile (parade)
la fiesta del barrio (neighbor-hood [block] party)
los fuegos artificiales (fireworks)
el globo (balloon)

B. Hablando de fiestas

PASO 1   ¿Cuáles de estas fiestas le gustan a Ud.? ¿Cuáles no le gustan? Explique por qué. Compare sus respuestas con las (*those*) de sus compañeros de clase.

MODELO: el Cuatro de Julio → Me gusta mucho el Cuatro de Julio porque vemos fuegos artificiales en el parque y…

1. el Cuatro de Julio
2. el Día de Acción de Gracias
3. el Día de San Patricio
4. la Noche Vieja
5. el Día de la Raza
6. el Día de los Enamorados

PASO 2   Ahora piense en su fiesta favorita. Puede ser una de la lista del **Paso 1** o una del **Vocabulario útil** de la página 209. Piense en cómo celebra Ud. esa fiesta, para explicárselo (*explain it*) luego a un compañero / una compañera de clase. Debe pensar en lo siguiente.

• los preparativos que Ud. hace de antemano (*beforehand*)
• la ropa especial que lleva
• las comidas o bebidas especiales que compra o prepara
• el lugar donde se celebra
• los adornos especiales que hay

EMOCIONES Y CONDICIONES

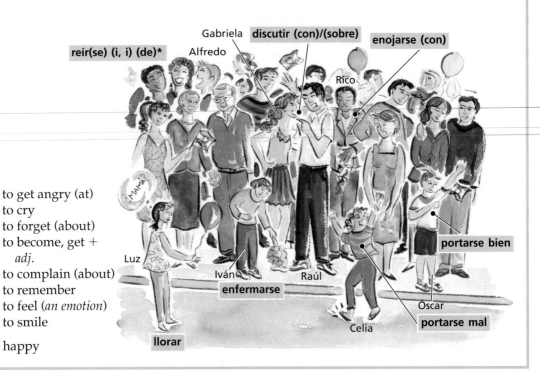

enojarse (con)	to get angry (at)
llorar	to cry
olvidar(se) (de)	to forget (about)
ponerse	to become, get +
(irreg.) + adj.	*adj.*
quejarse (de)	to complain (about)
recordar (ue)	to remember
sentir(se) (ie, i)	to feel *(an emotion)*
sonreír(se) (i, i)*	to smile
feliz	happy

NOTA COMUNICATIVA

Being Emphatic

To emphasize the quality described by an adjective or an adverb, speakers of Spanish often add **-ísimo/a/os/as** (adjectives) or **-ísimo** (adverbs) to it. This change adds the idea *extremely* (*exceptionally; very, very; super*) to the quality expressed. You have already used one emphatic adverb of this type: **Me gusta muchísimo.**

Estos entremeses son **dificilísimos** de preparar.   *These hors d'œuvres are very, very hard to prepare.*
Durante la época navideña, los niños son **buenísimos.**   *At Christmastime, kids are extremely good.*

- If the word ends in a consonant, **-ísimo** is added to the singular form: **difícil → dificilísimo** (and any accents on the word stem are dropped).
- If the word ends in a vowel, the final vowel is dropped before adding **-ísimo: bueno → buenísimo** (and any accents on the word stem are dropped).
- Spelling changes occur when the final consonant of an adjective is **c, g,** or **z: riquísimo, larguísimo, felicísimo.**

---

*The verbs **reír** and **sonreír** are e → i stem-changing verbs, but due to the double vowels, accents are required for all present tense forms: (son)río, (son)ríes, (son)ríe, (son)reímos, (son)reís, (son)ríen.*

Palabras útiles

avergonzado/a (*embarrassed*)
contento/a
feliz/triste
furioso/a
nervioso/a
serio/a

■ Conversación

A. Reacciones. ¿Cómo reacciona o cómo se pone Ud. en estas situaciones? Use estos adjetivos o cualquier otro, y también los verbos que describen las reacciones emocionales. No se olvide de usar las formas enfáticas cuando sea (*whenever it is*) apropiado.

1. Es Navidad y alguien le hace a Ud. un regalo carísimo.
2. Es su cumpleaños y sus padres/hijos no le regalaron nada.
3. Ud. da una fiesta en su casa pero los invitados no se divierten. Nadie se ríe ni sonríe.
4. Hay un examen importante hoy, pero Ud. no estudió anoche.
5. Ud. acaba de terminar un examen difícil/fácil y cree que lo hizo bien/mal.
6. En un examen de química, Ud. no puede recordar una fórmula muy importante.
7. Ud. cuenta un chiste (*joke*) pero nadie se ríe.
8. Un amigo tiene un problema grave (*serious*) y necesita su ayuda.
9. Llueve todo el día.
10. Ud. no sabe la respuesta, pero el profesor le pide que hable.
11. Ud. sabe la respuesta y levanta la mano, pero el profesor no le presta atención.
12. Ud. quiere bañarse y no hay agua caliente.
13. Ud. está solo/a en casa y oye un ruido.
14. Ud. le pide a alguien que no fume, pero la persona sigue fumando.

B. ¿Son buenos todos los días festivos? Los días festivos pueden ser difíciles para muchas personas. Para Ud., ¿son ciertas o falsas las siguientes oraciones? Cambie las oraciones falsas para que sean (*so that they are*) ciertas. Luego compare sus respuestas con las de sus compañeros de clase.

EN LAS FIESTAS DE FAMILIA

1. Toda o casi toda mi familia, incluyendo a mis tíos, primos, abuelos, etcétera, se reúne por lo menos (*at least*) una vez al año.
2. Las fiestas de familia me gustan muchísimo.
3. Hay un pariente que siempre se queja de algo.
4. Uno de mis parientes siempre me hace preguntas indiscretas.
5. Alguien siempre bebe/come demasiado (*too much*) y luego se enferma.
6. A todos les gustan los regalos que reciben.
7. Todos lo pasan bien en las fiestas de familia.

LOS DÍAS FESTIVOS EN GENERAL

8. La Navidad / La Fiesta de las Luces es esencialmente una excusa para gastar dinero.
9. La época de fiestas en noviembre y diciembre es triste y deprimente (*depressing*) para mí.
10. Sólo las personas que practican una religión deben tener vacaciones en los días de fiestas religiosas.
11. Las vacaciones de primavera son para divertirse muchísimo. De hecho (*In fact*), son las mejores vacaciones del año.
12. Debería haber (*There should be*) más días festivos... por lo menos uno al mes.

Need more practice?

- Workbook/Laboratory Manual
- Interactive CD-ROM
- Online Learning Center (www.mhhe.com/quetal7)

23 Talking About the Past (2) Irregular Preterites

La fiesta de la Noche Vieja

Conteste las siguientes preguntas sobre esta fiesta.

1. ¿Quién *estuvo* hablando por teléfono?
2. ¿Quién *dio* la fiesta?
3. ¿Quién no *pudo* ir a la fiesta?
4. ¿Quién *puso* su copa de champán en el televisor?
5. ¿Quién *hizo* mucho ruido?
6. ¿Quiénes no *quisieron* beber más?
7. ¿Quiénes *vinieron* con sus niñas?
8. ¿Quiénes le *trajeron* un regalo al anfitrión (*host*)?

¿Y Ud.?

¿Estuvo alguna vez en una fiesta como esta? (...estuve...) ¿Tuvo que salir temprano o se quedó hasta después de la medianoche (*midnight*)? (...tuve...) ¿Le trajo algo al anfitrión / a la anfitriona? (...traje...)

PAST ------------------- Present ------------------ Future
preterite
present
present progressive
formal commands

• You have already learned the irregular preterite forms of **dar, hacer, ir,** and **ser.** The following verbs are also irregular in the preterite. Note that the first and third person singular endings, which are the only irregular ones, are unstressed, in contrast to the stressed endings of regular preterite forms.

estar	
est**uve**	est**uvimos**
est**uviste**	est**uvisteis**
est**uvo**	est**uvieron**

estar:	estuv-	⎫ -e
poder:	pud-	-iste
poner:	pus-	-o
querer:	quis-	-imos
saber:	sup-	-isteis
tener:	tuv-	-ieron
venir:	vin-	⎭

• When the preterite verb stem ends in **-j-,** the **-i-** of the third person plural ending is omitted: **dijeron, trajeron.**

decir:	**dij-**	⎫ -e, -iste, -o, -imos, -isteis, **-eron**
traer:	**traj-**	⎭

• The preterite of **hay (haber)** is **hubo** (*there was/were*).

Hubo un accidente ayer en el centro.
There was an accident yesterday downtown.

Changes in Meaning

Several of the following Spanish verbs have an English equivalent in the preterite tense that is different from that of the infinitive.

	Infinitive Meaning	Preterite Meaning
saber	to know (*facts, information*)	to find out, learn
	Ya lo sé. *I already know it.*	Lo **supe** ayer. *I found it out (learned it) yesterday.*
conocer	to know, be familiar with (*people, places*)	to meet (*for the first time*)
	Ya la conozco. *I already know her.*	La **conocí** ayer. *I met her yesterday.*
querer	to want	to try
	Quiero hacerlo hoy. *I want to do it today.*	**Quise** hacerlo ayer. *I tried to do it yesterday.*
no querer	not to want	to refuse
	No quiero hacerlo hoy. *I don't want to do it today.*	**No quise** hacerlo anteayer. *I refused to do it the day before yesterday.*
poder	to be able to (*do something*)	to succeed (*in doing something*)
	Puedo leerlo *I can (am able to) read it.*	**Pude** leerlo ayer. *I could (and did) read it yesterday.*
no poder	not to be able, capable (*of doing something*)	to fail (*in doing something*)
	No puedo leerlo. *I can't (am not able to) read it.*	**No pude** leerlo anteayer. *I couldn't (did not) read it the day before yesterday.*

■ Práctica

AUTOPRUEBA

Give the correct irregular preterite forms.

1. (yo) saber
2. (ellos) tener
3. (tú) venir
4. (él) poner
5. (nosotros) querer
6. (Ud.) poder

Answers: 1. supe 2. tuvieron 3. viniste 4. puso 5. quisimos 6. pude

A. ¡Anticipemos! La última Noche Vieja. Piense en lo que Ud. hizo la Noche Vieja del año pasado e indique si las siguientes oraciones son ciertas o falsas para Ud.

1. Fui a una fiesta en casa de un amigo / una amiga.
2. Di una fiesta en mi casa.
3. No estuve con mis amigos, sino (*but rather*) con la familia.
4. Quise ir a una fiesta, pero no pude.
5. Les dije «¡Feliz Año Nuevo!» a muchas personas.
6. Conocí a algunas personas.
7. Tuve que preparar la comida de esa noche.
8. Me puse ropa elegante esa noche.
9. Pude quedarme despierto/a (*awake*) hasta la medianoche.
10. No quise bailar. Me sentía (*I felt*) mal.

CAPÍTULO 8

PASO 2

B. Una Nochebuena en casa de los Ramírez. Describa lo que pasó en casa de los Ramírez, haciendo el papel (*playing the role*) de uno de los hijos. Haga oraciones en el pretérito según las indicaciones, usando el sujeto pronominal cuando sea necesario.

1. todos / estar / en casa / abuelos / antes de / nueve
2. (nosotros) poner / mucho / regalos / debajo / árbol
3. tíos y primos / venir / con / comida y bebidas
4. yo / tener / que / ayudar / a / preparar / comida
5. haber / cena / especial / para / todos
6. más tarde / alguno / amigos / venir / a / cantar / villancicos (*carols*)
7. niños / ir / a / alcoba / a / diez / y / acostarse
8. niños / querer / dormir / pero / no / poder
9. a / medianoche / todos / decir / «¡Feliz Navidad!»
10. al día siguiente / todos / decir / que / fiesta / estar / estupendo

Need more practice?

- Workbook/Laboratory Manual
- Interactive CD-ROM
- Online Learning Center (www.mhhe.com/quetal7)

■ Conversación

A. ¡Un viaje de sueños (*dream*)! Conteste las siguientes preguntas sobre un viaje de sueños. Debe inventar una historia muy extraordinaria o fantástica. Puede ser de un viaje que a Ud. le gustaría hacer, de un viaje hecho (*taken*) por un amigo o de un viaje totalmente imaginario. ¡Sea creativo/a! Luego cuénteles su historia a sus compañeros de clase. ¿Quién inventó la mejor historia?

1. ¿Adónde fue de viaje? ¿Cómo fue (modo de transporte)? ¿Con quién(es) fue?
2. ¿Cuánto tiempo estuvo allí? ¿Dónde se alojó (*did you stay*)?
3. ¿A qué persona famosa o interesante conoció allí? ¿Qué le dijo a esa persona cuando la conoció? ¿Supo algo interesante de esa persona?
4. ¿Qué cosa divertida (*enjoyable*) hizo durante el viaje? ¿Qué no pudo hacer?
5. ¿Qué recuerdos (*souvenirs*) trajo a casa?

B. Entrevista

1. ¿En qué mes conociste al profesor / a la profesora de español? ¿A quién(es) más conociste ese mismo (*same*) día? ¿Tuviste que hablar español el primer día de clase? ¿Qué les dijiste a tus amigos después de esa primera clase? ¿Qué les vas a decir hoy?
2. El año pasado, ¿dónde pasaste la Nochebuena? ¿el Día de Acción de Gracias? ¿Dónde estuviste durante las vacaciones de primavera? ¿Ya hiciste planes para estas ocasiones este año? ¿Dónde piensas estar?
3. ¿Alguien te dio una fiesta de cumpleaños este año? (¿O le diste una fiesta a alguien?) ¿Fue una fiesta de sorpresa? ¿Dónde fue? ¿Qué te trajeron tus amigos? ¿Qué te regalaron tus parientes? ¿Alguien te hizo un pastel? ¿Qué te dijeron todos? ¿Y qué les dijiste tú? ¿Quieres que te den otra fiesta para tu próximo cumpleaños?

PASO 2

24 Talking About the Past (3) Preterite of Stem-Changing Verbs

La quinceañera de Lupe Carrasco

Imagine los detalles de la fiesta de Lupe cuando cumplió quince años.

1. Lupe *se vistió* con

   ☐ un vestido blanco muy elegante.
   ☐ una camiseta y *jeans*.
   ☐ el vestido de novia (*wedding gown*) de su abuela.

2. Cortando el pastel de cumpleaños, Lupe

   ☐ *empezó* a llorar.   ☐ *rió* mucho.
   ☐ *sonrió* para una foto.

3. Lupe *pidió* un deseo (*wish*) al cortar el pastel. Ella

   ☐ les dijo a todos su deseo.
   ☐ *prefirió* guardarlo en secreto.

4. En la fiesta *sirvieron*

   ☐ champán y refrescos.   ☐ sólo té y café.
   ☐ refrescos.

5. Todos *se divirtieron* mucho en la fiesta.
   Los invitados *se despidieron* (*said goodbye*) a la(s) _____.

¿Y Ud.?

¿Recuerda qué hizo cuando cumplió quince años? ¿Pidió muchos regalos? (...pedí...) ¿Se divirtió? (...me divertí...) ¿Cómo se sintió? (...me sentí...)

PAST		Present		Future
preterite		present		
		present progressive		
		formal commands		

A. In **Capítulo 7** you learned that the **-ar** and **-er** stem-changing verbs have no stem change in the preterite (or in the present participle).

recordar (ue)		perder (ie)	
recordé	recordamos	perdí	perdimos
recordaste	recordasteis	perdiste	perdisteis
recordó	recordaron	perdió	perdieron
	recordando		perdiendo

B. The **-ir** stem-changing verbs do have a stem change in the preterite, but only in the third person singular and plural, where the stem vowels **e** and **o** change to **i** and **u**, respectively. This is the same change that occurs in the present participle of **-ir** stem-changing verbs.

pedir (i, i)		dormir (ue, u)	
pedí	pedimos	dormí	dormimos
pediste	pedisteis	dormiste	dormisteis
pidió	pidieron	durmió	durmieron
	pidiendo		durmiendo

C. Here are some **-ir** stem-changing verbs. You already know or have seen many of them. The reflexive meaning, if different from the nonreflexive meaning, is in parentheses.

 Note the simplification:
ri-ió → rió; ri-ieron → rieron
son-ri-ió → sonrió; son-ri-ieron → sonrieron

¡Adiós!

despedirse (i, i) (de)

conseguir (i, i) (g)	*to get, obtain*
conseguir + *inf.*	*to succeed in (doing something)*
divertir(se) (ie, i)	*to entertain (to have a good time)*
dormir(se) (ue, u)	*to sleep (to fall asleep)*
morirse (ue, u)	*to die*
pedir (i, i)	*to ask for; to order*

preferir (ie, i)	*to prefer*
reír(se) (i, i)	*to laugh*
sentir(se) (ie, i)	*to feel (an emotion)*
servir (i, i)	*to serve*
sonreír(se) (i, i)	*to smile*
sugerir (ie, i)	*to suggest*
vestir(se) (i, i)	*to dress (to get dressed)*

AUTOPRUEBA

Complete the verbs with preterite stems.

1. nos div____rtimos
2. se d____rmieron
3. tú s____rviste

4. se v____stió
5. yo sug____rí
6. Uds. p____dieron

Answers: 1. divertimos 2. durmieron 3. serviste 4. vistió 5. sugerí 6. pidieron

---

■ Práctica

A. ¡Anticipemos! ¿Quién lo hizo? ¿Ocurrieron algunas de estas cosas en clase la semana pasada? Conteste con el nombre de la persona apropiada. Si nadie lo hizo, conteste con **Nadie...**

1. _____ se vistió de una manera muy elegante.
2. _____ se vistió de una manera rara (*strange*).
3. _____ se durmió en clase.
4. _____ le pidió al profesor / a la profesora más tarea.
5. _____ se sintió muy contento/a.
6. _____ se divirtió muchísimo, riendo y sonriendo.
7. _____ no sonrió ni siquiera (*not even*) una vez.
8. _____ sugirió tener la clase afuera.
9. _____ prefirió no contestar ninguna pregunta.

PASO 2

Need more practice?

- Workbook/Laboratory Manual
- Interactive CD-ROM
- Online Learning Center
  (www.mhhe.com/quetal7)

B. Historias breves. Cuente las siguientes historias breves en el pretérito. Luego continúelas, si puede.

1. **En un restaurante:** Juan (sentarse) a la mesa. Cuando (venir) el camarero, le (pedir) una cerveza. El camarero no (recordar) lo que Juan (pedir) y le (servir) una Coca-Cola. Juan no (querer) beber la Coca-Cola. Le (decir) al camarero: «Perdón, señor. Le (pedir: *yo*) una cerveza.» El camarero le (contestar): «_____.»

2. **Un día típico:** Rosa (acostarse) temprano y (dormirse) en seguida.[a] (Dormir) bien y (despertarse) temprano. (Vestirse) y (salir) para la universidad. En el autobús (ver) a su amigo José y los dos (sonreír) pero no (hablarse[b]). A las nueve _____.

3. **Dos noches diferentes:** Yo (vestirse), (ir) a una fiesta, (divertirse) mucho y (volver) tarde a casa. Mi compañero de cuarto (decidir) quedarse en casa y (ver) la televisión toda la noche. No (divertirse) nada. (Perder) una fiesta excelente y lo (sentir) mucho. Yo _____.

[a]en... *immediately*   [b]*to talk to each other*

■ Conversación

Una entrevista indiscreta

PASO 1   Lea las siguientes preguntas y piense en cómo va a contestarlas. Debe contestar algunas preguntas con información falsa.

1. ¿A qué hora se durmió anoche?
2. En alguna ocasión, ¿perdió Ud. mucho dinero? ¿Lo encontró (*did you find*) por fin?
3. ¿Cuánto dejó de propina (*tip*) la última vez que comió en un restaurante?
4. Alguna vez, ¿se despidió Ud. de alguien tardísimo?
5. ¿Se rió alguna vez al oír una noticia (*piece of news*) trágica?
6. ¿Con qué programa de televisión se divirtió mucho el año pasado / la semana pasada... pero se avergüenza (*you're ashamed*) de admitirlo?

PASO 2   Use las preguntas para entrevistar a un compañero / una compañera de clase. Luego cuénteles a todos algunas de las respuestas de su compañero/a. La clase va a decidir si la información es cierta o falsa.

MODELO: E1: ¿A qué hora te dormiste anoche?
            E2: Me dormí a las tres de la mañana y me levanté a las siete.
            E1: Alicia se durmió a las tres y se levantó a las siete.
         CLASE: No es cierto.
            E2: ¡Sí, es cierto! (Tienes razón. / No es cierto.)

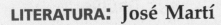

Voces de Cuba

LITERATURA: José Martí

Sobre el autor: *José Martí nació en la Habana, Cuba, pero se exilió a los 17 años por su oposición a la dominación colonial de España. Martí se considera uno de los grandes escritores del mundo hispano. Murió en una de las primeras batallas por la independencia de Cuba del dominio español.*

José Martí
(1853–1895)

XXXIX tomado de *Versos sencillos* (1891)

Cultivo una rosa blanca
en junio como enero
para el amigo sincero
que me da su mano franca.[a]

Y para el cruel que me arranca[b]
el corazón[c] con que vivo,
cardo[d] ni ortiga[e] cultivo;
cultivo la rosa blanca.

[a]mano... *open (sincere) hand* [b]*uproots, tears out* [c]*heart* [d]*thistle* [e]*nettle*

MÚSICA: El son

El son, que se desarrolló[a] en las comunidades rurales del este de Cuba, es uno de los estilos[b] de música cubana más viejos. Muchos lo consideran como el abuelo de todas las otras formas musicales caribeñas. El uso de las «inspiraciones», o sea,[c] llamada y respuesta,[d] revela[e] su origen africano.

[a]se... *developed* [b]*styles* [c]o... *in other words* [d]llamada... *call and response (a performance style in which one performer listens to another performer sing or play a few bars of music, then responds with his or her own voice or instrument)* [e]*shows*

Septeto Santiaguero es un conjunto cubano sonero[f] muy conocido que da conciertos por toda Latinoamérica y Europa. Su nombre «septeto» se refiere a la instrumentación de siete instrumentos, y «santiaguero» se refiere a su origen de la ciudad de Santiago, Cuba. Los instrumentos principales de este septeto son: la guitarra, el tres,[g] el bongó,[h] los claves,[i] las maracas, el contrabajo[j] y la trompeta.

[f]conjunto... *"son" band* [g]*type of guitar* [h]*bongo drum* [i]*two sticks used together as a percussion instrument* [j]*double bass*

Los tambores[k] batá son tres: el iyá, el itólele y el okónkolo. Los batá, muy presentes en la música popular de Cuba como el son, tienen su origen en la santería[l] y las ceremonias religiosas de los afrocubanos.

[k]*drums* [l]*syncretic religion that combines West African religious practices with Catholic traditions and that is primarily practiced in Caribbean nations*

25 Expressing Direct and Indirect Objects Together **Double Object Pronouns**

Berta habla de la fiesta que Anita hizo para sus amigos.

Preparé unos entremeses y *se los* llevé a Anita para la fiesta.

Me encantó el disco compacto que Anita tocó en la fiesta. Por eso Anita *me lo* prestó para escuchar más tarde.

Sergio sacó muchas fotos en la fiesta y *nos las* mostró en la computadora.

Comprensión: ¿Cierto o falso?

1. ¿Los entremeses? Berta se los llevó a Anita.
2. ¿El disco compacto? Sergio se lo prestó a Berta.
3. ¿Las fotos? Anita se las mostró a todos.

Order of Pronouns

When both an indirect and a direct object pronoun are used in a sentence, the indirect object pronoun (**I**) precedes the direct (**D**): **ID.** Note that nothing comes between the two pronouns. The position of double object pronouns with respect to the verb is the same as that of single object pronouns.

—¿Tienes el trofeo?
Do you have the trophy?

—Sí, acaban de dár**melo.**
Yes, they just gave it to me.

—Mamá, ¿está listo el almuerzo?
Mom, is lunch ready?

—**Te lo** preparo ahora mismo.
I'll get it ready for you right now.

Le(s) → se

A. When both the indirect and the direct object pronouns begin with the letter **l,** the indirect object pronoun always changes to **se.** The direct object pronoun does not change.

Le regaló unos zapatos.   *He gave her some shoes.*
Se los regaló.   *He gave them to her.*

Les mandamos una invitación.   *We sent you an invitation.*
Se la mandamos.   *We sent it to you.*

B. Since **se** can stand for **le** (*to/for you* [sing.], *him, her*) or **les** (*to/for you* [pl.], *them*), it is often necessary to clarify its meaning by using **a** plus the pronoun objects of prepositions.

Se lo escribo (**a Uds., a ellos, a ellas...**).
I'll write it to (you, them . . .).

Se las doy (**a Ud., a él, a ella...**).
I'll give them to (you, him, her . . .).

■ Práctica

A. ¡Anticipemos! Lo que se oye en casa. ¿A qué se refieren las siguientes oraciones? Fíjese en (*Note*) los pronombres y en el sentido (*meaning*) de la oración.

1. __ No **lo** prendan (*switch on*). Prefiero que los niños lean o que jueguen.
2. __ ¿Me **la** pasas? Gracias.
3. __ Tengo muchas ganas de comprárme**los** todos. Me encanta esa música.
4. __ ¿Por qué no se **las** mandas a los abuelos? Les van a gustar muchísimo.
5. __ Tengo que reservárte**los** hoy mismo, porque se va a terminar (*expire*) la oferta especial de Aeroméxico.
6. __ Yo se **la** organicé a Lupe para su cumpleaños. Antonio y Diego le hicieron un pastel.

a. unas fotos
b. la ensalada
c. unos billetes de avión para Guadalajara
d. la fiesta
e. el televisor
f. los discos compactos de Luis Miguel

B. En la mesa. Imagine que Ud. acaba de comer pero todavía tiene hambre. Pida más comida, según el modelo. Fíjese en el uso del tiempo presente como sustituto para el mandato.

MODELO: ensalada → ¿Hay más *ensalada*? ¿Me *la* pasas, por favor?

1. pan   2. tortillas   3. tomates   4. fruta   5. vino   6. jamón

C. En el aeropuerto. Cambie los sustantivos a pronombres para evitar (*avoid*) la repetición.

1. ¿La hora de la salida? Acaban de decirnos la hora de la salida.
2. ¿El horario? Sí, léame el horario, por favor.
3. ¿Los boletos? No, no tiene que darle los boletos aquí.
4. ¿El equipaje? Claro que le guardo el equipaje.
5. ¿Los pasajes? Ya te compré los pasajes.
6. ¿El puesto? No te preocupes. Te puedo guardar el puesto.
7. ¿La clase turística? Sí, les recomiendo la clase turística, señores.
8. ¿La cena? La asistente de vuelo nos va a servir la cena en el avión.

Need more practice?
- Workbook/Laboratory Manual
- Interactive CD-ROM
- Online Learning Center (www.mhhe.com/quetal7)

■ Conversación

A. Regalos especiales

PASO 1   The drawings in **Grupo A** show the presents that a number of people have just received. They were given by the people in **Grupo B.** Can you match the presents with the giver? Make as many logical guesses as you can.

GRUPO A

Ⓐ Estela   Ⓑ Maritere   Ⓓ Rigoberto

Ⓒ

Carlos y Juanita

GRUPO B

Ⓐ Pilar   Ⓑ Jorge

Ⓒ

Ⓓ la Sra. Santana

Raúl

PASO 2   Now compare your matches with those of a partner.

MODELO: ¿Quién le regaló (mandó, dio) la computadora a Maritere?
Se la regaló (mandó, dio) _____.

B. ¿Quién le regaló eso?

PASO 1   Haga una lista de los cinco mejores regalos que Ud. ha recibido (*have received*) en su vida. Si no sabe cómo expresar algo, pregúnteselo a su profesor(a).

PASO 2   Ahora déle a un compañero / una compañera su lista. Él/Ella le va a preguntar: **¿Quién te regaló _____?** Use pronombres en su respuesta. **¡OJO!** Fíjese en estas formas plurales (**ellos**): **regalaron, dieron, mandaron.**

MODELO: E1: ¿Quién te regaló los aretes?
E2: Mis padres me los regalaron.

En los Estados Unidos y el Canadá

El Día de César Chávez

Desde el año 2000, el líder sindical[a] mexicoamericano César Chávez (1927–1993) tiene **un día festivo en su honor en el estado de California.** El lunes o el viernes alrededor del[b] 31 de marzo, los colegios y otros organismos[c] pueden cerrar para honrar[d] a **Chávez** y **el movimiento en defensa de los trabajadores agrícolas**[e] que él defendió.

César Chávez

«[César Chávez] debe ser honrado porque su trabajo formó la América en la que hoy vivimos. Su vida nos dio a todos **el coraje**[f] y **la esperanza**[g] de que podemos hacer una diferencia. En su vida, nos enseñó que es importante **llevar una vida moral y responsable.**»

[a]*union* [b]*alrededor... around the* [c]*institutions* [d]*honor* [e]*trabajadores... farm workers* [f]*courage* [g]*hope*

UN POCO DE TODO

Lengua y cultura: Más días festivos. Complete the following paragraphs with the correct form of the words in parentheses, as suggested by the context. When two possibilities are given in parentheses, select the correct word. Use the preterite of the infinitives in italics.

Los días festivos son muy importantes en el mundo hispano, pero varían mucho de país en país y de pueblo en pueblo.

La fiesta de la Virgen de Guadalupe

En (alguno¹) países hispánicos (los/las²) días de varios santos (ser/estar³) fiestas nacionales. El día 12 (de/del⁴) diciembre los mexicanos (conmemorar⁵) a la santa patrona de México, la Virgen de Guadalupe. (Mucho⁶) mexicoamericanos celebran (este⁷) fiesta también. Se cree que la Virgen María se le (*aparecer*⁸) (a/de⁹) Juan, (un/una¹⁰) humilde pastor,ᵃ en el pueblo (a/de¹¹) Guadalupe. La Virgen (*dejar*¹²)ᵇ su imagen en un rebozoᶜ que todavía se puede (ver¹³) en su Basílicaᵈ en la Ciudad de México.

ᵃshepherd ᵇto leave ᶜshawl ᵈlarge church

Una bandera (banner) *típica durante la fiesta de la Virgen de Guadalupe*

La fiesta de San Fermín

No (todo¹⁴) las fiestas hispánicas (ser/estar¹⁵) religiosas. Esta fiesta de Pamplona (España) lleva (el/la¹⁶) nombre de un santo y (ser/estar¹⁷) de origen religioso, pero es esencialmente secular. Durante diez días —entre (el/la¹⁸) 7 y (el/la¹⁹) 14 de julio— se interrumpe la rutina diaria (del / de la²⁰) ciudad. (Llegar²¹) personas de todas partes de España e inclusiveᵃ de (otro²²) países para beber, cantar, bailar... y (pasarlo²³) (bien/bueno²⁴). Todas las mañanas algunos torosᵇ (correr²⁵) sueltosᶜ por la calleᵈ de la Estafeta, en dirección (al / a la²⁶) plaza de toros.ᵉ (Alguno²⁷) personas atrevidasᶠ (correr²⁸) delante de ellos. No (haber²⁹) dudaᵍ de que (este³⁰) demostración de valorʰ (ser/estar³¹) bastante peligrosa.ⁱ Luego por (el/la³²) tarde se celebra una corridaʲ en la famosa plaza de toros que (*describir*³³) Ernest Hemingway en (su³⁴) novela *The Sun Also Rises*. En Pamplona todavía (ser/estar³⁵) posible (hablar³⁶) con personas que (saber/conocer³⁷) a este famoso escritor estadounidense.

ᵃeven ᵇbulls ᶜcorrer... to run free ᵈstreet ᵉplaza... bullring ᶠdaring ᵍdoubt ʰcourage
ⁱbastante... quite dangerous ʲbullfight

Resources for Review and Testing Preparation

- Workbook/Laboratory Manual
- Interactive CD-ROM
- Online Learning Center
  (www.mhhe.com/quetal7)

Comprensión: ¿Cierto o falso? Corrija las oraciones falsas.

1. Todas las fiestas hispánicas son religiosas.
2. Sólo los mexicanos celebran la fiesta de la Virgen de Guadalupe.
3. La fiesta de San Fermín es esencialmente para los niños.
4. Algunos españoles todavía recuerdan a Hemingway.

VIDEOTECA

Entrevista cultural: Cuba

Rocío García nació en Cuba pero ahora vive y trabaja en México. En esta entrevista, Rocío describe su trabajo. También habla de unas costumbres cubanas. Antes de ver el vídeo, lea el siguiente fragmento de la entrevista.

ENTREVISTADORA: Rocío, ¿en dónde trabajas?

ROCÍO: Trabajo en una tienda que vende artículos típicos de fiesta, como son globos, serpentinas[a]... Y tiene una sección especial para artículos típicos de fiestas mexicanas, que es en la que nos encontramos.

ENTREVISTADORA: ¿Cómo se celebran los cumpleaños en Cuba?

ROCÍO: En Cuba hacemos una gran fiesta. Hay payasos,[b] globos, *cake*, piñatas, refrescos —todo para que los niños la pasen bien. Y jugamos mucho con ellos para que disfruten[c] ese día.

[a]*streamers* [b]*clowns* [c]*they enjoy*

Ahora vea el vídeo y conteste las siguientes preguntas basándose en la entrevista.

1. ¿Dónde trabaja Rocío?
2. ¿Qué se vende allí?
3. ¿Cómo son las fiestas de cumpleaños en Cuba?
4. ¿Cómo se celebra la Navidad en Cuba?
5. ¿Cuál es el día festivo preferido de Rocío?

Entre amigos: ¡Comemos «las uvas de la suerte (*the lucky grapes*)»!

Rubén, Miguel, Tané y Karina preparan las decoraciones para una fiesta, y hablan de las tradiciones navideñas (*Christmas traditions*) de sus países. En su opinión, ¿de qué van a hablar? Antes de mirar el vídeo, lea las preguntas a continuación. Mientras mire el vídeo, trate de entender la conversación en general y fíjese en la información sobre los días festivos. Luego mire el vídeo una segunda vez, fijándose en la información que necesita para contestar las preguntas.

1. ¿Qué van a hacer Miguel y Rubén con los adornos (*decorations*)?
2. ¿Qué hacen en España durante los días de Navidad?
3. ¿Cuándo comen «las uvas de la suerte» en España?
4. ¿Qué hacen en Venezuela para la Navidad?
5. ¿Y qué hacen en Cuba para la Navidad?

ENFOQUE CULTURAL

 Cuba

LOS ESTADOS UNIDOS
(Florida)

GOLFO DE
MÉXICO

OCÉANO
ATLÁNTICO

Estrecho de Florida

ISLAS BAHAMAS

La Habana

C U B A

• Camagüey

• Santiago

MAR CARIBE

HAITÍ

¡Fíjese!

- Cuba obtuvo[a] su independencia de España en 1898, tras[b] la guerra de Cuba.[c] Los Estados Unidos ayudó a Cuba en esta guerra.
- Después de la revolución socialista cubana en 1959, hubo un éxodo de cubanos a los Estados Unidos. La mayor parte de ellos se estableció en Florida, con la esperanza[d] de volver muy pronto a su isla. Pero empezó el milenio y todavía[e] Fidel Castro, el primer líder de la revolución, gobierna a Cuba.
- Los días festivos oficiales de Cuba incluyen el Aniversario del triunfo de la Revolución o el Día de la Liberación (1° de enero), el Día Internacional de los Trabajadores (1° de mayo), las Celebraciones por el Día de la Rebeldía Nacional (25–27 de julio) y el Inicio de las guerras de Independencia (10 de octubre). Al tomar[f] el control del poder de Cuba, Castro declaró el país oficialmente ateo[g] y prohibió que practicantes religiosos participaran en el gobierno. En 1992, Castro levantó esa prohibición. En 1997, un poco antes de la visita del Papa Juan Pablo II a Cuba, la Navidad, que por casi cuarenta años no fue un día festivo oficial, fue celebrada[h] pública y oficialmente.
- El régimen de Castro ha reducido[i] el analfabetismo[j] a menos de 5 por ciento y ha reformado el sistema educativo con resultados admirables.

Pero la situación económica del país es difícil. Con la caída[k] de la Unión Soviética, Cuba perdió fondos de apoyo[l] indispensables. El embargo económico de los Estados Unidos también sigue afectando las condiciones de vida[m] de los cubanos.

[a]*obtained* [b]*after* [c]*guerra… Spanish-American War* [d]*hope* [e]*still* [f]*Al… Upon taking* [g]*atheist* [h]*celebrated* [i]*ha… has reduced* [j]*illiteracy* [k]*fall* [l]*fondos… economic assistance* [m]*condiciones… living conditions*

Personas famosas: Nicolás Guillén

Nicolás Guillén (1902–1989), poeta cubano de origen africano y europeo, es quizás[a] el poeta que mejor refleja la influencia africana en la cultura hispana. El lenguaje, los mitos[b] y las leyendas afro-cubanos aparecen en su obra. Sus temas incluyen la injusticia social y una crítica al colonialismo.

[a]*perhaps* [b]*myths*

*Nicolás Guillén
(1902–1989)*

Learn more about Cuba with the Video, the Interactive CD-ROM, and the Online Learning Center (www.mhhe.com/quetal7).

PASO FINAL

A CONVERSAR

¿Cómo celebraron Uds. los días festivos?

PASO 1 En una hoja de papel aparte, prepare un cuadro (*grid*) como el siguiente. Primero, escoja cuatro de los días festivos de la lista en la página 209. Luego escríbalos en el cuadro. Deje espacios en blanco para escribir el nombre de una persona y sus respuestas breves a tres preguntas.

MODELO:

día festivo	el Día de San Patricio	la Noche Vieja	el cumpleaños	el Cinco de Mayo
persona				
actividades				

PASO 2 Apunte (*Jot down*) tres preguntas que Ud. puede hacerles a sus compañeros sobre cómo celebraron estos días festivos el año pasado.

MODELO: El año pasado, ¿qué hiciste en la Noche Vieja? ¿Te reuniste con amigos en algún lugar especial? ¿Lo pasaste bien o mal?

PASO 3 Formen parejas para hacer y contestar las tres preguntas sobre el primer día festivo en el cuadro. Después de hacer y contestar esas tres preguntas, formen parejas con otras personas para hacer y contestar las preguntas del siguiente día festivo. En total, van a formar cuatro parejas diferentes para hacer y contestar las preguntas sobre los cuatro días festivos. Escriban los nombres de sus compañeros y sus respuestas debajo del día festivo correspondiente para recordar con quiénes hablaron y qué dijeron.

MODELO: la Noche Vieja →
Felipe: Salió con su novia. Se reunieron con unos amigos en un bar. Lo pasaron muy bien.

PASO 4 Escoja uno de los días festivos y cuéntele a la clase cómo lo celebró la persona que contestó sus preguntas.

En resumen

GRAMÁTICA

To review the grammar points presented in this chapter, refer to the indicated grammar presentations. You'll find further practice of these structures in the Workbook/Laboratory Manual, on the Interactive CD-ROM, and on the *¿Qué tal?* Online Learning Center (www.mhhe.com/quetal7).

23 Talking About the Past (2)—Irregular Preterites

Do you know how to conjugate the verbs that are irregular in the preterite? How does the preterite change the meaning of **saber, conocer, querer,** and **poder?**

24 Talking About the Past (3)—Preterite of Stem-Changing Verbs

You should know the stem-changing patterns for **-ir** verbs like **pedir, sentir,** and **dormir.**

25 Expressing Direct and Indirect Objects Together—Double Object Pronouns

Do you know in which order the direct and indirect object pronouns occur when they are used together in Spanish? You should also know where to place the pronouns and when an accent is required on the verb forms.

VOCABULARIO

Practice this vocabulary with digital flash cards on the Online Learning Center (www.mhhe.com/quetal7).

Los verbos

conseguir (i, i) (g)	to get, obtain
conseguir + *inf.*	to succeed in (*doing something*)
despedirse (i, i) (de)	to say good-bye (to), take leave (of)
encontrar (ue)	to find
morirse (ue, u)	to die
reaccionar	to react
sugerir (ie, i)	to suggest

Los días festivos y las fiestas

el anfitrión / la anfitriona	host, hostess
el chiste	joke
el deseo	wish
el día festivo	holiday
los entremeses	hors d'œvres
el/la invitado/a	guest
el pastel de cumpleaños	birthday cake
la sorpresa	surprise

Repaso: el cumpleaños, el dinero, el refresco

cumplir años	to have a birthday
dar (*irreg.*) una fiesta	to give a party
faltar (a)	to be absent (from), not attend
gastar	to spend (*money*)
hacer (*irreg.*) una fiesta	to have a party
pasarlo bien/mal	to have a good/bad time
reunirse (me reúno) (con)	to get together (with)

Repaso: celebrar, divertirse (ie, i), regalar

Emociones y condiciones

discutir (con)/(sobre)	to argue (with)/(about)
enfermarse	to become sick
enojarse (con)	to get angry (at)
llorar	to cry
olvidarse (de)	to forget (about)
ponerse (*irreg.*) + *adj.*	to become, get + *adj.*
portarse bien/mal	to behave well/badly
quejarse (de)	to complain (about)
recordar (ue)	to remember
reír(se) (i, i) (de)	to laugh (about)
sentirse (ie, i)	to feel (*an emotion*)
sonreír(se) (i, i)	to smile

Los sustantivos

el hecho	fact, event
la medianoche	midnight
la noticia	piece of news

Los adjetivos

avergonzado/a	embarrassed
feliz (*pl.* **felices**)	happy
raro/a	strange

Algunos días festivos

la Navidad	Christmas
la Noche Vieja	New Year's Eve
la Nochebuena	Christmas Eve
la Pascua (Florida)	Easter

Palabras adicionales

¡felicitaciones!	congratulations!
gracias por	thanks for
por lo menos	at least
ser (*irreg.*) **en** + *place*	to take place at/in (*place*)
ya	already

El tiempo libre

Fuegos artificiales (Fireworks) al final de un festival de teatro, en la Plaza de Bolívar en Bogotá, Colombia

Pasatiempos... *Pastimes, fun activities, and hobbies*

PASATIEMPOS, DIVERSIONES Y AFICIONES°

- Nina
- visitar un museo
- ir (*irreg.*) al cine/ a ver una película
- Sara
- pasear en bicicleta
- Eva
- Irene
- correr
- Emilio
- patinar en línea
- Rita
- dar (*irreg.*) un paseo
- Felipe
- Julio
- hacer (*irreg.*) un *picnic*
- Leona
- jugar (ue) (gu) a las cartas
- Andrés
- montar a caballo

Los pasatiempos

los ratos libres	spare (free) time
dar (*irreg.*)/**hacer** (*irreg.*) **una fiesta**	to give a party
hacer (*irreg.*) *camping*	to go camping
hacer (*irreg.*) **planes para** + *inf.*	to make plans to (*do something*)
ir (*irreg.*)…	to go . . .
a una discoteca / a un bar	to a disco / to a bar
al teatro / a un concierto	to the theater / to a concert
jugar (ue) (gu) al ajedrez	to play chess
tomar el sol	to sunbathe
aburrirse	to get bored
ser (*irreg.*) **aburrido/a, divertido/a**	to be boring, fun

Los deportes

el ciclismo	bicycling
el fútbol	soccer
el fútbol americano	football
el/la jugador(a)	player
la natación	swimming
esquiar (esquío)	to ski
nadar	to swim
patinar	to skate

Cognados: el basquetbol, el béisbol, el golf, el hockey, el tenis, el vólibol

entrenar	to practice, train
ganar	to win
jugar (ue) (gu) al + *sport*	to play (*a sport*)
perder (ie)	to lose
practicar (qu)	to participate (*in a sport*)
ser (*irreg.*) **aficionado/a (a)**	to be a fan (of)

Conversación

A. ¿Cómo pasan estas personas su tiempo libre?

PASO 1 ¿Qué cree Ud. que hacen las siguientes personas para divertirse en un sábado típico? Use su imaginación pero manténgase (*keep yourself*) entre los límites de lo posible.

1. una persona rica que vive en Nueva York
2. un grupo de amigos que trabajan en una fábrica (*factory*) de Detroit
3. un matrimonio joven con poco dinero y dos niños pequeños

PASO 2 ¿Cómo se divierten los jóvenes españoles? Este recorte (*clipping*) de una revista española indica el tiempo medio (*average*) que los jóvenes españoles dedican a sus aficiones. ¿Puede explicar en español lo que significan los términos **Tomar copas** y **prensa**? ¿A qué tipos de «**Juegos**» cree Ud. que se refiere el recorte?

PASO 3 Indique el número de minutos que Ud. les dedica a estas aficiones cada día. ¿Qué diferencia hay entre Ud. y los jóvenes españoles?

TIEMPO QUE DEDICAN A SUS AFICIONES	
(Media de minutos diarios)	
Ver la televisión	**120**
Tomar copas	**60**
Pasear	**22**
Leer libros	**15**
Escuchar música	**15**
Oír la radio	**8**
Hacer deporte	**9**
Practicar *hobbies*	**8**
Leer la prensa	**6**
«Juegos»	**4**

B. ¿Cierto o falso? Corrija (*Correct*) las oraciones falsas según su opinión.

1. Ver un partido (*match, game*) de fútbol en la televisión es más aburrido que ir al cine.
2. Lo paso mejor con mi familia que con mis amigos.
3. Las actividades educativas me gustan más que las deportivas (*sporting*).
4. Odio el béisbol tanto como el fútbol.

NOTA CULTURAL

El fútbol, el béisbol y el basquetbol

Sin duda,[a] el deporte más popular en los países hispánicos es **el fútbol.*** La **Copa Mundial** de fútbol es el evento deportivo más popular del mundo. Este **torneo internacional** ocurre cada cuatro años y tiene más **espectadores** que cualquier[b] otro evento deportivo. Por ejemplo, en 2002, más de un billón de televidentes miraron el partido final de la Copa Mundial mientras el mismo año, 132 millones miraron el *Super Bowl* de los Estados Unidos. Como es un deporte tan popular, en todas las ciudades hispanas hay muchos **campos**[c] de **fútbol.** Los niños y los adultos van a jugar siempre que pueden.[d]

Un partido de la Copa Mundial entre el Brasil y Honduras

El béisbol también es muy popular, sobre todo en el Caribe. Hay muchos hispanos en **las ligas profesionales** de los Estados Unidos. El puertorriqueño Roberto Clemente fue el primer jugador hispano elegido al *Baseball Hall of Fame* en 1973.

Otro deporte muy popular es **el basquetbol** o **el baloncesto.** En los Juegos Olímpicos de verano de 2004, la Argentina se llevó la medalla de oro[e] después de derrotar[f] a Italia. En la Asociación Nacional de Basquetbol (*NBA*) de los Estados Unidos hay varios jugadores hispanos, entre ellos Emanuel Ginobili, Eduardo Nájera, Pau Gasol y Felipe Arroyo.

---

[a]*doubt* [b]*any* [c]*fields* [d]siempre... *whenever they can* [e]se... *took the gold medal* [f]*defeating*

---

*Remember that **fútbol** *is soccer, not U.S.-style football.*

Los… *Household chores*

LOS QUEHACERES DOMÉSTICOS°

Algunos aparatos domésticos

la cafetera	coffeemaker
el horno de	microwave
microondas	oven
la tostadora	toaster

Los quehaceres domésticos

dejar (en…)	to leave behind (in [*a place*])
lavar (los platos, la ropa)	to wash (the dishes, the clothes)
limpiar la casa (entera)	to clean the (whole) house
poner (*irreg.*) **la mesa**	to set the table
quitar la mesa	to clear the table
sacudir los muebles	to dust the furniture

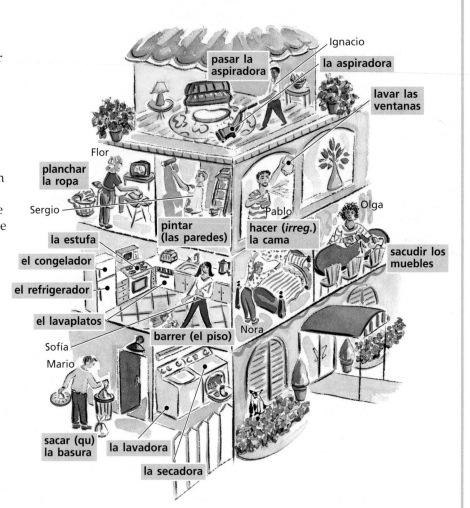

Ignacio

pasar la aspiradora

la aspiradora

lavar las ventanas

Flor

planchar la ropa

Sergio

Pablo

Olga

pintar (las paredes)

hacer (*irreg.*) **la cama**

la estufa

el congelador

el refrigerador

sacudir los muebles

el lavaplatos

barrer (el piso)

Nora

Sofía
Mario

sacar (qu) la basura

la lavadora

la secadora

Vocabulario útil

Here are some alternative phrases related to household chores and appliances that are used in some parts of the Spanish-speaking world. This vocabulary is for your information only and will not be actively practiced in *¿Qué tal?*

hacer (*irreg.*) **la cama** → **tender (ie) la cama**
lavar los platos → **fregar (ie) (gu) los platos**
sacar (qu) la basura → **tirar la basura**
sacudir los muebles → **quitar el polvo** (literally, *to remove the dust*)

el congelador → **la nevera**
la estufa → **la cocina** (**el horno** is generally used for *oven*)
el refrigerador → **el frigorífico, la refrigeradora**

■ Conversación

A. Los quehaceres. ¿En qué cuarto o parte de la casa se hacen las siguientes actividades? Hay más de una respuesta en muchos casos.

1. Se hace la cama en _____.
2. Se saca la basura de _____ y se deja en _____.
3. Se sacude los muebles de _____.
4. Uno se baña en _____. Pero es mejor que uno bañe al perro en _____.
5. Se barre el piso de _____.
6. Se pasa la aspiradora en _____.
7. Se lava y se seca la ropa en _____. La ropa se plancha en _____.
8. Se usa la cafetera en _____.

NOTA COMUNICATIVA

Talking About Obligation

You already know several ways to express the obligation to carry out particular activities.

Tengo que		I have to	
Necesito	barrer el suelo.	*I need to*	*sweep the floor.*
Debo		*I should*	

Of the three, **tener que** + *infinitive* expresses the strongest sense of obligation.

The concept *to be someone's turn or responsibility* (to do something) is expressed in Spanish with the verb **tocar** plus an indirect object.

—¿**A quién le toca** lavar los platos esta noche?
—**A mí me toca** solamente sacar la basura.
  Creo que **a papá le toca** lavar los platos.

Whose turn is it to wash the dishes tonight?
I only have to take out the garbage. I think it's Dad's turn to wash the dishes.

B. ¿A quién le toca?

PASO 1 ¿Mantiene Ud. su casa en orden? ¿Con qué frecuencia hace Ud. los siguientes quehaceres? Complete el siguiente formulario. Si Ud. vive en una residencia estudiantil, imagine que vive en una casa o en un apartamento.

0	= nunca
1	= a veces
2	= frecuentemente
3	= todos los días

1. _____ lavar las ventanas
2. _____ hacer las camas
3. _____ poner la mesa
4. _____ preparar la comida
5. _____ sacudir los muebles
6. _____ lavar los platos
7. _____ limpiar la casa entera
8. _____ sacar la basura
9. _____ pasar la aspiradora
10. _____ limpiar la estufa
11. _____ planchar la ropa
12. _____ barrer el piso

_____ TOTAL

PASO 2 Ahora hable con un compañero / una compañera sobre sus hábitos domésticos. Básense en el formulario del **Paso 1.** Luego hablen de los quehaceres domésticos para hoy, mañana o esta semana.

MODELO: lavar las ventanas →
    E1: ¿Con qué frecuencia lavas las ventanas?
    E2: Nunca las lavo.
    E1: ¿Qué te toca hacer en casa hoy (mañana, esta semana)?

Need more practice?

■ Workbook/Laboratory Manual
■ Interactive CD-ROM
■ Online Learning Center (www.mhhe.com/quetal7)

¿Recuerda Ud.?

In **Capítulos 7** and **8,** you learned the forms and some uses of the preterite. Before you learn the other simple past tense, you might want to review the forms of the preterite in those chapters. The verbs in the following sentences are in the preterite. Can you identify any words in the sentences that emphasize the completed nature of the actions expressed by the verbs?

1. Me levanté a las seis esta mañana.
2. Ayer fui al cine con un amigo.
3. Pinté las paredes de la cocina la semana pasada.

26 Descriptions and Habitual Actions in the Past Imperfect of Regular and Irregular Verbs

En su clase de antropología, Diego habla de los aztecas

Diego, un estudiante de California que estudia en México, da un informe sobre los aztecas.

«Los aztecas construyeron grandes pirámides para sus dioses. En lo alto de cada pirámide *había* un templo donde *tenían* lugar las ceremonias y *se ofrecían* los sacrificios. Las pirámides *tenían* muchísimos escalones, y *era* necesario subirlos todos para llegar a los templos.

Cerca de muchas pirámides *había* un terreno como el de una cancha de basquetbol. Allí *se celebraban* partidos que *eran* parte de una ceremonia. Los participantes *jugaban* con una pelota de goma dura, que sólo *podían* mover con las caderas y las rodillas... »

Comprensión: ¿Cierto o falso?

1. Los aztecas creían en un solo dios.
2. Las pirámides aztecas tenían una función religiosa.
3. Los aztecas practicaban un deporte similar al basquetbol.

In his anthropology class, Diego talks about the Aztecs   *Diego, a student from California who is studying in Mexico, is giving a report on the Aztecs. "The Aztecs constructed large pyramids for their gods. At the top of each pyramid there was a temple where ceremonies took place and sacrifices were offered. The pyramids had many, many steps, and it was necessary to climb them all in order to get to the temples.*

"Close to many pyramids there was an area of land like that of a basketball court. Ceremonial matches were celebrated there. The participants played with a ball made of hard rubber that they could only move with their hips and knees . . . "

You have already learned to use the *preterite* (**el pretérito**) to express events in the past. The *imperfect* (**el imperfecto**) is the second simple past tense in Spanish. In contrast to the preterite, which is used when you view actions or states of being as begun or completed in the past, the imperfect tense is used when you view past actions or states of being as habitual or as "in progress." The imperfect is also used for describing the past.

The imperfect has several English equivalents. For example, **hablaba,** the first person singular of **hablar,** can mean *I spoke, I was speaking, I used to speak,* or *I would speak* (when *would* implies a repeated action). Most of these English equivalents indicate that the action was still in progress or was habitual, except for *I spoke,* which can correspond to either the preterite or the imperfect.

PAST ------------------- Present ------------------- Future
preterite	present
imperfect	present progressive
	formal commands

Forms of the Imperfect

hablar		comer		vivir	
hablaba	hablábamos	comía	comíamos	vivía	vivíamos
hablabas	hablabais	comías	comíais	vivías	vivíais
hablaba	hablaban	comía	comían	vivía	vivían

- Stem-changing verbs do not show a change in the imperfect. The imperfect of **hay** is **había** (*there was, there were, there used to be*).

Pronunciation Hint: Remember that the pronunciation of a **b** between vowels, such as in the imperfect ending **-aba,** is pronounced as a fricative [ƀ] sound.

In the other imperfect forms, it is important not to pronounce the ending **-ía** as a diphthong, but to pronounce the **i** and the **a** in separate syllables (the accent mark over the **í** helps remind you of this).

Imperfect of stem-changing verbs = no change

almorzar (ue) → almorzaba
perder (ie) → perdía
pedir (i, i) → pedía

Imperfect of **hay** = **había**

- Only three verbs are irregular in the imperfect: **ir, ser,** and **ver.**

ir		ser		ver	
iba	íbamos	era	éramos	veía	veíamos
ibas	ibais	eras	erais	veías	veíais
iba	iban	era	eran	veía	veían

PASO 2

Uses of the Imperfect

Note the following uses of the imperfect. If you have a clear sense of when and where the imperfect is used, understanding where the preterite is used will be easier. When talking about the past, the preterite *is* used when the imperfect *isn't*. That is an oversimplification of the uses of these two past tenses, but at the same time it is a general rule of thumb that will help you out at first.

The imperfect has the following uses.

- To describe *repeated habitual actions* in the past

Siempre **nos quedábamos** en aquel hotel.
We always stayed (used to stay, would stay) at that hotel.

Todos los veranos **iban** a la costa.
Every summer they went (used to go, would go) to the coast.

- To describe an *action that was in progress* (*when something else happened*)

Pedía la cena.
She was ordering dinner.

- To describe two *simultaneous past actions in progress*, with **mientras**

Tú **leías mientras** Juan **escribía** la carta.
You were reading while Juan was writing the letter.

- To describe ongoing *physical, mental,* or *emotional states* in the past

Estaban muy distraídos.
They were very distracted.

La **quería** muchísimo.
He loved her a lot.

- To tell *time* in the past and to *express age* with **tener**

OJO Just as in the present, the singular form of the verb **ser** is used with one o'clock, the plural form from two o'clock on.

Era la una. / **Eran** las dos.
It was one o'clock. / It was two o'clock.

Tenía 18 años.
She was 18 years old.

- To form a *past progressive:* imperfect of **estar** + *present participle**

Note that the simple imperfect—**cenábamos, estudiabas**—could also be used in the example sentences to express the ongoing actions. The use of the progressive emphasizes that the action was actually in progress.

Estábamos cenando a las diez.
We were having dinner at ten.

¿No **estabas estudiando**?
Weren't you studying?

---

*A progressive tense can also be formed with the preterite of **estar: Estuvieron cenando** hasta las doce. The use of the progressive with the preterite of **estar,** however, is relatively infrequent, and it will not be practiced in ¿Qué tal?*

■ Práctica

A. ¡Anticipemos! Mi niñez (*childhood*)

PASO 1 Indique si las siguientes oraciones eran ciertas o falsas para Ud. cuando tenía 10 años.

	C	F
1. Estaba en el cuarto grado (*fourth grade*).	☐	☐
2. Me acostaba a las nueve todas las noches.	☐	☐
3. Los sábados me levantaba temprano para mirar los dibujos animados (*cartoons*).	☐	☐
4. Mis padres me pagaban por los quehaceres que hacía: cortar el césped (*cutting the grass*), lavar los platos…	☐	☐
5. Me gustaba acompañar a mi madre/padre al supermercado.	☐	☐
6. Le pegaba (*I hit*) a mi hermano/a con frecuencia.	☐	☐
7. Tocaba un instrumento musical en la orquesta de la escuela.	☐	☐
8. Mis héroes eran personajes (*characters*) de los dibujos animados como Superman y Kim Possible.	☐	☐

PASO 2 Ahora corrija las oraciones que son falsas para Ud.

MODELO: 2. Es falso. Me acostaba a las diez, no a las nueve.

B. Cuando Tina era niña… Describa la vida de Tina cuando tenía 6 años, haciendo oraciones según las indicaciones.

De niña, la vida de Tina era muy diferente.

1. todos los días / asistir / a / escuela primaria
2. por / mañana / aprender / a / leer / y / escribir / en / pizarra
3. a / diez / beber / leche / y / dormir / un poco
4. ir / a / casa / para / almorzar / y / regresar / a / escuela
5. estudiar / geografía / y / hacer / dibujos
6. jugar / con / compañeros / en / patio / de / escuela
7. camino de (*on the way*) casa / comprar / dulces / y / se los / comer
8. frecuentemente / pasar / por / casa / de / abuelos
9. cenar / con / padres / y / ayudar / a / lavar / platos
10. mirar / tele / un rato / y / acostarse / a / ocho

Palabras útiles

el timbre (doorbell)

discutir (to argue)
ladrar (to bark)
pelear (to fight)
sonar (ue)* (to ring; to sound)

C. El trabajo de niñera (baby-sitter)

PASO 1 El trabajo de niñera puede ser muy pesado (*difficult*), pero cuando los niños son traviesos (*mischievous*), también puede ser peligroso (*dangerous*). ¿Qué estaba pasando cuando la niñera perdió por fin la paciencia? Describa todas las acciones que pueda, usando **estaba(n)** + **-ndo.**

MODELO: Cuando la niñera perdió la paciencia... →
el bebé estaba llorando.

Cuando la niñera perdió la paciencia...

PASO 2 De joven (*As a youth*), ¿trabajaba Ud. de niñero/a? ¿Tuvo alguna vez una mala experiencia? Complete la siguiente oración, si puede, usando un verbo en el pretérito.

MODELO: Una vez, cuando yo estaba (leyendo, mirando la tele, hablando con un amigo / una amiga...), el niño / la niña...

Need more practice?

- Workbook/Laboratory Manual
- Interactive CD-ROM
- Online Learning Center (www.mhhe.com/quetal7)

■ Conversación

Entrevista. ¡Qué cambio! Hágale las siguientes preguntas a un compañero / una compañera de clase. Él/Ella va a pensar en las costumbres que tenía a los 14 años, es decir, cuando estaba en el noveno (*ninth*) o décimo (*tenth*) grado.

1. ¿Qué te gustaba comer? ¿Y ahora?
2. ¿Qué programa de televisión no te perdías nunca? ¿Y ahora?
3. ¿Qué te gustaba leer? ¿Y ahora?
4. ¿Qué hacías los sábados por la noche? ¿Y ahora?
5. ¿Qué deportes te gustaba practicar? ¿Y ahora?
6. ¿Con quién discutías mucho? ¿Y ahora?
7. ¿A quién te gustaba molestar (*to annoy*)? ¿Y ahora?

---

*Although **sonar** *is a stem-changing verb* (**o** → **ue**), *remember that the stem of present participles does not change with* **-ar** *verbs* (**sonando**).

¿Recuerda Ud.?

Before beginning **Gramática 27,** review comparisons, which were introduced in **Capítulo 5.** How would you say the following in Spanish?

1. I work as much as you do.
2. I work more/less than you do.
3. Bill Gates has more money than I have.

4. My housemate has fewer things than I do.
5. I have as many friends as you do.
6. My computer is worse/better than this one.

27 Expressing Extremes Superlatives

¡El número uno!

Jennifer López

Enrique Iglesias   Ricky Martin

¿Está Ud. de acuerdo con las opiniones expresadas en estas oraciones?

1. Jennifer López es *la* mujer *más bella* (*beautiful*) *del* mundo.
2. Enrique Iglesias es *el mejor* cantante (*singer*) *de* su familia.
3. Ricky Martin es *el* puertorriqueño *más conocido* (*well-known*) *de* hoy.

¿Y Ud.?

Ahora le toca a Ud. formular su propia (*own*) opinión.

1. El/La cantante hispánico/a más popular del momento es _____.
2. La mejor actriz del momento es _____.
3. La música popular más interesante es _____.

The *superlative* (**el superlativo**) is formed in English by adding *-est* to adjectives or by using expressions such as *the most* and *the least* with the adjective. In Spanish, this concept is expressed in the same way as the comparative but is always accompanied by the definite article. In this construction **mejor** and **peor** tend to precede the noun; other adjectives follow. *In* or *at* is expressed with **de.**

OJO The superlative forms **-ísimo/a/os/as** cannot be used with this type of superlative construction.

el/la/los/las + *noun* + **más/menos** + *adjective* + **de**

El basquetbol es **el deporte más interesante del** mundo.
Basketball is the most interesting sport in the world.

el/la/los/las + **mejor(es)/peor(es)** + *noun* + **de**

Son **los mejores** refrigeradores **de** aquella tienda.
They are the best refrigerators at that store.

superlative = adjective or adverb phrase used to compare three or more nouns or actions

■ Práctica

A. ¡Anticipemos! ¿Está Ud. de acuerdo o no?

PASO 1 Indique si Ud. está de acuerdo o no con las siguientes oraciones.

	SÍ	NO
1. El descubrimiento (*discovery*) científico más importante del siglo XX fue la vacuna (*vaccine*) contra la poliomielitis.	☐	☐
2. La persona más influyente (*influential*) del mundo es el presidente de los Estados Unidos.	☐	☐
3. El problema más serio del mundo es la deforestación de la región del Amazonas.	☐	☐
4. El día festivo más divertido del año es la Noche Vieja.	☐	☐
5. La mejor novela del mundo es *Don Quijote de la Mancha.*	☐	☐
6. El animal menos inteligente de todos es el avestruz (*ostrich*).	☐	☐
7. El peor mes del año es enero.	☐	☐
8. La ciudad más contaminada de los Estados Unidos es Los Ángeles.	☐	☐

PASO 2 Para cada oración que no refleja su opinión, invente otra oración.

MODELO: 4. No estoy de acuerdo. Creo que el día festivo más divertido del año es el Cuatro de Julio.

B. Superlativos.
Expand the information in these sentences based on the model. Then, if you can, restate each sentence with true information at the beginning.

MODELO: Es una estudiante muy *trabajadora.* (la clase) →
Es *la* estudiante *más trabajadora de la clase.* →
Carlota es la estudiante más trabajadora de la clase.

1. Es un día festivo muy *divertido.* (el año)
2. Es una clase muy *interesante.* (todas mis clases)
3. Es una persona muy *inteligente.* (todos mis amigos)
4. Es una ciudad muy *grande.* (los Estados Unidos / el Canadá)
5. Es un estado muy *pequeño* / una provincia muy *pequeña.* (los Estados Unidos / el Canadá)
6. Es un metro muy *rápido.* (el mundo)
7. Es una residencia muy *ruidosa* (*noisy*). (la universidad)
8. Es una montaña muy *alta.* (el mundo)

Need more practice?

- Workbook/Laboratory Manual
- Interactive CD-ROM
- Online Learning Center (www.mhhe.com/quetal7)

■ Conversación

Entrevista. With another student, ask and answer questions based on the following phrases. Then report your opinions to the class. Report any disagreements as well.

MODELO: E1: Shakira es la mujer más guapa del mundo.
E2: Estoy de acuerdo / No estoy de acuerdo. Para mí Salma Hayek es la más guapa.

1. la persona más guapa del mundo
2. la noticia más seria de esta semana
3. un libro interesantísimo y otro pesadísimo (*very boring*)
4. el mejor restaurante de la ciudad y el peor
5. el cuarto más importante de la casa y el menos importante
6. un plato riquísimo y otro malísimo
7. un programa de televisión interesantísimo y otro pesadísimo
8. un lugar tranquilísimo, otro animadísimo y otro peligrosísimo (*very dangerous*)
9. la canción (*song*) más bonita del año y la más fea
10. la mejor película/canción del año y la peor

En los Estados Unidos y el Canadá

Peloteros hispanos

Si a Ud. le gusta el béisbol, seguro que conoce los nombres de muchos **beisbolistas, o peloteros, de origen hispano.** Sólo tiene que mirar las listas de los jugadores de los Yanquis de Nueva York, los Azulejos[a] de Toronto, los Expos de Montreal, los Medias Rojas de Boston o los Rancheros de Texas, sólo por nombrar algunos de los equipos[b] más famosos, para ver cuántos nombres hispanos hay. El 30 por ciento de todos los jugadores de la Liga Mayor de Béisbol (LMB) y el 50 por ciento de los jugadores de las ligas menores son hispanos o de origen hispano.

Varios países hispanos tienen sus **propias[c] ligas de béisbol** y «exportan» a jugadores de béisbol a los Estados Unidos y al Canadá. Esos países hispanos son principalmente los **países caribeños:** Puerto Rico, la República Dominicana, Cuba y Venezuela, además de[d] México. Por ejemplo, al principio[e] del año 2004, setenta y tres peloteros de los treinta equipos principales **habían nacido** en[f] la República Dominicana.

¿Cuántos beisbolistas reconoce Ud. de esta lista? ¿Puede añadir otros nombres?

Estadounidenses de nacimiento: Alex Rodríguez (A-Rod) y Nomar Garcíaparra

Dominicanos: Sammy Sosa, Alfonso Soriano, Tony Batista y Vladimir Guerrero

Alex Rodríguez (A-Rod) durante un partido contra los Azulejos de Toronto

Cubanos: Rafael Palmeiro y José Canseco

Mexicanos: Erubiel Durazo y Juan Castro

Puertorriqueños: Jorge Posada y Carlos Delgado

Panameño: Mariano Rivera

[a]*Blue Jays* [b]*teams* [c]*own* [d]*además... in addition to* [e]*al... at the beginning* [f]*habían... were from*

Voces de Colombia

LITERATURA: Gabriel García Márquez

Gabriel García
Márquez
(1928–)

Sobre el autor: *Gabriel José García Márquez nació en Aracataca, en el norte de Colombia. Empezó su vida profesional como periodista. Vivió casi toda su vida de adulto fuera de Colombia, en Europa y México. Recibió el Premio Nóbel de Literatura en 1982 por su novela* Cien años de soledad. *Sus novelas y cuentos combinan lo fantástico y lo real, un estilo que se llama el realismo mágico. El siguiente fragmento es de* Cien años de soledad *(1967).*

Muchos años después, frente al pelotón de fusilamiento,[a] el coronel Aureliano Buendía había de[b] recordar aquella tarde remota en que su padre lo llevó a conocer el hielo.[c] Macondo era entonces una aldea[d] de veinte casas de barro[e] y cañabrava[f] construidas a la orilla[g] de un río de aguas diáfanas que se precipitaban por un lecho[h] de piedras pulidas,[i] blancas y enormes como huevos prehistóricos.

[a]pelotón… *firing squad* [b]había… *would* [c]*ice* [d]*village* [e]*mud* [f]*cane* [g]*bank* [h]*bed* [i]piedras… *polished rocks*

....

MÚSICA: El vallenato

el acordeón

la caja

la guacharaca

El vallenato, de raíces[a] africanas, nació hace unos cien años[b] en Valledupar, un pueblo en el norte de Colombia. Tiene cuatro ritmos básicos: el son (el ritmo más lento), el paseo (el ritmo intermedio), el merengue (un ritmo más alegre y acelerado) y la puya (el ritmo más rápido de los cuatro). La letra[c] de esta música generalmente trata[d] el amor[e] por una mujer o por la tierra[f] y sus costumbres.[g]

[a]*roots* [b]nació… *was born about one hundred years ago* [c]*lyrics* [d]*deal with* [e]*love* [f]*land* [g]*customs*

El vallenato se toca con tres instrumentos básicos: el acordeón, la caja[h] y la guacharaca,[i] pero estos pueden ir acompañados[j] de otros instrumentos.

[h]*type of drum* [i]*wooden percussion stick* [j]ir… *be accompanied*

Carlos Vives es el «embajador universal» del vallenato y es muy popular dentro y fuera de[k] Colombia. En 1993, causó gran sensación[l] con su música, que toma mucho de la tradición del vallenato. El estilo de Vives combina el vallenato con ritmos pop, rock, cumbia[m] y son.

[k]dentro… *in and outside of* [l]causó… *he made a big splash* [m]*another popular, traditional Colombian music style*

28 Getting Information **Summary of Interrogative Words**

Este es un anuncio de un restaurante de Connecticut.

1. ¿*Cómo* se llama el restaurante?
2. ¿En *qué* ciudad de Connecticut está?
3. ¿*Cuáles* son las especialidades de este restaurante?

¿Y Ud.?

¿Cuántas preguntas más puede Ud. hacer sobre este restaurante, basándose en el anuncio?

¿Cómo?	How?	**¿Dónde?**	Where?
¿Cuándo?	When?	**¿De dónde?**	From where?
¿A qué hora?	At what time?	**¿Adónde?**	Where (to)?
¿Qué?	What? Which?	**¿Cuánto/a?**	How much?
¿Cuál(es)?	What? Which one(s)?	**¿Cuántos/as?**	How many?
¿Por qué?	Why?	**¿Quién(es)?**	Who?
		¿De quién(es)?	Whose?

You have been using interrogative words to ask questions and get information since the beginning of *¿Qué tal?* The chart shows all of the interrogatives you have learned so far. Be sure that you know what they mean and how they are used. If you are not certain, the index and end-of-book vocabularies will help you find where they are first introduced. Only the specific uses of **¿qué?** and **¿cuál?** represent new information.

Using ¿qué? and ¿cuál?

• **¿Qué?** asks for a definition or an explanation.

¿Qué es esto?
What is this?

¿Qué quieres?
What do you want?

¿Qué tocas?
What (instrument) do you play?

- **¿Qué?** can be directly followed by a noun.

  ¿Qué traje necesitas?
  What (Which) suit do you need?

  ¿Qué playa te gusta más?
  What (Which) beach do you like most?

  ¿Qué instrumento musical tocas?
  What (Which) musical instrument do you play?

- **¿Cuál(es)?** expresses *what?* or *which?* in all other cases.

  ¿Cuál es la clase más grande?
  What (Which) is the biggest class?

  ¿Cuáles son tus actrices favoritas?
  What (Which) are your favorite actresses?

  ¿Cuál es la capital del Uruguay?
  What is the capital of Uruguay?

  ¿Cuál es tu teléfono?
  What is your phone number?

OJO The **¿cuál(es)?** + *noun* structure is not used by most speakers of Spanish: *¿Cuál de los dos libros quieres?* (*Which of the two books do you want?*) BUT *¿Qué libro quieres?* (*Which [What] book do you want?*)

AUTOPRUEBA

Match each word to the kind of information it asks for.

1. ¿Cuándo?   a. un lugar
2. ¿Dónde?   b. un número o una cantidad
3. ¿Qué?   c. una definición
4. ¿Cuánto?   d. la hora

Answers: 1. d 2. a 3. c 4. b

Need more practice?

- Workbook/Laboratory Manual
- Interactive CD-ROM
- Online Learning Center (www.mhhe.com/quetal7)

■ Práctica

¿Qué o cuál(es)?

1. ¿_____ es esto? —Un lavaplatos.
2. ¿_____ son los Juegos Olímpicos? —Son un conjunto (*group*) de competiciones deportivas.
3. ¿_____ es el quehacer que más te gusta? —Lavar los platos.
4. ¿_____ bicicleta vas a usar? —La de mi hermana.
5. ¿_____ son los cines más modernos? —Los del centro.
6. ¿_____ vídeo debo sacar? —El nuevo de Salma Hayek.
7. ¿_____ es una cafetera? —Es un aparato que se usa para preparar el café.
8. ¿_____ es tu padre? —En la foto, es el hombre a la izquierda del coche.

■ Conversación

Entrevista: Datos (*Information*) **personales.** Primero, forme preguntas para averiguar datos (*find out facts*) de un compañero / una compañera de clase. Se puede usar más de una palabra interrogativa para conseguir la información. (Debe usar las formas de **tú.**) Luego, entreviste a su compañero/a usando las preguntas.

MODELO: su dirección (*address*) → ¿Cuál es tu dirección? (¿Dónde vives?)

1. su teléfono
2. su dirección
3. su cumpleaños
4. la ciudad en que nació (*he/she was born*)
5. su número de seguro (*security*) social
6. la persona en que más confía (*he/she trusts*)
7. su tienda favorita
8. la fecha de su próximo examen

UN POCO DE TODO

Lengua y cultura: Diversiones familiares en Colombia. Complete the following passages with the correct forms of the words in parentheses, as suggested by the context. When two possibilities are given in parentheses, select the correct word. **¡OJO!** As you conjugate verbs in this activity, put the infinitives preceded by *I* in the imperfect.

Mayra y Joaquín son dos colombianos que llegaron recientemente a los Estados Unidos. Los dos (ser / estar[1]) de Cartagena, una gran ciudad colombiana y puerto[a] que (ser / estar[2]) en el mar Caribe. De niña, Mayra (*I:* vivir[3]) en la parte más antigua de la ciudad, el Centro Amurallado[b] colonial. En cambio,[c] la familia de Joaquín (*I:* tener[4]) un apartamento en Bocagrande, el sector más moderno de Cartagena. La manera de (divertirse[5]) cada uno[d] en su país los fines de semana era diferente.

En Cartagena, Mayra y su familia (*I:* ir[6]) con mucha frecuencia a la playa de La Boquilla* los fines de semana y (*I:* pasar[7]) todo el día (*pres. part.:* nadar[8]). Por la noche iban a un restaurante a (comer[9]) mariscos y a (*I:* bailar[10]) la cumbia. Por su parte, a Joaquín (se / le[11]) (*I:* gustar[12]) pasear por las fortalezas y las viejas y enormes murallas[e] de la ciudad. ¿(Saber / Conocer[13]) Uds. que (alguno[14]) de (ese[15]) murallas miden veinte metros de ancho[f] por veinte metros de alto? ¡(Ser / Estar[16]) realmente impresionantes!

Joaquín y Mayra (ser / estar[17]) de acuerdo en que, al visitar[g] Cartagena, es necesario ir también al centro comercial Las Bóvedas[†] y a la isla Barú.[‡] Allí, en las aguas del Parque Natural Corales del Rosario, (son / hay[18]) unos bancos de coral[h] muy bonitos. ¡Qué chévere![i]

Las Bóvedas en Cartagena, Colombia

[a]*port* [b]*Centro... Walled Center* [c]*En... On the other hand* [d]*cada... each of them* [e]*walls* [f]*de... wide* [g]*al... when one visits* [h]*bancos... coral reefs* [i]*¡Qué... How cool!*

Comprensión: Ahora y entonces. Conteste las preguntas en español.

1. ¿De qué ciudad son Mayra y Joaquín? ¿De qué partes de esa ciudad son?
2. ¿Qué sabe Ud. de la vida de ellos?
3. ¿Cómo pasaba Mayra los fines de semana en Cartagena?
4. Y Joaquín, ¿qué hacía él los fines de semana?

Resources for Review and Testing Preparation

- Workbook/Laboratory Manual
- Interactive CD-ROM
- Online Learning Center (www.mhhe.com/quetal7)

---

*La Boquilla, a fishing village outside Cartagena, has a long secluded beach with restaurants and bars.

[†]*Las Bóvedas (The Vaults) were barracks and storerooms built by the Spanish into the outer walls of the old city. Twenty-two of the dungeonlike rooms have been turned into small, upscale shops.*

[‡]*Barú Island, approximately ten minutes by motorboat from Cartagena, offers white sand beaches, crystal clear water, and big coral reefs.*

VIDEOTECA

Entrevista cultural: Colombia

Mauricio Tautiba es un colombiano apasionado de los deportes. Él habla en la entrevista de su equipo y de sus esperanzas para el futuro. Antes de ver el vídeo, lea el siguiente fragmento de la entrevista.

ENTREVISTADORA: Me dicen que juegas fútbol.* ¿Es cierto?

MAURICIO: Sí, juego fútbol, eh, inclusive juego en una liga todos los fines de semana.

ENTREVISTADORA: Y ¿es bueno tu equipo?

MAURICIO: Sí, muy bueno. La temporada[a] pasada ganamos casi todos los partidos, pero desafortunadamente no fuimos campeones.

[a]*season*

Ahora vea el vídeo y conteste las siguientes preguntas basándose en la entrevista.

1. ¿A qué deporte se dedica Mauricio?
2. ¿Con qué frecuencia lo practica y juega?
3. ¿Qué otros deportes practica?
4. ¿Juega bien o mal el equipo de Mauricio?
5. ¿Qué espera hacer Mauricio en el futuro?

Entre amigos: ¿Sabes bailar salsa?

Rubén, Karina, Miguel y Tané hacen planes para el fin de semana. Quieren ir a un club que se llama Mamá Rumba. En su opinión, ¿de qué van a hablar? Antes de mirar el vídeo, lea las preguntas a continuación. Mientras mire el vídeo, trate de entender la conversación en general y fíjese en la información sobre los planes de los amigos para el fin de semana. Luego mire el vídeo una segunda vez, fijándose en la información que necesita para contestar las preguntas.

1. Según Karina, ¿qué tipo de lugar es Mama Rumba?
2. ¿Le gusta a Miguel ir a Mama Rumba? ¿Por qué?
3. ¿Sabe bailar salsa Rubén?
4. ¿Por qué no debe preocuparse (*worry*) Rubén?
5. ¿Qué van a hacer los amigos el domingo?

---

*Some Spanish speakers omit the **al** *after* **jugar** *when talking about playing sports:* **jugar fútbol** *vs.* **jugar al fútbol.**

ENFOQUE CULTURAL

 Colombia

¡Fíjese!

- Colombia obtuvo su independencia de España en 1819, bajo la dirección de Simón Bolívar. Bolívar fue declarado el primer presidente de la independiente República de la Gran Colombia.
- Colombia produce más oro que cualquier[a] otro país sudamericano y tiene los yacimientos[b] de platino[c] más grandes del mundo. Las esmeraldas también son un producto minero importante.
- Aunque el café es reconocido[d] como el producto agrícola principal de exportación de Colombia, en los años noventa lo sobrepasó[e] el petróleo como primer producto de exportación.
- Aproximadamente un 14 por ciento de la población colombiana es de origen africano.
- Las misteriosas estatuas de piedra de San Agustín fueron creadas por una cultura indígena de la cual[f] se sabe muy poco. Se cree que las estatuas son del siglo VI (sexto) antes de Cristo. Una de las estatuas representa un pájaro con una serpiente en el pico,[g] imagen muy similar a la de una leyenda azteca.

[a]any [b]deposits [c]platinum [d]recognized [e]surpassed [f]de… of which
[g]beak

Personas famosas: Juanes

Juanes es un fenómeno colombiano en el mundo de la música. Nacido[a] en Medellín, Colombia, Juanes fundó el grupo Ekhymosis a los 14 años. El grupo se desintegró después de doce años y Juanes empezó su carrera como solista con el álbum *Fíjate bien*.[b] En los últimos años, Juanes ha ganado[c] varios premios[d] latinoamericanos e internacionales, entre ellos nueve Grammy Latinos, cinco Premios MTV y seis Premios Lo Nuestro. En 2002 tenía siete nominaciones en los Grammy Latino y salió de las ceremonias en Los Ángeles con tres Grammys: Mejor Canción Rock, Mejor Nuevo Artista y Mejor Solista Vocal para Álbum en Rock. En su gira[e] por Colombia en la primavera de 2003, dedicó su concierto en Bogotá a las víctimas de la violencia y a los que tratan de proteger[f] los derechos[g] y la vida de los colombianos.

[a]Born [b]Fíjate… *Pay close attention* [c]ha… *has won* [d]*prizes* [e]*tour*
[f]tratan… *try to protect* [g]*rights*

Estatuas de piedra, de San Agustín

Learn more about Colombia with the Video, the Interactive CD-ROM, and the Online Learning Center (www.mhhe.com/quetal7).

PASO 4

PASO FINAL

 A LEER

ESTRATEGIA: Recognizing Derivative Adjectives

In previous chapters of *¿Qué tal?,* you learned to recognize cognates, word endings, and new words that are related to familiar words. In this chapter, you will learn about derivative adjectives, a large group of adjectives derived from verbs. These adjectives end in **-ado/a** or **-ido/a.** You can often guess their meaning if you know the related verb. For example: **conocer** (*to know*) → **conocido** (*known, famous*); **preparar** (*to prepare*) → **preparado** (*prepared*).

In the following reading there are several **-do** adjectives. Try to guess their meaning based on the related verb and the context.

Noctámbulos

Las ciudades españolas se están adaptando con rapidez a la llamada «sociedad de las veinticuatro horas». Cualquier[a] necesidad puede ser cubierta[b] a cualquiera hora. Esto es algo que en países como Estados Unidos, Holanda o Canadá hace tiempo que es[c] una realidad, pero en España es ahora cuando se está produciendo el *boom* de las empresas de servicios veinticuatro horas. Es lo que llamamos la «sociedad de las veinticuatro horas». Ya no sólo basta con[d] poder comer de madrugada,[e] bien sea en un restaurante o pidiendo que nos lleven la comida a casa. Por eso la <u>oferta</u> se está <u>ampliando</u> notablemente. En los «*work center*» se puede <u>realizar</u> todo tipo de trabajos a cualquier hora, desde una simple fotocopia a una presentación completa en «PowerPoint».

[a]*Any* [b]*covered, taken care of* [c]*hace... for some time has been* [d]*Ya... It's no longer enough* [e]*de... late at night*

Un gimnasio que está abierto las veinticuatro horas, en Barcelona, España

Una cerrajería (locksmith) *que ayuda a sus clientes a cualquier hora del día, en Madrid, España*

Pero no son los únicos servicios que podemos encontrar de noche. Ya hay gimnasios <u>abiertos</u> hasta la madrugada y videoclubes nocturnos que incluyen cajeros expendedores[f] de películas que funcionan las veinticuatro horas. Pero, por supuesto, también podemos <u>hacer la compra</u> de madrugada en un supermercado. De hecho,[g] en una encuesta[h] realizada en Reino Unido[i] más de un millón de personas declaró que sólo podía hacer la compra a partir de[j] las diez de la noche. En plena era de las comunicaciones[k] no podíamos dejar de mencionar los cibercafés, que en algunos casos abren hasta bien entrada la madrugada.[l]

En total, entre un 10 y un 20 por ciento de la población activa, en función de los distintos sectores de producción, realiza toda o parte de su jornada laboral[m] por la noche. En España, son casi 2 millones de personas las que trabajan de noche, sin olvidarnos de quienes optan por el ocio:[n] el 63 por ciento de los jóvenes dedican su tiempo libre a salir de noche, porcentaje que se va reduciendo con la edad.

[f]cajeros... *dispensing machines* [g]De... *In fact* [h]*survey* [i]Reino... *United Kingdom* [j]a... *después de*
[k]En... *At the height of the communications age* [l]hasta... *well into the early morning* [m]jornada... *work day* [n]*leisure*

Comprensión

A. ¿Cierto o falso? Prepárese para explicar sus respuestas.

1. La sociedad española está cambiando para aceptar un horario mucho más flexible y adaptable.
2. La variedad de empresas que abren las veinticuatro horas en España está limitada.
3. También hay servicios para los que salen a divertirse hasta bien entrada la madrugada.

B. Palabras relacionadas

PASO 1   ¿De qué verbos se derivan los siguientes adjetivos del artículo?

1. llamada _____
2. realizada _____
3. entrada _____

PASO 2   Hay dos formas derivadas irregulares en la lectura. ¿Puede identificar los verbos de que se derivan estas palabras?

1. cubierta _____
2. abriertos _____

 A ESCRIBIR

A. ¿Y Ud.? ¿Qué servicios de las veinticuatro horas necesita o usa Ud.? ¿Cuáles son algunos de los servicios disponibles (*available*) para los estudiantes de esta universidad? ¿Tiene su comunidad muchos servicios abiertos las veinticuatro horas o hasta muy tarde? Describa brevemente los servicios de su universidad y/o comunidad y explique cuáles usa Ud. y por qué.

B. La sociedad de las 24 horas. La llamada «sociedad de las veinticuatro horas» es bastante común en este país. Esto se ve en los horarios de muchos restaurantes, gimnasios, tiendas, talleres y otras empresas. De hecho, hay una cadena (*chain*) de clubes de salud que se llama *24 Hour Fitness*. ¿Cree Ud. que este cambio social es bueno o malo? ¿Por qué? Escriba una breve composición de 150 palabras que presente las ventajas (*advantages*) y desventajas de este fenómeno. Dé ejemplos específicos.

GRAMÁTICA

To review the grammar points presented in this chapter, refer to the indicated grammar presentations. You'll find further practice of these structures in the Workbook/Laboratory Manual, on the Interactive CD-ROM, and on the *¿Qué tal?* Online Learning Center (www.mhhe.com/quetal7).

26 Descriptions and Habitual Actions in the Past—Imperfect of Regular and Irregular Verbs

You should know the imperfect forms of all verbs. What are the three verbs that are irregular in the imperfect?

27 Expressing Extremes—Superlatives

Do you know how to express that something is *the best* or *the most*?

28 Getting Information—Summary of Interrogative Words

You should know how to form questions with question words and how to express English *what?* with **¿qué?** or **¿cuál?**

VOCABULARIO

Practice this vocabulary with digital flash cards on the Online Learning Center (www.mhhe.com/quetal7).

Los verbos

aburrirse	to get bored
dejar (en)	to leave (behind) (in [*a place*])
pegar (gu)	to hit
pelear	to fight
sonar (ue)	to ring; to sound

jugar (ue) (gu) a las cartas	to play cards
ser (*irreg.*) aburrido/a / divertido/a	to be boring/fun
visitar un museo	to visit a museum

Repaso: dar (*irreg.*) / hacer (*irreg.*) una fiesta, hacer (*irreg.*) *camping*, jugar (ue) (gu) al ajedrez, tomar el sol

Pasatiempos, diversiones y aficiones

la afición	pastime, fun activity, hobby
el deporte	sport
la diversión	entertainment, amusement
el pasatiempo	pastime, hobby
los ratos libres	spare (free) time
dar (*irreg.*) un paseo	to take a walk
hacer (*irreg.*) un *picnic*	to have a picnic
hacer (*irreg.*) planes para + *inf.*	to make plans to (*do something*)
ir (*irreg.*)...	to go . . .
al cine / a ver una película	to the movies / to see a movie
a una discoteca / a un bar	to a disco / to a bar
al teatro / a un concierto	to the theater / to a concert

Los deportes

el ciclismo	bicycling
el fútbol	soccer
el fútbol americano	football
el/la jugador(a)	player
la natación	swimming
el partido	match, game

Cognados: el basquetbol, el béisbol, el golf, el hockey, el tenis, el vólibol

correr	to run; to jog
entrenar	to practice, train
esquiar (esquío)	to ski
ganar	to win
montar a caballo	to ride a horse
pasear en bicicleta	to ride a bicycle
patinar	to skate
patinar en línea	to rollerblade

ser (*irreg.*) **aficionado/**
  a (a)   to be a fan (of)

Repaso: jugar (ue) (gu) (al) (*sport*), nadar, perder
  (ie), practicar (qu)

Algunos aparatos domésticos

la aspiradora	vacuum cleaner
la cafetera	coffeemaker
el congelador	freezer
la estufa	stove
el horno de microondas	microwave oven
la lavadora	washing machine
el lavaplatos	dishwasher
el refrigerador	refrigerator
la secadora	clothes dryer
la tostadora	toaster

Los quehaceres domésticos

barrer (el piso)	to sweep (the floor)
hacer (*irreg.*) la cama	to make the bed
lavar (las ventanas, los platos, la ropa)	to wash (the windows, the dishes, the clothes)
limpiar la casa (entera)	to clean the (whole) house
pasar la aspiradora	to vacuum
pintar (las paredes)	to paint (the walls)
planchar la ropa	to iron clothing
poner (*irreg.*) la mesa	to set the table
quitar la mesa	to clear the table

sacar (qu) la basura	to take out the trash
sacudir los muebles	to dust the furniture

Otros sustantivos

el aparato doméstico	home appliance
la costumbre	custom, habit
la dirección	address
la escuela	school
el grado	grade, year (*in school*)
el/la niñero/a	baby-sitter
la niñez	childhood
el quehacer doméstico	household chore

Adjetivos

deportivo/a	sporting, sports (*adj.*); sports-loving
pesado/a	boring; difficult

Palabras adicionales

de joven	as a youth
de niño/a	as a child
mientras	while
tocarle (qu) a uno	to be someone's turn

Repaso: ¿a qué hora?, ¿adónde?, ¿cómo?, ¿cuál(es)?,
  ¿cuándo?, ¿cuánto/a?, ¿cuántos/as?, ¿de dónde?,
  ¿de quién(es)?, ¿dónde?, ¿por qué?, ¿qué?,
  ¿quién(es)?

La salud°

°**La...** *Health*

Un farmacéutico y su cliente, en una farmacia en Venezuela

La… Health and well-being

LA SALUD Y EL BIENESTAR°

dormir (ue, u) lo suficiente

comer equilibradamente

hacer (*irreg.*) ejercicios aeróbicos

el cerebro

el cerebro

la cabeza

la boca

la garganta

los pulmones

Josefa

el estómago

Enrique

correr

caminar

el corazón

Laura

la rueda de molino

El cuerpo humano

el diente	tooth
la nariz	nose
el oído	inner ear
el ojo	eye
la oreja	(outer) ear

Para cuidar de la salud

cuidarse	to take care of oneself
dejar de + *inf.*	to stop (*doing something*)
hacer (*irreg.*) **ejercicio**	to exercise; to get exercise
llevar gafas / lentes de contacto	to wear glasses / contact lenses
llevar una vida sana/tranquila	to lead a healthy/calm life
practicar (qu) deportes	to practice, play sports

■ Conversación

A. Asociaciones ¿Qué partes del cuerpo humano asocia Ud. con las siguientes palabras? A veces hay más de una respuesta posible.

1. un ataque
2. comer
3. cantar
4. las gafas

5. pensar
6. la digestión
7. el amor
8. fumar

9. la música
10. el perfume
11. un beso (*kiss*)
12. una flor

B. Más asociaciones. ¿Qué palabras asocia Ud. con las siguientes partes del cuerpo?

1. los ojos   **3.** la boca   **5.** el estómago
2. los dientes   **4.** el oído   **6.** la nariz

C. Hablando de la salud

PASO 1   ¿Qué significan para Ud. las siguientes oraciones?

MODELO: Se debe comer equilibradamente. →
Eso quiere decir (*means*) que es necesario comer muchas
verduras, que… También significa que no debemos comer
muchos dulces o…

<table><tr><td>**Palabras y frases útiles**</td></tr><tr><td>**Eso quiere decir…**
Esto significa que…
También…</td></tr></table>

1. Se debe dormir lo suficiente todas las noches.
2. Hay que hacer ejercicio.
3. Es necesario llevar una vida tranquila.
4. En general, uno debe cuidarse mucho.
5. Es importante llevar una vida sana.

PASO 2   ¿Lleva Ud. una vida sana? Dígale a un compañero / una compañera cómo vive, usando frases del **Paso 1** y del **Vocabulario.**

MODELO: Creo que llevo una vida sana porque como una dieta
equilibrada. No como muchos dulces, excepto en los días
festivos como la Navidad…

PASO 3   Ahora cambie su narración para describir lo que hacía de niño/a. ¿Qué hacía y qué *no* hacía Ud.? Debe organizar las ideas lógicamente.

MODELO: De niño, no llevaba una vida muy sana. Comía muchos dulces.
También odiaba las frutas y verduras…

NOTA CULTURAL

La medicina en los países hispanos

Los hispanos pueden **consultar a otros profesionales de la salud,** además de los médicos, especialmente **en relación con enfermedades** que no son graves. La gente consulta a los **farmacéuticos** con frecuencia, pues estos son profesionales con un riguroso entrenamiento universitario en farmacología. Además, **hay farmacias en cada barrio,** lo cual hace que haya[a] una relación bien establecida entre los farmacéuticos y sus clientes.

En las ciudades y pueblos hispanos siempre hay algunas farmacias abiertas a todas las horas del día. Se establecen horarios de turnos, y la farmacia que está abierta a horas en que las otras están cerradas se llama **farmacia de guardia.** Se puede saber cuáles son las farmacias de guardia a través del periódico o simplemente yendo a la farmacia más cercana, donde siempre hay una lista de todas las farmacias.

Otros profesionales al cuidado de la salud muy solicitados son los **practicantes,** que son enfermeros o estudiantes de medicina con varios años de estudio, que están capacitados[b] para poner inyecciones o hacer visitas a domicilio para **tratamientos sencillos.**

Finalmente, se debe mencionar la relativa popularidad de **remedios tradicionales,** como la homeopatía. Aunque hay expertos homeópatas con años de entrenamiento, también existe un repertorio popular de **remedios naturales** básicos para enfermedades o molestias[c] cotidianas, conocimientos[d] que se transmiten de generación a generación.

[a]lo… *which creates*   [b]*trained*   [c]*nuisances*   [d]*knowledge*

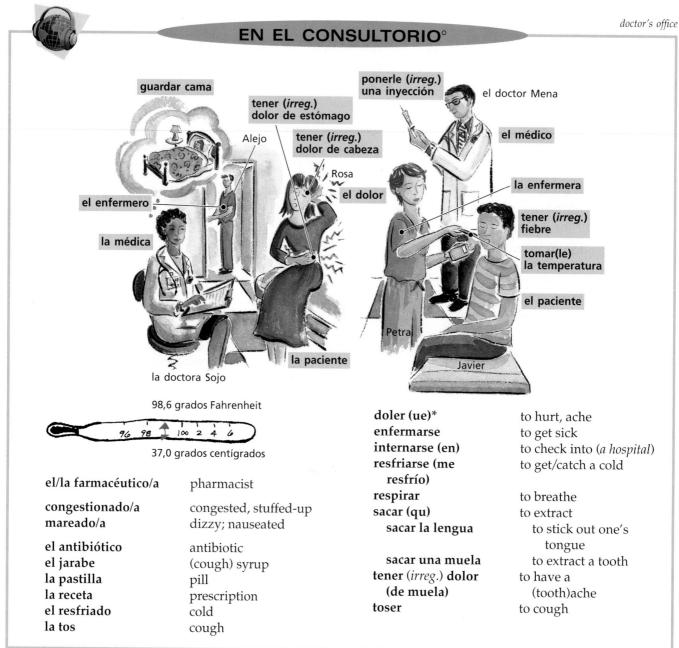

EN EL CONSULTORIO° *doctor's office*

guardar cama

tener (*irreg.*)
dolor de estómago

Alejo

tener (*irreg.*)
dolor de cabeza

Rosa

el dolor

el enfermero

la médica

la doctora Sojo

la paciente

ponerle (*irreg.*)
una inyección   el doctor Mena

el médico

la enfermera

tener (*irreg.*)
fiebre

tomar(le)
la temperatura

el paciente

Petra

Javier

98,6 grados Fahrenheit

96 98 100 2 4 6

37,0 grados centígrados

el/la farmacéutico/a	pharmacist
congestionado/a	congested, stuffed-up
mareado/a	dizzy; nauseated
el antibiótico	antibiotic
el jarabe	(cough) syrup
la pastilla	pill
la receta	prescription
el resfriado	cold
la tos	cough

doler (ue)*	to hurt, ache
enfermarse	to get sick
internarse (en)	to check into (*a hospital*)
resfriarse (me resfrío)	to get/catch a cold
respirar	to breathe
sacar (qu)	to extract
sacar la lengua	to stick out one's tongue
sacar una muela	to extract a tooth
tener (*irreg.*) dolor (de muela)	to have a (tooth)ache
toser	to cough

■ **Conversación**

A. Estudio de palabras.   Complete las siguientes oraciones con una palabra de la misma (*same*) familia que la palabra en letras cursivas (*italics*).

1. Si me *resfrío,* tengo _____.
2. La *respiración* ocurre cuando alguien _____.
3. Si me _____, estoy *enfermo/a.* Un(a) _____ me toma la temperatura.
4. Cuando alguien *tose,* se oye una _____.
5. Si me *duele* el estómago, tengo un _____ de estómago.

———————————

*Doler *is used like* gustar: Me duele la cabeza. Me duelen los ojos.*

B. Situaciones. Describa Ud. la situación de estas personas. ¿Dónde y con quiénes están? ¿Qué síntomas tienen? ¿Qué van a hacer?

1.  2.  3.

1. Anamari está muy bien de salud. Nunca le duele(n) _____. Nunca tiene _____. Siempre _____. Más tarde, ella va a _____.
2. Martín tiene _____. Debe _____. El dentista va a _____. Después, Martín va a _____.
3. A Inés le duele(n) _____. Tiene _____. El médico y la enfermera van a _____. Luego, Inés tiene que _____.

NOTA COMUNICATIVA

The Good News . . . The Bad News . . .

To describe general qualities or characteristics of something, use **lo** with the masculine singular form of an adjective.

lo bueno / lo malo   lo más importante   lo mejor / lo peor   lo mismo

This structure has a number of English equivalents, especially in colloquial speech.

lo bueno = the good thing/part/news, what's good

C. Ventajas y desventajas. (*Advantages and Disadvantages.*) Casi todas las cosas tienen un aspecto bueno y otro malo.

PASO 1   ¿Qué es lo bueno y lo malo (o lo peor y lo mejor) de las siguientes situaciones?

1. tener un resfriado
2. ir a una universidad cerca/lejos del hogar familiar (*family home*)
3. tener hijos cuando uno es joven (entre 18 y 25 años)
4. ser muy rico
5. ir a un consultorio médico
6. ir al consultorio de un dentista

PASO 2   Compare sus respuestas con las de sus compañeros. ¿Dijeron algo que Ud. no consideró?

Need more practice?

- Workbook/Laboratory Manual
- Interactive CD-ROM
- Online Learning Center (www.mhhe.com/quetal7)

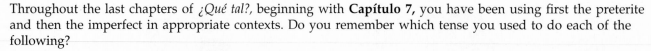

¿Recuerda Ud.?

Throughout the last chapters of *¿Qué tal?*, beginning with **Capítulo 7,** you have been using first the preterite and then the imperfect in appropriate contexts. Do you remember which tense you used to do each of the following?

1. to tell what you did yesterday
2. to tell what you used to do when you were in grade school
3. to explain the situation or condition that caused you to do something
4. to tell what someone did as the result of a situation
5. to talk about the way things used to be
6. to describe an action that was in progress

If you understand those uses of the preterite and the imperfect, the following summary of their uses will not contain much that is new information for you.

29 Narrating in the Past **Using the Preterite and the Imperfect**

En el consultorio de la Dra. Méndez

Marta, la hija de Lola y Manolo, se siente mal y su madre la lleva al consultorio de la Dra. Méndez.

DRA. MÉNDEZ: ¿Cuándo *empezó* a sentirse mal su hija?
LOLA: Ayer por la tarde. *Estaba* congestionada, *tosía* mucho y *se quejaba* de que le *dolían* el cuerpo y la cabeza.
DRA. MÉNDEZ: ¿Y le *notó* algo de fiebre?
LOLA: Sí. Por la noche le *tomé* la temperatura y *tenía* treinta y ocho grados.
DRA. MÉNDEZ: A ver… Tal vez necesito ponerle una inyección…
MARTA: Eh… bueno… ¡Creo que ahora me encuentro un poco mejor!

Comprensión

In the preceding dialogue, locate all of the verbs that do the following.

1. indicate actions
2. indicate conditions or descriptions

When speaking about the past in English, you choose different past tense forms to use, depending on the context: *I wrote letters, I was writing letters, I used to write letters,* and so on. Similarly, you can use either the preterite or the imperfect in many Spanish sentences, depending on the meaning you wish to convey. Often the question is: How do you view the action or state of being?

In Dr. Méndez's office *Marta, Lola and Manolo's daughter, feels sick, and her mother takes her to Dr. Méndez's office.* DR. MÉNDEZ: *When did your daughter begin to feel ill?* LOLA: *Yesterday afternoon. She was stuffed up, she was coughing a lot, and she was complaining that her body and head were hurting.* DR. MÉNDEZ: *And did you note any fever?* LOLA: *Yes. At night I took her temperature and it was thirty-eight degrees.* DR. MÉNDEZ: *Let's see . . . Perhaps I'll need to give her a shot . . .* MARTA: *Um . . . well . . . I think I feel a little bit better now!*

PAST	-------------------- Present -------------------- Future
preterite	**present**
imperfect	**present progressive**
	formal commands

Preterite	Imperfect
• beginning/end of past action	• habitual/repeated action
• completed action	• progress of a past action
• series of completed actions	• background details
• interrupt**ing** action	• interrupt**ed** action
• the action on the "stage"	• the backdrop (setup) of the "stage"

Beginning/End vs. Habitual

Use the preterite to . . .

• tell about the beginning or the end of a past action.

El sábado pasado, el partido de fútbol **empezó** a la una. **Terminó** a las cuatro. El entrenador **habló** a las cinco.
Last Saturday, the soccer game began at one. It ended at four. The coach spoke (began to speak) at five.

Use the imperfect to . . .

• talk about the habitual nature of an action (something you always did).

Había un partido todos los sábados. Muchas personas **jugaban** todas las semanas.
There was a game every Saturday. Many people played every week.

Completed vs. Ongoing

Use the preterite to . . .

• express an action that is viewed as completed.

El partido **duró** tres horas. **Ganaron** Los Lobos, de Villalegre.
The game lasted three hours. The Lobos of Villalegre won.

Use the imperfect to . . .

• tell what was happening when another action took place and tell about simultaneous events (with **mientras** = *while*).

Yo no vi el final del partido. **Estaba** en la cocina cuando **terminó.**
I didn't see the end of the game. I was in the kitchen when it ended.
Mientras mi amigo **veía** el partido, **hablaba** con su novia.
While my friend was watching the game, he was talking with his girlfriend.

Series of Completed Actions vs. Background

Use the preterite to . . .

- express a series of completed actions.

Durante el partido, los jugadores **corrieron, saltaron** y **gritaron.**
During the game, the players ran, jumped, and shouted.

Use the imperfect to . . .

- give background details of many kinds: time, location, weather, mood, age, physical and mental characteristics.

Llovía un poco durante el partido. Todos los jugadores **eran** jóvenes; **tenían** 17 ó 18 años. ¡Y todos **esperaban** ganar!
It rained a little bit during the game. All the players were young; they were 17 or 18 years old. And all of them hoped to win!

Changes in Meaning

Remember that, when used in the preterite, **saber, conocer, querer,** and **poder** have English equivalents different from that of the infinitives (see **Capítulo 8**). In the imperfect, the English equivalents of these verbs do not differ from the infinitive meanings.

Anoche **conocí** a Roberto.
*Last night I **met** Roberto.*

¿Anoche? Yo pensaba que ya lo **conocías.**
*Last night? I thought you already **knew** him.*

Interrupt**ing** vs. Interrupt**ed**

The preterite and the imperfect frequently occur in the same sentence. In the first sentence the imperfect tells what was happening when another action—conveyed by the preterite—broke the continuity of the ongoing activity. In the second sentence, the preterite reports the action that took place because of a condition—described by the imperfect—that was in progress or in existence at that time.

Miguel **estudiaba** cuando **sonó** el teléfono.
Miguel was studying when the phone rang.

Olivia **comió** tanto porque **tenía** mucha hambre.
Olivia ate so much because she was very hungry.

Action vs. the Stage (Background)/Conditions/Ongoing

The preterite and imperfect are also used together in the presentation of an event. The preterite narrates the action while the imperfect sets the stage, describes the conditions that caused the action, or emphasizes the continuing nature of a particular action.

Era un día hermoso. **Hacía** mucho sol pero no **hacía** mucho calor. Como no **tenía** que trabajar en la oficina, **compré** unas flores de primavera y **salí** vestida de camiseta y pantalones cortos para trabajar todo el día en el jardín.
It was a beautiful day. It was very sunny but it wasn't very hot. Since I didn't have to work in the office, I bought some spring flowers and I went out dressed in a T-shirt and shorts to work in the garden all day.

■ Práctica

A. En el consultorio. What did your doctor do the last time you had an appointment with him or her? Assume that you had the following conditions and match them with the appropriate procedure.

CONDICIONES: (yo / amí)

1. _____ Tenía mucho calor y temblaba.
2. _____ Me dolía la garganta.
3. _____ Tenía un poco de congestión en el pecho (*chest*).
4. _____ Creía que estaba anémico/a.
5. _____ No sabía lo que tenía.
6. _____ Necesitaba medicinas.
7. _____ Sólo necesitaba un chequeo (*checkup*) rutinario.

ACCIONES: El médico…

a. me hizo muchas preguntas.
b. me escribió una receta.
c. me tomó la temperatura.
d. me auscultó (*listened to*) los pulmones y el corazón.
e. me analizó la sangre (*blood*).
f. me hizo sacar la lengua.
g. me hizo toser.

NOTA COMUNICATIVA

Words and Expressions That Indicate the Use of Preterite and Imperfect

Certain words and expressions are frequently associated with the preterite, others with the imperfect.

Some words often associated with the preterite are:

> **ayer, anteayer** (*the day before yesterday*), **anoche** (*last night*)
> **una vez, dos veces** (*twice*)…
> **el año pasado, el lunes pasado…**
> **de repente** (*suddenly*)

Some words often associated with the imperfect are:

> **todos los días, todos los lunes…**
> **siempre, frecuentemente**
> **mientras**
> **de niño/a, de joven**

Some English equivalents also associated with the imperfect are:

> *was _____ -ing, were _____ -ing* (in English)
> *used to, would* (when *would* implies *used to* in English)

As you continue to practice preterite and imperfect, these expressions can help you determine which tense to use.

These words do not *automatically* cue either tense, however. The most important consideration is the meaning that the speaker wishes to convey.

Ayer cenamos temprano.	*Yesterday we had dinner early.*
Ayer cenábamos cuando Juan llamó.	*Yesterday we were having dinner when Juan called.*
Jugaba al fútbol **de niño.**	*He played soccer as a child.*
Empezó a jugar al fútbol **de niño.**	*He began to play soccer as a child.*

B. Pequeñas historias. Complete the following brief paragraphs with the appropriate phrases from the lists. Before you begin, it is a good idea to look at the drawing that accompanies each paragraph and to scan through the complete paragraph to get the gist of it, even though you may not understand everything the first time you read it.

1. estaba leyendo había   salí   tenía
 estaban apagadas[a] me levanté se apagaron[b]

Eran las once de la noche cuando ¡de repente ＿＿＿[1] todas las luces[c] de la casa! Puse el libro que ＿＿＿[2] en la mesa y ＿＿＿[3] para investigar la causa del incidente. La verdad es que ＿＿＿[4] mucho miedo. ＿＿＿[5] a la calle y vi que ＿＿＿[6] las luces de todo el barrio.[d] En ese momento me di cuenta[e] que ＿＿＿[7] un problema con la electricidad en toda la ciudad.

[a]out [b]se... went out [c]lights [d]neighborhood [e]me... I realized

2. dio   estaba   intentaba[a] tomarle puso
 esperaba examinó llegó   se sintió

La niña tosía mientras que la enfermera ＿＿＿[1] la temperatura. La madre de la niña ＿＿＿[2] pacientemente. Por fin ＿＿＿[3] la médica. Le ＿＿＿[4] la garganta a la niña, le ＿＿＿[5] una inyección y le ＿＿＿[6] a su madre una receta para un jarabe. La madre todavía ＿＿＿[7] muy preocupada, pero inmediatamente después que la médica le habló, ＿＿＿[8] más tranquila.

[a]tried to

C. Rubén y Soledad. Read the following paragraph at least once to familiarize yourself with the sequence of events, and look at the drawing. Then reread the paragraph, giving the proper form of the verbs in parentheses in the preterite or the imperfect, according to the needs of each sentence and the context of the paragraph as a whole.

Rubén estaba estudiando cuando Soledad entró en el cuarto. Le (preguntar[1]) a Rubén si (querer[2]) ir al cine con ella. Rubén le (decir[3]) que sí porque se (sentir[4]) un poco aburrido con sus estudios. Los dos (salir[5]) en seguida[a] para el cine. (Ver[6]) una película cómica y (reírse[7]) mucho. Luego, como (hacer[8]) frío, (entrar[9]) en su café favorito, El Gato Negro, y (tomar[10]) un chocolate. (Ser[11]) las dos de la mañana cuando por fin (regresar[12]) a casa. Soledad (acostarse[13]) inmediatamente porque (estar[14]) cansada, pero Rubén (empezar[15]) a estudiar otra vez.

[a]en... right away

Comprensión. Now answer the following questions based on the paragraph about Rubén and Soledad. ¡OJO! A question is not always answered in the same tense as that in which it is asked. Remember this, especially when you are asked to explain why something happened.

1. ¿Qué hacía Rubén cuando Soledad entró?
2. ¿Qué le preguntó Soledad a Rubén?
3. ¿Por qué dijo Rubén que sí?
4. ¿Les gustó la película? ¿Por qué?
5. ¿Por qué tomaron un chocolate?
6. ¿Regresaron a casa a las tres?
7. ¿Qué hicieron cuando llegaron a casa?

D. Caperucita Roja

PASO 1 Retell this familiar story, based on the drawings, sentences, and cues that accompany each drawing, using the imperfect or preterite of the verbs in parentheses. Add as many details as you can. Using context, try to guess the meaning of words that are glossed with ¿ ?.

Vocabulario útil

abalanzarse (c) sobre (to pounce on)
avisar (to warn)
dispararle (to shoot at [*someone/something*])
enterarse de (to find out about)
esconderse (to hide)
huir (huyó) (to flee)
querer (*irreg.*) (to love)
saltar (to jump)

1.  2.  3.

1. Érase una vez[a] una niña hermosa que (llamarse[1]) Caperucita Roja. Todos los animales del bosque[b] (ser[2]) sus amigos y Caperucita Roja los (querer[3]) mucho.
2. Un día su mamá le (decir[4]): —Lleva en seguida esta jarrita de miel[c] a casa de tu abuelita. Ten cuidado[d] con el lobo[e] feroz.
3. En el bosque, el lobo (salir[5]) a hablar con la niña. Le (preguntar[6]): —¿Adónde vas, Caperucita? Esta le (contestar[7]) dulcemente:[f] —Voy a casa de mi abuelita.

4.  5.  6.  7.

4. —Pues, si vas por este sendero,[g] vas a llegar antes, (decir[8]) el malvado[h] lobo. Él (irse[9]) por otro camino más corto.
5. El lobo (llegar[10]) primero a la casa de la abuelita y (entrar[11]) silenciosamente. La abuelita (tener[12]) mucho miedo. (*Ella:* Saltar[13]) de la cama y (correr[14]) a esconderse.
6. Caperucita Roja (llegar[15]) por fin a la casa de la abuelita. (*Ella:* Encontrar[16]) a su «abuelita», que (estar[17]) en la cama. Le (decir[18]): —¡Qué dientes tan largos tienes! —¡Son para comerte mejor!— (decir[19]) su «abuelita».
7. Una ardilla[i] del bosque (enterarse[20]) del peligro. Por eso (avisar[21]) a un cazador.[j]

[a]¿ ? [b]¿ ? [c]*jarrita... jar of honey* [d]*Ten... Be careful* [e]¿ ? [f]*sweetly* [g]*path* [h]¿ ? [i]¿ ? [j]¿ ?

8.  9.  10.

8. El lobo (saltar[22]) de la cama y (abalanzarse[23]) sobre Caperucita. Ella (salir[24]) de la casa corriendo y pidiendo socorro[k] desesperadamente.
9. El cazador (ver[25]) lo que (ocurrir[26]). (*Él:* Dispararle[27]) al lobo y le (hacer[28]) huir.
10. Caperucita (regresar[29]) a la casa de su abuelita. La (*ella:* abrazar[30]) y le (prometer[31]) escuchar siempre los consejos de su mamá.

[k]*help*

PASO 2 Hay varias versiones del cuento de Caperucita Roja. La que Ud. acaba de leer termina felizmente, pero otras no. Con otros dos compañeros, vuelva a contar la historia, empezando por el dibujo número 7. Inventen un diálogo más largo entre Caperucita y el lobo y cambien por completo el final del cuento.

Más vocabulario útil

atacar (qu) (to attack)
comérselo/la (to eat something up)
matar (to kill)

Need more practice?

- Workbook/Laboratory Manual
- Interactive CD-ROM
- Online Learning Center (www.mhhe.com/quetal7)

■ Conversación

A. **El primer día.** Dé Ud. sus impresiones del primer día de clases en la universidad. Use estas preguntas como guía.

1. ¿Cuál fue la primera clase? ¿A qué hora era la clase y dónde era?
2. ¿Vino a clase con alguien? ¿Ya tenía su libro de texto o lo compró después?
3. ¿Qué hizo Ud. después de entrar en la sala de clase? ¿Qué hacía el profesor / la profesora?
4. ¿A quién conoció Ud. aquel día? ¿Ya conocía a algunos miembros de la clase? ¿A quiénes?
5. ¿Aprendió Ud. mucho durante la clase? ¿Ya sabía algo de esa materia?
6. ¿Le gustó el profesor / la profesora? ¿Por qué sí o por qué no? ¿Cómo era?
7. ¿Cómo se sentía durante la clase? ¿Nervioso/a? ¿aburrido/a? ¿cómodo/a?
8. ¿Les dio tarea el profesor / la profesora? ¿Pudo Ud. hacerla fácilmente?
9. Su primera impresión de la clase y del profesor / de la profesora, ¿fue válida o cambió con el tiempo? ¿Por qué?

B. Entrevista. Unas preguntas sobre el pasado

PASO 1   Con un compañero / una compañera, haga y conteste las siguientes preguntas.

¿Cuántos años tenías cuando... ?

1. aprendiste a pasear en bicicleta
2. hiciste tu primer viaje en avión
3. tuviste tu primera cita (*date*)
4. empezaste a afeitarte
5. conseguiste tu licencia de manejar (*driver's license*)
6. abriste una cuenta corriente (*checking account*)
7. dejaste de crecer (*grow*)

PASO 2   Con otro compañero / otra compañera, haga y conteste estas preguntas.

¿Cuántos años tenías cuando tus padres... ?

1. te dejaron cruzar la calle (*street*) solo/a
2. te permitieron ir de compras a solas (*alone*)
3. te dejaron acostarte después de las nueve
4. te dejaron quedarte en casa sin niñero/a
5. te permitieron usar la estufa
6. te dejaron ver una película «*R*»
7. te dejaron conseguir un trabajo

PASO 3   Ahora, en grupos de cuatro, comparen sus respuestas. ¿Son muy diferentes las respuestas que dieron? ¿Quién del grupo tiene los padres más estrictos? ¿los menos estrictos?

En los Estados Unidos y el Canadá

Edward James Olmos: Actor y activista de la comunidad

El conocido **actor** de origen mexicano, Edward James Olmos (Los Ángeles, 1947–), tiene en su historia profesional papeles inolvidables[a] como el de Jaime Escalante en *Stand and Deliver* y el de policía en la famosa película cultista[b] *Blade Runner*. Además es un reconocido[c] **productor** y fue **director** y **guionista**[d] de la película *American Me*, sobre las pandillas[e] de Los Ángeles. Ha recibido los premios[f] Golden Globe y Emmy.

Pero el Sr. Olmos no es sólo un artista sino también un destacado[g] **líder de la**

Edward James Olmos

comunidad latina en los Estados Unidos. Su **trabajo humanitario** y **comunitario** demuestra[h] un profundo compromiso[i] a favor de **la juventud** y **la salud** y contra la violencia de las pandillas y el racismo. Entre los muchos cargos que ha desempeñado[j] están los de embajador[k] de los Estados Unidos en UNICEF, portavoz[l] nacional de la Fundación Juvenil contra la Diabetes, de la Fundación Alerta contra el SIDA[m] y del Registro de Votantes. Además es miembro del comité de varios hospitales para niños y también del Concejo Nacional de Adopción.

[a]papeles... *unforgettable roles* [b]*cult* [c]*well-known* [d]*scriptwriter* [e]*gangs* [f]Ha... *He has received the awards* [g]*distinguished* [h]*shows* [i]*commitment* [j]Entre... *Among the many positions he has held* [k]*ambassador* [l]*spokesperson* [m]Fundación... *AIDS Awareness Foundation*

LITERATURA: Rómulo Gallegos

Rómulo Gallegos
(1884–1969)

Sobre el autor: *Rómulo Gallegos nació en Caracas, Venezuela. En su novela más conocida,* Doña Bárbara, *el paisaje*[a] *de los llanos*[b] *venezolanos es el protagonista. Esto es un reflejo de la lucha*[c] *del hombre contra el enorme poder*[d] *de la naturaleza en América. El argumento*[e] *de la novela presenta la lucha entre la barbarie,*[f] *representada por doña Bárbara, y la civilización, representada por el personaje Santos Luzardo. El siguiente fragmento es de la novela* Doña Bárbara (*1*[a] *Parte Cap. VIII*) (*1929*).

La llanura[g] es bella y terrible a la vez; en ella caben[h] holgadamente,[i] hermosa vida y muerte[j] atroz; esta[k] acecha[l] por todas partes, pero allí nadie le teme.[m]

[a]*landscape* [b]*plains* [c]*struggle* [d]*power* [e]*plot* [f]*barbarism* [g]*plain* [h]*fit* [i]*comfortably* [j]*death* [k]*she (the latter)* [l]*lies in wait* [m]*tiene miedo*

MÚSICA: El joropo

el arpa llanera

maracas

cuatro

la bandola llanera

El joropo es considerado como la música y baile nacionales de Venezuela. Originalmente, «el joropo» era un evento rural de baile, música de cuerdas[a] y canciones. Ahora este nombre puede referirse a la música, al baile o a una reunión[b] social celebrada con música y baile. El joropo se toca y se baila en varios festivales y celebraciones.

[a]*música... string music* [b]*get-together*

Los instrumentos principales del joropo son el arpa llanera,[c] la bandola llanera,[d] el cuatro[e] y las maracas. Son instrumentos tradicionales de los llaneros, que eran los «*cowboys*» venezolanos. Generalmente, tres músicos tocan estos instrumentos básicos del joropo y una cuarta[f] persona canta, siguiendo[g] la música del arpa.

[c]*arpa... plains harp (folk harp with 32 strings, descended from the Spanish harp and used in the plains regions of Venezuela and Colombia)* [d]*four-stringed guitar with a rounded body* [e]*four-stringed guitar* [f]*fourth* [g]*following*

El baile, que tiene muchos pasos y movimientos rápidos, es complicado y bastante[g] difícil de aprender. Se dice que la intención de esta danza es dramatizar el dominio del hombre sobre la mujer: él dirige,[h] y ella lo sigue en todo.

[g]*rather* [h]*leads*

¿Recuerda Ud.?

Before learning how to express reciprocal actions, review the reflexive pronouns (**Gramática 13**), then provide the correct reflexive pronouns for the following sentences.

1. _____ levanté a las ocho y media.
2. Laura _____ puso el vestido.
3. Mis amigos y yo _____ sentamos en un café.
4. ¿Prefieres duchar_____ o bañar_____?

---

30 ## Expressing *each other* Reciprocal Actions with Reflexive Pronouns

Rosa y Casandra

Rosa y Casandra *se conocen* bien. Son compañeras de cuarto. *Se ven* todos los días y *se encuentran* después de clase para hablar.

¿Qué hacen Rosa y Casandra en esta escena? *Se besan* en la mejilla.*

¿Y Ud.?

Cuando Ud. y sus amigos se encuentran, ¿cómo se saludan (*do you greet other*)?

The plural reflexive pronouns, **nos, os,** and **se,** can be used to express *reciprocal actions* (**las acciones recíprocas**). Reciprocal actions are usually expressed in English with *each other* or *one another*.

Nos queremos.

Nos queremos.	*We love each other.*
¿**Os** ayudáis?	*Do you help one another?*
Se miran.	*They're looking at each other.*

AUTOPRUEBA

Give the correct pronoun to express a reciprocal action.

1. _____ miramos   4. _____ conocen
2. _____ pelearon   5. _____ llamaban
3. _____ veíais   6. _____ saludamos

Answers: 1. nos 2. se 3. os 4. se 5. se 6. nos

**As in many cultures, in Spain and Latin America kissing on the cheek is a common form of greeting and leave-taking. In Hispanic cultures, women kiss each other on the cheek, and men and women kiss each other on the cheek. The number of kisses varies from country to country. In Spain, two kisses (one on each cheek) is common. In much of Latin America, only one kiss, usually on the right cheek, is the norm.*

Rosa and Casandra *Rosa and Casandra know each other well. They are roommates. They see each other every day and they meet each other after class to talk. What are Rosa and Casandra doing in this scene? They are kissing each other on the cheek.*

■ **Práctica**

A. **¡Anticipemos! Buenos amigos.** Indique las oraciones que describen lo que hacen Ud. y un buen amigo / una buena amiga para mantener su amistad (*friendship*).

1. ☐ Nos vemos con frecuencia.
2. ☐ Nos conocemos muy bien. No hay secretos entre nosotros.
3. ☐ Nos respetamos mucho.
4. ☐ Nos ayudamos con cualquier (*any*) problema.
5. ☐ Nos escribimos cuando no estamos en la misma ciudad.
6. ☐ Nos hablamos por teléfono con frecuencia.
7. ☐ Nos decimos la verdad siempre, sea esta (*be it*) bonita o fea.
8. ☐ Cuando estamos muy ocupados, no importa si no nos hablamos por mucho tiempo.

B. **¿Qué se hacen?** Describa las siguientes relaciones familiares o sociales, haciendo oraciones completas con una palabra o frase de cada grupo.

MODELO: Los buenos amigos se conocen bien.

los buenos amigos
los parientes
los esposos
los padres y los niños
los amigos que no viven en la misma ciudad
los profesores y los estudiantes
los compañeros de cuarto/casa

+ (no) +

verse con frecuencia
quererse, respetarse
ayudarse (con los quehaceres domésticos, con los problemas económicos, con los problemas personales)
hablarse (todos los días, con frecuencia, sinceramente)
llamarse por teléfono, escribirse (con frecuencia)
mirarse (en la clase, con cariño [*affection*])
necesitarse
conocerse bien
saludarse (en la clase, con cariño), darse la mano

Need more practice?

- Workbook/Laboratory Manual
- Interactive CD-ROM
- Online Learning Center (www.mhhe.com/quetal7)

■ **Conversación**

Entrevista

1. ¿Con qué frecuencia se ven tú y tu novio/a (esposo/a, mejor amigo/a)? ¿Cuánto tiempo hace que (*How long has it been that*) se conocen? ¿Con qué frecuencia se dan regalos? ¿se escriben? ¿se telefonean? ¿Te gusta que se vean tanto (tan poco)?
2. ¿Con qué frecuencia se ven tú y tus abuelos/primos? ¿Por qué se ven Uds. tan poco (tanto)? ¿Cómo se mantienen en contacto? En la sociedad norteamericana, ¿los parientes se ven con frecuencia? En tu opinión, ¿es esto común entre los hispanos?

UN POCO DE TODO

Lengua y cultura: La leyenda del Lago de Maracaibo. Complete the following legend with the correct form of the word in parentheses, as suggested by the context. The verbs will be in the preterite or imperfect. When two possibilities are given, select the correct word.

En una tribu indígena de Venezuela, había una vez[a] un cacique[b] que se llamaba Zapara. Este[c] tenía una hija, Maruma, que (ser[1]) muy bonita. Al padre y a la hija (se/les[2]) (gustar[3]) pasar tiempo juntos andando por el bosque.[d]

Un día Zapara (comprender[4]) que su hija ya (ser[5]) una mujer y (se / le[6]) (decir[7]): «Debes escoger[e] esposo, pues ya tienes edad[f] para formar una familia. Pero (su / tu[8]) esposo debe ser guerrero,[g] como todos los hombres de nuestra familia.» Maruma (ponerse[9]) triste porque debía separarse de su padre para casarse.[h]

Un día, mientras su padre (estar[10]) ausente visitando otras tribus, Maruma (salir[11]) sola a cazar[i] en el bosque. Estaba a punto de dispararle a un ciervo,[j] cuando (un / —[12]) otro cazador[k] (matar[13])[l] al animal. El otro cazador era un joven guapo y simpático. Maruma (ponerse[14]) muy enojada[m] y le gritó:[n] «¿Quién te (dar[15]) permiso para cazar en este bosque?» El joven le contestó: «El ciervo es para (tú / ti[16]). Sólo quiero conocerte. Me llamo Tamaré.» A partir de ese día[o] los (joven[17]) (hacerse[18])[p] amigos. Pronto se enamoraron.[q]

Pero el joven no era guerrero y por eso el padre de Maruma (enojarse[19]) mucho cuando (saber[20]) que ella (querer[21]) casarse con él. Se enfadó tanto[r] que la naturaleza reaccionó y (haber[22]) grandes terremotos[s] e inundaciones[t]: las aguas cubrieron[u] las tierras del cacique Zapara y también a su hija con su amado,[v] formando así el Lago de Maracaibo. Zapara se convirtió en una de sus pequeñas islas.

[a]había... *once upon a time there was* [b]*leader* [c]*He* [d]*forest* [e]*choose* [f]ya... *you're old enough* [g]*a warrior* [h]*get married* [i]*hunt* [j]Estaba... *She was about to shoot a deer* [k]*hunter* [l]*to kill* [m]ponerse... *to become very angry* [n]le... *she shouted at him* [o]A... *From that day on* [p]*to become* [q]se... *they fell in love* [r]Se... *He was so angry* [s]*earthquakes* [t]*floods* [u]*covered* [v]*beloved*

Un residente del Lago de Maracaibo en su lancha (boat)

Comprensión: ¿Qué sabe Ud.? Conteste las siguientes preguntas en español.

1. ¿Quién era Zapara?
2. ¿Qué debía hacer su hija?
3. ¿De quién estaba enamorada (*in love*) Maruma?
4. ¿Por qué se enfadó Zapara?
5. ¿Cómo se formó el Lago de Maracaibo?

Resources for Review and Testing Preparation

- Workbook/Laboratory Manual
- Interactive CD-ROM
- Online Learning Center (www.mhhe.com/quetal7)

VIDEOTECA

Entrevista cultural: Venezuela

Sabina García es una estudiante venezolana. En esta entrevista, ella comenta sus estudios y sus hábitos personales. Sabina hace mucho para mantener un buen estado de salud. Antes de ver el vídeo, lea el siguiente fragmento de la entrevista.

ENTREVISTADORA: ¿Qué estudias?
SABINA: Estudio relaciones internacionales. Considero que actualmente[a] las relaciones internacionales son un campo muy importante en el mundo y se han desarrollado[b] con gran rapidez.
ENTREVISTADORA: ¿Cómo cuidas de tu salud?
SABINA: Trato de alimentarme sanamente, comiendo frutas, verduras, fibra principalmente y me acuesto temprano.

[a]*currently* [b]*se… they have developed*

Ahora vea el vídeo y conteste las siguientes preguntas basándose en la entrevista.

1. ¿Qué estudia Sabina?
2. ¿Por qué estudia esta carrera?
3. ¿Qué come Sabina?
4. ¿Qué más hace Sabina para cuidarse?
5. ¿Qué hace para aliviarse el estrés?

Entre amigos: ¡Yo sí hago ejercicio!

Tané, Karina, Rubén y Miguel visitan un mercado de pulgas (*flea market*) y hablan del ejercicio. En su opinión, ¿qué preguntas se van a hacer? Antes de mirar el vídeo, lea las preguntas a continuación. Mientras mire el vídeo, trate de entender la conversación en general y fíjese en la información sobre el ejercicio que hacen los amigos. Luego mire el vídeo una segunda vez, fijándose en la información que necesita para contestar las preguntas.

1. ¿Hace ejercicio Karina? ¿Qué tipo de ejercicio hace?
2. ¿Y Tané? ¿Qué tipo de ejercicio hace ella?
3. ¿Quiénes no tienen mucho tiempo para hacer ejercicio?
4. ¿Qué está haciendo Miguel mientras hablan del ejercicio?
5. ¿Cuántas veces por semana va Miguel al gimnasio?

ENFOQUE CULTURAL

 Venezuela

¡Fíjese!

Por su variedad de climas, Venezuela le ofrece al turista atracciones diversas. El clima venezolano varía entre el clima templado de las regiones andinas y el clima tropical de los llanos[a] y la costa. De hecho, el clima es agradable la mayor parte del año. Entre las atracciones turísticas hay lo siguiente.

- las hermosas[b] playas tropicales de la Isla Margarita y la costa caribeña
- la famosa catarata[c] Salto Ángel que, siendo dieciséis veces más alta que las cataratas del Niágara, es considerada la más alta del mundo
- la belleza[d] colonial de Ciudad Bolívar y Coro
- la progresiva y cosmopolita ciudad de Caracas y las majestuosas montañas andinas

[a]*plains* [b]*beautiful* [c]*waterfall* [d]*beauty*

Personas famosas: Simón Bolívar

Simón Bolívar (1783–1830) nació en Caracas. La fecha de su cumpleaños, el 24 de julio, es hoy día una fiesta nacional en Venezuela. Bolívar, llamado «el Libertador», ocupa un puesto[a] importante tanto en la historia de Venezuela como en la historia de Colombia, el Perú, el Ecuador y Bolivia por ser el personaje principal en las luchas[b] por la independencia de estos países. Bolívar, influenciado por las ideas de Jean Jacques Rousseau[c] y por la lucha de las colonias estadounidenses contra Inglaterra en el siglo XVIII, soñaba con[d] una América hispánica unida, sueño que nunca vio realizado.[e]

[a]*position* [b]*struggles* [c]*French writer and philosopher (1712–1778) whose ideas helped spark the French Revolution* [d]*soñaba... dreamed about* [e]*achieved*

La estatua de Simón Bolívar en la Plaza Bolívar de Ciudad Bolívar

Learn more about Venezuela with the Video, the Interactive CD-ROM, and the Online Learning Center (www.mhhe.com/quetal7).

PASO FINAL

 A CONVERSAR

En la farmacia

Como Ud. leyó en la **Nota cultural** de este capítulo, en muchos países hispanos la gente puede consultar a un farmacéutico / una farmacéutica en vez de ir al médico. La persona enferma describe sus síntomas y el farmacéutico / la farmacéutica o (*either*) le receta un medicamento apropiado o le manda a ver al médico.

PASO 1 En una hoja de papel aparte, prepare un cuadro como el siguiente. En su cuadro, escriba los síntomas y los posibles tratamientos para las enfermedades en los espacios en blanco.

enfermedad	una infección de garganta	un resfriado	una migraña
síntomas			
tratamientos			

PASO 2 Con un compañero / una compañera, prepare una escena entre una persona enferma y un farmacéutico / una farmacéutica. Escojan el papel que quieren hacer e improvisen una escena basándose en los cuadros del **Paso 1.** Su escena debe incluir saludos, una descripción de los síntomas, las recomendaciones médicas y una despedida.

MODELO: E1: Buenos días, Sr. Maldonado.
E2: Buenos días, Sra. Velázquez. ¿En qué le puedo servir?
E1: Me siento muy mal hoy. No sé qué me pasa.
E2: ¿Qué síntomas tiene?…

PASO 3 Cambien papeles e improvisen la escena otra vez.

GRAMÁTICA

To review the grammar points presented in this chapter, refer to the indicated grammar presentations. You'll find further practice of these structures in the Workbook/Laboratory Manual, on the Interactive CD-ROM, and on the *¿Qué tal?* Online Learning Center (www.mhhe.com/quetal7).

29 Narrating in the Past—Using the Preterite and the Imperfect

Do you know which tense to use to express habitual or repeated actions? Which tense should be used to express the beginning or end of an action?

30 Expressing *each other*—Reciprocal Actions with Reflexive Pronouns

Which reflexive pronouns are used in reciprocal constructions?

VOCABULARIO   Practice this vocabulary with digital flash cards on the Online Learning Center (www.mhhe.com/quetal7).

Los verbos

encontrarse (ue) (con)	to meet (*someone somewhere*)
saludarse	to greet each other

La salud y el bienestar

el bienestar	well-being
la rueda de molino	treadmill
la salud	health
caminar	to walk
cuidarse	to take care of oneself
dejar de + *inf.*	to stop (*doing something*)
doler (ue)	to hurt, ache
encontrarse (ue)	to be, feel
examinar	to examine
guardar cama	to stay in bed
hacer (*irreg.*) ejercicios aeróbicos	to do aerobics
internarse (en)	to check into (*a hospital*)
llevar una vida sana/tranquila	to lead a healthy/calm life
ponerle (*irreg.*) una inyección	to give (someone) a shot, injection
resfriarse (me resfrío)	to get/catch a cold
respirar	to breathe
sacar (qu)	to extract
sacar la lengua	to stick out one's tongue
sacar una muela	to extract a tooth

tener (*irreg.*) dolor de	to have a pain in
tener dolor de cabeza	to have a headache
tener dolor de estómago	to have a stomachache
tener dolor de muela	to have a toothache
tomar(le) la temperatura	to take someone's temperature
toser	to cough

Repaso: comer, correr, dormir (ue, u), enfermarse, hacer (*irreg.*) ejercicio, practicar (qu) deportes

Algunas partes del cuerpo humano

la boca	mouth
la cabeza	head
el cerebro	brain
el corazón	heart
el cuerpo	body
el diente	tooth
el estómago	stomach
la garganta	throat
la muela	tooth; molar
la nariz	nose
el oído	inner ear
el ojo	eye
la oreja	(outer) ear
los pulmones	lungs
la sangre	blood

Las enfermedades y los tratamientos

el chequeo	checkup
el consultorio	(medical) office
el dolor (de)	pain, ache (in)
la farmacia	pharmacy
la fiebre	fever
las gafas	glasses
el jarabe	(cough) syrup
los lentes de contacto	contact lenses
la pastilla	pill
la receta	prescription
el resfriado	cold
el síntoma	symptom
la tos	cough

Cognados: el antibiótico, la medicina
Repaso: llevar

El personal médico

el/la enfermero/a	nurse
el/la farmacéutico/a	pharmacist
el/la paciente	patient

Cognado: el/la dentista
Repaso: el/la médico/a

Otros sustantivos

la desventaja	disadvantage
la ventaja	advantage

Los adjetivos

congestionado/a	congested, stuffed up
mareado/a	dizzy; nauseated
mismo/a	same
pasado/a	past, last

Palabras adicionales

anoche	last night
anteayer	the day before yesterday
de repente	suddenly
dos veces	twice
en seguida	right away
equilibradamente	in a balanced way
eso quiere decir...	that means . . .
lo bueno	the good thing, news
lo malo	the bad thing, news
lo suficiente	enough

Repaso: ayer, de joven, de niño/a, mientras, siempre, una vez

Presiones de la vida° moderna

°life

Dos estudiantes en el campus de la Universidad de Puerto Rico, en Río Piedras

CULTURA

- **Nota cultural:** Palabras y frases para momentos difíciles
- **En los Estados Unidos y el Canadá:** La impresionante variedad de la música latina
- **Voces** de Puerto Rico
    - Literatura: Rosario Ferré
    - Música: La bomba y la plena
- **Videoteca**
    - Entrevista cultural: Puerto Rico
    - Entre amigos: ¡Estoy superestresada!
- **Enfoque cultural:** Puerto Rico
- **A leer:** Divórciate del estrés

VOCABULARIO

- Las presiones de la vida estudiantil
- ¡La profesora Martínez se levantó con el pie izquierdo!

GRAMÁTICA

31 Another Use of **se**

32 ¿**Por** o **para**?

LAS PRESIONES DE LA VIDA ESTUDIANTIL

el calendario

el horario

la llave

el despertador

la calificación

la tarjeta de identificación

el examen

sufrir (muchas) presiones

acordarse (ue) (de)	to remember	**la fecha límite**	deadline
entregar (gu)	to turn, hand in	**el informe (oral/**	(oral/written) report
estacionar	to park	**escrito)**	
llegar (gu) a tiempo/	to arrive on time/late	**la prueba**	quiz; test
tarde		**la tarea**	homework
olvidarse (de)	to forget	**el trabajo**	job, work; report,
pedir (i, i) disculpas	to apologize		(piece of) work
recoger (j)*	to collect; to pick up	**de tiempo completo/**	full/part time
sacar (qu) buenas/	to get good/bad	**parcial**	
malas notas	grades		
ser (*irreg.*) **flexible**	to be flexible	**Discúlpeme.**	Pardon me.
sufrir	to suffer		I'm sorry.
		¡Lo siento (mucho)!	Pardon me!
el estrés	stress		I'm (very) sorry!
la (falta de)	(lack of) flexibility	**Perdón.**	Pardon me.
flexibilidad			I'm sorry.

---

*Note the present indicative conjugation of **recoger: recojo, recoges, recoge, recogemos, recogéis, recogen.**

Conversación

A. Asociaciones

PASO 1 ¿Qué palabras asocia Ud. con estos verbos? Pueden ser sustantivos, antónimos o sinónimos.

1. estacionar	**4.** entregar	**7.** pedir	**10.** perder
2. recoger	**5.** sacar	**8.** llegar a tiempo	**11.** ser feliz
3. acordarse	**6.** sufrir	**9.** abrir	**12.** ser flexible

PASO 2 ¿Qué palabras y/o situaciones asocia Ud. con los siguientes sustantivos?

1. el calendario	**6.** el horario	**10.** las disculpas
2. el despertador	**7.** los informes	**11.** las presiones
3. las calificaciones	**8.** la llave	**12.** la flexibilidad
4. el estrés	**9.** la tarjeta de	**13.** la prueba
5. la fecha límite	identificación	**14.** el trabajo

B. Situaciones

PASO 1 La primera lista que Ud. va a leer consta de (*consists of*) preguntas o comentarios hechos por varias personas. La segunda lista incluye las respuestas de otras personas. Decida qué respuesta corresponde a cada comentario.

1. ____ —Anoche no me acordé de poner el despertador.

2. ____ —No puedes estacionar el coche aquí. No tienes permiso de estacionamiento para esta zona.

3. ____ —¿Sacaste una buena nota en la prueba?

4. ____ —Ramiro no tiene buen aspecto (*doesn't look right*). Creo que algo le causa mucho estrés.

5. ____ —Aquí tiene mi trabajo escrito sobre el Mercado Común.

a. —Pues estoy cansado de buscar estacionamiento por todo el *campus*. Lo voy a dejar aquí.

b. —¿Lo olvidaste otra vez? ¿A qué hora llegaste a la oficina?

c. —Pero la fecha límite era ayer. Es la última vez que acepto un informe suyo (*of yours*) tarde.

d. —Muy buena, pero no la esperaba. No tuve tiempo de estudiar.

e. —Es porque tiene un trabajo de tiempo completo, y también toma tres cursos este semestre.

PASO 2 Ahora, con un compañero / una compañera, invente un contexto para cada diálogo. ¿Dónde están las personas que hablan? ¿En casa? ¿en una oficina? ¿en clase? ¿Quiénes son?

MODELO: **1.** → Las personas que hablan están en el trabajo (la oficina). Probablemente están almorzando. Son compañeros de trabajo; no son buenos amigos…

C. Los años estudiantiles, ¿una época (*period, time*) **maravillosa?** Con frecuencia se oye a las personas mayores hablar de los años universitarios con nostalgia: años de libertad, sin responsabilidades, sin las tensiones propias de la vida laboral y familiar. ¿Ve Ud. así la época universitaria? Con un compañero / una compañera, comente este tema. Pueden usar las siguientes preguntas como guía (*guide*).

1. ¿Sufren muchas presiones los estudiantes universitarios? ¿Por qué? ¿Qué les causa estrés?
2. ¿Son más divertidos los años universitarios que los años de la escuela secundaria?
3. ¿Le preocupa a Ud. el costo de la matrícula? Para Ud. o para su familia, ¿es difícil pagarla?
4. ¿Piensa Ud. que la vida va a ser mejor después de graduarse en la universidad? ¿Por qué sí o por qué no?

con... *on the wrong side of the bed*

¡LA PROFESORA MARTÍNEZ SE LEVANTÓ CON EL PIE IZQUIERDO!°

doler(le) (ue) la cabeza

la cabeza

la mano

Le **duele** la cabeza.

equivocarse (qu) (de)

CABALLEROS   DAMAS

el brazo

Estaba **distraída** y **se equivocó de** puerta.

darse (*irreg.*) **contra la silla**

darse (*irreg.*) **en la pierna**

lastimarse la pierna

los dedos (de la mano)

Se lastimó cuando **se pegó contra** la silla.

caerse (*irreg.*)*

el pie

la pierna

romper

La profesora **se cayó*** y **rompió** los lentes.

Note that the first person singular of* **caer *is irregular:* **caigo.** *The present participle is* **cayendo.**

Accidentes		pegarse (gu) en/con/ contra	to run, bump into
darse (*irreg.*) **en/con/ contra**	to hit (*a part of one's body*); to run into / bump against	**el dedo del pie**	toe
		Fue sin querer.	It was unintentional.
doler (ue)	to hurt, ache	**distraído/a**	absentminded
equivocarse (qu) (de)	to be wrong, make a mistake (about)	**torpe**	clumsy
hacerse (*irreg.*) **daño**	to hurt oneself	**¡Qué torpe!**	How clumsy!

▓ Conversación

NOTA CULTURAL

Palabras y frases para momentos difíciles

Hay muchas expresiones para **ocasiones de mala suerte**[a] **o de presión.** Varían mucho de región en región y de país en país. Estas son algunas de las más comunes.

Para expresar dolor, sorpresa o compasión

¡Ay!	Ah! Ouch!	**¿Qué le vamos a hacer?**	What can you do?
¡Uy!	Oops! Oh!	**¡No me digas!**	You're kidding! (You don't say!)
¡No puede ser!	That can't be!	**¡Qué mala suerte!**	What bad luck!
¡Cuánto lo siento!	I'm so sorry!		

Para dar ánimo[b]

¡Venga!	Come on!	**¡No es para tanto!**	It's not so bad!
¡Órale! (*Mex.*)	Come on!	**¡Anímate!**	Cheer up!

---

[a]*luck*   [b]*Para... To cheer (someone up)*

A. Posibilidades. ¿Qué puede Ud. hacer o decir —o qué le puede pasar— en cada situación?

MODELO: Ud. se da contra el escritorio de otro estudiante y se lastima el pie. →
—¡Ay! ¡Qué torpe soy!

1. A Ud. le duele mucho la cabeza.
2. Ud. le pega a otra persona sin querer.
3. Ud. se olvida del nombre de otra persona.
4. Ud. está muy distraído/a y no mira por dónde camina (*you're walking*).
5. Ud. se lastima la mano (el pie).
6. Su amigo está nervioso porque se dio contra la profesora antes de clase.

PASO 1

B. Accidentes y tropiezos (*mishaps*). ¿Le pasaron a Ud. alguna vez las siguientes cosas? Complete las oraciones con información verdadera para Ud. Si nunca le pasó nada de esto, invente una situación que podría haber ocurrido (*could have happened*). Luego, con un compañero / una compañera, haga y conteste preguntas basadas en estas oraciones.

MODELO: ¿Te caíste por las escaleras ayer? ¿Te hiciste daño?

1. Me caí por las escaleras (*stairs*) y _____.
2. No me acordé de hacer la tarea para la clase de _____.
3. Me equivoqué cuando _____.
4. El despertador sonó, pero _____.
5. No pude encontrar _____.
6. Me di con _____ y me lastimé _____.
7. Pasó la fecha límite para entregar un informe y _____.
8. Caminaba un poco distraído/a y _____.

NOTA COMUNICATIVA

More on Adverbs

You already know the most common Spanish adverbs: words like
bien/mal, mucho/poco, siempre/nunca...

Adverbs that end in *-ly* in English usually end in **-mente** in Spanish. The suffix **-mente** is added to the feminine singular form of adjectives. Note that the accent mark on the stem word (if there is one) is retained.

ADJECTIVE	ADVERB	ENGLISH
rápida	**rápida**mente	*rapidly*
fácil	**fácil**mente	*easily*
paciente	**paciente**mente	*patiently*

Adjetivos

constante	posible
directo	puntual
fácil	rápido
inmediato	total
paciente	tranquilo

C. ¡Seamos (*Let's be*) **lógicos!** Complete estas oraciones lógicamente con adverbios basados en los siguientes adjetivos.

1. La familia está esperando _____ en la cola.
2. Hay examen mañana y tengo que empezar a estudiar _____.
3. ¿Las enchiladas? Se preparan _____.
4. ¿Qué pasa? Estoy _____ confundido/a (*confused*).
5. Cuando mira la tele, mi hermanito cambia el canal _____.
6. Es necesario que las clases empiecen _____.

D. Entrevista. Con un compañero / una compañera, haga y conteste las siguientes preguntas.

MODELO: E1: ¿Qué haces pacientemente?
E2: Espero pacientemente a mi esposo cuando se viste para salir. ¡Lo hace muy lentamente (*slowly*)!

1. ¿Qué haces rápidamente?
2. ¿Qué te toca hacer inmediatamente?
3. ¿Qué hiciste (comiste,...) solamente una vez que te gustó muchísimo (no te gustó nada)?
4. ¿Qué haces tú fácilmente que es difícil para otras personas?
5. ¿Qué hace constantemente tu compañero/a de casa (amigo/a, esposo/a,...) que te molesta (*bothers*) muchísimo?

Need more practice?

- Workbook/Laboratory Manual
- Interactive CD-ROM
- Online Learning Center
  (www.mhhe.com/quetal7)

31 Expressing Unplanned or Unexpected Events Another Use of *se*

Un día fatal

Diego y Antonio son compañeros de cuarto. Hoy todo les salió mal.

A Diego *se le cayó* la taza de café.

También *se le perdió* la cartera.

A Antonio *se le olvidaron* sus libros y su trabajo cuando fue a clase.

También *se le perdieron* las llaves de su apartamento.

¿Y Ud.?

¿Le pasaron a Ud. las mismas cosas —o cosas parecidas (*similar*)— esta semana? Conteste, completando las oraciones.

1. *Se me perdieron / No se me perdieron* las llaves de mi coche/casa.
2. *Se me olvidó / No se me olvidó* una reunión importante.
3. *Se me cayó / No se me cayó* una taza de café.
4. *Se me rompió / No se me rompió* un objeto de valor (*value*) sentimental.

A. Unplanned or unexpected events (*I dropped . . . , We lost . . . , You forgot . . .*) are frequently expressed in Spanish with **se** and a third person form of the verb. In this structure, the occurrence is viewed as happening *to* someone—the unwitting "victim" of the action.

The chart on page 282 illustrates the different parts and word order of this structure. Note:

- The "victim" is indicated by an indirect object pronoun.
- As with the verb **gustar,** the **a** + *noun* phrase is required in sentences that express the "victim" as a noun. The **a** + *pronoun* phrase is often used to clarify or emphasize meaning when the "victim" is expressed as a pronoun.
- The subject of the verb is the thing that is dropped, broken, forgotten, and so on.
- The subject usually follows the verb in this structure.

Se me cayó el papel.
I dropped the paper. (The paper was dropped by me.)

Se le olvidaron las llaves.
He forgot the keys. (The keys were forgotten by him.)

Se te olvidó llamar a tu hija.
You forgot to call your daughter. (Calling your daughter was forgotten by you.)

a + Noun / (a + Pronoun)	se	Indirect Object Pronoun	Verb	Subject
(A mí)	Se	me	cayó	la taza de café.
¿(A ti)	Se	te	perdió	la cartera?
A Antonio	se	le	olvidaron	los apuntes.

The verb agrees with the grammatical subject of the Spanish sentence (**la taza, la cartera, los apuntes**), not with the indirect object pronoun. **No** immediately precedes **se**.

A Diego *se le perdió la cartera.*
Diego lost his wallet. (Diego's wallet got lost on him.)

A Antonio *no se le olvidaron los apuntes.*
Antonio didn't forget his notes. (Antonio's notes were not forgotten by him.)

B. Here are some verbs frequently used in this construction.

Note: In this structure **quedar** can mean *to have* (something left [over]) or *to leave* (something behind).

Note: Although all indirect object pronouns can be used in this construction, this section will focus on the first, second, and third person singular forms (**se me…, se te…, se le…**).

acabar	*to finish; to run out of*
olvidar	*to forget*
perder (ie)	*to lose*

caer

romper

quedar

A Miguel no le queda mucha Coca-Cola. (*Miguel doesn't have much Coke left.*)

C. In general, this structure is used to emphasize the accidental nature of an event. When the speaker wishes to emphasize *who* committed the act, or that the act was intentional, that person becomes the subject of the verb and the **se** structure is not used. Compare the sentences at the right.

Se me rompió el plato.
The plate broke on me. (accidentally)

(Yo) Rompí el plato.
I broke the plate. (emphasizes either who broke the plate or the intentionality of the act)

AUTOPRUEBA

Match the following sentences.

1. _____ No encuentro las llaves.
2. _____ Tu calculadora no funciona.
3. _____ Paco no entregó la tarea.
4. _____ Necesito comprar leche.

a. Se te rompió.
b. Se me acabó.
c. Se me perdieron.
d. Se le olvidó.

Answers: 1. c 2. a 3. d 4. b

▪ Práctica

A. ¡Anticipemos! ¡Qué mala memoria! Hortensia sufre muchas presiones en su vida. Por eso cuando se fue de vacaciones al Perú, estaba tan distraída que se le olvidó hacer muchas cosas importantes antes de salir. Empareje (*Match*) los lapsos de Hortensia con las consecuencias.

LAPSOS	CONSECUENCIAS
1. _____ Se le olvidó cerrar la puerta de su casa.	**a.** Va a perder el trabajo.
2. _____ Se le olvidó pagar las cuentas (*bills*).	**b.** No la van a dejar entrar en el Perú.
3. _____ Se le olvidó pedirle a alguien que cuidara a (*to take care of*) su perro.	**c.** Le van a suspender el servicio de la luz (*electricity*) y de gas... ¡y cancelar sus tarjetas de crédito!
4. _____ Se le olvidó cancelar el periódico.	**d.** Alguien le va a robar el televisor.
5. _____ Se le olvidó pedirle permiso a su jefa (*boss*).	**e.** ¡«King» se va a morir de hambre!
6. _____ Se le olvidó llevar el pasaporte.	**f.** No va a tener dónde alojarse (*to stay*).
7. _____ Se le olvidó hacer reserva en un hotel.	**g.** Todos van a saber que no está en casa.

B. ¡Desastres por todas partes (*everywhere*)!

PASO 1 ¿Es Ud. una persona distraída o torpe? Indique las oraciones que se apliquen (*apply*) a Ud. Puede cambiar algunos de los detalles de las oraciones si es necesario.

1. ☐ Con frecuencia se me caen los libros (los platos,...).
2. ☐ Se me pierden constantemente las llaves (los calcetines,...).
3. ☐ A menudo (*Often*) se me olvida apagar (*to turn off*) la computadora (la luz,...).
4. ☐ Siempre se me rompen las gafas (las lámparas,...).
5. ☐ De vez en cuando (*From time to time*) se me quedan los libros (los cuadernos,...) en la clase.
6. ☐ Se me olvida fácilmente mi horario (el teléfono de algún amigo,...).

PASO 2 ¿Es Ud. igual ahora que cuando era más joven? Complete cada oración del **Paso 1** para describir cómo era de niño/a. No se olvide de usar el imperfecto en sus oraciones.

MODELO: De niño/a, (no) se me caían los libros con frecuencia.

PASO 3 Ahora compare sus respuestas con las de un compañero / una compañera. ¿Quién es más distraído/a o torpe ahora? ¿Quién lo era de niño/a?

Need more practice?

▪ Workbook/Laboratory Manual
▪ Interactive CD-ROM
▪ Online Learning Center (www.mhhe.com/quetal7)

■ Conversación

Pablo tuvo una mañana fatal

PASO 1 Complete la siguiente descripción de lo que le pasó a Pablo ayer.
Use expresiones con **se**.

Pablo tuvo una mañana fatal. Primero (olvidar¹) poner el despertador.
Se levantó tarde y se vistió rápidamente. No cerró bien su maletín;ᵃ por
eso (caer²) unos papeles importantes. Recogió los papeles y subió al
coche. Salió rápido pero después de cinco minutos, (acabar³) la gasolina
y se le paróᵇ el coche. Dejó el coche en la calle y decidió ir caminando.
Llevaba el maletín en una mano y las llaves y un documento urgente en
la otra. Desafortunadamente,ᶜ mientras caminaba, (perder⁴) el
documento. Cuando llegó a la oficina, buscó a su jefeᵈ para entregarle el
documento pero no podía encontrar el documento entre sus papeles.
Cansado y enojado, cerró el maletín sin cuidado y (romper⁵) los lentes.

ᵃ*briefcase* ᵇ*se… (the car) stopped on him* ᶜ*Unfortunately* ᵈ*boss*

PASO 2 Ahora, con un compañero / una compañera, describa una mañana o
un día fatal que Ud. tuvo. Trate de incluir expresiones con **se**.

MODELO: El primer día de clases, se me olvidó poner el despertador, y
llegué tarde a clase. Luego…

En los Estados Unidos y el Canadá

La impresionante variedad de la música latina

Es difícil hablar de «música latina»
porque hay una inmensa **variedad**. La
música de España y de toda Latinoamérica cuenta conᵃ **diversos orígenes**
que luego **se mezclan.**ᵇ La música de
los españoles y portugueses llegó al
Nuevo Mundo, pero pronto se mezcló
con fuertes **tradiciones indígenas.**
Cuando los conquistadores trajeron
esclavosᶜ **africanos** al Nuevo Mundo, estos trajeron
consigoᵈ sus propias tradiciones musicales, que influyeron
en varios tipos de música que hoy consideramos música
hispánica.

Hoy día, **los artistas hispanos** de los Estados Unidos
son cada vez más conocidos, no sólo como representan-
tes de la música latina, sino también en las áreas del rock,
pop, hip hop y jazz. Como ejemplo, podemos nombrar,
entre muchos, a los neoyorquinos de origen puertorri-

Tito Puente (1923–2000)

queño Jennifer López y Marc
Anthony, al mexicoamericano Carlos
Santana, a la colombiana Shakira, al
español Enrique Iglesias y al pianista
dominicano Michel Camilo.

La salsa es uno de los tipos de
música hispana más reconocidos. Es
una mezcla de **ritmos afrocaribeños**
que fue creada en Nueva York por
músicos hispanos en los años sesenta
y setenta del siglo XX. La salsa es muy
variada, pero siempre tiene una
característica clara: es muy **bailable.** Uno de los nombres
más asociados con la salsa es Tito Puente, el famoso
percusionista. Carlos Santana grabó su versión de la
composición de Puente, «Oye ¿cómo va?» e introdujo a
Puente y un estilo de música hispánica no sólo a una
nueva generación, sino también al público no hispano.

ᵃ*cuenta… has* ᵇ*se… are combined* ᶜ*slaves* ᵈ*with them*

LITERATURA: Rosario Ferré

Sobre la autora: *Rosario Ferré nació en Ponce, Puerto Rico. Además de biografías, crítica literaria y poesía, escribe también ficción en español y en inglés. Actualmente enseña en la Universidad de Puerto Rico y contribuye en el periódico* San Juan Star. *El siguiente fragmento es del ensayo: «De cómo dejarse caer de la sartén al fuego[a]»,* Sitio a eros: Trece ensayos *(1980).*

A lo largo del tiempo, las mujeres narradoras han escrito[b] por múltiples razones: Emily Brontë escribió para demostrar la naturaleza revolucionaria de la pasión; Virginia Woolf para exorcizar su terror a la locura y a la muerte; Joan Didion escribe para descubrir lo que piensa y cómo piensa; Clarisse Lispector descubre en su escritura una razón para amar y ser amada. En mi caso, escribir es una voluntad a la vez constructiva y destructiva; una posibilidad de crecimiento[c] y de cambio.[d]

Rosario Ferré
(1938–)

[a]*de... from the frying pan into the fire*   [b]*han... have written*   [c]*growth*   [d]*change*

MÚSICA: La bomba y la plena

los tambores bomba

el güiro

las pleneras   las maracas

Los dos estilos de música puertorriqueña más conocidos son la bomba y la plena. Se asocian tanto que a veces se oye decir «bombayplena» como una sola palabra. Aunque[a] son diferentes, los dos estilos se derivan de tradiciones africanas. Su interpretación[b] incluye una danza y los dos son una especie de conversación entre los participantes. Los instrumentos principales de la bomba son dos tambores[c] bomba (el burlador y el subidor), la cuá[d] y las maracas. La plena se toca con tres pleneras[e] y un güiro.[f]

[a]*Although*   [b]*performance*   [c]*drums*   [d]*percussion instrument made of bamboo and played with two sticks*   [e]*percussion instruments, very similar to a tambourine, without the cymbals*   [f]*rasping percussion instrument often made from a gourd*

En la bomba, el músico que toca el burlador establece un ritmo constante. El músico que toca la otra bomba, el subidor, «dialoga» con la persona que baila e intenta interpretar el ritmo de sus pasos o su danza.

La plena es una «conversación» entre dos cantantes. El cantante principal echa una frase[g] y uno o dos de los otros cantantes contestan, todo al ritmo[h] de las pleneras. La plena se conoce también como el «periódico cantao[i]» porque es un comentario sobre eventos, elecciones y escándalos corrientes.[j]

[g]*echa... sings out a phrase*   [h]*al... to the rhythm*   [i]*abbreviated form of* cantado (sung), *past participle of the verb* cantar   [j]*recent*

¿Recuerda Ud.?

Before beginning **Gramática 32,** review what you have learned about prepositional pronouns. The first and second person singular pronouns differ from subject pronouns; the rest are identical to subject pronouns. Then give the prepositional pronouns that correspond to the following persons.

1. Pepe: de _____
2. Lisa y yo: después de _____
3. tú: para _____
4. yo: de _____
5. Ud.: con _____
6. Juan y Olga: para _____

---

32   *¿Por o para?* **A Summary of Their Uses**

¿Qué se representa?

a.   b.   c.

Comprension:

Empareje (*Match*) cada dibujo con la oración que le corresponde.

1. _____ Caminamos *para* el parque.
2. _____ Ayer compramos el regalo *por* la abuela.
3. _____ Paseamos *por* el parque.
4. _____ El regalo es *para* Eduardo.

d.

You have been using the prepositions **por** and **para** throughout your study of Spanish. Although most of the information in this section will be a review, you will also learn some new uses of **por** and **para**.

Por

The preposition **por** has the following English equivalents.

• *by, by means of*	Vamos **por** avión (tren, barco,...). *We're going by plane (train, ship, . . .).* Nos hablamos **por** teléfono mañana. *We'll talk by (on the) phone tomorrow.*
• *through, along*	Me gusta pasear **por** el parque y **por** la playa. *I like to stroll through the park and along the beach.*
• *during, in* (time of day)	Trabajo **por** la mañana. *I work in the morning.*
• *because of, due to*	Estoy nervioso **por** la entrevista. *I'm nervous because of the interview.*
• *for = in exchange for*	Piden 1.000 dólares **por** el coche. *They're asking $1,000 for the car.* Gracias **por** todo. *Thanks for everything.*
• *for = for the sake of, on behalf of*	Lo hago **por** ti. *I'm doing it for you (for your sake).*
• *for = duration* (often omitted)	Vivieron allí (**por**) un año. *They lived there for a year.*

Por is also used in a number of fixed expressions.

por Dios	for heaven's sake
por ejemplo	for example
por eso	that's why
por favor	please
por fin	finally
por lo general	generally, in general
por lo menos	at least
por primera/ última vez	for the first/ last time
por si acaso	just in case
¡por supuesto!	of course!
por todas partes	everywhere

Para

Although **para** has many English equivalents, including *for*, it always has the underlying purpose of referring to a goal or destination.

- *in order to* + infinitive

  Regresaron pronto **para** estudiar.
  They returned soon (in order) to study.

  Estudian **para** conseguir un buen trabajo.
  They're studying (in order) to get a good job.

- *for* = destined for, to be given to

  Todo esto es **para** ti.
  All this is for you.

  Le di un libro **para** su hijo.
  I gave her a book for her son.

- *for* = by (deadline, specified future time)

  Para mañana, estudien **por** y **para**.
  *For tomorrow, study **por** and **para**.*

  La composición es **para** el lunes.
  The composition is for Monday.

- *for* = toward, in the direction of

  Salió **para** el Ecuador ayer.
  She left for Ecuador yesterday.

- *for* = to be used for

  El dinero es **para** la matrícula.
  The money is for tuition.

  OJO Compare the example at the right to **un vaso de agua** = a glass (full) of water.

  Es un vaso **para** agua.
  It's a water glass.

- *for* = as compared with others, in relation to others

  Para mí, el español es fácil.
  For me, Spanish is easy.

  Para (ser) extranjera, habla muy bien el inglés.
  For (being) a foreigner, she speaks English very well.

- *for* = in the employ of

  Trabajan **para** el gobierno.
  They work for the government.

AUTOPRUEBA

Indicate whether you would use **por** or **para.**

1. _____ to travel to a place
2. _____ to travel through a place
3. _____ to travel by plane
4. _____ to work for someone (a company)
5. _____ to work for someone (on behalf of)
6. _____ to last for a period of time
7. _____ to be due by a certain time

Answers: 1. para 2. por 3. por 4. por 5. para 6. por 7. para

■ Práctica

A. Preguntas

PASO 1 Complete las siguientes preguntas con **por** y **para**.

1. ¿_____ quién trabaja Ud.? ¿Le pagan a Ud. bien?
2. ¿_____ dónde tiene que manejar (*drive*) para llegar a la universidad?
3. ¿Cuánto pagó Ud. _____ su carro/bicicleta?
4. ¿_____ qué es la llave grande que Ud. tiene?
5. ¿_____ qué profesión estudia Ud.? ¿_____ cuántos años tiene que estudiar?
6. ¿_____ cuándo necesita Ud. volver a casa hoy?

PASO 2 Ahora, conteste las preguntas del **Paso 1**. Invente la información necesaria.

B. ¿Por o para? Complete los siguientes diálogos y oraciones con **por** o **para**.

1. Los Sres. Arana salieron _____ el Perú ayer. Van _____ avión, claro, pero luego piensan viajar en coche _____ todo el país. Van a estar allí _____ dos meses. Va a ser una experiencia extraordinaria _____ toda la familia.
2. Mi prima Graciela quiere estudiar _____ (ser) doctora. _____ eso trabaja _____ un médico _____ la mañana; tiene clases _____ la tarde.
3. —¿ _____ qué están Uds. aquí todavía? Yo pensaba que iban a dar un paseo _____ el parque. —Íbamos a hacerlo, pero no fuimos, _____ la nieve.
4. Este cuadro fue pintado (*was painted*) por Picasso _____ expresar los desastres de la guerra (*war*). _____ muchos críticos de arte, es la obra maestra (*masterpiece*) de este artista.
5. La «Asociación Todo _____ Ellos» trabaja _____ las personas mayores, _____ ayudarlos cuando lo necesitan. ¿Trabaja Ud. _____ alguna asociación de voluntarios? ¿Qué tuvo que hacer _____ inscribirse (*sign up*)?

■ Conversación

Entrevista. Hágale preguntas a su profesor(a) para saber la siguiente información.

1. la tarea para mañana y para la semana que viene
2. lo que hay que estudiar para el próximo examen
3. si para él/ella son interesantes o aburridas las ciencias
4. la opinión que tiene de la pronunciación de Uds., para ser principiantes
5. qué deben hacer Uds. para mejorar su pronunciación del español
6. por cuánto tiempo deben Uds. practicar el español todos los días

Need more practice?

■ Workbook/Laboratory Manual
■ Interactive CD-ROM
■ Online Learning Center (www.mhhe.com/quetal7)

PASO 3

UN POCO DE TODO

Lengua y cultura: Un poco de historia de Puerto Rico. Complete the following passages with the correct forms of the words in parentheses, as suggested by the context. When two possibilities are given in parentheses, select the correct word. **¡OJO!** As you conjugate verbs in this activity, use the present tense unless otherwise indicated in the parentheses. If you see *P/I*, you will choose between the preterite and the imperfect; *comm.* means to use an **Ud./Uds.** command; and *prog.* stands for the present/past progressive.

¿Qué saben Uds. de la historia de Puerto Rico? ¿Muy poco? Pues no (*comm. Uds.:* preocuparse[1]). Aquí tienen (algún / alguna[2]) información.

Originalmente, en Puerto Rico (*P/I,* vivir[3]) los indígenas[a] taínos y caribes, que (*P/I,* extenderse[4]) por gran parte de las costas caribeñas. En (esto/estas[5]) costas del Mar Caribe (ser/estar[6]) las islas Antillas, que se dividen en Antillas Mayores y Antillas Menores. Las Antillas Mayores (ser/estar[7]) las islas de Puerto Rico, Cuba, Jamaica y Española (la República Dominicana y Haití).

Cristóbal Colón (*P/I,* llegar[8]) a Puerto Rico en su segundo viaje a América. (Se/Le[9]) dice que el jefe[b] de los taínos, que (*P/I,* tener[10]) el título de cacique, (*P/I,* recibir[11]) a Colón con un collar de oro.[c] (Por/Para[12]) eso Colón pensó que (*P/I,* haber[13]) mucho oro en la isla, pero no (*P/I,* tener[14]) (razón/sueño[15]). De todas formas,[d] los españoles explotaron la isla intensamente. En poco tiempo, la población taína prácticamente (*P/I,* desaparecer[16]) debido a[e] tres factores: (el/la[17]) explotación de la tierra, las rebeliones de los nativos y las enfermedades que los españoles traían consigo[f] que (*P/I,* ser[18]) nuevas (por/para[19]) los taínos. La población africana, que los españoles importaron como esclavos,[g] (*P/I,* empezar[20]) a llegar en el siglo[h] XVI.

En el siglo XIX, mientras toda Latinoamérica (*P/I,* tener[21]) guerras[i] contra España y (*prog.,* obtener[22]) su independencia, las islas antillanas no (*P/I,* independizarse[23]). En 1898 Puerto Rico (*P/I,* convertirse[24]) en una colonia de los Estados Unidos, después de que España (*P/I,* perder[25]) la guerra que en los Estados Unidos (*P/I,* llamarse[26]) *the Spanish American War.*

En 1917, los puertorriqueños fueron declarados ciudadanos[j] (estadounidense[27]), y desde 1953 su país es un Estado Libre Asociado de los Estados Unidos. Esto quiere decir que aunque[k] no es independiente, tiene plena[l] autonomía interna.

[a]*Indians, indigenous peoples* [b]*chief* [c]*collar... gold necklace* [d]*De... In any case* [e]*debido... due to* [f]*with them* [g]*slaves* [h]*century* [i]*wars* [j]*citizens* [k]*although* [l]*full*

La estatua de Cristóbal Colón en la Plaza de Colón, en San Juan, Puerto Rico

Resources for Review and Testing Preparation

- Workbook/Laboratory Manual
- Interactive CD-ROM
- Online Learning Center (www.mhhe.com/quetal7)

Comprensión. Conteste las preguntas en español.

1. ¿Dónde están las Antillas?
2. ¿Cuáles son las Antillas Mayores?
3. ¿Quiénes eran los habitantes originales de Puerto Rico?
4. ¿Qué otros grupos raciales había en la Isla?
5. ¿Desde cuándo es Puerto Rico territorio de los Estados Unidos?
6. ¿Cuál es la situación política actual (*current*) de Puerto Rico?

Un paso más   PASO 4

VIDEOTECA

Entrevista cultural: Puerto Rico

Antonio Solórzano es un estudiante puertorriqueño. Aquí describe su rutina diaria. También habla de las presiones que sufre y de lo que hace para disminuir el estrés. Antes de ver el vídeo, lea el siguiente fragmento de la entrevista.

ENTREVISTADORA: ¿Qué estudias?

ANTONIO: Estudio antropología.

ENTREVISTADORA: Antonio, ¿cómo es para ti un día típico?

ANTONIO: Pues un día típico para mí es despertarme temprano para ir a la universidad y,… este, estar allí casi todo el día. Y después en la tarde irme al trabajo como hasta las seis y media de la tarde, estudiar un rato cuando llego a mi casa y después irme en la noche a hacer ejercicio.

Ahora vea el vídeo y conteste las siguientes preguntas basándose en la entrevista.

1. ¿Dónde vive y estudia Antonio?
2. ¿Qué hace por la tarde, generalmente?
3. Según Antonio, ¿qué presiones sufren los estudiantes?
4. ¿Qué hace Antonio todos los días para aliviar el estrés?
5. Y los fines de semana, ¿qué hace?

Entre amigos: ¡Estoy superestresada!

Karina, Miguel, Tané y Rubén hablan del estrés y de las presiones de la vida diaria. En su opinión, ¿de qué van a hablar? Antes de mirar el vídeo, lea las preguntas a continuación. Mientras mire el vídeo, trate de entender la conversación en general y fíjese en la información sobre los exámenes, las clases y el trabajo. Luego mire el vídeo una segunda vez, fijándose en la información que necesita para contestar las preguntas.

1. ¿Cuántas horas por semana trabaja Rubén?
2. ¿Por qué está estresada Karina?
3. ¿Tiene Tané buenas o malas notas?
4. ¿Qué clase le da más dificultades a Tané?
5. ¿Qué tipo de ayuda le ofrece Miguel a Tané?

ENFOQUE CULTURAL

 Puerto Rico

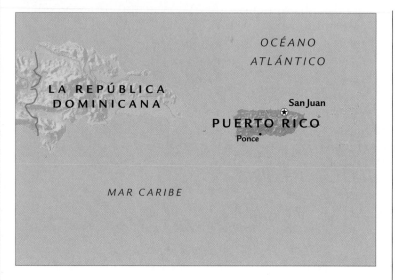

OCÉANO ATLÁNTICO

LA REPÚBLICA DOMINICANA

San Juan

PUERTO RICO

Ponce

MAR CARIBE

¡Fíjese!

- Puerto Rico ha estado relacionado[a] políticamente con los Estados Unidos desde la Guerra Hispano-norteamericana de 1898, año en que España perdió las ultimas colonias de su imperio. En 1952, Puerto Rico se convirtió en Estado Libre Asociado. Bajo[b] este sistema de gobierno, los puertorriqueños son ciudadanos[c] estadounidenses. Sin embargo, los que viven en la Isla no pueden votar por el presidente de los Estados Unidos aunque deben servir en el ejército[d] de ese país en caso de guerra.

- Otro nombre de Puerto Rico es Borinquen y los puertorriqueños se conocen también como boricuas. Estas palabras originaron en el lenguaje de los indios taínos. Los taínos llegaron a la Isla en el siglo[e] XIII pero su cultura casi desapareció con la llegada de los españoles en 1493.

- El Parque Nacional del Yunque, ubicado[f] en una montaña de 1.065 metros de altura que está al noreste de la Isla, es pequeño cuando se compara a otros bosques[g] nacionales, pero es el único bosque *tropical* del sistema de Bosques Nacionales de los Estados Unidos.

[a]ha... has been associated [b]Under [c]citizens [d]army [e]century [f]located [g]forests

Personas famosas: Alonso Ramírez

En 1690 se publicó en México la primera novela del Nuevo Mundo, *Infortunios*[a] *de Alonso Ramírez*. Aunque esta obra[b] se atribuyó al mexicano Carlos Sigüenza y Góngora, hoy se cree que el verdadero[c] autor fue el mismo Alonso Ramírez del título. También se cree que la obra no es ficticia, sino autobiográfica: la vida de un puertorriqueño que se cría[d] en la Isla, viaja a México y tiene aventuras en muchas partes del Mar Pacífico. Sus aventuras incluyen batallas contra piratas, una estadía[e] en una isla desierta y muchos otros eventos interesantísimos. Es una novela que vale la pena[f] leer.

[a]Misfortunes [b]work [c]real [d]se... is brought up [e]stay
[f]que... that is worthwhile

Una calle en el viejo San Juan

Learn more about Puerto Rico with the Video, the Interactive CD-ROM, and the Online Learning Center (www.mhhe.com/quetal7).

A LEER

REPASO DE ESTRATEGIAS: Guessing the Content of a Passage

In previous reading sections, you have learned several different strategies to improve your comprehension of a text. Whenever you can, it's a good idea to utilize as many of these strategies as possible. Of course, not all texts will lend themselves to the application of all strategies. For example, there might be limited visual cues such as photos to help you anticipate what the reading is about. In those instances, what else can you rely on to make predictions about the content? One strategy is to identify the source of the passage (see **Sobre la lectura**). And, of course, the title often reveals a great deal about the content of a passage. Take a look at the title of the reading that follows and the accompanying photo. What do you think this article is about?

1. Divorce rates in Spanish-speaking countries
2. The relationship between divorce and stress
3. Advice for reducing stress

If you picked number 3, you were right! The following article offers suggestions and techniques for reducing stress and enjoying a calmer life.

Sobre la lectura... Esta lectura es parte de un artículo que se publicó en la revista hispana *Nuestra Gente.* Esta revista presenta artículos de interés sobre una gran variedad de temas: cine, música, cocina y otros.

Divórciate del estrés

<u>Convivimos</u> tanto con el estrés que hasta parece un miembro de la familia. Lo llevamos al trabajo, a las tiendas, a la lavandería,[a] a veces hasta nos acostamos y <u>amanecemos</u> con él. Pero es un compañero de muchos disfraces.[b] Nos mantiene en movimiento diario, pero aparece como dolor de cabeza, nudos[c] de músculos en el cuello,[d] ratos de <u>olvido</u>, cansancio o enojo.

Cinco pasos hacia una vida más tranquila

¡Córrele![e]

O hasta puedes decir «¡camínale!» si prefieres pues también te servirá.[f] Es decir, si notas que se te viene encima el maldito estrés, ponte los tenis, y ¡a la calle! Una simple <u>caminata</u> o <u>corrida</u> de veinte minutos diarios hace milagros.[g] Hasta los científicos han comprobado[h] que el ejercicio diario —aunque corto— sí reduce sustancialmente los niveles de estrés.

Respira profundamente

Uno de los mejores y más sencillos pasos a tomar para reducir el estrés es cuidar de tu respiración, según el Centro Médico Arnot Ogden de El-mira, Nueva York. Cuando te afecta el estrés, tu respiración <u>se acorta</u> y

Correr o caminar veinte minutos todos los días reduce el estrés.

---

[a]*lugar público donde se puede lavar la ropa* [b]*disguises* [c]*knots* [d]*neck* [e]*Run!* [f]*te... it (walking) will work for you* [g]*miracles, wonders* [h]*han... have proven*

es poco <u>profunda</u> debido al efecto que producen los músculos tensos. Cada vez que te sientas tenso, concéntrate unos segundos en tu respiración y profundízala. Tu corazón te lo agradecerá.[i]

Un <u>spa</u> en tu propia casa

Aunque sea un día a la semana —o al mes— aparta[j] una hora —o más— para ti mismo. <u>Prende</u> una vela[k] de aroma tranquilizante, llena la <u>tina del baño</u> con un delicioso jabón y tómate un té caliente de manzanilla,[l] vainilla o canela.[m]

Come de manera saludable

Una buena dieta baja en <u>grasas</u>, alta en fibra y que incluye comer vegetales y frutas diariamente ayuda no sólo al cuerpo sino al estado mental. Cuando <u>ingerimos</u> en exceso comida grasosa y azucarada[n] —los famosos alimentos vacíos de nutrición que suelen aparecer en nuestras cocinas— el cuerpo protesta de diversas formas. Las enfermedades que pueden aparecer a la larga[o] como la obesidad, el alto colesterol y enfermedades del corazón son aun otras y muy serias fuentes de estrés.

Convierte estos pasos en una rutina diaria

Poco a poco —¡y sin estresarte!— incorpora estos pasos a la rutina de tus días y noches. No hay que hacerlo de un jalón.[p] Comienza al paso que puedas, <u>incrementando</u> gradualmente para que poco a poco se conviertan en algo cotidiano[q] y <u>esperado.</u> Verás[r] que dentro de poco tu cara sonriente y tranquila lo dirá todo:[s] ¿Estrés? ¿De qué hablas? ■

[i]te... *will thank you for it* [j]*set aside* [k]*candle* [l]*chamomile* [m]*cinnamon* [n]*sweetened, containing sugar* [o]a... *over time* [p]de... *all at once* [q]*diario* [r]*You'll see* [s]lo... *will say it all*

Comprensión

A. Consejos. De los siguientes consejos para reducir el estrés, ¿cuáles *no* se mencionan en el artículo?

1. comer bien
2. escuchar música
3. hacer ejercicio

4. controlar la respiración
5. practicar yoga
6. beber bastante agua

B. Síntomas y soluciones

PASO 1   Identifique tres síntomas del estrés, según la lectura.

1. _____
2. _____
3. _____

PASO 2   Ahora haga una lista de posibles soluciones para el estrés. Indentifique las soluciones que Ud. prefiere o que cree que son más efectivos. ¿Puede añadir (*add*) otra solución no mencionada en el artículo?

 A ESCRIBIR

Ud. y el estrés. La lectura presenta varias sugerencias para reducir el estrés, pero claro que no es una lista definitiva. Seguro que hay otros métodos también. Cuando Ud. se siente estresado/a, ¿qué hace para bajar el nivel de estrés? ¿Tiene alguna técnica en particular? Escriba un breve ensayo de 100 palabras en el cual describa cómo responde Ud. al estrés y qué hace para aliviarlo (*alleviate it*).

En resumen

GRAMÁTICA

To review the grammar points presented in this chapter, refer to the indicated grammar presentations. You'll find further practice of these structures in the Workbook/Laboratory Manual, on the Interactive CD-ROM, and on the *¿Qué tal?* Online Learning Center (www.mhhe.com/quetal7).

31 Expressing Unplanned or Unexpected Events—Another Use of **se**

Do you know how to use **se** to express unplanned or unexpected events?

32 ¿**Por** o **para**?—A Summary of Their Uses

Do you know the difference between **por** and **para** and when to use one or the other?

VOCABULARIO
Practice this vocabulary with digital flash cards on the Online Learning Center (www.mhhe.com/quetal7).

Los verbos

acabar	to finish; to run out of
apagar (gu)	to turn off
quedar	to remain, be left

Repaso: olvidar, perder (ie)

Presiones de la vida estudiantil

la calificación	grade
el despertador	alarm clock
el estrés	stress
la (falta de) flexibilidad	(lack of) flexibility
la fecha límite	deadline
el horario	schedule
el informe (oral/escrito)	(oral/written) report
la llave	key
la nota	grade
la presión	pressure
la prueba	quiz; test
la tarjeta de identificación	identification card
el trabajo	job, work; report, (piece of) work
de tiempo completo/parcial	full time/part time

Cognado: el calendario
Repaso: el examen, la tarea

acordarse (ue) (de)	to remember
entregar (gu)	to turn, hand in

estacionar	to park
recoger (j)	to collect; to pick up
sacar (qu)	to get (*grades*)
sufrir	to suffer
(muchas) presiones	to be under (a lot of) pressure

Repaso: llegar (gu) a tiempo / tarde, olvidarse de

Más partes del cuerpo humano

el brazo	arm
el dedo (de la mano)	finger
el dedo del pie	toe
la mano	hand
el pie	foot
la pierna	leg

Repaso: la cabeza

Accidentes

caer (*irreg.*)	to fall
caerse	to fall down
darse (*irreg.*) en/con/contra	to run, bump into
equivocarse (qu) (de)	to be wrong, make a mistake (about)
hacerse (*irreg.*) **daño**	to hurt oneself
lastimarse	to injure oneself
levantarse con el pie izquierdo	to get up on the wrong side of the bed
pedir (i, i) disculpas	to apologize

pegarse (gu) en/con/contra	to hit (*a part of one's body*); to run into/bump against
romper	to break

Repaso: doler (ue)

Discúlpeme.	Pardon me. I'm sorry.
Fue sin querer.	It was unintentional.
¡Lo siento (mucho)!	Pardon me! I'm (very) sorry!
¡Qué mala suerte!	What bad luck!

Repaso: perdón

Los adjetivos

distraído/a	absentminded
escrito/a	written
estudiantil	(of) student(s)
torpe	clumsy
universitario/a	(of the) university

Cognado: flexible

Otros sustantivos

la época	era, time (*period*)
la luz (*pl.* **luces**)	light; electricity

Repaso: la vida

Palabras adicionales

-mente	-ly (*adverbial suffix*)
por Dios	for heaven's sake
por ejemplo	for example
por primera/ última vez	for the first/last time
por si acaso	just in case
¡por supuesto!	of course!
por todas partes	everywhere
¡qué + *adj.*!	how + *adj.*!

Repaso: gracias por, por eso, por favor, por fin, por la mañana/tarde/noche, por lo general, por lo menos

La calidad de la vida

Las terrazas de Machu Picchu, Perú

TENGO... NECESITO... QUIERO...

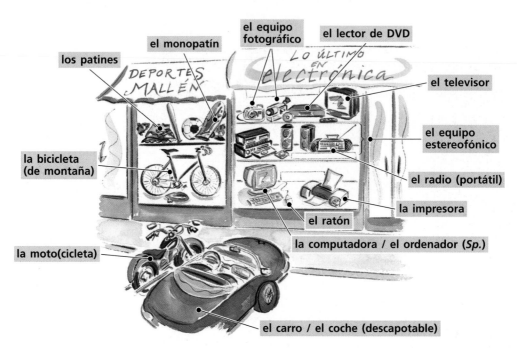

el equipo fotográfico

el monopatín

el lector de DVD

los patines

DEPORTES MALLÉN

LO ÚLTIMO EN electrónica

el televisor

la bicicleta (de montaña)

el equipo estereofónico

el radio (portátil)

la impresora

el ratón

la computadora / el ordenador (*Sp.*)

la moto(cicleta)

el carro / el coche (descapotable)

La electrónica

la cinta	tape
el contestador automático	answering machine
el correo electrónico	e-mail
el disco duro	hard drive
la grabadora	(tape) recorder/player
la Red	Net
navegar (gu) la Red	to surf the Net
la videocasetera	videocassette recorder/player (VCR)

Cognados: la cámara (de vídeo), el CD-ROM, el control remoto, el disco compacto (el CD), el disco de computadora, el DVD, el fax, el *iPod*, la memoria, el módem, el teléfono (celular), el *walkman*

Verbos útiles

cambiar (de canal, de cuarto, de ropa...)	to change (channels, rooms, clothing . . .)
conseguir (i, i) (g)	to get, obtain
copiar / hacer (*irreg.*) **copia**	to copy
fallar	to "crash" (*of computers*)
funcionar	to work, function; to run (*machines*)
grabar	to record; to tape
guardar	to keep, to save (*documents*)
imprimir	to print
manejar	to drive; to operate (*a machine*)
obtener (*irreg.*)	to get, obtain
sacar (qu) fotos	to take photos

En el trabajo

el aumento	raise
el/la jefe/a	boss
el sueldo	salary

■ Conversación

A. Ud. y los aparatos

PASO 1 ¿Qué se usa en estas situaciones? Con un compañero / una compañera, conteste las preguntas. Luego piense en cuatro situaciones similares. Uno/a de Uds. da la descripción y el otro / la otra identifica el aparato.

1. para mandar copias de documentos no originales que deben llegar inmediatamente
2. para grabar un programa de televisión cuando no podemos verlo a la hora de su emisión
3. para cambiar el programa de la tele sin levantarse del sillón
4. para recibir llamadas telefónicas cuando no estamos en casa
5. para escuchar música mientras hacemos ejercicio

PASO 2 Para Ud., ¿son ciertas o falsas las siguientes oraciones?

1. Entiendo cómo funcionan los aparatos.
2. Aprendí con facilidad a usar la computadora.
3. No me puedo imaginar la vida sin los aparatos electrónicos modernos.
4. Para mí, el vehículo es una expresión de la personalidad.
5. Una vez me falló la computadora y perdí unos documentos y archivos (*files*) muy importantes.
6. Uso la videocasetera para ver películas, pero no sé grabar.
7. Me gusta navegar la red porque encuentro mucha información.

B. ¿Qué vehículos... ? ¿Qué vehículo piensa Ud. que deben tener y usar las siguientes personas? ¿Qué vehículo(s) tiene Ud.? ¿Es lo más apropiado para su vida? ¿Por qué? ¿Qué vehículo le gustaría tener?

1. una persona joven que vive en Key West, una isla soleada e informal en el sur de Florida
2. una familia con tres hijos
3. un estudiante de artes liberales que vive en este *campus*
4. unos chicos que pasan gran parte de su tiempo libre en la playa y en el *boardwalk*
5. un matrimonio jubilado (*retired*) que vive en Nueva Inglaterra

C. ¿Necesidad o lujo (*luxury*)?

PASO 1 ¿Considera Ud. que las siguientes posesiones son un lujo o una necesidad de la vida moderna? Indique si Ud. tiene este aparato o vehículo. Luego, dé tres cosas más que Ud. considera necesarias en la vida moderna.

MODELO: un televisor → Para mí, un televisor es una necesidad. Tengo uno. (No tengo uno ahora.)

1. un contestador automático
2. una videocasetera
3. el equipo estereofónico
4. una computadora
5. un coche
6. una bicicleta
7. un *iPod*
8. un teléfono celular

PASO 2 Para terminar, entreviste a un compañero / una compañera para saber si está de acuerdo con Ud. y si tiene las mismas posesiones.

MODELO: el televisor → E1: ¿El televisor?
E2: Yo lo considero un lujo y por eso no tengo uno.

La... *Housing*

LA VIVIENDA°

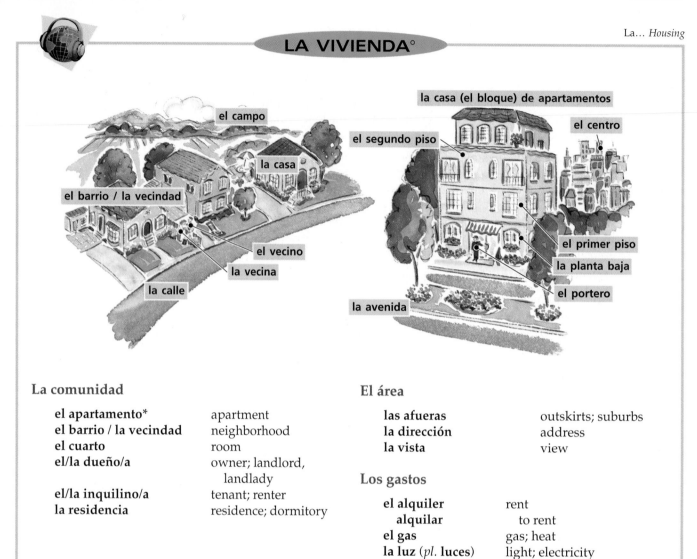

el campo

la casa (el bloque) de apartamentos

el centro

el segundo piso

la casa

el barrio / la vecindad

el vecino

la vecina

el primer piso

la planta baja

el portero

la calle

la avenida

La comunidad

el apartamento*	apartment
el barrio / la vecindad	neighborhood
el cuarto	room
el/la dueño/a	owner; landlord, landlady
el/la inquilino/a	tenant; renter
la residencia	residence; dormitory

El área

las afueras	outskirts; suburbs
la dirección	address
la vista	view

Los gastos

el alquiler	rent
alquilar	to rent
el gas	gas; heat
la luz (*pl.* **luces**)	light; electricity

■ Conversación

A. Definiciones. Dé las definiciones de las siguientes palabras.

MODELO: la residencia →
Es un lugar donde viven muchos estudiantes. Por lo general está situada en el *campus* universitario.

Frases útiles

Es una persona que...
Es un lugar donde...
Es una cosa que...

1. el inquilino
2. el centro
3. el alquiler
4. el portero
5. la vecina

6. la dueña
7. la dirección
8. las afueras
9. el barrio
10. la casa

11. la avenida
12. el campo
13. la planta baja
14. la vista
15. la luz

*****El apartamento** *is used throughout Latin America and the Caribbean.* **El departamento** *is used in Mexico, Peru, and other Latin American countries, but* **el piso** *is the word most commonly used in Spain.*

NOTA CULTURAL

Los barrios y las familias

En los pueblos pequeños del mundo es común que **los parientes** de una familia **vivan en la misma calle,** o por lo menos, en el mismo barrio. También es común que la madre o la abuela de la familia prepare la comida para que **todos los familiares** que viven cerca **vengan a comer juntos.**[a]

Las personas que viven en apartamentos a veces mantienen **una relación muy unida** con **sus vecinos.** En una casa de apartamentos típica, muchos se consideran como una gran familia. Hay un ambiente familiar entre los vecinos aunque[b] no sean parientes.

A veces por necesidad o simplemente para seguir[c] una carrera,[d] unos **dejan su comunidad** y se mudan[e] a otra ciudad o a otro país.

Una familia hispana durante una comida típica

[a]*together*   [b]*although*   [c]*follow*   [d]*career, profession*   [e]*se... move*

B. A buscar vivienda

PASO 1   Lea los tres anuncios de viviendas en el Perú y conteste las siguientes preguntas.

1. ¿Qué tipo de vivienda aparece (*appears*) en cada anuncio? ¿Son para comprar o alquilar?
2. ¿Cuántos dormitorios tiene cada vivienda?
3. ¿Cree Ud. que estas viviendas son para familias con mucho o poco dinero?

PASO 2   **Entrevista.** Con un compañero / una compañera, hable sobre el tipo de vivienda que prefieren.

1. Como estudiante universitario, ¿prefieres vivir en el *campus* o fuera del *campus*? ¿en una residencia o en una casa o apartamento de alquiler con otras personas?
2. ¿Prefieres vivir en la planta baja o en los pisos más altos?
3. Si alquilas tu vivienda, ¿prefieres que el alquiler incluya (*include*) todos los gastos o prefieres pagar la luz y el gas por separado?
4. Si pudieras (*If you could*) escoger, ¿qué te gustaría más, tener un apartamento pequeño en un barrio elegante del centro o una casa grande en las afueras?
5. ¿Qué tipo de vecinos te gusta tener?

CUZCO

Alquilo casa. Barrio residencial. Semi-amueblada[a] con teléfono. Informes Teléf. Cuzco: 084-226752. Lima: 774153 (horario 2 a 5 p.m.)

[a]*Partially furnished*

CHACARILLA DEL ESTANQUE

Departamentos exclusivos, diseño especial, 3 dormitorios, comedor de diario, área de servicio, totalmente equipados. Desde $41.500. Buenas facilidades.

Av. Buena Vista N° 230 (a 2 Cdras. de Velasco Aslete) Tels. 458107 – 357743

DEPARTAMENTOS MONTERRICO

Finos departamentos de 3 dormitorios, 3½ baños, sala de estar,[b] 1 ó 2 cocheras,[c] acabados de primera,[d] verlos todos los días en: Domingo de la Presa 165, espalda cuadra 12 Av. Primavera.

[b]*sala... living room; sitting room*   [c]*1 ó 2... one- or two-car garage*   [d]*acabados... first-class finishing details*

Need more practice?

- Workbook/Laboratory Manual
- Interactive CD-ROM
- Online Learning Center (www.mhhe.com/quetal7)

¿Recuerda Ud.?

In **Gramática 19** you learned about **Ud.** and **Uds.** (formal) commands. Remember that object pronouns (direct, indirect, reflexive) must follow and be attached to affirmative commands; they must precede negative commands.

AFFIRMATIVE: Háblele Ud.   Duérmase.   Dígaselo Ud.

NEGATIVE: No le hable Ud.   No se duerma.   No se lo diga Ud.

¿Cómo se dice en español?

1. Bring me the book. (**Uds.**)
2. Don't give it (*m.*) to her. (**Uds.**)
3. Sit here, please. (**Ud.**)
4. Don't sit in that chair! (**Ud.**)
5. Tell them the truth. (**Uds.**)
6. Tell it (*f.*) to them now! (**Uds.**)
7. Never tell it (*f.*) to her. (**Uds.**)
8. Take care of yourself. (**Ud.**)
9. Lead a healthy life. (**Ud.**)
10. Listen to me. (**Ud.**)
11. Wake up earlier. (**Ud.**)
12. Get dressed quickly. (**Uds.**)
13. Enjoy yourself with your friends. (**Ud.**)
14. Don't give it (*m.*) to them now. (**Uds.**)

33   Influencing Others   *Tú* (Informal) Commands

¡Marta, tu cuarto es un desastre!

El padre de Marta está enojado.

«¡Marta, qué desordenado está tu cuarto! Por favor, *arréglalo* antes de jugar con tus amigos. *Guarda* la ropa limpia en tu armario, *pon* la ropa sucia en el cesto, *haz* la cama, *recoge* los libros del piso y *ordénalos* en los estantes… Y no *dejes* los zapatos por todas partes… ¡Es muy peligroso!»

Comprensión

¿Quién diría (*would say*) lo siguiente, Marta o Manolo, su padre?

1. No te enojes… Ya voy a arreglarlo todo.
2. Hazlo inmediatamente… ¡antes de salir a jugar!
3. Dime, ¿por qué tengo que hacerlo ahora mismo?
4. La próxima vez, ¡no dejes tu cuarto en estas condiciones!

> Informal commands (**los mandatos informales**) are used with persons whom you would address as **tú**.

Past	------------------------	PRESENT	----------------------	Future
preterite		present indicative		
imperfect		present progressive		
		formal commands		
		informal commands		

Marta, your room is a disaster!   *Marta's father is angry. "Marta, what a messy room you have! Please straighten it up before you go out to play with your friends. Put your clean clothes away in the closet, put your dirty clothes in the hamper, make your bed, pick your books up off of the floor and arrange them on the shelves… And don't leave your shoes lying around everywhere… It's very dangerous!"*

Negative *tú* Commands

	-ar verbs		*-er/-ir* verbs	
No hables.	Don't speak.	**No comas.**	Don't eat.
No cantes.	Don't sing.	**No escribas.**	Don't write.
No juegues.	Don't play.	**No pidas.**	Don't order.

A. Like **Ud.** commands (**Gramática 19**), the negative **tú** commands are expressed using the "opposite vowel": **no hable Ud., no hables (tú).** The pronoun **tú** is used only for emphasis.

No cantes **tú** tan fuerte.
*Don't **you** sing so loudly.*

B. As with negative **Ud.** commands, object pronouns—direct, indirect, and reflexive—precede negative **tú** commands.

No lo mires.   **No les** escribas.   **No te** levantes.
Don't look at him.   Don't write to them.   Don't get up.

Affirmative *tú* Commands

	-ar verbs		*-er/-ir* verbs	
Habla.	Speak.	**Come.**	Eat.
Canta.	Sing.	**Escribe.**	Write.
Juega.	Play.	**Pide.**	Order.

A. Unlike the other command forms you have learned, most affirmative **tú** commands have the same form as the third person singular of the present indicative.* Some verbs have irregular affirmative **tú** command forms.

decir:	di	salir:	sal
hacer:	haz	ser:	sé
ir:	ve	tener:	ten
poner:	pon	venir:	ven

Spelling Hint: One-syllable words, like the affirmative **tú** commands of some verbs (**decir, ir, tener,…**) do not need an accent mark: **di, ve, ten,…** Exceptions to this rule are those forms that could be mistaken for other words, like the command of **ser** (**sé**), which could be mistaken for the pronoun **se.**

Sé puntual pero **ten** cuidado.
Be there on time, but be careful.

OJO The affirmative **tú** commands for **ir** and **ver** are identical: **ve.** Context will clarify meaning.

¡**Ve** esa película!   **Ve** a casa ahora mismo.
See that movie!   Go home right now.

*As you know, there are two different moods in Spanish: the indicative mood (the one you have been using, which is used to state facts and ask questions) and the subjunctive mood (which is used to express more subjective actions or states). Beginning with **Gramática 34,** you will learn more about the subjunctive mood.

PASO 2

B. As with affirmative **Ud.** commands, object and reflexive pronouns follow affirmative **tú** commands and are attached to them. Accent marks are necessary except when a single pronoun is added to a one-syllable command.

Dile la verdad.
Tell him the truth.

Léela, por favor.
Read it, please.

Póntelos.
Put them on.

AUTOPRUEBA

Choose the correct command form for each sentence.

1. _____me qué quieres.
2. No _____ al parque sola.
3. No le _____ nada de la fiesta.
4. _____te un abrigo.
5. _____ a la tienda.
6. No _____ eso en mi cama.

a. di
b. digas
c. pon
d. pongas
e. vayas
f. ve

Answers: 1. a 2. e 3. b 4. c 5. f 6. d

NOTA COMUNICATIVA

Vosotros Commands

In **Capítulo 1,** you learned about the pronoun **vosotros/vosotras** that is used in Spain as the plural of **tú.** Here is information about forming **vosotros** commands, for recognition only.

- Affirmative **vosotros** commands are formed by substituting **-d** for the final **-r** of the infinitive. There are no irregular affirmative **vosotros** commands.

  hablar → hablad
  comer → comed
  escribir → escribid

- Negative **vosotros** commands are expressed with the present subjunctive. (You will learn more about the present subjunctive in the next and subsequent grammar sections.)

  no habléis
  no comáis
  no escribáis

- Placement of object pronouns is the same as for all other command forms.

  Decídmelo.
  No me lo digáis.

■ Práctica

A. ¡Anticipemos! Recuerdos de la niñez

PASO 1 Indique los mandatos afirmativos que Ud. oía con frecuencia cuando era niño/a. Después de leerlos todos, indique los dos que oía más. ¿Hay entre estos algún mandato que Ud. no oyera (*heard*) nunca?

1. _____ Limpia tu cuarto.
2. _____ Cómete el desayuno.
3. _____ Haz la tarea.
4. _____ Cierra la puerta.
5. _____ Bébete la leche.
6. _____ Lávate las manos.
7. _____ Dime la verdad.
8. _____ Quítate el *walkman*.
9. _____ Guarda tu bicicleta en el garaje.

 OJO

Note in **Práctica A** the use of the reflexive pronoun with the verbs **comer** and **beber**. This use of the reflexive means *to eat up* and *to drink up*, respectively.

Cómete las zanahorias.
Eat up your carrots.

No **te bebas** la leche tan rápido.
Don't drink up your milk so fast.

PASO 2   Ahora indique los mandatos negativos que escuchaba con frecuencia. Debe indicar también los dos que oía más. ¿Hay alguno que no oyera (*heard*) nunca?

1. ____ No cruces la calle solo/a.
2. ____ No juegues con cerillas (*matches*).
3. ____ No comas dulces antes de cenar.
4. ____ No me digas mentiras (*lies*).
5. ____ No les des tanta comida a los peces.

6. ____ No hables con personas desconocidas (*strangers*).
7. ____ No dejes el monopatín en el jardín.
8. ____ No cambies los canales tanto.
9. ____ No digas tonterías (*silly things*).

B. Julita, la mal educada

PASO 1   Los Sres. Villarreal no están contentos con el comportamiento de su hija Julita. Continúe los comentarios de ellos con mandatos informales lógicos según cada situación. Siga los modelos.

MODELOS: *Hablaste* demasiado (*too much*) ayer. → No *hables* tanto hoy, por favor.
Dejaste tu ropa en el suelo anoche. → No la *dejes* allí hoy, por favor.

1. También *dejaste* tus libros en el suelo (*floor*).
2. ¿Por qué *regresaste* tarde a casa hoy después de las clases?
3. ¿Por qué *vas* al parque todas las tardes?
4. No es bueno que *mires* la televisión constantemente. ¿Y por qué quieres *ver* todos esos programas de detectives?
5. ¿Por qué le *dices* mentiras (*lies*) a tu papá?
6. Siempre *te olvidas* de sacar la basura, que es tu único quehacer.
7. Ay, hija, no te comprendemos. ¡*Eres* tan insolente!

PASO 2   La pobre Julita también escucha muchos mandatos de su maestra en clase. Invente Ud. esos mandatos según las indicaciones.

1. llegar / a / escuela / puntualmente
2. quitarse / abrigo / y / sentarse
3. sacar / libro de matemáticas / y / abrirlo / en / página diez
4. leer / nuevo / palabras / y / aprenderlas / para mañana
5. venir / aquí / a / hablar conmigo / sobre / este / composición

Need more practice?

- Workbook/Laboratory Manual
- Interactive CD-ROM
- Online Learning Center (www.mhhe.com/quetal7)

▪ Conversación

A. **Entre compañeros de casa.**   Con un compañero / una compañera, haga una lista de los cinco mandatos que se oyen con más frecuencia en su casa (apartamento, residencia). Piensen no sólo en los mandatos que Uds. escuchan sino (*but*) también en los que Uds. les dan a los demás (*others*).

Frases útiles		
apagar (gu) la **computadora** **contestar el teléfono** **lavar los platos** **no hacer** (*irreg.*) **ruido**	**no ser** (*irreg.*)... **así** (like that), **bobo/a** (dumb), **impaciente,** **impulsivo/a, loco/a,** **pesado/a,** **precipitado/a** (hasty)	**prestarme dinero** **poner** (*irreg.*) **la tele** **sacar** (qu) **la basura** **¿ ?**

PASO 2

B. Situaciones. ¿Qué consejos les daría (*would you give*) a las siguientes personas si fueran (*they were*) sus amigos? Déles a todos consejos en forma de mandatos informales.

1. Celia siempre tiene mucha energía los viernes y le encanta ir al cine o salir a bailar. Pero a su novio no le gusta salir mucho los viernes porque está cansado después de una larga semana de trabajo.

2. Nati tiene 19 años. El próximo año quiere vivir en un apartamento ecónomico en un barrio estudiantil con cuatro amigos (dos de ellos son hombres). Pero los padres de Nati son muy tradicionales y no les va a gustar la situación.

3. Su abuelo va a comprarse su primera computadora y necesita su opinión y experiencia. Tiene muchas preguntas, desde qué tipo debe comprar hasta cómo usarla eficientemente. Él quiere una computadora para conectarse con unos amigos jubilados (*retired*) que ahora viven en otro estado, para navegar la Red y para realizar el sueño de su vida: escribir la historia de la llegada de sus padres a este país.

4. Mariana es una *yuppi*. Gana (*She makes*) muchísimo dinero pero trabaja demasiado. Duerme poco y bebe muchísimo café para seguir despierta (*awake*). No come bien y jamás hace ejercicio. Acaba de comprarse una agenda electrónica (*PDA*) para llevar su trabajo a todas partes.

En los Estados Unidos y el Canadá

Las computadoras y la comunidad hispana

El acceso a las computadoras entre la comunidad hispana es **mayor ahora** que hace diez años.[a] En un estudio del Departamento de Comercio de los Estados Unidos, con datos del año 2001, se ve que el 49 por ciento de los hispanos de este país usa una computadora. Sin embargo, este aumento es **una mejora**[b] **relativa,** pues la diferencia en cuanto al[c] uso de computadoras entre los hispanos y los no hispanos también creció.[d] Aún[e] más significativa es la diferencia en el porcentaje de hispanos **con acceso al Internet en sus hogares**[f] comparado con el de la población no hispana.

	1997	2001
uso de computadoras		
hispanos	38%	49%
no hispanos	54%	66%
uso del Internet		
hispanos	11%	22%
no hispanos	32%	54%

¿Por qué estas diferencias? Esencialmente por **razones económicas.** Es evidente que las personas que ganan más dinero pueden comprar más computadoras y tecnología, y por ahora hay muchos hispanos que no tienen suficientes

ingresos[g] para estar al día[h] con **los avances tecnológicos.**

En el futuro, será[i] necesario que las computadoras y el Internet se hagan accesibles[j] a más hispanos. Son herramientas[k] necesarias para **la educación, el trabajo, la comunicación** y sobre todo para **la información.** Casi todos los periódicos

En Chicago, Illinois

principales de los países hispanos se publican ahora en el Internet. A través de[l] las publicaciones ciberespaciales, los hispanos pueden leer las noticias en español y hasta[m] pueden leer las noticias de su país o ciudad natal. También pueden participar en comunicaciones con **la comunidad hispana** del Internet.

[a]hace... *ten years ago* [b]*improvement* [c]en... *regarding the* [d]*grew* [e]*Still* [f]*homes* [g]*income* [h]al... *up-to-date* [i]*it will be* [j]*available* [k]*tools* [l]A... *Through* [m]*even*

34 Expressing Subjective Actions or States Present Subjunctive: An Introduction

Una decisión importante

José Miguel habla con Gustavo de cámaras digitales

JOSÉ MIGUEL: Quiero comprar una cámara digital. No tengo mucho dinero, pero *es posible que* un amigo me *preste* el dinero que necesito.

GUSTAVO: Pues yo acabo de comprar una cámara digital. Está muy bien y no era muy cara.

JOSÉ MIGUEL: *¿Me recomiendas que compre* alguna marca en particular?

GUSTAVO: Realmente, todas las marcas conocidas tienen buenos productos. *Yo te sugiero que mires* los anuncios en los periódicos y *que busques* las mejores ofertas.

JOSÉ MIGUEL: *Me alegro de que sepas* tanto de electrónica. *¿Me permites que vea* tu cámara?

GUSTAVO: Claro, voy por ella.

Comprensión: ¿Cierto o falso?

1. José Miguel quiere que su mamá le preste dinero.
2. Gustavo le recomienda a José Miguel que compre una cámara de una marca específica.
3. Gustavo le sugiere a José Miguel que primero vaya a muchas tiendas.
4. José Miguel quiere que Gustavo le enseñe su cámara nueva.

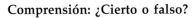

Past ------------------- PRESENT ------------------- Future		
preterite	**present indicative**	
imperfect	**present progressive**	
	formal commands	
	informal commands	
	present subjunctive	

An important decision José Miguel is talking to Gustavo about digital cameras. JOSÉ MIGUEL: *I want to buy a digital camera. I don't have a lot of money, but it's possible that a friend will lend me the money I need.* GUSTAVO: *Well, I just bought a digital camera. It's very nice and it wasn't expensive.* JOSÉ MIGUEL: *Do you recommend that I buy a particular brand?* GUSTAVO: *To tell the truth, all of the well-known brands have good products. I suggest that you check out the ads in the newspapers and that you look for the best deals.* JOSÉ MIGUEL: *I'm glad you know so much about electronic equipment. Can I see your camera?* GUSTAVO: *Of course, I'll go get it.*

Present Subjunctive: An Introduction

A. Except for command forms, all the verb forms you have learned so far in *¿Qué tal?* are part of the *indicative mood* (**el modo indicativo**). In both English and Spanish, the indicative is used to state facts and to ask questions; it objectively expresses actions or states of being that are considered true by the speaker.

INDICATIVE:

¿Vienes a la fiesta?
Are you coming to the party?

Prefiero llegar temprano a casa.
I prefer getting home early.

B. Both English and Spanish have another verb system called the *subjunctive mood* (**el modo subjuntivo**). The subjunctive is used to express more subjective or conceptualized actions or states. These include things that the speaker wants to happen or wants others to do, events to which the speaker reacts emotionally, things that are as yet unknown, and so on.

SUBJUNCTIVE:

Espero que **vengas** a la fiesta.
I hope (that) you are coming to the party.

Prefiero que **llegues** temprano a casa.
I prefer that you be home early.

C. Sentences in English and Spanish may be simple or complex. A simple sentence is one that contains a single verb.

Complex sentences are comprised of two or more *clauses* (**las cláusulas**), each containing a conjugated verb. There are two types of clauses: main (independent) clause and subordinate (dependent) clause. *Independent clauses* (**las cláusulas principales**) contain a complete thought and can stand alone. *Dependent clauses* (**las cláusulas subordinadas**) contain an incomplete thought and cannot stand alone. Dependent clauses require an independent clause to form a complete sentence.

When the subjects of the clauses in a complex sentence are different, the subjunctive is often used in the subordinate clause in Spanish. Note that subordinate clauses are linked by the conjunction **que,** which is never optional (as it is in English).

SIMPLE SENTENCE:

Vienes a la fiesta.   Alicia está en casa.
You are coming to the party.   *Alicia is at home.*

COMPLEX SENTENCE:

INDICATIVE

MAIN CLAUSE		SUBORDINATE CLAUSE
Ella sabe	que	vienes a la fiesta.
She knows	*(that)*	*you are coming to the party.*
Miguel piensa	que	Alicia está en casa.
Miguel thinks	*(that)*	*Alicia is at home.*

SUBJUNCTIVE

MAIN CLAUSE		SUBORDINATE CLAUSE
Quiere	que	**vengas** a la fiesta.
She wants	*(for)*	*you to come to the party.*
Miguel espera	que	Alicia **esté** en casa.
Miguel hopes	*(that)*	*Alicia is at home.*
Duda	que	**vengas** a la fiesta.
She doubts	*(that)*	*you are coming to the party.*

When there is no change of subject in the sentence, the infinitive follows the conjugated verb and no conjunction is necessary. In this type of sentence, the infinitive functions as a direct object of the conjugated verb.

Quiero ir a la fiesta.
I want to go to the party.

D. Three of the most common uses of the subjunctive are to express influence, emotion, and doubt or denial. These are signaled in the previous examples by the verb forms **quiere, espera,** and **duda.**

Forms of the Present Subjunctive

Many Spanish command forms that you have already learned are part of the subjunctive. The **Ud./Uds.** command forms are highlighted in the following box. What you have learned about forming these commands will help you learn the forms of the present subjunctive.

	hablar	**comer**	**escribir**	**volver**	**decir**
Singular	hable	coma	escriba	vuelva	diga
	hables	comas	escribas	vuelvas	digas
	hable	coma	escriba	vuelva	diga
Plural	hablemos	comamos	escribamos	volvamos	digamos
	habléis	comáis	escribáis	volváis	digáis
	hablen	coman	escriban	vuelvan	digan

A. The personal endings of the present subjunctive are added to the first person singular of the present indicative minus its **-o** ending. **-Ar** verbs add endings with **-e,** and **-er/-ir** verbs add endings with **-a.**

-ar → -e
-er/-ir → -a

present indicative **yo** stem =
present subjunctive stem

B. **-Car, -gar,** and **-zar** verbs have a spelling change in all persons of the present subjunctive to preserve the **-c-, -g-,** and **-z-** sounds.

-car: c → qu
-gar: g → gu
-zar: z → c

	buscar		**pagar**		**empezar**	
busque	busquemos	pague	paguemos	empiece	empecemos
busques	busquéis	pagues	paguéis	empieces	empecéis
busque	busquen	pague	paguen	empiece	empiecen

C. Verbs with irregular **yo** forms show the irregularity in all persons of the present subjunctive.

conocer:	**cono**zca,...	salir:	**sal**ga,...
decir:	**di**ga,...	tener:	**ten**ga,...
hacer:	**ha**ga,...	traer:	**trai**ga,...
oír:	**oi**ga,...	venir:	**ven**ga,...
poner:	**pon**ga,...	ver:	**ve**a,...

D. A few verbs have irregular present subjunctive forms.

dar:	**dé, des, dé, demos, deis, den**
estar:	**esté,...**
haber (hay):	**haya**
ir:	**vaya,...**
saber:	**sepa,...**
ser:	**sea,...**

E. **-Ar** and **-er** stem-changing verbs follow the stem-changing pattern of the present indicative.

pensar (ie):

p**ie**nse	pensemos
p**ie**nses	penséis
p**ie**nse	p**ie**nsen

poder (ue):

p**ue**da	podamos
p**ue**das	podáis
p**ue**da	p**ue**dan

F. **-Ir** stem-changing verbs show a stem change in the four forms that have a change in the present indicative. In addition, however, they show a second stem change in the **nosotros** and **vosotros** forms, similar to the present progressive tense.

-ir stem-changing verbs (**nosotros, vosotros**):
o → u, e → i

dormir (ue, u):

d**ue**rma	d**u**rmamos
d**ue**rmas	d**u**rmáis
d**ue**rma	d**ue**rman

pedir (i, i):

p**i**da	p**i**damos
p**i**das	p**i**dáis
p**i**da	p**i**dan

preferir (ie, i):

pref**ie**ra	pref**i**ramos
pref**ie**ras	pref**i**ráis
pref**ie**ra	pref**ie**ran

AUTOPRUEBA

Complete each verb form with the correct letters to form the subjunctive.

1. conocer: cono_____amos
2. decir: di_____an
3. sacar: sa_____es

4. entregar: entre_____en
5. conseguir: consi_____an
6. morir: m_____ramos

Answers: 1. conozcamos 2. digan 3. saques 4. entreguen 5. consigan 6. muramos

■ Práctica

A. ¡Anticipemos! La vida tecnológica. Indique si está de acuerdo o no con las siguientes oraciones.

1. En la vida actual es absolutamente necesario tener una computadora.
2. Yo quiero comprarme una computadora nueva, pero no creo que pueda hacerlo inmediatamente.
3. Hoy día (*These days*) es posible comprar una buena computadora portátil por $1.000.
4. Es horrible que la tecnología cambie tan rápidamente; nadie puede aprender a este ritmo.
5. Prefiero que la gente no dependa tanto de la tecnología.
6. Es ridículo que tantas personas usen un teléfono celular.
7. Dudo que el precio de las llamadas de los teléfonos celulares baje más en los próximos dos años.
8. Espero que mi compañero/a de casa (esposo/a, hijo/a) cambie el mensaje del contestador automático.

B. Su trabajo actual. Use frases de la lista a la derecha para completar las oraciones de modo (*in such a way*) que se refieran a su situación laboral actual. (Siempre hay más de una respuesta posible.) Si Ud. no trabaja ahora, no importa. ¡Invéntese una respuesta!

1. _____ El jefe quiere que _____.
2. _____ También espera que _____.
3. _____ Y duda que _____.
4. _____ Prohíbe (*He forbids*) que _____.
5. _____ En el trabajo, es importante que _____.
6. _____ Yo espero que _____.
7. _____ No quiero que _____.
8. _____ Es difícil que _____.

a. a veces trabajemos los fines de semana
b. todos lleguemos a tiempo
c. hablemos por teléfono con los amigos
d. me den un aumento de sueldo
e. nos paguen más a todos
f. no usemos el *fax* para asuntos (*matters*) personales
g. me den un trabajo de tiempo completo algún día
h. no perdamos mucho tiempo charlando (*chatting*) con los demás
i. fumemos en la oficina
j. tengamos muchas fechas límites
k. me den otro proyecto (*project*)
l. ¿ ?

Need more practice?

- Workbook/Laboratory Manual
- Interactive CD-ROM
- Online Learning Center (www.mhhe.com/quetal7)

■ Conversación

A. ¿Puede Ud. substituir en la ausencia de su profesor(a)? Demuéstrele a su profesor(a) que Ud. lo/la conoce bien, formando oraciones como las que dice él/ella en clase. (Sólo tiene que cambiar el infinitivo.)

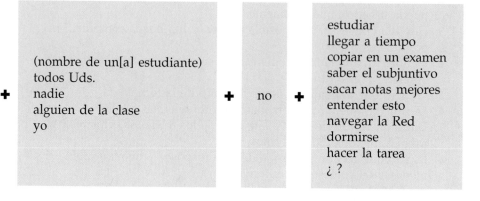

Quiero que
Espero que
Prohíbo que
Dudo que
Es necesario que
Me alegro de (*I'm glad*) que
No creo que
Recomiendo que

+

(nombre de un[a] estudiante)
todos Uds.
nadie
alguien de la clase
yo

+ no **+**

estudiar
llegar a tiempo
copiar en un examen
saber el subjuntivo
sacar notas mejores
entender esto
navegar la Red
dormirse
hacer la tarea
¿ ?

B. Consejos para comprar y usar la tecnología de multimedia

PASO 1 Complete las siguientes recomendaciones. Use el subjuntivo del verbo entre paréntesis y complete cada recomendación según su opinión y sus conocimientos (*knowledge*).

Recomiendo que…

MODELO: (encontrar) [un amigo / un experto / ¿ ?] para ayudarlo/la a montar (*set up*) la computadora →
Recomiendo que *encuentre un experto* para ayudarlo/la a montar la computadora.

1. (ir) a [nombre de una tienda de computadoras] para comprar la computadora
2. (comprar) [marca y modelo de computadora]
3. (mirar) revistas especializadas, como [nombre de revista]
4. (no) (pagar) más de $ _____
5. (no) (usar) [marca o tipo de *software*]
6. (estar) seguro/a de que la computadora tenga [módem / impresora en colores / ¿ ?]
7. (poner) la computadora en [lugar]

PASO 2 Ahora, explique por qué hizo las recomendaciones del **Paso 1**.

MODELO: Recomiendo que encuentre un experto para ayudarlo/la a montar la computadora *porque es difícil hacerlo*.

PASO 3 Compare sus respuestas con las de algunos compañeros para ver si están de acuerdo. ¿Quién sabe más del tema en la clase?

Voces del Perú

LITERATURA: Mario Vargas Llosa

Sobre el autor: *Jorge Mario Pedro Vargas Llosa nació y estudió en el Perú, pero ha vivido[a] en varios países. En los años 90, se trasladó[b] a España, donde consiguió ciudadanía[c] española. Ha sido[d] profesor visitante en universidades de los Estados Unidos, Latinoamérica y Europa. El siguiente fragmento es de la novela:* La tía Julia y el escribidor *(1977).*

En ese tiempo remoto, yo era muy joven y vivía con mis abuelos en una quinta[e] de paredes blancas de la calle Ocharán, en Miraflores. Estudiaba en San Marcos, Derecho,[f] creo, resignado a ganarme más tarde la vida con una profesión liberal, aunque, en el fondo,[g] me hubiera gustado[h] más llegar a ser un escritor. Tenía un trabajo de título pomposo, sueldo modesto, apropiaciones ilícitas[i] y horario elástico: director de Informaciones de Radio Panamericana. Consistía en recortar las noticias interesantes que aparecían en los diarios[j] y maquillarlas[k] un poco para que se leyeran[l] en los boletines.

Mario Vargas Llosa
(1936–)

[a]ha... *he has lived* [b]se... *he moved* [c]*citizenship* [d]Ha... *He has been* [e]*casa* [f]*Law* [g]en... *deep down* [h]me... *I would have liked* [i]apropiaciones... *crooked deals* [j]*periódicos* [k]*editing them* [l]*para... so that they could be read*

MÚSICA: El huayno

El huayno es una música tradicional del Perú y el baile andino más típico. Su sonido[a] es inconfundible,[b] como lo es[c] su baile, caracterizado por pequeños saltos.[d] El nombre «huayno» refleja el origen precolombino de esta forma musical; viene de la palabra quechua **wayna,** que significa «joven».

[a]*sound* [b]*unmistakable* [c]como... *as is* [d]*jumps, hops*

la quena

el charango

Originalmente, el huayno era una danza indígena rítmica acompañada de instrumentos precolombinos como la quena.[e] Con la llegada[f] de los españoles, el huayno se modificó para incluir instrumentos de cuerda.[g] La quena es un instrumento de viento[h] indígena del Perú, típica de la música de los Andes. Hoy el huayno también se toca con el charango (un instrumento andino de diez cuerdas), el arpa[i] y el violín.

[e]*Andean flute* [f]*arrival* [g]instrumentos... *stringed instruments* [h]instrumento... *wind instrument* [i]*harp*

«Tres de mayo» es una canción huayno típica. La fecha, el tres de mayo, es una referencia a un festival nacional peruano.

Tres de mayo

En una noche de tres de mayo
Tuve la suerte de conocerte[j]
Tuve la suerte de haberte querido.[k]

Cuando decías olvidaremos[l]
Olvidaremos todo lo pasado[m]
Huaycheña[n] todo lo pasado
Huaycheña todo lo pasado.

[j]Tuve... *I was lucky to meet you* [k]de... *to have loved you* [l]*we will forget* [m]lo... *what has happened* [n]*Mujer joven*

35 **Expressing Desires and Requests** Use of the Subjunctive: Influence

1. **2.** **3.**

Comprensión:

Escoja la oración que describa cada dibujo.

1. _____ **a.** Quiero aprender las formas del subjuntivo.
   b. Quiero que nosotros *aprendamos* juntos las formas del subjuntivo.
2. _____ **a.** Insisto en hablar con Jorge.
   b. Insisto en que tú *hables* con Jorge.
3. _____ **a.** Es necesario arreglar esta habitación.
   b. Es necesario que tú *arregles* esta habitación.

A. So far, you have learned to identify the subjunctive by the features listed at the right.

The subjunctive:

- appears in a subordinate (dependent) clause.
- has a different subject from the one in the main (independent) clause.
- is preceded by **que.**

B. In addition, the use of the subjunctive is associated with the presence of a number of concepts or conditions that trigger the use of it in the dependent clause. The concept of influence is one trigger for the subjunctive in a dependent clause. When the speaker wants something to happen, he or she tries to influence the behavior of others, as in these sentences.

The verb in the main clause is, of course, in the indicative, because it is a fact that the subject of the sentence wants something. The subjunctive occurs in the dependent clause.

MAIN (INDEPENDENT) CLAUSE		SUBORDINATE (DEPENDENT) CLAUSE
Yo **quiero**	**que**	tú **pagues** la cuenta.
I want		*you to pay the bill.*
La profesora **prefiere**	**que**	los estudiantes no **lleguen** tarde.
The professor prefers	*that*	*students don't arrive late.*

C. **Querer** and **preferir** are not the only verbs that can express the main subject's desire to influence what someone else thinks or does. There are many other verbs of influence, some very strong and direct, some very soft and polite.

STRONG	SOFT
insistir en	desear
mandar (*to order*)	pedir (i, i)
permitir (*to permit*)	recomendar (ie)
prohibir (prohíbo)	sugerir (ie, i)

D. An impersonal generalization of influence or volition can also be the main clause that triggers the subjunctive. Some examples of this appear at the right.

Es necesario que…	Es importante que…
Es urgente que…	Es mejor que…

▓ Práctica

A. ¡Anticipemos! En la tienda de aparatos electrónicos. Imagine que Ud. y un amigo están en una tienda de aparatos electrónicos. Ud. quiere comprarse un televisor pero no sabe cuál; por eso su amigo lo/la acompaña. ¿Quién dice las siguientes oraciones, Ud., su amigo o el vendedor (*salesperson*)?

1. Prefiero que busques un televisor en varias tiendas; así puedes comparar precios.
2. Quiero que el televisor tenga pantalla plana (*flat screen*).
3. Recomiendo que no le digas cuánto dinero quieres gastar.
4. Insisto en que Ud. vea este modelo. ¡Es lo último!
5. Prefiero que me muestre otro modelo más barato.
6. Es mejor que vayamos a buscar en otra tienda. Estos televisores son muy caros.
7. Quiero que lo sepa: Este es uno de los mejores en el mercado.

B. Expectativas de la educación

PASO 1 ¿Qué expectativas de la educación tienen los profesores, los estudiantes y los padres de los estudiantes? Forme oraciones según las indicaciones y añada (*add*) palabras cuando sea necesario.

1. todos / profesores / querer / que / estudiantes / llegar / clase / a tiempo
2. profesor(a) de / español / preferir / que / (nosotros) ir / con frecuencia / laboratorio de lenguas
3. profesores / prohibir / que / estudiantes / traer / comida / y / bebidas / clase
4. padres / de / estudiantes / desear / que / hijos / asistir a / clases
5. estudiantes / pedir / que / profesores / no darles / mucho / trabajo
6. también / (ellos) querer / que / haber / más vacaciones
7. padres / insistir en / que / hijos / sacar / buenas / notas

PASO 2 Y Ud., ¿qué quiere que hagan los profesores? Invente tres oraciones más para indicar sus deseos.

AUTOPRUEBA

Check off the sentences that have subordinate clauses in the subjunctive.

1. ☐ Quiero ir a la tienda
2. ☐ Prohíben que los estudiantes usen calculadoras.
3. ☐ Es urgente que vayas ahora.
4. ☐ Sé que estudias mucho.
5. ☐ ¿Quieres que te lo diga todo?

Answers: 2, 3, 5

Need more practice?

■ Workbook/Laboratory Manual
■ Interactive CD-ROM
■ Online Learning Center (www.mhhe.com/quetal7)

■ Conversación

A. ¿Qué quieres? Con un compañero/una compañera, hable de lo que Ud. quiere, prefiere, permite, etcétera, que otras personas hagan. Para formar las preguntas y oraciones, combinen palabras de las tres listas, o usen la imaginación. Luego, hablen de las cosas que otras personas quieren, prefieren, permiten, etcétera, que Uds. hagan.

MODELOS: E1: ¿Qué quieres que haga tu padre?
           E2: Quiero que mi padre me compre una computadora.

           E1: ¿Qué quieren tus hijos que hagas?
           E2: Quieren que yo compre una computadora nueva.

| querer
preferir
insistir en
mandar
permitir
prohibir
recomendar | **+** | padre/madre
amigos/as
hermano/a
profesor(a)
novio/a
esposo/a
compañero/a de cuarto
hijo/a
hijos | **+** | comprarme… (un televisor, rosas, ¿ ?)
visitarme… (mañana, el jueves, ¿ ?)
invitarme… (al cine, a cenar, ¿ ?)
(no) dar tarea… (hoy, mañana, ¿ ?)
ayudarme con… (los quehaceres, la tarea, ¿ ?)
salir con… (otra persona, mi amigo, ¿ ?)
llamarme… (todos los días, el viernes, ¿ ?)
explicarme… (la gramática, ¿ ?)
¿ ? |

B. Entrevista. Complete las siguientes oraciones lógicamente… ¡y con sinceridad! Luego, entreviste a un compañero / una compañera para saber cómo él/ella completó las oraciones.

MODELO: ¿En qué insisten tus padres?

1. Mis padres (hijos, abuelos,…) insisten en que (yo) _____.
2. Mi mejor amigo/a (esposo/a, novio/a,…) desea que (yo) _____.
3. Prefiero que mis amigos _____.
4. No quiero que mis amigos _____.
5. Es urgente que (yo) _____.
6. Es necesario que mi mejor amigo/a (esposo/a, novio/a,…) _____.

UN POCO DE TODO

Lengua y cultura: Una visita a Lima. Complete the following messages with the correct forms of the words in parentheses, as suggested by the context. When two possibilities are given in parentheses, select the correct word. ¡OJO! As you conjugate verbs in this activity, use the present tense unless otherwise indicated in parentheses. If you see *P/I,* you will choose between the preterite and the imperfect; *comm.* means to use a command; *prog.* stands for the present/past progressive, and *subj.* stands for the present subjunctive.

Marcia Hilbert, de Chicago, y su amiga limeña,[a] Matilde O'Hara, se conocieron hace un mes[b] por el Internet. (Escribirse[1]) regularmente (por/para[2]) correo electrónico, y parece que cada día (descubrir[3]) una

[a]de Lima, Perú   [b]hace… *a year ago*

nueva cosa que (tener[4]) en común. Quieren conocerse en persona y Matilde (sugerir[5]) que Marcia (*subj.*, venir[6]) a Lima para (saber/conocer[7]) la capital del Perú. Los siguientes correos electrónicos son los últimos mensajes que se mandaron.

Querida Marci:

¿Cómo estás, amiga? Aquí todo (seguir[8]) más o menos igual. Es diciembre y (*yo:* alegrarse[9]) de que ya (*subj., nosotros:* ser/estar[10]) en verano. Ahora, la garúa[c] que cubre[d] (este[11]) ciudad por muchos días del año (levantarse[12]), y (*nosotros:* ir[13]) a la playa casi todas las tardes. Muy pronto, todo el mundo (ir[14]) a (ser/estar[15]) ocupadísimo en (prepararse[16]) para las festividades del 18 de enero, aniversario de la fundación de Lima por Francisco Pizarro en 1535. Oye, (*yo:* tener[17]) una idea fabulosa. ¿Por qué no (*Uds.:* venir[18]) a Lima para entonces? Me gustaría mucho (verte[19]) y compartir contigo toda la gala del aniversario de esta ciudad. (*comm., Tú:* Preguntarles[20]) a (tu[21]) padres, y (*comm.,* escribirme[22]) pronto.

Un abrazo,

Tu amiga Mati

Querida Mati:

Chica, una noticia maravillosa. Ayer, mamá y yo (*prog.,* hablar[23]) de tu correo electrónico. Mamá visitó Perú en 1980 y tiene (mucho[24]) ganas de volver (a/de[25]) Lima para el Aniversario. ¡Fíjate[e] que (*nosotras:* ir[26]) a vernos en poco más de un mes!

Muchos abrazos,

Marci

Hola Marci:

¡Qué suerte loca! ¿Sabes? Mis tíos viven en los Estados Unidos pero (tener[27]) un apartamento aquí en Lima. Sólo (lo/la[28]) usan cuando (venir[29]) de visita. Mi tío le (*P/I:* decir[30]) a papá que Uds. (poder[31]) quedarse en el apartamento en enero. ¡(*comm., Tú:* Escribirme[32]) tu respuesta pronto!

Abrazos,

Mati

Hola Mati:

¡Qué buenas noticias! El ofrecimiento de quedarnos en el apartamento de los inquilinos es estupendo. Mamá y yo (lo/la[33]) aceptamos con mucho gusto. ¡(*Nosotros:* Salir[34]) (por/para[35]) Lima en tres semanas!

Tu amiga loca de felicidad,

Marci

Una procesión durante las festividades del aniversario de la fundación de Lima

[c]*coastal fog* [d]*covers* [e]*Just think (figurative)*

Comprensión: Una reorganización. The following series of events from the above e-mails is out of order. Rearrange the statements so they will be in chronological order.

1. Matilde invita a Marcia y a la familia de ella a visitar Lima.
2. Marcia y su mamá aceptan la oferta de quedarse en el apartamento.
3. Matilde y Marcia se conocen por correo electrónico.
4. La garúa de Lima se levanta, y todos van a la playa.
5. La madre de Marcia quiere hacer el viaje a Lima.

Resources for Review and Testing Preparation

- Workbook/Laboratory Manual
- Interactive CD-ROM
- Online Learning Center (www.mhhe.com/quetal7)

VIDEOTECA

Entrevista cultural: El Perú

Valdemar de Icasa es un estudiante peruano que trabaja en una tienda. Habla con la entrevistadora de las cosas que se venden en la tienda y de los productos que son más populares. Antes de ver el vídeo, lea el siguiente fragmento de la entrevista.

ENTREVISTADORA: …Y ¿te gusta tu trabajo?

VALDEMAR: Sí, me gusta mucho, eh… digamos, lo único que no me gusta es que gasto mucho de mi… de mi sueldo, en… en comprar equipo de lo mismo que vendemos nosotros.[a] Por ejemplo la semana pasada me compré una cámara digital muy bonita. Pero bueno, salvo[b] eso, no… no pienso quedarme mucho tiempo en este trabajo.

[a]equipo… *the kind of equipment we sell here*   [b]*except for*

Ahora vea el vídeo y conteste las siguientes preguntas basándose en la entrevista.

1. ¿De dónde es Valdemar?
2. ¿Dónde trabaja Valdemar?
3. Según él, ¿cuáles son los productos más populares ahora?
4. ¿Qué problema menciona relativo al trabajo?
5. ¿Qué estudia Valdemar?

Entre amigos: Me tiras un correo, ¿eh?

Karina, Tané, Rubén y Miguel hablan de los aparatos electrónicos y de su uso. En su opinión, ¿qué preguntas se van a hacer? Antes de mirar el vídeo, lea las preguntas a continuación. Mientras mire el vídeo, trate de entender la conversación en general y fíjese en la información sobre las computadoras y otros aparatos electrónicos. Luego mire el vídeo una segunda vez, fijándose en la información que necesita para contestar las preguntas.

1. ¿Qué hace Karina en la computadora?
2. ¿Para qué usa Tané una computadora?
3. ¿Cuál es la dirección electrónica de Tané?
4. ¿Tiene Karina un sitio web?
5. Según Rubén, ¿qué efecto tiene él en los aparatos electrónicos?

ENFOQUE CULTURAL

El Perú

¡Fíjese!

- El Lago Titicaca, que queda entre Bolivia y el Perú, es el lago más grande de Sudamérica y es la ruta de transporte principal entre estos dos países.
- Cientos de años antes de la llegada[a] de los españoles, la agricultura de los indígenas del Perú ya era muy sofisticada. Hace más de 2.000 años,[b] los indígenas ya construían terrazas para sembrar en las faldas[c] de los Andes. Muchas de estas terrazas se usan todavía.
- Uno de los cultivos[d] más importantes de los incas es la papa, que originó en la región cerca del Lago Titicaca. La papa es una de las pocas plantas que puede subsistir[e] en altitudes de más de 13.000 pies y en regiones frías y áridas.

[a]arrival [b]Hace... More than 2,000 years ago [c]para... so that they could plant on the slopes [d]crops [e]survive

Civilizaciones indígenas: La cultura inca

Cuando los españoles llegaron al Perú en 1532, los incas ya dominaban una gran zona de Sudamérica, desde Colombia hasta Chile, y desde el Pacífico hasta las selvas[a] del este. A partir del siglo XIII,[b] muchos otros pueblos indígenas de la inmensa región vivían bajo[c] el dominio de los incas. La capital del imperio era Cuzco.

La palabra *inca* significa *rey* o *príncipe*[d] en quechua, lengua que todavía se habla en el Perú. Bajo el inca, había un gobierno de poder[e] absoluto y un sistema burocrático y social muy complejo.

El imperio inca se destacó[f] por la arquitectura, la ingeniería[g] y las técnicas de cultivo. También estableció un sistema de correo[h] y un censo de la población. Tras la conquista[i] de los incas por los españoles Pizarro y Almagro, el Perú y su capital Lima se convirtieron en un centro fundamental de las colonias españolas en América. Lima fue fundada por Pizarro en 1535.

[a]jungles [b]A... Beginning in the 13th century [c]under [d]rey... king or prince [e]power [f]se... distinguished itself [g]engineering [h]mail delivery [i]Tras... After the conquest

Cuzco, Perú

Learn more about Peru with the Video, the Interactive CD-ROM, and the Online Learning Center (www.mhhe.com/quetal7).

PASO FINAL

A CONVERSAR

Buscando apartamento

PASO 1   Lea los avisos (*ads*) de los apartmentos para alquilar y escoja el apartmento que Ud. prefiere.

**3 dorm.
1 baño.**

Cerca del parque y centro comercial. Planta Baja. $900.

1.

Zona residencial excelente. 3 dorm. 2 baños. Garaje gratis. Sala grande. $1000.

2.

¡Cocina para gourmet!

2 dorm. 1 baño. Autobús. Amueblado. Portero. $825.

3.

PASO 2   En grupos de tres, imaginen que necesitan alquilar un apartamento juntos. Indiquen dónde prefieren vivir y por qué. Traten de comenzar sus oraciones con frases como **Prefiero que... , Recomiendo que... , Es mejor/ bueno que...** o **Es importante que...** Después, cada grupo debe escoger uno de los apartamentos.

> MODELO: Recomiendo que alquilemos el apartamento número dos porque tiene una sala grande. También es bueno que haya dos baños.

PASO 3   Cada grupo debe inventar más información sobre el apartamento que escogió. La información puede incluir: dónde está el apartamento, cuánto es el alquiler, si se permiten animales, si está en una casa particular o en una casa de apartamentos, si se incluye la luz en el alquiler, etcétera.

> MODELO: El alquiler es setecientos dólares al mes. La luz no está incluida.

PASO 4   Cada grupo debe improvisar una escena entre dos personas que buscan apartamento y el dueño / la dueña que lo alquila, basándose en los avisos y la información que inventaron.

> MODELO   E1: ¿Dónde está el apartamento?
> E2: Está en el centro, en una zona muy bonita.

GRAMÁTICA

To review the grammar points presented in this chapter, refer to the indicated grammar presentations. You'll find further practice of these structures in the Workbook/Laboratory Manual, on the Interactive CD-ROM, and on the *¿Qué tal?* Online Learning Center (www.mhhe.com/quetal7).

33 Influencing Others—**Tú** (Informal) Commands

Do you know how to give orders to friends and children in Spanish? How do you tell them what not to do?

34 Expressing Subjective Actions or States—Present Subjunctive: An introduction

Do you understand how to form the present subjunctive?

35 Expressing Desires and Requests—Use of the Subjunctive: Influence

You should be able to express what you want or need someone else to do without using a direct command.

VOCABULARIO
Practice this vocabulary with digital flash cards on the Online Learning Center (www.mhhe.com/quetal7).

Los verbos

alegrarse (de)	to be happy (about)
arreglar	to straighten (up); to fix, repair
dudar	to doubt
esperar	to hope
haber (*infinitive form* *of* **hay**)	(there is, there are)
insistir (en)	to insist (on)
mandar	to order
permitir	to permit, allow
prohibir (prohíbo)	to prohibit, forbid

Repaso: conseguir (i, i) (g), desear, pedir (i, i), preferir (ie, i), querer (*irreg.*), recomendar (ie), sacar (qu) fotos, sugerir (ie, i)

Vehículos

la bicicleta (de montaña)	(mountain) bike
el carro (descapotable)	(convertible) car
el monopatín	skateboard
la moto(cicleta)	motorcycle; moped
los patines	roller skates
manejar	to drive; to operate (*a machine*)

Repaso: el coche

La electrónica

el archivo	(computer) file
el canal	channel
el contestador automático	answering machine
el correo electrónico	e-mail
el disco duro	hard drive
el equipo estereofónico/ fotográfico	stereo/photography equipment
la grabadora	(tape) recorder/player
la impresora	printer
el lector de DVD	DVD player
el ordenador (*Sp.*)	computer
el ratón	mouse
la Red	Net
la videocasetera	videocassette recorder/player (VCR)
cambiar (de)	to change
copiar	to copy
fallar	to "crash" (*of computers*)
funcionar	to work, function; to run (*machines*)
grabar	to record; to tape
guardar	to keep; to save (*documents*)
hacer (*irreg.*) **copia**	to copy

imprimir	to print
navegar (gu) la Red	to surf the Net
obtener (*irreg.*)	to get, obtain

Cognados: la cámara (de vídeo), el CD-ROM, la computadora, el control remoto, el disco compacto (el CD), el disco de computadora, el DVD, el fax, el *iPod*, la memoria, el módem, el radio (portátil) / la radio,* el teléfono celular, el *walkman*

Repaso: la cinta, el televisor

En el trabajo

el aumento	raise
el/la jefe/a	boss
el sueldo	salary

La vivienda

las afueras	outskirts; suburbs
el alquiler	rent
la avenida	avenue
el barrio	neighborhood
el bloque de apartamentos	apartment building
la calle	street
el campo	countryside
el *campus*	(university) campus
la casa de apartamentos	apartment building

la comunidad	community
el/la dueño/a	landlord, landlady
el gas	gas; heat
el gasto	expense
el/la inquilino/a	tenant; renter
el piso	floor (*of a building*)
el primer piso	second floor
el segundo piso	third floor
la planta baja	ground floor
el/la portero/a	building manager; doorman
la vecindad	neighborhood
el/la vecino/a	neighbor
la vista	view
alquilar	to rent

Cognado: el área (*but* las áreas)
Repaso: el apartamento, la casa, el centro, el cuarto, la dirección, el/la dueño/a (*owner*), la luz, la residencia

Otros sustantivos

el lujo	luxury
la mentira	lie

Palabras adicionales

los/las demás	others
demasiado	too much

**El radio *is the apparatus;* la radio *is the medium.*

El arte y la cultura

Unos residentes de Quito, Ecuador, que miran obras de arte en el Parque de la Alameda

LAS ARTES*

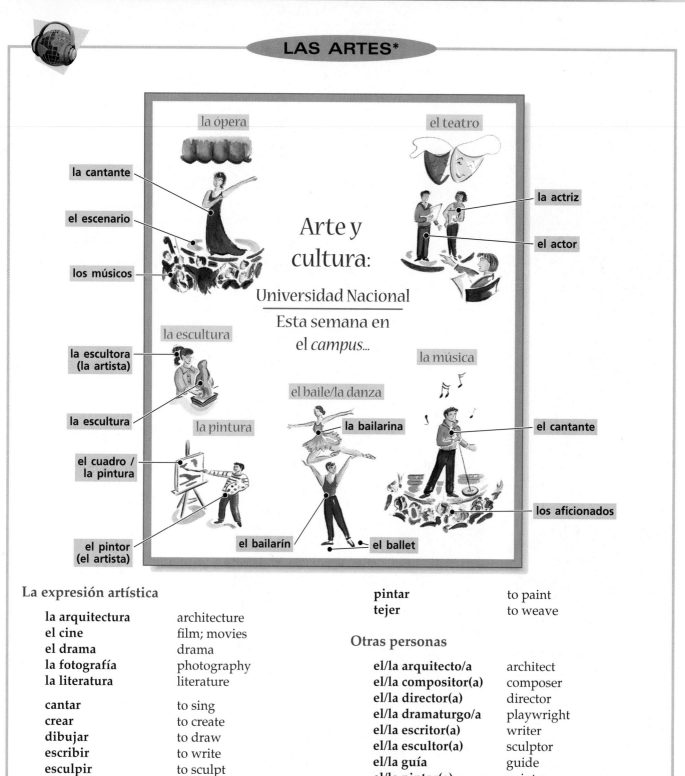

la ópera

el teatro

la cantante

el escenario

los músicos

Arte y
cultura:

Universidad Nacional

Esta semana en
el *campus...*

la actriz

el actor

la escultura

la escultora
(la artista)

la escultura

la pintura

el cuadro /
la pintura

el pintor
(el artista)

la música

el baile/la danza

la bailarina

el cantante

los aficionados

el bailarín

el ballet

La expresión artística

la arquitectura	architecture
el cine	film; movies
el drama	drama
la fotografía	photography
la literatura	literature
cantar	to sing
crear	to create
dibujar	to draw
escribir	to write
esculpir	to sculpt

pintar	to paint
tejer	to weave

Otras personas

el/la arquitecto/a	architect
el/la compositor(a)	composer
el/la director(a)	director
el/la dramaturgo/a	playwright
el/la escritor(a)	writer
el/la escultor(a)	sculptor
el/la guía	guide
el/la pintor(a)	painter
el/la poeta	poet

*The word **arte** is both masculine and feminine. The masculine articles and adjectives are normally used with **arte** in the singular while the feminine ones are used in the plural. Note that **las artes** often refers to "the arts" in general: Guillermo es estudiante **del arte moderno.** Me gustan mucho **las artes gráficas.**

La tradición cultural

la artesanía	arts and crafts
la cerámica	pottery; ceramics
las ruinas	ruins
los tejidos	woven goods

Otras palabras útiles

la canción	song
el guión	script
la obra (de arte)	work (of art)
la obra maestra	masterpiece

■ Conversación

A. Obras de arte. Primero, diga qué tipo de arte representan las siguientes obras. Luego, dé otros ejemplos de obras en cada una de las categorías artísticas que Ud. mencionó.

1. la catedral de Notre Dame y la de Santiago de Compostela
2. los murales de Diego Rivera
3. las estatuas griegas y romanas
4. *El lago de los cisnes* (*Swan Lake*) y *El amor brujo* (*Love, the Magician*)
5. *El ciudadano Kane*
6. *La Bohème* y *La Traviata*
7. las pirámides (*pyramids*) aztecas y mayas
8. *Don Quijote*
9. la Torre Eiffel de París
10. la *Mona Lisa* de Leonardo da Vinci
11. «*El cuervo* (*The Raven*)» de Edgar Allen Poe
12. las imágenes de Ansel Adams
13. las canciones de Norah Jones
14. *El mago* (*The Wizard*) *de Oz* (¡**OJO!** Hay dos respuestas posibles.)

B. ¿Qué hacen?

PASO 1   Forme oraciones completas, emparejando palabras de cada columna. Hay más de una posibilidad en algunos casos.

MODELO: La compositora escribe canciones.

la compositora la artesana la actriz el director el músico el bailarín el dramaturgo la pintora el escritor la arquitecta el poeta	**+**	escribe baila esculpe toca compone (*composes*) interpreta diseña pinta mira trabaja dirige (*directs*) teje	**+**	novelas canciones en el ballet cerámica edificios y casas papeles (*roles*) en la televisión guiones tejidos con actores obras de teatro cuadros instrumentos musicales poesía

PASO 2   Ahora, con dos o tres compañeros, dé nombres de artistas en cada categoría, ya sean (*whether they be*) hombres o mujeres. ¿Cuántos artistas hispanos pueden nombrar?

NOTA CULTURAL

La Guinea Ecuatorial

Este país hispanohablante, el único del **continente africano,** se encuentra **en la costa atlántica.** La Guinea Ecuatorial, algo más grande que El Salvador, tiene un área de **28.051 kilómetros cuadrados** incluyendo sus **cinco islas habitadas** y **un clima tropical,** cálido[a] y lluvioso. Su historia colonial es evidente en su **variedad lingüística.** Las lenguas oficiales son el español y el francés, y además se hablan un inglés criollo, el fang, el bubi y el ibo, entre otras lenguas.

Piruchi Apo Botupá (a la izquierda) y su sobrina Paloma Loribó (a la derecha), de Las Hijas del Sol

La Guinea Ecuatorial **se independizó de España** en 1968 y poco después cayó bajo la represión de **una dictadura brutal.** Desde 1979 el país vive otra forma de dictadura, **una supuesta**[b] **democracia** en la cual el pueblo[c] vota, pero no se permiten partidos[d] de oposición. Sus reservas de gas natural y de petróleo no son suficientes para elevar el nivel de vida[e] de este **país en vías de desarrollo.**[f]

Pero la Guinea Ecuatorial tiene otro recurso natural que atrae la atención mundial, sobre todo entre los aficionados a la música internacional. **Las Hijas del Sol,** una tía y su sobrina, **cantantes** de la isla Bioko, saltaron a la fama[g] en 1992 al ganar un premio[h] en España por su música tradicional. Estas talentosas mujeres produjeron unos seis **discos** en diez años e hicieron numerosas **giras,**[i] cantando solas o con otros músicos como Rita Marley y Mano Negra. También han aparecido[j] en **películas.** Empezaron a cantar siempre **a capela,** sobre temas de su cultura, en su lengua natal—el bubi. Poco a poco incorporaron más **instrumentos musicales,** más español y temas más universales. Su cuarto disco lleva el título de *Pasaporte Mundial,* del cual ellas dicen: «Para vivir necesitas un pasaporte mundial, y para nosotras, ese pasaporte es el valor[k] que se necesita para enfrentarse a[l] todos los problemas».

---

[a]*hot* [b]*supposed* [c]*people* [d]*(political) parties* [e]*nivel... standard of living* [f]*en... developing* [g]*saltaron... suddenly became famous* [h]*prize, award* [i]*tours* [j]*han... they have appeared* [k]*bravery* [l]*enfrentarse... face*

NOTA COMUNICATIVA

Más sobre los gustos y preferencias

Here are some additional verbs to talk about what you like and don't like.

• The following two verbs are used like **gustar.**

aburrir	**Me aburre** el ballet moderno. *Modern ballet bores me.*
agradar	Pero **me agrada** el ballet folklórico. *But I like (I am pleased by) folkloric dances.*

• This verb functions as a transitive verb (one that can take a direct object).

apreciar	**Aprecio** mucho la arquitectura precolombina. *I really appreciate pre-Columbian architecture.*

C. Preferencias personales

PASO 1   ¿Le gusta el arte? ¿Asiste a funciones culturales de vez en cuando (*from time to time*) o no asiste a esas funciones nunca? ¡Diga la verdad! (En otras actividades va a hablar de lo que prefiere en general.)

MODELO: asistir a los ballets clásicos →
Me gusta mucho asistir a los ballets clásicos.
(No me agrada para nada asistir a los ballets clásicos. Es aburrido.)
(Me aburre asistir a los ballets clásicos. Prefiero ir a la ópera.)

Palabras útiles	
aburrir	gustar
agradar	interesar
apreciar	preferir (ie, i)
encantar	

1. asistir a los ballets clásicos
2. ir a los museos de arte moderno
3. asistir a funciones teatrales
4. ver obras maestras en los museos grandes
5. ir a conciertos de música clásica
6. asistir a lecturas de poesía en un café
7. ver películas extranjeras
8. asistir a la ópera

PASO 2   Ahora entreviste a un compañero / una compañera para saber cuáles son sus preferencias con respecto a este tema.

MODELO: E1: ¿Te gusta ir a los museos de arte moderno?
E2: Sí, me gusta muchísimo. Voy siempre que puedo (*whenever I can*).

D. Entrevista

1. ¿Tienes talento artístico? ¿Para qué? ¿Qué te gusta crear? ¿Cuándo empezaste a desarrollar (*develop*) esta actividad? ¿Tienes aspiraciones de dedicarte a esa actividad profesionalmente? ¿Cuáles son las ventajas y las desventajas de esa ocupación?
2. Si crees que no posees ningún talento artístico en particular, ¿sientes alguna atracción por el arte? ¿Qué tipo de arte en particular? ¿Por qué te gusta tanto?
3. ¿Te gusta ir a los mercados de artesanía? ¿Qué compras allí? Cuando vas de viaje, ¿te interesa saber cuáles son los trajes (*outfits*) y la música tradicionales del lugar que visitas? ¿Coleccionas obras de artesanía? ¿Qué coleccionas?
4. ¿Qué funciones teatrales te gustan? ¿Hay muchas oportunidades en esta ciudad / este pueblo (*town*) para asistir a interpretaciones (*performances*) de baile, música o drama? ¿Qué tipo de interpretaciones te gustan más?
5. ¿Tienes un pintor favorito / una pintora favorita? ¿Quién es? ¿Te gusta más la pintura abstracta o la figurativa?
6. Para ti, ¿qué es más importante, que un edificio sea elegante o práctico? ¿Qué tipo de arquitectura te gusta más? ¿Te gusta la arquitectura de esta universidad?
7. Para ti, ¿qué es más importante en una película, el guión, la dirección o la actuación? ¿Quiénes son tus actores favoritos? ¿Tienes algún director favorito o alguna directora favorita? ¿Quién es?

PASO 1

RANKING THINGS: ORDINALS

primer(o/a)	first	**sexto/a**	sixth
segundo/a	second	**séptimo/a**	seventh
tercer(o/a)	third	**octavo/a**	eighth
cuarto/a	fourth	**noveno/a**	ninth
quinto/a	fifth	**décimo/a**	tenth

- Ordinal numbers are adjectives and must agree in number and gender with the nouns they modify. Ordinals usually precede the noun: **la cuarta lección, el octavo ejercicio.**
- Like **bueno,** the ordinals **primero** and **tercero** shorten to **primer** and **tercer,** respectively, before masculine singular nouns: **el primer niño, el tercer mes.**
- Ordinal numbers are frequently abbreviated with superscript letters that show the adjective ending: **las 1as lecciones, el 1^{r} grado, el 5° estudiante.**

■ Conversación

A. Mis actividades favoritas

PASO 1   Piense en lo que le gusta hacer en su tiempo libre en cuanto a (*regarding*) actividades culturales. Luego ponga en el orden de su preferencia (del 1 al 10) las siguientes actividades.

_____ ir al cine
_____ ir a ver películas extranjeras o clásicas
_____ ir a museos
_____ asistir a conciertos de música clásica/rock
_____ leer poesía
_____ bailar en una discoteca
_____ ver programas de televisión
_____ ver obras teatrales
_____ leer una novela
_____ ¿ ?

PASO 2   Ahora cuéntele a un compañero / una compañera sus cinco actividades favoritas. Use números ordinales.

MODELO: Mi actividad favorita es ir a ver películas clásicas. Mi segunda actividad favorita es…

B. Preguntas

1. ¿Es Ud. estudiante de cuarto año?
2. ¿Es este su segundo semestre/trimestre de español?
3. ¿A qué hora es su primera clase los lunes? ¿y su segunda clase?
4. ¿Vive Ud. en una casa de apartamentos o en una residencia? ¿En qué piso vive? Si vive en una casa, ¿en qué piso está su alcoba?

Need more practice?

- Workbook/Laboratory Manual
- Interactive CD-ROM
- Online Learning Center (www.mhhe.com/quetal7)

36 Expressing Feelings Use of the Subjunctive: Emotion

Diego y Lupe escuchan un grupo de mariachis

DIEGO: Ay, ¡cómo me encanta esta música!

LUPE: *Me alegro de que te guste.*

DIEGO: Y yo *me alegro de que estemos* aquí. ¿Sabes el origen de la palabra **mariachi**?

LUPE: No… ¿Lo sabes tú?

DIEGO: Bueno, una teoría es que viene del siglo XIX, cuando los franceses ocuparon México. Ellos contrataban a grupos de músicos para tocar en las bodas. Y como los mexicanos no podían pronunciar bien la palabra francesa *mariage*, pues acabaron por decir **mariachi.** Y de allí viene el nombre de los grupos.

LUPE: ¡Qué fascinante! *Me sorprende que sepas* tantos datos interesantes de nuestra historia.

DIEGO: Pues, todo buen antropólogo debe saber un poco de historia también, ¿no?

México, D.F.

Comprensión

1. Lupe se alegra de que _____.
2. Y Diego se alegra de que _____.
3. A Lupe le sorprende que _____.

MAIN (INDEPENDENT) CLAUSE		SUBORDINATE (DEPENDENT) CLAUSE
first subject + *indicative* (expression of emotion)	**que**	second subject + *subjunctive*

A. Expressions of emotion are those in which speakers express their feelings: *I'm glad you're here; It's good that they can come.* Such expressions of emotion are followed by the subjunctive mood in the subordinate (dependent) clause in Spanish.

Esperamos que Ud. **pueda** asistir.
We hope (that) you'll be able to come.

Tengo miedo de que mi abuelo **esté** muy enfermo.
I'm afraid (that) my grandfather is very ill.

Es una lástima que no **den** aumentos este año.
It's a shame (that) they're not giving raises this year.

Diego and Lupe are listening to a mariachi group DIEGO: *Oh, how I love this music!* LUPE: *I'm glad you like it.* DIEGO: *And I'm glad we're here. Do you know the origin of the word **mariachi**?* LUPE: *No . . . Do you?* DIEGO: *Well, one theory is that it comes from the nineteenth century, when the French occupied Mexico. They used to hire musical groups to play at weddings. And because the Mexicans couldn't correctly pronounce the French word* mariage, *they ended up saying **mariachi.** And so that's where the name of the groups comes from.* LUPE: *How fascinating! I'm surprised you know so much interesting information about our history.* DIEGO: *Well, all good anthropologists should also know a little bit of history, shouldn't they?*

B. Some common expressions of emotion are found in the list and drawing at the right.

alegrarse (de)	*to be happy* (*about*)
esperar	*to hope*
sentir (ie, i)	*to regret; to feel sorry*
tener miedo (de)	*to be afraid* (*of*)

temer: Temo que María **se caiga** durante el baile.
I'm afraid that María will fall during the dance.

At the right are some common expressions of emotion used with indirect object pronouns. Not all Spanish expressions of emotion are given here. Remember that any expression of emotion is followed by the subjunctive in the dependent clause when there is a change in subject.

me (te, le,...)	*I'm (you're, he's . . .)*
gusta que	*glad that*

Me molesta que **fumen** en la galería.
It bothers me that they smoke in the gallery.

Nos sorprende que este cantante **tenga** tanto éxito.
It surprises us that this singer is so successful.

C. When a new subject is introduced after a generalization of emotion, it is followed by the subjunctive in the subordinate (dependent) clause. Here are some general expressions of emotion.

es extraño que...	it's strange that . . .
es increíble que...	it's incredible that . . .
es mejor/bueno/ malo que...	it's better/good/ bad that . . .
es ridículo que...	it's ridiculous that . . .
es terrible que...	it's terrible that . . .
es una lástima que...	it's a shame that . . .
es urgente que...	it's urgent that . . .
¡qué extraño que... !	how strange that . . . !
¡qué lástima que... !	what a shame that . . . !

■ Práctica

A. Opiniones sobre el cine

PASO 1 **¡Anticipemos!** ¿Ciertas o falsas?

1. Me molesta que muchas películas sean tan violentas.
2. Es ridículo que algunos actores ganen (*earn*) tanto dinero.
3. Espero que salgan más actores asiáticos e hispanos en las películas.
4. Temo que muchas actrices no desempeñen (*play*) papeles inteligentes.
5. Es increíble que gasten millones de dólares en hacer películas.
6. Me sorprende que Julia Roberts sea tan famosa.

PASO 2   Ahora invente oraciones sobre lo que Ud. quiere o no quiere que pase con respecto al cine. Use las oraciones del **Paso 1** como base.

MODELO: **1.** Quiero que las películas sean menos violentas.

NOTA COMUNICATIVA

Expressing Wishes with *ojalá*

The word **ojalá** is invariable in form and means *I wish* or *I hope*. It is used with the subjunctive to express wishes or hopes. The use of **que** with it is optional.

¡Ojalá (que) yo **gane** la lotería algún día!	*I hope (that) I win the lottery some day!*
¡Ojalá (que) haya paz en el mundo algún día!	*I hope (that) there will be peace in the world some day!*
Ojalá (que) no **pierdan** tu equipaje.	*I hope (that) they don't lose your luggage.*

Ojalá can also be used alone as an interjection in response to a question.

—¿Te va a ayudar Julio a estudiar para el examen?
—**¡Ojalá!**

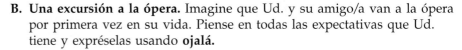

Need more practice?

■ Workbook/Laboratory Manual
■ Interactive CD-ROM
■ Online Learning Center
  (www.mhhe.com/quetal7)

B. Una excursión a la ópera. Imagine que Ud. y su amigo/a van a la ópera por primera vez en su vida. Piense en todas las expectativas que Ud. tiene y exprésalas usando **ojalá.**

MODELO: las entradas (*tickets*) / no costar mucho →
Ojalá que las entradas no cuesten mucho.

1. el escenario / ser / extravagante
2. haber / subtítulos / en inglés
3. el director (*conductor*) / estar / preparado
4. los cantantes / saber / sus papeles
5. nuestros asientos / no estar / lejos del escenario
6. (nosotros) llegar / a tiempo

■ Conversación

A. Situaciones. Las siguientes personas están pensando en otra persona o en algo que van a hacer. ¿Qué emociones sienten? ¿Qué temen? Con un compañero / una compañera, conteste las preguntas según los dibujos.

1. Jorge piensa en su amiga Estela. ¿Por qué piensa en ella? ¿Dónde está? ¿Qué siente Jorge? ¿Qué espera? ¿Qué espera Estela? ¿Espera que la visiten los amigos? ¿que le manden algo?

2. Fausto quiere comer fuera esta noche. ¿Quiere que alguien lo acompañe? ¿Dónde espera que cenen? ¿Qué teme Fausto? ¿Qué le parecen (*seem*) los precios del restaurante?

3. ¿Dónde quiere pasar las vacaciones Mariana? ¿Espera que alguien la acompañe? ¿Dónde espera que pasen los días? ¿Qué teme Mariana? ¿Qué espera?

B. ¿Qué le molesta más? The following phrases describe aspects of university life. React to them, using phrases such as: **Me gusta que...,** **Me molesta que...,** **Es terrible que...**

MODELO: Gastan mucho/poco dinero en construir nuevos edificios. →
Me molesta que gasten mucho dinero en construir nuevos edificios.

1. Se pone mucho énfasis en los deportes.
2. Pagamos mucho/poco por la matrícula.
3. Se ofrecen muchos/pocos cursos en mi especialización (*major*).
4. Es necesario estudiar ciencias/lenguas para graduarse.
5. Hay muchos/pocos requisitos (*requirements*) para graduarse.
6. En general, hay mucha/poca gente (*people*) en las clases.

LITERATURA: Jorge Icaza

Sobre el autor: *Jorge Icaza nació en Icuña, Ecuador. Empezó su carrera como actor y dramaturgo, pero cuando las autoridades censuraron su drama,* El dictador, *abrió una librería y empezó a escribir novelas. Su novela* Huasipungo (1934) *es la novela ecuatoriana más famosa y una de las novelas indigenistas más importantes de Latinoamérica. El siguiente fragmento es de esa novela.*

Jorge Icaza
(1906–1978)

—Nu han de robar[a] así nu más[b] a taita[c] Andrés Chiliquinga— concluyó el indio, rascándose[d] la cabeza, lleno de un despertar[e] de oscuras e indefinidas venganzas.[f] Ya le era imposible dudar de la verdad del atropello[g] que invadía el cerro.[h] Llegaban… Llegaban más pronto de lo que él pudo imaginarse. Echarían abajo su techo,[i] le quitarían la tierra.[j] Sin encontrar[k] una defensa posible, acorralado[l] como siempre, se puso pálido, con la boca semiabierta, con los ojos fijos,[m] con la garganta anudada.[n] ¡No!

[a]*Nu… They will not rob* [b]*nu… ever again* [c]*abuelo* [d]*scratching* [e]*lleno… overcome by an awakening* [f]*oscuras… dark and vague vengeance* [g]*attack, assault* [h]*hill* [i]*Echarían… They would tear down his roof (house)* [j]*le… they would take away his land* [k]*Sin… Without finding* [l]*corralled* [m]*fixed* [n]*con… with a lump in his throat*

MÚSICA: Rumillajta

el bombo

el charango

las quenas

las zampoñas

Rumillajta es un conjunto[a] boliviano que interpreta[b] música y canciones andinas. Su nombre en quechua significa «ciudad de piedras[c]». Sus cinco músicos son de la ciudad de La Paz, donde viven y trabajan, aunque[d] hacen giras[e] internacionales. La meta[f] del conjunto, además de[g] crear música bella,[h] es promover[i] la cultura andina y sus valores sociales y espirituales de interdependencia y cooperación.

[a]*group* [b]*performs* [c]*stones* [d]*although* [e]*tours* [f]*goal* [g]*además… in addition to* [h]*beautiful* [i]*to promote*

Los músicos de Rumillajta fabrican sus propios[j] instrumentos tradicionales, como son las zampoñas,[k] quenas,[l] bombos[m] y charangos.[n] Los miembros del grupo dicen que su música tiene tres cualidades importantes: un vínculo[o] profundo con la naturaleza,[p] una melancolía que refleja la experiencia del pueblo[q] y una energía vital que llega al[r] corazón de los oyentes.[s]

[j]*own* [k]*panpipes* [l]*Andean flutes* [m]*large drums* [n]*type of guitar* [o]*link* [p]*nature* [q]*common people* [r]*llega… reaches* [s]*listeners*

37 Expressing Uncertainty Use of the Subjunctive: Doubt and Denial

Mire Ud. la pintura detenidamente (*carefully*) y luego complete las siguientes oraciones de acuerdo con su opinión.

Vocabulario útil

la alegría (happiness)
la esperanza (hope)
los guardias (guardsmen)
el miedo (fear)
la tristeza (sadness)

Comprensión

1. *Es posible que* los miembros de esta familia tengan (miedo / esperanza).
   Estoy seguro/a de que no tienen (miedo / esperanza).
2. Creo que los colores representan (la alegría / la tristeza).
   Dudo que representen (la alegría / la tristeza).
3. *Es probable que* los guardias estén (enojados / contentos).
   Estoy seguro/a de que no están (enojados / contentos).

Familia andina, por Héctor Poleo
(venezolano, 1918–1989)

MAIN (INDEPENDENT) CLAUSE		SUBORDINATE (DEPENDENT) CLAUSE
first subject + *indicative* (expression of doubt or denial)	**que**	second subject + *subjunctive*

A. Expressions of doubt and denial are those in which speakers express uncertainty or negation. Such expressions, however strong or weak, are followed by the subjunctive in the dependent clause in Spanish.

No creo que **sean** sus cuadros.
I don't believe they're her paintings.

Es imposible que ella **esté** en el escenario.
It's impossible for her to be on the stage.

B. Some expressions of doubt and denial appear at the right. Not all Spanish expressions of doubt are given here. Remember that any expression of doubt is followed by the subjunctive in the dependent clause.

no creer	*to disbelieve*
dudar	*to doubt*
negar (ie) (gu)	*to deny*
no estar seguro/a (de)	*to be unsure (of)*

Creer and **estar seguro/a** are usually followed by the indicative in affirmative statements because they do not express doubt, denial, or negation. Compare these examples.

Estamos seguros de (Creemos) que el concierto **es** hoy.
We're sure (We believe) that the concert is today.

No estamos seguros de (No creemos) que el concierto **sea** hoy.
We're not sure (We don't believe) that the concert is today.

C. When a new subject is introduced after a generalization of doubt, the subjunctive is used in the dependent clause. Some generalizations of doubt and denial are included at the right.

es posible que...	it's possible that . . .
es imposible que...	it's impossible that . . .
es probable que...	it's probable (likely) that . . .
es improbable que...	it's improbable (unlikely) that . . .
no es cierto que...	it's not certain that . . .
no es seguro que...	it's not a sure thing that . . .
no es verdad que...	it's not true that . . .

 Generalizations that express certainty are not followed by the subjunctive but by the indicative: **Es verdad que cocina bien. No hay duda de que Julio lo paga.**

■ Práctica

Opiniones distintas. Imagine que Ud. y un amigo / una amiga están en un museo arqueológico. En este momento están mirando una figura. Desafortunadamente, no hay ningún letrero (*sign*) cerca de Uds. para indicar lo que representa la figura. Haga oraciones completas según las indicaciones. Añada palabras cuando sea necesario.

Habla Ud.:

1. creo / que / ser / figura / de / civilización / maya
2. es cierto / que / figura / estar / hecho (*made*) / de oro
3. es posible / que / representar / dios (*god, m.*) / importante
4. no estoy seguro/a de / que / figura / ser / auténtico

Habla su amigo/a:

5. no creo / que / ser / figura / de / civilización / maya
6. creo / que / ser / de / civilización / tolteca
7. estoy seguro/a de / que / estar / hecho / de bronce
8. creo / que / representar / víctima [*m.*] / de / sacrificio humano

Need more practice?

- Workbook/Laboratory Manual
- Interactive CD-ROM
- Online Learning Center (www.mhhe.com/quetal7)

■ Conversación

A. ¿Una ganga? Imagine que Ud. va a un mercado al aire libre. Encuentra algunos objetos de artesanía muy interesantes que parecen ser de origen azteca... ¡y son baratísimos! ¿Cómo reacciona Ud.?

Empiece sus oraciones con estas frases.

Vocabulario útil
el calendario (calendar)
la joyería (jewelry)
la máscara (mask)
auténtico/a (authentic)
falsificado/a (forged)

1. ¡Es imposible que... !
2. No creo que...
3. Dudo muchísimo que...
4. Estoy seguro/a de que...
5. Es improbable que...

NOTA COMUNICATIVA

Verbs that Require Prepositions

You learned in earlier chapters that when two verbs occur in a series (one right after the other), the second verb is usually the infinitive.

Prefiero *cenar* a las siete.   *I prefer to eat at seven.*

Some Spanish verbs, however, require that a preposition or other word be placed before the second verb (still the infinitive). You have already used many of the important Spanish verbs that have this feature.

• The following verbs require the preposition **a** before an infinitive.

aprender a	empezar (ie) (c) a	invitar a	venir (*irreg.*) a
ayudar a	enseñar a	ir (*irreg.*) a	volver (ue) a

Mis padres me **enseñaron a bailar.**   *My parents taught me to dance.*

• These verbs or verb phrases require **de** before an infinitive.

acabar de	dejar de	tener (*irreg.*) ganas de
acordarse (ue) de	olvidarse de	tratar de (*to try to*)

Siempre **tratamos de llegar** puntualmente.   *We always try to arrive on time.*

• **Insistir** requires **en** before an infinitive.

Insisten en venir esta noche.   *They insist on coming over tonight.*

• Two verbs require **que** before an infinitive: **haber que, tener que.**

Hay que ver el nuevo museo.   *It's necessary to see the new museum.*

B. ¿Qué piensa Ud. del futuro?

PASO 1   Haga oraciones con frases de cada columna para expresar su opinión sobre lo que le puede ocurrir a Ud. en los próximos cinco años. **¡OJO!** No se olvide de usar el subjuntivo después de expresiones de duda o negación.

En los próximos cinco años...

| (no) creo que...
 (no) dudo que...
 es (im)posible que...
 (no) estoy seguro/a de que...
 (no) es cierto que... | **+** | (yo) { ir a <br> aprender a <br> empezar a <br> dejar de <br> tratar de <br> volver a | **+** | ser famoso/a <br> estar casado/a <br> ganar la lotería <br> jugar a la lotería <br> pintar cuadros <br> fumar <br> tener hijos <br> terminar mis estudios <br> esculpir
 ¿ ? |

PASO 2   Compare sus respuestas con las de uno o dos compañeros. ¿Cuántas respuestas similares hay? ¿Cuántas diferentes?

En los Estados Unidos y el Canadá

Carlos Santana y la Fundación Milagro[a]

El legendario **guitarrista** Carlos Santana nació en Autlán, México. Luego su familia se trasladó[b] de allí a Tijuana y más tarde a San Francisco, donde Carlos y su hermano Jorge empezaron a tener sus primeros seguidores.[c] Santana **se hizo famoso en el Festival de Woodstock** en 1969 con un increíble solo de guitarra. Después tuvo una serie de éxitos,[d] entre ellos su inolvidable **interpretación** en 1971 de **la canción** de Tito Puente, **«Oye cómo va».** En 1999, Santana creó una sensación con su **disco compacto** *Supernatural,* en el que tocó con una variedad de artistas norteamericanos e hispanos para crear una obra rica en estilo y composición. Este esfuerzo de Santana le ganó varios *Grammys* en 2000.

Carlos Santana

Santana es una persona profundamente **dedicada a la comunidad,** especialmente **a los niños.** Junto con su esposa Deborah, Santana creó **la Fundación Milagro,** una organización educativa para niños y jóvenes. La Fundación Milagro contribuye con dinero a otras organizaciones comunitarias sin fines lucrativos[e] en San Francisco y sus alrededores.[f] El propósito es **ayudar a la juventud[g] del área** por medio de programas de salud, educación y arte. Puede encontrar más información sobre la Fundación en su página web en el Internet.

[a]*Miracle* [b]*se... moved* [c]*followers* [d]*successes* [e]*sin... nonprofit* [f]*surrounding areas* [g]*youth*

UN POCO DE TODO

Lengua y cultura: El cuadro *Guernica* de Picasso. En esta actividad hay información sobre el famoso cuadro del pintor español Picasso, *Guernica*, que está en el Museo Nacional Centro de Arte Reina Sofía, en Madrid, España. Un guía les habla sobre el cuadro. Complete el siguiente diálogo con la forma correcta de los verbos entre paréntesis. Cuando se den dos posibilidades, escoja la palabra correcta.

Guernica, *por Pablo Picasso (español, 1881–1973)*

GUÍA: (Pasar[1]) Uds. por aquí, por favor. También les pido que (dejar[2]) suficiente espacio para todos. Y bien, aquí estamos (delante/detrás[3]) de *Guernica,* la obra maestra pintada por Picasso. (Ser[4]) obvio que el cuadro (representar[5]) los horrores de la guerra,[a] ¿no? En 1937 Picasso (pintar[6]) este cuadro como reacción al bombardeo[b] (del / de la[7]) ciudad de Guernica durante la Guerra Civil Española. Por razones políticas, (durante / encima de[8]) la dictadura[c] de Franco,[d] el cuadro (fue/estuvo[9]) muchos años en el Museo de Arte Moderno de Nueva York. Pero por deseo expreso del pintor, el cuadro (trasladarse[10])[e] a España después de la muerte de Franco...

UD.: Yo dudo que (este/esto[11]) cuadro (ser[12]) una obra maestra. Creo que no (ser[13]) nada bonito. ¡No hay colores en él!

SU AMIGO: Yo no (creer[14]) que todos los cuadros (tener[15]) que (ser[16]) bonitos. Para mí, la falta de color (servir[17]) para expresar el dolor y el desastre... (Por/Para[18]) eso, uno (poder[19]) sentir el mensaje de la destrucción de la guerra en la pintura.

[a]*war* [b]*bombing* [c]*dictatorship* [d]Francisco Franco (1892–1975), dictador de España desde 1939 hasta su muerte [e]*to be moved*

Comprensión. ¿Quién pudo haber dicho (*could have said*) lo siguiente, el guía, Ud. o su amigo?

1. Yo prefiero los cuadros en colores.
2. Ahora voy a mostrarles una obra maestra de la pintura española.
3. No me molesta que esta pintura esté pintada en blanco y negro.
4. Quiero que todos me sigan y que se pongan delante del cuadro.

Resources for Review and Testing Preparation

- Workbook/Laboratory Manual
- Interactive CD-ROM
- Online Learning Center (www.mhhe.com/quetal7)

VIDEOTECA

Entrevista cultural: Bolivia

Juan Prudencio, un joven artista boliviano, habla de su trabajo artístico y de su familia. Antes de ver el vídeo, lea el siguiente fragmento de la entrevista.

ENTREVISTADORA: Y ¿qué pintas?

JUAN: Pinto cuadros abstractos. Pinto cosas que tienen que ver con mis emociones o con la manera en que yo veo las… la situación actual[a] en el mundo.

[a]*current*

Ahora vea el vídeo y conteste las siguientes preguntas basándose en la entrevista.

1. ¿Cómo son los cuadros que Juan pinta?
2. ¿Cómo reaccionan los padres de Juan a su trabajo artístico?
3. Y ¿cómo responden sus hermanos a sus obras?

Entrevista cultural: El Ecuador

Álvaro Montealbán, un estudiante ecuatoriano, habla del arte y de sus planes profesionales. Antes de ver el vídeo, lea el siguiente fragmento de la entrevista.

ENTREVISTADORA: Álvaro, ¿qué planes tienes para el futuro?

ÁLVARO: Para el futuro pienso desarrollarme profesionalmente y hacer un museo o una galería de arte. En un futuro más a largo plazo[a] trabajaré[b] …eh… por montarme[c] mi propia galería de arte.

[a]*más… more long term*   [b]*I will work*   [c]*establish, open*

Ahora vea el vídeo y conteste las siguientes preguntas basándose en la entrevista.

1. ¿Por qué estudia Álvaro la historia del arte?
2. ¿Qué quiere hacer Álvaro en el futuro?

Entre amigos: ¿Y qué pintores te gustan?

Tané, Karina, Rubén y Miguel hablan del arte. En su opinión, ¿qué preguntas se van a hacer? Antes de mirar el vídeo, lea las preguntas a continuación. Mientras mire el vídeo, fíjese en la información sobre el arte y los artistas. Luego mire el vídeo una segunda vez, fijándose en la información que necesita para contestar las preguntas.

1. ¿Qué pintor le gusta a Rubén? ¿Qué tipo de arte le gusta a Tané? Y a Miguel, ¿qué música le gusta?
2. ¿Cómo describe Tané la ópera? Y ¿qué dice Rubén de la ópera?

━━━━ ENFOQUE CULTURAL ━━━━

Bolivia y el Ecuador

¡Fíjese!

- Bolivia formó parte del antiguo imperio inca. Aproximadamente el 55 por ciento de la población boliviana actual es de origen indígena.
- Bolivia fue nombrada[a] en honor a Simón Bolívar, quien luchó por la independencia del país.
- A 12.000 pies de altura, La Paz es la capital más alta del mundo.
- Las Islas Galápagos pertenecen[b] al Ecuador y son de origen volcánico. Fueron descubiertas[c] en 1535, por el español Berlanga. Berlanga las llamó las Islas Encantadas[d] porque las fuertes corrientes[e] marinas confundían a los navegantes[f] como si fuera por[g] acto de magia. Trescientos años más tarde, el biólogo Charles Darwin llegó a las islas a bordo del barco *HMS Beagle*. De sus investigaciones de las plantas y animales de cuatro de las islas resultaron sus ideas sobre la evolución y su famoso libro, *El origen de las especies*. Darwin teorizó que los animales y las plantas cambian y se adaptan a su medio ambiente.[h]

[a]*fue… was named* [b]*belong* [c]*Fueron… They were discovered* [d]*Enchanted* [e]*currents* [f]*sailors* [g]*como… as if by* [h]*medio… environment*

Personas famosas: Oswaldo Guayasamín

Oswaldo Guayasamín (1919–1999) fue un pintor ecuatoriano cuyo[a] arte es un testimonio del sufrimiento[b] humano y de la vida difícil de los indios y los pobres de su país. Guayasamín se inspiró en los símbolos y motivos de los pueblos precolombinos y en el arte colonial del Ecuador.

[a]*whose* [b]*suffering*

Madre y niño, por Oswaldo Guayasamín

Learn more about Bolivia and Ecuador with the Video, the Interactive CD-ROM, and the Online Learning Center (www.mhhe.com/quetal7).

A LEER

REPASO DE ESTRATEGIAS: Guessing the Content of a Passage

Look at the photographs that accompany the reading. Read the title of the passage also. Based on these clues, what do you think the article is going to be about? How do you know? What important information do the photos and the title provide? Remember to always look for these types of visual and textual clues as a useful strategy to facilitate comprehension when reading in a second language (or even in your first language).

> **Sobre la lectura…** Este artículo es de la revista hispana *Cristina*, que publica la famosa cubanoamericana Cristina Saralegui. Frecuentemente comparada con Oprah Winfrey, Saralegui también tiene un *talk show* en español y un sitio web. Su sitio web es cristinaonline.com.

El arte de la Talavera

La cerámica que hoy conocemos como Talavera proviene[a] del pueblo español de Talavera de la Reina, situado en la provincia de Toledo. Los árabes se establecieron en la Península Ibérica en el siglo[b] VI, y trajeron consigo[c] sus técnicas artísticas para <u>moldear</u> la cerámica. Pintar <u>adornos</u> azules en cerámicas blancas, un distintivo[d] de Talavera, se debe a la influencia árabe en este arte.

Cerámica mexicana Talavera auténtica

Un grupo de artesanos de Talavera de la Reina trajo la técnica de Talavera con sus raíces árabes a Puebla, México, ciudad que se ha convertido en[e] el centro de este arte. Inicialmente, el propósito fue crear lozas[f] y murales en las iglesias y monasterios católicos, para adornar los templos religiosos.

La cerámica de Talavera se convirtió en una verdadera pieza de colección, porque recibe múltiples influencias. Además de la árabe y española, les debe[g] a italianos y chinos, convirtiéndose así en una de las más famosas del mundo.

El arte y sus técnicas iban trasladándose[h] de un lugar a otro. Así llega también a México la influencia que ejerció la técnica italiana del artista Francisco Niculoso en la cerámica Talavera, conocida también como cerámica italiana Majólica. De ahí es

que <u>surge</u> el uso del verde, negro y amarillo intenso. En las piezas de la cerámica mexicana Talavera de finales del siglo XVII se aprecia este baño de nuevos colores, lo que hace preciosos[i] los adornos.

En México, la Talavera también se enriqueció de lo oriental, por el arte chino que se recibió a través de Filipinas. Algunas piezas orientales fueron copiadas por los artesanos mexicanos. De esta forma, surgen las figuras orientales, las cerámicas de animales y los diseños florales.

La Talavera mexicana es una técnica que, aunque[j] llegó de España en el siglo XVI, se depuró[k] en el siglo XVIII. Se <u>agregaron</u> otros colores como el morado, que junto al azul convencional, el amarillo y el verde, le impartieron muchísima personalidad.

La Talavera se puso[l] tan de moda que fue necesaria una ordenanza con los requisitos[m] estéticos y de manufactura. En México una pieza siempre debe incluir el color azul y estar firmada[n] por el artesano para evitar[o] la falsificación. Este tipo de cerámica también se subdivide en [categorías:] fina, semifina y para el uso diario.

[a]viene [b]*century* [c]*with them* [d]característica [e]*se… has become*
[f]porcelana [g]*les… it owes a debt* [h]*moving* [i]*valuable* [j]*although*
[k]*se… se refinó* [l]*se… became* [m]estipulaciones [n]*signed* [o]*avoid*

Es importante que, al comprar^p una pieza, le preguntes al artesano si es posible darle un uso práctico, como usarla de vajilla,^q lavar en lavadora de platos automática y poner en el microondas, porque algunas piezas son sólo decorativas. ■

^pal... *upon purchasing*   ^qde... *as dishes*

Comprensión

A. Preguntas.   Conteste las siguientes preguntas.

1. ¿En que país tiene su origen la cerámica Talavera?
2. ¿Qué culturas influyen en el arte de la Talavera?
3. ¿Cuáles son algunos de los colores tradicionales de la cerámica Talavera, y cuál es el color esencial?

B. ¿Cierto o falso?   Conteste según la lectura y corrija las oraciones falsas.

1. La cerámica Talavera puede usarse tanto para ocasiones formales como informales.
2. La Talavera siempre tiene diseños geográficos.
3. El arte de la Talavera llegó a América cuando los árabes conquistaron México.

 A ESCRIBIR

La expresión artística.   Muchas personas se expresan mediante (*by means of*) el arte en sus varias formas. Es decir, el arte no se limita solamente a la pintura y la escultura. El arte puede tomar varias formas: la música, la escritura, el diseño de ropa o muebles, etcétera. ¿Qué «arte» usa Ud. para expresar su personalidad? Escriba un breve ensayo para explicar cómo se expresa Ud. por medio del arte. Ideas para considerar:

- el medio artístico (la música, etcétera)
- cómo el arte expresa sus emociones y personalidad
- si sus preferencias con respecto a la expresión artística están cambiando o si son siempre las mismas

Cuando termine su ensayo, entrégueselo a su profesor(a). El profesor / La profesora se lo va a presentar al resto de la clase para ver si entre todos pueden adivinar quién es el autor / la autora.

GRAMÁTICA

To review the grammar points presented in this chapter, refer to the indicated grammar presentations. You'll find further practice of these structures in the Workbook/Laboratory Manual, on the Interactive CD-ROM, and on the *¿Qué tal?* Online Learning Center (www.mhhe.com/quetal7).

36 Expressing Feelings—Use of the Subjunctive: Emotion

You should know how and when to use the subjunctive in a dependent clause when the main clause of a sentence expresses emotion.

37 Expressing Uncertainty—Use of the Subjunctive: Doubt and Denial

You should know how and when to use the subjunctive in a dependent clause when the main clause of a sentence expresses doubt or denial.

VOCABULARIO

Practice this vocabulary with digital flash cards on the Online Learning Center (www.mhhe.com/quetal7).

Los verbos

aburrir	to bore
agradar	to please
apreciar	to appreciate
negar (ie) (gu)	to deny
parecer (zc)	to seem
representar	to represent
sentir (ie, i)	to regret; to feel sorry
temer	to fear
tratar de + *inf.*	to try to (*do something*)

Repaso: alegrarse (de), creer, dudar, esperar, gustar, tener (*irreg.*) miedo de

La expresión artística

el baile	dance
el cuadro	painting (*piece of art*)
la danza	dance
la escultura	sculpture
la fotografía	photography
la pintura	painting (*general; piece of art; the art form*)

Cognados: la arquitectura, el arte (*but* las artes), el ballet, el drama, la música, la ópera
Repaso: el cine, la foto(grafía) (photo[graph]), la literatura, el teatro

crear	to create
desempeñar	to play, perform (*a part*)
dibujar	to draw
esculpir	to sculpt
tejer	to weave

Repaso: cantar, escribir, pintar

Los artistas

el actor / la actriz	actor, actress
el bailarín / la bailarina	dancer
el/la cantante	singer
el/la compositor(a)	composer
el/la director(a)	director; conductor
el/la dramaturgo/a	playwright
el/la escritor(a)	writer
el/la escultor(a)	sculptor
el/la músico	musician
el/la pintor(a)	painter

Cognados: el/la arquitecto/a, el/la artista, el/la poeta
Repaso: el/la aficionado/a

La tradición cultural

la artesanía	arts and crafts
la cerámica	pottery; ceramics
los tejidos	woven goods

Cognado: las ruinas

Otros sustantivos

la canción	song
el escenario	stage
la gente	people
el/la guía	guide
el guión	script
la obra (de arte)	work (of art)
la obra maestra	masterpiece
el papel	role

Los adjetivos

clásico/a	classic(al)
folklórico/a	folkloric
moderno/a	modern

Los números ordinales

primer(o/a)
segundo/a
tercer(o/a)
cuarto/a
quinto/a
sexto/a
séptimo/a
octavo/a
noveno/a
décimo/a

Palabras adicionales

es extraño que	it's strange that
¡qué extraño que...!	how strange that ...!
es...	it's ...
cierto que	certain that
imposible que	impossible that
(im)probable que	(un)likely, (im)probable that
increíble que	incredible that
ridículo que	ridiculous that
seguro que	a sure thing that
terrible que	terrible that
urgente que	urgent that
es una lástima que	it's a shame that
¡qué lástima que...!	what a shame that ...!
hay que + *inf.*	it is necessary to (*do something*)
me (te, le,...) molesta que	it bothers me (you, him, ...) that
me (te, le,...) sorprende que	it surprises me (you, him, ...) that
ojalá (que)	I hope, wish (that)

Repaso: es posible que, es mejor/bueno/malo que, es verdad que, estar seguro/a (de) que

La naturaleza y el medio ambiente°

°**La...** *Nature and the environment*

CULTURA

- **Nota cultural:** Programas medioambientales
- **En los Estados Unidos y el Canadá:** Lugares con nombres españoles
- **Voces** de la Argentina
  - **Literatura:** Alfonsina Storni
  - **Música:** El tango
- **Videoteca**
  - **Entrevista cultural:** La Argentina
  - **Entre amigos:** Nuestro pequeño grano de arena
- **Enfoque cultural:** La Argentina

VOCABULARIO

- La naturaleza y el medio ambiente
- Los coches

GRAMÁTICA

38 Past Participle Used As an Adjective

39 Perfect Forms: Present Perfect Indicative and Present Perfect Subjunctive

Las cataratas del Iguazú, en la Argentina

LA NATURALEZA Y EL MEDIO AMBIENTE

la contaminación (del aire)

el aire puro

la montaña

el árbol

el rascacielos

la fábrica

el caballo

el río

la agricultora

el agricultor

la finca

la vaca

el lago

el toro

el pez (*pl.* peces)

el animal	domesticated	la falta	lack; absence
doméstico	animal; pet	el gobierno	government
el animal salvaje	wild animal	la población	population
la ballena	whale	los recursos	natural resources
el bosque	forest	naturales	
el/la campesino/a	farm worker; peasant		
el campo	countryside; field	Cognados: el elefante, el gorila	
la ciudad	city		
la energía	energy	acabar	to finish; run out (of)
eléctrica	electric		(use up completely)
nuclear	nuclear	conservar	to save, conserve
solar	solar	construir (y)*	to build
la escasez	lack; shortage	contaminar	to pollute
(*pl.* escaseces)		desarrollar	to develop
la especie (en peligro	(endangered)	destruir (y)*	to destroy
de extinción)	species	proteger (j)	to protect

*Note the present indicative conjugation of **construir: construyo, construyes, construye, construímos, construís, construyen. Destruir** is conjugated like **construir.**

Más vocabulario

el delito	crime	**el transporte público**	public transportation
el ritmo (acelerado) de la vida	(fast) pace of life	**la violencia**	violence
los servicios públicos	public services	**bello/a**	beautiful
		denso/a	dense

■ Conversación

A. ¿La ciudad o el campo?

1. El aire es más puro y hay menos contaminación.
2. La naturaleza es más bella.
3. El ritmo de la vida es más acelerado.
4. Hay más delitos.
5. Los servicios financieros y legales son más asequibles (*available*).
6. Hay pocos medios de transporte públicos.
7. La población es menos densa.
8. Hay escasez de viviendas.

NOTA CULTURAL

Programas medioambientales

Muchos países del mundo se encuentran en la posición de **equilibrar**[a] la **protección** del medio ambiente con los objetivos del **desarrollo económico**. En muchos casos, **la explotación de recursos naturales** es la **mayor fuente de ingreso**[b] para la economía de un país. Pero los gobiernos latinoamericanos están conscientes de la necesidad de **proteger** el medio ambiente y de **conservar** los recursos naturales, y están haciendo lo posible por hacerlo. Los siguientes son algunos de los muchos **programas medioambientales** que se encuentran en los países hispanohablantes.

- En la Ciudad de México, existe un programa permanente de **restricción vehicular** que se llama Hoy no circula.[c] Los coches no deben circular un día por semana. El día está determinado por el **último número de la placa**.[d] El propósito de este programa es controlar **la emisión de contaminantes**. Programas semejantes a Hoy no circula existen también en otros países como Chile y la Argentina.
- En México, España y otros países existen programas de **separación de basura**. Se depositan materiales distintos en recipientes[e] de colores diferentes, desde el papel y el cartón, el vidrio,[f] el metal y el plástico, hasta la materia orgánica y los desechos[g] sanitarios.

Madrid, España

---

[a]*needing to balance* [b]*fuente… source of income* [c]*Hoy… Today (these) don't drive.*
[d]*license plate* [e]*containers* [f]*glass* [g]*waste*

B. Problemas del mundo en que vivimos. Con un compañero / una compañera, dé sus reacciones a las siguientes opiniones. Puede usar las expresiones útiles para aclarar (*clarify*) su posición con respecto a cada tema. ¡OJO! Todas las expresiones requieren el uso del subjuntivo, porque expresan deseos e influencia.

1. Para conservar energía debemos reciclar todo lo posible.
2. Es mejor calentar las casas con estufas de leña (*wood stoves*) que con gas o electricidad.
3. Se debe crear más parques urbanos, estatales y nacionales.
4. La protección del medio ambiente no debe impedir la explotación de los recursos naturales.
5. Para evitar (*avoid*) la contaminación urbana, debemos limitar el uso de los coches y no usarlos algunos días de la semana, como se hace en otros países.
6. El gobierno debe ponerles multas (*fines*) muy graves a las compañías e individuos que causan la contaminación.
7. El desarrollo de las tecnologías promueve (*promotes*) el ritmo tan acelerado de nuestra vida.
8. Los países desarrollados están destruyendo los recursos naturales de los países más pobres.

Expresiones útiles

Es / Me/Nos parece...
  fundamental que...
  importantísimo que...
  ridículo que...
  ¿ ?
Me opongo / Nos oponemos a que (*I am / We are against*)...
No creo/creemos que...

En ECOPETROL tenemos conciencia ambiental y social. Nuestra planeación incluye siempre los estudios de localización e impacto ambiental, buscando no perturbar la naturaleza y la vida de las poblaciones vecinas a nuestras futuras operaciones. En esta planeación el trabajo con la comunidad es indispensable.

**Nuestro propósito:
Una mejor convivencia**

EMPRESA COLOMBIANA DE PETROLEOS
ECOPETROL

C. Un recurso natural importante

PASO 1 Lea este anuncio de una empresa (compañía) colombiana y conteste las preguntas.

1. ¿Qué tipo de negocio cree Ud. que es Ecopetrol? ¿Qué produce?
2. ¿Qué asuntos (*matters*) son de mayor interés para esta empresa? ¿El tránsito? ¿la deforestación? ¿las poblaciones humanas? ¿otros asuntos?
3. ¿Le parece que la foto que han elegido (*they chose*) para el anuncio es buena para la imagen de la empresa? ¿Por qué?
4. El sustantivo **convivencia** se relaciona con el verbo **vivir** y contiene la preposición **con**. ¿Qué cree Ud. que significa **convivencia**?
5. ¿Sabe Ud. cuáles son algunos de los países que producen lo mismo que Ecopetrol?

Vocabulario útil

la energía eólica (wind energy)
la energía hidráulica (hydraulic energy)

PASO 2 Hay varias formas de energía. ¿Las conoce Ud. bien? Diga a qué tipo de energía corresponde cada descripción.

1. Es la energía más usada en los hogares (*homes*).
2. Según los expertos, es la forma de energía más limpia; es decir, es la que menos contaminación produce.
3. Puede ser la forma de energía más eficiente, pero también la más peligrosa (*dangerous*).
4. Esta energía viene del viento; por eso sólo se puede desarrollar en lugares específicos.
5. Para producir esta forma de energía son necesarios los ríos y las cataratas (*waterfalls*).

LOS COCHES

En la gasolinera Gómez

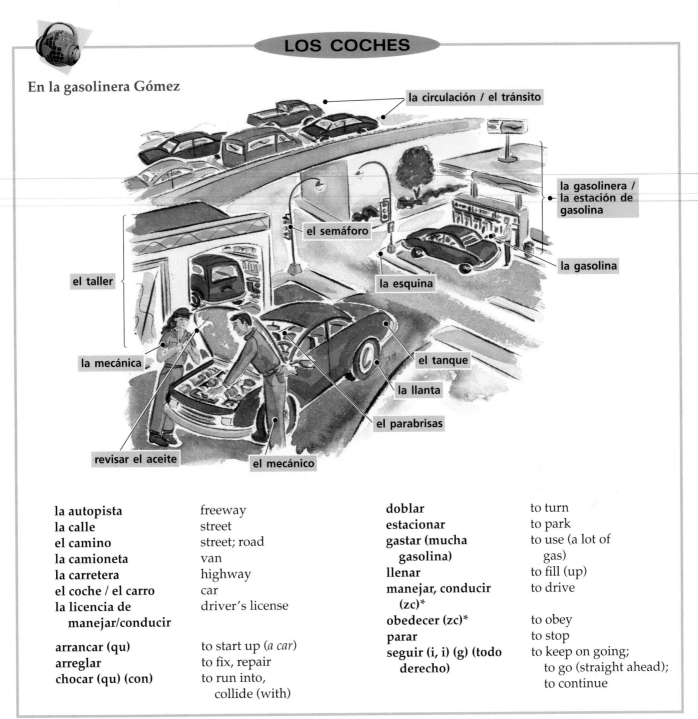

la circulación / el tránsito

la gasolinera / la estación de gasolina

el semáforo

la gasolina

el taller

la esquina

la mecánica

el tanque

la llanta

el parabrisas

revisar el aceite

el mecánico

la autopista	freeway	**doblar**	to turn
la calle	street	**estacionar**	to park
el camino	street; road	**gastar (mucha**	to use (a lot of
la camioneta	van	**gasolina)**	gas)
la carretera	highway	**llenar**	to fill (up)
el coche / el carro	car	**manejar, conducir**	to drive
la licencia de	driver's license	**(zc)***	
manejar/conducir		**obedecer (zc)***	to obey
		parar	to stop
arrancar (qu)	to start up (*a car*)	**seguir (i, i) (g) (todo**	to keep on going;
arreglar	to fix, repair	**derecho)**	to go (straight ahead);
chocar (qu) (con)	to run into, collide (with)		to continue

*Like the verb **conocer,** **conducir** *and* **obedecer** *have a spelling change in the* **yo** *form of the present indicative:* **conozco, conduzco, obedezco.** *This spelling change is also used in all forms of the present subjunctive.*

■ Conversación

A. Definiciones

PASO 1 Busque Ud. la definición de las palabras de la columna de la derecha.

1. ___ Se pone en el tanque.
2. ___ Se llenan de aire.
3. ___ Lubrica el motor.
4. ___ Es necesaria para arrancar el motor.
5. ___ Cuando se llega a una esquina, hay que hacer esto o seguir todo derecho.
6. ___ No contiene aire suficiente y por eso es necesario cambiarla.
7. ___ Es un camino público ancho (*wide*) donde los coches circulan rápidamente.
8. ___ Se usan para parar el coche.
9. ___ El policía nos la pide cuando nos para en el camino.
10. ___ Allí se revisan y se arreglan los coches.

a. los frenos (*brakes*)
b. doblar
c. la carretera
d. la batería
e. el taller
f. una llanta desinflada (*flat*)
g. la gasolina
h. las llantas
i. el aceite
j. la licencia

PASO 2 Ahora, siguiendo el modelo de las definiciones anteriores, ¿puede Ud. dar una definición de las siguientes palabras?

1. el semáforo
2. la circulación
3. estacionar
4. gastar gasolina
5. la gasolinera
6. la autopista

B. Entrevista: Un conductor (*driver*) responsable

PASO 1 Entreviste a un compañero / una compañera de clase para determinar con qué frecuencia hace las siguientes cosas.

1. dejar la licencia en casa cuando va a manejar
2. acelerar (*to speed up*) cuando ve a un policía
3. manejar después de tomar bebidas alcohólicas
4. respetar o exceder el límite de velocidad
5. estacionar el coche donde dice «Prohibido estacionar»
6. revisar el nivel (*level*) del aceite y la batería
7. seguir todo derecho a toda velocidad cuando no sabe llegar a su destino
8. rebasar (*to pass*) tres carros a la vez (*at the same time*)

Need more practice?

- Workbook/Laboratory Manual
- Interactive CD-ROM
- Online Learning Center (www.mhhe.com/quetal7)

PASO 2 Ahora, con el mismo compañero / la misma compañera, haga una lista de diez cosas que hace —o no hace— un conductor responsable. Pueden usar frases del **Paso 1**, si quieren.

PASO 3 Ahora, analice Ud. sus propias (*own*) costumbres y cualidades como conductor(a). ¡Diga la verdad! ¿Es Ud. un conductor / una conductora responsable? ¿Cuál de los dos es el mejor conductor / la mejor conductora?

38 *Más descripciones* Past Participle Used as an Adjective

Algunos refranes y dichos en español

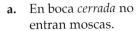

a. En boca *cerrada* no entran moscas.

b. Estoy tan *aburrido* como una ostra.

c. Cuando está *abierto* el cajón, el más *honrado* es ladrón.

Comprensión

Empareje estas oraciones con el refrán o dicho que explican.

1. _____ Es posible que una persona honrada caiga en la tentación de hacer algo malo si la oportunidad se le presenta.
2. _____ Hay que ser prudente. A veces es mejor no decir nada para evitar (*avoid*) problemas.
3. _____ Las ostras ejemplifican el aburrimiento (*boredom*) porque llevan una vida tranquila… siempre igual.

Forms of the Past Participle

A. The past participle of most English verbs ends in *-ed*.

to walk → *walked*   *to close* → *closed*

Many, however, are irregular.

to sing → **sung**   *to write* → **written**

In Spanish, the *past participle* (**el participio pasado**) is formed by adding **-ado** to the stem of **-ar** verbs, and **-ido** to the stem of **-er** and **-ir** verbs. An accent mark is used on the past participle of **-er/-ir** verbs with stems ending in **-a, -e,** or **-o.**

> **past participle** = the form of a verb used with **haber** in Spanish and *to have* in English to form perfect tenses

hablar	comer	vivir
hablado	comido	vivido
(*spoken*)	(*eaten*)	(*lived*)

caer → **caído**	oír → **oído**
creer → **creído**	(son)reír → **(son)reído**
leer → **leído**	traer → **traído**

A few Spanish proverbs and sayings   **1.** *Into a closed mouth no flies enter.* **2.** *I am as bored as an oyster.*
3. *When the (cash) drawer is open, the most honest person is (can become) a thief.*

PASO 2

Pronunciation hint: The Spanish **d** between vowels, as found in past participle endings, is pronounced as the fricative [ð] (see **Pronunciación** in **Capítulo 6**, Workbook/Laboratory Manual).

B. The Spanish verbs at the right have irregular past participles.

abrir:	**abierto**	morir:	**muerto**
cubrir (*to cover*):	**cubierto**	poner:	**puesto**
		resolver:	**resuelto**
decir:	**dicho**	romper:	**roto**
descubrir:	**descubierto**	ver:	**visto**
escribir:	**escrito**	volver:	**vuelto**
hacer:	**hecho**		

The Past Participle Used as an Adjective

A. In both English and Spanish, the past participle can be used as an adjective to modify a noun. Like other Spanish adjectives, the past participle must agree in number and gender with the noun modified.

Viven en una casa **construida** en 1920.
They live in a house built in 1920.

El español es una de las lenguas **habladas** en los Estados Unidos y en el Canadá.
Spanish is one of the languages spoken in the United States and in Canada.

B. The past participle is frequently used with **estar** to describe conditions that are the result of a previous action.

El lago **está contaminado.**
The lake is polluted.

Todos los peces **estaban cubiertos** de crudo.
All the fish were covered with crude oil.

OJO

English past participles often have the same form as the past tense.

*I **closed** the book.*

*The thief stood behind the **closed** door.*

The Spanish past participle is never identical in form or use to a past tense. Compare the sentences at the right.

Cerré la puerta. Ahora la puerta está **cerrada.**
*I **closed** the door. Now the door is **closed.***

Resolvieron el problema. Ahora el problema está **resuelto.**
*They **solved** the problem. Now the problem is **solved.***

AUTOPRUEBA

Give the infinitive of the past participles.

1. estudiadas
2. leído
3. vistos
4. dicha
5. abiertas
6. bebido

Answers: 1. estudiar 2. leer 3. ver 4. decir 5. abrir 6. beber

---

■ Práctica

A. En este momento...

PASO 1 **¡Anticipemos!** En este momento, ¿son ciertas o falsas las siguientes oraciones con relación a su sala de clase?

1. La puerta está abierta.
2. Las luces están apagadas.
3. Las ventanas están cerradas.
4. Algunos libros están abiertos.
5. Los estudiantes están sentados.
6. Hay algo escrito en la pizarra.
7. Una silla está rota.
8. Hay carteles y anuncios colgados en la pared.
9. Un aparato está enchufado.
10. Las persianas (*blinds*) están bajadas.

Palabras útiles
colgar (ue) (gu) (to hang)
enchufar (to plug in)
prender (to turn on [*lights or an appliance*])

PASO 2 Ahora describa el estado de las siguientes cosas en su casa (cuarto, apartamento).

1. las luces
2. la cama
3. el televisor
4. las ventanas
5. la puerta
6. las cortinas (*curtains*)

B. Situaciones.
¿Cuál es la situación en este momento? Conteste según el modelo.

MODELO: Natalia les tiene que *escribir* una *tarjeta* (*card*) a sus abuelos. →
La *tarjeta* no está *escrita* todavía.

1. Los Sres. García deben *abrir* la *tienda* más temprano. ¡Ya son las nueve!
2. Pablo tiene que *cerrar* las *ventanas*; entra un aire frío.
3. Los niños siempre esperan que la *tierra* se *cubra* de nieve para la Navidad.
4. Delia debe *poner* la *mesa*. Los invitados llegan a las nueve y ya son las ocho.
5. Claro está que la contaminación va a contribuir a la *destrucción* de la *capa de ozono*.
6. Es posible que los ingenieros *descubran* el *error* en la construcción del reactor nuclear.
7. Se debe *resolver* pronto el *problema* de la escasez de energía.

Need more practice?
- Workbook/Laboratory Manual
- Interactive CD-ROM
- Online Learning Center (www.mhhe.com/quetal7)

■ Conversación

¡Ojo alerta! Hay por lo menos cinco cosas que difieren (*are different*) entre un dibujo y el otro. Con un compañero / una compañera, encuéntralos todas. Use participios pasados como adjetivos cuando pueda.

Ⓐ

Ⓑ

En los Estados Unidos y el Canadá

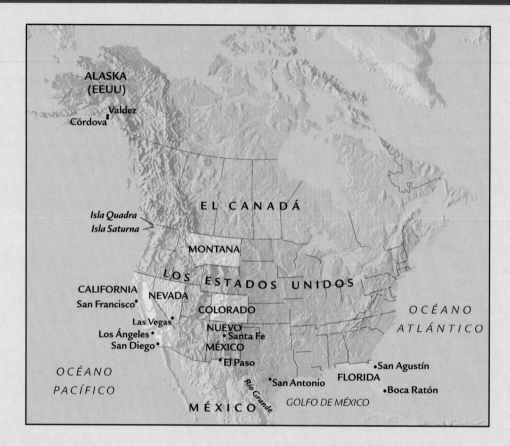

Lugares con nombres españoles

La **geografía de Norteamérica** está llena de **nombres que dejaron los españoles,** los primeros europeos que exploraron y se establecieron en estas tierras. Varios **estados** de los Estados Unidos tienen nombres españoles, por ejemplo: Colorado (*de color rojo*), Nevada (*cubierta de nieve*), Montana (*de la palabra «montaña»*), Florida (*con flores*) y Nuevo México. Numerosas **ciudades** estadounidenses también llevan nombres de origen español.

St. Augustine: Esta ciudad de Florida, establecida en 1564, lleva el nombre de la **misión** San Agustín. Es la ciudad más antigua de Norteamérica fuera de[a] México.

Santa Fe: El nombre original y completo de la capital de Nuevo México es la **Villa Real de la Santa Fe** de San Francisco de Asís. Santa Fe, el nombre usado hoy, significa *Holy Faith*. Es la capital más antigua de los Estados Unidos (establecida en 1607).

Sarasota: Esta ciudad fue nombrada en honor de la **hija del gobernador de Florida,** Sara de Soto.

Las Vegas: El nombre de esta ciudad en Nevada significa *fertile plains*.

Los Angeles: En 1781 los españoles fundaron el Pueblo de Nuestra Señora la Reina de Los Ángeles de Porciúncula, en California. Hoy es la segunda ciudad más grande de los Estados Unidos.

Fresno: Esta ciudad de California fue nombrada por sus **árboles,** los fresnos.[b]

Los españoles también exploraron la **costa pacífica** hasta Alaska, donde hay muchos nombres de influencia española: el Cabo[c] Blanco, en Oregón; el Cabo de Álava, en Washington; las ciudades de Valdez y Córdova y el Glaciar Malaspina, en Alaska. En Canadá están los estrechos[d] de Juan de Fuca y de Laredo, y las islas Quadra, Saturna, Galiano, Gabriola, Aristazábal y Flores, todos en la costa de la Columbia Británica.

[a]fuera... *outside of* [b]*ash trees* [c]*Cape* [d]*straits*

Voces de la Argentina

LITERATURA: Alfonsina Storni

Sobre la autora: *Alfonsina Storni nació en Sala Capriasca, Suiza, pero vivió en la Argentina casi toda la vida, una vida llena de desilusiones y obstáculos. Storni era —y sufría los problemas de— una mujer intelectual a principios del siglo XX. El poema «Cuadrados*[a] *y ángulos» es de la colección* El dulce daño *(1918).*

Alfonsina Storni
(1892–1938)

Casas enfiladas,[b] casas enfiladas,
casas enfiladas.
Cuadrados, cuadrados, cuadrados.
Casas enfiladas.
Las gentes ya tienen el alma[c] cuadrada,
Ideas en fila[d]
y ángulos en la espalda.
Yo misma he vertido[e] ayer una lágrima,[f]
Dios mío, cuadrada.

[a]*Squares* [b]*in a straight row* [c]*soul* [d]*en… in single file* [e]*he… have shed* [f]*tear*

·······································

MÚSICA: El tango

El tango es uno de los bailes más populares de la Argentina, pero su historia no está muy clara. Muchos creen que se originó en la Argentina entre los negros que habían sido importados[a] como esclavos. Estos[b] llamaban «tangó» al tambor,[c] al baile y al espacio en que se bailaba. El tango evolucionó y llegó a su forma moderna en los barrios pobres de Buenos Aires. Originalmente, el baile representaba la lucha[d] entre una prostituta y su chulo,[e] y por muchos años tuvo mala fama[f] y hasta[g] se consideraba escandaloso.

[a]*habían… had been imported* [b]*They (The slaves)* [c]*drum* [d]*struggle* [e]*pimp* [f]*mala… a bad reputation* [g]*even*

Para tocar el tango, se usan muchos instrumentos, pero el principal,[h] introducido durante la «italianización*» del tango, es el bandoneón, un tipo de acordeón.

[h]*el… the main one (instrument)*

El cantante de tango más famoso fue Carlos Gardel (1890–1935), quien se hizo estrella[i] de cine en Hollywood cantando tangos en varias películas. Murió trágicamente en un accidente de avión con otro grande del tango, el compositor Alfredo Lepera.

[i]*se… became a star*

*This term refers to the late nineteenth century and early twentieth century, during which many Italians immigrated to Argentina, especially to Buenos Aires. The addition of the mandolin and the **bandoneón** (accordion) to the instrumentation of the tango reflects the Italian influence.*

39 ¿Qué has hecho? Perfect Forms: Present Perfect Indicative and Present Perfect Subjunctive

Una llanta desinflada

MANOLO: ¡Ay, qué mala suerte!

LOLA: ¿Qué pasa?

MANOLO: Parece que el coche tiene una llanta desinflada. Y como no hay ningún taller por aquí, tengo que cambiarla yo mismo.

LOLA: *¿Has cambiado* una llanta alguna vez?

MANOLO: No. Siempre *he llevado* el coche a un taller cuando hay problemas.

LOLA: Pues, yo nunca *he cambiado* una llanta tampoco. Pero te puedo ayudar, si quieres.

MANOLO: Gracias. ¡Espero que la llanta de recambio* no esté desinflada también!

¿Y Ud.? ¿Ha... ?

1. cambiado una llanta desinflada
2. revisado el nivel del aceite de su coche
3. arreglado otras cosas del coche
4. tenido un accidente con el coche
5. excedido el límite de velocidad en la autopista

Present Perfect Indicative

PAST ------------------- Present ------------------- Future	
preterite	**present indicative**
imperfect	**present progressive**
present perfect	**formal commands**
present perfect subjunctive	**informal commands**
	present subjunctive

he hablado	*I have spoken*	**hemos** hablado	*we have spoken*
has hablado	*you have spoken*	**habéis** hablado	*you (pl.) have spoken*
ha hablado	*you have spoken, he/she has spoken*	**han** hablado	*you (pl.) / they have spoken*

A flat tire   MANOLO: *Aw, what bad luck!*   LOLA: *What's wrong?*   MANOLO: *It seems the car has a flat tire. And, since there aren't any repair shops around here, I have to change it myself.*   LOLA: *Have you ever changed a flat tire before?*   MANOLO: *No. I've always taken the car to a repair shop when there are problems.*   LOLA: *Well, I've never changed a tire either. But I can help you, if you want.*   MANOLO: *Thanks. I hope that the spare tire isn't flat, too!*

Other terms for spare tire in Spanish are **la llanta de respuesto and **la quinta llanta**.*

A. In English, the present perfect is a compound tense consisting of the present tense form of the verb *to have* plus the past participle: *I have written, you have spoken,* and so on.

In the Spanish *present perfect indicative* (**el presente perfecto del indicativo**), the past participle is used with present tense forms of **haber,** the equivalent of English *to have* in this construction.

In general, the use of the Spanish present perfect parallels that of the English present perfect.

No **hemos estado** aquí antes.
We haven't been here before.

Me he divertido mucho.
I've had a very good time.

Ya le **han escrito** la carta.
They've already written her the letter.

 OJO Haber, an auxiliary verb, is not interchangeable with **tener.**

B. The form of the past participle never changes with **haber,** regardless of the gender or number of the subject. The past participle always appears immediately after the appropriate form of **haber** and is never separated from it. Object pronouns and **no** are always placed directly before the form of **haber.**
[Práctica A–B]

Ella **ha cambiado** una llanta desinflada varias veces.
She's changed a flat tire several times.

Todavía **no le** han revisado el aceite al coche.
They still haven't checked the car's oil.

C. The present perfect form of **hay** is **ha habido** (*there has/have been*).

 OJO Remember that **acabar** + **de** + *infinitive*—not the present perfect tense—is used to state that something *has just occurred.*

Ha habido un accidente.
There's been an accident.

Acabo de mandar la carta.
I've just mailed the letter.

Present Perfect Subjunctive

The *present perfect subjunctive* (**el perfecto del subjuntivo**) is formed with the present subjunctive of **haber** plus the past participle. It is used to express *I have spoken* (*written,* and so on) when the subjunctive is required. Although its most frequent equivalent is *I have* plus the past participle, its exact equivalent in English depends on the context in which it occurs.

Note in the model sentences at the right that the English equivalent of the present perfect subjunctive can be expressed as a simple or as a compound tense: *did/have done; came/have come; built/have built.*
[Práctica C]

haya hablado	hayamos hablado
hayas hablado	hayáis hablado
haya hablado	hayan hablado

Es posible que lo **haya hecho.**
It's possible (that) he may have done (he did) it.

Me alegro de que **hayas venido.**
I'm glad (that) you've come (you came).

Es bueno que lo **hayan construido.**
It's good (that) they built (have built) it.

AUTOPRUEBA

Give the correct form of **haber.**

INDICATIVE **1.** yo _____   **2.** Uds. _____   **3.** nosotros _____

SUBJUNCTIVE **4.** tú _____   **5.** Ud. _____   **6.** ellos _____

Answers: 1. he 2. han 3. hemos 4. hayas 5. haya 6. hayan

■ **Práctica**

A. El pasado y el futuro

PASO 1 **¡Anticipemos!** Indique las actividades que Ud. ha hecho en el pasado.

1. _____ He hecho un viaje a Europa.
2. _____ He montado a camello (*camel*).
3. _____ He tomado una clase de informática.
4. _____ He buceado (*gone scuba diving*).
5. _____ He ido de safari a África.
6. _____ He comprado un coche.
7. _____ He preparado una comida italiana.
8. _____ He ocupado un puesto (*position*) político.
9. _____ He tenido una mascota.
10. _____ He escrito un poema.
11. _____ He visto una película de Almodóvar.
12. _____ He leído un periódico en español.
13. _____ Me he puesto un sombrero para ir a clase.
14. _____ Me he roto el brazo o la pierna.

PASO 2 Ahora, entre las cosas que Ud. no ha hecho, ¿cuáles le gustaría hacer? Conteste, siguiendo los modelos.

MODELOS: Nunca he montado a camello, pero me gustaría hacerlo.
(Nunca he montado a camello y no me interesa hacerlo.)

B. El coche de Carmina. Carmina acaba de comprarse un coche usado. Describa lo que le ha pasado a Carmina, según el modelo.

MODELO: ir a la agencia de compra-venta de coches →
Ha ido a la agencia de compra-venta de coches.

1. pedirle ayuda a su padre
2. hacer preguntas acerca de (*about*) los diferentes coches
3. ver uno bastante barato
4. revisar las llantas
5. conducirlo como prueba
6. regresar a la agencia
7. decidir comprarlo
8. comprarlo
9. volver a casa
10. llevar a sus amigas al cine en su coche

C. ¡No lo creo! ¿Tienen espíritu aventurero sus compañeros de clase? ¿Llevan una vida interesante? ¿O están tan aburridos como una ostra? ¡A ver!

PASO 1 **¡Anticipemos!** De cada par de oraciones, indique la que (*the one that*) expresa su opinión acerca de los estudiantes de esta clase.

1. ☐ Creo que alguien en esta clase ha visto las pirámides de Egipto.
   ☐ Es dudoso que alguien haya visto las pirámides de Egipto.
2. ☐ Estoy seguro/a de que por lo menos uno de mis compañeros ha escalado una montaña alta.
   ☐ No creo que nadie haya escalado una montaña alta.
3. ☐ Creo que alguien ha viajado haciendo autostop.
   ☐ Dudo que alguien haya hecho autostop en un viaje.
4. ☐ Creo que alguien ha practicado el paracaidismo.
   ☐ Es improbable que alguien haya practicado el paracaidismo.

Vocabulario útil

escalar (to climb)
hacer (*irreg.*) **autostop** (to hitchhike)
el paracaidismo (skydiving)

5. ☐ Estoy seguro/a de que alguien ha tomado el metro en Nueva York a medianoche.
☐ No creo que nadie haya tomado el metro neoyorquino a medianoche.

PASO 2 Ahora escuche mientras el profesor / la profesora pregunta si alguien ha hecho estas actividades. ¿Tenía Ud. razón en el **Paso 1**?

Need more practice?
- Workbook/Laboratory Manual
- Interactive CD-ROM
- Online Learning Center (www.mhhe.com/quetal7)

Conversación

A. ¿Verdad o mentira?

PASO 1 Invente Ud. tres oraciones sobre cosas que ha hecho y no ha hecho en su vida. Dos oraciones deben ser verdaderas y una debe ser una mentira.

MODELO: *He hecho* un viaje a Sudamérica.
Nunca *he conocido* a mis primos.
He visto muchas películas en español.

PASO 2 Lea sus oraciones a unos compañeros o a la clase entera. Ellos van a tratar de encontrar la mentira.

MODELO: Creo que *has hecho* un viaje a Sudamérica y que *has visto* muchas películas en español. Dudo que no *hayas conocido* a tus primos.

NOTA COMUNICATIVA

Talking About What You Had Done

Use the past participle with the imperfect form of **haber** (**había, habías,...**) to talk about what you had—or had not—done before a given time in the past. This form is called the *past perfect* (**el pluscuamperfecto**).

Antes de graduarme en la escuela secundaria, no **había estudiado** español.

Before graduating from high school, I hadn't studied Spanish.

Antes de 1985, siempre **habíamos vivido** en Kansas.

Before 1985, we had always lived in Kansas.

B. Entrevista. Use the following cues to interview a classmate about his or her activities before coming to this campus.

MODELO: ¿qué? / no haber aprendido a hacer antes del año pasado →
E1: ¿Qué no *habías aprendido* a hacer antes del año pasado?
E2: Pues… no *había aprendido* a nadar. Aprendí a nadar este año en mi clase de natación.

1. ¿qué? / no haber aprendido a hacer antes del año pasado
2. ¿qué materia? / no haber estudiado antes del año pasado
3. ¿qué deporte? / haber practicado mucho
4. ¿qué viaje? / haber hecho varias veces
5. ¿qué libro importante? / no haber leído
6. ¿qué decisión? / no haber tomado
7. ¿ ?

PASO 3

C. Dos dibujos, un punto de vista. Un español hizo el dibujo de la izquierda; un argentino, el de la derecha. Pero los dos comentan el mismo tema.

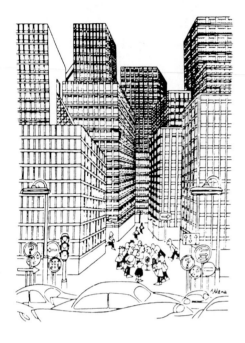

Palabras útiles			
el arado (plow)	la flor	la mecanización	el tractor
la deshumanización	la gente	la mula	

© Joaquín Salvador, Lavado (QUINO), *Esto no es todo,* Ediciones de la Flor, © 2001.

PASO 1 Conteste estas preguntas sobre el dibujo de la izquierda.

1. Describa la ciudad que se ve en el dibujo.
2. ¿Qué ha descubierto la gente? ¿Por qué mira con tanto interés?
3. Para construir esta ciudad, ¿qué han hecho? ¿Qué han destruido?

PASO 2 Conteste estas preguntas sobre el dibujo de la derecha.

1. ¿Qué se ha comprado el agricultor de la izquierda? ¿Qué ha vendido?
2. ¿Qué es «más moderno», según el otro agricultor?
3. ¿Qué desventaja tiene el tractor?

PASO 3 Ahora explique su reacción personal a estos dos dibujos. ¿Son chistosos (*funny*)? ¿serios?

UN POCO DE TODO

Lengua y cultura: ¿Glaciares en la Argentina? Complete the following dialogue and article with the correct forms of the words in parentheses, as suggested by the context. When two possibilities are given in parentheses, select the correct word. **¡OJO!** When **haber** appears in parentheses followed by an infinitive, you will decide whether to use present perfect indicative or subjunctive. You will also need to decide between using present tense indicative or subjunctive with several other infinitives.

En la clase de Geografía mundial, todos los estudiantes se han reunido en grupos de tres para investigar la geografía de uno de los países de Sudamérica. Luego deben hacer una presentación «PowerPoint» con la intención de mostrar(les/los[1]) a sus compañeros de clase lo que el grupo (haber descubrir[2]) del país que seleccionaron. Milton, Marisol y Petra están (tratado/tratando[3]) de terminar su informe sobre la Argentina.

MARISOL: Bueno, ya tenemos muchos datos sobre las ciudades argentinas y las famosas Pampas.[a] Es suficiente, ¿no creen Uds.?

MILTON: Creo que sí. Y (*yo/me*[4]) encanta que (*tú:* haber encontrar[5]) esos artículos que (comparar[6]) históricamente la figura del gaucho con la del «cowboy» del oeste de los Estados Unidos. Y a (tú/ti[7]), ¿qué te (parecer[8]), Petra?

PETRA: Pues, yo no (encontrarse[9]) totalmente satisfecha[b] con la presentación. Sí, sí, estoy de acuerdo en que está muy bien (escrito[10]), pero esa información no tiene (algo/nada[11]) de nuevo. Yo (haber oír[12]) hablar de las Pampas, de los gauchos y de la ciudad de Buenos Aires desde que estaba en la escuela primaria. Quiero que (*nosotros:* presentar[13]) algo diferente, algo menos común...

MARISOL: ¿Qué (*tú:* sugerir[14]), entonces?

PETRA: Miren este párrafo breve que tengo. Es un resumen de un artículo que encontré en el Internet. Sugiero que lo (*nosotros:* poner[15]) al final de la presentación.

MILTON: De acuerdo. Pero quiero que (*nosotros:* entregar[16]) el informe hoy. A ver... ¿qué dice tu párrafo?

Un turista en el Parque Nacional Los Glaciares, Argentina

El párrafo:

Y, finalmente, atención ecoturistas extremistas:

Vengan (a / —[17]) ver el Parque Nacional Los Glaciares, en la Patagonia, en el sur de la Argentina. El gobierno argentino (*P/I,* crear[18]) este parque en 1937, y en 1982 el parque (*P/I,* ser[19]) designado Patrimonio Natural de la Humanidad por la UNESCO. Allí, en las 600.000 hectáreas[c] del parque, pueden explorar unos glaciares (impresionante[20]). Se calcula que aproximadamente 200 de esos glaciares (salir[21]) de los campos de hielo[d] que dominan este parque. Con (alguno[22]) precauciones, es posible que los ecoturistas aventureros (escalar[23])[e] unas montañas de hielo precipitosas como el Cerro Torre, un desafío[f] para los mejores alpinistas profesionales. Es fascinante encontrar una geografía tan variada dentro de un solo país.

[a]*grassy plains of Argentina* [b]*satisfied* [c]*hectares (2.47 acres)* [d]*campos... ice fields* [e]*to climb* [f]*challenge*

Comprensión: ¿Cierto o falso? Corrija las oraciones falsas.

1. Todos los estudiantes de la clase de Geografía mundial van a preparar un informe sobre la Argentina.
2. Milton, Marisol y Petra necesitan empezar su informe sobre la Argentina.
3. Marisol ha encontrado unos artículos sobre el gaucho y el «cowboy».
4. Petra no está contenta porque dice que la información es incorrecta.
5. Petra les trae un párrafo que ella ha escrito con información que encontró en el Internet.
6. El Parque Nacional Los Glaciares es un pequeño parque al sur de Buenos Aires.

Resources for Review and Testing Preparation

- Workbook/Laboratory Manual
- Interactive CD-ROM
- Online Learning Center (www.mhhe.com/quetal7)

VIDEOTECA

Entrevista cultural: La Argentina

Natalia D'Ángelo es una estudiante de la Argentina. Habla de sus estudios, pero se enfoca en el medio ambiente. Antes de ver el vídeo, lea el siguiente fragmento de la entrevista.

ENTREVISTADORA: ¿Perteneces tú[a] a alguna asociación?

NATALIA: En la universidad estamos trabajando en una asociación para proteger la biodiversidad de una zona de la Argentina que se llama la Patagonia.

ENTREVISTADORA: ¿Nos puedes hablar un poco más sobre la Patagonia?

NATALIA: Sí, la Patagonia es un territorio muy extenso que es todo el sur de Argentina y es una zona muy poco poblada, con actividades que están centradas principalmente en la pesca[b] y en el turismo.

[a]Perteneces… *Do you belong*   [b]*fishing*

Ahora vea el vídeo y conteste las siguientes preguntas, basándose en la entrevista.

1. ¿Dónde estudia Natalia?
2. ¿En qué se especializa?
3. Según Natalia, ¿se preocupan mucho o poco los estudiantes por los problemas ecológicos?
4. ¿Cómo pueden participar los estudiantes en actividades ecológicas?
5. ¿Qué es la Patagonia?

Entre amigos: Nuestro pequeño grano de arena (*grain of sand*)

Miguel, Tané, Rubén y Karina hablan del medio ambiente. En su opinión, ¿qué preguntas se van a hacer? Antes de mirar el vídeo, lea las preguntas a continuación. Mientras mire el vídeo, trate de entender la conversación en general y fíjese en la información sobre la ecología, la naturaleza y el medio ambiente. Luego mire el vídeo una segunda vez, fijándose en la información que necesita para contestar las preguntas.

1. ¿Qué tipo de coche está manejando Miguel?
2. ¿Por qué no tiene Miguel su propio (*own*) coche?
3. ¿Qué tipo de coche tiene Karina?
4. ¿Cómo sugiere Karina cuidar el medio ambiente?
5. ¿Qué opinión tiene Rubén de las fábricas?

CAPÍTULO 14

PASO 4

ENFOQUE CULTURAL

 La Argentina

¡Fíjese!

- La inmigración de europeos en el siglo XIX ha tenido un papel decisivo en la formación de la población de la Argentina (así como en la del Uruguay). En 1856 la población argentina era de 1.200.000 habitantes; para 1930, 10.500.000 extranjeros habían entrado en la Argentina por el puerto[a] de Buenos Aires. La mitad[b] estaba formada por italianos, una tercera parte por españoles, y el resto estaba formado principalmente por alemanes y eslavos. Muchos de los que llegaron fueron trabajadores temporales que, tarde o temprano, regresaron a Europa. El resto, sin embargo, se estableció permanentemente, porque el gobierno quería estimular la inmigración para poblar la Pampa. Pero muchos, acostumbrados a la vida urbana, se quedaron en Buenos Aires.

- Buenos Aires es una ciudad con una población de más de 13.000.000 de habitantes, lo cual supone[c] el 30 por ciento de la población del país. Es el centro cultural, comercial, industrial y financiero, así como el puerto principal de la Argentina. A las personas de Buenos Aires se les llama «porteños», derivado de la palabra «puerto».

[a]port [b]half [c]lo... which constitutes

Personas famosas: Mercedes Sosa

Mercedes Sosa (1935–) es probablemente la cantante argentina más conocida del mundo. Es también una de las figuras más prominentes del canto nuevo, una forma de música de protesta que surgió[a] en la Argentina en los años 60 y se hizo muy popular en otras partes de Latinoamérica. Hace unos cuarenta años que[b] Sosa canta,[c] sola y con otros artistas, en su país y en todos los continentes. Ha grabado[d] más de treinta discos y sus conciertos son muy concurridos.[e] Sosa tiene una voz fuerte y dramática y su repertorio incluye canciones folklóricas de la Argentina y toda Latinoamérica. Las canciones pueden ser alegres o trágicas, pero siempre son bellas y conmovedoras.[f] De 1979 a 1982, años de un régimen dictatorial en la Argentina, Sosa vivió en el exilio, porque el gobierno argentino no la permitía cantar en la Argentina. Pero volvió, triunfante, en 1982.

[a]sprang up [b]Hace... For some forty years [c]has been singing [d]recorded [e]well attended [f]moving

La Plaza de Mayo, que data de 1580, año de la fundación de Buenos Aires

Learn more about Argentina with the Video, the Interactive CD-ROM, and the Online Learning Center (www.mhhe.com/quetal7).

Paso 4 Enfoque cultural trescientos sesenta y tres **363**

PASO FINAL

A CONVERSAR

¿Somos buenos o malos conductores?

PASO 1   Con un compañero / una compañera, haga y conteste preguntas basadas en el siguiente cuadro. Utilice el presente perfecto en sus preguntas y respuestas y marque el cuadro según las respuestas de su compañero/a. También añada (*add*) al cuadro otro problema relacionado con los coches.

> MODELO: E1: ¿Has superado (*Have you exceeded*) el límite de velocidad recientemente?
>
> E2: Sí, (No, no) he superado el límite de velocidad recientemente.

	sí	no
chocar con otro coche		
superar el límíte de velocidad		
pasarse (*to run*) un semáforo en rojo		
desobedecerle a un policía		
¿?		

PASO 2   Ahora, entre todos, hablen de sus compañeros/as. En general, ¿son Uds. buenos o malos conductores? Deben marcar la información en un cuadro como el del **Paso 1.** Incluyan los problemas que añadieron al cuadro.

> MODELOS: ¿Quiénes han chocado con otro coche recientemente? →
> Tom ha chocado con otro coche este mes.

PASO 3   Calculen el porcentaje de personas que contestaron **sí** a cada pregunta del **Paso 1.** Reaccionen a los porcentajes con las siguientes frases. **¡OJO!** Las frases requieren el uso del subjuntivo.

> Es bueno/malo que…
> Me alegra / No me alegra que…
> Me sorprende que / No me sorprende que…

> MODELO: Siete de veintiún estudiantes han superado recientemente el límite de velocidad. → El 33 por ciento de la clase ha superado recientemente el límite de velocidad.
> E1: No me sorprende que el 33 por ciento de la clase haya superado el límite de velocidad.

GRAMÁTICA

To review the grammar points presented in this chapter, refer to the indicated grammar presentations. You'll find further practice of these structures in the Workbook/Laboratory Manual, on the Interactive CD-ROM, and on the *¿Qué tal?* Online Learning Center (www.mhhe.com/quetal7).

38 **Más descripciones**—Past Participle Used As an Adjective

Do you know how to form past participles? You should remember that past participles that are used as adjectives agree with the noun they describe.

39 **¿Qué has hecho?**—Perfect Forms: Present Perfect Indicative and Present Perfect Subjunctive

How do you express that you have done something? Do you know how to say that you're happy or sad that someone else did or has done something?

VOCABULARIO

Practice this vocabulary with digital flash cards on the Online Learning Center (www.mhhe.com/quetal7).

Los verbos

cubrir	to cover
descubrir	to discover
evitar	to avoid
resolver (ue)	to solve, resolve

El medio ambiente

la escasez (*pl.* **escaseces**)	lack; shortage
la fábrica	factory
el gobierno	government
el medio ambiente	environment (*natural*)
la naturaleza	nature
la población	population
los recursos naturales	natural resources

Cognados: el aire, la energía eléctrica (nuclear, solar)

Repaso: la contaminación, la falta

acabar	to run out (of), use up completely
conservar	to save, conserve
construir (y)	to build
contaminar	to pollute
desarrollar	to develop
destruir (y)	to destroy
proteger (j)	to protect
reciclar	to recycle

¿La ciudad o el campo?

el/la agricultor(a)	farmer
el/la campesino/a	farm worker; peasant
el campo	countryside; field
el delito	crime
la finca	farm
el rascacielos	skyscraper
el ritmo	rhythm, pace
el transporte	(means of) transportation

Cognados: el servicio, la violencia
Repaso: la ciudad, la vida

Los animales

el animal doméstico	domesticated animal; pet
el animal salvaje	wild animal
la ballena	whale
el caballo	horse
la especie (en peligro de extinción)	(endangered) species
el pez (*pl.* **peces**)	fish
el toro	bull
la vaca	cow

Cognados: el elefante, el gorila

El paisaje

el árbol	tree
el bosque	forest
el lago	lake
el paisaje	countryside
el río	river

Repaso: la montaña

Los coches

el aceite	oil
la estación de gasolina	gas station
los frenos	brakes
la gasolinera	gas station
la llanta (desinflada)	(flat) tire
el/la mecánico/a	mechanic
el nivel	level
el parabrisas	windshield
el taller	(repair) shop
el tanque	tank

Cognados: la batería, la gasolina
Repaso: la camioneta, el carro, el coche

arrancar (qu)	to start up (*a car*)
gastar	to use (*gas*)
llenar	to fill (up)
revisar	to check

Repaso: arreglar

En el camino

la autopista	freeway
el camino	street; road

la carretera	highway
la circulación	traffic
el/la conductor(a)	driver
la esquina	(street) corner
la licencia de manejar/conducir	driver's license
el límite de velocidad	speed limit
el/la policía	police officer
el semáforo	traffic signal
el tránsito	traffic

Repaso: la calle

chocar (qu) (con)	to run into, collide (with)
conducir (zc)	to drive
doblar	to turn
obedecer (zc)	to obey
parar	to stop
seguir (i, i) (g)	to keep on going; to go; to continue

Repaso: estacionar, manejar

todo derecho	straight ahead

Los adjetivos

acelerado/a	fast, accelerated
bello/a	beautiful
puro/a	clean; pure

Cognados: denso/a, público/a

La vida social y la vida afectiva°

°*emotional*

Unos novios en el Parque Forestal de Santiago, Chile

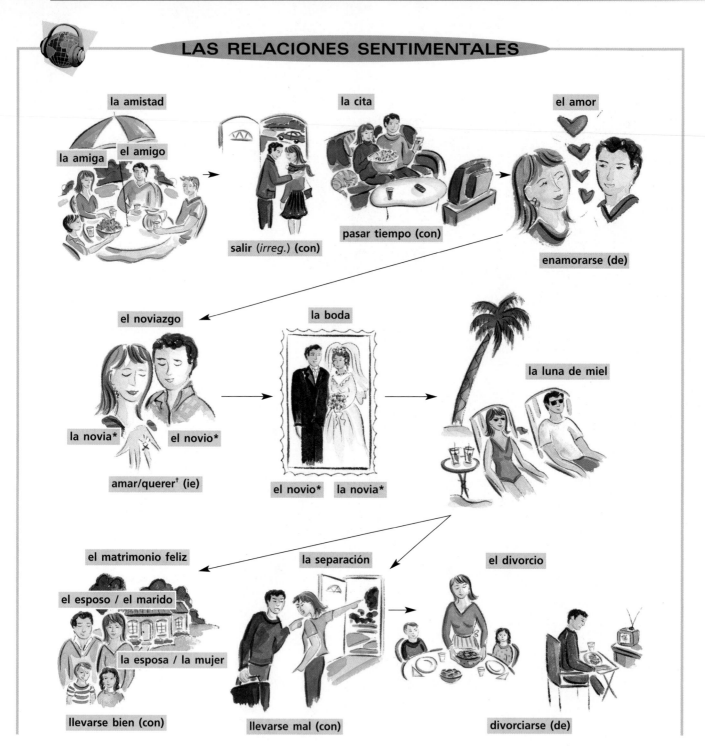

LAS RELACIONES SENTIMENTALES

la amistad

la amiga   el amigo

salir *(irreg.)* (con)

la cita

pasar tiempo (con)

el amor

enamorarse (de)

el noviazgo

la novia*   el novio*

amar/querer† (ie)

la boda

el novio*   la novia*

la luna de miel

el matrimonio feliz

el esposo / el marido

la esposa / la mujer

llevarse bien (con)

la separación

llevarse mal (con)

el divorcio

divorciarse (de)

---

*El novio / La novia *can mean* boyfriend/girlfriend, fiancé(e), *or* groom/bride.
†Amar *and* querer *both mean* to love, *but* amar *can imply more passion in some dialects.*

la pareja	(married) couple; partner	**amistoso/a**	friendly
el/la viudo/a	widower/widow	**cariñoso/a**	affectionate
		casado/a* (con)	married (to)
casarse (con)	to marry	**divorciado/a (de)**	divorced (from)
pelear (con)	to fight (with)	**enamorado/a† (de)**	in love (with)
romper (con)	to break up (with)	**recién casado/a (con)**	newlywed (to)
separarse (de)	to separate (from)	**soltero/a***	single, not married

■ Conversación

A. Definiciones. Empareje las palabras con sus definiciones. Luego, para cada palabra definida, dé un verbo y también el nombre de una persona asociada con esa relación social. Hay más de una respuesta posible en cada caso.

1. _____ el matrimonio
2. _____ el amor
3. _____ el divorcio
4. _____ la boda
5. _____ la amistad

a. Es una relación cariñosa entre dos personas. Se llevan bien y se hablan con frecuencia.

b. Es el posible resultado de un matrimonio, cuando los esposos no se llevan bien.

c. Es una relación sentimental, apasionada, muy especial, entre dos personas. Puede llevar al (*lead to*) matrimonio.

d. Es una ceremonia religiosa o civil en la que (*which*) la novia a veces lleva un vestido blanco.

e. Es una relación legal entre dos personas que viven juntas (*together*) y que a veces tienen hijos.

B. ¡Seamos lógicos! Complete las oraciones lógicamente.

1. Mi abuelo es el _____ de mi abuela.
2. Muchos novios tienen un largo _____ antes de la boda.
3. María y Julio tienen una _____ el viernes para comer en un restaurante. Luego van a bailar.
4. La _____ de Juan y Pati es el domingo a las dos de la tarde, en la iglesia (*church*) de San Martín.
5. En una _____, ¿quién debe comprar los boletos, el hombre o la mujer?
6. La _____ entre los ex esposos es imposible. No pueden ser amigos.
7. ¡El _____ es ciego (*blind*)!
8. Para algunas personas, el _____ es un concepto anticuado. Prefieren vivir juntos, sin casarse.
9. Algunas parejas modernas no quieren gastar su dinero en una _____.
10. ¿Cree Ud. que es posible el _____ a primera vista (*at first sight*)?

---

*In the activities of **Capítulo 2,** *you began to use* **ser casado/a.** *A variation of this phrase is* **estar casado/a. Estar casado/a** *means to be married;* **ser casado/a** *means to be a married person.* **Ser soltero/a** *is used exclusively to describe an unmarried person.*

†**(Mi) Enamorado/a** *can also mean (my) boyfriend/girlfriend.*

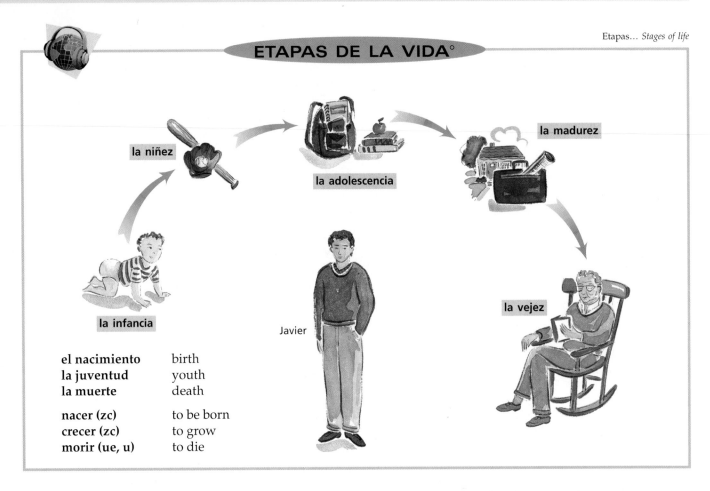

Etapas... *Stages of life*

ETAPAS DE LA VIDA°

la niñez

la adolescencia

la madurez

la infancia

Javier

la vejez

el nacimiento	birth
la juventud	youth
la muerte	death
nacer (zc)	to be born
crecer (zc)	to grow
morir (ue, u)	to die

NOTA CULTURAL

¿Amigos, novios, prometidos... ?

Dos palabras españolas que no tienen equivalente exacto en inglés son **amigo** y **novio**. En el mundo hispánico la palabra «amigo» se usa casi exclusivamente para indicar una relación de amistad fraternal. Normalmente no tiene ninguna connotación romántica. Palabras como **mi pareja, mi enamorado/a** y **mi chico/a** denotan una relación romántica entre dos personas y, por lo tanto, son equivalentes a *boyfriend/girlfriend*. En la mayoría de los países sólo se usan las palabras **novio/a** y **prometido/a** después de formalizarse las relaciones y hacer planes para contraer matrimonio.

friend	*girlfriend/boyfriend*	*fiancée/fiancé*	*bride/groom*

amiga/amigo   novia/novio

Unos novios en Chile

Capítulo 15 • La vida social y la vida afectiva

Conversación

A. Etapas de la vida. Relacione las siguientes palabras y frases con las distintas etapas de la vida de una persona. **¡OJO!** Hay más de una posible relación en algunos casos.

1. el amor
2. los nietos
3. los juguetes (*toys*)
4. no poder comer sin ayuda

5. los hijos en la universidad
6. los granos (*pimples*)
7. la universidad
8. la boda

B. Entrevista

1. ¿Son bastante (*rather*) importantes en tu vida los amigos? ¿Quién es tu mejor amigo/a? ¿En qué año lo/la conociste? ¿Crecieron Uds. juntos/as? Es decir, ¿se han conocido desde la niñez? ¿desde la adolescencia? ¿Por qué te llevas bien con esa persona?

2. ¿Quieres casarte algún día? (¿Ya te casaste?) ¿Te gusta la idea de tener una boda grande? (¿Tuviste una boda grande?) ¿Piensas hacer un viaje de luna de miel? (¿Hiciste un viaje de luna de miel?) ¿Adónde?

3. ¿Qué es lo bueno de estar casado? ¿y lo malo? ¿Qué es lo bueno de ser soltero? ¿y lo malo?

4. ¿En qué década del siglo (*century*) pasado naciste? ¿Has visto muchos cambios desde entonces (*then*)? ¿Cuáles son? ¿Cómo piensas pasar tu vejez? (Si ya eres una persona madura, ¿cómo pasas tu tiempo?)

5. ¿Has sido afectado/a personalmente por la muerte de alguien? ¿Quién murió? ¿Cómo te sentiste? ¿Tienes buenos recuerdos (*memories*) de esa persona? ¿Cuáles son?

C. Una receta para unas buenas relaciones. Piense en su propio (*own*) matrimonio o en el de sus padres / unos amigos. O, si lo prefiere, piense en sus relaciones con su mejor amigo/a o en las de un par de amigos que Ud. tiene. En su opinión, ¿cuáles son los ingredientes necesarios para un buen matrimonio o una buena amistad?

Need more practice?

- Workbook/Laboratory Manual
- Interactive CD-ROM
- Online Learning Center (www.mhhe.com/quetal7)

PASO 1 Haga una lista de los cinco ingredientes más esenciales. Los ingredientes pueden expresarse con una palabra o una frase.

PASO 2 Compare su lista con las de otros tres estudiantes. ¿Coinciden en la selección de algunos ingredientes? Hablen de todos los ingredientes y hagan una lista de los cinco más importantes.

PASO 3 Ahora comparen los resultados de todos los grupos. ¿Han contestado todos más o menos de la misma manera?

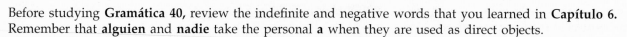
¿Recuerda Ud.?

Before studying **Gramática 40,** review the indefinite and negative words that you learned in **Capítulo 6.** Remember that **alguien** and **nadie** take the personal **a** when they are used as direct objects.

Busco **a alguien** de la familia.	*I'm looking for someone from the family.*
No veo **a nadie** en el salón de baile.	*I don't see anyone in the dance hall.*

Give the opposite of the following words. **1.** nada **2.** algunos **3.** alguien

40 ¿Hay alguien que... ? ¿Hay un lugar donde... ? Subjunctive After Nonexistent and Indefinite Antecedents

Un buen lunes

© Joaquín Salvador Lavado
(QUINO), *Toda Mafalda,*
Ediciones de la Flor © 1993

^a*eres*

Mafalda tiene un padre que la quiere, la protege y que pasa mucho tiempo con ella. Por eso, Mafalda ve a su padre como un hombre que ahora es más guapo que cuando era joven. Todos los niños *necesitan padres que los quieran, los cuiden y que pasen* tiempo con ellos.

Comprensión

¿Quién lo dice o piensa, el padre de Mafalda u otro pasajero en el autobús?

1. No hay nadie en este autobús que sea más feliz que yo.
2. Tengo una hija que es una maravilla, ¿verdad?
3. En camino al trabajo no hay nada que me haga sonreír.

A. In English and Spanish, statements or questions that give or ask for information about a person, place, thing, or idea often contain two clauses.

Each of the example sentences contains a main clause (*I have a car; Is there a house for sale*). In addition, each sentence also has a subordinate clause (*that gets good mileage; that is closer to the city*) that modifies a noun in the main clause: *car, house.*

I have a **car** *that gets good mileage.*
Is there a **house** for sale *that is closer to the city*?

A good Monday Mafalda has a father who loves her, protects her, and spends a lot of time with her. That's why Mafalda sees her father as a man who is now more handsome than when he was young. All children need parents who love them, take care of them, and spend time with them.

The noun (or pronoun) modified is called the *antecedent* (**el antecedente**) of the subordinate clause, and the clause itself is called an adjective clause because—like an adjective—it modifies a noun (or pronoun).

> **antecedent** = the word, noun, or phrase referred to by a pronoun or clause

B. Sometimes the antecedent of an adjective clause is something that, in the speaker's mind, does not exist or whose existence is indefinite or uncertain.

NONEXISTENT ANTECEDENT

There is *nothing* that you can do.

INDEFINITE ANTECEDENT

We need *a car* that will last us for years. (We don't have one yet.)

In these cases, the subjunctive must be used in the adjective (subordinate) clause in Spanish.

Note in the examples that adjective clauses that describe a place can be introduced with **donde...** as well as with **que...**

EXISTENT ANTECEDENT

Hay algo aquí que me **interesa.**
There is something here that interests me.

NONEXISTENT ANTECEDENT

No veo nada que me **interese.**
I don't see anything that interests me.

DEFINITE ANTECEDENT

Hay muchos restaurantes donde **sirven** comida mexicana auténtica.
There are a lot of restaurants where they serve authentic Mexican food.

INDEFINITE ANTECEDENT

Buscamos un restaurante donde **sirvan** comida chilena auténtica.
We're looking for a restaurant where they serve authentic Chilean food.

OJO The dependent adjective clause structure is often used in questions to find out about someone or something the speaker does not know much about. Note, however, that the indicative is used to answer the question if the antecedent is known to the person who answers.

INDEFINITE ANTECEDENT

¿Hay algo aquí que te **guste?**
Is there anything here that you like?

DEFINITE ANTECEDENT

Sí, **hay varias bolsas** que me **gustan.**
Yes, there are several purses that I like.

OJO The personal **a** is not used with direct object nouns that refer to hypothetical persons. Compare the use of the indicative and the subjunctive in the sentences at the right.

NONEXISTENT ANTECEDENT

Busco **un señor** que **sepa** francés.
I'm looking for a man who knows French.

EXISTENT ANTECEDENT

Busco **al señor** que **sabe** francés.
I'm looking for the man who knows French.

■ Práctica

A. ¡Anticipemos! Hablando de gente que conocemos. En su familia, ¿hay personas que tengan las siguientes características? Indique la oración apropiada en cada par de oraciones.

TENGO UN PARIENTE…	NO TENGO NINGÚN PARIENTE…
1. ☐ que habla alemán.	☐ que hable alemán.
2. ☐ que vive en el extranjero.	☐ que viva en el extranjero.
3. ☐ que es dueño de un restaurante.	☐ que sea dueño de un restaurante.
4. ☐ que sabe tocar el piano.	☐ que sepa tocar el piano.
5. ☐ que es médico/a.	☐ que sea médico/a.
6. ☐ que se lleva mal conmigo.	☐ que se lleve mal conmigo.
7. ☐ que está divorciado/a.	☐ que esté divorciado/a.
8. ☐ que trabaja en la televisión.	☐ que trabaje en la televisión.
9. ☐ que es viudo/a.	☐ que sea viudo/a.
10. ☐ que se casa este año.	☐ que se case este año.

B. Las preguntas de Carmen

PASO 1 Carmen acaba de llegar aquí de otro estado. Necesita tener información sobre la universidad y la ciudad. Haga las preguntas de Carmen según el modelo.

MODELO: restaurantes / sirven comida latinoamericana →
¿Hay restaurantes que *sirvan* (donde *sirvan*) comida latinoamericana?

1. librerías / venden libros usados
2. tiendas / se puede comprar revistas de Latinoamérica
3. cafés cerca de la universidad / se reúnen muchos estudiantes
4. apartamentos cerca de la universidad / son buenos y baratos
5. cines / pasan (*they show*) películas en español
6. un gimnasio en la universidad / se juega al ráquetbol
7. parques / la gente corre o da paseos
8. museos / hacen exposiciones de arte latinoamericano

PASO 2 ¿Cierto o falso?

1. A Carmen no le interesa la cultura hispánica.
2. Carmen es deportista.
3. Es posible que sea estudiante.
4. Este año piensa vivir con unos amigos de sus padres.

PASO 3 Ahora conteste las preguntas de Carmen con información verdadera sobre la ciudad donde Ud. vive y su universidad.

Need more practice?

- Workbook/Laboratory Manual
- Interactive CD-ROM
- Online Learning Center (www.mhhe.com/quetal7)

■ Conversación

A. Una encuesta. ¿Qué sabe Ud. de los compañeros de su clase de español? Pregúnteles a los miembros de la clase si saben hacer lo siguiente o a quién le ocurre lo siguiente. Deben levantar la mano sólo los que puedan contestar afirmativamente. Luego la persona que hizo la pregunta debe hacer un comentario apropiado. Siga el modelo.

MODELO: hablar chino →
En esta clase, ¿hay alguien que hable chino?
(*Nadie levanta la mano.*) No hay nadie que hable chino.
(*Alguien levanta la mano.*) Hay una persona que habla chino.

1. hablar ruso
2. saber tocar la viola
3. conocer a un actor / una actriz
4. saber preparar comida vietnamita
5. tener su cumpleaños hoy
6. escribir poemas
7. vivir en las afueras
8. ¿ ?

B. Entrevista. With another student, ask and answer the following questions. Then report any interesting details to the class.

1. ¿Hay alguien en tu vida que te quiera locamente?
2. ¿Hay algo que te importe más que los estudios universitarios?
3. ¿Con qué tipo de persona te gusta salir / pasar tiempo?
4. Para el semestre/trimestre que viene, ¿qué clases buscas? ¿Una que empiece a las ocho de la mañana?
5. ¿Tienes algún amigo o alguna amiga de la escuela secundaria que esté casado/a? ¿que tenga hijos? ¿que esté divorciado/a?
6. **¡OJO!** Unas preguntas indiscretas: ¿Has conocido recientemente a alguien que te haya gustado mucho? ¿de quien te hayas enamorado? ¿Hay algún pariente con quien te lleves muy mal? ¿o muy, muy bien?

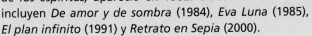

En los Estados Unidos y el Canadá

Isabel Allende: Novelista chilena

Es posible que la chilena Isabel Allende (1942–) sea **la escritora hispánica más conocida de Norteamérica.** Sobrina del presidente de Chile, Salvador Allende, quien fue derrocado[a] violentamente y murió en 1973, Isabel viene de **una familia que tiene un pasado muy interesante.** Este pasado, con su mezcla[b] de lo familiar y lo político, aparece como uno de los elementos más salientes[c] de sus novelas. Estas se caracterizan también por el uso del «**realismo mágico**», técnica literaria en que elementos fantásticos se entretejen[d] con aspectos de la vida diaria. Su primera novela, *La casa de los espíritus,* apareció en 1982. Otras incluyen *De amor y de sombra* (1984), *Eva Luna* (1985), *El plan infinito* (1991) y *Retrato en Sepia* (2000).

Isabel Allende

La vida de Allende no ha sido fácil. Después de los eventos políticos en que murió su tío, tuvo que **abandonar su país** con sus hijos pequeños. Vivió por un tiempo en Venezuela y hoy **reside en los Estados Unidos con su segundo esposo. Perdió a su segunda hija,** Paula, después de una larga y trágica enfermedad, cuando esta tenía 28 años. A ella le dedicó un libro en el que[e] cuenta la historia de la familia a la vez que narra los cambios que sufre la escritora a consecuencia del trauma de la enfermedad de su hija. Pero los contratiempos[f] no parecen detener a la incansable Isabel Allende.

[a]*overthrown* [b]*mixture* [c]*prominent* [d]*se... are interwoven* [e]*en... in which* [f]*mishaps, disappointments*

Voces de Chile

LITERATURA: Gabriela Mistral

Gabriela Mistral
(1889–1957)

Sobra la autora: *Gabriela Mistral nació en Vicuña, Chile. Publicó sus primeros versos a los 15 años. Fue maestra y cónsul de Chile en varios países. Participó en la asamblea de las Naciones Unidas y publicó varias colecciones de poesía. En 1945 le otorgaron el Premio Nóbel de Literatura por sus versos líricos. Murió en Nueva York. Los siguientes versos son del poema, «Puertas», Lagar (1954).*

Entre los gestos[a] del mundo
recibí el que dan las puertas.
En la luz yo las he visto
o selladas[b] o entreabiertas[c]
y volviendo sus espaldas[d]
del color de la vulpeja.[e]
¿Por qué fue que las hicimos
para ser sus prisioneras?

[a]*gestures* [b]*cerradas* [c]*half-open, ajar* [d]*volviendo... turning a cold shoulder* [e]*vixen (female fox)*

MÚSICA: El canto nuevo y Víctor Jara

Víctor Jara también colaboró con Quilapayún, el conjunto[d] que le dio impulso popular y comercial al nuevo canto. El nombre Quilapayún es una palabra mapuche[e] que significa «tres barbas[f]».

[d]*band* [e]*grupo indígena de Chile* [f]*beards*

Víctor Jara (1932–1973) fue uno de los compositores más representativos del canto nuevo chileno, un movimiento musical que surgió[a] en Chile y la Argentina en los años 60 y 70. El canto nuevo (o la nueva canción) expresa la lucha[b] de los latinoamericanos por la libertad y contra la opresión. Jara fue el Embajador Cultural de Chile durante la breve presidencia del socialista Salvador Allende, quien celebró su victoria en las elecciones bajo una bandera[c] que decía: «No puede haber revolución sin canciones».

[a]*emerged* [b]*struggle* [c]*flag*

Durante el golpe de estado[g] en el cual[h] murió Salvador Allende, se oía al pueblo[i] cantar los versos de la canción «El pueblo unido»,* de Sergio Ortega (1938–2003), un compositor importante del canto nuevo. «El pueblo unido» se considera como el himno[j] de la resistencia del pueblo chileno.

Y ahora el pueblo
que se alza[k] en la lucha
con voz[l] de gigante

gritando: ¡Adelante![m]
¡El pueblo unido
jamás será[n] vencido[o]!

(de «El pueblo unido», de Sergio Ortega)

[g]*golpe... coup d'etat* [h]*el... which* [i]*people* [j]*hymn* [k]*se... rises up* [l]*voice* [m]*Onward!* [n]*will be* [o]*overcome*

During this military coup, Víctor Jara was arrested, tortured, and murdered. El canto nuevo, which had been the voice of the people protesting bad government, became even more representative of the struggle of the Chilean people for justice and liberty.

41 *Lo hago para que tú...* **Subjunctive After Conjunctions of Contingency and Purpose**

Maneras de amar

a.   b.   c.

¿A qué dibujo corresponde cada una de las siguientes oraciones? ¿Quién las dice?

1. _____ Aquí tienes la tarjeta de crédito, pero úsala sólo *en caso de que haya una emergencia*, ¿eh?
2. _____ Escúchame bien. No vas a salir *antes de que termines* la tarea.
3. _____ Quiero casarme contigo *para que estemos* siempre juntos *y no salgas más* con Raúl.

Comprensión

1. En el dibujo **a,** es obvio que el chico _____. Es normal que la madre _____.
2. En el dibujo **b,** está claro que la chica _____. Por eso el padre se siente _____ (adjetivo).
3. En el dibujo **c,** creo que el chico _____. No estoy seguro/a de que la chica _____. Pienso que esta pareja es muy joven para _____.

A. When one action or condition is related to another—*x* will happen provided that *y* occurs; we'll do *z* unless *a* happens—a relationship of *contingency* is said to exist: one thing is contingent, or depends, on another.

   The Spanish *conjunctions* (**las conjunciones**) at the right express relationships of contingency or purpose. The subjunctive always occurs in subordinate clauses introduced by these conjunctions.

a menos que	unless
antes (de) que	before
con tal (de) que	provided (that)
en caso de que	in case
para que	so that

conjunction = a word or phrase that connects words, phrases, or clauses

B. Note that these conjunctions introduce subordinate clauses in which the events have not yet materialized; the events are conceptualized, not real-world, events.

Voy **con tal de que** ellos me **acompañen.**
I'm going, provided (that) they go with me.

En caso de que llegue Juan, dile que ya salí.
In case Juan arrives, tell him that I already left.

C. When there is no change of subject in the sentence, Spanish more frequently uses the prepositions **antes de** and **para,** plus an infinitive, instead of the corresponding conjunctions plus the subjunctive. Compare the sentences at the right.

PREPOSITION (one subject)	Estoy aquí **para aprender.** *I'm here to (in order to) learn.*
CONJUNCTION (two subjects)	Estoy aquí **para que Uds. aprendan.** *I'm here so that you will learn.*
PREPOSITION (one subject)	Voy a comer **antes de salir.** *I'm going to eat before leaving.*
CONJUNCTION (two subjects)	Voy a comer **antes de que salgamos.** *I'm going to eat before we leave.*

AUTOPRUEBA

Match each conjunction with its correct meaning in English.

1. _____ para que
2. _____ antes de que
3. _____ con tal de que
4. _____ a menos que
5. _____ en caso de que

a. unless
b. before
c. provided that
d. in case
e. so that

Answers: 1. e 2. b 3. c 4. a 5. d

■ Práctica

A. ¡Anticipemos! ¿Es Ud. un buen amigo / una buena amiga? La amistad es una de las relaciones más importantes de la vida. Indique si las siguientes oraciones son ciertas o falsas para Ud. con respecto a sus amigos. **¡OJO!** No todas las características son buenas. Hay que leer con cuidado.

	C	F
1. Les hago muchos favores a mis amigos, con tal que ellos después me ayuden a mí.	☐	☐
2. Les ofrezco consejos a mis amigos para que tomen buenas decisiones.	☐	☐
3. Les presto dinero a menos que yo sepa que no me lo pueden devolver.	☐	☐
4. Les traduzco el menú en los restaurantes mexicanos en caso de que no sepan leer español.	☐	☐
5. Los llevo a casa cuando beben, para que no tengan accidentes de coche.	☐	☐

B. Un fin de semana en las montañas. Hablan Manolo y Lola. Use la conjunción entre paréntesis para unir las oraciones, haciendo todos los cambios necesarios.

1. No voy. Dejamos a la niña con los abuelos. (a menos que)
2. Vamos solos a las montañas. Pasamos un fin de semana romántico. (para que)
3. Esta vez voy a aprender a esquiar. Tú me enseñas. (con tal de que)
4. Vamos a salir temprano por la mañana. Nos acostamos tarde la noche anterior. (a menos que)
5. Es importante que lleguemos a la estación (*resort*) de esquí. Empieza a nevar. (antes de que)
6. Deja la dirección y el teléfono del hotel. Tus padres nos necesitan. (en caso de que)
7. No vamos a regresar. Nos hemos cansado de esquiar. (antes de que)

Need more practice?

- Workbook/Laboratory Manual
- Interactive CD-ROM
- Online Learning Center (www.mhhe.com/quetal7)

■ Conversación

A. Situaciones. Cualquier acción puede justificarse. Con un compañero / una compañera o con un grupo de estudiantes, dé una explicación para las siguientes situaciones. Luego comparen sus explicaciones con las de otro grupo.

1. Los padres trabajan mucho para (que)…
2. Los profesores les dan tarea a los estudiantes para (que)…
3. Los dueños de los equipos deportivos profesionales les pagan mucho a algunos jugadores para (que)…
4. Las películas extranjeras se doblan (*are dubbed*) para (que)…
5. Los padres castigan (*punish*) a los niños para (que)…
6. Las parejas se divorcian para (que)…
7. Los jóvenes forman pandillas (*gangs*) para (que)…

NOTA COMUNICATIVA

¿Para qué… ? / ¿Por qué… ? and *para que / porque*

English usage offers a general guideline for knowing when to use **¿Para qué… ?** versus **¿Por qué… ?** and **para que** versus **porque**. **¿Por qué… ?** asks *Why . . . ?*, in the general sense, but if the question is specifically asking *For what reason / purpose?* something is for, use **¿Para qué… ?**

¿Por qué te casaste con él?	*Why did you marry him?*
¿Para qué te casaste con él?	*For what reason did you marry him?*
¿Para qué es el anillo?	*What (purpose) is the ring for?*

The conjunction **porque** means *because* in English, when *because* serves as a conjunction between two clauses. The adverbial conjunction **para que,** on the other hand, means *in order that* or *so that*.

Me casé con él **porque** lo quiero.	*I married him because I love him.*
Me voy a casar con él **para que** mis padres nos acepten.	*I'm going to marry him so that my parents accept us.*

B. La boda. Julia y Salvador se casan este año y quieren una gran boda. Todos los parientes tienen preguntas. Con un compañero / una compañera, haga y conteste las siguientes preguntas, imaginando que uno/a de Uds. es Julia o Salvador. Si quieren, pueden usar las sugerencias entre paréntesis.

MODELO: ¿Por qué se casan en enero? (el invierno) →
Nos casamos en enero porque nos gusta el invierno.

1. ¿Para qué son las velas (*candles*)? (la ceremonia)
2. ¿Por qué quieren mandar trescientas invitaciones? (todos nuestros amigos y parientes / asistir)
3. ¿Por qué van a mandar las invitaciones con cuatro meses de anticipación (*ahead*)? (todos los invitados / poder hacer planes para asistir)
4. ¿Por qué buscan un salón tan grande para la recepción después de la boda? (haber música y baile)
5. ¿Por qué quieren contratar un grupo latino de música? (todos / bailar)

PASO 3

UN POCO DE TODO

Lengua y cultura: ¿Cómo se divierten los hispanos? Complete the following passages with the correct forms of the words in parentheses, as suggested by the context. When two possibilities are given in parentheses, select the correct word. **¡OJO!** As you conjugate verbs in this activity, you will decide whether to use the subjunctive mood (the present or present perfect tense) or the indicative mood (the present, the present perfect, the preterite, or the imperfect tense). The context of the passages will give clues to help you choose, and occasionally clues in italics will guide you in choosing a tense or mood.

Como Ud. sabe, hay semejanzas y diferencias entre las culturas hispana y norteamericana. En cuanto a[a] las diversiones, la verdad es (que / lo que[1]), en general, no hay (mucho[2]) diferencia entre la manera de divertirse de los (joven[3]) hispanos y los norteamericanos. Es normal que los muchachos y muchachas—chicos y chicas en España, gallos y gallas en Chile, patojos y patojas en Guatemala, (por / para[4]) ejemplo—(ir[5]) a bailar por la noche a las discotecas y clubes y que (bailar[6]) casi hasta el amanecer.[b] La música (ser / estar[7]) una de las grandes aficiones de todos, y (a / —[8]) los muchachos especialmente les (gusta / gustan[9]) también mirar los partidos deportivos. En años recientes, el concepto de los centros comerciales (llegar[10]) a las ciudades hispánicas. En estos centros (haber[11]) tiendas y restaurantes que (le / les[12]) (interesar[13]) a la gente joven. Con frecuencia también hay cines y hasta (grande[14]) supermercados.

Pero hay algo que sí es diferente entre las dos culturas, y es la costumbre del paseo. Consiste en andar por distracción[c] o por hacer ejercicio, particularmente al aire libre. Para dar un paseo, tradicionalmente la gente de todas las edades (ir[15]) a una plaza o a otro lugar céntrico a pasar un rato. Allí (por / para[16]) la tarde, (relajarse[17]) y (encontrarse[18]) con amigos y familiares. Hoy día, como[d] las ciudades son más grandes, el paseo no (concentrarse[19]) en un solo[e] lugar, pero la costumbre (seguir[20]) existiendo de igual forma.

Hay que recordar que el paseo no (se / —[21]) considera como una actividad deportiva sino[f] social. El paseo *no* se compara con el *hiking* norteamericano. Para expresar esa idea, se (poder[22]) decir «dar / hacer una caminata por el bosque o la montaña». Pero (ese[23]) actividad no es muy típico de la cultura hispana, a menos que los que[g] la practican (ser[24]) jóvenes con tendencia al naturismo.[h]

Cuatro muchachas chilenas que pasan un rato juntas en un parque, en Valparaíso, Chile

[a]En... *As far as . . . are concerned* [b]el... *dawn* [c]*amusement* [d]*since* [e]*single* [f]*but rather* [g]los... *those who* [h]actividades recreativas en la naturaleza

Comprensión. Conteste las preguntas en español.

1. Según la información en los párrafos, ¿cuáles son algunas de las diferencias y semejanzas entre la forma de divertirse de los jóvenes en las culturas hispánicas y en la norteamericana?
2. ¿Qué palabras se usan para expresar «muchachos y muchachas» en varios países hispánicos?
3. ¿Qué ventajas ve Ud. en la costumbre hispana del paseo? ¿Y qué desventajas ve? ¿En qué sentido puede un hispano sentirse incómodo en una ciudad norteamericana en cuanto a las formas de divertirse de este país?

Resources for Review and Testing Preparation

- Workbook/Laboratory Manual
- Interactive CD-ROM
- Online Learning Center (www.mhhe.com/quetal7)

VIDEOTECA

Entrevista cultural: Chile

Jorge Balmaceda es chileno. Habla de su trabajo y de sus clientes. ¡Le encanta su profesión! Antes de ver el vídeo, lea el siguiente fragmento de la entrevista.

JORGE: Me encanta mi trabajo, sobre todo sacar fotos en bodas. Me encanta fotografiar a la novia, al novio, a los padrinos, amigos y familiares. Es una fiesta bastante feliz. Me encanta retratarla.[a]

ENTREVISTADORA: Y ¿es siempre agradable, o de vez en cuando encuentras dificultades o problemas?

JORGE: Porque [la novia] no se siente bien, porque no le quedó bien[b] el vestido o porque el peinado[c] no le gusta como le quedó.

[a]portraying it in photos   [b]no… didn't fit well   [c]hairdo

Ahora vea el vídeo y conteste las siguientes preguntas basándose en la entrevista.

1. ¿Cuál es la profesión de Jorge?
2. ¿A qué eventos sociales debe asistir?
3. ¿Qué problemas ocurren en su trabajo?
4. ¿Cuáles de las celebraciones le parecen más felices a Jorge?
5. ¿Por qué le gusta su trabajo?

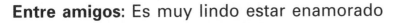

Entre amigos: Es muy lindo estar enamorado

Miguel, Tané, Rubén y Karina hablan de las relaciones sentimentales. En su opinión, ¿qué preguntas se van a hacer? Antes de mirar el vídeo, lea las preguntas a continuación. Mientras mire el vídeo, trate de entender la conversación en general y fíjese en la información sobre los novios y las relaciones. Luego mire el vídeo una segunda vez, fijándose en la información que necesita para contestar las preguntas.

1. ¿Cuándo rompieron Miguel y su novia? (Hace… [. . . ago.])
2. Según Karina, ¿qué es importante en una relación amorosa?
3. ¿Dónde vive el novio de Tané?
4. ¿Qué planes tienen Tané y su novio para el futuro?
5. ¿Sabe Tané cuántos hijos quiere tener?

Chile

¡Fíjese!

- El nombre de Chile se deriva de la palabra indígena *chilli*, que significa «lugar donde termina la tierra».
- Chile es uno de los países más modernos e industrializados de Sudamérica. Durante la colonización de Sudamérica, los españoles no tenían mucho interés en Chile. Los Andes dificultaban los viajes al país y, como no habían encontrado allí oro como en el Perú, los colonizadores pensaban que la tierra de Chile tenía poco valor. Esto es irónico porque hoy la minería del cobre[a] es la industria más importante del país, y Chile es uno de los mayores exportadores de cobre del mundo.
- Aunque Chile sufrió una crisis económica en los años 70, a finales del siglo XX muchos lo llamaban «el jaguar económico de Latinoamérica». La calidad de la vida en Chile es una de las mejores entre los países hispánicos. La natalidad[b] ha bajado drásticamente y la esperanza de vida al nacer es de aproximadamente 80 años. Con una tasa de alfabetización[c] de casi el 95 por ciento, Chile tiene un estable sistema de escuelas y universidades.

[a]*copper* [b]*birthrate* [c]*tasa... literacy rate*

Lugares famosos: La geografía chilena

Se puede dividir Chile en tres regiones principales. El norte de Chile principalmente consiste en 600 millas (1.000 kilómetros) del desierto Atacama. Aunque el desierto tiene un clima moderado, es uno de los lugares más áridos del mundo. En algunas partes del desierto, no hay evidencia ninguna de pluviosidad.[a]

El centro de Chile se extiende unas mil millas (1.600 kilómetros). Mucho del centro consiste en el Valle de Chile entre los Andes y la Cordillera de la Costa. Es la región más poblada de Chile y el centro agrícola del país.

El sur de Chile es una región escabrosa.[b] Aquí los Andes descienden al océano para formar fiordos e islas y se encuentran los glaciares de la Tierra del Fuego, que Chile comparte con la Argentina.

[a]*rainfall* [b]*rugged*

Un viñedo (vineyard) *chileno, con los Andes al fondo* (in the background)

Learn more about Chile with the Video, the Interactive CD-ROM, and the Online Learning Center (www.mhhe.com/quetal7).

PASO FINAL

A LEER

ESTRATEGIA: Using Graphics to Get Information

Reading graphics such as tables and pie charts requires as much concentration as, if not more than, any other reading since a lot information is often summarized in a compact space. Paying attention to the head of a section as well as to the categories within the graphic can help you to focus on important parts of the information presented.

The following chart provides a summary of statistical information regarding how males and females in Spain spend their time each day. As you read and analyze the information in the chart, remember to rely on all of the visual clues that you can to facilitate your comprehension.

Sobre la lectura... La lectura, o mejor dicho, el gráfico, es del periódico *El País,* de España. Es parte de un artículo más largo que da los resultados de una encuesta (*survey*), entre más de 23.000 personas a partir de (*older than*) 10 años de edad, que estudia las actividades a que dedican su tiempo los españoles.

Una encuesta revela que las mujeres españolas dedican el triple de tiempo que los varones al hogar y la familia

Encuesta sobre el empleo del tlempo

PORCENTAJE DE PERSONAS OUE REALIZAN LA ACTIVIDAD EN EL TRANSCURSO DEL DÍA Y PROMEDIO DE TIEMPO DIARIO DEDICADO A LA ACTIVIDAD POR DICHAS PERSONAS

	Ambos sexos		Varones		Mujeres	
Actividades principales	% de personas	Duración media diaria	% de personas	Duración media diaria	% de personas	Duración media diaria
Cuidados personales	100,0	11:22	100,0	11:24	100,0	11:20
Trabajo	34,3	7:43	43,5	8:18	26,0	6:51
Estudios	15,0	5:25	14,9	5:32	15,2	5:19
Hogar y familia	82,0	3:44	70,1	2:06	92,7	4:50
Trabajo voluntario y reuniones	12,7	1:45	9,9	1:51	15,2	1:42
Vida social y diversión	64,4	2:03	64,3	2:08	64,5	1:58
Deportes y actividades al aire libre	37,8	1:54	40,6	2:11	35,4	1:36
Aflclones y juegos	17,3	1:45	22,5	1:55	12,7	1:30
Medios de comunicación	87,7	2:42	88,0	2:54	87,5	2:31
Trayectos y tlempo no especificado	84,6	1:24	87,3	1:27	82,2	1:21

DISTRIBUCIÓN DE ACTIVIDADES EN UN DíA PROMEDIO (por sexo)

	Varones	Mujeres
Cuidados personales (Incluye comer y dormir)	11:24	11:20
Trabajo y estudios	4:26	2:35
Hogar y familia	1:29	4:29
Trabajo voluntario y reuniones	0:11	0:16
Tiempo libre	6:16	4:13
Trayectos y tlempo no especificado	1:16	1:07

Fuente:INE EL PAÍS

Comprensión

A. ¿Cierto o falso? Conteste según el gráfico. Corrija las oraciones falsas.

1. Hay un alto nivel de voluntarismo entre los dos sexos en España.
2. Los hombres y las mujeres dedican más o menos el mismo tiempo a las tareas domésticas, al cuidado (*care*) de los niños y a otras responsabilidades de hogar.
3. Parece que el tiempo libre es más importante para las mujeres que para los hombres.
4. Ambos (*Both*) sexos dedican la mayoría de su tiempo al trabajo y los estudios.

Una madre que acompaña a sus hijas a la escuela, en Lima, Perú

B. Preguntas. Conteste según el gráfico.

1. ¿Cuánto tiempo dedican cada día los hombres y las mujeres, respectivamente, a los deportes y otras actividades físicas?
2. ¿Cuántos minutos de diferencia hay entre el tiempo dedicado a los estudios por los hombres y el tiempo dedicado por las mujeres?
3. Apunte las tres actividades a las que las mujeres, típicamente, dedican más tiempo. ¿Y los hombres?
4. ¿Cree Ud. que un gráfico que compara las actividades de los hombres con las de las mujeres en este país sería (*would be*) muy diferente? Explique.

A ESCRIBIR

A. Una encuesta entre amigos. Ud. va a hacer una encuesta entre ocho amigos (cuatro hombres y cuatro mujeres) para determinar cuánto tiempo dedican cada día a cinco actividades: el cuidado personal, el trabajo, los estudios, la vida social y los deportes. Organice los resultados en un gráfico. Luego prepare un breve informe para resumir la información y también para comparar su estudio con el estudio español.

B. ¿Y Ud.? Ahora, analice las actividades a las que Ud. dedica el tiempo. Puede usar las diez categorías del gráfico de la lectura o puede usar las cinco actividades de **Actividad A** en **A escribir.** Haga un gráfico para analizar la información. Luego, escriba un breve informe para comparar sus resultados con los de la lectura y/o de la **Actividad A.**

Comiendo tapas (appetizers), *en San Sebastián, España*

En resumen

GRAMÁTICA

To review the grammar points presented in this chapter, refer to the indicated grammar presentations. You'll find further practice of these structures in the Workbook/Laboratory Manual, on the Interactive CD-ROM, and on the *¿Qué tal?* Online Learning Center (www.mhhe.com/quetal7).

40 **¿Hay alguien que... ? ¿Hay un lugar donde... ?** —Subjunctive After Nonexistent and Indefinite Antecedents

You should know how to use the subjunctive in two-clause sentences when the antecedent is nonexistent or indefinite.

41 **Lo hago para que tú...** —Subjunctive After Conjunctions of Contingency and Purpose

You should know how and when to use the subjunctive after certain conjunctions of contingency and purpose.

VOCABULARIO
Practice this vocabulary with digital flash cards on the Online Learning Center (www.mhhe.com/quetal7).

Las relaciones sentimentales

la amistad	friendship
el amor	love
la boda	wedding (ceremony)
la cita	date
la luna de miel	honeymoon
el marido	husband
el matrimonio	marriage; married couple
la mujer	wife
la novia	fiancée; bride
el noviazgo	engagement
el novio	fiancé; groom
la pareja	(married) couple; partner
el/la viudo/a	widower/widow

Cognados: el divorcio, la separación
Repaso: el/la amigo/a, el/la esposo/a, el/la novio/a (boy/girlfriend)

amar	to love
casarse (con)	to marry
divorciarse (de)	to get divorced (from)
enamorarse (de)	to fall in love (with)
llevarse bien/mal (con)	to get along well/poorly (with)
pasar tiempo (con)	to spend time (with)
querer (ie)	to love
romper (con)	to break up (with)
separarse (de)	to separate (from)

Repaso: pelear (con), salir (*irreg.*) **con**

amistoso/a	friendly
divorciado/a (de)	divorced (from)
enamorado/a (de)	in love (with)
recién casado/a (con)	newlywed (to)

Repaso: cariñoso/a, casado/a (con), feliz, soltero/a

Etapas de la vida

la etapa	stage (*period of time*)
la juventud	youth
la madurez	middle age
la muerte	death
el nacimiento	birth
la vejez	old age

Cognados: la adolescencia, la infancia
Repaso: la niñez

crecer (zc)	to grow
nacer (zc)	to be born

Repaso: morir (ue, u)

Conjunciones

a menos que	unless
antes (de) que	before
con tal (de) que	provided (that)
en caso de que	in case
para que	so that

Palabras adicionales

a primera vista	at first sight
bastante	rather, sufficiently; enough
juntos/as	together
propio/a	own

¿Trabajar para vivir o vivir para trabajar?

Mujeres profesionales que caminan por la Puerta de la Ciudadela, en Montevideo, Uruguay

Vocabulario

trades

PROFESIONES Y OFICIOS°

el contador / la contadora

el maestro / la maestra

el médico / la médica

el periodista / la periodista

el cocinero / la cocinera

el peluquero / la peluquera

Profesiones

el/la abogado/a	lawyer
el/la bibliotecario/a	librarian
el/la consejero/a	counselor
el/la enfermero/a	nurse
el hombre / la mujer de negocios	businessperson
el/la ingeniero/a	engineer
el/la sicólogo/a	psychologist
el/la siquiatra	psychiatrist
el/la trabajador(a) social	social worker
el/la traductor(a)	translator

Oficios

el/la cajero/a	cashier; teller
el/la comerciante	merchant; shopkeeper
el/la criado/a	servant
el/la dependiente/a	clerk
el/la obrero/a	worker, laborer
el/la plomero/a	plumber
el soldado / la mujer soldado	soldier
el/la técnico/a	technician
el/la vendedor(a)	salesperson

Cognados: el/la analista de sistemas, el/la dentista, el/la electricista, el/la fotógrafo/a, el/la mecánico/a, el/la profesor(a), el/la programador(a), el/la secretario/a, el/la veterinario/a

In the preceding chapters of *¿Qué tal?* you learned to use a number of the words for professions and trades that are listed here. You will practice all of these words in the following activities. However, you may also want to learn new terms that are particularly important or interesting to you. If the vocabulary needed to describe your career goal is not listed here, look it up in a dictionary or ask your instructor.

■ Conversación

A. ¿A quién necesita Ud.? ¿A quién debe llamar o con quién debe consultar en estas situaciones? Hay más de una respuesta posible en algunos casos.

1. La tubería (*plumbing*) de la cocina no funciona bien.
2. Ud. acaba de tener un accidente automovilístico; el otro conductor dice que Ud. tuvo la culpa (*blame*).
3. Por las muchas tensiones y presiones de su vida profesional y personal, Ud. tiene serios problemas afectivos (*emotional*).
4. Ud. quiere que alguien lo/la ayude con los quehaceres domésticos porque no tiene mucho tiempo para hacerlos.
5. Ud. quiere que alguien le construya un muro (*wall*) en el jardín.
6. Ud. conoce todos los detalles de un escándalo en el gobierno de su ciudad y quiere divulgarlos.

B. Asociaciones. ¿Qué profesiones u oficios asocia Ud. con estas frases? Con un compañero / una compañera, consulte la lista de profesiones y oficios y use las siguientes palabras también. Hagan asociaciones rápidas. ¡No lo piensen demasiado!

1. creativo/rutinario
2. muchos/pocos años de preparación
3. mucho/poco salario
4. mucha/poca responsabilidad
5. mucho/poco prestigio
6. flexibilidad/«de nueve a cinco»
7. mucho/poco tiempo libre
8. peligroso (*dangerous*)/seguro
9. en el pasado, sólo para hombres/mujeres
10. todavía, sólo para hombres/mujeres

Profesiones y oficios

el actor / la actriz	el/la detective
el/la arquitecto/a	el/la niñero/a
el/la asistente de vuelo	el/la pintor(a)
el *barman*	el/la poeta
el/la camarero/a	el policía /
el/la carpintero/a	la mujer policía
el/la chófer	el/la político/a
el/la consejero/a	el/la presidente/a
el cura (*priest*) / el/la	el/la senador(a)
pastor(a) protestante /	
el/la rabino/a	

C. ¿Qué preparación se necesita para ser... ? Imagine que Ud. es consejero universitario / consejera universitaria. Explíquele a un(a) estudiante qué cursos debe tomar para prepararse para las siguientes carreras. Use el **Vocabulario útil** y la lista de cursos académicos del **Capítulo 1.** Piense también en el tipo de experiencia que debe obtener.

1. traductor(a) en la ONU (Organización de las Naciones Unidas)
2. reportero/a en la televisión, especializado/a en los deportes
3. contador(a) para un grupo de abogados
4. periodista para una revista de ecología
5. trabajador(a) social, especializado/a en los problemas de los ancianos
6. maestro/a de primaria, especializado/a en la educación bilingüe

Vocabulario útil

las **comunicaciones**
la **contabilidad** (accounting)
el **derecho** (law)
la **gerontología**
la **ingeniería**
el *marketing*/**mercadeo**
la **organización administrativa**
la **pedagogía/enseñanza**
la **retórica** (speech)
la **sociología**

D. Entrevista. Con un compañero / una compañera, haga y conteste preguntas para averiguar (*find out*) la siguiente información.

1. lo que hacían sus abuelos
2. la profesión u oficio de sus padres
3. si tiene un amigo o pariente que tenga una profesión extraordinaria o interesante y el nombre de esa profesión
4. lo que sus padres (su esposo/a) quiere(n) que Ud. sea (lo que Ud. quiere que sean sus hijos)
5. lo que Ud. quiere ser (lo que sus hijos quieren ser)
6. la carrera para la cual (*which*) se preparan muchos de sus amigos (los hijos de sus amigos)

EL MUNDO DEL TRABAJO

el/la aspirante	candidate; applicant	**el/la gerente**	manager
el currículum	résumé	**el puesto**	job; position
la dirección de personal	personnel office, employment office	**el salario / el sueldo**	salary
el/la director(a) de personal	personnel director	**caerle** (*irreg.*) **bien/ mal a alguien**	to make a good/bad impression on someone
la empresa	corporation; business	**dejar**	to quit
el/la entrevistador(a)	interviewer	**renunciar (a)**	to resign (from)

■ Conversación

A. Definiciones. Dé definiciones de las siguientes palabras y frases.

MODELO: la empresa →
una compañía grande, como la IBM o Ford

1. el currículum
2. dejar un puesto
3. la aspirante
4. el gerente
5. el sueldo
6. llenar una solicitud

B. En busca de un puesto. Imagine que Ud. solicitó un puesto el mes pasado. Usando los números del 1 al 7 para cada sección, indique en qué orden ocurrió lo siguiente. El número 1 ya está indicado.

ANTES DE LA ENTREVISTA

a. _____ Fue a la biblioteca para informarse sobre la empresa: su historia, dónde tiene sucursales (*branches*), etcétera.

b. _____ Ud. llenó la solicitud tan pronto como la recibió y se la mandó, con el currículum, a la empresa.

c. __1__ En la oficina de empleos de su universidad, Ud. leyó un anuncio para un puesto en su especialización.

d. _____ Le dijo que le iba a mandar una solicitud para que la llenara (*you could fill it out*) y también le pidió que mandara (*you send*) su currículum.

e. _____ Llamó al teléfono que se dio el anuncio y habló con un secretario en la dirección de personal.

f. _____ La mañana de la entrevista, Ud. se levantó temprano, se vistió con cuidado y salió temprano para la empresa para llegar puntualmente.

g. _____ En una semana lo/la llamaron para arreglar una entrevista.

EL DÍA DE LA ENTREVISTA Y EN ADELANTE (*ON*)

a. _____ Se despidió de Ud. cordialmente, diciendo que lo/la iba a llamar en una semana.

b. _____ Por fin, el secretario le dijo que Ud. se iba a entrevistar con (*were going to be interviewed by*) la directora de personal.

c. _____ Cuando por fin lo/la llamó la directora, ¡fue para ofrecerle el puesto!

d. __1__ Mientras esperaba en la dirección de personal, Ud. estaba nerviosísimo/a.

e. _____ La directora le hizo una serie de preguntas: cuándo se iba a graduar, qué cursos había tomado, etcétera.

f. _____ Al entrar en la oficina de la directora, Ud. la saludó con cortesía, tratando de caerle bien desde el principio.

g. _____ También le pidió que hablara (*you speak*) un poco en español, ya que la empresa tiene una sucursal en Santiago, Chile.

NOTA CULTURAL

Los nombres de las profesiones

En el mundo de habla española **hay poco acuerdo** sobre las palabras que deben usarse para **referirse a las mujeres que ejercen ciertas profesiones.** En gran parte, eso se debe al hecho de que, en muchos de estos países, **las mujeres acaban de empezar a ejercer esas profesiones;** por eso el idioma todavía está cambiando para acomodarse a esa nueva realidad. **En la actualidad se emplean,** entre otras, **las siguientes formas.**

Una científica en su laboratorio

- Se usa el artículo **la** con los sustantivos que terminan en **-ista.**

  el dentista → **la** dent**ista**

- En otros casos se usa una forma femenina.

  el médico → **la** médic**a**　　el trabajador → **la** trabajador**a**

- Se usa la palabra **mujer** con el nombre de la profesión.

  el policía → **la mujer** policía　　el soldado → **la mujer** soldado

Escuche lo que dice cualquier[a] persona con quien Ud. habla español para saber las formas que él o ella usa. No se trata de[b] formas correctas o incorrectas, sólo de usos y costumbres locales.

___

[a]*any*　[b]*No… It's not a question of*

PASO 1

UNA CUESTIÓN DE DINERO

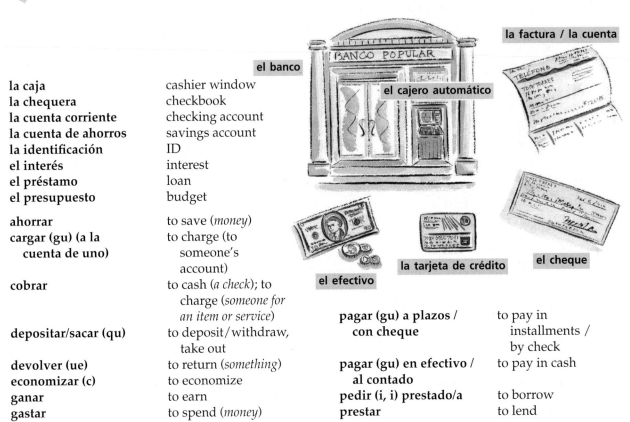

la factura / la cuenta

el banco

el cajero automático

la caja	cashier window
la chequera	checkbook
la cuenta corriente	checking account
la cuenta de ahorros	savings account
la identificación	ID
el interés	interest
el préstamo	loan
el presupuesto	budget
ahorrar	to save (*money*)
cargar (gu) (a la cuenta de uno)	to charge (to someone's account)
cobrar	to cash (*a check*); to charge (*someone for an item or service*)
depositar/sacar (qu)	to deposit/withdraw, take out
devolver (ue)	to return (*something*)
economizar (c)	to economize
ganar	to earn
gastar	to spend (*money*)

la tarjeta de crédito

el cheque

el efectivo

pagar (gu) a plazos / con cheque	to pay in installments / by check
pagar (gu) en efectivo / al contado	to pay in cash
pedir (i, i) prestado/a	to borrow
prestar	to lend

■ Conversación

A. El mes pasado. Piense en sus finanzas personales del mes pasado. ¿Fue un mes típico? ¿Tuvo dificultades al final del mes o todo le salió bien?

PASO 1 Indique las respuestas apropiadas para Ud.

	¡CLARO QUE SÍ!	¡CLARO QUE NO!
1. Hice un presupuesto al principio del mes.	☐	☐
2. Deposité más dinero en el banco del que (*than what*) saqué.	☐	☐
3. Saqué dinero del cajero automático sin apuntar (*writing down*) la cantidad en mi chequera.	☐	☐
4. Pagué todas mis cuentas a tiempo.	☐	☐
5. Saqué un préstamo (Le pedí dinero prestado al banco) para pagar mis cuentas.	☐	☐
6. Tomé el autobús en vez de (*instead of*) usar el coche, para economizar un poco.	☐	☐
7. Gasté mucho dinero en diversiones.	☐	☐
8. Saqué el saldo (*I balanced*) de mi chequera sin dificultades.	☐	☐

	¡CLARO QUE SÍ!	¡CLARO QUE NO!
9. Le presté dinero a un amigo.	☐	☐
10. Usé mis tarjetas de crédito sólo en casos de urgencia.	☐	☐

PASO 2   Vuelva a mirar sus respuestas. ¿Fue el mes pasado un mes típico? Pensando todavía en sus respuestas, sugiera tres cosas que Ud. debe hacer para mejorar su situación económica.

MODELO: Debo hacer un presupuesto mensual.

B. Diálogos

PASO 1   Empareje las preguntas de la izquierda con las respuestas de la derecha.

1. _____ ¿Cómo prefiere Ud. pagar?

2. _____ ¿Hay algún problema?

3. _____ Me da su identificación, por favor. Necesito verla para que pueda cobrar su cheque.

4. _____ ¿Quisiera (*Would you like*) usar su tarjeta de crédito?

5. _____ ¿Va a depositar este cheque en su cuenta corriente o en su cuenta de ahorros?

6. _____ ¿Adónde quiere Ud. que mandemos la factura?

a. En la cuenta de ahorros, por favor.

b. Me la manda a la oficina, por favor.

c. No, prefiero pagar al contado.

d. Sí, señorita. Ud. me cobró demasiado por el jarabe.

e. Aquí la tiene Ud. Me la va a devolver pronto, ¿verdad?

f. Cárguelo a mi cuenta, por favor.

Need more practice?

- Workbook/Laboratory Manual
- Interactive CD-ROM
- Online Learning Center (www.mhhe.com/quetal7)

PASO 2   Ahora, con un compañero / una compañera, invente un contexto posible para cada diálogo. ¿Dónde están las personas que hablan? ¿En un banco? ¿en una tienda? ¿Quiénes son? ¿Clientes? ¿cajeros? ¿dependientes?

C. Situaciones.

Con un compañero / una compañera, describa lo que pasa en los siguientes dibujos. Usen las preguntas a continuación como guía.

¿Quiénes son estas personas?   ¿Cómo van a pagar?

¿Dónde están?   ¿Qué van a hacer después?

¿Qué van a comprar?

1.   **2.**   **3.**   **4.**

¿Recuerda Ud.?

Before studying the future tense in **Gramática 42**, review **Gramática 3** (**Capítulo 1**) and **Gramática 10** (**Capítulo 3**), where you learned ways of expressing future actions. Then indicate which of the following sentences can be used to express a future action.

1. Trabajé hasta las dos.
2. Trabajo a las dos.
3. Voy a trabajar a las dos.
4. Trabajaba a las dos.
5. Estoy trabajando.
6. He trabajado a las dos.

42   Talking About the Future   Future Verb Forms

¿Cómo va a ser su vida dentro de diez años? ¿Está de acuerdo con las primeras cinco oraciones? Conteste sí o no. Luego, complete las últimas dos con información verdadera —¡o por lo menos deseable!

1. *Viviré* en otra ciudad / otro país.
2. *Estaré* casado/a.
3. *Tendré* uno o más hijos (nietos).
4. *Seré* dueño/a de mi propia casa.
5. *Llevaré* una vida más tranquila.
6. *Trabajaré* como _____ (nombre de profesión).
7. *Ganaré* por lo menos _____ dólares al año.

The future tense expresses things or events that *will* or *are going* to happen.

Past -------------------	Present -------------------	FUTURE
preterite	present indicative	future
imperfect	present progressive	
present perfect	formal commands	
present perfect subjunctive	informal commands	
	present subjunctive	

A. In English, the future is formed with the auxiliary verbs *will* or *shall*. *I **will**/**shall*** speak.

In Spanish, the *future* (**el futuro**) is a simple verb form (only one word). It is formed by adding future endings to the infinitive. No auxiliary verbs are needed.

Future verb endings.
-é	-emos
-ás	-éis
-á	-án

hablar		comer		vivir	
hablaré	hablaremos	comeré	comeremos	viviré	viviremos
hablarás	hablaréis	comerás	comeréis	vivirás	viviréis
hablará	hablarán	comerá	comerán	vivirá	vivirán

B. The verbs on the right are the most common Spanish verbs that are irregular in the future. The future endings are attached to their irregular stems.

Note that the future of **hay (haber)** is **habrá** (*there will be*).*

decir: diré, dirás, dirá, diremos, diréis, dirán

decir:	**dir-**	
haber (hay):	**habr-**	
hacer:	**har-**	-é
poder:	**podr-**	-ás
poner:	**pondr-**	-á
querer:	**querr-**	-emos
saber:	**sabr-**	-éis
salir:	**saldr-**	-án
tener:	**tendr-**	
venir:	**vendr-**	

C. Compare the use of the indicative and subjunctive present tense forms to express the immediate future.

OJO When the English *will* refers not to future time but to the willingness of someone to do something, Spanish uses the verb **querer,** not the future.

Llegaré a tiempo.
I'll arrive on time.

Llego a las ocho mañana. ¿Vienes a buscarme?
I'll arrive at 8:00 tomorrow. Will you come to pick me up?

No creo que Pepe **llegue** a tiempo.
I don't think Pepe will arrive on time.

¿**Quieres** cerrar la puerta, por favor?
Will you please close the door?

---

*The future forms of the verb **haber** are used to form the future perfect tense (**el futuro perfecto**), which expresses what *will have* occurred at some point in the future.

Para mañana, ya **habré hablado** con Miguel.   *By tomorrow, I will have spoken with Miguel.*

You will find a more detailed presentation of these forms in Appendix 3, Additional Perfect Forms (Indicative and Subjunctive).

PASO 2

■ Práctica

A. ¡Anticipemos! Mis compañeros de clase. ¿Cree Ud. que conoce bien a sus compañeros de clase? ¿Sabe lo que les va a pasar en el futuro? Vamos a ver.

PASO 1 Indique si las siguientes oraciones serán ciertas para Ud. algún día.

	SÍ	NO
1. Seré profesor(a) de idiomas.	☐	☐
2. Me casaré (Me divorciaré) dentro de tres años.	☐	☐
3. Me mudaré (*I will move*) a otro país.	☐	☐
4. Compraré un coche deportivo.	☐	☐
5. Tendré una familia muy grande (mucho más grande).	☐	☐
6. Asistiré a una escuela de estudios graduados.	☐	☐
7. Visitaré Latinoamérica.	☐	☐
8. Estaré en bancarrota (*bankruptcy*).	☐	☐
9. Estaré jubilado/a (*retired*).	☐	☐
10. No tendré que trabajar porque seré rico/a.	☐	☐

PASO 2 Ahora, para cada oración del **Paso 1,** indique el nombre de una persona de la clase para quien Ud. cree que la oración es cierta. Puede ser un compañero / una compañera de clase o su profesor(a).

PASO 3 Ahora compare sus predicciones con las respuestas de estas personas. ¿Hizo Ud. predicciones correctas?

B. ¿Qué harán en los próximos diez años? Haga oraciones sobre lo que harán las siguientes personas en los próximos diez años, usando frases de cada grupo.

yo tú nosotros (los estudiantes de esta clase) el/la profesor(a) mi padre/madre / mis padres/hijos mi mejor amigo/a ¿ ?	**+** (no) **+**	tener uno o dos hijos jubilarse (*to retire*) querer cambiar de trabajo ganar mucho/poco dinero saber hablar español perfectamente venir a esta universidad poder hacer lo que quiera dar clases de… decir que… trabajar en… poner mucho dinero mensualmente en la cuenta del banco ser dueño/a de… ir/viajar a… ¿ ?

C. Mi amigo Gregorio

PASO 1 Describa Ud. las siguientes cosas que hará su compañero Gregorio. Luego indique si Ud. hará lo mismo (**Yo también… Yo tampoco…**) u otra cosa.

> MODELO: no / gastar / menos / mes →
> Gregorio no *gastará* menos este mes. Yo tampoco *gastaré* menos.
> (Yo sí *gastaré* menos este mes. ¡Tengo que ahorrar!)

1. pagar / tarde / todo / cuentas
2. tratar / adaptarse a / presupuesto
3. volver / hacer / presupuesto / próximo mes
4. no / depositar / nada / en / cuenta de ahorros
5. quejarse / porque / no / tener / suficiente dinero
6. seguir / usando / tarjetas / crédito
7. pedirles / dinero / a / padres
8. buscar / trabajo / de tiempo parcial

PASO 2 ¿Cuál de las siguientes oraciones describe mejor a su amigo?

- Gregorio es muy responsable en cuanto a (*regarding*) asuntos de dinero. Es un buen modelo para imitar.
- Gregorio tiene que aprender a ser más responsable con su dinero.

Need more practice?

- Workbook/Laboratory Manual
- Interactive CD-ROM
- Online Learning Center
  (www.mhhe.com/quetal7)

■ Conversación

A. **Ventajas y desventajas.** What can you do to get extra cash or to save money? The first three possibilities are shown in the following drawings. What are the advantages and disadvantages of each suggestion?

> MODELO: dejar de tomar tanto café →
> Si dejo de tomar tanto café, ahorraré sólo un poco de dinero. Estaré menos nervioso/a, pero creo que será más difícil despertarme por la mañana.

1. pedirles dinero a mis amigos o parientes
2. cometer un robo
3. alquilar unos cuartos de mi casa a otras personas
4. dejar de fumar / beber cerveza / tomar tanto café
5. buscar un trabajo de tiempo parcial
6. vender mi coche / televisor
7. comprar muchos billetes de lotería
8. estudiar más
9. invertir mis ahorros en bonos y acciones (*stocks and bonds*)

B. El mundo en el año 2500.   ¿Cómo será el mundo del futuro? Haga una lista de temas o cosas que Ud. cree que van a ser diferentes en el año 2500. Por ejemplo: el transporte, la comida, la vivienda… Piense también en temas globales: la política, los problemas que presenta la capa de ozono…

Ahora, a base de su lista, haga una serie de predicciones para el futuro.

MODELO: La gente comerá (Comeremos) comidas sintéticas.

Vocabulario útil

la colonización	**el transbordador espacial** (space shuttle)
la energía nuclear/solar	**la vida artificial**
el espacio	
los OVNIs (Objetos Volantes No Identificados)	**diseñar** (to design)
el planeta	**eliminar**
la pobreza (poverty)	**intergaláctico/a**
el robot	**interplanetario/a**
el satélite	**sintético/a**

NOTA COMUNICATIVA

Expressing Conjecture

Estela, en el aeropuerto	Cecilia, en la carretera
¿Dónde **estará** Cecilia?	*I wonder where Cecilia is. (Where can Cecilia be?)*
¿Qué le **pasará**?	*I wonder what's up with her. (What can be wrong?)*
Estará en un lío de tráfico.	*She's probably (must be) in a traffic jam. (I bet she's in a traffic jam.)*

The future can also be used in Spanish to express probability or conjecture about what is happening now. This use of the future is called the *future of probability* (**el futuro de probabilidad**). Note in the preceding examples that the English cues for expressing probability (*probably, I bet, must be, I wonder . . . , Where can . . .* , and so on) are not directly expressed in Spanish. Their sense is conveyed in Spanish by the use of the future form of the verb.

C. Predicciones. ¿Quiénes serán las siguientes personas? ¿Qué estarán haciendo? ¿Dónde estarán? Invente todos los detalles que pueda sobre los siguientes dibujos.

1.

2.

3.

4.

En los Estados Unidos y el Canadá

El creciente mercado hispánico

¿Qué tienen en común Ford, Chevrolet, Sprint, Dockers, United Health y Toys "Я" Us? Pues, como muchas compañías norteamericanas, **tienen activas campañas publicitarias para atraer al mercado hispánico nacional.** Con más de 40 millones de hispanos, según el censo estadounidense del año 2004, los Estados Unidos ocupa **el cuarto puesto**[a] entre las naciones que tienen una población hispanohablante (se calcula que podría[b] ser **la segunda** o **tercera nación** en los próximos quince años, por delante de España). La población hispana de los Estados Unidos se traduce en[c] **un mercado de más de 600.000 millones de**[d] **dólares.**

CNN en español, HBO Latino y *People en español* se dirigen a[e] la variada comunidad hispana de los Estados

Unidos. Muchos programas y publicaciones se originan en la Florida, entre ellos *Latin Trade,* una **revista mensual**[f] de **negocios** y **economía** referente a Norteamérica en relación con todos los países hispánicos. El ámbito de lectores[g] de *Latin Trade* incluye a hispanos de todo el mundo, un grupo de más de 400 millones de personas.

Desgraciadamente,[h] **la importancia numérica de los hispanos,** más del 12 por ciento de la población de los Estados Unidos, **no se ve reflejada**[i] **en el mundo de la comunicación, de la política ni de los negocios.** Es este el gran reto[j] para los hispanos de este país.

[a]*position* [b]*it could* [c]*se... translates into* [d]*600.000... seiscientos millones de (600 billion)* [e]*se... target* [f]*monthly* [g]*ámbito... readership* [h]*Unfortunately* [i]*no... is not reflected* [j]*challenge*

Voces del Uruguay y del Paraguay

LITERATURA: Horacio Quiroga

Horacio Quiroga
(1878– 1937)

Sobre el autor: *Horacio Silvestre Quiroga nació en Salto, Uruguay. En 1899 fundó la* Revista de Salto, *y en 1900 viajó a París con otros jóvenes intelectuales. Volvió al Uruguay pero, después de matar[a] accidentalmente a un amigo, se trasladó a la Argentina. En 1935 publicó* Más allá, *su último libro de cuentos antes de morir. El siguiente fragmento es del cuento «El hijo»,* Más allá *(1935).*

Es un poderoso[b] día de verano en Misiones, con todo el sol, el calor y la calma que puede deparar[c] la estación. La naturaleza plenamente[d] abierta, se siente satisfecha de sí. Como el sol, el calor y la calma ambiente, el padre abre también su corazón a la naturaleza.

—Ten cuidado, chiquito —dice a su hijo; abreviando[e] en esa frase todas las observaciones del caso y que su hijo comprende perfectamente.

—Sí, papá —responde la criatura[f] mientras coge la escopeta[g] y carga de cartuchos[h] los bolsillos de su camisa, que cierra con cuidado.

[a]*killing* [b]*powerful* [c]*traer* [d]*completely, fully* [e]*abbreviating* [f]*niño* [g]*shotgun* [h]*carga… fills with cartridges*

MÚSICA: El candombe y el arpa paraguaya

El candombe es una música basada en los ritmos de tambores.[a] Fue creado[b] por los afro-uruguayos de Montevideo en el siglo[c] XVIII y con gran influencia del tamborileo[d] bantú de África. La música y el baile candombe son esenciales en la celebración del Carnaval en Montevideo y son una de las principales atracciones turísticas del país. Este carnaval tiene mucho en común con otras celebraciones carnavalescas, como las de Río de Janeiro y Nueva Orleáns. La comparsa[e] se prepara todo el año para perfeccionar su traje, sus ritmos y su baile.

[a]*drums* [b]*created* [c]*century* [d]*drumming* [e]*dance troupe*

Aunque[f] la mayoría de los paraguayos son mestizos y de fuerte ascendencia indígena, la música del Paraguay es de carácter europeo. El instrumento nacional del Paraguay es el arpa, que los jesuitas* hicieron popular en la cuenca[g] del Paraná.

[f]*Although* [g]*river basin*

---

*Beginning in the late sixteenth century, the Jesuits established missions in Paraguay along the Paraná River to convert the Guaraní people. Some of the priests brought musical instruments, such as the harp. Paraguay continues to be an internationally recognized center for making harps.

Gramática

43 Expressing Future or Pending Actions Subjunctive and Indicative After Conjunctions of Time

Antes de la entrevista

La mamá de Tomás le habla *antes de que salga* para entrevistarse.

SRA. LÓPEZ: ¿Estás listo para la entrevista?

TOMÁS: Sí. ¿Estoy elegante?

SRA. LÓPEZ: Muy elegante. Recuerda, *cuando llegues a la oficina,* no te olvides de darle la mano a la directora de personal.

TOMÁS: Claro, mamá. No te preocupes.

SRA. LÓPEZ: *Y tan pronto como te sientes,* entrégale el currículum.

TOMÁS: Mamá, se lo daré *después de que ella me lo pida.* Cálmate. Yo soy la persona que va a entrevistarse.

SRA. LÓPEZ: Está bien. Pero llámame *tan pronto como termines* la entrevista.

Comprensión: ¿Cierto o falso?

1. La Sra. López tiene una entrevista hoy.
2. La Sra. López le da consejos a su hijo.
3. Es obvio que Tomás está nervioso.
4. A Tomás le gustan los consejos de su madre.

A. The subjunctive is often used in Spanish in adverbial clauses, which function like adverbs, telling when the action of the main verb takes place. Such adverbial clauses are introduced by conjunctions (see **Capítulo 15**).

Lo veré **mañana.** (adverb)
I'll see him tomorrow.

Lo veré **cuando venga mañana.** (adverbial clause)
I'll see him when he comes tomorrow.

> **adverb** = a word that describes a verb, adjective, or another adverb, that is, a word that tells when, how, where, or how much something takes place
>
> **conjunction** = a word or phrase that connects words, phrases, or clauses

B. Future events are often expressed in Spanish in two-clause sentences that include conjunctions of time such as those on the right.

antes (de) que	before
cuando	when
después (de) que	after
en cuanto	as soon as
hasta que	until
tan pronto como	as soon as

Before the interview   Tomás's mom talks to him before he leaves for his interview.   SRA LÓPEZ: Are you ready for the interview?   TOMÁS: Yes. Do I look elegant?   SRA. LÓPEZ: Very elegant. Remember, when you get to the office, don't forget to shake hands with the personnel director.   TOMÁS: Of course, Mom. Don't worry.   SRA. LÓPEZ: And as soon as you sit down, give her your resume.   TOMÁS: Mom, I'll give it to her after she asks for it. Calm down. I'm the one who's going to be interviewed.   SRA. LÓPEZ: OK. But call me as soon as you finish the interview.

C. The subjunctive is used in a subordinate clause after these conjunctions of time to express a future action or state of being—that is, one that is still pending or has not yet occurred from the point of view of the main verb. This use of the subjunctive is very frequent in conversation in phrases such as the examples on the right.

    The events in the subordinate clause are imagined—not real-world—events. They haven't happened yet.

Cuando **sea** grande/mayor…
When I'm older . . .

Cuando **tenga** tiempo…
When I have the time . . .

Cuando **me gradúe**…
When I graduate . . .

D. When the present subjunctive is used in this way to express pending actions, the main-clause verb is in the present indicative or future.

PENDING ACTION (SUBJUNCTIVE)

Pagaré las cuentas **en cuanto reciba** mi cheque.
I'll pay the bills as soon as I get my check.

Debo depositar el dinero **tan pronto como** lo **reciba**.
I should deposit the money as soon as I get it.

E. However, the indicative (not the present subjunctive) is used after conjunctions of time to describe a habitual action or a completed action in the past. Compare the following.

HABITUAL ACTIONS (INDICATIVE)

Siempre **pago** las cuentas **en cuanto recibo** mi cheque.
I always pay bills as soon as I get my check.

Deposito el dinero **tan pronto como** lo **recibo**.
I deposit the money as soon as I receive it.

COMPLETED PAST ACTION (INDICATIVE):

El mes pasado **pagué** las cuentas **en cuanto recibí** mi cheque.
Last month I paid my bills as soon as I got my check.

Deposité el dinero **tan pronto como** lo **recibí**.
I deposited the money as soon as I got it.

Siempre me ducho **antes de que se despierten** mis hijos.
I always shower before my kids wake up.

OJO The subjunctive is always used with **antes (de) que.** (See **Capítulo 15.**)

AUTOPRUEBA

Indicate which sentences express a pending action and thus require the subjunctive in Spanish.

1. I'll call as soon as I get home.
2. We interview applicants only after we contact their references.
3. Many students apply for graduate school as soon as they begin their senior year.
4. They won't deposit this check until you sign it.

Answers: 1, 4

■ Práctica

A. Decisiones económicas

PASO 1   Lea las siguientes oraciones sobre Rigoberto y decida si se trata de una acción habitual o de una acción que no ha pasado todavía. Luego indique la frase que mejor complete la oración.

1. Rigoberto se va a comprar una computadora en cuanto…
   a. el banco le dé el préstamo.
   b. el banco le da el préstamo.
2. Siempre usa su tarjeta de crédito cuando…
   a. no tenga efectivo.
   b. no tiene efectivo.
3. Al principio del mes saca el saldo (*he balances*) de su cuenta corriente después de que…
   a. reciba el estado de cuentas (*statement*).
   b. recibe el estado de cuentas.
4. Piensa abrir una cuenta de ahorros tan pronto como…
   a. consiga un trabajo.
   b. consigue un trabajo.
5. No puede pagar sus cuentas este mes hasta que…
   a. su hermano le devuelva el dinero que le prestó.
   b. su hermano le devuelve el dinero que le prestó.

PASO 2   Ahora describa cómo lleva Ud. sus propios asuntos económicos, completando las siguientes oraciones semejantes.

1. Voy a comprarme _____ en cuanto el banco me dé un préstamo.
2. Cuando no tengo efectivo, siempre uso _____.
3. Después de que el banco me envía el estado de cuentas, yo siempre

   _____.
4. Tan pronto como consiga un trabajo, voy a _____.
5. No te presto más dinero hasta que tú me _____ el dinero que me debes.
6. Este mes, voy a _____ antes de que se me olvide.

B. Algunos momentos en la vida.

Las siguientes oraciones describen algunos aspectos de la vida de Mariana en el pasado, en el presente y en el futuro. Lea cada grupo de oraciones para tener una idea general del contexto. Luego dé la forma apropiada de los infinitivos.

1. Hace cuatro años,[a] cuando Mariana (graduarse) en la escuela secundaria, sus padres (darle) un reloj. El año que viene, cuando (graduarse) en la universidad, (darle) un coche.
2. Cuando (ser) niña, Mariana (querer) ser enfermera. Luego, cuando (tener) 18 años, (decidir) que quería estudiar computación. Cuando (terminar) su carrera este año, yo creo que (poder) encontrar un buen trabajo como programadora.
3. Generalmente Mariana no (escribir) cheques hasta que (tener) los fondos en su cuenta corriente. Este mes tiene muchos gastos, pero no (ir) a pagar ninguna cuenta hasta que le (llegar) el cheque de su trabajo de tiempo parcial.

[a]Hace… *Four years ago*

C. Hablando de dinero: Planes para el futuro. Complete las siguientes oraciones con el presente del subjuntivo de los verbos indicados.

1. Voy a ahorrar más dinero en cuanto…
   darme (ellos) un aumento de sueldo (*raise*)
   dejar (yo) de gastar tanto
2. Pagaré todas mis cuentas tan pronto como…
   tener el dinero para hacerlo
   ser absolutamente necesario
3. El semestre/trimeste que viene, pagaré la matrícula después de que…
   cobrar mi cheque en el banco
   (¿quién?) mandarme un cheque
4. No podré pagar el alquiler hasta que…
   sacar dinero de mi cuenta de ahorros
   depositar el dinero en mi cuenta corriente
5. No voy a jubilarme hasta que mis hijos…
   terminar sus estudios universitarios
   casarse

D. Planes para una boda. Use las conjunciones entre paréntesis para unir cada oración con la frase que la sigue. Haga todos los cambios necesarios. **¡OJO!** No se usa el subjuntivo en todos los casos. Tenga cuidado con las formas verbales.

MODELO: Miguel quiere casarse con Carmen. / él: conseguir un trabajo
(tan pronto como) →
Miguel quiere casarse con Carmen tan pronto como él consiga un trabajo.

1. Carmen quiere esperar. / ella: graduarse en la universidad (hasta que)
2. Miguel se lo va a decir a los padres de Carmen. / (ellos) llegar a la ciudad (tan pronto como)
3. Los padres de Carmen siempre quieren ver a Miguel. / él: visitar a su hija (cuando)
4. Los padres se van a alegrar. / (ellos) oír las noticias (en cuanto)
5. Miguel y Carmen van a Acapulco en su luna de miel. / (ellos) tener dinero (cuando)
6. Todos nosotros les vamos a dar una fiesta. / (ellos) regresar de su viaje (después de que)

Need more practice?

- Workbook/Laboratory Manual
- Interactive CD-ROM
- Online Learning Center
  (www.mhhe.com/quetal7)

■ Conversación

A. Descripciones. Describa Ud. los dibujos, completando las oraciones e inventando un contexto para las escenas. Luego describa su propia vida.

1. Pablo va a estudiar hasta que _____.

   Esta noche yo voy a estudiar hasta que _____.

   Siempre estudio hasta que _____.
   Anoche estudié hasta que _____.

2. Los Sres. Castro van a cenar tan pronto como _____.

   Esta noche voy a cenar tan pronto como _____.
   Siempre ceno tan pronto como _____.
   Anoche cené tan pronto como _____.

3. Lupe va a viajar al extranjero en cuanto _____.

   En cuanto yo gane la lotería, voy a _____.
   En cuanto tengo el dinero, siempre _____.
   De niño/a, _____ en cuanto tenía el dinero.

B. Reacciones. ¿Cómo reaccionará o qué hará cuando ocurran los siguientes acontecimientos? Complete las oraciones con el futuro.

1. Cuando colonicemos otro planeta, _____.
2. Cuando descubran algo para curar el cáncer, _____.
3. Cuando haya una mujer presidenta, _____.
4. Cuando me jubile, _____.
5. Cuando yo sea anciano/a, _____.
6. Cuando me gradúe, _____.
7. Antes de graduarme,…
8. Después de conseguir mi primer/próximo trabajo,…
9. En cuanto tenga suficiente dinero,…
10. Antes de tener hijos…

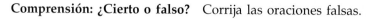
UN POCO DE TODO

Lengua y cultura: ¿Cómo se ganan la vida (*earn a living*) **los estudiantes?**
Complete the following paragraphs with the correct form of the words in
parentheses, as suggested by the context. When two possibilities are given
in parentheses, select the correct word. Use an adverb derived from the
adjectives in italics.

La preocupación por el dinero es algo compartido[a] por los estudiantes
en todo el mundo. En (el/la[1]) mayor parte de los países de habla
española, (el/la[2]) sistema universitario es gratuito.[b] Sin embargo, hay
(de/que[3]) tener dinero para los (gastar/gastos[4]) personales y también
para (el/la[5]) cine y otras diversiones.

Aquí, algunos estudiantes hispanos contestan la pregunta: ¿Cómo
(te/se[6]) ganaba Ud. la vida cuando era estudiante?

Una joven de México: A los 13 años, (*yo:* empezar[7]) a trabajar en una
oficina. Así (*yo:* poder[8]) pagar la colegiatura[c] de mis estudios. (*Yo:*
Trabajar[9]) de día y (estudiar[10]) de noche.

Un joven uruguayo: Cuando (*yo:* ser/estar[11]) estudiante, me (ganar[12]) la
vida como fotógrafo. (*Yo:* Sacar[13]) fotos de bodas, bautismos, fiestas de
cumpleaños. (*Yo:* Trabajar[14]) en cualquier ocasión y en cualquier sitio.

Una mujer española: (*Yo:* Ayudar[15]) a enseñar a párvulos.[d]

Algunos estudiantes (ofrecer[16]) los siguientes comentarios adicionales.

Una joven chilena: Los padres (*normal*[17]) mantienen a sus hijos
(*económico*[18]). Pero muchos chicos (trabajar[19]) de todas maneras. Las
chicas (cuidar[20]) niños o (ayudar[21]) en casa y los chicos (trabajar[22]) en
talleres. Si los padres tienen dinero, es raro que los hijos (trabajar[23])
hasta que no (terminar[24]) su carrera.[e]

Un joven argentino: En la Argentina, la enseñanza universitaria
(ser/estar[25]) gratuita. De todos modos, los estudiantes siempre
(necesitar[26]) tener más de un trabajo y los padres los ayudan con lo que
pueden. Muchos estudiantes no (irse[27]) a otras ciudades a (estudiar[28]).
(*Ellos:* Vivir[29]) con (su[30]) padres y estudian en (el/la[31]) universidad más
cercana.

[a]*shared* [b]*free* [c]*fees* [d]*tots* [e]*studies*

Comprensión: ¿Cierto o falso? Corrija las oraciones falsas.

1. El sistema universitario es gratuito en muchos países hispánicos.
2. Los estudiantes hispanos nunca tienen que trabajar.
3. Generalmente los padres mantienen a sus hijos mientras estos son
   estudiantes.

*Una maestra con sus estudiantes en
una escuela de México, D.F.*

**Resources for Review and
Testing Preparation**

- Workbook/Laboratory Manual
- Interactive CD-ROM
- Online Learning Center
  (www.mhhe.com/quetal7)

VIDEOTECA

Entrevista cultural: El Uruguay

María Dioni es del Uruguay; es consejera para estudiantes universitarios. María describe su trabajo. Antes de ver el vídeo, lea el siguiente fragmento de la entrevista.

MARÍA: Mi trabajo principal es ayudar a los estudiantes a prepararse para buscar trabajo. Muchos estudiantes no tienen experiencia con el proceso de buscar trabajo: las solicitudes, las entrevistas y las negociaciones, por ejemplo.

Ahora vea el vídeo y conteste las siguientes preguntas basándose en la entrevista.

1. ¿Cuáles son las responsabilidades de María?
2. ¿Qué necesitan saber los estudiantes para buscar trabajo?

Entrevista cultural: El Paraguay

La paraguaya Sonia Sancho tiene un puesto administrativo con una compañía en México. Ella comenta su trabajo y algunos de los errores cometidos por los solicitantes. Antes de ver el vídeo, lea el siguiente fragmento de la entrevista.

ENTREVISTADORA: ¿Es difícil su trabajo?
SONIA: Un poco, porque no todas las solicitudes son seleccionadas para una entrevista, y no todas las personas que vienen a una entrevista obtienen un trabajo.

Ahora vea el vídeo y conteste las siguientes preguntas basándose en la entrevista.

1. ¿Cuál es el trabajo de Sonia? ¿Por qué le parece difícil, a veces?
2. ¿Cuál es uno de los errores que se hacen con las solicitudes?

Entre amigos: ¿A qué hora es la entrevista?

Karina, Tané, Miguel y Rubén hablan del trabajo y de las entrevistas. En su opinión, ¿qué preguntas se van a hacer? Antes de mirar el vídeo, lea las preguntas a continuación. Mientras mire el vídeo, trate de entender la conversación en general y fíjese en la información sobre las entrevistas y los planes futuros de los amigos. Luego mire el vídeo una segunda vez, fijándose en la información que necesita para contestar las preguntas.

1. ¿Por qué está tan bien vestido Rubén? ¿Está tranquilo o nervioso?
2. ¿Qué quiere hacer Miguel después de graduarse?

ENFOQUE CULTURAL

  ### El Uruguay y el Paraguay

¡Fíjese!

- Aproximadamente el 45 por ciento de la población uruguaya vive en Montevideo.
- Para los uruguayos, la educación primaria, secundaria y universitaria es gratuita.[a] La tasa de alfabetización[b] es de un 96 por ciento, una de las más altas de Latinoamérica.
- El Paraguay es uno de los dos países latinoamericanos sin costa marítima (el otro es Bolivia). Por eso, sus numerosos ríos navegables tienen gran importancia económica para el país.
- La ciudad de Asunción, en el Paraguay, la primera ciudad permanente en la región del Río de la Plata, fue fundada por los españoles en 1537.
- La represa[c] hidroeléctrica de Itaipú, terminada en 1982, es la más grande y potente del mundo. Fue construida en la frontera entre el Paraguay, la Argentina y el Brasil con la ayuda financiera del Brasil. La represa suministra[d] casi el 80 por ciento de la energía del Paraguay, y más o menos el 25 por ciento de la energía del Brasil.

[a]free [b]tasa… rate of literacy [c]dam [d]supplies

Civilizaciones indígenas: El guaraní

El Paraguay es el único país latinoamericano que tiene dos lenguas oficiales, una de ellas indígena. El 90 por ciento de la población paraguaya habla guaraní (sólo el 75 por ciento habla español). Hoy hay literatura, música y hasta páginas web en guaraní.

Guaraní significa guerrero[a] en esa lengua, nombre que recuerda las disputas de los diversos grupos étnicos guaraníes contra el poderoso imperio inca.

[a]warrior

Asunción, Paraguay

Learn more about Uruguay and Paraguay with the Video, the Interactive CD-ROM, and the Online Learning Center (www.mhhe.com/quetal7).

A CONVERSAR

Un futuro imaginado

PASO 1   En una hoja de papel aparte, prepare un cuadro como el siguiente. Apunte brevemente sus respuestas en los espacios en blanco. Si el nombre de la profesión que a Ud. le interesa no está en este capítulo, búsquelo en un diccionario. Use su imaginación: ¡el futuro está lleno de posibilidades!

MODELO:

	Mi trabajo	**Mi vivienda / El lugar**	**Mis vacaciones**
En cinco años...	cocinera	apartamento / Nueva York	ninguna
En diez años...	dueña de un restaurante elegante	casa / California	una isla en el Caribe
En quince años...			

PASO 2   Con un compañero / una compañera, hable de su futuro. Deben hacer las predicciones indicadas (hasta quince años), pero pueden hablar de un futuro aun (*even*) más distante si quieren. Utilicen verbos en el futuro en sus preguntas y respuestas.

MODELO: E1: ¿Qué trabajo tendrás en cinco años?
E2: Seré cocinera, pero sólo de tiempo parcial. Trabajaré por la noche mientras estudio para la maestría (*master's*) en negocios. Quiero ser dueña de un restaurante. Será bueno tener experiencia en restaurantes, pero también será importante saber mucho de los negocios. ¿Y tú?
E1: Me graduaré en dos años, así que (*so*) en cinco años ya seré trabajador social. Trabajaré con jóvenes delincuentes en Los Ángeles. Muchos de mis familiares son de esa área. ¿Y tú? ¿Dónde vivirás?
E2: Viviré en un apartamento en Nueva York, cerca de la universidad...

PASO 3 Entre todos, hablen de los planes de sus compañeros. Pueden comparar los planes de sus compañeros con sus propios planes. Usen verbos en el futuro para describir los planes. Deben marcar la información en la pizarra en un cuadro como el del **Paso 1.**

MODELO: E1: En cinco años, Marsha será cocinera de tiempo parcial. Vivirá en un apartamento en Nueva York, cerca de la universidad donde estudiará para su maestría en negocios. Quiere ser dueña de un restaurante y necesitará la experiencia en restaurantes y la preparación en negocios.

PASO 4 Después de apuntar la información en la pizarra, comparen los planes y las carreras. Traten de hacer algunas generalizaciones sobre la clase, pero hablen también de puntos específicos. ¿Quiénes tendrán las carreras más interesantes? ¿más exigentes (*demanding*)? ¿Quiénes tendrán que pasar más tiempo estudiando y preparándose para su profesión? ¿En qué partes del país (del mundo) vivirá la mayoría de Uds.? ¿Quiénes tendrán las vacaciones más divertidas? ¿originales? Deben expresar sus opiniones y defenderlas si no están de acuerdo.

MODELO: E1: Marsha tendrá una carrera exigente porque en diez años será dueña de un restaurante. Los restaurantes representan mucho trabajo y Marsha no tendrá mucho tiempo para las vacaciones.

E2: Bill tendrá la carrera más exigente porque será trabajador social y trabajará con jóvenes delincuentes...

GRAMÁTICA

To review the grammar points presented in this chapter, refer to the indicated grammar presentations. You'll find further practice of these structures in the Workbook/Laboratory Manual, on the Interactive CD-ROM, and on the *¿Qué tal?* Online Learning Center (www.mhhe.com/quetal7).

42 Talking About the Future—Future Verb Forms

You should know how to form and when to use the future tense, including all irregular forms.

43 Expressing Future or Pending Actions—Subjunctive and Indicative After Conjunctions of Time

Do you know how to express actions that will take place only after something else takes place? What are the conjunctions that you can use for this?

VOCABULARIO

Practice this vocabulary with digital flash cards on the Online Learning Center (www.mhhe.com/quetal7).

Los verbos

jubilarse	to retire
mudarse	to move (*residence*)

Profesiones y oficios

el/la abogado/a	lawyer
el/la cajero/a	cashier; teller
el/la cocinero/a	cook; chef
el/la comerciante	merchant; shopkeeper
el/la contador(a)	accountant
el/la criado/a	servant
el hombre / la mujer de negocios	businessperson
el/la ingeniero/a	engineer
el/la maestro/a	schoolteacher
el/la obrero/a	worker, laborer
el/la peluquero/a	hairstylist
el/la periodista	journalist
el/la plomero/a	plumber
el/la sicólogo/a	psychologist
el/la siquiatra	psychiatrist
el soldado / la mujer soldado	soldier
el/la técnico/a	technician
el/la trabajador(a) social	social worker
el/la traductor(a)	translator
el/la vendedor(a)	salesperson

Cognados: el/la analista de sistemas, el/la electricista, el/la fotógrafo/a, el/la programador(a), el/la veterinario/a

Repaso: el/la bibliotecario/a, el/la consejero/a, el/la dentista, el/la dependiente/a, el/la enfermero/a, el/la mecánico/a, el/la médico/a, el/la profesor(a), el/la secretario/a

El mundo del trabajo

el/la aspirante	candidate; applicant
el currículum	resumé
la dirección de personal	personnel office, employment office
el/la director(a) de personal	personnel director
la empresa	corporation; business
la entrevista	interview
el/la entrevistador(a)	interviewer
el/la gerente	manager
el oficio	trade (*profession*)
el puesto	job; position
el salario	salary
la solicitud	application (*form*)
la sucursal	branch (office)

Repaso: el sueldo, el teléfono

caerle (*irreg.*) bien/ mal a alguien	to make a good/bad impression on someone
dejar	to quit

entrevistar	to interview
escribir en la computadora	to key, type (in)
graduarse (me gradúo) (en)	to graduate (from)
llenar	to fill out (*a form*)
renunciar (a)	to resign (from)

Repaso: contestar

Una cuestión de dinero

el aumento de sueldo	raise
el banco	bank
la caja	cashier window
el cajero automático	automatic teller machine (ATM)
el cheque	check
la chequera	checkbook
la cuenta corriente	checking account
la cuenta de ahorros	savings account
el efectivo	cash
la factura	bill
la identificación	ID
el interés	interest
el préstamo	loan
el presupuesto	budget

Repaso: la cuenta, la tarjeta de crédito

ahorrar	to save (*money*)
cargar (gu)	to charge (*to an account*)
cobrar	to cash (*a check*); to charge (*someone for an item or service*)

depositar	to deposit
devolver (ue)	to return (*something*)
economizar (c)	to economize
ganar	to earn
pedir (i, i) prestado/a	to borrow
sacar (qu)	to withdraw, take out
sacar el saldo	to balance a checkbook

Repaso: gastar, pagar (gu), prestar

a plazos	in installments
al contado	in cash
con cheque	by check
en efectivo	in cash

Conjunciones

después (de) que	after
en cuanto	as soon as
hasta que	until
tan pronto como	as soon as

Repaso: antes (de) que, cuando

Palabras adicionales

al principio de	at the beginning of
en vez de	instead of

En la actualidad

Partidaria (Supporter) de Eduardo Estrella, el candidato del Partido Reformista Social Cristiano, para la presidencia de la República Dominicana en 2004

LAS NOTICIAS

el reportero

Y ahora, **el canal** 45 les ofrece a Uds. el NOTICIERO 45, con los últimos **eventos** del **mundo**…

El asesinato de **un dictador**

La huelga de obreros

La guerra en el Oriente Medio

La erupción de un volcán en Centroamérica

Bombas en un avión

El choque de trenes

el acontecimiento	event, happening	**comunicarse (qu) (con)**	to communicate (with)
el desastre	disaster	**enterarse (de)**	to find out, learn (about)
la esperanza	hope, wish	**informar**	to inform
el medio de comunicación	means of communication	**mantener** (*irreg.*) **la paz**	to maintain, keep peace
la paz (*pl.* **paces**)	peace	**ofrecer (zc)**	to offer
la prensa	press; news media	**vivir en paz**	to live in peace
el/la testigo	witness		

Cognados: el ataque (terrorista), el terrorismo, el/la terrorista, la víctima

■ Conversación

A. ¿Cómo se entera Ud.? El público utiliza diferentes medios para enterarse de los acontecimientos locales, nacionales e internacionales. ¿Cómo se entera Ud. de las noticias?

PASO 1 Indique con qué frecuencia utiliza los siguientes medios.

	TODOS LOS DÍAS	DE 3 A 5 VECES POR SEMANA	DE 1 A 2 VECES POR SEMANA	CASI NUNCA
1. Leo un periódico local.	☐	☐	☐	☐
2. Leo un periódico nacional.	☐	☐	☐	☐
3. Leo una revista.	☐	☐	☐	☐
4. Leo las noticias en el Internet.	☐	☐	☐	☐
5. Miro el noticiero local.	☐	☐	☐	☐
6. Miro el noticiero nacional.	☐	☐	☐	☐
7. Miro CNN.	☐	☐	☐	☐
8. Escucho la radio.	☐	☐	☐	☐

PASO 2 Compare sus respuestas con las de sus compañeros. ¿Cuál es el medio preferido por la mayoría de Uds. para informarse?

B. Definiciones. ¿Qué palabra se asocia con cada definición?

1. _____ un programa que nos informa de lo que pasa en nuestro mundo
2. _____ una persona que está presente durante un acontecimiento y lo ve todo
3. _____ un medio importantísimo de comunicación
4. _____ una persona que nos informa de los acontecimientos
5. _____ una persona que gobierna un país de una forma absoluta
6. _____ una persona que emplea la violencia para cambiar el mundo según sus deseos
7. _____ cuando los obreros se niegan a (*refuse*) trabajar
8. _____ la frecuencia en que se transmiten y se reciben los programas de televisión
9. _____ la confrontación armada entre dos o más países

a. el noticiero
b. la guerra
c. el/la terrorista
d. el/la dictador(a)
e. el canal
f. el/la testigo
g. el/la reportero/a
h. la huelga
i. la prensa

C. Uds. y la televisión. Con un compañero / una compañera, diga si está de acuerdo con las siguientes opiniones. Si no están de acuerdo, hagan los cambios necesarios para expresar su opinión. En cualquier caso, intenten dar un ejemplo que justifique su punto de vista.

1. Los reporteros de la televisión nos informan imparcialmente de los acontecimientos.
2. Por lo general ofrecen los programas más interesantes en el canal de televisión pública.
3. En este país la prensa es irresponsable. Nos da sólo los detalles que apoyan (*support*) sus ideas políticas.
4. Las telenovelas (*soap operas*) reflejan la vida tal (*just*) como es.
5. Los anuncios son sumamente (*extremely*) informativos y más interesantes que muchos programas.
6. Me gusta que los reporteros y meteorólogos cuenten chistes (*jokes*) durante el noticiero.

EL GOBIERNO Y LA RESPONSABILIDAD CÍVICA

el rey

la reina

el dictador

el político

votar

la ciudadana

el ciudadano

el ejército

el deber	responsibility; obligation	**la ley**	law
los/las demás	others, other people	**la política**	politics
el derecho	right	**el servicio militar**	military service
la (des)igualdad	(in)equality		
la dictadura	dictatorship	**durar**	to last
la discriminación	discrimination	**obedecer (zc)**	to obey

■ Conversación

A. ¡Peligro! (*Jeopardy!*)   ¿Cuánto sabe Ud. de la historia y la política? Conteste rápidamente con la información necesaria y en forma de pregunta. Use las preguntas a la derecha.

¿Quién/Qué es... ?

1. _____ Fue un dictador argentino que tenía una esposa famosa.
2. _____ Se llama Elizabeth y vive en Buckingham Palace.
3. _____ Es una famosa película de Orson Welles, y su protagonista se llama Kane.
4. _____ Fue un presidente estadounidense que se opuso a (*opposed*) la esclavitud de los negros.
5. _____ En algunos países, es un deber de los hombres de cierta edad. Generalmente, tienen que entrar en el ejército por dos años, más o menos.
6. _____ Es la forma de gobierno que existe en España.
7. _____ Existe cuando muchas personas no tienen los mismos derechos que los demás.
8. _____ Es un deber de los ciudadanos en una democracia.

a. el servicio militar
b. la reina de Inglaterra
c. votar
d. la monarquía parlamentaria
e. *El ciudadano Kane* (*Citizen Kane*)
f. la discriminación
g. Juan Perón
h. Abraham Lincoln

NOTA CULTURAL

La mayoría de edad en los países hispánicos

En el mundo hispánico los jóvenes se consideran legalmente adultos, es decir, **alcanzan**[a] **la mayoría de edad, a los 18 años.** Al cumplir los 18 años, los jóvenes hispanos pueden **participar en la política y pueden votar.** En varios países los hombres de 18 años también tienen la responsabilidad de inscribirse[b] en **el servicio militar.** En Colombia, los jóvenes pueden inscribirse en el servicio militar a los 16 años. La selección de los conscriptos[c] generalmente se hace mediante[d] una lotería. Recientemente, las mujeres mexicanas y argentinas también pueden inscribirse en el servicio militar, un hecho[e] sin precedentes en Latinoamérica.

Una licencia de conducir argentina

A los 18 años, los jóvenes hispanos pueden obtener su **licencia de manejar.** Sin embargo, algunos jóvenes en ciertos países no esperan hasta los 18 años. A los 16 años solicitan un **permiso especial para menores de edad** para operar un vehículo.

Otro aspecto importante al llegar a la mayoría de edad es el consumo de alcohol. **La edad límite para tomar bebidas alcohólicas** varía entre los 18 y 21 años. En Ecuador, por ejemplo, la edad límite es de 21 años. En algunos países hay menos restricciones sociales sobre el alcohol.

---

[a]*they reach*   [b]*de... of registering*   [c]*draftees*   [d]*by means of*   [e]*evento*

B. Asociaciones.   ¿Qué cosas, personas o ideas asocia Ud. con las siguientes palabras?

1. el deber
2. el ejército
3. la política
4. la ley
5. la monarquía
6. la dictadura

C. Opiniones.   ¿Qué piensan Uds. de las siguientes ideas? Den su opinión, empezando con una de las **Expresiones útiles.**

1. En este país consumimos demasiada energía.
2. La paz mundial completa es (im)posible.
3. En este país, la igualdad de todos los ciudadanos es una realidad, no sólo una esperanza.
4. Los policías, los bomberos (*firefighters*) y los médicos no tienen derecho a declararse en huelga.
5. El servicio militar obligatorio es necesario para formar un ejército.
6. El mundo de la política está lleno de gente (des)honesta.
7. La edad permitida para tomar bebidas alcohólicas debe ser la misma que la edad para votar.
8. Hay muchos países que tienen dictadores.

Expresiones útiles

Dudo que…
(No) Creo que…
Es probable que…
Es bueno/malo que…
Es una lástima que…
Es increíble que…
Me parece terrible/buena idea que…

Need more practice?

■ Workbook/Laboratory Manual
■ Interactive CD-ROM
■ Online Learning Center (www.mhhe.com/quetal7)

¿Recuerda Ud.?

In **Gramática 44,** you will learn about and begin to use the forms of the past subjunctive. As you learn this new tense, you will be continually using the past tense forms you have already learned along with the new material, so this section presents many opportunities for review.

To learn the forms of the past subjunctive, you will need to know the forms of the preterite well, especially the third person plural.

- Regular **-ar** verbs end in **-aron** and regular **-er/-ir** verbs in **-ieron** in the third person plural of the preterite.
- Stem-changing **-ir** verbs show the second change in the third person.

  servir (i, i) ⟶ **sirvieron**   **dormir (ue, u)** ⟶ **durmieron**

- Verbs with a stem ending in a vowel change the **i** to **y.**

  leyeron, cayeron, construyeron

- Many common verbs have irregular stems in the preterite.

  quisieron, hicieron, dijeron, and so on

- Four common verbs are totally irregular in this tense.

  ser/ir ⟶ **fueron**   **dar** ⟶ **dieron**   **ver** ⟶ **vieron**

The following brief exercises will help you get started.

A. Give the third person plural of the preterite for these infinitives.

1. hablar	**5.** perder	**9.** estar	**13.** traer	**17.** decir
2. comer	**6.** dormir	**10.** tener	**14.** dar	**18.** creer
3. vivir	**7.** reír	**11.** destruir	**15.** saber	**19.** ir
4. jugar	**8.** leer	**12.** mantener	**16.** vestirse	**20.** poder

B. You will often use the imperfect indicative in structures that trigger the past subjunctive. The forms of the imperfect indicative are relatively regular. Only three verbs have irregular imperfect forms: **ir, ser,** and **ver.** Give their first person singular and plural forms.

---

44 *¡No queríamos que fuera así!* Past Subjunctive

¡Qué pena que no *nos lleváramos* bien!

Elisa habla con su madre sobre su niñez.

MARÍA: ¿No recuerdas? ¡Qué mala memoria!

ELISA: Pero, mamá, ¿tú permitías que yo *hablara* así? ¡Qué falta de respeto hacia ti!

It's a shame we didn't get along! Elisa talks to her mother about her childhood. MARÍA: *You don't remember? What a bad memory!* ELISA: *But, Mom, did you let me talk that way? What a lack of respect for you!*

MARÍA: Eras muy cabezuda. No había nadie que *pudiera* contigo. ¡Cómo discutíamos! Tú creías que siempre tenías razón. Era imposible que *te equivocaras*. Tampoco querías que te *dijeran* lo que debías hacer.

ELISA: Bueno, por lo menos ahora no soy así. Digo, no tanto…

MARÍA: Sí, pero de todos modos, es necesario que una buena periodista sea un poco terca.

ELISA: Estoy de acuerdo. Es probable que, sin esa cualidad mía, yo no hubiera obtenido ese puesto.

¿Y Ud.?

Hace diez años (*Ten years ago*)…

1. ¿era difícil que Ud. hablara con sus padres sobre algún tema? ¿Cuál?
2. ¿con quién era imposible que Ud. se pusiera de acuerdo?
3. ¿con quién era imposible que Ud. se comunicara?
4. ¿contra qué orden de sus padres era común que Ud. protestara?

Cuando Ud. era niño/a…

5. ¿era probable que discutiera con alguien en la escuela primaria o en el barrio? ¿Con quién?
6. ¿dónde le prohibían sus padres que jugara?
7. ¿qué era obligatorio que comiera o bebiera?
8. ¿de qué temía que sus padres se enteraran?

Although Spanish has two simple indicative past tenses (preterite and imperfect), it has only one simple subjunctive past tense, the *past subjunctive* (**el imperfecto del subjuntivo**). Generally speaking, this tense is used in the same situations as the present subjunctive but, of course, when talking about past events. The exact English equivalent depends on the context in which it is used.

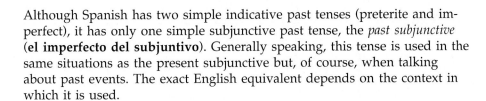

PAST	Present	Future
preterite	present indicative	future
imperfect	present progressive	
present perfect	formal commands	
present perfect subjunctive	informal commands	
past subjunctive	present subjunctive	

MARÍA: You were very stubborn. No one could change your mind. How we used to argue! You thought you were always right. It was impossible that you could ever make a mistake. Nor did you want anyone to tell you what to do. ELISA: Well, at least I'm not like that now. I mean, not as much . . . MARÍA: Yes, but, in any case, it's necessary for a good journalist to be a little bit stubborn. ELISA: I agree. It's likely that, without that quality of mine, I wouldn't have gotten that job.

Forms of the Past Subjunctive

A. The past subjunctive endings **-a, -as, -a, -amos, -ais, -an** are identical for **-ar, -er,** and **-ir** verbs. These endings are added to the third person plural of the preterite, minus its **-on** ending. For this reason, the forms of the past subjunctive reflect the irregularities of the preterite.

PAST SUBJUNCTIVE ENDINGS	
-a	-amos
-as	-ais
-a	-an

Past Subjunctive of Regular Verbs*

hablar: hablar~~on~~		comer: comier~~on~~		vivir: vivier~~on~~	
hablara	habláramos	comiera	comiéramos	viviera	viviéramos
hablaras	hablarais	comieras	comierais	vivieras	vivierais
hablara	hablaran	comiera	comieran	viviera	vivieran

B. Stem-changing verbs

-Ar and **-er** verbs: no change

-Ir verbs: all persons of the past subjunctive reflect the vowel change in the third person plural of the preterite.

empezar (ie): empezar~~on~~ → **empezara, empezaras,...**
volver (ue): volvier~~on~~ → **volviera, volvieras,...**
dormir (ue, u): durmier~~on~~ → **durmiera, durmieras,...**
pedir (i, i): pidier~~on~~ → **pidiera, pidieras,...**

C. Spelling changes

All persons of the past subjunctive reflect the change from **i** to **y** between two vowels.

i → y (caer, construir, creer, destruir, leer, oír)

creer: creyer~~on~~ →

creyera	creyéramos
creyeras	creyerais
creyera	creyeran

D. Verbs with irregular preterites

dar: dier~~on~~ →

diera	diéramos
dieras	dierais
diera	dieran

decir:	dijer~~on~~ → **dijera**	poner:	pusier~~on~~ → **pusiera**
estar:	estuvier~~on~~ → **estuviera**	querer:	quisier~~on~~ → **quisiera**
haber:	hubier~~on~~ → **hubiera**	saber:	supier~~on~~ → **supiera**
hacer:	hicier~~on~~ → **hiciera**	ser:	fuer~~on~~ → **fuera**
ir:	fuer~~on~~ → **fuera**	tener:	tuvier~~on~~ → **tuviera**
poder:	pudier~~on~~ → **pudiera**	venir:	vinier~~on~~ → **viniera**

*An alternative form of the past subjunctive (used primarily in Spain) ends in **-se: hablase, hablases, hablase, hablásemos, hablaseis, hablasen.** This form will not be practiced in ¿Qué tal?

Uses of the Past Subjunctive

A. The past subjunctive usually has the same applications as the present subjunctive, but it is used for past events. Compare these pairs of sentences.

Quiero que **se enteren** esta tarde.
I want them to find out this afternoon.

Quería que **se enteraran** por la tarde.
I wanted them to find out in the afternoon.

Siente que no **estén** allí esta noche.
He's sorry (that) they aren't there tonight.

Sintió que no **estuvieran** allí anoche.
He was sorry (that) they weren't there last night.

Dudamos que **mantengan** la paz.
We doubt that they will keep the peace.

Dudábamos que **mantuvieran** la paz.
We doubted that they would keep the peace.

B. Remember that the subjunctive is used after
(1) expressions of *influence, emotion,* and *doubt;*
(2) *nonexistent* and *indefinite* antecedents; and
(3) *conjunctions* of *contingency and purpose,* as well as those of *time.*

(1) ¿**Era necesario** que **regatearas**?
Was it necessary for you to bargain?

(1) **Sentí** que no **tuvieran** tiempo para ver Granada.
I was sorry that they didn't have time to see Granada.

(2) **No había nadie** que **pudiera** resolverlo.
There wasn't anyone who could (might have been able to) resolve it.

(3) Los padres **trabajaron para que** sus hijos **asistieran** a la universidad.
The parents worked so that their children could (might) go to the university.

(3) Anoche, **íbamos** a salir **en cuanto llegara** Felipe.
Last night, we were going to leave as soon as Felipe arrived.

C. The past subjunctive of the verb **querer** is often used to make a request sound more polite.

Quisiéramos hablar con Ud. en seguida.
We would like to speak with you immediately.

Quisiera un café, por favor.
I would like a cup of coffee, please.

AUTOPRUEBA

Change the following verbs from the present subjunctive to the past subjunctive.

1. quiera   **3.** salgan   **5.** esté
2. tengamos   **4.** sepas   **6.** traigas

Answers: 1. quisiera 2. tuviéramos 3. salieran 4. supieras 5. estuviera 6. trajeras

PASO 2

■ Práctica

A. ¡Anticipemos! Si pudiera volver... ¿Le gusta la idea de volver a la escuela secundaria? ¿O prefiere la vida de la universidad?

PASO 1 Lea las siguientes oraciones e indique las que son verdaderas para Ud. Cambie las oraciones falsas para que expresen su propia experiencia.

En la escuela secundaria...

1. ☐ era obligatorio que yo asistiera a todas mis clases.
2. ☐ mis padres insistían en que yo estudiara mucho.
3. ☐ era necesario que yo trabajara para que pudiera asistir a la universidad algún día.
4. ☐ no había ninguna clase que me interesara.
5. ☐ sacaba buenas notas para que mis padres me dieran dinero.
6. ☐ era necesario que volviera a casa a una hora determinada, aun (*even*) en los fines de semana.
7. ☐ mis padres me exigían que limpiara mi cuarto cada semana.
8. ☐ mis padres no permitían que saliera con alguna persona o con los miembros de ciertos grupos.

PASO 2 Ahora considere sus respuestas. ¿Realmente era mejor la vida en la escuela secundaria? ¿Le gustaría regresar a esa época? Explique.

B. Escenas históricas

PASO 1 La gente emigra por varias razones. Complete las siguientes oraciones con la forma correcta del infinitivo. Luego, si puede, nombre un grupo que emigró por la razón citada.

1. Las leyes de su país de origen no permitían que este grupo (practicar) libremente su religión.
2. Algunas personas esperaban que (haber) oro y plata en América.
3. El rey no quería que estos criminales (seguir) viviendo en su país.
4. Estos inmigrantes buscaban un país donde (haber) paz y esperanza.
5. Este grupo buscaba un país donde no (tener) que pasar hambre.

PASO 2 Dé una breve descripción del pasado histórico de los Estados Unidos, haciendo oraciones según las indicaciones. Empiece en el pasado. Desde el número 8, las oraciones se refieren al presente.

1. indios / temer / que / colonos / quitarles / toda la tierra
2. colonos / no / gustar / que / ser necesario / pagarle / impuestos / rey
3. parecía imposible / que / joven república / tener éxito (*success*)
4. los del sur / no / gustar / que / gobernarlos / los del norte
5. abolicionistas / no / gustar / que / algunos / no / tener / mismo / libertades
6. era necesario / que / declararse / en huelga / obreros / para / obtener / alguno / derechos
7. era terrible / que / haber / dos / guerra / mundial
8. para que / nosotros / vivir / en paz / es cuestión de / aprender / comunicarse
9. también / es necesario / que / haber / leyes / que / garantizar / derechos

C. Y ahora, la niñez. ¿Qué quería Ud. de la vida cuando era niño/a? ¿Y qué querían los demás que Ud. hiciera? Conteste, haciendo oraciones con una frase de cada grupo.

1. Mis padres (no) querían que yo… 2. Mis maestros me pedían que… 3. Yo buscaba amigos que… 4. Me gustaba mucho que nosotros…	ir a la iglesia / al templo con ellos portarse bien, ser bueno/a estudiar mucho, hacer la tarea todas las noches, sacar buenas notas ponerse ropa vieja para jugar, jugar en la calle, pelear con mis amigos mirar mucho la televisión, leer muchas tiras cómicas, comer muchos dulces vivir en nuestro barrio, asistir a la misma escuela, tener muchos juguetes, ser aventureros ir de vacaciones en verano, pasar todos juntos los días feriados, tener un árbol de Navidad muy alto

+

D. El noticiero de las seis. En las noticias los reporteros nos informan de los acontecimientos del día, pero a veces también ofrecen sus propias opiniones. Lea las siguientes oraciones y cámbielas al pasado. Debe usar el imperfecto del primer verbo en cada oración y luego el imperfecto del subjuntivo en la segunda parte.

1. «Los obreros quieren que les den un aumento de sueldo.»
2. «Es posible que los trabajadores sigan en huelga hasta el verano.»
3. «Es necesario que las víctimas reciban atención médica en la Clínica del Sagrado Corazón.»
4. «Los terroristas piden que los oficiales no los persigan.»
5. «Es necesario que el gobierno informe a todos los ciudadanos del desastre.»
6. «El presidente y los directores prefieren que la nueva fábrica se construya en México.»
7. «Temo que el número de votantes sea muy bajo en las próximas elecciones.»

Need more practice?

■ Workbook/Laboratory Manual
■ Interactive CD-ROM
■ Online Learning Center (www.mhhe.com/quetal7)

■ Conversación

A. Entrevista

1. ¿A qué le tenías miedo cuando eras pequeño/a? ¿Era probable que ocurrieran las cosas que temías? ¿Temías a veces que tus padres te castigaran (*punish*)? ¿Lo merecías a veces? ¿Era necesario que siempre los obedecieras? ¿Qué te prohibían que hicieras?
2. ¿Qué tipo de clases buscabas para este semestre/trimestre? ¿Clases que fueran fáciles? ¿interesantes? ¿Las encontraste? ¿Han sido las clases tal como las esperabas? ¿Qué tipo de clases vas a buscar para el semestre/trimestre que viene?
3. ¿Qué buscaban los primeros inmigrantes que vinieron a los Estados Unidos? ¿Buscaban un lugar donde pudieran practicar su religión? ¿un lugar donde hubiera abundancia de recursos naturales? ¿menos restricciones? ¿más libertad política y personal? ¿más respeto por los derechos humanos? ¿menos gente? ¿más espacio?

—Verás, quisiera un vaso de agua. Pero no te molestes, porque ya no tengo sed. Sólo quisiera saber si, en el caso de que tuviese otra vez sed, podría (*I could*) venir a pedirte un vaso de agua.

B. Situaciones. El niño del dibujo sabe que está molestando a sus padres cuando los despierta pidiendo ahora un vaso de agua que no quiere pero que podría (*he might*) querer más tarde. Por eso les habla de una forma muy cortés: «quisiera un vaso de agua… quisiera saber… ». Con un compañero / una compañera, explique cómo podrían Uds. pedir de una forma muy cortés lo que necesitan en las siguientes situaciones. ¿Qué dirían para conseguirlo?

1. Ud. quiere tener el número de teléfono de un chico / una chica que acaba de conocer. Habla con un amigo de él / una amiga de ella.
2. En un restaurante, el camarero no lo/la atiende como debe. Ud. no quiere perder la paciencia con él, pero quiere el café que le pidió hace diez minutos (*ten minutes ago*)… y la cuenta.
3. Uds. quieren saber cuándo es el examen final en esta clase y qué va a incluir.
4. Ud. necesita una extensión para el próximo examen de español.
5. Ud. piensa que va a necesitar una extensión para el próximo proyecto.
6. Ud. necesita una carta de recomendación del profesor / de la profesora.
7. Ud. quiere hablar con el rector / la rectora de la universidad para invitarlo/la a cenar en su residencia con motivo de pedirle algo especial.

NOTA COMUNICATIVA

I wish I could . . . I wish they would . . .

There are many ways to express wishes in Spanish. As you know, one of the most common is **ojalá (que)**. Used alone, **¡Ojalá!** means *I hope so!* It can also be used with the present or past subjunctive to mean *I hope . . . !* or *I wish . . .*

¡Ojala (que) la guerra **acabe** pronto!	*I hope (that) the war will be over soon!*

The past subjunctive following **ojalá** is one of the most frequent uses of those verb forms. Here **ojalá** expresses *I wish*.

Ojalá (que) pudiera acompañarlos, pero no es posible.	*I wish (that) I could go with you, but it's not possible.*

C. ¡Ojalá! Complete las oraciones lógicamente.

1. Ojalá que (yo) tuviera _____.
2. Ojalá que pudiera _____.
3. Ojalá inventaran una máquina que _____.
4. Ojalá solucionaran el problema de _____.
5. Ojalá que en esta universidad fuera posible _____.

LITERATURA: Manuel del Cabral

Sobre el autor: *Manuel del Cabral nació en Santiago de los Caballeros, República Dominicana. Estudió derecho,[a] pero prefirió escribir. También sirvió de diplomático de la República Dominicana en Nueva York y en varios países latinoamericanos. En su poesía aparece el tema del negro caribeño. Murió en Santo Domingo en 1999. El siguiente poema, «Sobre el agua», es de la colección* Color de agua *(1932).*

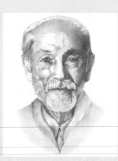

Manuel del Cabral
(1907–1999)

Agua tan pura que casi
no se ve en el vaso de agua.

Del otro lado está el mundo.
De este lado, casi nada...

Un agua pura, tan limpia
que da trabajo mirarla.

AGUA

La del río, ¡qué blanda![b]
Pero qué dura[c] es ésta:
¡La que cae de los párpados[d]
es un agua que piensa!

[a]*law* [b]*soft* [c]*hard* [d]*eyelids*

MÚSICA: El merengue

El merengue es la música y danza nacional de la República Dominicana. El festival del Merengue se celebra en Santo Domingo las dos últimas semanas de julio.

el güiro

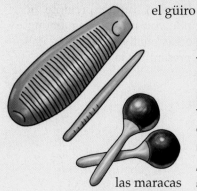

las maracas

Dos de los instrumentos típicos del merengue son las maracas y el güiro.[a] El acordeón o el saxofón típicamente acompaña el ritmo animado del merengue.

[a]*rasping percussion instrument, often made from a gourd*

Juan Luis Guerra es un compositor y cantante del merengue. Promueve[b] las tradiciones musicales de su país y también usa su música para hacer crítica social. Su canción «El costo de la vida» es una protesta contra la pobreza[c] de los países latinoamericanos. Ha ganado muchos premios, incluso[d] tres Grammy Latinos en 2000 por su álbum *Ni es lo mismo ni es igual*.

[b]*He promotes* [c]*poverty* [d]*including*

En los Estados Unidos y el Canadá

Los medios de comunicación en español

A la creciente[a] población hispánica (más de 40 millones) en los Estados Unidos se le ofrece[b] cada vez **más variedad en los mundos del entretenimiento[c] y la información.** Hoy día se puede comprar la revista *People en español* en cualquier lugar del país donde haya población hispanohablante. *Latin Trade,* una revista de economía y comercio que cubre los intereses de toda Latinoamérica, también tiene un ámbito[d] nacional.

Las ciudades con una gran concentración de hispanos tienen sus **propios periódicos en español.** Algunos de los muchos son el *Diario de las Américas* y el *Nuevo Herald* de Miami, *LA Opinión* de Los Ángeles, *La Prensa* de Minnesota, *La Semana* de Boston, *La Raza* de Chicago y *El Canillita* de Connecticut. Muchas ciudades tienen hasta varias[e] estaciones de radio y televi-

Unas publicaciones hispánicas en Nueva York

sión, como WSKQ-FM, WPAT-FM y WXTV-TV en Nueva York y KLEY-FM y KWEX-TV en San Antonio. El grupo Televisa es **la empresa más grande de medios de comunicación,** con participación en programas de televisión, revistas, servicios de televisión por satélite y por cable, radio, etcétera. **La cadena[f] de televisión** Univisión es **la más popular en los Estados Unidos,** con una difusión del 97 por ciento de los hogares[g] hispanos.

Últimamente,[h] **la televisión satelital** ha añadido aun[i] más opciones a la oferta de entretenimientos para los hispanohablantes. A través de ella[j] no sólo se pueden ver las cadenas más famosas de México y los Estados Unidos, como Univisión, Telefutura y CNN en español, sino que se ven canales de toda Hispanoamérica y España.

[a]*growing* [b]*se... is offered* [c]*entertainment* [d]*market* [e]*hasta... as many as several* [f]*channel* [g]*residences* [h]*Lately* [i]*even* [j]*A... Through it*

UN POCO DE TODO

Lengua y cultura: Maneras de practicar el español fuera (*outside of*) **de clase**

Complete the following dialogue with the correct form of the words in parentheses, as suggested by the context. When two possibilities are given in parentheses, select the correct word.

¡OJO! When you conjugate verbs in this activity, you will often have to decide whether to use the subjunctive mood (present, present perfect, or past) or the indicative mood (present, present perfect, future, preterite, or imperfect). The context of the passage will guide you in choosing among the indicative verb tenses, and you will also occasionally see clues in italics to show you which tense to use. Start in the present tense.

Claro está que Ud. habla español en clase. También es probable que lo (hablar[1]) con su profesor(a) cada vez que lo/la (ver[2]) en el *campus*. Pero (por/para[3]) hablar español con soltura[a] Ud. tiene que practicar (tanto/más[4]).

«¡Ojalá que (*yo: poder*[5]) practicar español fuera de clase!» ¿(*pres. perf., Decir*[6]) Ud. eso alguna vez? Pues hay muchas maneras de hacerlo. Por ejemplo, los compañeros y compañeras de una misma clase de español siempre pueden hablar español cuando (verse[7]) para no (perder[8]) (ninguno[9]) oportunidad de (practicar[10]).

Pero hablar con los compañeros de estudio no es lo (único/unica[11]) que un estudiante puede hacer fuera de clase. Es buena idea que (*Ud.: mirar*[12]) la televisión o (escuchar[13]) la radio en español. ¿(Qué/Cuál[14]) programa? Realmente (ese/eso[15]) no importa: se puede mirar una telenovela[b] o escuchar (un/una[16]) programa de noticias. Lo importante es (dedicar[17]) un rato[c] a escuchar español auténtico con frecuencia. Muchas personas (encontrar[18]) muy frustrante esta actividad (por qué/porque[19]) no pueden comprenderlo todo. Hay que recordar que no es necesario (entender[20]) cada palabra que se oye. Para los estudiantes principiantes[d] es suficiente identificar el tema y (alguno[21]) palabras o expresiones. Si Ud. escucha español habitualmente en los medios de comunicación, seguro que (*fut., aprender*[22]) mucho… y rápidamente.

Otra actividad útil es leer el periódico o una revista de actualidad en español. Puesto que[e] hay muchos hispanohablantes en este país, es relativamente fácil (seguir/conseguir[23]) algo que leer en español en muchos lugares. Y si esto no es fácil en el lugar donde Ud. vive, (*comm., Ud.: buscar*[24]) en el Internet; en (el/la[25]) Red hay miles de páginas con información de todo tipo en español. Por ejemplo, si le gusta viajar, (*comm., Ud.: consultar*[26]) las páginas relacionadas con el turismo en los países donde se habla español.

Finalmente, (*comm., Ud.: recordar*[27]) su propia comunidad. Es muy posible que Ud. (vivir[28]) en una ciudad o estado en que (hay/haya[29]) una comunidad hispana. Si hay una comunidad hispana, entonces[f] (*fut., tener*[30]) restaurantes y tiendas. ¿(Porque/Por qué[31]) no visita una de esas tienda o supermercados hispanos para que (*Ud.: ver*[32]) las cosas que se venden allí? ¡Leer una lista de ingredientes en cualquier producto es ya[g] un ejercicio de lectura!

El noticiero de un canal de televisión en San Antonio, Texas

[a]hablar… *speak Spanish fluently* [b]*soap opera* [c]*un… a bit of time* [d]*beginning* [e]*Puesto… Since* [f]*then* [g]*actually*

Comprensión. Conteste las preguntas en español.

1. Además de hablar español con sus compañeros en clase, ¿qué otras opciones tiene Ud. para practicar el idioma fuera de la clase?
2. ¿Es buena o mala la idea de mirar la televisión en español? ¿Qué tipo de programas se recomienda ver?
3. ¿Es necesario que un estudiante entienda cada palabra de lo que oye o mira en los medios de comunicación en español?
4. ¿Qué tipo de lecturas puede Ud. conseguir en español para practicar más?
5. ¿Qué posibilidades de hablar español existen en la mayoría de las comunidades? ¿Existen en la de Ud. (*yours*)?

Resources for Review and Testing Preparation

- Workbook/Laboratory Manual
- Interactive CD-ROM
- Online Learning Center (www.mhhe.com/quetal7)

VIDEOTECA

Entrevista cultural: La República Dominicana

Una estudiante dominicana, Milstry del Orbe, habla de la carrera profesional que quiere seguir. Además, comenta los problemas del mundo contemporáneo que ella considera más graves. Antes de ver el vídeo, lea el siguiente fragmento de la entrevista.

ENTREVISTADORA: ¿Por qué te interesa esa carrera?

MILSTRY: Creo que es muy importante poder informar a la gente, a la juventud,[a] de lo que acontece[b] en otros… en otros países en el momento y en el lugar exacto de donde… de donde ocurre.

ENTREVISTADORA: ¿Cuáles son los problemas mundiales más graves hoy en día?

MILSTRY: Pues hoy en día considero que hay muchísimos problemas graves, entre ellos problemas de enfermedades como el SIDA,[c] que todavía no se le ha podido encontrar cura. Problemas de terrorismo, problemas de medio ambiente, destrucción del medio ambiente.

[a]*young people* [b]*happens* [c]*AIDS*

Ahora vea el vídeo y conteste las siguientes preguntas basándose en la entrevista.

1. ¿Qué estudia Milstry?
2. ¿Por qué ha escogido esta profesión?
3. Según Milstry, ¿cuál es uno de los problemas graves en el mundo de hoy? ¿Y otro de los problemas?

Entre amigos: ¡Por eso sí protestaría!

Tané, Karina, Rubén y Miguel hablan de las manifestaciones y las protestas. En su opinión, ¿qué van a decir sobre estos temas? Antes de mirar el vídeo, lea las preguntas a continuación. Mientras mire el vídeo, trate de entender la conversación en general y fíjese en la información sobre las manifestaciones y protestas. Luego mire el vídeo una segunda vez, fijándose en la información que necesita para contestar las preguntas.

1. ¿De dónde viene Miguel con la pancarta (*banner*)?
2. ¿Por qué va a protestar Tané?
3. ¿Por qué no va a protestar Karina?
4. ¿Por qué protestaría (*would protest*) Rubén?
5. Al final, ¿qué sugiere hacer Tané?

ENFOQUE CULTURAL

 La República Dominicana

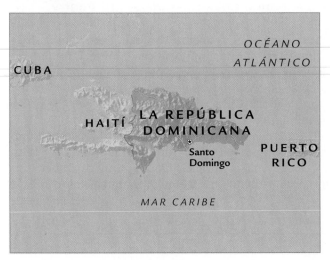

¡Fíjese!

- España le cedió[a] a Francia, en 1697, el tercio occidental[b] de La Española. Por esta razón, este territorio, el actual país de Haití, tiene una cultura y un idioma diferentes a los de la República Dominicana.
- El merengue es el baile nacional de la República Dominicana. Hay dos leyendas sobre el origen del baile. Según la primera leyenda, el baile se originó entre los esclavos que tenían que arrastrar[c] una pierna porque la tenían encadenada[d] con la pierna de otro esclavo. La segunda leyenda atribuye el baile a un héroe que regresó de una batalla con una pierna herida. El pueblo, para mostrar su empatía, bailó durante las celebraciones cojeando[e] y arrastrando un pie. En Santo Domingo se celebra el Festival del Merengue, diez días de música, bailes, espectáculos, ferias y festejos en las calles.

El Convento Dominico en Santo Domingo

[a]*ceded* [b]*tercio... western third* [c]*drag* [d]*chained* [e]*limping*

Lugares famosos: Santo Domingo

La ciudad de Santo Domingo fue fundada en 1496 por Bartolomé Colón, hermano de Cristóbal Colón. Esta capital, establecida a orillas del río Ozama y el mar Caribe, es la primera ciudad europea del Hemisferio Occidental. La zona original de Santo Domingo se conoce como la Ciudad Colonial y está rodeada[a] de antiguos muros.[b] La UNESCO designó a Santo Domingo como la cuna[c] de la civilización europea en América, porque es aquí donde se encuentra la primera catedral del Nuevo Mundo, así como el primer monasterio, el primer hospital, la primera universidad, los primeros palacios de estilo europeo y la primera corte de justicia. A Santo Domingo también se le llamaba la Atenas[d] del Nuevo Mundo por la actividad intelectual que había en la universidad y otras instituciones.

En 1992, la UNESCO designó la Ciudad Colonial Patrimonio de la Humanidad[e] por sus riquezas arquitectónicas e históricas que datan del siglo XVI. Las imponentes casas e iglesias de piedra fueron cuidadosamente colocadas[f] en forma octogonal. El plan de la ciudad fue diseñado y trazado[g] en 1502 y sirvió de patrón[h] para otras ciudades establecidas por los españoles en el Nuevo Mundo. Hoy por muchas de las calles de la Ciudad Colonial se encuentran pintorescos cafés y bares, pequeños hoteles y conocidos restaurantes, discotecas y tiendas.

[a]*surrounded* [b]*walls* [c]*cradle, birthplace* [d]*Athens* [e]*Patrimonio... World Heritage Site* [f]*placed* [g]*laid out* [h]*model*

Learn more about the Dominican Republic with the Video, the Interactive CD-ROM, and the Online Learning Center (www.mhhe.com/quetal7).

PASO FINAL

A LEER

ESTRATEGIA: Using Language Cues to Understand Poetry

Part of the meaning of a poem can be conveyed through grammatical structures. The particular grammatical forms in a poem can convey information or contribute to its unique mood. For example, a poem written primarily in the imperfect may convey a sense of timelessness or of things recurring in the poet's personal history. The use of the preterite may give you the feeling that the moment was fleeting, perhaps all too fleeting.

As you read the following poem, note the instances of the past subjunctive that you have learned in this chapter. Why do you think the poet chose this form? What or how does it make you feel? Do you think the poem would be different if the poet had chosen a different grammatical form?

Cubanita descubanizada

Cubanita descubanizada
quién te pudiera recubanizar.
Quién supiera devolverte
el ron[a] y la palma,[b]
el alma y el son.[c]

Cubanita descubanizada,
tú que pronuncias todas las eses*
y dices ómnibus[d] y autobús
quién te pudiera
quién te supiera
si te quisieras recubanizar.

[a]*rum* [b]*palm tree* [c]*el... the soul and the sound (the* son *is also a popular Cuban dance)* [d]*synonym for* autobús *(the author is referring to the rich lexical variety that exists in Cuban Spanish, but that in this case signals a departure from its local, rural roots)*

---

*In general, Cuban Spanish is characterized by a lack of pronunciation of the letter **s** when found in certain positions within a word.*

Comprensión

A. Definiciones. El autor toma libertades poéticas en su poema e inventa palabras que sirven para expresar sus ideas. Con un compañero / una compañera, trate de definir las siguientes palabras inventadas por Pérez Firmat. Comparen sus definiciones con las de otra persona en la clase.

- descubanizada
- recubanizar

B. Interpretación. ¿Cuál cree Ud. que es el punto de vista del narrador del poema? ¿Tiene una actitud positiva hacia la vida en el extranjero? ¿Qué mensaje intenta expresar? ¿Qué elementos de la poesía comunican este mensaje?

A ESCRIBIR

A. ¿El bilingüismo o no? El tema de la inmigración es uno que provoca mucha reacción en este país. A continuación hay dos puntos de vista contrarios. Escoja una de estas posturas y escriba un breve informe en el que presenta y apoya su opinión.

1. El bilingüismo y el biculturalismo enriquecen la vida de este país.
2. Los inmigrantes a este país deben asimilarse por completo a la lengua, a la vida y a la cultura.

B. Una experiencia personal. Escriba una breve composición sobre la experiencia de inmigrar a los Estados Unidos o al Canadá. Puede escribir desde el punto de vista de un(a) pariente o un amigo / una amiga, o puede tomar la perspectiva de una persona imaginaria. Explique cuándo se inmigró, por qué y con quién. También incluya información sobre el lugar al que llegó, cómo se sentía en aquel entonces (*back then*) y cómo se siente ahora.

En resumen

GRAMÁTICA

To review the grammar points presented in this chapter, refer to the indicated grammar presentation. You'll find further practice of these structures in the Workbook/Laboratory Manual, on the Interactive CD-ROM, and on the *¿Qué tal?* Online Learning Center (www.mhhe.com/quetal7).

44 **¡No queríamos que fuera así!**—Past Subjunctive

You should know the forms of the past subjunctive and when to use it.

VOCABULARIO

Practice this vocabulary with digital flash cards on the Online Learning Center (www.mhhe.com/quetal7).

Las noticias

el acontecimiento	event, happening
el asesinato	assassination
el choque	collision
el desastre	disaster
la esperanza	hope, wish
la guerra	war
la huelga	strike (*labor*)
el medio de comunicación	means of communication
las noticias	(evening) news
el noticiero	newscast
la paz (*pl.* paces)	peace
la prensa	press; news media
el/la testigo	witness

Cognados: el ataque (terrorista), la bomba, la erupción, el evento, el/la reportero/a, el terrorismo, el/la terrorista, la víctima
Repaso: el canal, el mundo, el/la obrero/a

comunicarse (qu) (con)	to communicate (with)
enterarse (de)	to find out, learn (about)
informar	to inform
mantener (*irreg.*)	to maintain, keep

Repaso: ofrecer (zc), vivir

El gobierno y la responsabilidad cívica

el/la ciudadano/a	citizen
el deber	responsibility; obligation
el derecho	right
la (des)igualdad	(in)equality
el/la dictador(a)	dictator
la dictadura	dictatorship
la discriminación	discrimination
el ejército	army
la ley	law
la libertad	liberty, freedom
la política	politics
el/la político/a	politician
el rey / la reina	king/queen
el servicio militar	military service

Repaso: los/las demás, el gobierno

apoyar	to support
castigar (gu)	to punish
durar	to last
gobernar (ie)	to govern, rule
votar	to vote

Repaso: obedecer (zc)

En el extranjero°

°En... *Abroad*

La Giralda de Sevilla, España, una torre campanaria (bell tower) construida en 1184 como parte de una mezquita (mosque) musulmana

LUGARES Y COSAS EN EL EXTRANJERO

el champú
la pastelería
la farmacia
el jabón
la papelería
la oficina de correos
la pasta dental
el papel para cartas
el quiosco
el café
el paquete
el estanco
la parada del autobús
el correo
el sello
la tarjeta postal
el sobre

el batido	*drink similar to a milkshake*	**el fósforo**	match
una copa / un trago	drink (*alcoholic*)	**el pastelito**	small pastry
la estación del metro	subway stop	**la revista**	magazine

■ Conversación

A. **¿Cierto o falso?** Corrija las oraciones falsas. (Sugerencia: Lea primero la **Nota cultural** en la página 436.)

1. Se puede comprar batidos y pastelitos en una pastelería.
2. Si yo quisiera tomar una copa, iría (*I would go*) a un quiosco.
3. Se va a una papelería para mandar paquetes.
4. Es más rápido ir a pie que tomar el metro.
5. Se va a un café a comprar champú.
6. Si yo necesitara pasta dental, iría a la oficina de correos.
7. Se puede comprar fósforos en un estanco.
8. Un batido se hace con vino.

B. **En el extranjero.** Con un compañero / una compañera, conteste con oraciones completas.

1. ¿Dónde se compra el champú? ¿el jabón?
2. ¿Cuál es la diferencia entre una farmacia de este país y una farmacia en el extranjero?
3. ¿Dónde se puede comprar sellos? (dos lugares)
4. Si se necesitan cigarrillos o fósforos, ¿adónde se va?
5. ¿Qué es un quiosco? ¿Qué cosas se venden allí?
6. ¿Qué venden en una papelería?

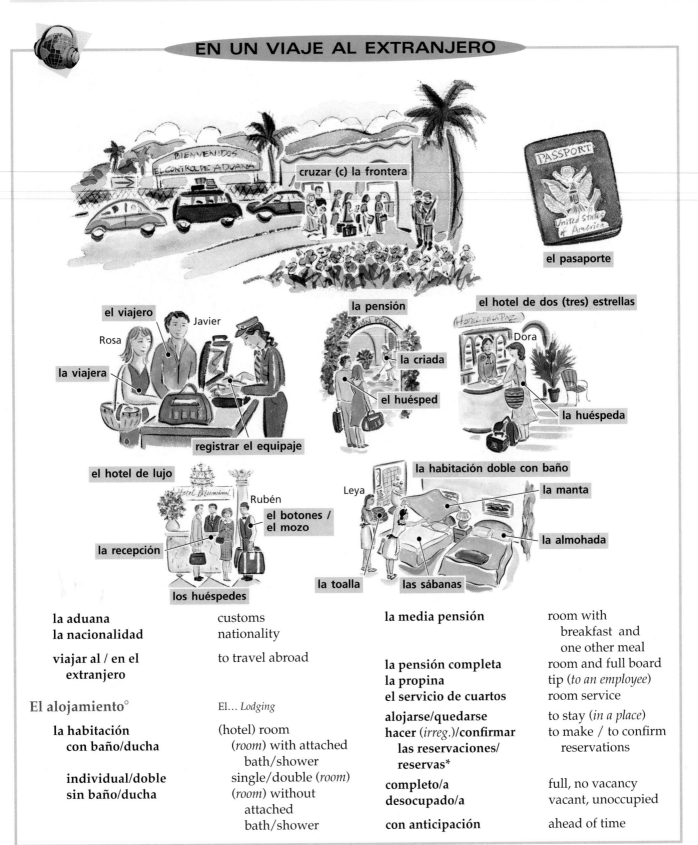

EN UN VIAJE AL EXTRANJERO

cruzar (c) la frontera

el pasaporte

el viajero
Rosa
Javier
la viajera
la criada
la pensión
el huésped
el hotel de dos (tres) estrellas
Dora
la huéspeda
registrar el equipaje

el hotel de lujo
Rubén
el botones / el mozo
la recepción
los huéspedes

Leya
la habitación doble con baño
la manta
la almohada
la toalla
las sábanas

la aduana	customs	**la media pensión**	room with breakfast and one other meal
la nacionalidad	nationality		
viajar al / en el extranjero	to travel abroad	**la pensión completa**	room and full board
		la propina	tip (*to an employee*)
		el servicio de cuartos	room service
El alojamiento°	El... *Lodging*	**alojarse/quedarse**	to stay (*in a place*)
la habitación	(hotel) room	**hacer** (*irreg.*)/**confirmar las reservaciones/ reservas***	to make / to confirm reservations
con baño/ducha	(*room*) with attached bath/shower		
individual/doble	single/double (*room*)	**completo/a**	full, no vacancy
sin baño/ducha	(*room*) without attached bath/shower	**desocupado/a**	vacant, unoccupied
		con anticipación	ahead of time

*****La reserva** is used in Spain for a reservation (for accommodations). **La reservación** is widely used in other parts of the Spanish-speaking world.

NOTA CULTURAL

De compras en el extranjero

Aunque^a **los nombres** de muchos lugares y tiendas del mundo hispánico **se parecen** a los de este país, **no siempre son iguales los productos** que en ellos se venden. Tome en cuenta sobre todo las siguientes diferencias.

- En **las farmacias** no venden la variedad de cosas —dulces, tarjetas postales, etcétera— que se venden en las farmacias de los EE.UU.* y el Canadá. Por lo general, sólo se venden medicinas y productos para **la higiene personal** como jabón, pasta dental, champú…
- En **los estancos**, además de productos tabacaleros, se venden **sellos**, así que^b uno no tiene que ir a una oficina de correos para comprarlos. También se venden **sobres** y **tarjetas postales** en los estancos.
- En **los quioscos** se vende una **gran variedad** de cosas: periódicos, revistas, libros, etcétera, pero también lápices, papel para cartas…

Un quiosco en Madrid, España

^a*Although*   ^basí… *so*

■ Conversación

A. Definiciones

PASO 1   Empareje las personas con la descripción apropiada.

1. _____ el huésped
2. _____ el recepcionista
3. _____ el botones
4. _____ la turista
5. _____ la inspectora de aduanas
6. _____ el viajero

a. la persona que nos ayuda con el equipaje en un hotel
b. la persona que se aloja en un hotel o una pensión
c. una persona que va de un lugar a otro
d. alguien que viaja para ver otros lugares
e. la persona que nos registra las maletas y toma la declaración en la aduana
f. la persona que nos atiende en la recepción de un hotel

PASO 2   Defina las siguientes palabras en español.

1. la aduana
2. el pasaporte
3. la pensión completa
4. la frontera
5. la propina
6. el formulario de inmigración

---

*EE.UU. is one way to abbreviate **Estados Unidos**. **E.U.** and **USA** are also used.*

B. En la aduana. ¿Ha viajado Ud. al extranjero? ¿Sabe Ud. lo que pasa en la aduana? Aunque (*Although*) no lo haya hecho, va a poder contestar las preguntas de esta actividad, pues se trata de (*it's a question of*) utilizar el sentido común. De las siguientes acciones, ¿cuáles pueden causar problemas en la aduana?

1. ☐ ser cortés con el inspector
2. ☐ no tener el pasaporte (o el visado necesario)
3. ☐ tener toallas de su hotel en las maletas
4. ☐ esconder (*hiding*) artículos de contrabando en su equipaje, con la esperanza que el inspector no los encuentre
5. ☐ quejarse del gobierno del país del inspector
6. ☐ intentar cruzar la frontera con un pasaporte falsificado
7. ☐ traficar en drogas
8. ☐ tratar de distraer al inspector mientras este (*he*) registra sus maletas

C. Cuando Ud. viaja...

PASO 1   Lea la lista de acciones típicas de los viajeros. ¿Hace Ud. lo mismo cuando viaja? Indique las acciones que son verdaderas para Ud.

1. ☐ Hago una reserva en un hotel con un mes de anticipación.
2. ☐ Confirmo la reserva antes de salir de viaje.
3. ☐ Voy al banco a conseguir cheques de viajero (*traveler's checks*).
4. ☐ Alquilo un coche.
5. ☐ Me alojo en un hotel de lujo.
6. ☐ Pido que el mozo me suba las maletas.
7. ☐ Llamo al servicio de cuartos en vez de comer en el restaurante.
8. ☐ Le dejo una propina a la criada el último día de mi estancia (*stay*).

PASO 2   Ahora piense en su último viaje. ¿Hizo Ud. las cosas de la lista del **Paso 1**? Conteste según el modelo y cambie los detalles de esas oraciones por los que en realidad ocurrieron en su viaje.

MODELO: La última vez que hice un viaje... →
           Hice una reserva en un hotel, pero con sólo dos días de anticipación.

D. Situaciones. Con un compañero / una compañera, haga el papel de un viajero / una viajera o del / de la recepcionista de un hotel.

PASO 1   El/La recepcionista le pregunta al viajero / a la viajera que acaba de llegar:

- si tiene una reserva
- cuánto tiempo piensa quedarse
- el tipo de habitación reservada o deseada
- la forma de pago

PASO 2   El huésped / La huéspeda pide los siguientes servicios:

- el desayuno en su cuarto
- más toallas/jabón
- información sobre lugares turísticos de interés

Need more practice?

- Workbook/Laboratory Manual
- Interactive CD-ROM
- Online Learning Center (www.mhhe.com/quetal7)

PASO 3   Por fin, el huésped / la huéspeda pasa por la recepción para pagar la cuenta. Encuentra los siguientes errores en su cuenta.

- Le cobraron por un desayuno que no tomó.
- Le cobraron por cuatro noches en vez de tres.
- Le cobraron por una llamada a larga distancia que nunca hizo.

¿Recuerda Ud.?

In **Gramática 42** you learned the forms and uses of the future tense. Can you provide the correct future forms of the following verbs?

1. (yo) viajar   **3.** (tú) ir   **5.** (nosotros) hacer
2. (ellos) beber   **4.** (Ud.) venir   **6.** (ella) poner

Review all of the future forms before studying the conditional tense in **Gramática 45.** Also note that you learned a conditional expression in **Capítulo 7: me gustaría(n).** What is the English equivalent of the following sentence?

Me gustaría visitar el museo esta tarde.

45 Expressing What You Would Do **Conditional Verb Forms**

La fantasía de Yolanda Torres-Luján

Yolanda es una mujer de negocios muy ocupada. Sufre muchas presiones y está muy cansada. Le *gustaría* ir de vacaciones.

«Con tres días de vacaciones, simplemente *dormiría* todo el día. No *haría* más que comer y dormir. Con una semana de vacaciones, *iría* a la playa, *tomaría* el sol todo el día y *tomaría* copas tropicales en bares elegantes. Con un mes de vacaciones... *descansaría* una semana en casa y luego *viajaría* por Europa.»

¿Y Ud.?

¿Sufre muchas presiones? ¿Le gustaría ir de vacaciones? ¿Qué haría en las vacaciones? Haga oraciones con las siguientes indicaciones. Use **no** cuando sea necesario.

MODELO: dormir todo el día → *Dormiría* todo el día.

1. ir a la playa
2. tomar el sol
3. tomar copas tropicales en bares elegantes

4. descansar una semana
5. viajar por Europa
6. ¿ ?

The fantasy of Yolanda Torres-Luján   Yolanda is a very busy businesswoman. She's under a lot of pressure, and she's very tired. She would like to go on vacation. "With three days of vacation, I would simply sleep all day. I wouldn't do anything but eat and sleep. With a week of vacation, I would go to the beach, sunbathe all day, and have tropical drinks in elegant bars. With a month of vacation . . . I would rest at home a week and then I would travel through Europe."

The phrase **me gustaría…** expresses what you *would like to* (do, say, and so on). **Gustaría** is a conditional verb form, part of a system that will allow you to talk about what you and others *would* (do, say, buy, and so on) in a given situation.

Past	Present	FUTURE
preterite	present indicative	future
imperfect	present progressive	conditional
present perfect	formal commands	
present perfect subjunctive	informal commands	
past subjunctive	present subjunctive	

A. Like the English future, the English conditional is formed with an auxiliary verb: *I would speak, I would write.*

The Spanish *conditional* (**el condicional**), like the Spanish future, is a simple verb form (only one word). It is formed by adding conditional endings to the infinitive. No auxiliary verbs are needed.

CONDITIONAL ENDINGS

-ía	-íamos
-ías	-íais
-ía	-ían

hablar		comer		vivir	
hablaría	hablaríamos	comería	comeríamos	viviría	viviríamos
hablarías	hablaríais	comerías	comeríais	vivirías	viviríais
hablaría	hablarían	comería	comerían	viviría	vivirían

B. Verbs that form the future on an irregular stem use the same stem to form the conditional.

Note that the conditional of **hay (haber)** is **habría** (*there would be*).*

decir: diría, dirías, diría, diríamos, diríais, dirían

decir:	dir-	
haber (hay):	habr-	
hacer:	har-	-ía
poder:	podr-	-ías
poner:	pondr-	-ía
querer:	querr-	-íamos
saber:	sabr-	-íais
salir:	saldr-	-ían
tener:	tendr-	
venir:	vendr-	

---

*The conditional forms of the verb **haber** are used to form the conditional perfect tense (**el condicional perfecto**), which expresses what would have occurred at some point in the past.

Habríamos tenido que buscarla en el aeropuerto.

*We **would have had** to pick her up at the airport.*

You will find a more detailed presentation of these forms in Appendix 3, Additional Perfect Forms (Indicative and Subjunctive).

C. The conditional expresses what you would do in a particular situation, given a particular set of circumstances.

—¿**Hablarías** español en el Brasil?
Would you speak Spanish in Brazil?

—No. **Hablaría** portugués.
No. I would speak Portuguese.

 When *would* implies *used to* in English, use the imperfect in Spanish.

Íbamos a la playa todos los veranos.
We would go (used to go) to the beach every summer.

■ **Práctica**

AUTOPRUEBA

Provide the missing letters for the following verbs in the conditional.

1. salir: sal____ía
2. hacer: ha____íamos
3. querer: que____ías
4. decir: d____ían
5. tener: ten____ía
6. poder: po____ía

Answers: 1. saldría 2. haríamos 3. querrías 4. dirían 5. tendría 6. podría

A. ¡Anticipemos! ¿Qué haría Ud.?

PASO 1   Imagine que hace un viaje a España. Complete las siguientes oraciones de manera que (*so that*) correspondan a la realidad y a lo que a Ud. le gustaría hacer. ¡Es una gran oportunidad de demostrarles a sus compañeros y a su profesor(a) su conocimiento (*knowledge*) sobre la vida y la cultura españolas!

1. Hablaría _____.
2. Comería _____ y bebería _____.
3. Iría a _____ y allí vería _____.
4. No podría irme sin antes visitar _____.
5. Me compraría _____.
6. Me divertiría mucho _____ (**Sugerencia:** Se puede usar un gerundio: **-iendo** o **-ando**.)

PASO 2   Claro que durante un viaje no sólo se hacen actividades culturales. Las oraciones a continuación muestran actividades típicas durante un viaje, pero Ud. debe completarlas con algunos detalles.

1. Yo haría el viaje a España con _____.
2. Tendría que sacar muchas fotos para mostrárselas a _____.
3. Le(s) mandaría tarjetas postales a _____.
4. Querría _____ durante el viaje, pero probablemente no lo haría.
5. Conocería a _____.

PASO 3   Ahora con un compañero / una compañera, haga una lista similar a las del **Paso 1** y el **Paso 2,** pero sobre otro país hispánico.

B. ¿Es posible escapar?   Cuente Ud. la fantasía de esta trabajadora social, dando la forma condicional de los verbos.

Necesito salir de todo esto... Creo que me (gustar[1]) ir a Puerto Rico o a algún otro lugar exótico del Caribe... No (trabajar[2])... (Poder[3]) nadar todos los días... (Tomar[4]) el sol en la playa... (Comer[5]) platos exóticos... (Ver[6]) bellos lugares naturales... El viaje (ser[7]) ideal...

   Pero..., tarde o temprano, (tener[8]) que volver a lo de siempre... a los rascacielos de la ciudad... al tráfico... al medio ambiente contaminado... al mundo del trabajo... (Poder[9]) usar mi tarjeta de crédito, como dice el anuncio —pero ¡(tener[10]) que pagar después!

Comprensión: ¿Cierto, falso o no lo dice? Corrija las oraciones falsas.

1. Esta persona trabaja en una ciudad grande.
2. No le interesan los deportes acuáticos.
3. Puede pagar este viaje de sueños (*dreams*) al contado.
4. Tiene un novio con quien quisiera hacer el viaje.

C. ¿Qué harías si pudieras?

PASO 1 Con un compañero / una compañera, haga y conteste preguntas según el modelo. Pueden cambiar los detalles, si quieren.

MODELO: estudiar árabe / japonés →
E1: ¿Estudiarías *árabe*?
E2: No. Estudiaría *japonés*.

1. estudiar italiano / chino
2. renunciar a un puesto sin avisar / con dos semanas de anticipación
3. hacer un viaje a España / la Argentina
4. salir de casa sin apagar el estéreo / las luces
5. seguir un presupuesto rígido / flexible
6. gastar menos en ropa / libros
7. poner el aire acondicionado en invierno / verano
8. alquilar un coche de lujo / económico

PASO 2 Ahora sigan con el mismo modelo, pero inventen las respuestas.

1. dejar de estudiar / ¿ ?
2. vivir en otra ciudad / ¿ ?
3. ser presidente/a de los Estados Unidos / primer ministro (primera ministra) del Canadá / ¿ ?
4. gustarle conocer a una persona famosa / ¿ ?

Need more practice?

- Workbook/Laboratory Manual
- Interactive CD-ROM
- Online Learning Center (www.mhhe.com/quetal7)

Conversación

A. Entrevista. ¿Cómo será su futuro? ¿Qué hará? ¿Qué haría? Con otro/a estudiante, haga y conteste las siguientes preguntas.

MODELO: E1: ¿Dejarás de fumar algún día? →
E2: No. No dejaré de fumar nunca. No puedo.
(Creo que sí. Dejaré de fumar algún día.)

PREGUNTAS CON EL FUTURO

1. ¿Te graduarás en esta universidad (o en otra)?
2. ¿Vivirás en esta ciudad después de graduarte?
3. ¿Buscarás un puesto aquí?
4. ¿Cuántos niños (nietos) crees que tendrás algún día?

PREGUNTAS CON EL CONDICIONAL

1. ¿Te casarías con una persona de otro país?
2. ¿Podrías estar contento/a sin la televisión?
3. ¿Serías capaz de (*capable of*) ahorrar el 10 por ciento de tu salario?
4. ¿Podrías vivir sin las tarjetas de crédito?

NOTA COMUNICATIVA

If I were you, I would . . .

Both English and Spanish use clauses to speculate about likely or unlikely situations. These are called *if* or **si** clauses.

- The present indicative after **si** presents a situation that is likely to occur. It is followed or preceded by a clause in the indicative or by a command.

  LIKELY

  Si **ahorro** suficiente dinero, **iré** de vacaciones a España.

  If I save enough money, I will go to Spain on vacation.

- The imperfect subjunctive after **si** introduces an unlikely event. The preceding or following clause includes a verb in the conditional.

  UNLIKELY

  Si **tuviera** dinero suficiente, le **daría** la vuelta al mundo.

  If I had enough money, I would go around the world.

B. Circunstancias. Con un compañero / una compañera, haga y conteste preguntas según los modelos.

PASO 1 ¿Qué haces si... ?

MODELO: ¿Qué haces si... ? / haces tu maleta para un viaje pero no toda la ropa que deseas llevar cabe (*fits*) en la maleta →
E1: ¿Qué haces si haces tu maleta para un viaje pero no toda la ropa que deseas llevar cabe en la maleta?
E2: Si hago mi maleta pero no toda la ropa cabe en la maleta, trato de llevar menos ropa / busco una maleta más grande.

¿Qué haces si... ?

1. tu primera clase es a las nueve de la mañana y te despiertas a las 8:50
2. tu mejor amigo/a (novio/a, esposo/a, hijo/a) tiene un resfriado muy fuerte
3. es viernes por la noche y no tienes ningún plan para divertirte esa noche
4. se te pierde la llave de tu cuarto/casa

PASO 2 ¿Qué harías si... ?

MODELO: ¿Qué harías si... ? / en una lotería ganaras un viaje al extranjero a cualquier (*any*) país del mundo →
E1: ¿Qué harías si en una lotería ganaras un viaje al extranjero a cualquier país del mundo?
E2: Si en una lotería ganara un viaje al extranjero a cualquier país del mundo, tendría que decidirme entre España y el Perú. Primero, buscaría información en el Internet.

¿Qué harías si... ?

1. alguien te dejara una herencia (*inheritance*) de dos millones de dólares
2. pudieras hacer lo que quisieras en este momento
3. tuvieras un solo (*single*) deseo para todo el mundo
4. pudieras dar la fiesta de tus sueños (*dreams*)

Voces de España

LITERATURA: Juan Ramón Jiménez

Sobre el autor: *Juan Ramón Jiménez nació en Moguer, en la provincia de Andalucía, España. Estudió derecho,[a] pero se interesó más en la poesía y la pintura. Llegó a ser un poeta prolífico, y escribió varios libros. Le otorgaron[b] el Premio Nóbel de Literatura en 1956. El siguiente poema, «El viaje definitivo», es del libro de poesías* Canción *(1936).*

Juan Ramón Jiménez
(1881–1958)
y su esposa Zenobia

El viaje definitivo

Y yo me iré. Y se quedarán los pájaros
cantando;
y se quedará mi huerto,[c] con su verde árbol,
y con su pozo[d] blanco.

Todas las tardes, el cielo será azul y plácido;
y tocarán, como esta tarde están tocando,
las campanas del campanario.[e]

Se morirán aquellos que me amaron;
y el pueblo se hará nuevo cada año;
y en el rincón[f] aquel de mi huerto florido y encalado,[g]
mi espíritu errará,[h] nostálgico…

Y yo me iré; y estaré solo, sin hogar,[i] sin árbol
verde, sin pozo blanco,
sin cielo azul y plácido…
Y se quedarán los pájaros cantando.

[a]*law* [b]*they awarded* [c]*jardín* [d]*well* [e]*campanas… bells of the bell tower* [f]*corner* [g]*whitewashed* [h]*will wander* [i]*home*

MÚSICA: Los romances

El romance es una canción narrativa que trata aventuras, amores y lamentaciones líricas. Esta forma oral de la Edad Media[a] se cantaba en todas partes de España, para propagar[b] noticias, recordar la historia, celebrar eventos y entretener.[c]

El Quarteto Medieval de Urueña se dedica a la interpretación de la música antigua de España.

El prisionero

Que por mayo era, por mayo,
cuando hace la calor,
cuando los trigos encañan[d]
y están los campos en flor,

cuando canta la calandria[e]
y responde el ruiseñor,[f]
cuando los enamorados
van a servir al amor;

sino yo,[g] triste, cuitado,[h]
que vivo en esta prisión;
que no sé cuándo es de día
ni cuándo las noches son,

sino[i] por una avecilla[j]
que me canta al albor.[k]
Matómela un ballestero;[l]
déle Dios mal galardón.[m]

[a]*Edad… Middle Ages (roughly spanning from the fifth through the fifteenth centuries)* [b]*spread* [c]*entertain* [d]*cuando… when the wheat forms stalks* [e]*lark (bird)* [f]*nightingale* [g]*sino… but not I* [h]*forlorn* [i]*except* [j]*little bird* [k]*dawn* [l]*Matómela… A crossbowman shot it* [m]*reward*

Ziryab fue innovador de instrumentos como el laúd, un ancestro de la guitarra española. Nació en lo que hoy es Irak, se trasladó[n] a España en el siglo[o] IX y llegó a ser[p] una figura muy importante en la fusión de varios aspectos de las culturas ibérica y árabe, incluyendo la música.

[n]*se… moved* [o]*century* [p]*llegó… became*

En los Estados Unidos y el Canadá

Churrísimo

¿Sabe Ud. qué son **los churros**? Son **pedacitos de masa**[a] **frita** que se comen solos con azúcar o mojados[b] en el café o el chocolate caliente. Son originarios **de España**, pero se encuentran **por toda Latinoamérica**. Y ahora también se pueden conseguir en el Canadá, gracias a la cadena[c] Churrísimo.

El dueño de la cadena es Moses Bendayan, un venezolano-canadiense de origen sefardí. **Los sefardíes** son descendientes de los judíos que vivieron en España hasta el siglo[d] XVI. En la cultura sefardí todavía se conservan las tradiciones culinarias de la época de su vida

Churros y chocolate

española, y su lengua es una mezcla de hebreo con español.

Según el Sr. Bendayan, los churros son **exitosos**[e] en el Canadá por dos **razones principales**: a los canadienses les gustan mucho **las meriendas y comidas entre horas**, y **el chocolate caliente** —el compañero por excelencia de los churros— **es ideal en su clima frío**. Además,[f] el Sr. Bendayan señala[g] que el mercado norteamericano anglosajón es un público con curiosidad por los gustos[h] nuevos, y tiene en la actualidad[i] un interés especial en todo lo hispano. ¡Que los disfruten![j]

[a]pedacitos… *little pieces of dough* [b]*dunked*
[c]*(restaurant) chain* [d]*century* [e]*successful* [f]*In addition*
[g]*notes* [h]*tastes* [i]en… *currently* [j]¡Que… *Enjoy them!*

UN POCO DE TODO

Lengua y cultura: Un viaje por España.   Complete the following passages with the correct forms of the words in parentheses, as suggested by the context. When two possibilities are given in parentheses, select the correct word. **¡OJO!** As you conjugate verbs in this activity, sometimes you will have to decide which mood (subjunctive or indicative) and tense to use according to context.

Seguro que a Ud. le interesa conocer España algún día. Cuando (ir[1]) Ud. a España por primera vez, ¿qué (*cond.,* deber[2]) visitar? Una pregunta difícil de contestar, porque (es/hay[3]) una inmensa cantidad de lugares recomendables. Todo depende de lo que le guste (a/—[4]) Ud. y del tiempo que (tener[5]).

(Por/Para[6]) empezar, España es tan grande (que/como[7]) Texas, y eso quiere decir que las distancias de un punto a otro del país (ser/estar[8]) considerables. Recuerde que en España hay muestras[a] de su rica y antiquísima[b] historia de más de 2.000 años (por/para[9]) todas partes del país. Finalmente, a causa de la diversidad cultural y geográfica del país, cada región parece (ser[10]) un país diferente. España tiene las montañas más altas (de/que[11]) Europa, después de los Alpes; islas en el Mediterráneo y en la costa africana; una región celta; una gran zona que muestra la larga influencia musulmana[c] en el pasado; una zona desértica; zonas de (gran/grande[12]) actividad agrícola y miles de kilómetros de costa de todo tipo. ¡Es imposible que alguien no (encontrar[13]) (algo/algún[14]) de su interés!

[a]*examples* [b]*very old* [c]*Islamic*

El otro día (le/se[15]) pedimos a una (español/ española[16]), Patricia, que nos (recomendar[17]) un itinerario para un (primer/primero[18]) viaje a España. Nos (*ella:* sugerir[19]) que antes de todo (*nosotros:* escoger[20])[d] el clima que preferimos (fresco o caluroso), el tipo de paisaje (más o menos urbano, en las montañas o donde hay playa). Después nos aseguró que no (*ella:* conocer/saber[21]) a (nadie/alguien[22]) que no (pensar[23]) que España es un país interesante y (muy/mucho[24]) bello. Otro español, Jesús, (nos/—[25]) (decir[26]) que, (por/para[27]) él, es importante (pasar[28]) tiempo suficiente en los lugares que se visitan; cree que no (ser[29]) bueno ver demasiados lugares en poco tiempo. Por eso, él nos recomienda que no (*nosotros:* tratar[30]) (a/de[31]) ver media España en una semana o diez días, sino que[e] (escoger[32]) una zona del país para conocer(lo/la[33]) bien.

Un puerto en Palma de Mallorca, en las Islas Baleares

¿Tiene Ud. ahora una idea de lo que le (gustar[34]) ver en España?

[d]*to choose* [e]*sino... but rather that*

Comprensión.   Las siguientes oraciones son falsas. Corríjalas.

1. En España, hay pocos lugares recomendables para los turistas.
2. España es un país recién fundado.
3. Todas las regiones de España se parecen; no hay diferencia entre ellas.
4. Los árabes vivieron en España, pero sin gran impacto cultural.
5. España casi no tiene costas.
6. A las personas que conoce Patricia, les parece que España es un país muy aburrido.
7. Jesús recomienda verlo todo... ¡y muy rápidamente!

Resources for Review and Testing Preparation

- Workbook/Laboratory Manual
- Interactive CD-ROM
- Online Learning Center (www.mhhe.com/quetal7)

PASO 4 Un paso más

VIDEOTECA

Entrevista cultural: España

Margarita Durán es una española que trabaja en el negocio de su familia. En esta entrevista, habla del negocio y de los clientes. Antes de ver el vídeo, lea el siguiente fragmento de la entrevista.

ENTREVISTADORA: ¿De dónde vienen sus huéspedes?

MARGARITA: Por lo general nuestros huéspedes vienen de muchas partes del mundo. Generalmente predominan los alemanes; también tenemos ingleses, franceses y muchos norteamericanos. Eh, las parejas jóvenes son nuestros huéspedes más frecuentes, y eh, normalmente ellos nos solicitan habitaciones que den aᵃ la ciudad, que tengan una vista bonita pero que al mismo tiempo sean tranquilas, y esto para nosotros es una contradicción, porque todas las habitaciones que dan a la calle siempre van a tener algún ruido.

ᵃden... *open to, overlook*

Ahora vea el vídeo y conteste las siguientes preguntas basándose en la entrevista.

1. ¿De dónde es Margarita?
2. ¿Cuál es el negocio de su familia?
3. ¿Cuáles son las responsabilidades de los miembros de la familia?
4. ¿Quiénes son los clientes, generalmente?
5. ¿Qué opinión tiene Margarita de su trabajo? ¿Por qué?

Entre amigos: Tengo mi pasaje a San Francisco.

Miguel, Karina, Rubén y Tané hablan de las vacaciones. En su opinión, ¿qué van a decir sobre este tema? Antes de mirar el vídeo, lea las preguntas a continuación. Mientras mire el vídeo, trate de entender la conversación en general y fíjese en la información sobre las vacaciones y los arreglos (*arrangements*). Luego mire el vídeo una segunda vez, fijándose en la información que necesita para contestar las preguntas.

1. ¿Para qué necesita Rubén folletos (*brochures*) de viaje?
2. ¿Adónde piensa ir de vacaciones Miguel? ¿Ha decidido?
3. ¿Qué sugiere Karina que busquen en un hotel? Y Rubén, ¿qué sugiere?
4. ¿Qué ha comprado Tané?
5. ¿Qué le sugiere Miguel a Tané?

ENFOQUE CULTURAL

 España

¡Fíjese!

- España es un país donde muchas culturas se han encontrado a través de[a] la historia. Sin embargo fueron los romanos los que marcaron el principio de la historia de la España que hoy conocemos, pues ellos introdujeron el latín a la península durante su dominio (desde el año 200 a.C.[b] hasta la invasión de los visigodos, un pueblo germánico, en el 419 d.C.[c]).
- El latín es la lengua madre del español y también del catalán, el gallego y el portugués. La otra lengua que se habla en la península, el vasco, es una lengua ancestral de origen desconocido: ni siquiera es[d] una lengua indoeuropea.
- España no fue siempre un solo país. De hecho,[e] España se unificó en el siglo XV cuando los Reyes Católicos, Isabel y Fernando, monarcas de dos reinos[f] independientes, se casaron. Su campaña[g] de unificación terminó en 1492 con la conquista del reino musulmán[h] de Granada.
- Los árabes vivieron en España durante ocho siglos, hasta su expulsión, junto con los judíos, en el año 1492.

[a]a... *throughout*   [b]a.C.... *antes de Cristo*   [c]d.C.... *después de Cristo*
[d]ni... *it is not even*   [e]De... *In fact*   [f]*kingdoms*   [g]*campaign*   [h]*Moslem*

Personas famosas: Pedro Almodóvar

Las películas del cineasta[a] Pedro Almodóvar (1951–) han tenido y siguen teniendo un éxito enorme dentro y fuera de España, y Almodóvar es el director de cine español más conocido de las últimas décadas. Con temas que satirizan actitudes tradicionales respecto a la familia, la religión, el machismo y la moralidad convencional, sus películas presentan una sociedad española moderna y cambiante.[b]

Muchas de sus películas se pueden conseguir en las bibliotecas públicas y universitarias, así como en los videoclubs de este país: *Mujeres al borde de un ataque de nervios, La ley del deseo, ¿Qué he hecho yo para merecer esto?, ¡Átame!,*[c] *Kika, La flor de mi secreto, Todo sobre mi madre* y *Hable con ella.* Las útimas dos fueron ganadoras del Óscar: *Todo sobre mi madre* para la mejor película extranjera (1999) y *Hable con ella* para el mejor guión[d] original (2002).

[a]*director de cine*   [b]*changing*   [c]*Tie Me Up! Tie Me Down!*   [d]*screenplay*

El escudo (shield) *de Fernando e Isabel*

Learn more about Spain with the Video, the Interactive CD-ROM, and the Online Learning Center (www.mhhe.com/quetal7).

PASO FINAL

A CONVERSAR

Improvisación turística

Si Ud. viaja a un país hispanohablante algún día, tendrá la oportunidad de hablar español. Imagine que Ud. es turista en un país hispanohablante. ¿Qué diría en las siguientes situaciones?

PASO 1 Formen grupos de tres o cuatro personas. Escojan una de las siguientes situaciones para improvisar. Lean la situación y escriban en una hoja de papel aparte un esquema (*outline*) de la improvisación.

> MODELO: en el aeropuerto → saludarse; pedir los pasaportes; preguntar y contestar por qué vienen a este país...

Lugar	Situación	Personajes (*Characters*)
En el aeropuerto	pasar por el control de pasaportes y por la aduana	uno o dos turistas, el/la agente que revisa los pasaportes, el/la agente de aduana
En el hotel	pedir una habitación y pedirle al botones que lleve las maletas a la habitación	uno o dos turistas, el/la recepcionista del hotel, el botones
En la calle	pedirles direcciones a algunas personas	uno o dos turistas, las personas del grupo

PASO 2 Cada miembro del grupo debe escoger un personaje y prepararse para la improvisación, haciendo apuntes sobre las posibles preguntas que necesitará hacer y contestar.

> MODELO: agente de aduana → preguntarles si tienen algo que declarar; preguntarles si llevan plantas o productos orgánicos...

PASO 3 Improvisen la escena varias veces, modificándola si es necesario. Luego, presenten su escena improvisada a la clase.

> MODELO: E1: Sus pasaportes, por favor. Gracias. ¿De dónde vienen?
> E2: Venimos de los Estados Unidos.
> E1: ¿Y por qué vienen a México?
> E3: Estamos de vacaciones. Vamos a ir a la playa...

GRAMÁTICA

To review the grammar points presented in this chapter, refer to the indicated grammar presentation. You'll find further practice of these structures in the Workbook/Laboratory Manual, on the Interactive CD-ROM, and on the *¿Qué tal?* Online Learning Center (www.mhhe.com/quetal7).

45 Expressing What You Would Do—Conditional Verb Forms

Do you know how to form the conditional tense? When would you use the conditional in Spanish?

VOCABULARIO

Practice this vocabulary with digital flash cards on the Online Learning Center (www.mhhe.com/quetal7).

Lugares y cosas en el extranjero

el batido	*drink similar to a milkshake*
el champú	shampoo
una copa	drink (*alcoholic*)
el correo	mail
la oficina de correos	post office
la estación del metro	subway stop
el estanco	tobacco stand/shop
el fósforo	match
el jabón	soap
el papel para cartas	stationery
la papelería	stationery store
el paquete	package
la parada del autobús	bus stop
la pasta dental	toothpaste
la pastelería	pastry shop
el pastelito	small pastry
el quiosco	kiosk
el sello	(postage) stamp
el sobre	envelope
un trago	drink (*alcoholic*)

Cognado: el café
Repaso: la farmacia, la revista, la tarjeta postal

En un viaje al extranjero

la aduana	customs
el cheque de viajero	traveler's check
el extranjero	abroad
el formulario	form (*to fill out*)
la frontera	border
el/la viajero/a	traveler

Cognados: la nacionalidad, el pasaporte
Repaso: el equipaje

cruzar (c)	to cross
registrar	to search, examine

Repaso: viajar

El alojamiento

la almohada	pillow
el alojamiento	lodging
el botones	bellhop
la criada	maid
la estancia	stay (*in a place*)
la habitación	(hotel) room
con baño/ducha	(*room*) with attached bath/shower
individual/doble	single/double (*room*)
sin baño/ducha	(*room*) without attached bath/shower
el hotel (de lujo)	(luxury) hotel
el hotel de dos (tres) estrellas	two (three) star hotel
el/la huésped(a)	(hotel) guest
la manta	blanket
el mozo	bellhop
la pensión	boardinghouse
pensión completa	room and full board
media pensión	room with breakfast and one other meal
la propina	tip (*to an employee*)
la recepción	front desk
las reservas	reservations
las sábanas	sheets
el servicio de cuartos	room service
la toalla	towel

Cognado: las reservaciones

alojarse	to stay (*in a place*)
confirmar	to confirm

Repaso: quedarse

completo/a	full, no vacancy
desocupado/a	vacant, unoccupied

con anticipación	ahead of time

Glossary of Grammatical Terms

ADJECTIVE A word that describes a noun or pronoun.	una casa **grande** *a **big** house* Ella es **inteligente.** *She is **smart.***
Demonstrative adjective An adjective that points out a particular noun.	**este** chico, **esos** libros, **aquellas** personas ***this** boy, **those** books, **those** people (over there)*
Interrogative adjective An adjective used to form questions.	¿**Qué** cuaderno? ***Which** notebook?* ¿**Cuáles** son los carteles que buscas? ***What (Which)** posters are you looking for?*
Possessive adjective (unstressed) An adjective that indicates possession or a special relationship.	**sus** coches ***their** cars* **mi** hermana ***my** sister*
Possessive adjective (stressed) An adjective that more emphatically describes possession.	Es **una** amiga **mía.** *She's **my** friend.	She's a friend **of mine.*** Es **un** coche **suyo.** *It's **her** car.	It's a car **of hers.***
ADVERB A word that describes an adjective, a verb, or another adverb.	Él es **muy** alto. *He is **very** tall.* Ella escribe **bien.** *She writes **well.*** Van **demasiado** rápido. *They are going **too** quickly.*
ARTICLE A determiner that sets off a noun. **Definite article** An article that indicates a specific noun.	**el** país *the country* **la** silla *the chair* **las** mujeres *the women*
Indefinite article An article that indicates an unspecified noun.	**un** chico *a boy* **una** ciudad *a city* **unas** zanahorias *(**some**) carrots*

CLAUSE   A construction that contains a subject and a verb.

Main (Independent) clause   A clause that can stand on its own because it expresses a complete thought.

Busco una muchacha.
I'm looking for a girl.

Si yo fuera rica, **me compraría una casa.**
If I were rich, **I would buy a house.**

Subordinate (Dependent) clause   A clause that cannot stand on its own because it does not express a complete thought.

Busco a la muchacha **que juega al tenis.**
*I'm looking for the girl **who plays tennis.***

Si yo fuera rica, me compraría una casa.
If I were rich, I would buy a house.

COMPARATIVE   The form of adjectives and adverbs used to compare two nouns or actions.

Luis es **menos hablador** que Julián.
*Luis is **less talkative** than Julián.*

Él corre **más rápido** que Julián.
*He runs **faster** than Julián.*

CONJUGATION   The different forms of a verb for a particular tense or mood. This is a present indicative conjugation.

(yo) hablo	(nosotros/as) hablamos
(tú) hablas	(vosotros/as) habláis
(Ud.) habla	(Uds.) hablan
(él/ella) habla	(ellos/as) hablan

I speak	*we speak*
you (fam. sing.) speak	*you (fam. pl.) speak*
you (form. sing.) speak	*you (form. pl.) speak*
he/she speaks	*they speak*

CONJUNCTION   An expression that connects words, phrases, or clauses.

Cristóbal **y** Diana
*Cristóbal **and** Diana*

Hace frío, **pero** hace buen tiempo.
*It's cold, **but** it's nice out.*

DIRECT OBJECT   The noun or pronoun that receives the action of a verb.

Veo **la caja.**
*I see **the box.***

La veo.
*I see **it.***

GENDER   A grammatical category of words. In Spanish, there are two genders: masculine and feminine.

	Masculine	Feminine
Articles and Nouns:	**el** disco compacto	**la** cinta
Pronouns:	**él**	**ella**
Adjectives:	bonit**o**, list**o**	bonit**a**, list**a**
Past Participles:	El informe está **escrito.**	La composición está **escrita.**

IMPERATIVE   *See* Mood.

IMPERFECT (*IMPERFECTO*)   In Spanish, a verb tense that expresses a past action with no specific beginning or ending.

Nadábamos con frecuencia.
*We **used to swim** often.*

IMPERSONAL CONSTRUCTION   One that contains a third person singular verb but no specific subject in Spanish. The subject of English impersonal constructions is generally *it*.

Es importante que...
It is important that . . .

Es necesario que...
It is necessary that . . .

A-2

INDICATIVE *See* Mood.

INDIRECT OBJECT The noun or pronoun that indicates for whom or to whom an action is performed. In Spanish, the indirect object pronoun must always be included, even when the indirect object pronoun is explicitly stated.

Marcos **le** da el suéter a **Raquel.** / Marcos **le** da el suéter.
*Marcos gives the sweater **to Raquel.** / Marcos gives **her** the sweater.*

INFINITIVE The form of a verb introduced in English by *to: to play, to sell, to come.* In Spanish dictionaries, the infinitive form of the verb appears as the main entry.

Luisa va a **comprar** un periódico.
*Luisa is going **to buy** a newspaper.*

MOOD A set of categories for verbs indicating the attitude of the speaker toward what he or she is saying.

Imperative mood A verb form expressing a command.

¡**Ten** cuidado!
Be careful!

Indicative mood A verb form denoting actions or states considered facts.

Voy a la biblioteca.
I'm going to the library.

Subjunctive mood A verb form, uncommon in English, used primarily in subordinate clauses after expressions of desire, doubt, or emotion. Spanish constructions with the subjunctive have many possible English equivalents.

Quiero que **vayas** inmediatamente.
*I want you **to go** immediately.*

NOUN A word that denotes a person, place, thing, or idea. Proper nouns are capitalized names.

abogado, ciudad, periódico, libertad, Luisa
lawyer, city, newspaper, freedom, Luisa

NUMBER

Cardinal number A number that expresses an amount.

una silla, **tres** estudiantes
one chair, three students

Ordinal number A number that indicates position in a series.

la **primera** silla, el **tercer** estudiante
*the **first** chair, the **third** student*

PAST PARTICIPLE The form of a verb used in compound tenses (*see* Perfect Tenses). Used with forms of *to have* or *to be* in English and with **ser, estar,** or **haber** in Spanish.

comido, terminado, perdido
eaten, finished, lost

PERFECT TENSES Compound tenses that combine the auxiliary verb **haber** with a past participle.

Present perfect indicative This form uses a present indicative form of **haber.** The use of the Spanish present perfect generally parallels that of the English present perfect.

No **he viajado** nunca a México.
*I've never **traveled** to Mexico.*

Past perfect indicative   This form uses **haber** in the imperfect tense to talk about something that had or had not been done before a given time in the past.

Antes de 2004, **no había estudiado** español.
*Before 2004, **I hadn't studied** Spanish.*

Present perfect subjunctive   This form uses the present subjunctive of **haber** to express a present perfect action when the subjunctive is required.

¡Ojalá que Marisa **haya llegado** a su destino!
*I hope Marisa **has arrived** at her destination!*

PERSON   The form of a pronoun or verb that indicates the person involved in an action.

	Singular	Plural
First Person	*I* / yo	*we* / nosotros/as
Second Person	*you* / tú, Ud.	*you* / vosotros/as, Uds.
Third Person	*he, she* / él, ella	*they* / ellos, ellas

PREPOSITION   A word or phrase that specifies the relationship of one word (usually a noun or pronoun) to another. The relationship is usually spatial or temporal.

a la escuela
to school

cerca de la biblioteca
near the library

con él
with him

antes de la medianoche
before midnight

PRETERITE (*PRETÉRITO*)   In Spanish, a verb tense that expresses a past action with a specific beginning and ending.

Salí para Roma el jueves.
I left for Rome on Thursday.

PRONOUN   A word that refers to a person (I, you) or that is used in place of one or more nouns.

Demonstrative pronoun   A pronoun that singles out a particular person, place, thing, or idea.

Aquí hay dos libros. **Este** es interesante, pero **ese** es aburrido.
*Here are two books. **This one** is interesting, but **that one** is boring.*

Interrogative pronoun   A pronoun used to ask a question.

¿**Quién** es él?   ¿**Qué** prefieres?
Who is he?   *What do you prefer?*

Object pronoun   A pronoun that replaces a direct object noun or an indirect object noun. Both direct and indirect object pronouns can be used together in the same sentence. However, when the pronouns **le** or **les** are used with **lo, la, los,** or **las,** they change to **se.**

Si **me** llamas más tarde, **te** doy el número de David.
*If you call **me** later, I'll give **you** David's (phone) number.*

Veo a **Alejandro. Lo** veo.
*I see **Alejandro**. I see **him**.*

Le doy el libro **a Juana.**
*I give the book **to Juana**.*

Se lo doy (**a ella**).
*I give **it** to **her**.*

Reflexive pronoun   A pronoun that represents the same person as the subject of the verb.

Me miro en el espejo.
*I look at **myself** in the mirror.*

Relative pronoun   A pronoun that introduces a dependent clause and denotes a noun already mentioned.

El hombre con **quien** hablaba era mi vecino.
*The man with **whom** I was talking was my neighbor.*

Aquí está el bolígrafo **que** buscas.
*Here is the pen (**that**) you are looking for.*

Subject pronoun   A pronoun representing the person thing, or idea performing the action of a verb.

Lucas y Julia juegan al tenis.
***Lucas and Julia** are playing tennis.*

Ellos juegan al tenis.
***They**'re playing tennis.*

SUBJECT   The word(s) denoting the person, place, thing, or idea performing an action or existing in a state.

Sara trabaja aquí.
***Sara** works here.*

¡**Buenos Aires** es una ciudad magnífica!
***Buenos Aires** is a great city!*

Mis **libros** y mi **computadora** están allí.
*My **books** and my **computer** are over there.*

SUBJUNCTIVE   *See* Mood.

SUPERLATIVE   The form of adjectives or adverbs used to compare three or more nouns or actions. In English, the superlative is marked by *most, least,* or *-est.*

Escogí el vestido **más caro.**
*I chose **the most expensive** dress.*

Ana es la persona **menos habladora** que conozco.
*Ana is **the least talkative** person I know.*

TENSE   The form of a verb indicating time: present, past, or future.

Raúl **era, es** y siempre **será** mi mejor amigo.
*Raúl **was, is,** and always **will be** my best friend.*

VERB   A word that reports an action or state.

Ella **llegó.**
*She **arrived.***

Ella **estaba** cansada.
*She **was** tired.*

Auxiliary verb   A verb in conjuction with a participle to convey distinctions of tense and mood. In Spanish, one auxiliary verb is **haber.**

Han viajado por todas partes del mundo.
*They **have** traveled everywhere in the world.*

Reflexive verb   A verb whose subject and object are the same.

Él **se corta** la cara cuando **se afeita.**
*He **cuts himself** when he shaves (**himself**).*

APPENDIX 2

Using Adjectives as Nouns

Nominalization means using an adjective as a noun. In Spanish, adjectives can be nominalized in a number of ways, all of which involve dropping the noun that accompanies the adjective, then using the adjective in combination with an article or other word. One kind of adjective, the demonstrative, can simply be used alone. In most cases, these usages parallel those of English, although the English equivalent may be phrased differently from the Spanish.

Article + Adjective

Simply omit the noun from an *article + noun + adjective* phrase.

el **libro** azul → **el azul** (*the blue one*)
la **hermana** casada → **la casada** (*the married one*)
el **señor** mexicano → **el mexicano** (*the Mexican one*)
los **pantalones** baratos → **los baratos** (*the inexpensive ones*)

You can also drop the first noun in an *article + noun + de + noun* phrase.

la **casa** de Julio → **la de Julio** (*Julio's*)
los **coches** del Sr. Martínez → **los del Sr. Martínez** (*Mr. Martínez's*)

In both cases, the construction is used to refer to a noun that has already been mentioned. The English equivalent uses *one* or *ones*, or a possessive without the noun.

—¿Necesitas el libro grande?
—No. Necesito **el pequeño.**
Do you need the big book?
No. I need the small one.

—¿Usamos el coche de Ernesto?
—No. Usemos **el de Ana.**
Shall we use Ernesto's car?
No. Let's use Ana's.

Note that in the preceding examples the noun is mentioned in the first part of the exchange (**libro, coche**) but not in the response or rejoinder.

Note also that a demonstrative can be used to nominalize an adjective: **este rojo** (*this red one*), **esos azules** (*those blue ones*).

Lo + Adjective

As seen in **Capítulo 10, lo** combines with the masculine singular form of an adjective to describe general qualities or characteristics. The English equivalent is expressed with words like *part* or *thing*.

lo mejor   *the best thing (part), what's best*
lo mismo   *the same thing*
lo cómico   *the funny thing (part), what's funny*

Article + Stressed Possessive Adjective

The stressed possessive adjectives—but not the unstressed possessives—can be used as possessive pronouns: **la maleta suya** → **la suya.** The article and the possessive form agree in gender and number with the noun to which they refer.

Este es mi **banco.** ¿Dónde está **el suyo?**
This is my bank. Where is yours?

Sus **bebidas** están preparadas; **las nuestras,** no.
Their drinks are ready; ours aren't.

No es **la maleta** de Juan; es **la mía.**
It isn't Juan's suitcase; it's mine.

Note that the definite article is frequently omitted after forms of **ser: ¿Esa maleta? Es suya.**

Demonstrative Pronouns

When the demonstrative adjective is used alone, without a noun, it is a demonstrative pronoun. An accent mark can be added to the demonstrative pronoun to distinguish it from the demonstrative adjectives (**éste, ése, aquél**).

Necesito este diccionario y **ese (ése).**
I need this dictionary and that one.

Estas señoras y **aquellas (aquéllas)** son las hermanas de Sara, ¿no?
These women and those (over there) are Sara's sisters, aren't they?

It is acceptable in modern Spanish, per the **Real Academia Española,** to omit the accent on demonstrative pronouns when context makes the meaning clear and no ambiguity is possible.

Additional Perfect Forms (Indicative and Subjunctive)

Some indicative verb tenses have corresponding perfect forms in the indicative and subjunctive moods. Here is the present tense system.

el presente:	yo hablo, como, pongo
el presente perfecto:	yo he hablado, comido, puesto
el presente perfecto de subjuntivo:	yo haya hablado, comido, puesto

Other indicative forms that you have learned also have corresponding perfect indicative and subjunctive forms. Here are the most important ones, along with examples of their use. In each case, the tense or mood is formed with the appropriate form of **haber.**

El pluscuamperfecto del subjuntivo

yo:	hubiera hablado, comido, puesto
tú:	hubieras hablado, comido, puesto
Ud./él/ella:	hubiera hablado, comido, puesto
nosotros:	hubiéramos hablado, comido, puesto
vosotros:	hubierais hablado, comido, puesto
Uds./ellos/ellas:	hubieran hablado, comido, puesto

These forms correspond to **el presente perfecto del indicativo** (**Capítulo 14**). These forms are most frequently used in **si** clause sentences, along with the conditional perfect. See examples below in the *Si clause* section.

El futuro perfecto

yo:	habré hablado, comido, puesto
tú:	habrás hablado, comido, puesto
Ud./él/ella:	habrá hablado, comido, puesto
nosotros:	habremos hablado, comido, puesto
vosotros:	habréis hablado, comido, puesto
Uds./ellos/ellas:	habrán hablado, comido, puesto

These forms correspond to **el futuro** (**Capítulo 16**) and are most frequently used to tell what *will have already happened* at some point in the future. (In contrast, the future is used to tell what *will happen.*)

Mañana **hablaré** con Miguel.
I'll speak with Miguel tomorrow.

Para las tres, ya **habré hablado** con Miguel.
By 3:00, I'll already have spoken to Miguel.

El año que viene **visitaremos** a los nietos.
We'll visit our grandchildren next year.

Para las Navidades, ya **habremos visitado** a los nietos.
We'll already have visited our grandchildren by Christmas.

El condicional perfecto

yo:	habría hablado, comido, puesto
tú:	habrías hablado, comido, puesto
Ud./él/ella:	habría hablado, comido, puesto
nosotros:	habríamos hablado, comido, puesto
vosotros:	habríais hablado, comido, puesto
Uds./ellos/ellas:	habrían hablado, comido, puesto

These forms correspond to **el condicional** (**Capítulo 18**). These forms are frequently used to tell what *would have happened* at some point in the past. (In contrast, the conditional tells what one *would do.*)

Yo **hablaría** con Miguel.
I would speak with Miguel (if I were you, at some point in the future).

Yo **habría hablado** con Miguel.
I would have spoken with Miguel (if I had been you, at some point in the past).

***Si* Clause: Sentences About the Past**

You have learned (**Capítulo 18**) to use the past subjunctive and conditional to speculate about the present in **si** clause sentences: what *would happen* if a particular event *were* (or *were not*) to occur.

Si **tuviera** el tiempo, **aprendería** francés.
If I had the time, I would learn French (in the present or at some point in the future).

The perfect forms of the past subjunctive and the conditional are used to speculate about the past: what *would have happened* if a particular event *had* (or *had not*) occurred.

En la escuela superior, si **hubiera tenido** el tiempo, **habría aprendido** francés.
In high school, if I had had the time, I would have learned French.

Verbs

A. Regular Verbs: Simple Tenses

INFINITIVE PRESENT PARTICIPLE PAST PARTICIPLE	INDICATIVE					SUBJUNCTIVE		IMPERATIVE
	Present	Imperfect	Preterite	Future	Conditional	Present	Imperfect	
hablar hablando hablado	hablo hablas habla hablamos habláis hablan	hablaba hablabas hablaba hablábamos hablabais hablaban	hablé hablaste habló hablamos hablasteis hablaron	hablaré hablarás hablará hablaremos hablaréis hablarán	hablaría hablarías hablaría hablaríamos hablaríais hablarían	hable hables hable hablemos habléis hablen	hablara hablaras hablara habláramos hablarais hablaran	habla tú, no hables hable Ud. hablemos hablen
comer comiendo comido	como comes come comemos coméis comen	comía comías comía comíamos comíais comían	comí comiste comió comimos comisteis comieron	comeré comerás comerá comeremos comeréis comerán	comería comerías comería comeríamos comeríais comerían	coma comas coma comamos comáis coman	comiera comieras comiera comiéramos comierais comieran	come tú, no comas coma Ud. comamos coman
vivir viviendo vivido	vivo vives vive vivimos vivís viven	vivía vivías vivía vivíamos vivíais vivían	viví viviste vivió vivimos vivisteis vivieron	viviré vivirás vivirá viviremos viviréis vivirán	viviría vivirías viviría viviríamos viviríais vivirían	viva vivas viva vivamos viváis vivan	viviera vivieras viviera viviéramos vivierais vivieran	vive tú, no vivas viva Ud. vivamos vivan

B. Regular Verbs: Perfect Tenses

INDICATIVE										SUBJUNCTIVE			
Present Perfect		Past Perfect		Preterite Perfect		Future Perfect		Conditional Perfect		Present Perfect		Past Perfect	
he	hablado	había	hablado	hube	hablado	habré	hablado	habría	hablado	haya	hablado	hubiera	hablado
has	comido	habías	comido	hubiste	comido	habrás	comido	habrías	comido	hayas	comido	hubieras	comido
ha	vivido	había	vivido	hubo	vivido	habrá	vivido	habría	vivido	haya	vivido	hubiera	vivido
hemos		habíamos		hubimos		habremos		habríamos		hayamos		hubiéramos	
habéis		habíais		hubisteis		habréis		habríais		hayáis		hubierais	
han		habían		hubieron		habrán		habrían		hayan		hubieran	

C. Irregular Verbs

INFINITIVE PRESENT PARTICIPLE PAST PARTICIPLE	INDICATIVE					SUBJUNCTIVE		IMPERATIVE
	Present	Imperfect	Preterite	Future	Conditional	Present	Imperfect	
andar andando andado	ando	andaba	anduve	andaré	andaría	ande	anduviera	
	andas	andabas	anduviste	andarás	andarías	andes	anduvieras	anda tú, no andes
	anda	andaba	anduvo	andará	andaría	ande	anduviera	ande Ud.
	andamos	andábamos	anduvimos	andaremos	andaríamos	andemos	anduviéramos	andemos
	andáis	andabais	anduvisteis	andaréis	andaríais	andéis	anduvierais	anden
	andan	andaban	anduvieron	andarán	andarían	anden	anduvieran	
caer cayendo caído	caigo	caía	caí	caeré	caería	caiga	cayera	
	caes	caías	caíste	caerás	caerías	caigas	cayeras	cae tú, no caigas
	cae	caía	cayó	caerá	caería	caiga	cayera	caiga Ud.
	caemos	caíamos	caímos	caeremos	caeríamos	caigamos	cayéramos	caigamos
	caéis	caíais	caísteis	caeréis	caeríais	caigáis	cayerais	caigan
	caen	caían	cayeron	caerán	caerían	caigan	cayeran	

C. Irregular Verbs (continued)

INFINITIVE PRESENT PARTICIPLE PAST PARTICIPLE	INDICATIVE					SUBJUNCTIVE		IMPERATIVE
	Present	Imperfect	Preterite	Future	Conditional	Present	Imperfect	
dar dando dado	doy das da damos dais dan	daba dabas daba dábamos dabais daban	di diste dio dimos disteis dieron	daré darás dará daremos daréis darán	daría darías daría daríamos daríais darían	dé des dé demos deis den	diera dieras diera diéramos dierais dieran	da tú, no des dé Ud. demos den
decir diciendo dicho	digo dices dice decimos decís dicen	decía decías decía decíamos decíais decían	dije dijiste dijo dijimos dijisteis dijeron	diré dirás dirá diremos diréis dirán	diría dirías diría diríamos diríais dirían	diga digas diga digamos digáis digan	dijera dijeras dijera dijéramos dijerais dijeran	di tú, no digas diga Ud. digamos digan
estar estando estado	estoy estás está estamos estáis están	estaba estabas estaba estábamos estabais estaban	estuve estuviste estuvo estuvimos estuvisteis estuvieron	estaré estarás estará estaremos estaréis estarán	estaría estarías estaría estaríamos estaríais estarían	esté estés esté estemos estéis estén	estuviera estuvieras estuviera estuviéramos estuvierais estuviera	está tú, no estés esté Ud. estemos estén
haber habiendo habido	he has ha hemos habéis han	había habías había habíamos habíais habían	hube hubiste hubo hubimos hubisteis hubieron	habré habrás habrá habremos habréis habrán	habría habrías habría habríamos habríais habrían	haya hayas haya hayamos hayáis hayan	hubiera hubieras hubiera hubiéramos hubierais hubieran	

C. Irregular Verbs (continued)

INFINITIVE PRESENT PARTICIPLE PAST PARTICIPLE	INDICATIVE						SUBJUNCTIVE		IMPERATIVE
	Present	Imperfect	Preterite	Future	Conditional		Present	Imperfect	
hacer haciendo hecho	hago haces hace hacemos hacéis hacen	hacía hacías hacía hacíamos hacíais hacían	hice hiciste hizo hicimos hicisteis hicieron	haré harás hará haremos haréis harán	haría harías haría haríamos haríais harían		haga hagas haga hagamos hagáis hagan	hiciera hicieras hiciera hiciéramos hicierais hicieran	haz tú, no hagas haga Ud. hagamos hagan
ir yendo ido	voy vas va vamos vais van	iba ibas iba íbamos ibais iban	fui fuiste fue fuimos fuisteis fueron	iré irás irá iremos iréis irán	iría irías iría iríamos iríais irían		vaya vayas vaya vayamos vayáis vayan	fuera fueras fuera fuéramos fuerais fueran	ve tú, no vayas vaya Ud. vayamos vayan
oír oyendo oído	oigo oyes oye oímos oís oyen	oía oías oía oíamos oíais oían	oí oíste oyó oímos oísteis oyeron	oiré oirás oirá oiremos oiréis oirán	oiría oirías oiría oiríamos oiríais oirían		oiga oigas oiga oigamos oigáis oigan	oyera oyeras oyera oyéramos oyerais oyeran	oye tú, no oigas oiga Ud. oigamos oigan
poder pudiendo podido	puedo puedes puede podemos podéis pueden	podía podías podía podíamos podíais podían	pude pudiste pudo pudimos pudisteis pudieron	podré podrás podrá podremos podréis podrán	podría podrías podría podríamos podríais podrían		pueda puedas pueda podamos podáis puedan	pudiera pudieras pudiera pudiéramos pudierais pudieran	

C. Irregular Verbs (continued)

INFINITIVE / PRESENT PARTICIPLE / PAST PARTICIPLE	INDICATIVE					SUBJUNCTIVE		IMPERATIVE
	Present	Imperfect	Preterite	Future	Conditional	Present	Imperfect	
poner / poniendo / puesto	pongo / pones / pone / ponemos / ponéis / ponen	ponía / ponías / ponía / poníamos / poníais / ponían	puse / pusiste / puso / pusimos / pusisteis / pusieron	pondré / pondrás / pondrá / pondremos / pondréis / pondrán	pondría / pondrías / pondría / pondríamos / pondríais / pondrían	ponga / pongas / ponga / pongamos / pongáis / pongan	pusiera / pusieras / pusiera / pusiéramos / pusierais / pusieran	pon tú, no pongas / ponga Ud. / pongamos / pongan
querer / queriendo / querido	quiero / quieres / quiere / queremos / queréis / quieren	quería / querías / quería / queríamos / queríais / querían	quise / quisiste / quiso / quisimos / quisisteis / quisieron	querré / querrás / querrá / querremos / querréis / querrán	querría / querrías / querría / querríamos / querríais / querrían	quiera / quieras / quiera / queramos / queráis / quieran	quisiera / quisieras / quisiera / quisiéramos / quisierais / quisieran	quiere tú, no quieras / quiera Ud. / queramos / quieran
saber / sabiendo / sabido	sé / sabes / sabe / sabemos / sabéis / saben	sabía / sabías / sabía / sabíamos / sabíais / sabían	supe / supiste / supo / supimos / supisteis / supieron	sabré / sabrás / sabrá / sabremos / sabréis / sabrán	sabría / sabrías / sabría / sabríamos / sabríais / sabrían	sepa / sepas / sepa / sepamos / sepáis / sepan	supiera / supieras / supiera / supiéramos / supierais / supieran	sabe tú, no sepas / sepa Ud. / sepamos / sepan
salir / saliendo / salido	salgo / sales / sale / salimos / salís / salen	salía / salías / salía / salíamos / salíais / salían	salí / saliste / salió / salimos / salisteis / salieron	saldré / saldrás / saldrá / saldremos / saldréis / saldrán	saldría / saldrías / saldría / saldríamos / saldríais / saldrían	salga / salgas / salga / salgamos / salgáis / salgan	saliera / salieras / saliera / saliéramos / salierais / salieran	sal tú, no salgas / salga Ud. / salgamos / salgan

C. Irregular Verbs (*continued*)

INFINITIVE PRESENT PARTICIPLE PAST PARTICIPLE	INDICATIVE						SUBJUNCTIVE		IMPERATIVE
	Present	Imperfect	Preterite	Future	Conditional		Present	Imperfect	
ser siendo sido	soy eres es somos sois son	era eras era éramos erais eran	fui fuiste fue fuimos fuisteis fueron	seré serás será seremos seréis serán	sería serías sería seríamos seríais serían		sea seas sea seamos seáis sean	fuera fueras fuera fuéramos fuerais fueran	sé tú, no seas sea Ud. seamos sean
tener teniendo tenido	tengo tienes tiene tenemos tenéis tienen	tenía tenías tenía teníamos teníais tenían	tuve tuviste tuvo tuvimos tuvisteis tuvieron	tendré tendrás tendrá tendremos tendréis tendrán	tendría tendrías tendría tendríamos tendríais tendrían		tenga tengas tenga tengamos tengáis tengan	tuviera tuvieras tuviera tuviéramos tuvierais tuvieran	ten tú, no tengas tenga Ud. tengamos tengan
traer trayendo traído	traigo traes trae traemos traéis traen	traía traías traía traíamos traíais traían	traje trajiste trajo trajimos trajisteis trajeron	traeré traerás traerá traeremos traeréis traerán	traería traerías traería traeríamos traeríais traerían		traiga traigas traiga traigamos traigáis traigan	trajera trajeras trajera trajéramos trajerais trajeran	trae tú, no traigas traiga Ud. traigamos traigan
venir viniendo venido	vengo vienes viene venimos venís vienen	venía venías venía veníamos veníais venían	vine viniste vino vinimos vinisteis vinieron	vendré vendrás vendrá vendremos vendréis vendrán	vendría vendrías vendría vendríamos vendríais vendrían		venga vengas venga vengamos vengáis vengan	viniera vinieras viniera viniéramos vinierais vinieran	ven tú, no vengas venga Ud. vengamos vengan

C. Irregular Verbs (*continued*)

INFINITIVE PRESENT PARTICIPLE PAST PARTICIPLE	INDICATIVE						SUBJUNCTIVE		IMPERATIVE
	Present	Imperfect	Preterite	Future	Conditional		Present	Imperfect	
ver viendo visto	veo ves ve vemos veis ven	veía veías veía veíamos veíais veían	vi viste vio vimos visteis vieron	veré verás verá veremos veréis verán	vería verías vería veríamos veríais verían		vea veas vea veamos veáis vean	viera vieras viera viéramos vierais vieran	ve tú, no veas vea Ud. veamos vean

D. Stem-Changing and Spelling Change Verbs

INFINITIVE PRESENT PARTICIPLE PAST PARTICIPLE	INDICATIVE						SUBJUNCTIVE		IMPERATIVE
	Present	Imperfect	Preterite	Future	Conditional		Present	Imperfect	
pensar (ie) pensando pensado	pienso piensas piensa pensamos pensáis piensan	pensaba pensabas pensaba pensábamos pensabais pensaban	pensé pensaste pensó pensamos pensasteis pensaron	pensaré pensarás pensará pensaremos pensaréis pensarán	pensaría pensarías pensaría pensaríamos pensaríais pensarían		piense pienses piense pensemos penséis piensen	pensara pensaras pensara pensáramos pensarais pensaran	piensa tú, no pienses piense Ud. pensemos piensen
volver (ue) volviendo vuelto	vuelvo vuelves vuelve volvemos volvéis vuelven	volvía volvías volvía volvíamos volvíais volvían	volví volviste volvió volvimos volvisteis volvieron	volveré volverás volverá volveremos volveréis volverán	volvería volverías volvería volveríamos volveríais volverían		vuelva vuelvas vuelva volvamos volváis vuelvan	volviera volvieras volviera volviéramos volvierais volvieran	vuelve tú, no vuelvas vuelva Ud. volvamos vuelvan

D. Stem-Changing and Spelling Change Verbs (continued)

INFINITIVE PRESENT PARTICIPLE PAST PARTICIPLE	INDICATIVE					SUBJUNCTIVE		IMPERATIVE
	Present	Imperfect	Preterite	Future	Conditional	Present	Imperfect	
dormir (ue, u) durmiendo dormido	duermo duermes duerme dormimos dormís duermen	dormía dormías dormía dormíamos dormíais dormían	dormí dormiste durmió dormimos dormisteis durmieron	dormiré dormirás dormirá dormiremos dormiréis dormirán	dormiría dormirías dormiría dormiríamos dormiríais dormirían	duerma duermas duerma durmamos durmáis duerman	durmiera durmieras durmiera durmiéramos durmierais durmieran	duerme tú, no duermas duerma Ud. durmamos duerman
sentir (ie, i) sintiendo sentido	siento sientes siente sentimos sentís sienten	sentía sentías sentía sentíamos sentíais sentían	sentí sentiste sintió sentimos sentisteis sintieron	sentiré sentirás sentirá sentiremos sentiréis sentirán	sentiría sentirías sentiría sentiríamos sentiríais sentirían	sienta sientas sienta sintamos sintáis sientan	sintiera sintieras sintiera sintiéramos sintierais sintieran	siente tú, no sientas sienta Ud. sintamos sientan
pedir (i, i) pidiendo pedido	pido pides pide pedimos pedís piden	pedía pedías pedía pedíamos pedíais pedían	pedí pediste pidió pedimos pedisteis pidieron	pediré pedirás pedirá pediremos pediréis pedirán	pediría pedirías pediría pediríamos pediríais pedirían	pida pidas pida pidamos pidáis pidan	pidiera pidieras pidiera pidiéramos pidierais pidieran	pide tú, no pidas pida Ud. pidamos pidan
reír (i, i) riendo reído	río ríes ríe reímos reís ríen	reía reías reía reíamos reíais reían	reí reíste rio reímos reísteis rieron	reiré reirás reirá reiremos reiréis reirán	reiría reirías reiría reiríamos reiríais reirían	ría rías ría riamos riáis rían	riera rieras riera riéramos rierais rieran	ríe tú, no rías ría Ud. riamos rían

D. Stem-Changing and Spelling Change Verbs (*continued*)

INFINITIVE PRESENT PARTICIPLE PAST PARTICIPLE	INDICATIVE					SUBJUNCTIVE		IMPERATIVE
	Present	Imperfect	Preterite	Future	Conditional	Present	Imperfect	
seguir (i, i) (g) siguiendo seguido	sigo sigues sigue seguimos seguís siguen	seguía seguías seguía seguíamos seguíais seguían	seguí seguiste siguió seguimos seguisteis siguieron	seguiré seguirás seguirá seguiremos seguiréis seguirán	seguiría seguirías seguiría seguiríamos seguiríais seguirían	siga sigas siga sigamos sigáis sigan	siguiera siguieras siguiera siguiéramos siguierais siguieran	sigue tú, no sigas siga Ud. sigamos sigan
construir (y) construyendo construido	construyo construyes construye construimos construís construyen	construía construías construía construíamos construíais construían	construí construiste construyó construimos construisteis construyeron	construiré construirás construirá construiremos construiréis construirán	construiría construirías construiría construiríamos construiríais construirían	construya construyas construya construyamos construyáis construyan	construyera construyeras construyera construyéramos construyerais construyeran	construye tú, no construyas construya Ud. construyamos construyan
producir (zc) produciendo producido	produzco produces produce producimos producís producen	producía producías producía producíamos producíais producían	produje produjiste produjo produjimos produjisteis produjeron	produciré producirás producirá produciremos produciréis producirán	produciría producirías produciría produciríamos produciríais producirían	produzca produzcas produzca produzcamos produzcáis produzcan	produjera produjeras produjera produjéramos produjerais produjeran	produce tú, no produzcas produzca Ud. produzcamos produzcan

This **Spanish-English Vocabulary** contains all the words that appear in the text, with the following exceptions: (1) most close or identical cognates that do not appear in the chapter vocabulary lists; (2) most conjugated verb forms; (3) diminutives ending in **-ito/a;** (4) absolute superlatives in **-ísimo/a;** and (5) most adverbs in **-mente.** Active vocabulary is indicated by the number of the chapter in which a word or given meaning is first listed (**P=Preliminar**); vocabulary that is glossed in the text is not considered to be active vocabulary and is not numbered. Only meanings that are used in the text are given. The **English-Spanish Vocabulary** is based on the chapter lists of active vocabulary.

The gender of nouns is indicated, except for masculine nouns ending in **-o** and feminine nouns ending in **-a.** Stem changes and spelling changes are indicated for verbs: **dormir (ue, u); llegar (gu).** Because **ch** and **ll** are no longer considered separate letters, words beginning with **ch** and **ll** are found as they would be found in English. The letter **ñ** follows the letter **n: añadir** follows **anuncio,** for example. The following abbreviations are used:

adj.	adjective	*ind. art.*	indefinite article	*pl.*	plural
adv.	adverb	*inf.*	infinitive	*poss.*	possessive
Arg.	Argentina	*interj.*	interjection	*p.p.*	past participle
C.A.	Central America	*inv.*	invariable form	*prep.*	preposition
coll.	colloquial	*i.o.*	indirect object	*pron.*	pronoun
conj.	conjunction	*irreg.*	irregular	*refl. pron.*	reflexive pronoun
d.o.	direct object	*L.A.*	Latin America	*s.*	singular
def. art.	definite article	*m.*	masculine	*sl.*	slang
f.	feminine	*Mex.*	Mexico	*Sp.*	Spain
fam.	familiar	*n.*	noun	*sub. pron.*	subject pronoun
form.	formal	*obj. (of prep.)*	object (of a preposition)	*Uru.*	Uruguay
gram.	grammatical term				

Spanish–English Vocabulary

A

a to (P); at (*with time*) (P); **a base de** based on; **a bordo** on board; **a consecuencia de** as a consequence of; **a continuación** following, below; **a diferencia de** unlike; **a favor de** in favor of; with the aid of; **a finales de** at the end of; **a la(s)...** at . . . (*hour*) (P); **a la derecha (de)** to the right (of) (5); **a la izquierda (de)** to the left (of) (5); **a la plancha** grilled; **a la vez** at the same time; **a larga distancia** long-distance; **a largo plazo** long-term; **a lo largo de** along; throughout; **a menos que** *conj.* unless (15); **a menudo** often; **a partir de** as of; from (*this moment, date on*); **a pesar de** in spite of; **a pie** on foot; **a plazos** in installments (16); **a primera vista** at first sight (15); **a principios de** at the beginning of; **¿a qué hora?** at what time? (P); **a raíz de** as a result of; because of; **a sus órdenes** at your service; **a tiempo** on time (7); **a veces** sometimes, at times (2); **a ver** let's see

abajo below, underneath

abalanzarse (c) (sobre) to pounce (on)

abandonar to abandon; to leave

abanicar (qu) to fan

abarcar (qu) to comprise; to encompass

abecedario alphabet

abierto/a (*p.p. of* **abrir**) open (5); opened

abogado/a lawyer (16)

abolicionista *n. m., f.* abolitionist

abrazar (c) to embrace, hug

abreviar to abbreviate

abrigo coat (3)

abril *m.* April (5)

abrir (*p.p.* **abierto**) to open (2)

absoluto/a absolute; **en absoluto** at all

abstracto/a abstract

abuelo/a grandfather/grandmother (2)

abuelos *m. pl.* grandparents (2)

abundancia abundance

aburrido/a bored (5); **ser** (*irreg.*) **aburrido/a** to be boring (9)

aburrir to bore (13); **aburrirse** to get bored (9)

abuso abuse

acabar to finish (11); to run out of (11); to use up completely (14); **acabar de** + *inf.* to have just (*done something*) (6); **acabar por** + *inf.* to end up by (*doing something*)

academia: Real Academia Española Royal Spanish Academy

académico/a *adj.* academic

acaso: por si acaso just in case (11)

accesible accessible
acceso access
accidentalmente accidentally
accidente *m.* accident
acción *f.* action; **Día** (*m.*) **de Acción de Gracias** Thanksgiving
acecho/a: estar (*irreg.*) **acecho/a** to be lying in wait; to watch, be on the lookout
aceite *m.* oil (14); **aceite de oliva** olive oil; **revisar el aceite** to check the oil (14)
aceituna olive
acelerado/a fast (14), accelerated (14)
acelerar to speed up
acento accent
aceptar to accept
acerca de *prep.* about, concerning
aclaración *f.* clarification
aclarar to clarify
acogedor(a) welcoming
acomodarse (a) to adapt oneself (to)
acompañar to accompany; to go with
acondicionado/a: aire (*m.*) **acondicionado** air conditioning
aconsejable advisable
aconsejar to advise
acontecimiento event (17), happening *n.* (17)
acordarse (ue) (de) to remember (11)
acordeón *m.* accordion
acorralado/a corralled; frightened
acortarse to become, get shorter
acostarse (ue) to go to bed (4)
acostumbrarse a to become accustomed to, get used to
acreedor(a) worthy, deserving
acrílico acrylic
actitud *f.* attitude
actividad *f.* activity
activista *n. m., f.* activist
activo/a active
acto act
actor *m.* actor (13)
actriz *f.* (*pl.* **actrices**) actress (13)
actual *adj.* current, present-day
actualidad *f.* present time
actuar (actúo) to act
acuario aquarium; **Acuario** Aquarius
acuático/a: deportes (*m. pl.*) **acuáticos** water sports
acuerdo agreement; **de acuerdo** agreed; **de acuerdo con** in accordance with; **(no) estoy de acuerdo** I (don't) agree (2); **ponerse** (*irreg.*) **de acuerdo** to reach an agreement
adaptación *f.* adaptation

adaptar to adapt; **adaptarse (a)** to adapt oneself (to)
adarga leather shield
adecuado/a appropriate
adelante let's go; **de ahora en adelante** from now on
adelanto advance
adelgazar (c) to lose weight
además *adv.* moreover; **además de** *prep.* besides
adicional additional
adiós bye (P), good-bye (P)
adivinanza riddle
adivinar to guess
adjetivo adjective
administración *f.* administration; **administración de empresas** business administration (1)
administrado/a administered
administrativo/a administrative
admirar to admire
admitir to admit; to accept
adolescencia adolescence (15)
¿adónde? where (to)? (3)
adopción *f.* adoption
adoquinado/a cobblestoned
adorado/a adored
adorno decoration
adquirir (ie) to acquire
adquisitivo/a purchasing, buying
aduana *s.* customs (18); **inspector(a) de aduanas** customs inspector
adulto/a adult
adverbio adverb
aeróbico/a: hacer (*irreg.*) **ejercicios aeróbicos** to do aerobics (10)
aeropuerto airport (7)
afectar to affect
afectivo/a emotional
afectuoso/a affectionate
afeitadora razor
afeitarse to shave oneself (4)
afición *f.* pastime (9), fun activity (9), hobby (9)
aficionado/a fan; **ser** (*irreg.*) **aficionado/a (a)** to be a fan (of) (9)
afirmación *f.* statement
afirmar to affirm, state
africano/a *n., adj.* African
afrocaribeño/a *adj.* Afro-Caribbean
afrocubano/a *adj.* Afro-Cuban
afuera *adv.* outside, outdoors (5)
afueras *n. f. pl.* suburbs (12), outskirts (12)
agencia agency; **agencia de viajes** travel agency (7)

agenda agenda; date book; **agenda de teléfonos** address/telephone book; **agenda digital/electrónica** electronic calendar, date book
agente (*m., f.*): **agente de viajes** travel agent (7)
ágil agile
agosto August (5)
agotar to use up
agradable pleasant
agradar to please (13)
agradecer (zc) to thank; to be grateful
agradecido/a grateful
agravar to make worse
agregar (gu) to add
agresividad *f.* aggressiveness
agresivo/a aggressive
agrícola *adj. m., f.* agricultural; **trabajador(a) agrícola** farm worker
agricultor(a) farmer (14)
agricultura agriculture
agroturismo agrotourism (*farm stays*)
agroturista *n. m., f.* agrotourist
agua *f.* (*but* **el agua**) water (6); **agua dulce** fresh water; **agua mineral** mineral water (6); **cama de agua** waterbed (4); **huevo pasado por agua** poached egg
aguacate *m.* avocado
aguantar to stand, tolerate
aguar (agüe) to spoil (*a party*)
agudo/a sharp
ahí there
ahora now (1); **ahora mismo** right now; at once; **de ahora en adelante** from now on
ahorrar to save (*money*) (16)
ahorros (*m. pl.*): **cuenta de ahorros** savings account (16)
aire *m.* air; (14); **aire acondicionado** air conditioning; **aire puro** clean air (14); **al aire libre** outdoors; **contaminación** (*f.*) **del aire** air pollution (14)
ajedrez *m.* chess (4)
ajillo: al ajillo in garlic sauce
ajo garlic; **diente** (*m.*) **de ajo** garlic clove
al (*contraction of* **a** + **el**) to the (3); **al** + *inf.* upon, while, when + *verb form*; **al aire libre** outdoors; **al ajillo** in garlic sauce; **al alza** on the rise; **al borde de** on the verge of; **al contado** in cash (16); **al contrario** on the contrary; **al este/ norte/oeste/sur** to the east/north/west/ south (5); **al fondo** in the background; **al lado de** *prep.* alongside of (5); beside; next to; **al principio (de)** at the beginning of (16); **al revés** backward

ala *f.* (*but* **el ala**) wing
alarma alarm
albor *m.* dawn
álbum *m.* album
alcance *m.* reach
alcanzar **(c)** to reach
alce *m.* elk, moose
alcoba bedroom (4)
alcohol *m.* alcohol
alcohólico/a *adj.* alcoholic
aldea village
alegrarse **(de)** to be happy (about) (12)
alegre happy (5)
alemán *m.* German (*language*) (1)
alemán, alemana *n., adj.* German (2);
    perro pastor alemán German Shepherd
Alemania Germany
alergia allergy; **tener** (*irreg.*) **alergia a** to
    be allergic to
alérgico/a: **ser** (*irreg.*) **alérgico/a a** to be
    allergic to
alerta: **ojo alerta** eagle eye; **Fundación**
    (*f.*) **Alerta contra el SIDA** AIDS
    Awareness Foundation
alertar to warn
alfabetización *f.* literacy
alfabetizado/a alphabetized
alfabeto alphabet
alfombra rug (4)
alfombrado/a carpeted
algo something (3), anything (3)
algodón *m.* cotton (3); **es de algodón** it's
    made of cotton (3)
alguien someone (6), anyone (6)
algún, alguno/a(s) some (6); any (6); **algún**
    día some day; **alguna vez** once; ever
alimentar to feed
aliviar to relieve, alleviate
alivio relief
allá over there; **más allá** further, farther;
    más allá de beyond, farther than
allí (over) there (3)
alma *f.* (*but* **el alma**) soul
almacén *m.* department store (3)
almacenamiento storage
almendra almond
almohada pillow (18)
almorzar **(ue) (c)** to have lunch (4)
almuerzo lunch (6)
aló hello
alojamiento lodging (18)
alojarse to stay (*in a place*) (18)
alpinismo: **hacer** (*irreg.*) **alpinismo** to
    mountain climb
alquilar to rent (12)

alquiler *m.* rent (12)
alrededor de *prep.* around; about
alrededores *m. pl.* surroundings
alteración *f.* irregularity
alternativa *n.* alternative
altitud *f.* altitude
alto/a tall (2); high; **clase** (*f.*) **alta** upper
    class
altura height, altitude; **ponerse** (*irreg.*) **a**
    la altura de to compete on the same
    level as
alza: **al alza** on the rise
alzarse **(c)** to rise up
ama (*f.* [*but* **el ama**]) **de casa** homemaker
amable kind (2), nice (2)
amado/a *adj.* beloved
amanecer **(zc)** to wake up
amar to love (15)
amarillo/a yellow (3)
Amazonas *m. s.* Amazon
Amazonia Amazon (*Basin*)
amazónico/a *adj.* Amazonian
ambiental environmental (*pertaining to*
    surroundings)
ambiente *m.* atmosphere, environment;
    medio ambiente environment
    (*nature*) (14)
ámbito scope
amenazador(a) threatening
América Central Central America
americano/a *n., adj.* American; **fútbol**
    (*m.*) **americano** football (9)
amigo/a friend (1)
amistad *f.* friendship (15)
amistoso/a friendly (15)
amor *m.* love (15)
amplio/a large, spacious
amueblado/a furnished
analfabetismo illiteracy
análisis *m. inv.* analysis
analista (*m., f.*) **de sistemas** systems
    analyst (16)
analizar **(c)** to analyze
anaranjado/a orange *adj.* (3)
ancho/a wide; **de ancho** in width
anciano/a *n.* old person; *adj.* old; ancient
andar (*irreg.*) to walk; **andar en bicicleta**
    to ride a bicycle; **rueda de andar**
    treadmill
andino/a *adj.* Andean
anémico/a anemic
anfitrión, anfitriona host(ess) (8)
anglohablante *m., f.* English-speaker
angula eel
ángulo angle

animado/a lively; animated; **dibujos** (*m.*
    pl.) **animados** cartoons
animal *m.* animal (14); **animal doméstico**
    domesticated animal (14), pet (14);
    animal salvaje wild animal (14)
ánimo: **dar** (*irreg.*) **ánimo** to cheer; **estado**
    de ánimo state of mind
aniversario anniversary
anoche *adv.* last night (10)
anotar to jot down
ansiedad *f.* fatigue; restlessness; worry;
    nervousness
Antártida Antarctica
ante *prep.* before; in front of; **ante todo**
    above all; first of all
anteayer *adv.* the day before yesterday (10)
antecedente *m.* antecedent
antemano: **de antemano** beforehand
anterior previous, preceding
antes *adv.* before; **antes de** *prep.* before
    (4); **antes de Cristo (a.C.)** before Christ
    (B.C.); **antes (de) que** *conj.* before (15)
antibiótico antibiotic (10)
anticipación (*f.*): **con anticipación** in
    advance (18), ahead of time (18); **de**
    anticipación ahead
anticipar to anticipate
anticuado/a antiquated, old-fashioned
antigüedad *f.* antiquity; advanced age; *pl.*
    antiques
antiguo/a old; ancient; former
antipático/a unpleasant (2)
antirrevolucionario/a *n.*
    counterrevolutionary
antónimo antonym
antropología anthropology
antropólogo/a anthropologist
anual annual, yearly
anudado/a knotted
anunciar to announce (7)
anuncio announcement; advertisement
añadidura: **de añadidura** on the side
añadir to add
año year (5); **cumplir años** to have a
    birthday (8); **de los últimos años** in
    recent years; **Día** (*m.*) **del Año Nuevo**
    New Year's Day; **el año pasado** last
    year; **Feliz Año Nuevo** Happy New
    Year; **los años sesenta, ochenta,…** the
    sixties, eighties, . . .; **pasar… años** to be
    more than . . . years old; **tener** (*irreg.*)**…**
    años to be . . . years old (2)
apagado/a out; turned off (*lights*)
apagar **(gu)** to turn off (11); **apagarse** to
    go out (*lights*)

aparato appliance; **aparato doméstico** home appliance (9); **aparato electrónico** electronic device

aparcar (qu) to park

aparecer (zc) to appear

aparentemente apparently

apariencia appearance

apartamento apartment (1); **casa/ bloque** (*m.*) **de apartamentos** apartment building (12)

apartar to separate

aparte *adv.* apart, separately

apasionado/a passionate

apellido last name, surname

apenas hardly

apendicitis *f. inv.* appendicitis

aperitivo aperitif; appetizer

apilado/a piled up

apinado/a tightly arranged

apio celery

aplicar (qu) to apply

apoyar to support (17)

apoyo support; **fondos** (*m. pl.*) **de apoyo** economic assistance

apreciar to appreciate (13)

aprender to learn (2); **aprender a** + *inf.* to learn how to (*do something*)

apretado/a tight

apropiado/a appropriate

aprovechar (de) to make use (of), avail oneself (of); **que aproveche** enjoy your meal

aproximadamente approximately

apuntar to write down

apuntes *m. pl.* notes

apurarse to hurry (up)

aquel, aquella *dem. adj.* that (*over there*) (3); *dem. pron.* that one (*over there*) (3)

aquello *dem. pron.* that (3); that thing

aquellos/as *dem. adj.* those (*over there*) (3); *dem. pron.* those (ones) (*over there*) (3)

aquí here (1)

árabe *m.* Arabic (*language*)

árabe *n., adj. m., f.* Arab

arado plow

árbol *m.* tree (14)

archipiélago archipelago

archivo (computer) file (12)

ardilla squirrel

área *f.* (*but* **el área**) area (12)

arena sand

arete *m.* earring (3)

argentino/a *n., adj.* Argentine

argumento argument; plot (*of a play, book*)

árido/a dry, arid

arma *f.* (*but* **el arma**) weapon

armado/a armed

armario closet (4)

arpa *f.* (*but* **el arpa**) harp

arqueológico/a archeological

arquitecto/a architect (13)

arquitectónico/a *adj.* architectural

arquitectura architecture (13)

arrancar (qu) to start up (*a car*) (14); to pull out, wrench

arrastrar to drag

arreglar to fix (12); to repair (12); to straighten (up) (12)

arriba *adv.* above; up

arrogante arrogant

arroz *m.* (*pl.* **arroces**) rice (6)

arte *f.* (*but* **el arte**) art (1); **obra de arte** work of art (13)

artesanía *s.* arts and crafts (13)

artículo article

artificial: fuegos (*m. pl.*) **artificiales** fireworks

artista *m., f.* artist (13)

artístico/a artistic

arvejas *f. pl.* green peas (6)

arzobispo archbishop

asado/a roasted (6); **pollo asado** roast chicken (6)

asamblea assembly

ascensor *m.* elevator

asco: dar (*irreg.*) **asco** to make sick

asegurar to assure; **asegurarse** to make sure

asequible available

asesinado/a murdered

asesinato assassination (17); murder

asesoramiento advice

así thus, so; **así como** as well as; **así que** therefore, consequently, so

asiático/a *adj.* Asian

asiento seat (7)

asimilarse to assimilate

asistente *m., f.* assistant; **asistente de vuelo** flight attendant (7); **asistente del profesor** teaching assistant

asistir (a) to attend (*a class, function*) (2), to go to (*a class, function*) (2)

asma *f.* (*but* **el asma**) asthma

asociación *f.* association

asociado/a: estado libre asociado commonwealth

asociar to associate

aspecto aspect; appearance; **no tener** (*irreg.*) **buen aspecto** to not look right

aspiración *f.* aspiration

aspiradora vacuum cleaner (9); **pasar la aspiradora** to vacuum (9)

aspirante *m., f.* candidate (16), applicant (16)

aspirina aspirin

astronauta *m., f.* astronaut

astronomía astronomy

asumir to assume

asunto question, matter

atacar (qu) to attack

ataque *m.* attack (17); **ataque de nervios** nervous breakdown; **ataque terrorista** terrorist attack (17)

atar to tie

atención *f.* attention; **atención médica** healthcare

atender (ie) to attend to; to serve

ateo/a *adj.* atheist

atlántico/a: Océano Atlántico Atlantic Ocean

atleta *m., f.* athlete

atlético/a athletic

átono/a *gram.* unstressed

atracción *f.* attraction; **parque** (*m.*) **de atracciones** amusement park

atractivo/a attractive

atraer (*like* **traer**) to attract

atrapado/a trapped

atrás *adv.* back, backward; behind

atrasado/a: estar (*irreg.*) **atrasado/a** to be late (7)

atrevido/a daring

atribuir (y) to attribute

atropello assault, attack; abuse, outrage

atroz (*pl.* **atroces**) atrocious, brutal

atún *m.* tuna (6)

auditivo/a: comprensión (*f.*) **auditiva** listening comprehension

aumentar to increase

aumento increase; raise (12); **aumento de sueldo** raise (*in salary*) (16)

aun *adv.* even

aún *adv.* still, yet

aunque although

auscultar to listen (*with a stethoscope*)

ausencia absence

ausente absent

autenticidad *f.* authenticity

auténtico/a authentic

auto car; **auto chocador de choque** bumper car

autobiografía autobiography

autobiográfico/a autobiographical

autobús *m.* bus (7); **estación** (*f.*) **de autobuses** bus station (7); **ir** (*irreg.*) **en autobús** to go/travel by bus (7); **parada del autobús** bus stop (18)

autoestima self-esteem

automático/a: cajero automático automatic teller machine (16); **contestador** (*m.*) **automático** answering machine (12)

automovilístico/a *adj.* automobile

autónomo/a autonomous

autopista freeway (14)

autoprueba self-test

autor(a) author

autoridad *f.* authority

autostop (*m.*)**: hacer** (*irreg.*) **autostop** to hitchhike

avanzado/a advanced

avenida avenue (12)

aventura adventure

aventurero/a adventurous

aventurismo adventure tourism

aventurista *m., f.* adventure tourist

avergonzado/a embarrassed (8)

avergonzarse (me avergüenzo) (c) to be ashamed

averiguar (averiguo) to find out

aves *f. pl.* fowl

avestruz *m.* (*pl.* **avestruces**) ostrich

avión *m.* airplane (7); **ir** (*irreg.*) **en avión** to go/travel by plane (7)

avisar to warn

aviso warning

¡ay! *interj.* ah!; ouch!

ayer yesterday (4)

ayuda help

ayudante *m., f.* assistant

ayudar to help (6)

azafrán *m.* saffron

azteca *n., adj. m., f.* Aztec

azúcar *m.* sugar

azucarado/a sweetened; containing sugar

azul blue (3)

B

bailable danceable

bailar to dance (1)

bailarín, bailarina dancer (13)

baile *m.* dance (13)

bajado/a lowered

bajar to carry down; to lower; to go down; **bajar de** to get down from (*a vehicle*) (7); to get off (*a vehicle*) (7)

bajo *n.* bass (*music*)

bajo *prep.* under

bajo/a *adj.* low; short (*in height*) (2); **planta baja** ground floor (12)

balance *m.* balance

balboa Panamanian monetary unit

balcón *m.* balcony

ballena whale (14)

ballestero crossbowman

ballet *m.* ballet (13)

banana banana (6)

bancarrota bankruptcy

banco bank (16)

banda band

banderilla *Sp.* appetizer

bandoneón *m.* large concertina

banquero/a banker

bañar to bathe; **bañarse** to take a bath (4)

bañera bathtub (4)

baño bathroom (4); **habitación** (*f.*) **con/sin baño** room with(out) attached bath (18); **traje** (*m.*) **de baño** swimsuit (3)

bar *m.* bar (9); club; **ir** (*irreg.*) **a un bar** to go to a bar (9)

barato/a inexpensive (3)

barbacoa barbecue

barca small boat

barcaza barge

barco boat (7), ship (7); **ir** (*irreg.*) **en barco** to go/travel by boat (7)

barra bar, railing

barrer (el piso) to sweep (the floor) (9)

barrera barrier

barriga belly

barril *m.* barrel

barrio neighborhood (12)

barro clay

basar to base, support (*an opinion*); **basarse en** to base one's ideas, opinions on

base *f.* base, foundation; basis; **a base de** based on

básico/a basic

basílica basilica

basquetbol *m.* basketball (9)

bastante *adv.* enough (15); rather (15), sufficiently (15)

bastar to be enough

basura trash; **sacar (qu) la basura** to take out the trash (9)

basurero wastebasket

bata robe

batá: tambores (*m. pl.*) **batá** *set of drums used in Cuban music*

batalla battle

batería battery (14)

batido *drink similar to a milkshake* (17)

bautismo baptism

bebé *m., f.* baby

beber to drink (2)

bebida drink (6), beverage (6)

beca scholarship

béisbol *m.* baseball (9)

belleza beauty

bello/a beautiful (14); **Bella Durmiente** Sleeping Beauty

besar to kiss

beso kiss

biblioteca library (1)

bibliotecario/a librarian (1)

bicicleta (de montaña) (mountain) bike (12); **andar** (*irreg.*)**/montar en bicicleta** to ride a bicycle; **montañismo en bicicleta** mountain biking; **pasear en bicicleta** to ride a bicycle (9)

biculturalismo biculturalism

bidón (*m.*) *drum made of an oil drum*

bien *adv.* well (P); **caerle** (*irreg.*) **bien a alguien** to make a good impression on someone (16); **estar** (*irreg.*) **bien** to be comfortable (*temperature*) (5); **llevarse bien (con)** to get along well (with) (15); **muy bien** fine (P), very well (P); **pasarlo bien** to have a good time (8); **quedarle bien** to fit well; **salir** (*irreg.*) **bien** to turn out well

bienestar *m.* well-being (10)

bienvenido/a welcome

bilingüe bilingual

bilingüismo bilingualism

billete *m.* ticket (7); **billete de ida** one-way ticket (7); **billete de ida y vuelta** round-trip ticket (7)

biodiversidad *f.* biodiversity

biografía biography

biología biology

biólogo/a biologist

bisonte *m.* bison, buffalo

bistec *m.* steak (6)

blanco/a white (3); **espacio en blanco** blank space; **vino blanco** white wine (6)

blancura whiteness

bloque (*m.*) **de apartamentos** apartment building (12)

blusa blouse (3)

bobo/a dumb, stupid

boca mouth (10)

boda wedding (ceremony) (15); **lista de bodas** bride's registry

bodegón *m.* inexpensive restaurant, tavern

boicoteo boycott

boleto ticket (7); **boleto de ida** one-way ticket (7); **boleto de ida y vuelta** round-trip ticket (7)
bolígrafo pen (1)
bolívar *m.* Venezuelan monetary unit
boliviano/a *n., adj.* Bolivian
bolsa purse (3)
bolsillo pocket
bomba bomb (17); *traditional music from Puerto Rico*
bombardeo bombing
bombero/a firefighter
bombilla lightbulb
bonito/a pretty (2)
borde: al borde de on the verge of
bordo: a bordo on board
boricua *n., adj. m., f.* Puerto Rican
Borinquén *f. indigenous name for Puerto Rico*
bosque *m.* forest (14); **bosque primario** old-growth forest
bota boot (3)
botella bottle
botones *m. inv.* bellhop (18)
brasileño/a *n., adj.* Brazilian
bravura fierceness; bravery
brazo arm (11)
breve *adj.* brief
brindar to offer
británico/a *adj.* British
bronce *m.* bronze
bronquitis *f. inv.* bronchitis
bruja witch
brujo warlock; magician
bucanero/a buccaneer, pirate
bucear to scuba dive; to snorkle
buen, bueno/a *adj.* good (2); **buenas noches** good evening (P); good night (P); **buenas tardes** good afternoon (P); **buenos días** good morning (P); **hace buen tiempo** it's good weather (5); **lo bueno** the good thing, news (10); **muy buenas** good afternoon/evening (P)
bueno... *interj.* well . . . (2)
buque (*m.*) **petrolero** oil tanker
burbuja bubble
burlador *m. one of two **bomba** drums*
burocrático/a bureaucratic
busca: en busca de in search of
buscar (qu) to look for (1)
butaca seat (*in a theater*)

C

caballero knight; gentleman
caballo horse (14); **montar a caballo** to ride a horse (9)
caber *irreg.* to fit
cabeza head (10); **doler(le) (ue) la cabeza** to have a headache (11); **dolor** (*m.*) **de cabeza** headache (10)
cabezudo/a stubborn
cabina cabin (*on a ship*) (7)
cabo cape (*geography*)
cacique *m.* chief
cada *inv.* each (4), every (4); **cada vez más** increasingly
cadena channel (*television*); chain
cadera hip
caer *irreg.* to fall (11); **caerle bien/mal a alguien** to make a good/bad impression on someone (16); **caerse** to fall down (11)
café *m.* café (18); coffee (1); **(de) color café** brown (3)
cafeína caffeine
cafetera coffee pot, coffeemaker (9)
cafetería cafeteria (1)
caída fall (*accident*)
caja box; cashier window (16); *type of drum*
cajero automático ATM (16); automatic teller machine (16)
cajero/a cashier (16); teller (16)
calabaza gourd
calamar *m.* squid
calandria lark (*bird*)
calcetín *m.* (*pl.* **calcetines**) sock (3)
calculadora calculator (1)
calcular to calculate
cálculo calculus; calculation
calendario calendar (11)
calentar (ie) to heat
calidad *f.* quality
cálido/a hot
caliente hot
calificación *f.* grade (11)
calle *f.* street (12)
callos (*m. pl.*) **a la madrileña** tripe Madrid–style
calma calm
calor *m.* heat; **hace calor** it's hot (5); **tener** (*irreg.*) **(mucho) calor** to be (very) warm, hot (5)
caloría calorie
calzas *f. pl.* stockings
cama (de agua) (water)bed (4); **guardar cama** to stay in bed (10); **hacer** (*irreg.*) **la cama** to make the bed (9); **tender (ie) la cama** to make the bed
cámara camera (12); **cámara de vídeo** video camera (12)

camarero/a waiter, waitress (6)
camarógrafo/a cameraman/woman
camarones *m. pl.* shrimp (6)
cambiante changing
cambiar to change; **cambiar (de canal/cuarto/ropa)** to change (channels/rooms/clothes) (12)
cambio change; **en cambio** on the other hand, on the contrary
camello camel
caminar to walk (10)
caminata walk
camino way; road (14), street (14); **camino de** on the way (to); **Camino Real** Royal Highway
camión *m.* truck
camioneta station wagon (7)
camisa shirt (3)
camiseta T-shirt (3)
campana bell
campanada stroke, ringing of a bell
campanario bell tower
campaña campaign; **tienda de campaña** tent (7)
campeón, campeona champion
campeonato championship
campesino/a farm worker (14), peasant (14)
camping *m.* campground (7); **hacer** (*irreg.*) **camping** to go camping (7)
campo field (14); countryside (12); **mozo de campo y plaza** farmhand
campus *m. inv.* (university) campus (12)
canadiense *n., adj. m., f.* Canadian
canal *m.* canal; channel (12); **cambiar de canal** to change channels (12)
cancelar to cancel
cáncer *m.* cancer
cancha court (*sports*)
canción *f.* song (13)
candidato/a candidate
canela cinnamon
cansado/a tired (5)
cansancio fatigue, weariness
cansarse to get tired
cantante *m., f.* singer (13)
cantar *m.* song
cantar to sing (1)
cantidad *f.* quantity
canto song
capa de ozono ozone layer
capacidad *f.* ability
capacitación *f.* training
capacitado/a trained

capaz (*pl.* **capaces**) able
Caperucita Roja Little Red Ridinghood
capital *f.* capital city (5)
capítulo chapter
Capricornio Capricorn
capturado/a captured
cara face; **plantar cara a** to confront
característica *n.* characteristic
caracterizar (c) to characterize
caramelo candy
carcajadas (*f. pl.*): **reírse (i, i) (me río) a carcajadas** to laugh one's head off
cardinal: punto cardinal cardinal direction (5)
carga charge; payload (*ammunition*)
cargar (gu) to charge (*to an account*) (16); to carry
cargo position, post; **estar** (*irreg.*) **a cargo** to be in control of
Caribe *m.* Caribbean
caribeño/a *n., adj.* Caribbean
cariño affection
cariñoso/a affectionate (5)
carne *f.* meat (6); flesh
carnero mutton
carnet *m.* identity card
caro/a expensive (3)
carpintero/a carpenter
carrera career; major (*academic*)
carreta wooden cart
carretera highway (14)
carro (descapotable) (convertible) car (12)
carta letter (2); **jugar (ue) (gu) a las cartas** to play cards (9); **papel** (*m.*) **de cartas** stationery (18)
cartel *m.* poster
cartera wallet (3); handbag (3)
cartón *m.* cardboard
cartucho cartridge
casa house (2), home (2); **ama** (*f.* [*but el ama*]) **de casa** homemaker; **casa de apartamentos** apartment building (12); **en casa** at home (1); **limpiar la casa (entera)** to clean the (whole) house (9); **regresar a casa** to go home (1)
casado/a married (2); **recién casado/a (con)** newlywed (to) (15)
casarse (con) to marry (15)
cascada waterfall
cascanueces *m. inv.* nutcracker
casero/a *adj.* home
casi almost (2); **casi nunca** almost never (2)
caso case; **caso de urgencia** emergency; **en caso de que** *conj.* in case (15)
castigar (gu) to punish (17)

catalán *m.* Catalan (*language*)
catálogo catalogue
catarata waterfall
catastrófico/a catastrophic
catedral *f.* cathedral
categoría category
católico/a *n., adj.* Catholic
catorce fourteen (P)
causa cause
causar to cause
caza hunting
cazador(a) hunter
cazuelita bowl
CD CD (12), compact disc (12)
CD-ROM *m.* CD-ROM (12)
ceder to cede
celebración *f.* celebration
celebrar to celebrate (5)
celular: teléfono celular cellular phone (12)
cementerio cemetery
cena dinner (6), supper (6)
cenar to have (eat) dinner, supper (6)
Cenicienta Cinderella
censo census
censurar to censure
centavo cent
centrado/a centered
central central; **América Central** Central America
céntrico/a central
centro center; downtown (3); **centro comercial** shopping mall (3)
Centroamérica Central America
centroamericano/a *n., adj.* Central American
ceño frown
cepillarse los dientes to brush one's teeth (4)
cerámica *s.* pottery (13); ceramics (13)
cerca *adv.* near, nearby, close; **cerca de** *prep.* close to (5); **de cerca** up close
cercanía closeness
cercano/a *adj.* close, near
cerdo pork; **chuleta de cerdo** pork chop (6)
cereal *m.* cereal (6)
cerebro brain (10)
ceremonia ceremony
cerilla *Sp.* match (*for lighting things*)
cero zero (P)
cerrado/a closed (5)
cerrar (ie) to close (4)
cerro hill
cervantino/a Cervantine (*pertaining to Miguel de Cervantes*)

cervecería beer hall
cerveza beer (1)
césped *m.* grass
cesto basket
ceviche *m. raw fish dish*
champán *m.* champagne
champanería champagne bar
champiñón *m.* mushroom (6)
champú *m.* shampoo (18)
chaperón, chaperona chaperone
chaqueta jacket (3)
charango *ten-string guitar-like instrument*
charlar to chat
chau good-bye
cheque *m.* check (16); **cheque de viajero** traveler's check (18); **pagar (gu) con cheque** pay by check (16); **talonario de cheques** *Sp.* checkbook
chequeo checkup (10)
chequera checkbook (16)
chicharrón *m.* pork flavorings
chico/a boy, girl
chileno/a *n., adj.* Chilean
chimenea chimney
chimpancé *m.* chimpanzee
chino Chinese (*language*)
chino/a *n., adj.* Chinese
chirimía *clarinet-type wind instrument*
chiste *m.* joke (8)
chistoso/a funny, amusing
chocador(a): auto chocador bumper car
chocar (qu) (con) to run into (14), to collide (with) (14)
chocolate *m.* chocolate; hot chocolate
chofer *m., f.* driver
choque *m.* collision (17); **auto de choque** bumper car; **choque** (*m.*) **de trenes** train wreck
chorizo sausage
chuleta rib steak; **chuleta de cerdo** pork chop (6)
chulo pimp
ciberespacial *adj.* cyberspace
ciberespacio *n.* cyberspace
ciclismo bicycling (9)
ciclo cycle
ciego/a blind
cielo heaven; sky
cien, ciento one hundred (2); **por ciento** percent
ciencia science; *pl.* (*academic discipline*) science (1); **ciencia ficción** science fiction; **ciencias políticas** *f. pl.* political science
científico/a *n.* scientist; *adj.* scientific

cierto/a true; certain, **en cierta medida** in some measure; **es cierto que** it's certain that (13)
cigarrillo cigarette
cilantro cilantro, fresh coriander
cinco five (P); **Cinco de Mayo** Mexican awareness celebration
cincuenta fifty (2)
cine *m.* movies (4); movie theater (4); **ir** (*irreg.*) **al cine** to go to the movies (9)
cineasta *m., f.* film director
cinta tape (3)
cinturón *m.* belt (3)
circuito circuit
circulación *f.* traffic (14)
circular to circulate; to move
círculo circle, ring
circunstancia circumstance
cisne *m.* swan
cita appointment; date (15)
citado/a quoted
ciudad *f.* city (2)
ciudadanía citizenship
ciudadano/a citizen (17)
ciudadela citadel
cívico/a civic (17)
civil: estado civil marital status
civilización *f.* civilization
claro *interj.* of course
claro/a clear
clase *f.* class(room) (1); **clase alta** upper class; **clase turística** tourist class (7); **compañero/a de clase** classmate (1); **primera clase** first class (7); **sala de clase** classroom
clásico/a classic(al) (13)
cláusula *gram.* clause; **cláusula nominal** noun clause
clave *adj. inv.* key
clave *m.* percussion stick (*used in Caribbean music*)
cliente *m., f.* client (1); customer
clima *m.* climate (5)
climatología climatology
clínica clinic
club *m.* club
coágulo clot
cobrar to cash (*a check*) (16); to charge (*someone for an item or service*) (16)
cobre *m.* copper; brass instrument
coche *m.* car (2); **coche deportivo** sports car; **coche descapotable** convertible car (12)
cochera garage

cocido/a: huevo cocido hard-boiled egg
cocina kitchen (4)
cocinar to cook (6)
cocinero/a cook (16), chef (16)
coco coconut
cóctel *m.* cocktail
coger (j) to catch; to seize, grab
cognado cognate
coherente coherent
coincidir to coincide; to agree
cojear to limp
cola line; **hacer** (*irreg.*) **cola** to stand in line (7)
colección *f.* collection
coleccionar to collect
colega *m., f.* colleague
colegiatura *s.* fees (*academic*)
colegio secondary school
colesterol *m.* cholesterol
colgar (ue) (gu) to hang
colocar (qu) to place
colombiano/a *n., adj.* Colombian
colón *m.* monetary unit of Costa Rica and El Salvador
colonia colony
colonialismo colonialism
colonizador(a) colonist
colonizar (c) to colonize
colono/a settler
color *m.* color (3); **(de) color café** brown (3); **¿de qué color es?** what color is it?
colorado/a red
columna column
comandante *m., f.* commander
combatir to fight, combat
combinación *f.* combination
combinar to combine
comedor *m.* dining room (4)
comentar to comment on; to discuss
comentario commentary
comenzar (ie) (c) to begin
comer to eat (2); **comer equilibradamente** to eat in a balanced way (10); **comérselo/la** to eat (*something*) up
comercial: centro comercial shopping mall (3)
comerciante *m., f.* merchant (16); shopkeeper (16)
cometer to commit
cómico/a funny; **tira cómica** comic strip
comida food (6); meal (6)
comisión *f.* commission
como like, as; **así como** as well as; **tal como** just as; **tan… como** as . . . as (5);

tan pronto como as soon as (16); **tanto como** as much as (5); **tanto/a(s)… como** as much/many . . . as (5)
¿cómo? how? (P); what? (P); **¿cómo es usted?** what are you (*form. s.*) like? (P); **¿cómo está(s)?** how are you? (P); **¿cómo se llama usted?** what's your (*form. s.*) name? (P); **¿cómo te llamas?** what's your (*fam. s.*) name? (P)
cómoda bureau (4), dresser (4)
cómodo/a comfortable (4)
compacto/a: disco compacto CD (12); compact disc (12)
compañero/a companion, friend; **compañero/a de clase** classmate (1); **compañero/a de cuarto** roommate (1)
compañía company
comparación *f.* comparison
comparar to compare
comparativo *gram.* comparative
comparsa dance troupe
compartir to share
compasión *f.* compassion
compatabilizar (c) to make compatible
compensar to compensate, make up for
competencia competition
competición *f.* competition
complacer (zc) to please
complejo/a complex
complementar to complement
complementario/a complementary
complemento *gram.* object; **complemento directo** direct object; **complemento indirecto** indirect object
completar to complete
completo/a complete; full (18), no vacancy (18); **pensión** (*f.*) **completa** room and full board (18); **por completo** completely; **trabajo de tiempo completo** full time work (11)
complexión *f.* body type/build
complicado/a complicated
complicar (qu) to complicate
componer (*like* **poner**) to compose
comportamiento behavior
composición *f.* composition
compositor(a) composer (13)
comprar to buy (1)
compras: de compras shopping (3); **ir** (*irreg.*) **de compras** to go shopping (3)
comprender to understand (2)
comprensión *f.* comprehension; **comprensión auditiva** listening comprehension

comprensivo/a understanding
comprobar (*like* **probar**) to prove
compromiso commitment
computación *f.* computer science (1)
computadora computer (12); **computadora portátil** laptop computer; **disco de computadora** computer disc (12); **escribir** (*p.p.* **escrito**) **en la computadora** to key in, type (16)
común common, usual, ordinary
comunicación *f.* communication; *pl.* communications (1); **medio de comunicación** means of communication (17); **medios** (*m. pl.*) **de comunicación** media
comunicarse (**qu**) (**con**) to communicate (with) (17)
comunicativo/a communicative
comunidad *f.* community (12)
comunitario/a *adj.* community
con with (1); **con anticipación** in advance (18), ahead of time (18); **con cheque** by check (16); **con cuidado** carefully; **con frecuencia** frequently (1); **con permiso** excuse me (P); pardon me (P); **con respecto a** with regard to, with respect to; **con tal (de) que** *conj.* provided that (15)
concentrarse to concentrate
concepción *f.* conception, idea
concepto concept, idea
concertar (**ie**) to arrange; to agree upon
conciencia conscience, moral awareness
concierto concert; **ir** (*irreg.*) **a un concierto** to go to a concert (9)
concluir (**y**) to conclude
conclusión *f.* conclusion
concordar (**ue**) (**con**) to correspond (to)
concurso contest
condición *f.* condition
condicional *m. gram.* conditional
conducir *irreg.* to drive (14); to conduct; **conducir a** to lead to; **licencia de conducir** driver's license (14)
conductor(a) driver (14)
conectar to connect
conexión *f.* connection
confección *f.* confection
conferencia lecture
conferenciante *m., f.* lecturer
confianza trust
confiar (**confío**) to trust
configurado/a configured
confirmación *f.* confirmation

confirmar to confirm (18)
confluencia coming together
confrontación *f.* confrontation
confundido/a confused
congelado/a frozen (5); very cold (5)
congelador *m.* freezer (9)
congestionado/a congested (10), stuffed up (10)
congreso congress
conjugar (**gu**) *gram.* to conjugate
conjunción *f. gram.* conjunction
conjunto group; band
conmemorar to commemorate
conmigo with me (5)
conocer (**zc**) to know (6), to be acquainted with (6); to meet
conocido/a known, famous
conocimiento knowledge
conquista conquest
conquistador(a) conqueror
consciente conscious, aware
conscripto draftee
consecuencia consequence; **a consecuencia de** as a consequence of
conseguir (*like* **seguir**) to get (8), to obtain (8); **conseguir** + *inf.* to succeed in (*doing something*) (8)
consejero/a advisor (1)
consejo (piece of) advice (6); council
conservación *f.* conservation
conservador(a) *n., adj.* conservative
conservar to save (14), to conserve (14)
considerar to consider
consigo with them
consistir en to consist of
constante *adj.* constant
constar de to consist of
constitución *f.* constitution
constitucional constitutional
constituir (**y**) to constitute; to be
construcción *f.* construction
constructivo/a constructive
construir (**y**) to build (14)
cónsul *m.* consul
consulta consultation
consultar to consult
consultorio (medical) office (10)
consumidor(a) consumer
consumir to consume
consumo consumption; use
contabilidad *f.* accounting
contable *m., f.* accountant
contacto contact; **lentes** (*m. pl.*) **de contacto** contact lenses (10); **llevar lentes de contacto** to wear contact

lenses (10); **mantenerse** (*like* **tener**) **en contacto** to keep in touch
contado: pagar (**gu**) **al contado** to pay in cash (16)
contador(a) accountant (16)
contaminación (*f.*) (**del aire**) (air) pollution (14); **hay** (**mucha**) **contaminación** there's (lots of) pollution (5)
contaminar to pollute (14)
contar (**ue**) to tell (7); **contar con** to count on
contemplar to contemplate
contemporáneo/a contemporary
contenido *s.* contents
contento/a content (5), happy (5)
contestador (*m.*) **automático** answering machine (12)
contestar el teléfono to answer the phone (16)
contexto context
contigo with you (5)
continente *m.* continent
continuación (*f.*): **a continuación** following, below
continuar (**continúo**) to continue
contra against; **en contra** opposed; **Fundación** (*f.*) **Alerta contra el SIDA** AIDS Awareness Foundation
contrabajo double bass (*instrument*)
contrabando contraband
contradicción *f.* contradiction
contraer (*like* **traer**) **matrimonio** to get married
contrario/a opposite; **al contrario** on the contrary; **lo contrario** the opposite
contrastar to contrast
contratar to contract
contratiempos *m. pl.* mishaps; disappointments
contrato contract
contribución *f.* contribution
contribuir (**y**) to contribute
control (*m.*) **de aduana** customs checkpoint; **control remoto** remote control (12); **pasar por el control de la seguridad** to go/pass through security (7)
controlar to control
convencer (**convenzo**) to convince
convencional conventional
conveniencia convenience
conveniente convenient
conversación *f.* conversation
conversar to talk, converse
convertir (**ie, i**) to change, convert; **convertirse en** to turn into

convivencia living together, cohabitation

convivir to live together

cónyuge *m., f.* spouse

cooperativo/a cooperative

copa glass; drink (*alcoholic*) (18); upper branches in a tree; **Copa Mundial** World Cup; **tomar una copa** to have a drink

copia: hacer (*irreg.*) **copia** to copy (12)

copiar to copy (12)

coquí *m.* frog (*found in the Caribbean*)

coraje *m.* courage

corazón *m.* heart (10)

corbata tie (3)

corcho cork

cordillera mountain range

córdoba *m.* monetary unit of Nicaragua

coro chorus

corona wreath

coronel *m.* colonel

correcto/a correct, right

corredor(a) *adj.* running

corregir (i, i) (j) to correct

correo mail (18); **correo electrónico** e-mail (12); **oficina de correos** post office (18)

correr to run (9); to jog (9); to flow (*water*)

corresponder to correspond

correspondiente corresponding

corresponsal *m., f.* (news) correspondent

corrida de toros bullfight

corrido *traditional song from Mexico, associated with the Mexican Revolution*

corriente (*adj.*): **cuenta corriente** checking account (16)

corriente *f.* current

cortar to cut

corte *m.* cut; *f.* court (of law)

cortés *m., f.* courteous

cortesía courtesy

cortina curtain

corto/a short (*in length*) (2); **pantalones** (*m. pl.*) **cortos** shorts

cosa thing (1)

cosechar to harvest

cosmopolita *adj. m., f.* cosmopolitan

costa coast

costar (ue) to cost; **¿cuánto cuesta?** how much does it cost? (3)

costarricense *n., adj. m., f.* Costa Rican

costero/a coastal

costilla rib

costo cost

costumbre *f.* custom (9); habit (9); **por costumbre** customarily

cotidiano/a everyday, daily

crear to create (13)

creatividad *f.* creativity

creativo/a creative

crecer (zc) to grow (15)

creciente growing

crecimiento growth

crédito credit; **tarjeta de crédito** credit card (6)

creencia belief

creer (y) (en) to think (2); to believe (in) (2)

criada maid (18)

criado/a servant (16)

criar (crío) to raise (*children*)

criatura child

crimen *m.* crime

criminal *n., adj. m., f.* criminal

criollo/a creole

crisis *f. inv.* crisis

cristal *m.* crystal

Cristo: antes de Cristo (a.C.) before Christ (B.C.); **después de Cristo (d.C.)** after Christ (A.D.)

crítica criticism

crítico/a *n.* critic; *adj.* critical

cronológico/a chronological

crudo *n.* crude (oil)

cruzar (c) to cross (18)

cuá *m. percussion instrument made of bamboo and played with two sticks*

cuaderno notebook (1)

cuadrado *n.* square

cuadrado/a *adj.* square(d)

cuadro chart; painting (*piece of art*) (13); square; **de cuadros** plaid

¿cuál(es)? what? (1); which? (1); **¿cuál es la fecha de hoy?** what's today's date? (5)

cualidad *f.* quality

cualquier *adj.* any

cualquiera *pron.* anyone; either

¿cuán? *adv.* how?

cuando when; **de vez en cuando** once in a while

¿cuándo? when? (1)

cuanto: en cuanto *conj.* as soon as (16); **en cuanto a** *prep.* regarding

¿cuánto/a? how much? (1); **¿cuánto cuesta?** how much does it cost? (3); **¿cuánto es?** how much is it? (3)

¿cuántos/as? how many? (1)

cuarenta forty (2)

cuarto *n.* room (1); one-fourth; quarter (of an hour); **cambiar de cuarto** to change rooms (12); **compañero/a de cuarto** roommate (1); **servicio de cuarto** room service (18); **y/menos cuarto** a quarter (fifteen minutes) after/to (*the hour*) (P)

cuarto/a *adj.* fourth (13)

cuatro four (P)

cuatro four-stringed guitar

cuatrocientos/as four hundred (3)

cubano/a *n., adj.* Cuban

cubanoamericano/a *adj.* Cuban American

cubierto/a (*p.p. of* **cubrir**) covered

cubito ice cube

cubo cube

cubrir (*p.p.* **cubierto**) to cover (14)

cuchara spoon

cucharada spoonful

cucharadita teaspoon

cuchillo knife

cuello neck

cuenca basin

cuenta account (16); (*for service*) bill (6), check (6); **cuenta corriente** checking account (16); **cuenta de ahorros** savings account (16); **darse** (*irreg.*) **cuenta (de)** to realize; **estado de cuentas** bank statement; **tomar en cuenta** to take into account

cuento story

cuerda string

cuero leather

cuerpo body (10)

cuesta: ¿cuánto cuesta? how much does it cost? (3)

cuestión *f.* question, matter

cuidado care; *interj.* careful; **con cuidado** carefully; **tener** (*irreg.*) **cuidado** to be careful

cuidadosamente carefully

cuidar(se) to take care of (oneself) (10); **¡hay que cuidarse!** you must take care of yourself!

cuitado/a forlorn

culinario/a culinary

culpa: tener (*irreg.*) **la culpa** to be guilty

cultista *adj. m., f.* cult member

cultivo cultivation, raising (*of crops*)

cultura culture

cumpleaños *m. inv.* birthday (5); **feliz cumpleaños** happy birthday; **pastel** (*m.*) **de cumpleaños** birthday cake (8)

cumplir años to have a birthday (8)

cuna cradle; birthplace

cuñado/a brother-in-law, sister-in-law
cupo quota, share
cura *m.* priest
curador(a) curator
curar(se) to heal, cure (oneself); **curarse de** to be cured of
currículum *m.* (*pl.* **currículos**) résumé (16)
cursar to study (*at a university*)
cursivo/a: letra cursiva *s.* italics
curso course
cuyo/a whose

D

dados *m. pl.* dice
dama woman
danza dance (13)
daño damage; **hacerse** (*irreg.*) **daño** to hurt oneself (11)
dar *irreg.* to give (7); **dar ánimo** to cheer; **dar asco** to make sick; **dar un paseo** to take a walk (9); **dar una fiesta** to give a party (8); **darle la gana** to feel like; **darse** to occur; **darse cuenta (de)** to realize; **darse en/contra/con** to run, bump into (11); **darse la mano** to shake hands; **darse la vuelta** to turn oneself around
datar (de) to date (from)
datos *m. pl.* information; facts
dé give (*form. command*)
de *prep.* of (P); from (P); **de acuerdo** agreed; **de acuerdo con** in accordance with; **de ahora en adelante** from now on; **de ancho** in width; **de antemano** beforehand; **de anticipación** ahead; **de añadidura** on the side; **de cerca** up close; **(de) color café** brown (3); **de compras** shopping (3); **de cuadros** plaid; **de desnudismo** nudist; **¿de dónde eres?** where are you (*fam. s.*) from? (P); **¿de dónde es usted?** where are you (*form. s.*) from? (P); **de guardia** on-call; **de hecho** in fact; **de ida** one-way (7); **de ida y vuelta** round-trip (7); **de joven** as a youth (9); **de la mañana/tarde/noche** in the morning/afternoon/evening (P); **de la noche** at night (P); **de largo** in length; **de los últimos años** in recent years; **de lujo** luxury (*adj.*) (18); **de lunares** polka-dotted; **de manera que** *conj.* so that, in such a way that; **de moda** in style; **de modo** in such a way; **de nada** you're welcome (P); **de niño/a** as a child (9); **de noche** at night; **de paso** passing through; **de primera** first-class; **¿de qué color es?** what color is it?; **¿de quién?** whose? (2); **de rayas** striped; **de repente** suddenly (10); **de tiempo completo/parcial** full time/part time (11); **de todas maneras** by all means; whatever happens; **de todo** everything (3); **de todos modos** anyway; **de última moda** the latest style (3); **de un jalón** all at once; **de vacaciones** on vacation (7); **de vez en cuando** once in a while; **de viaje** on a trip (7)
debajo de *prep.* below (5)
deber *n. m.* responsibility (17), obligation (17); *v.* **deber** (+ *inf.*) should, must, ought to (*do something*) (2); **deberse a** to be due to
debido a due to, because
débil weak
debilitamiento weakening, debilitation
década decade
decidir to decide
décimo/a tenth (13)
decir *irreg.* (*p.p.* **dicho**) to say (7); to tell (7); **es decir** that is to say; **eso quiere decir...** that means . . . (10)
decisión *f.* decision
decisivo/a decisive
declaración *f.* declaration
declarar to declare
decoración *f.* decoration
decorar to decorate
dedicarse (qu) a to dedicate oneself to
dedo (de la mano) finger (11); **dedo del pie** toe (11)
deducir *irreg.* to deduct
defecto defect
defender (ie) to defend
defensa defense
definición *f.* definition
definir to define
definitivo/a definitive
deforestación *f.* deforestation
deforestado/a deforested
deformación *f.* deformation
degustar to taste; to try, sample
dejar (en) to quit (16); **dejar** + *inf.* to allow, let (*something happen*); **dejar (en)** to leave (behind) (in [*a place*]) (9); **dejar de** + *inf.* to stop (*doing something*) (10)
del (*contraction of* **de** + **el**) of the (2); from the (2)
delante *adv.* before, in front, ahead; **delante de** *prep.* in front of (5)
delegación *f.* delegation
delegado/a delegate
deleitarse to take delight; to enjoy
deletrear to spell
delgado/a thin (2), slender (2)
delicioso/a delicious
delincuente delinquent
delito crime (14)
demás: los/las demás the others (12), the rest
demasiado *adv.* too, too much (12)
demasiado/a *adj.* too much; *pl.* too many
democracia democracy
demócrata *m., f.* Democrat
demográfico/a demographic
demonio devil, demon
demora delay (7)
demostración *f.* demonstration
demostrar (*like* **mostrar**) to show, demonstrate
demostrativo/a *gram.* demonstrative
denso/a dense (14)
dental: pasta dental toothpaste (18)
dentista *m., f.* dentist (10)
dentro *adv.* in, within, inside; **dentro de** *prep.* within; **dentro de poco** in a little while
denuncia accusation
deparar to supply
departamento department; *Sp.* apartment
depender (de) to depend (on)
dependiente/a clerk (1)
deporte *m.* sport (9); **deportes acuáticos** water sports; **practicar (qu) deportes** to practice, play sports (10)
deportista *m., f.* sports player
deportivo/a sports *adj.* (9), sporting *adj.* (9), sports-loving (9); **coche** (*m.*) **deportivo** sports car
depositar to deposit (16)
depósito deposit
deprimente depressing
depurar to refine
derecha *n.* right; right hand; **a la derecha (de)** to the right (of) (5)
derecho *n.* right (*legal*) (17); **todo derecho** straight ahead (14)
derivarse (de) to derive (from)
dermatológico/a dermatologic, skin
derretido/a melted
derrocado/a overthrown
derrotado/a defeated
desafortunadamente unfortunately
desagradable unpleasant

desaparecer (*like* **parecer**) to disappear
desarraigado/a uprooted
desarrollar to develop (14)
desarrollo development
desastre *m.* disaster (17)
desastroso/a disastrous
desayunar to have (eat) breakfast (6)
desayuno breakfast (4)
descansar to rest (4)
descanso rest
descapotable: carro/coche (*m.*)
   descapotable convertible car (12)
descender (ie) to descend
descendiente *m., f.* descendent
desconocido/a unknown
descortésmente discourteously,
   impolitely
describir (*like* **escribir**) to describe
descripción *f.* description
descubanizado/a less Cuban
descubierto/a (*p.p. of* **descubrir**)
   discovered
descubrimiento discovery
descubrir (*like* **cubrir**) to discover (14)
descuidado/a careless
desde *prep.* from (7); since; **desde
   entonces** from then on; **desde que**
   conj. since
deseable desirable
desear to want (1), to desire
desecho waste (product)
desempeñar to play (*a part*) (13), to
   perform (*a part*) (13); to hold, carry out
   (*a responsibility*)
deseo wish (8)
desequilibrio imbalance
desertización *f.* process of becoming a
   desert
desesperadamente desperately
desfile *m.* parade
desgracia disgrace
desgraciadamente unfortunately
deshumanización *f.* dehumanization
desierto *n.* desert
desierto/a *adj.* deserted
designar to designate
desigualdad *f.* inequality (17)
desilusión *f.* disillusion
desinflado/a flat; **llanta desinflada** flat
   tire (14)
desintegrarse to break up
desnudismo: de desnudismo nudist
desnudo/a nude, naked
desocupado/a vacant (18), unoccupied (18)
desordenado/a messy (5)

desorientar to disorient, confuse
despacio *adv.* slowly
despedirse (*like* **pedir**) **(de)** to say good-
   bye (to) (8); to take leave (of) (8)
despegar (gu) to take off (*airplane*)
desperdiciar to waste
despertador *m.* alarm clock (11)
despertarse (ie) (*p.p.* **despierto**) to wake
   up (4)
despierto/a (*p.p. of* **despertar**) awake
desplazamiento journey; move
desplegar(se) (ie) (gu) to unfold
después *adv.* after, afterwards; later;
   después de *prep.* after (4); **después de
   Cristo (d.C.)** after Christ (A.D.);
   después (de) que *conj.* after (16)
destacado/a distinguished
destacar (qu) to emphasize; to stand
   out; **destacarse** to distinguish
   oneself
desterrado/a exiled
destinar to designate, assign
destino destination
destreza skill
destrucción *f.* destruction
destructivo/a destructive
destructor(a) destructive
destruir (y) to destroy (14)
desventaja disadvantage (10)
detalle *m.* detail (6)
detective *m., f.* detective
detener (*like* **tener**) to detain
detenidamente carefully
determinar to determine
detestar to detest, hate
detrás de *prep.* behind (5)
devolver (*like* **volver**) to return
   (*something*) (16)
día *m.* day (1); **algún día** some day;
   buenos días good morning (P); **Día de
   Acción de Gracias** Thanksgiving; **Día
   de la Independencia** Independence
   Day; **Día de la Raza** Columbus Day
   (Hispanic Awareness Day); **día de la
   semana** weekday (4); **Día de los
   Enamorados** Valentine's Day; **Día de
   los Inocentes** April Fool's Day; **Día de
   los Reyes Magos** Day of the Magi
   (Three Kings); **Día de San Patricio** St.
   Patrick's Day; **Día del Año Nuevo**
   New Year's Day; **día del santo** saint's
   day; **día festivo** holiday (8); **Día
   Internacional de los Trabajadores**
   International Labor Day; **día laborable**
   workday; **hoy (en) día** nowadays,

these days; **ponerse** (*irreg.*) **al día** to
   get up-to-date; **¿qué día es hoy?** what
   day is today? (4); **todos los días** every
   day (1)
diabetes *f. inv.* diabetes
diablo devil
diáfano/a transparent
diagrama *m.* diagram
dialecto dialect
diálogo dialogue
diamante *m.* diamond
diario/a daily; **rutina diaria** daily
   routine (4)
diarrea diarrhea
dibujar to draw (13)
dibujo drawing; **dibujos animados**
   cartoons
diccionario dictionary (1)
dicho/a (*p.p. of* **decir**) said
diciembre *m.* December (5)
dictador(a) dictator (17)
dictadura dictatorship (17)
dictar to dictate
diecinueve nineteen (P)
dieciocho eighteen (P)
dieciséis sixteen (P)
diecisiete seventeen (P)
diente *m.* tooth (10); **cepillarse los
   dientes** to brush one's teeth (4); **diente
   de ajo** garlic clove
dieta diet; **estar** (*irreg.*) **a dieta** to be on a
   diet (6)
dietético/a *adj.* diet
diez ten (P)
diferencia difference; **a diferencia de**
   unlike
diferente different
diferir (ie, i) to differ
difícil difficult (5); hard (5)
dificultad *f.* difficulty
dificultar to make difficult
difundir to spread
difusión *f.* broadcasting
diga *interj.* hello (*on the telephone, Sp.*)
digestión *f.* digestion
digital: agenda digital electronic date
   book
dimensión *f.* dimension
Dinamarca Denmark
dinero money (1)
Dios *m. s.* God; **por Dios** for heaven's
   sake (11); *pl.* gods
diosa goddess
diplomático/a diplomatic
diptongo *gram.* diphthong

dirección *f.* address (9); **dirección de personal** personnel office (16), employment office (16)

directo/a direct; **complemento directo** *gram.* direct object pronoun

director(a) director (13); conductor (13); **director(a) de personal** personnel director (16)

dirigir (j) to direct; to target

disco disk; **disco compacto** CD (12), compact disc (12); **disco de computadora** computer disc (12); **disco duro** hard drive (12)

discoteca discotheque; **ir** (*irreg.*) **a una discoteca** to go to a disco (9)

discriminación *f.* discrimination (17)

disculpa apology, excuse; **pedir (i, i) disculpas** to apologize (11)

disculpar to excuse, pardon

discúlpeme pardon me (11); I'm sorry (11)

discutir (sobre) (con) to argue (with) (about) (8)

diseñador(a) designer

diseñar to design

diseño design

disfraz *m.* (*pl.* **disfraces**) disguise, costume; **fiesta de disfraz** costume party

disfrutar (de) to enjoy

disminuir (y) to lessen, diminish

disparar to shoot, fire

disparate *m.* silly thing; crazy idea

disponible available

disputa dispute, argument

distancia distance; **a/por larga distancia** long-distance

distante distant, far

distinguir (g) to distinguish

distinto/a different, distinct

distraer (*like* **traer**) to distract

distraído/a absentminded (11)

distribución *f.* distribution

distrito district

diversidad *f.* diversity

diversificar (qu) to diversify

diversión *f.* entertainment (9), amusement (9)

diverso/a diverse; various

divertido/a fun; **ser** (*irreg.*) **divertido/a** to be fun (9)

divertir (ie, i) to entertain; **divertirse** to have a good time (4), to enjoy oneself (4)

dividir to divide

divorciado/a (de) divorced (from) (15)

divorciarse (de) to get divorced (from) (15)

divorcio divorce (15)

divulgar (gu) to make known

doblar to turn (14); to dub (*movies*)

doble double; **habitación** (*f.*) **doble** double room (*in a hotel*) (18)

doce twelve (P)

dócil tame, docile

doctor(a) doctor

doctorado doctorate, Ph.D.

documentar to document

documento document

dólar *m.* dollar

doler (ue) to hurt (10), ache (10); **doler(le) la cabeza** to have a headache (11)

dolor *m.* pain, ache (10); **tener** (*irreg.*) **dolor de cabeza/estómago/muela** to have a headache/stomachache/toothache (10)

doméstico/a domestic; household; **animal** (*m.*) **doméstico** domesticated animal (14); pet (14); **aparato doméstico** home appliance (9); **quehacer** (*m.*) **doméstico** household chore (9)

domicilio home, residence

dominación *f.* domination

dominar to dominate

domingo Sunday (4)

dominicano/a *n., adj.* Dominican

dominio mastery

don *m. title of respect used with a man's first name*

donde where

¿dónde? where? (P); **¿de dónde eres?** where are you (*fam. s.*) from? (P); **¿de dónde es usted?** where are you (*form. s.*) from? (P)

doña *f. title of respect used with a woman's first name*

dorado/a golden

dormir (ue, u) to sleep (4); **dormir la siesta** to take a nap (4); **dormir lo suficiente** to sleep enough (10); **dormirse** to fall asleep (4)

dormitorio bedroom

dos two (P); **dos veces** twice (10); **hotel** (*m.*) **de dos estrellas** two-star hotel (18)

doscientos/as two hundred (3)

dosis *f. inv.* dose

drama *m.* drama (13)

dramático/a dramatic

dramaturgo/a playwright (13)

drásticamente drastically

droga drug; **traficar (qu) en drogas** to traffic in/deal drugs

dromedario dromedary (*camel*)

dualidad *f.* duality

ducha shower; **habitación** (*f.*) **con/sin ducha** room with/without attached shower (18)

ducharse to take a shower (4)

duda doubt; **no hay duda** there is no doubt; **sin duda** without a doubt

dudar to doubt (12)

dudoso/a doubtful

duende *m.* ghost; spirit

dueño/a owner (6); landlord, landlady (12)

dulce *adj.* sweet; **agua dulce** fresh water; **dulces** *n. m. pl.* sweets (6); candy (6)

dulzura sweetness

durante during (4)

durar to last (17)

durmiente: Bella Durmiente Sleeping Beauty

duro/a hard, firm; **disco duro** hard drive (12)

DVD *m.* DVD (12); **lector** (*m.*) **de DVD** DVD player (12)

E

e and (*used instead of* **y** *before words beginning with stressed* **i** *or* **hi,** *except* **hie-**)

echar to throw

ecología ecology

ecológico/a ecological

economía economy; *s.* economics (1)

económico/a economic

economizar (c) to economize (16)

ecosistema *m.* ecosystem

ecoturismo ecotourism

ecoturista *m., f.* ecotourist

ecuador *m.* equator

ecuatoriano/a *n., adj.* Ecuadorian

edad *f.* age; **Edad Media** Middle Ages

edificio building (1)

editor(a) editor

educación *f.* education

educado/a educated; polite; **mal educado/a** rude, bad-mannered

educativo/a educational

efectivo cash (16); **pagar (gu) en efectivo** to pay in cash (16)

efecto effect

eficiencia efficiency

eficiente efficient

Egipto Egypt

egoísta *m., f.* selfish

ejecutivo/a executive

ejemplar *m.* issue (*magazine*)

ejemplo example; **por ejemplo** for example (11)

ejercer (z) to practice (*a profession*)

ejercicio exercise (3); **hacer** (*irreg.*) **ejercicio** to exercise, get exercise (4); **hacer ejercicios aeróbicos** to do aerobics (10)

ejército army (17)

él *sub. pron.* he (1); *obj.* (*of prep.*) him

el *def. art. m. s.* the; **el primero de** the first of (*month*) (5)

elaborar to elaborate

elección *f.* election

electricidad *f.* electricity

electricista *m., f.* electrician (16)

eléctrico/a: energía eléctrica electric energy (14)

electrónica *s.* electronics

electrónico/a electronic; **agenda electrónica** electronic calendar; **aparato electrónico** electronic device; **correo electrónico** e-mail (12); **mensaje** (*m.*) **electrónico** e-mail message

electrostático/a electrostatic

elefante *m.* elephant (14)

elegancia elegance

elegante elegant

elegir (i, i) (j) to choose; to elect

elemento element

elevar to raise, elevate

eliminar to eliminate

ella *sub. pron.* she (1); *obj.* (*of prep.*) her

ellos/as *sub. pron.* they (1); *obj.* (*of prep.*) them

embajada embassy

embajador(a) ambassador

embarazada *n.* pregnant woman

embargo: sin embargo however (5), nevertheless

embotellamiento de tráfico traffic jam

embriagado/a drunk

emergencia emergency; **sala de emergencias** emergency room

emigrante *m., f.* emigrant

emigrar to emigrate

emisión *f.* emission; broadcast

emoción *f.* emotion (8)

emocional emotional

emocionante exciting

empanado/a breaded

empapelado/a (wall)papered

emparejar to match

emperador emperor

empezar (ie) (c) to begin (4); **empezar a** + *inf.* to begin to (*do something*) (4)

empleado/a employee

emplear to use; to employ

empleo employment

empresa company, corporation (16), business (16); **administración** (*f.*) **de empresas** business administration (1)

empresario/a businessman/woman

empuje *m.* push

en in (P); on (P); at (P); **en absoluto** at all; **en busca de** in search of; **en cambio** on the other hand, on the contrary; **en casa** at home (1); **en caso de que** *conj.* in case (15); **en cierta medida** in some measure; **en contra** opposed; **en cuanto** *conj.* as soon as (16); **en cuanto a** *prep.* regarding; **en efectivo** in cash (16); **en este momento** right now; **en exceso** to excess, excessively; **en fila** in single file; **en fin** in short; **en punto** exactly (*time*) (P); on the dot (*time*) (P); sharp (*time*) (P); **en realidad** in fact; **en resumen** in short; **en seguida** right away (10); **en vez de** instead of (16)

enamorado/a (de) in love (with) (15); **Día** (*m.*) **de los Enamorados** Valentine's Day

enamorarse (de) to fall in love (with) (15)

encabezado/a por headed by

encadenado/a chained

encalado/a whitewashed

encantado/a enchanted; delighted; nice/pleased to meet you (P)

encantador(a) enchanting; delightful

encantamiento enchantment

encantar to like very much (7), to love (7)

encañar to form stalks

encarar to confront, face up to

encargado/a person in charge

encargarse (gu) de to be in charge of

encender (ie) to turn on; to light

encendido/a lit up

encerado/a waxed

enchufar to plug in

encima de *prep.* on top of (5); in addition to

encontrar (ue) to find (8); **encontrarse** to be (10), to feel (10); **encontrarse con** to meet (*someone* [*somewhere*]) (10)

encuesta survey

energía energy (14); **energía eléctrica (nuclear, solar)** electric (nuclear, solar) energy (14)

enero January (5)

énfasis *m. inv.* emphasis

enfático/a emphatic

enfermarse to get sick (8)

enfermedad *f.* illness, sickness

enfermero/a nurse (10)

enfermo/a sick (5); **ponerse** (*irreg.*) **enfermo/a** to get sick

enfilado/a in a row

enfisema *m.* emphysema

enfocarse (qu) (en) to focus (on)

enfoque *m.* focus

enlace *m.* link

enlatado/a canned

enojado/a angry

enojarse (con) to get angry (at) (8)

enorme enormous

enriquecer (zc) to enrich

enrollado/a rolled up; in a roll

ensalada salad (6)

ensayo essay

enseñanza teaching

enseñar to teach (1)

entender (ie) to understand (4)

enterado/a informed

enterarse (de) to find out (17), to learn (about) (17)

entero/a entire; whole; **limpiar la casa entera** to clean the whole house (9)

entonces then, next; **desde entonces** from then on

entrada entrance; ticket

entrar to enter

entre between (5); among (5)

entreabierto/a half-open, ajar

entregar (gu) to turn in (11), to hand in (11)

entremeses *m. pl.* hors d'œuvres (8)

entrenamiento training

entrenar to practice (9), to train (9)

entretejer to interweave

entretener (*like* **tener**) to entertain

entretenimiento entertainment

entrevista interview (16); **tener** (*irreg.*) **una entrevista** to have an interview (16)

entrevistador(a) interviewer (16)

entrevistar to interview (16); **entrevistarse** to be interviewed

envase *m.* container

enviar (envío) to send

envidia envy

envuelto/a (*p.p. of* **envolver**) wrapped

eólico/a *adj.* wind

epifanía epiphany

episodio episode

época era, time (*period*) (11)

equilibradamente: comer equilibradamente to eat in a balanced way (10)

equilibrado/a balanced

equilibrar to balance

equilibrio balance

equipaje *m.* baggage (7), luggage (7); **facturar el equipaje** to check baggage (7)

equipo team; equipment; **equipo estereofónico/fotográfico** stereo/photography equipment (12)

equivalente *n. m.* equivalence; *adj.* equivalent

equivaler (*like* **valer**) to equal

equivocarse (qu) (de) to be wrong (about) (11), to make a mistake (about) (11)

érase una vez once upon a time

eres you (*fam. s.*) are (P)

errante wandering

error *m.* mistake, error

erupción *f.* eruption (17)

es he/she/it is (P); you (*form. s.*) are (P); **¿cómo es usted?** what are you (*form. s.*) like? (P); **¿cuánto es?** how much is it? (3); **es cierto/extraño/imposible/increíble/ridículo/seguro/terrible/una lástima/urgente que** it's certain, strange/impossible/incredible/ridiculous/a sure thing/terrible/a shame/urgent that (13); **es de…** it is made of . . . (3); **¡es de última moda!** it's the latest style! (3); **es decir** that is to say; **es (im)probable que** it's (un)likely, (im)probable that (13); **es la…** it's (*time*) (P)

escabroso/a rugged

escala stop; **hacer** (*irreg.*) **escalas** to make stops (7); **vuelo sin escalas** nonstop flight

escalar to climb

escaleras *f. pl.* stairs; **escaleras mecánicas** escalator

escalón *m.* step

escalopín *m.* breaded cutlet

escándalo scandal

escapar to escape

escaparate *m.* store (display) window

escasez *f.* (*pl.* **escaseces**) lack (14), shortage (14)

escaso/a scarce

escena scene

escenario stage (13)

esclavitud *f.* slavery

esclavo/a slave

escoger (j) to choose

esconder(se) to hide

escondido/a hidden

escopeta shotgun

escorpión *m.* scorpion

escribir (*p.p.* **escrito**) to write (2); **escribir en la computadora** to key in (16), to type (16); **máquina de escribir** typewriter

escrito/a (*p.p. of* **escribir**) written (11); **informe** (*m.*) **escrito** written report (11)

escritor(a) writer (13)

escritorio desk (1)

escritura writing

escuchar to listen (to) (1)

escudo shield

escuela school (9)

esculpir to sculpt (13)

esculsa canal lock

escultor(a) sculptor (13)

escultura sculpture (*general*) (13); (piece of) sculpture (13)

ese/a *dem. adj.* that (3); *dem. pron.* that one (3)

esencial essential

esfuerzo effort

eslavo/a *n.* Slav

esmeralda emerald

eso *dem. pron.* that (3); **eso quiere decir…** that means . . . (10); **por eso** therefore (1)

esos/as *dem. adj.* those (3); *dem. pron.* those (*ones*) (3)

espacial *adj.* space; **transbordador** (*m.*) **espacial** space shuttle

espacio *n.* space; **espacio en blanco** blank space

espacioso/a spacious

espalda back

espantoso/a frightening

España Spain

español *m.* Spanish (*language*) (1)

español(a) *n.* Spaniard; *adj.* Spanish (2); **de habla española** Spanish-speaking; **Real Academia Española** Royal Spanish Academy

espárragos *m. pl.* asparagus (6)

especial special

especialidad *f.* specialty

especialista *m., f.* specialist

especialización *f.* specialization

especializado/a en majoring in

especializarse (c) (en) to major (in)

especie (*f. s.*) **(en peligro de extinción)** (endangered) species (14)

específico/a specific

espectáculo spectacle; show

espectador(a) spectator

espera: sala de espera waiting room (7); **llamada en espera** call-waiting

esperanza hope (17), wish (17); **esperanza de vida** life expectancy

esperar to wait (for) (6); to expect (6); to hope (12)

espíritu *m.* spirit

espléndido/a splendid

esposo/a husband/wife (2); spouse

esqueleto skeleton

esquí *m.* skiing; **estación** (*f.*) **de esquí** ski resort

esquiar (esquío) to ski (9)

esquina (street) corner (14)

está (muy) nublado it's (very) cloudy (5), it's (very) overcast (5); **¿cómo está?** how are you (*form. s.*)? (P)

estable *adj.* stable

establecer (zc) to establish, set up; **establecerse** to settle, establish oneself

estación *f.* season (5); **estación de autobúses / del tren** bus/train station (7); **estación de esquí** ski resort; **estación de gasolina** gas station (14); **estación de metro** subway stop (18)

estacionamiento parking

estacionar to park (11)

estadía stay

estadística statistic

estado state (2); **estado civil** marital status; **estado de ánimo** state of mind; **estado de cuentas** bank statement; **estado libre asociado** commonwealth; **golpe de estado** coup d'etat

Estados (*m. pl.*) **Unidos** United States

estadounidense *adj. m., f.* U.S. (2)

estancia stay (*in a place*) (18)

estanco tobacco stand/shop (18)

estanque *m.* pond; reservoir

estante *m.* bookshelf (4)

estar *irreg.* to be (1); **¿cómo esta(s)?** how are you? (P); **estar a cargo (de)** to be in control (of); **estar a dieta** to be on a diet (6); **estar acecho/a** to be lying in wait; to watch, be on the lookout; **estar atrasado/a** to be late (7); **estar bien** to be comfortable (*temperature*) (5); **estar de mal humor** to be in a bad mood; **estar de vacaciones** to be on vacation (7); **estar en manos de** to belong to; **(no) estar de acuerdo** to (dis)agree; **no estar seguro/a (de)** to be (un)sure (of); **(no) estoy de acuerdo** I (don't) agree (2); **sala de estar** living room; sitting room

estás: ¿cómo estás? how are you (*fam. s.*) (P)

estatal *adj.* state (*pertaining to the government*)

estatua statue

este *n. m.* east (5)

este/a *dem. adj.* this (2); **esta noche** tonight (5); *dem. pron.* this one (3)

estéreo stereo

estereofónico/a: equipo estereofónico stereo equipment (12)

estereotipado/a stereotyped

estereotipo stereotype

estilo style

estimado/a esteemed

estimulante *m.* stimulant

estimular to stimulate

esto *dem. pron.* this (2)

estofado/a stewed

estómago stomach (10); **dolor** (*m.*) **de estómago** stomachache (10)

estos/as *dem. adj.* these (2); *dem. pron.* these (ones) (3)

estoy: (no) estoy de acuerdo I (don't) agree (2)

estrategia strategy

estrechar las manos to shake hands

estrecho/a close; tight; narrow

estrechos *m. pl.* straits (*geography*)

estrella star; **hotel** (*m.*) **de dos (tres) estrellas** two (three) star hotel (18)

estrés *m. s.* stress (11)

estresado/a stressed

estresarse to become stressed

estricto/a strict

estructura structure

estudiante *m., f.* student (1)

estudiantil *adj.* student (11), of students (11); **residencia estudiantil** dormitory (1)

estudiar to study (1)

estudio study

estudioso/a studious

estufa stove (9); **estufa de leña** wood stove

estupendo/a stupendous

etapa stage (*period of time*) (15)

etnia ethnic group

étnico/a ethnic

euro monetary unit of many European countries

europeo/a *n., adj.* European

evaluar (evalúo) to evaluate

evento event (17)

evidencia evidence

evidente evident

evitar to avoid (14)

evolución *f.* evolution

exacto/a exact

examen *m.* exam (3), test (3)

examinar to examine (10)

exceder to exceed

excelente excellent

excepto except

exceso excess; **en exceso** to excess, excessively; **tener** (*irreg.*) **exceso de peso** to be overweight

exclusivo/a exclusive

excursión *f.* excursion

excusa excuse

exhibición *f.* exhibition

exigente demanding

exigir (j) to demand

exiliarse to be exiled

existencia existence

existir to exist

éxito success; **tener** (*irreg.*) **éxito** to be successful

exitoso/a successful

éxodo exodus

exorcizar (c) to exorcize

exótico/a exotic

expectativa expectation

expendedor(a) *adj.* dispensing

experiencia experience

experimentar to experience

experimento experiment

experto expert

explicación *f.* explanation

explicar (qu) to explain (7)

exploración *f.* exploration

explorar to explore

explosión *f.* explosion

explosivo/a explosive

explotación *f.* exploitation; use

explotado/a exploited; used

exportación *f.* export

exportador(a) exporter

exposición *f.* show, exhibition

expresar to express

expresión *f.* expression

expreso/a express, exact

expuesto/a (*p.p. of* **exponer**) exposed; on display

expulsar to expel

expulsión *f.* expulsion

extender (ie) to extend

extenso/a extensive

exterior *adj.* outside

extinción (*f.*): **especie** (*f. s.*) **en peligro de extinción** endangered species (14)

extracción *f.* extraction

extraer (*like* **traer**) to extract

extranjero/a *n.* foreigner; *adj.* foreign (1); **lenguas** (*f. pl.*) **extranjeras** foreign languages (1)

extranjero *n.* abroad, overseas (18); **viajar al/en el extranjero** to travel abroad (18)

extraño strange; **es extraño que** it's strange that (13); **¡qué extraño que… !** how strange that . . . ! (13)

extraordinario/a extraordinary

extravagante extravagant

extremo/a extreme

extroversión *f.* extroversion

extrovertido/a extrovert

exuberancia exuberance

exuberante exuberant

F

fábrica factory (14)

fabricación *f.* making

fabricar (qu) to manufacture

fabuloso/a fabulous

fachada facade

fácil easy (5)

facilidad *f.* ease; facility; ability

facilitar to facilitate

factible feasible

factor *m.* factor

factura bill (16)

facturar to check (*baggage*) (7)

facultad *f.* department (*in a university*)

falda skirt (3)

fallar to "crash" (*of computers*) (12)

falsificado/a forged

falso/a false

falta lack (11); absence; **falta de flexibilidad** lack of flexibility (11)

faltar to be lacking; to be absent; **faltar (a)** to be absent (from) (8), to not attend (8)

familia family (2)

familiar *n. m.* relation, member of the family; *adj.* pertaining to a family

famoso/a famous

fantasía fantasy

fantástico/a fantastic

farmacéutico/a pharmacist (10)

farmacia pharmacy (10)

farmacología pharmacology

faro lighthouse

fascinante fascinating

fatal bad; unlucky

fatiga fatigue

favor *m.* favor; **a favor de** in favor of; with the aid of; **favor de** + *inf.* please (*do something*); **por favor** please (P); **si me hace el favor** if you would do me the favor

favorecer (zc) to favor

favorito/a favorite

fax *m.* fax (12)

fe *f.* faith

febrero February (5)

fecha date (*calendar*) (5); **¿cuál es la fecha de hoy?** what's today's date? (5); **fecha límite** deadline (11)

felicitaciones *f. pl. interj.* congratulations (8)

feliz (*pl.* **felices**) happy (8); **Feliz Año Nuevo** Happy New Year; **feliz cumpleaños** (*m. pl.*) happy birthday; **Feliz Navidad** (*f.*) Merry Christmas

femenino/a feminine

feminidad *f.* femininity

Fénix *m.* Phoenix

fenomenal phenomenal

fenómeno phenomenon

feo/a ugly (2)

feria fair, festival; **rueda de feria** Ferris wheel

feriado/a: día (*m.*) **feriado** holiday

feroz (*pl.* **feroces**) fierce

ferrocarril *m.* railroad

fértil fertile

festejos *m. pl.* public festivities

festival *m.* festival

festividad *f.* festivity

festivo/a: día (*m.*) **festivo** holiday (8)

fibra fiber

ficción *f.* fiction; **ciencia ficción** science fiction

fiebre *f.* fever (10); **tener** (*irreg.*) **fiebre** to have a fever (10)

fiel faithful (2)

fiesta party (1); **dar** (*irreg.*)/**hacer** (*irreg.*) **una fiesta** to give/have a party (8); **fiesta de disfraz** costume party; **fiesta de sorpresa** surprise party

figura figure

fijarse (en) to take note (of), pay attention (to)

fijo/a set; fixed; **precio fijo** fixed price (3)

fila line, row; **en fila** in single file

filete *m.* fillet

filmar to film

filosofía philosophy (1)

filtro filter

fin *m.* end; **en fin** in short; **fin de semana** weekend (1); **por fin** at last, finally (4);

sin fines de lucro not-for-profit; **sin fines lucrativos** nonprofit

final *n. m.* end; *adj.* final; **a finales de** at the end of

financiamiento financing

financiero/a financial

finanza finance

finca farm (14)

fino/a fine

fiordo fjord

firmar to sign

física *s.* physics (1)

físico/a physical

flaco/a skinny

flan *m.* (baked) custard (6)

flexibilidad *f.* flexibility (11); **falta de flexibilidad** lack of flexibility (11)

flexible flexible; **ser** (*irreg.*) **flexible** to be flexible (11)

flor *f.* flower (7)

florecer (zc) to flourish

florido/a: Pascua Florida Easter (8)

flota fleet

folklore *m.* folklore

folklórico/a folkloric (13)

folleto pamphlet

fondo fund; **al fondo** in the background; **fondos** (*m. pl.*) **de apoyo** economic assistance

fontanero/a *Sp.* plumber

forestal pertaining to forests or forestry

forma form; shape; **de todas formas** anyway

formación *f.* background

formar to form; **formar parte de** to be part of, a member of

formular to formulate

formulario form (*to fill out*) (18)

fortaleza fort

fósforo match (*for lighting things*) (18)

foto(grafía) photo(graph) (7); photography (13); **sacar (qu) fotos** to take photos (7)

fotografía photography (13)

fotográfico/a photographic; **equipo fotográfico** photography equipment (12)

fotógrafo/a photographer (16)

frágil fragile

fragmento fragment

francés *m.* French (*language*) (1)

francés, francesa *n., adj.* French (2)

franco/a free, open

frase *f.* phrase

frecuencia frequency; **con frecuencia** frequently (1)

frecuente frequent

fregar (ie) (gu) los platos to wash the dishes

frenar to brake

freno brake (14)

frente a facing, opposite

fresco/a fresh (6); cool (*weather*); **hace fresco** it's cool (*weather*) (5)

fresno ash tree

frialdad *f.* coldness

frigidez *f.* frigidity

frigorífico refrigerator

frijoles *m. pl.* beans (6)

frío *n.* cold(ness); *adj.* cold; **hace (mucho) frío** it's (very) cold (*weather*) (5); **tener** (*irreg.*) **(mucho) frío** to be (very) cold (5)

frito/a fried (6); **patata frita** French fried potato

frontera border (*political, geographical*) (18)

frugalidad *f.* frugality

fruncir (z) to knit (*brows*)

fruta fruit (6); **jugo de fruta** fruit juice (6)

frutal *adj.* fruit

fruto seco nut

fue sin querer it was unintentional (11)

fuego fire; **fuegos artificiales** fireworks

fuente *f.* source

fuera *adv.* outside

fuerte strong (6); heavy (*meal*) (6)

fuerza strength; force

fulano/a so-and-so (*person*)

fumador(a) smoker

fumar to smoke (7); **sección** (*f.*) **de (no) fumar** (non)smoking section (7)

función *f.* function

funcionar to work (12), to function (12); to run (*machines*) (12)

fundación *f.* foundation; **Fundación Alerta contra el SIDA** AIDS Awareness Foundation

fundar to found

furioso/a furious, angry (5)

fusilamiento shooting, execution; **pelotón** (*m.*) **de fusilamiento** firing squad

fútbol *m.* soccer (9); **fútbol americano** football (9)

futbolista *m., f.* soccer player

futuro *n.* future

futuro/a *adj.* future

G

gabrielino/a person from the San Gabriel mission

gafas *f. pl.* glasses (10); **llevar gafas** to wear glasses (10)

gajo branch (*of a tree*)

galante gallant

galardón *m.* reward

galería gallery

gallego/a *n.* Galician

galleta cookie (6)

gallina hen, chicken

gallinero chicken coop

gallo: misa del gallo Midnight Mass; **gallo/a** guy, gal (*sl., Chile*)

gamba *Sp.* shrimp

gana desire, wish; **darle** (*irreg.*) **la gana** to feel like; **tener** (*irreg.*) **ganas de** + *inf.* to feel like (*doing something*) (3)

ganar to earn (16); to win (9); **ganarse la vida** to earn a living

ganga bargain (3); **¡qué ganga!** what a bargain!

garaje *m.* garage (4)

garantizar (c) to guarantee

garawón *m. traditional drum of Central America*

garganta throat (10)

garífuna *m. s., pl. ethnic group from Nicaragua*

garúa coastal fog

gas *m.* gas (12); heat (12)

gasolina gasoline (14); **estación** (*f.*) **de gasolina** gas station (14)

gasolinera gas station (14)

gastar to spend (*money*) (8); to use (*gas*) (14); to expend

gasto expense (12)

gastronómico/a gastronomic

gato/a cat (2)

gazpacho *cold, tomato-based soup (Sp.)*

generación *f.* generation

general general; **por lo general** generally (4)

generalizar (c) to generalize

género genre

generoso/a generous

génesis *m. inv.* beginning

genio/a genius

gente *f. s.* people (13)

geografía geography

geográfico/a geographic

geoturismo geotourism

gerente *m., f.* manager (16)

germánico/a Germanic

gerontología gerontology

gerundio *gram.* gerund

gesto gesture

gigante *adj.* giant

gimnasio gymnasium

gira tour

glaciación *f.* glaciation

glaciar *m.* glacier

globo balloon

gobernador(a) governor

gobernar (ie) to govern (17), to rule (17)

gobierno government (14)

golf *m.* golf (9)

golpe (*m.*) **de estado** coup d'etat

gordo/a fat (2)

gorila *m.* gorilla (14)

gorra cap (3)

gozar (c) to enjoy

gozo joy

grabadora (tape) recorder/player (12)

grabar to record (12), to tape (12)

gracias thank you (P); **Día** (*m.*) **de Acción de Gracias** Thanksgiving; **gracias por** thanks for (8); **muchas gracias** thank you very much (P)

grado grade (*in school*) (9), year (*in school*) (9)

graduado/a *adj.* graduate

graduarse (me gradúo) (en) to graduate (from) (16)

gráfico *n.* graph, diagram

gráfico/a *adj.* graphic

gramática grammar

gran, grande big (2), large (2); great (2)

granada pomegranate

grandeza majesty, grandeur; greatness

granito granite

granja farm

grano pimple

grasa fat

grasoso/a fatty; greasy

gratuito/a free (of charge)

grave serious

Grecia Greece

griego/a *n., adj.* Greek

gripe *f.* flu

gris gray (3)

gritar to shout, yell

grotesco/a grotesque

gruñir to grunt; to growl

grupo group

guacamole *m.* avocado dip or side-dish

guacharaca *wooden percussion stick*

guanacaste: punto guanacaste *national dance of Costa Rica*

guapo/a handsome (2); good-looking (2)

guaraní *m.* Guarani (*L.A. indigenous language*)

guardar to save (*a place*) (7); to keep (12); to save (*documents*) (12); **guardar cama** to stay in bed (10)

guardia *m.* guard, guardsman; **de guardia** on-call

guatemalteco/a *n., adj.* Guatemalan

guerra war (17); **Segunda Guerra Mundial** World War II

guerrero/a warrior

gueto ghetto

guía *f.* guide(book); *m., f.* guide (*person*) (13)

guiado/a guided

guión *m.* script (13)

guionista *m., f.* scriptwriter

guisante *m.* green pea

guitarra guitar

guitarrista *m., f.* guitarist

gusta: ¿le gusta… ? do you (*form. s.*) like . . . ? (P); **sí, (no, no) me gusta…** yes, I do (no, I don't) like . . . (P); **¿te gusta… ?** do you (*fam. s.*) like . . . ? (P)

gustar to be pleasing (7)

me gustaría… I would (really) like (7)

gusto like, preference, taste; **mucho gusto** nice/pleased to meet you (P)

H

haber *irreg.* (*inf. of* **hay** there is, there are) have *auxilary with past participle* (12); **hay que** + *inf.* it's necessary to (*do something*) (13)

habilidad *f.* ability, skill

habilidoso/a skillful, clever

habitable habitable

habitación *f.* room; **habitación con/sin baño/ducha** room with(out) attached bath/shower (18); **habitación individual/doble** single/double room (*in a hotel*) (18); **servicio de habitación** *Sp.* room service

habitante *m., f.* inhabitant

habitar to live, reside

hábito habit, custom

hablante *m. f.* speaker

hablar to speak (1); to talk (1); **de habla española** Spanish-speaking; **hablar por teléfono** to talk on the phone (1)

hacer *irreg.* (*p.p.* **hecho**) to do (4); to make (4); **hace** + *period of time* + **que** + *present tense* to have been (*doing something*) for (*a period of time*); **hace** + *time time* ago; **hace (muy) buen/mal tiempo** it's (very) good/bad weather (5); **hace fresco** it's cool (*weather*) (5); **hace (mucho) frío/calor** it's (very) cold/hot (weather) (5); **hace (mucho) sol** it's (very) sunny (5); **hace (mucho) viento** it's (very) windy (5); **hacer**

hacer (*continued*)
   alpinismo to mountain climb; **hacer autostop** to hitchhike; **hacer** *camping* to go camping (7); **hacer cola** to stand in line (7); **hacer copia** to copy (12); **hacer ejercicio** to exercise (4), to get exercise; **hacer ejercicios aeróbicos** to do aerobics (10); **hacer escalas/paradas** to make stops (7); **hacer la cama** to make the bed (9); **hacer la(s) maleta(s)** to pack one's suitcase(s) (7); **hacer las cuentas** to pretend; **hacer planes para** + *inf.* to make plans to (*do something*) (9); **hacer preguntas** to ask questions; **hacer un** *picnic* to have a picnic (9); **hacer un viaje** to take a trip (4); **hacer una fiesta** to have/give a party (8); **hacer una pregunta** to ask a question (4); **hacer visitas** to visit; **hacerse** to become; **hacerse daño** to hurt oneself (11); **¿qué tiempo hace hoy?** what's the weather like today? (5); **si me hace el favor** if you would do me the favor
hacia toward
hacienda farm, ranch; country estate
hallar to find
hambre *f.* (*but* **el hambre**) hunger; **pasar hambre** to go hungry; **tener** (*irreg.*) **(mucha) hambre** to be (very) hungry (6)
hamburguesa hamburger (6)
harto/a fed up
hasta *adv.* even; *prep.* until (4); **hasta luego** see you later (P); **hasta mañana** see you tomorrow (P); **hasta pronto** see you soon; **hasta que** *conj.* until (16)
hay: (no) hay there is (not) (P); there are (not) (P); **hay (mucha) contaminación** there's (lots of) pollution (5); **hay que** + *inf.* it's necessary to (*do something*) (13); **¡hay que cuidarse!** you must take care of yourself!; **no hay de qué** you're welcome (P); **no hay duda** there is no doubt
hebreo/a *n.* Hebrew; **Pascua (de los hebreos)** Passover
hecho *n.* fact (8); deed; event (8); **de hecho** in fact
hecho/a (*p.p. of* **hacer**) made; done; taken
helado *n.* ice cream (6)
helado/a *adj.* frozen
hemisferio hemisphere
heredar to inherit
herido/a wounded
hermanastro/a stepbrother, stepsister

hermano/a brother/sister (2); **medio hermano/media hermana** half-brother / half-sister
hermoso/a beautiful
héroe *m.* hero
herramienta tool
hervir (ie, i) to boil
hidalgo nobleman; gentleman
hidráulico/a hydraulic
hidroeléctrico/a hydroelectric
hidrógeno hydrogen
hielo ice
hígado liver
higiénico/a hygienic, sanitary
hijastro/a stepson, stepdaughter
hijo/a son/daughter (2)
hijos *m. pl.* children (2)
himno hymn
hipopótamo hippopotamus
hipoteca mortgage
hispánico/a *adj.* Hispanic
hispano/a *n., adj.* Hispanic
hispanoamericano/a *n., adj.* Hispanic-American
hispanocanadiense *n., adj. m., f.* Hispanic-Canadian
hispanohablante *adj. m., f.* Spanish-speaking
historia story; history (1)
historiador(a) historian
histórico/a historic
hockey *m.* hockey (9)
hogar *m.* home; household
hoja leaf
hola hello (P)
Holanda Holland
holgadamente comfortably, easily
hombre *m.* man (1); **hombre de negocios** businessman (16)
homeopatía homeopathy
homeópato/a homeopathic
hondureño/a *n., adj.* Honduran
honesto/a honest
honor *n. m.* honor
honrar to honor
hora hour; time; **¿a qué hora?** at what time? (P); **¿qué hora es?** what time is it? (P)
horario schedule (11)
horneado/a baked
horno oven; **horno de microondas** microwave oven (9)
horóscopo horoscope
horror *m.* horror
hospedarse to stay (as a guest)

hospicio hospice
hospital *m.* hospital
hotel (*m.*) **(de lujo)** (luxury) hotel (18); **hotel de dos (tres) estrellas** two (three) star hotel (18)
hoy today (P); **¿cuál es la fecha de hoy?** what's today's date? (5); **hoy (en) día** nowadays, these days
huayno *traditional music and dance from Peru*
huelga strike (*labor*) (17)
huella footprint
huerto orchard; garden
hueso bone
huésped(a) (hotel) guest (18)
huevo egg (6); **huevo cocido** hard-boiled egg; **huevo tibio/pasado por agua** poached egg; **huevos revueltos** scrambled eggs
huir (y) to flee
humanidad *f.* humanity; *pl.* humanities (1)
humanitario/a humanitarian
humano/a *adj.* human; **ser** (*m.*) **humano** human being
humedad *f.* humidity
humilde humble
humo smoke
humor *m.* humor; mood; **estar** (*irreg.*) **de mal humor** to be in a bad mood
huracán *m.* hurricane

I

ibérico/a *adj.* Iberian
ida: de ida one-way (7); **de ida y vuelta** round-trip (7)
idealista *adj. m., f.* idealistic
idéntico/a identical
identidad *f.* identity; **tarjeta de identidad** identification card
identificación *f.* ID (16); **tarjeta de identificación** identification card (11)
identificado/a: objeto volante no identificado (OVNI) unidentified flying object (UFO)
identificar (qu) to identify
idioma *m.* language
iglesia church
ignorante ignorant
igual equal, same
igualdad *f.* equality (17)
igualmente likewise (P), same here (P)
ilegal illegal
iluminación *f.* lighting
imagen *f.* image
imaginación *f.* imagination

imaginar(se) to imagine
imaginario/a imaginary
imán *m.* magnet
imitar to imitate
impaciente impatient
impacto impact
impar uneven, odd (*with numbers*)
imparcialmente impartially
impedir (*like* **pedir**) to impede, hinder
imperfecto *gram.* imperfect (*past tense*)
imperio empire
impermeable *m.* raincoat (3)
imponente imposing; majestic
importación *f.* import
importancia importance
importante important
importar to matter, be important; **no me importa un pito** I don't care one bit
imposible impossible; **es imposible que** it's impossible that (13)
imprescindible essential, indispensable
impresión *f.* impression
impresionante impressive
impresora printer (12)
imprimir to print (12)
improbable unlikely; **es improbable que** it's improbable, unlikely that (13)
impuesto tax
impulsivo/a impulsive
inadecuado/a inadequate
inaugurar to inaugurate
inca *n. m., f.* Inca; *adj. m., f.* Incan
incidente *m.* incident
incluir (y) to include
inclusive *adj.* including
incluso *adv.* even; including
incomodar to make uncomfortable
inconcebible inconceivable
inconfundible unmistakeable
inconveniente *m.* drawback, difficulty
incorporar to incorporate
incorrecto/a incorrect
increíble incredible; **es increíble que** it's incredible that (13)
incrementar to increase
indefinido/a: artículo indefinido *gram.* indefinite article
independencia independence; **Día** (*m.*) **de la Independencia** Independence Day
independiente independent
indicación *f.* instruction; direction
indicar (qu) to indicate
indicativo *gram.* indicative
indiferencia indifference

indiferenciado/a undifferentiated
indígena *n. m., f.* indigenous person; *adj. m., f.* indigenous
indigenista pertaining to indigenous topics and themes
indio/a *n., adj.* Indian
indirecto/a: complemento indirecto *gram.* indirect object pronoun
indiscreto/a indiscreet
individual: habitación (*f.*) **individual** single room (*in a hotel*) (18)
individuo *n.* individual
indoeuropeo/a *adj.* Indo-European
industria industry
industrializado/a industrialized
inequívoco/a unmistakable, certain
infancia infancy (15)
infantil *adj.* child, children's
infección *f.* infection
inferior lower
infinitivo *gram.* infinitive
infinito/a infinite
influencia influence
influenciado/a influenced
influente influential
influir (y) to influence
infográfico graph (with information)
información *f.* information
informar to inform (17); **informarse (de)** to find out (about)
informática *s.* computer studies
informativo/a informative
informe *m.* (**oral/escrito**) (written/oral) report (11)
infortunio misfortune
infraestructura infrastructure
ingeniería engineering
ingeniero/a engineer (16)
ingenioso/a ingenious, clever
ingerir (ie, i) to ingest
Inglaterra England
inglés *m.* English (*language*) (1)
inglés, inglesa *n.* Englishman, Englishwoman; *adj.* English (2)
ingrediente *m.* ingredient
ingreso income
iniciar to begin, initiate
inicio beginning
injusticia injustice
inmediato/a immediate
inmenso/a huge, immense
inmigración *f.* immigration
inmigrante *m., f.* immigrant
inmigrar(se) to immigrate
inmortalizar (c) to immortalize

innecesario/a unnecessary
innumerable countless
inocente innocent; **Día** (*m.*) **de los Inocentes** April Fool's Day
inolvidable unforgettable
inquietante worrisome
inquilino/a tenant (12), renter (12)
insano/a insane; unhealthy
inscribirse (*p.p.* **inscrito**) to sign up, register
inscrito/a (*p.p. of* **inscribir**) registered
insistir (en) + *inf.* to insist (on) (12)
insolente insolent
insomnio insomnia
inspector(a) inspector; **inspector(a) de aduanas** customs inspector
inspiración *f.* inspiration
inspirarse en to be inspired by
instalación *f.* equipment
institución *f.* institution
instituto institute
instrumento instrument
intacto/a intact
integral *adj.* whole grain
integrar to integrate; to form, make up
integridad *f.* integrity
intelectual intellectual
inteligente intelligent (2)
intención *f.* intention
intensivo/a intensive
intentar to try
interactivo/a interactive
interés *m.* interest (16)
interesante interesting
interesar to interest; to be interesting (7)
intergaláctico/a intergalactic
interior *n.* interior; *adj.* inside, inner; interior; **ropa interior** underwear (3)
internacional international; **Día** (*m.*) **Internacional de los Trabajadores** International Labor Day
internarse (en) to check into (*a hospital*) (10)
Internet *m.* Internet
interno/a internal
interplanetario/a interplanetary
interpretación *f.* interpretation
interpretar to interpret; to perform
intérprete *m., f.* interpreter
interrogativo/a *gram.* interrogative
interrumpir to interrupt
intervención *f.* intervention
íntimamente intimately
intranquilidad *f.* uneasiness, restlessness
introducción *f.* introduction
introducir *irreg.* to introduce

intromisión *f.* intrusion
introversión *f.* introversion
introvertido/a introverted
inútilmente uselessly
invadir to invade
invasión *f.* invasion
invención *f.* invention
inventar to invent
investigación *f.* investigation
investigar (gu) to investigate
invierno winter (5)
invitación *f.* invitation
invitado/a guest (8)
invitar to invite (6)
involucrado/a involved
inyección (*f.*)**: ponerle** (*irreg.*) **una inyección** to give (someone) a shot, injection (10)
iPod **m.** iPod (12)
ir *irreg.* to go (3); **ir a** + *inf.* to be going to (*do something*) (3); **ir a una discoteca / un bar / un concierto** to go to a disco/bar/concert (9); **ir a ver una película** to go to see a movie (9); **ir al cine** to go to the movies (9); **ir al teatro** to go to the theater (9); **ir de compras** to go shopping (3); **ir de vacaciones** to go on vacation (7); **ir en autobús/avión/barco/tren** to go/travel by bus/plane/boat, ship/train (7); **irse** to leave
Irlanda Ireland
irónico/a ironic
irresponsable irresponsible
irritación *f.* irritation
isla island (5)
Islandia Iceland
isleta isle
istmo isthmus
Italia Italy
italiano Italian (*language*) (1)
italiano/a *n., adj.* Italian
itólele *m.* one of three *batá* drums
iyá *m.* one of three *batá* drums
izquierda *n.* left-hand side; **a la izquierda (de)** to the left (of) (5)
izquierdo/a *adj.* left (*direction*); **levantarse con el pie izquierdo** to get up on the wrong side of the bed (11)

J

jabón *m.* soap (18)
jalón (*m.*)**: de un jalón** all at once
jamás never (6), not ever
jamón *m.* ham (6)
Japón *m.* Japan

japonés *m.* Japanese (*language*)
japonés, japonesa *n., adj.* Japanese
jarabe *m.* (cough) syrup (10)
jardín *m.* yard (4)
jarrita jar
jeans **m. pl.** jeans (3)
jefe/a boss (12)
jerez *m.* (*pl.* **jereces**) sherry
jeroglífico/a *adj.* hieroglyphic
jipijapa Panama hat, straw hat
jirafa giraffe
joropo *traditional music and dance from Venezuela*
joven *n. m., f.* youth; *adj.* young (2); **de joven** as a youth (9)
joya jewel
joyería jewelry store
jubilado/a retired
jubilarse to retire (16)
judío/a Jewish person
juego game; **Juegos Olímpicos** Olympic Games
jueves *m. inv.* Thursday (4)
jugador(a) player (9)
jugar (ue) (gu) (al) to play (*a game, sport*) (4); **jugar a las cartas** to play cards (9); **jugar al ajedrez** to play chess
jugo (de fruta) (fruit) juice (6)
jugoso/a juicy
juguete *m.* toy
juicio: perder (ie) el juicio to go crazy
julio July (5)
jungla jungle
junio June (5)
juntarse to get together
junto a near, next to; **junto con** along with, together with
juntos/as *adj.* together (15)
justificar (qu) to justify
justo/a fair
juvenil *adj.* juvenile
juventud *f.* youth (15)
juzgado court
juzgar (gu) to judge

K

kilogramo kilogram
kilómetro kilometer
kiosco kiosk

L

la *def. art. f. s.* the (1); *d.o. f. s.* you (*form.*); her, it
labor *f.* work
laborable: día (*m.*) **laborable** workday

laboral *adj.* pertaining to work or labor
laboratorio laboratory
lado side; **al lado de** *prep.* alongside of (5); beside; next to; **por otro lado** on the other hand; **por un lado** on the one hand
ladrar to bark
lago lake (14)
lágrima tear
lámpara lamp (4)
lana wool (3); **es de lana** it's made of wool (3); **perro de lanas** poodle
langosta lobster (6)
lanza spear, lance
lápiz *m.* (*pl.* **lápices**) pencil (1)
largo (*n.*)**: de largo** in length
largo/a *adj.* long (2); **a largo plazo** long-term; **a lo largo de** along; throughout; **llamada a larga distancia** long-distance call
las *def. art. f. pl.* the; *d.o. f. pl.* you (*form.*); them; **a las...** at . . . (*hour*) (P); **las demás** others (12)
lástima shame; **es una lástima que** it's a shame that (13) **¡qué lástima que... !** what a shame that . . . ! (13)
lastimarse to injure oneself (11)
lata: ser (*irreg.*) **una lata** to be a pain, drag
latín *m.* Latin (*language*)
latino/a *adj.* Latin
Latinoamérica Latin America
latinoamericano/a *n., adj.* Latin American
latinocanadiense *adj. m., f.* Latin-Canadian
lavabo (bathroom) sink (4)
lavadora washing machine (9)
lavandería laundromat
lavaplatos *m. inv.* dishwasher (9)
lavar to wash; **lavar (las ventanas, los platos, la ropa)** to wash (the windows, the dishes, the clothes) (9)
le *i.o. s.* to/for you (*form.*), him, her, it; **¿le gusta... ?** do you (*form. s.*) like . . . ? (P); **le molesta/sorprende que** it bothers/surprises you (*form. s.*)/him/her that (13)
lección *f.* lesson
leche *f.* milk (6)
lecho bed
lechuga lettuce (6)
lector (*m.*) **de DVD** DVD player (12)
lector(a) reader
lectura reading

leer (y) to read (2)
legalizar (c) to legalize
legendario/a legendary
legislación *f.* legislation
lejos de *prep.* far from (5)
lempira *m.* monetary unit of Honduras
lengua language (1); tongue; **lenguas extranjeras** foreign languages (1); **sacar (qu) la lengua** to stick out one's tongue (10)
lenguado flounder
lenguaje *m.* language
lentamente slowly
lentes (*m. pl.*) **de contacto** contact lenses (10); **llevar lentes de contacto** to wear contact lenses (10)
leña: estufa de leña wood stove
les *i.o. pl.* to/for you (*form. pl.*); them
letanía litany
letra letter (*alphabet*); lyrics; **letra cursiva** *s.* italics
letrero sign
levantar to raise, lift; **levantar pesas** to lift weights; **levantarse** to get up (4); to stand up (4); **levantarse con el pie izquierdo** to get up on the wrong side of the bed (11)
leve light, slight
ley *f.* law (17)
leyenda legend
liberación *f.* liberation
libertad *f.* liberty (17), freedom (17)
libertador(a) liberator
libra pound
libre free; **al aire libre** outdoors; **estado libre asociado** commonwealth; **ratos** (*m. pl.*) **libres** spare (free) time (9)
librería bookstore (1)
libro book (1); **libro de texto** textbook (1)
licencia license; **licencia de conducir/ manejar** driver's license (14)
líder *m.* leader
liga league
ligero/a light(weight); light (6); not heavy (6)
limeño/a person from Lima, Peru
limitación *f.* limitation
limitar to limit
límite *m.* limit; **fecha límite** deadline (11); **límite de velocidad** speed limit (14)
limón *m.* lemon
limonada lemonade
limpiaparabrisas *m. inv.* windshield wiper

limpiar la casa (entera) to clean the (whole) house (9)
limpio/a clean (5)
lindo/a pretty, lovely
línea line; **patinar en línea** to rollerblade (9)
lingüístico/a linguistic
lío de tráfico traffic jam
líquido *n.* liquid
lírico/a lyrical
lista list; **lista de bodas** bride's registry
listo/a smart (2); clever (2); ready
literario/a literary
literatura literature (1)
llamada (telephone) call; **llamada a larga distancia** long-distance call; **llamada en espera** call-waiting
llamar to call (6); **¿cómo se llama usted?** what is your (*form. s.*) name? (P); **¿cómo te llamas?** what is your (*fam. s.*) name? (P); **llamarse** to be called (4); **me llamo…** my name is . . . (P)
llanero/a pertaining to the plains
llanta tire (14); **llanta de recambio** spare tire; **llanta desinflada** flat tire (14)
llanura *n.* plain
llave *f.* key (11)
llegada arrival (7)
llegar (gu) to arrive (6); **llegar a ser** to become; **llegar a tiempo** to arrive on time
llenar to fill (up) (14); **llenar la solicitud** to fill out the application (16)
lleno/a full
llevar to wear (3); to carry (3); to take (3); to lead; **llevar gafas/lentes de contacto** to wear glasses/contact lenses (10); **llevar puesto/a** to have on; **llevar una vida sana/tranquila** to lead a healthy/calm life (10); **llevarse bien/mal (con)** to get along well/poorly (with) (15)
llorar to cry (8)
llover (ue) to rain (5)
llueve it's raining (5)
lluvia rain
lluvioso/a rainy
lo *d.o. m. s.* you (*form.*); him, it; **lo bueno / lo malo** the good/bad thing, news (10); **lo contrario** the opposite; **lo mismo** the same thing; **lo que** what (4), that which; **¡lo siento (mucho)!** pardon me! (11), I'm (very) sorry! (11); **lo suficiente** enough (10)
lobo wolf

local *n. m.* stall (market); *adj.* local
localidad *f.* ticket (*to a movie, play*)
localización *f.* location
localizar (c) to locate
loco/a crazy (5)
locura madness, craziness
lógico/a logical
lograr to achieve
loma hill
Londres London
los *def. art. m. pl.* the; *d.o. m. pl.* you (*form.*); them; **los años sesenta, ochenta, …** the sixties, eighties, . . . ; **los demás** others (12); **los lunes, martes…** on Mondays, Tuesdays, . . . (4)
lotería lottery
loza porcelain
lubricar (qu) to lubricate
lucha struggle; fight
luchar to fight; to struggle
lucrativo/a: sin fines lucrativos nonprofit
lucro: sin fines de lucro not-for-profit
lúdico/a entertaining
luego *adv.* then (4); afterwards (4); **hasta luego** see you later (P)
lugar *m.* place (1); **ningún lugar** nowhere; **tener** (*irreg.*) **lugar** to take place
lujo luxury (12); **hotel** (*m.*) **de lujo** luxury hotel (18)
lujoso/a luxurious
luna moon; **luna de miel** honeymoon (15)
lunar (*m.*): **de lunares** polka-dotted
lunes *m. inv.* Monday (4); **los lunes** on Mondays (4)
lustroso/a shiny
Luxemburgo Luxembourg
luz *f.* (*pl.* **luces**) light (11); electricity (11)

M

machista *adj. m., f.* male; chauvinistic
madera wood
madrastra stepmother
madre *f.* mother (2)
madrileño/a: callos (*m. pl.*) **a la madrileña** tripe Madrid–style
madrugada dawn
madurez *f.* maturity (15)
maduro/a mature
maestro/a school teacher (16); **obra maestra** masterpiece (13)
magia magic
mágico/a magic
magnético/a magnetic

magnífico/a magnificent

mago wizard; **Día** (*m.*) **de los Reyes Magos** Day of the Magi (Three Kings)

maíz *m.* (*pl.* **maíces**) corn

majestuoso/a majestic

mal *n. m.* evil; illness, sickness; *adv.* badly; poorly (1); **caerle** (*irreg.*) **mal a alguien** to make a bad impression on someone (16); **llevarse mal (con)** to get along poorly (with) (15); **mal educado/a** rude, bad-mannered; **pasarlo mal** to have a bad time (8); **salir** (*irreg.*) **mal** to turn/come out badly

mal, malo/a *adj.* bad (2); **hace mal tiempo** it's bad weather (5); **lo malo** the bad thing, news (10); **¡qué mala suerte!** what bad luck! (11); **sacar (qu) malas notas** to get bad grades (11)

maldito/a accursed, awful

maleta suitcase (7); **hacer** (*irreg.*) **la(s) maleta(s)** to pack one's suitcase(s) (7)

maletero porter (7)

maletín *m.* briefcase

malvado/a wicked

mamá mother (2), mom (2)

mamífero mammal

manchego: queso manchego hard, white cheese (*from La Mancha, Spain*)

mandar to send (7); to order (*someone to do something*) (12)

mandato command

manejar to drive (12); to operate (*a machine*) (12); to manage; **licencia de manejar** driver's license (14)

manera way, manner; **de manera que** *conj.* so that, in such a way that; **de todas maneras** by all means; whatever happens

manifestación *f.* manifestation; demonstration

manjar *m.* delicacy

mano *f.* hand (11); **darse** (*irreg.*) **la mano** to shake hands; **dedo de la mano** finger (11); **estar** (*irreg.*) **en manos de** to belong to; **¡manos a la obra!** let's get to work!

manta blanket (18)

mantener (*like* **tener**) to maintain; to keep; **mantener la paz** to maintain, keep the peace (17); **mantenerse en contacto** to keep/stay in touch

mantequilla butter (6)

manzana apple (6)

manzanilla chamomile

mañana *n.* morning; *adv.* tomorrow (P); (*an hour*) **de la mañana** in the morning (P); **hasta mañana** see you tomorrow (P); **pasado mañana** day after tomorrow (4); **por la mañana** in the morning (1)

mapa *m.* map

mapuche *m.* Araucan (*indigenous language of S.A.*)

máquina machine; **máquina de escribir** typewriter

mar *m.* sea (7)

maratón *m.* marathon

maravilla wonder, marvel

maravilloso/a marvelous, wondrous

marca brand name

marcar (qu) to strike (*clock*); to mark

mareado/a dizzy (10); nauseated (10)

mareo dizziness

marido husband (15)

marihuana marijuana

marinado/a marinated

marino/a *adj.* sea

mariposa butterfly

mariscos *m. pl.* seafood; shellfish (6)

marítimo/a maritime; sea, marine

Marruecos *m.* Morocco

martes *m. inv.* Tuesday (4); **los martes** on Tuesdays (4)

marzo March (5)

más more (1); **cada vez más** increasingly; **más allá** further, farther; **más allá de** beyond, farther than; **más... que** more . . . than (5)

masa dough

máscara mask

mascota pet (2)

masculino/a masculine

masoquista *n. m., f.* masochist

matar to kill

matemáticas *f. pl.* mathematics (1)

materia (school) subject (1)

material *m.* material (3)

materialista *m., f.* materialistic

matrícula tuition (1)

matrimonio marriage (15); married couple (15); **contraer** (*like* **traer**) **matrimonio** to get married

máximo/a maximum

maya *n., adj. m., f.* Mayan

mayo May (5); **Cinco de Mayo** *Mexican awareness celebration*

mayor older (5); oldest; greater; greatest; **la mayor parte** most

mayoría majority

me *d.o.* me; *i.o.* to/for me; *refl. pron.* myself; **me gustaría...** I would (really) like . . . (7); **me llamo...** my name is . . .
(P); **me molesta/sorprende que** it bothers/surprises me that (13); **sí, (no, no) me gusta(n)...** yes, I do (no, I don't) like . . . (P)

mecánico/a *n.* mechanic (14); *adj.* mechanical; **escaleras** (*f. pl.*) **mecánicas** escalator

mecanización *f.* mechanization

media: media pensión *f.* room with breakfast and one other meal (18); **y media** half-past/30 minutes past (*the hour*) (P)

mediano/a medium; average

medianoche *f.* midnight (8)

mediante *prep.* by means of, through

medias *f. pl.* stockings (3)

medicina medicine (10)

médico/a *n.* (medical) doctor (2); *adj.* medical; **atención** (*f.*) **médica** healthcare

medida measure; **en cierta medida** in some measure

medio *n.* medium; means; **medio ambiente** environment (*nature*) (14); **medio de comunicación** means of communication (17); **medios de comunicación** media; **por medio de** by means of

medio/a *adj.* half; middle; average; **Edad** (*f.*) **Media** Middle Ages; **media hermana** half-sister; **media pensión** *f.* room with breakfast and one other meal (18); **medio hermano** half-brother; **Oriente** (*m.*) **Medio** Middle East

medioambiental environmental

mediodía *m.* noon

mediterráneo/a *adj.* Mediterranean

mejor better (5); best (5)

mejorar to improve

membrana membrane

memoria memory (12)

mencionar to mention

menor *m.* minor; *adj.* younger (5); youngest; less; least

menos less; least; minus; **a menos que** *conj.* unless (15); **menos cuarto (quince)** a quarter (fifteen minutes) to (*the hour*) (P); **menos... que** less . . . than (5); **por lo menos** at least (8)

mensaje *m.* message; **mensaje electrónico** e-mail message

mensual monthly

mensualidad *f.* monthly installment

menta mint

-mente *suffix* -ly (11)

mentira lie (12)

menú *m.* menu (6)

menudo: a menudo often

mercadeo marketing

mercado market(place) (3)

merecer (zc) to deserve

merengue *m. traditional music and dance from the Dominican Republic*

merienda snack

mes *m.* month (5)

mesa table (1); **poner** (*irreg.*) **la mesa** to set the table (9); **quitar la mesa** to clear the table (9); **uva de mesa** table grape

meseta plateau (*geography*)

mesita end table (4)

mesón *m.* tavern

mestizo/a mixed-race person

meta goal

metáfora metaphor

metereólogo/a meteorologist

método method

metro subway; meter; **estación** (*f.*) **de metro** subway stop (18)

metrópoli *f.* metropolis; capital city

mexicano/a *n., adj.* Mexican (2)

México Mexico

mexicoamericano/a *n., adj.* Mexican American

mezcla mixture

mezclar to mix

mí *obj.* (*of prep.*) me (5)

mi(s) *poss. adj.* my (2)

microondas (*f. pl.*): **horno de microondas** microwave oven (9)

miedo fear; **tener** (*irreg.*) **miedo (de)** to be afraid (of) (3)

miel *f.* honey; **luna de miel** honeymoon (15)

miembro member

mientras while (9); **mientras que** *conj.* while

miércoles *m. inv.* Wednesday (4)

migrante *adj.* migrant

mil *m.* thousand, one thousand (3); **dos mil** two thousand (3); **mil millón** (*m.*) billion

milagro miracle

milanesa cutlet

milenio millennium

miligramo milligram

militar: servicio militar military service (17)

milla mile

millón *m.* million, **un millón (de)** million (3); **dos millones** two million (3); **mil millón** billion

millonario/a millionaire

mineral: agua (*f.* [*but* **el agua**]) **mineral** mineral water (6)

minería mining

minero/a miner

minidiálogo minidialogue

minidrama *m.* minidrama

minifalda miniskirt

mínimo/a minimum

ministerio ministry

ministro/a: primer(a) ministro/a prime minister

minoría minority

minuto minute

mío/a(s) *poss. adj.* my; *poss. pron.* (of) mine

mirar to look at (2), to watch (2); **mirar la televisión** to watch television (2)

misa mass; **misa del gallo** Midnight Mass; **oficiar una misa** to celebrate a mass

misión *f.* mission

mismo *adv.* same (10); **ahora mismo** right now; at once

mismo/a *adj.* same; self; **lo mismo** the same thing

misterioso/a mysterious

mitad *f.* half

mito myth

mitología mythology

mixteca *m.* Mixtec (*indigenous language*)

mixteca *n., adj. m., f.* Mixtec

mochila backpack (1)

moda fashion; style; **de moda** in style; **¡es de última moda!** it's the latest style! (3)

modelo model

módem *m.* modem (12)

moderación *f.* moderation

moderado/a moderate

modernismo modernism

moderno/a modern (13)

modificación *f.* modification

modificar (qu) to modify

modismo idiom

modo way, manner; mode; *gram.* mood; **de modo** in such a way; **de todos modos** anyway; **modo (de transporte)** means (of transportation) (7)

molestar to bother, annoy; **me (te, le...) molesta que** it bothers me (you, him . . .) that (13)

molestia bother, annoyance

molido/a *adj.* ground (up)

molino: rueda de molino treadmill (10)

momento moment; **en este momento** right now

monarca *m., f.* monarch

monarquía monarchy

monasterio monastery

moneda currency; coin

monoparental *adj.* single-parent

monopatín *m..* skateboard (12)

monstruo monster

montaña mountain (7); **bicicleta de montaña** mountain bike (12); **montaña rusa** roller coaster

montañismo en bicicleta mountain biking

montar to set up; to ride; **montar a caballo** to ride a horse (9); **montar en bicicleta** to ride a bicycle

montón (*m.*): **un montón** a bunch

monumento monument

morado/a purple (3)

moralidad *f.* morality

morcilla blood sausage

moreno/a brunet(te) (2)

morirse (ue, u) (*p.p.* **muerto**) to die (8)

moro/a *n.* Moor; *adj.* Moorish

mostaza mustard

mostrar (ue) to show (7)

motivo reason, motive; motif

moto(cicleta) *f.* motorcycle (12); moped (12)

motor *m.* motor, engine

movimiento movement

mozo bellhop (18); **mozo de campo y plaza** farmhand

muchacho/a boy, girl (4)

muchísimo *adv.* an awful lot (7)

mucho *adv.* a lot, much (1); **¡lo siento mucho!** I'm very sorry!

mucho/a *adj.* a lot (of) (2); *pl.* many (2); **muchas gracias** thank you very much (P); **mucho gusto** pleased to meet you (P)

mucoso/a *adj.* mucous

mudanza *n.* move; moving

mudarse to move (*residence*) (16)

muebles *m. pl.* furniture (4); **sacudir los muebles** to dust the furniture (9)

muela tooth (10); molar (10), **sacar (qu) una muela** to extract a tooth (10); **tener** (*irreg.*) **dolor de muela** toothache (10)

muerte *f.* death (15)

muerto/a (*p.p. of* **morir**) dead; **muerto/a de risa** dying of laughter

mujer *f.* woman (1); wife (15); **mujer de negocios** businesswoman (16); **mujer soldado** female soldier (16)

mula mule

mulato/a mulatto

multa *n.* fine

multimillonario/a multimillionaire; billionaire

multinacional *f.* multinational company

mundial *adj.* world; **Copa Mundial** World Cup; **Segunda Guerra Mundial** World War II

mundo *n.* world (7)

muralismo muralism

murciélago bat

murmurar to murmur, whisper

muro wall

músculo muscle

museo museum; **visitar un museo** to visit a museum (9)

música music (13)

músico/a musician (13)

musulmán, musulmana *adj.* Moslem

muy very (1); **muy bien** fine (P), very well (P); **muy buenas** good afternoon/evening (P)

N

nacer (zc) to be born (15)

nacido/a born; **recién nacido/a** newborn

nacimiento birth (15)

nación *f.* nation; **Naciones** (*f. pl.*) **Unidas** United Nations

nacional national

nacionalidad *f.* nationality (18)

nada nothing (6), not anything (6); **de nada** you're welcome (P)

nadar to swim (7)

nadie no one (6), nobody (6), not anybody (6)

náhuatl *m. indigenous language of Central America*

naranja *n.* orange (6)

nariz *f.* nose (10); *pl.* **narices** nostrils

narración *f.* narration

narrador(a) narrator

narrar to narrate

natación *f.* swimming (9)

natal *adj.* native

natalidad *f.* birth

nativo/a *n.* native

natural: recursos (*m. pl.*) **naturales** natural resources (14)

naturaleza nature (14)

náuseas *f. pl.* nausea

navegación *f.* navigation; sailing

navegar (gu) to sail; to navigate; **navegar la Red** to surf the Net (12)

Navidad *f.* Christmas (8); **Feliz Navidad** Merry Christmas

navideño/a *adj.* Christmas; **tarjeta navideña** Christmas card

necesario/a necessary (2)

necesidad *f.* necessity

necesitar to need (1)

negación *f.* negation

negar (ie) (gu) to deny (13); **negarse a +** *inf.* to refuse to (*do something*)

negativa *n. gram.* negative

negativo/a *adj.* negative

negocio business; **hombre** (*m.*)/**mujer** (*f.*) **de negocios** businessperson (16)

negro/a *n.* black (person); *adj.* black (3)

neoyorquino/a *adj.* pertaining to New York

nervio: ataque (*m.*) **de nervios** nervous breakdown

nervioso/a nervous (5)

neutro/a neutral

nevado/a snow-covered

nevar (ie) to snow (5)

nevera refrigerator

ni neither; nor; not even; **ni... ni...** neither . . . nor . . .; **ni siquiera** not even

nicaragüense *n., adj. m., f.* Nicaraguan

nido nest

nieto/a grandson/granddaughter (2)

nietos *m. pl.* grandchildren (2)

nieva it's snowing (5)

nieve *f.* snow

ningún, ninguno/a no (6), none (6), not any (6); **ningún lugar** nowhere

niñero/a baby-sitter (9)

niñez *f.* (*pl.* **niñeces**) childhood (9)

niño/a small child; boy/girl; **de niño/a** as a child (9)

nitrógeno nitrogen

nivel *m.* level (14)

no no (P); not; **¿no?** right?, don't they (you, *and so on*) (3); **no estoy de acuerdo** I don't agree (2); **no hay** there is not/are not (P); **no hay de qué** you're welcome (P); **no hay duda** there is no doubt; **no, no me gusta(n)...** no, I don't like . . . (P); **no tener** (*irreg.*) **razón** to be wrong (3); **ya no** no longer

noche *f.* night; **buenas noches** good evening (P); good night (P); **de noche** at night; (*an hour*) **de la noche** in the evening (P); at night (P); **esta noche** tonight (5); **Noche Vieja** New Year's Eve (8); **por la noche** in the evening (1); at night (1)

Nochebuena Christmas Eve (8)

nombrar to name

nombre *m.* name

nominación *f.* nomination

nominado/a nominated

nominal: cláusula nominal *gram.* noun clause

noreste *m.* northeast

noria Ferris wheel

norma norm; standard

normalidad *f.* normality

norte *n., adj. m.* north (5)

Norteamérica North America

norteamericano/a *n., adj.* North American

nos *d.o. pron.* us; *i.o. pron.* to/for us; *refl. pron.* ourselves; **nos vemos** see you around (P)

nosotros/as *sub. pron.* we (1); *obj.* (*of prep.*) us

nota grade (11); note

notar to notice, note

noticia piece of news (8); *pl.* news (17)

noticiero newscast (17)

novecientos/as nine hundred (3)

novedades *f. pl.* news

novela novel

novelista *m., f.* novelist

noveno/a ninth (13)

noventa ninety (2)

noviazgo engagement (15)

noviembre *m.* November (5)

novio/a boyfriend/girlfriend (5); fiancé(e) (15); groom/bride (15); **vestido de novia** wedding gown

nublado/a cloudy; **está (muy) nublado** it's (very) cloudy (5)

nuclear: energía nuclear nuclear energy (14)

nudo knot

nuera daughter-in-law

nuestro/a(s) *poss. adj.* our (2); *poss. pron.* ours, of ours

nueve nine (P)

nuevo/a new (2); **Día** (*m.*) **del Año Nuevo** New Year's Day; **Feliz Año Nuevo** Happy New Year

numérico/a numerical

número number (2)

numeroso/a numerous

nunca never (2), not ever; **casi nunca** almost never (2)

nutrición *f.* nutrition

O

o or (P)

ó or (*between two numbers* [*digits*])

obedecer (zc) to obey (14)

obelisco obelisk

obesidad *f.* obesity

objetivo objective

objeto object; **objeto volante no identificado (OVNI)** unidentified flying object (UFO)

obligación *f.* obligation

obligatorio/a compulsory

obra (de arte) work (of art) (13); **¡manos a la obra!** let's get to work!; **obra maestra** masterpiece (13)

obrero/a worker (16), laborer (16)

observación *f.* observation

observar to observe

obstáculo obstacle

obtener (*like* **tener)** to get (12), to obtain (12)

obvio/a obvious

ocarina *potato-shaped wind instrument*

ocasión *f.* occasion

ocasionar to bring about

occidental western

océano ocean (7); **Océano Atlántico** Atlantic Ocean

ochenta eighty (2)

ocho eight (P)

ochocientos/as eight hundred (3)

ocio leisure time

ocioso/a leisurely

octavo/a eighth (13)

octubre *m.* October (5)

ocular *adj.* eye, pertaining to the eye

ocupación *f.* occupation

ocupado/a busy (5)

ocupar to occupy

ocurrir to occur, happen

odiar to hate (7)

oeste *m.* west (5)

oferta offer; sale, special

oficial *n., adj. m., f.* official

oficiar una misa to celebrate a mass

oficina office (1); **oficina de correos** post office (18); **oficina de personal** personnel office

oficio trade (*profession*) (16)

ofrecer (zc) to offer (7)

oído inner ear (10)

oír *irreg.* to hear (4)

ojalá (que) I wish (that) (13), I hope (that) (13)

ojo eye (10); **¡ojo!** watch out!; **ojo alerta** eagle eye

okónkolo *one of three* **batá** *drums*

olímpico/a: Juegos (*m. pl.*) **Olímpicos** Olympic Games

oliva olive; **aceite** (*m.*) **de oliva** olive oil

olla pot

olmeca *n., adj. m., f.* Olmec

olvidadizo/a forgetful

olvidar(se) (de) to forget (about) (8)

olvido forgetfulness; oblivion

ómnibus *m.* bus

once eleven (P)

onda wave; **¿qué onda?** *sl.* what's new?, what's happening?

ONU *f.* (**Organización de Naciones Unidas**) U.N. (United Nations)

opción *f.* option

ópera opera (13)

operación *f.* operation

operar to operate

opinar to think; to have, express an opinion

oponerse (*like* **poner)** to oppose

oportunidad *f.* opportunity

oposición *f.* opposition

optimista *adj. m., f.* optimist

opuesto/a (*p.p. of* **oponer**) opposite

oración *f.* sentence

oral: informe (*m.*) **oral** oral report (11)

órale *sl. Mex.* come on

orden *m.* order (*chronological*); *f.* order, command; **a sus órdenes** at your service

ordenado/a neat (5)

ordenador *m. Sp.* computer (12); **ordenador portátil** laptop computer

ordenar to put in order

oreja (outer) ear (10)

orgánico/a organic

organismo organism

organización *f.* organization

organizar (c) to organize

oriental eastern

Oriente (*m.*) **Medio** Middle East

origen *m.* origin

originar(se) to originate

originario/a originating; native

orilla shore; bank (*of a river*)

oriundo/a (de) native (of)

oro gold; **Ricitos de Oro** Goldilocks

orquesta orchestra

ortiga nettle

ortográfico/a *adj.* spelling, orthographic

os *d.o. pron.* you (*fam. pl.*); *i.o. pron.* to / for you (*fam. pl.*)

oscuro/a dark

oso bear; **oso pardo** grizzly bear

ostra oyster

otoño autumn (5), fall (5)

otorgar (gu) to grant

otro/a other (2), another (2); **otra vez** again; **por otra parte/otro lado** on the other hand

OVNI *m.* (**objeto volante no identificado**) UFO (unidentified flying object)

oxígeno oxygen

oye *interj.* listen; hey

oyente *m., f.* listener

ozono: capa de ozono ozone layer

P

paciencia patience

paciente *n. m., f.* patient (10); *adj.* patient

Pacífico/a Pacific (Ocean, Coast)

padecer (zc) to suffer

padrastro stepfather

padre *m.* father (2)

padres *m. pl.* parents (2)

padrino godfather

padrinos *m. pl.* godparents

paella *dish made with rice, shellfish, and often chicken, and flavored with saffron*

pagar (gu) to pay (1); **pagar a plazos** to pay in installments (16); **pagar al contado/en efectivo** to pay in cash (16); **pagar con cheque** to pay by check (16)

página page

país *m.* country (2)

paisaje *m.* countryside (14); landscape

pájaro bird (2)

palabra word (P)

palacio palace

pálido/a pale

palma palm tree

palo stick

palomino young dove

palomitas *f. pl.* popcorn

pampa plain (*geography, Arg.*)

pan *m.* bread (6); **pan tostado** toast (6)

panameño/a *n., adj.* Panamanian

pantalones *m. pl.* pants (3); **pantalones cortos** shorts

papá *m.* father (2), dad (2); **Papá Noel** Santa Claus

papa potato (6)

papel *m.* paper (1); role (*in a play*) (13); **papel para cartas** stationery (18)

papelería stationery store (18)

paquete *m.* package (18)

par *m.* pair (3)

para *prep.* (intended) for (2); in order to (2); **para + inf.** in order to (*do something*); **para que** *conj.* so that (15)

parabrisas *m. inv.* windshield (14)

paracaidismo skydiving

parada stop; **hacer** (*irreg.*) **paradas** to make stops (7); **parada de autobús** bus stop (18)

paraguas *m. inv.* umbrella

paraguayo/a *n., adj.* Paraguayan

parar to stop (14)

parcial: de tiempo parcial part time (11)

pardo/a brown; **oso pardo** grizzly bear

parecer (zc) to seem (13)

parecido/a similar

pared *f.* wall (4); **pintar las paredes** to paint the walls (9)

pareja (married) couple (15); partner (15)

paréntesis *m. inv.* parentheses

pariente *m., f.* relative (2)

parlamentario/a parliamentary

párpado eyelid

parque *m.* park (5); **parque de atracciones** amusement park

párrafo paragraph

parrandero/a party-loving

parroquiano/a client

parte *f.* part; **la mayor parte** most; **formar parte de** to be part of, a member of; **por otra parte** on the other hand; **por parte de** by; **por todas partes** everywhere (11)

participante *m., f.* participant

participar to participate

participativo/a participatory

participio *gram.* participle

partícula particle

particular particular; private

partida: punto de partida starting point

partido game (9), match (*sports*) (9)

partir: a partir de as of; from (*this moment, date on*)

párvulo tot

pasado *n.* past

pasado/a *adj.* last (10); past (10); **el año pasado** last year; **huevo pasado por agua** poached egg; **pasado mañana** day after tomorrow (4)

pasaje *m.* passage (7); ticket (7)

pasajero/a passenger (7)

pasaporte *m.* passport (18)

pasar to happen (5); to pass; to spend (*time*) (5); **pasar... años** to be more than . . . years old; **pasar hambre** to go hungry; **pasar la aspiradora** to vacuum (9); **pasar películas** to show movies; **pasar por el control de la seguridad** to go/pass through security (7); **pasar tiempo (con)** to spend time (with) (15); **pasarlo bien/mal** to have a good/bad time (8)

pasatiempo pastime (9), hobby (9)

Pascua (Florida) Easter (8); **Pascua (de los hebreos)** Passover

pasear to take a walk, stroll; to go for a ride; **pasear en bicicleta** to ride a bicycle (9)

paseo walk, stroll; **dar** (*irreg.*) **un paseo** to take a walk (9)

pasión *f.* passion

pasional passionate

pasivo/a passive

paso step; **de paso** passing through

pasta dental toothpaste (18)

pastel *m.* cake (6); pie (6); **pastel de cumpleaños** birthday cake (8)

pastelería pastry shop (18)

pastelito small pastry (18)

pastilla pill (10)

pastor(a) shepherd; **perro pastor alemán** German Shepherd

pata paw

patata potato *Sp.* (6); **patata frita** French fried potato (6)

patinar to skate (9); **patinar en línea** to rollerblade (9)

patines *n. m. pl.* roller skates (12)

patio patio (4); yard (4)

pato duck

patria homeland

patrón *m.* pattern

patrona: santa patrona patron saint

pavo turkey (6); **pavo real** peacock

paz *f.* (*pl.* **paces**) peace (17); **mantener** (*like* **tener**) **la paz** to maintain, keep the peace (17); **vivir en paz** to live in peace (17)

pecho chest

pechuga breast

pedagogía pedagogy

pedir (i, i) to ask for (4); to order (4); **pedir disculpas** to apologize (11); **pedir prestado/a** to borrow (16)

pegar (gu) to hit (9), strike; **pegarse en/con/contra** to hit (*a part of one's body*) (11); to run into (11), to bump against (11)

peinado hairdo

peinarse to comb one's hair (4)

pelado/a peeled

pelear to fight (9)

película movie (4), film; **ir** (*irreg.*) **a ver una película** to go to see a movie (9); **pasar películas** to show movies

peligro danger; jeopardy; **especie** (*f. s.*) **en peligro de extinción** endangered species (14)

peligroso/a dangerous

pelo hair; **tomarle el pelo** to pull someone's leg

pelota ball

pelotón (*m.*) **de fusilamiento** firing squad

peluquero/a hairstylist (16)

pena: ¡qué pena! what a shame!; **valer** (*irreg.*) **la pena** to be worthwhile, worth the trouble

pendencia quarrel, fight

péndulo pendulum

pensar (ie) to intend (4), to plan to (4); **pensar (en)** to think (about) (4)

pensión *f.* boardinghouse (18); **media pensión** room with breakfast and one other meal (18); **pensión completa** room and full board (18)

peor worse (5); worst

pepino cucumber

pequeño/a small (2)

percibido/a perceived

percusionista *m., f.* percussionist

perder (ie) to lose (4); to miss (*a function*) (4); **perder el juicio** to go crazy

pérdida loss

perdón pardon me (P), excuse me (P)

perezoso/a lazy (2)

perfecto/a perfect

periódico newspaper (2)

periodista *m., f.* journalist (16)

periodístico/a *adj.* journalistic

perjudicar (qu) to damage, hurt

permanente permanent

permiso permission; permit; **con permiso** excuse me (P)

permitir to permit (12), to allow (12)

pero but (P)

perpetuo/a perpetual

perro dog (2); **perro de lanas** poodle; **perro pastor alemán** German Shepherd

persa *adj. m., f.* Persian
perseguir (*like* **seguir**) to pursue
persona person (1)
personaje *m.* character (*in literature*)
personal (*m.*): **dirección** (*f.*) **de personal** personnel office (16); employment office (16); **director(a) de personal** personnel director (16); **oficina de personal** personnel office
personalidad *f.* personality
perspectiva perspective
persuadir to persuade
pertenecer (zc) a to belong to
perturbar to disturb
peruano/a *n., adj.* Peruvian
pesado/a boring (9); difficult (9); heavy
pesar to weigh; **a pesar de** in spite of
pesas: levantar pesas to lift weights
pesca fishing
pescado fish (*cooked*) (6)
peseta former monetary unit of Spain
pesimista *adj. m., f.* pessimist
peso weight; **tener** (*irreg.*) **exceso de peso** to be overweight
pesticida pesticide
petróleo petroleum, oil
petrolero/a *adj.* petroleum, oil; **buque** (*m.*) **petrolero** oil tanker
petrolífero/a *adj.* oil-bearing, oil
pez *m.* (*pl.* **peces**) fish (*animal*) (14)
pianista *m., f.* pianist
picnic: **hacer** (*irreg.*) **un** *picnic* to have a picnic (9)
pico beak
pie *m.* foot (11); **a pie** on foot; **dedo del pie** toe (11); **levantarse con el pie izquierdo** to get up on the wrong side of the bed (11); **poner** (*irreg.*) **pie en** to set foot on
piedra stone
piel *f.* skin
pierna leg (11)
pieza piece
píldora pill
piloto/a pilot
pimienta pepper
pingüino penguin
pintar (las paredes) to paint (the walls) (9)
pintor(a) painter (13)
pintoresco/a picturesque
pintura painting (*art form*) (13); (*general*) (13); (*piece of art*) (13); paint
pirámide *f.* pyramid
pirata *m., f.* pirate
Pirineos *m. pl.* Pyrenees

pisar to tread on, step on
piscina swimming pool (4)
piso floor; apartment (*Sp.*); **barrer el piso** to sweep the floor (9); **primer/segundo piso** second/third floor (first/second floor above ground floor) (12)
pistacho pistachio
pitar to whistle
pito: no me importa un pito I don't care one bit
pizarra chalkboard (1)
pizzería pizza parlor
placa license plate
placer *m.* pleasure
plan *m.* plan; **hacer** (*irreg.*) **planes para +** *inf.* to make plans to (*do something*) (9)
plancha: a la plancha grilled
planchar la ropa to iron clothing (9)
planeación *f.* plan
planear to plan
planeta *m.* planet
plano/a flat
planta plant; **planta baja** ground floor (12)
plantación *f.* plantation
plantar cara a to confront
plástico *n.* plastic
plata silver
plátano banana
platino platinum
plato dish (*of a meal*) (6); course (*of a meal*) (6); **platos** dishes, plates (4); **fregar (ie) (gu) los platos** to wash the dishes; **lavar los platos** to wash the dishes (9); **plato principal** entrée
playa beach (5)
plaza: plaza de toros bullring
plazo period, term; **a largo plazo** long-term; **pagar (gu) a plazos** to pay in installments (16)
plegaria prayer
plena *traditional music from Puerto Rico*
plenamente fully, completely
plenera *tambourine-like instrument*
plomero/a plumber (16)
pluralismo pluralism
pluviosidad *f.* rainfall
población *f.* population (14)
poblado/a populated
poblar to settle
pobre *n. m., f.* poor person; *adj.* poor (2)
pobreza poverty
poco *adv.* little (1); **dentro de poco** in a little while; **poco a poco** little by little; **un poco (de)** a little bit (of)
poco/a *adj.* little (3); *pl.* few

poder *v. irreg.* to be able to (3), can (3)
poder *n. m.* power
poderoso/a powerful
poema *m.* poem
poesía poetry
poeta *m., f.* poet (13)
poético/a poetic
policía *m., f.* police officer (14); *f.* police (force)
poliomielitis *f.* poliomyelitis (polio)
política *s.* politics (17)
político/a *n.* politician (17); *adj.* political; **ciencias** (*f. pl.*) **políticas** political science
pollo (asado) (roast) chicken (6)
pololo/a *sl.* (*Chile*) boyfriend/girlfriend
polvo: quitar el polvo to dust
poner *irreg.* (*p.p.* **puesto**) to put (4), to place (4); to turn on (*appliances*) (4); **poner la mesa** to set the table (9); **poner pie en** to set foot on; **ponerle +** *adj.* to make someone (*feel a certain way*); **ponerle una inyección** to give (someone) a shot, injection (10); **ponerse** to put on (*clothing*) (4); **ponerse +** *adj.* to become, get + *adj.* (8); **ponerse a la altura de** to compete on the same level as; **ponerse al día** to get up-to-date; **ponerse de acuerdo** to reach an agreement; **ponerse enfermo/a** to get sick
popularidad *f.* popularity
popularizar (c) to popularize
por *prep.* by; for (4); through; in (1); during (4); along; by way of; **por ciento** percent; **por completo** completely; **por costumbre** customarily; **por Dios** for heaven's sake (11); **por ejemplo** for example (11); **por eso** therefore (1); **por favor** please (P); **por fin** at last, finally (4); **por la mañana/tarde/noche** in/during the morning/afternoon/evening (1); **por la noche** at night (1); **por lo general** generally (4); **por lo menos** at least (8); **por medio de** by means of; **por otra parte/por otro lado** on the other hand; **por parte de** by; **por primera/última vez** for the first/last time (11); **¿por qué?** why? (2); **por si acaso** just in case (11); **¡por supuesto!** of course! (11); **por todas partes** everywhere (11); **por último** finally; **por un lado** on the one hand
¿por qué? why? (2)

porcentaje *m.* percentage
pordiosero/a beggar
porque because (2)
portarse to behave (8)
portátil: portable; **computadora/ ordenador** (*m.*) (*Sp.*) **portátil** laptop computer; **radio portátil** portable radio (12)
porteño/a person from Buenos Aires
portero/a building manager; doorman (12)
portugués *m.* Portuguese (*language*)
portugués, portuguesa *n., adj.* Portuguese
porvenir *m.* future
posada boarding house; inn
posesión *f.* possession
posesivo/a possessive
posgraduado/a *adj.* graduate; postgraduate
posibilidad *f.* possibility
posible possible (2)
posición *f.* position
postal: tarjeta postal postcard (7)
postre *m.* dessert (6)
postura stance
potencia power
potente strong
pozo well
práctica practice
practicar (qu) to practice (1); to participate (*in a sport*) (9); **practicar deportes** to practice, play sports (10)
práctico/a practical
precedente *m.* precedent
precio price (3); **precio fijo** fixed price (3), set price (3)
precioso/a precious
precipitado/a hasty
precipitarse to rush headlong
preciso/a exact, precise
precolombino/a pre-Columbian
predicción *f.* prediction
predominar to dominate
preferencia preference
preferible preferable
preferir (ie, i) to prefer (3)
pregunta question; **hacer** (*irreg.*) **preguntas** to ask questions; **hacer una pregunta** to ask a question (4)
preguntar to ask (a question) (6)
prehistórico/a prehistoric
prejuicio prejudice
prematuro/a premature
premio prize
prender to turn on (*lights, appliance*)

prensa press (17), news media (17)
prensado/a crushed
preocupación *f.* worry, concern
preocupado/a worried (5)
preocupante worrisome
preocuparse (por) to worry (about)
preparación *f.* preparation
preparar to prepare (6)
preparativo preparation
preposición *f. gram.* preposition
presa seizure; **ser** (*irreg.*) **presa de** to be a victim of
presea treasure
presencia presence
presentación *f.* presentation
presentar to present, introduce
presente *n. m.* present (*time*); *gram.* present tense
preservación *f.* preservation
presidencia presidency
presidencial presidential
presidente/a president
presidio fort
presión *f.* pressure; **sufrir (muchas) presiones** to be under (a lot of) pressure (11)
prestado/a: pedir (i, i) prestado/a to borrow (16)
préstamo loan (16)
prestar to lend (7)
prestigio prestige
prestigioso/a prestigious
presupuesto budget (16)
pretérito *gram.* preterite (*past tense*)
primario/a primary; **bosque** (*m.*) **primario** old-growth forest
primavera spring (5); **vacaciones** (*f. pl.*) **de primavera** spring break
primer, primero/a *adj.* first (13); **a primera vista** at first sight (15); **de primera** first-class; **el primero de** the first of (*month*) (5); **por primera vez** for the first time (11); **primer(a) ministro/a** prime minister; **primer piso** second floor (12); **primera clase** first class (7)
primero *adv.* first (4)
primo/a cousin (2)
principal main, principle; **plato principal** entrée
príncipe *m.* prince
principiante *m., f.* beginner
principio beginning; **a principios de** at the beginning of; **al principio de** at the beginning of (16)

prisa hurry *n.;* **tener** (*irreg.*) **prisa** to be in a hurry (3)
prisionero/a prisoner
privado/a private
privilegio privilege
probabilidad *f.* probability
probable: es probable que it's probable, likely that (13)
probar (ue) to try; to taste
problema *m.* problem
procesamiento processing
proceso process
producción *f.* production
producir *irreg.* to produce
producto product
productor(a) producer
profesión *f.* profession (16)
profesional professional
profesor(a) professor (1); **asistente** (*m., f.*) **del profesor** teaching assistant
profundidad *f.* depth
profundo/a deep
programa *m.* program
programador(a) programmer (16)
progresista *adj. m., f.* progressive
progresivo/a progressive
progreso progress
prohibición *f.* prohibition
prohibir (prohíbo) to forbid (12), to prohibit (12)
proliferación *f.* proliferation
promedio *n.* average
prometer to promise (7)
promover (ue) to promote
pronombre *m. gram.* pronoun
pronto soon; **hasta pronto** see you soon; **tan pronto como** as soon as (16)
pronunciación *f.* pronunciation
pronunciar to pronounce
propagar (gu) to spread (*news*)
propiedad *f.* property
propina tip (18)
propio/a *adj.* own (15)
proponer (like poner) to propose
proporcionar to provide
propósito purpose
protagonista *m., f.* protagonist
protección *f.* protection
proteger (j) to protect (14)
protestar to protest
proveer (like ver) to provide
provenir (like venir) to come from
proverbio proverb
providencia providence
provincia province

provocar (qu) to provoke, cause
proximidad *f.* closeness
próximo/a next (4)
proyecto project
prueba test (11); quiz (11)
psicología psychology
psicológico/a psychological
psiquiatra *m., f.* psychiatrist
psíquico/a *adj.* psychic
publicación *f.* publication
publicar (qu) to publish
publicidad *f.* publicity; advertising
público *n.* audience; public
público/a *adj.* public (14); **servicios** (*m. pl.*) **públicos** public services (14); **transporte** (*m.*) **público** public transportation (14)
pueblo town; people
puerta door (1)
puerto port (7)
puertorriqueño/a *n., adj.* Puerto Rican
pues *conj.* since, because, for; *adv.* then, well, all right
puesto *n.* job (16); position; place (*in line*) (7); **guardar un puesto** to save a place (7); **renunciar el puesto** to resign from a job, position (16)
puesto/a (*p.p. of* **poner**): **llevar puesto/a** to have on
pulgada inch
pulido/a polished
pulmón *m.* lung (10); **a todo pulmón** at the top of one's lungs
punto point; **en punto** exactly (*time*) (P); on the dot (*time*) (P); sharp (*time*) (P); **punto cardinal** cardinal direction; **punto de partida** starting point, point of departure; **punto de vista** point of view; **punto guanacaste** *national dance of Costa Rica*
puntual punctual
puro *n.* cigar
puro/a pure (14); clean (14); **aire** (*m.*) **puro** clean air (14)

Q

que that (2); which; who (2); **así que** therefore, consequently, so; **hasta que** *conj.* until (16); **hay que** + *inf.* it's necessary to (*do something*) (13); **lo que** what (4); that which; **más... que** more . . . than (5); **menos... que** less . . . than (5); **que aproveche** enjoy your meal; **ya que** since
¿qué? what? (P); which?; **¿a qué hora?** what time? (P); **¿de qué color es?** what color is it?; **¿por qué?** why?; **¿qué día es hoy?** what day is today?; **¿qué hora es?** what time is it? (P); **¿qué tal?** how are you doing? (P); **¿qué tiempo hace hoy?** what's the weather like today? (5)
¡qué + *adj.***!** how + *adj.*! (11); **¡qué** + *noun***!** what (a) + *noun*!; **¡qué extraño qué...!** how strange that . . . ! (13); **¡qué ganga!** what a bargain!; **¡qué lástima que...!** what a shame that . . . ! (13); **¡qué mala suerte!** what bad luck! (11); **¡qué pena!** what a shame!; **¡qué torpe!** how clumsy! (11)
quebranto misfortune
quechua *m.* Quechua (*indigenous language*)
quedar to remain (11); to be left (11); to be situated; **quedarle bien** to fit well; to look good (*on someone*); **quedarse** to stay, remain (*in a place*) (5)
quehacer *m.* chore; **quehacer doméstico** household chore (9)
quejarse (de) to complain (about) (8)
quemar to burn (up)
quena Andean flute
querella fight
querer *irreg.* to want (3); to love (15); **eso quiere decir...** that means . . . (10); **fue sin querer** it was unintentional (11)
querido/a dear (5)
queso cheese (6); **queso manchego** hard, white cheese (*from La Mancha, Spain*)
quetzal *m.* monetary unit of Guatemala
quiché *m.* Quiché (*indigenous language from Central America*)
quien who, whom
¿quién(es)? who? (1), whom? (1); **¿de quién?** whose? (2)
quiere: eso quiere decir... that means (10)
quieto/a still (*movement*)
quijongo *single-string bow with gourd resonator*
química chemistry (1)
quince fifteen (P); **y/menos quince** a quarter (fifteen minutes) after/to (*the hour*) (P)
quinceañera *young woman's fifteenth birthday party*
quinientos/as five hundred (3)
quinto/a fifth (13)
quiosco kiosk (18)
quitar to remove; **quitar la mesa** to clear the table (9); **quitar el polvo** to dust; **quitarse** to take off (*clothing*) (4)
quizás perhaps

R

rabino/a rabbi
racismo racism
radical *m. gram.* stem
radio *m.* (**portátil**) (portable) radio (*apparatus*) (12); *f.* radio (*medium*) (12)
radioyente *m., f.* radio listener; *m., pl.* radio audience
raíz *f.* (*pl.* **raíces**) root; **a raíz de** as a result of; because of
rama branch
rancho ranch
rapidez *f.* speed
rápido/a fast (6)
ráquetbol *m.* racketball
raro/a strange (8)
rascacielos *m. inv.* skyscraper (14)
rato *n.* while, short time; **ratos** (*m. pl.*) **libres** spare (free) time (9)
ratón *m.* mouse (12)
raya: de rayas striped
raza race; **Día** (*m.*) **de la Raza** Columbus Day (Hispanic Awareness Day)
razón *f.* reason; **no tener** (*irreg.*) **razón** to be wrong (3); **tener** (*irreg.*) **razón** to be right (3)
reacción *f.* reaction
reaccionar to react (8)
real real; royal; **Camino Real** Royal Highway; **pavo real** peacock; **Real Academia Española** Royal Spanish Academy
realidad *f.* reality; **en realidad** in fact
realismo realism
realista *adj. m., f.* realistic
realizar (c) to achieve, attain
rebajas *f. pl.* sales (3), reductions (3)
rebelde *n. m., f.* rebel; *adj.* rebellious
rebozo shawl
recado message
recambio: llanta de recambio spare tire
recepción *f.* front desk (18)
recepcionista *m., f.* receptionist
receta recipe; prescription (10)
recetar to prescribe (*medicine*)
rechazar (c) to reject
recibir to receive (2)
reciclaje *m.* recycling
reciclar to recycle (14)
recién *adv.* newly, recently; **recién casado/a (con)** newlywed (to) (15); **recién nacido/a** newborn
reciente recent
recinto enclosure, space
recipiente *m.* container

reciprocidad *f.* reciprocity
recíproco/a reciprocal
recoger (j) to collect (11); to pick up (11)
recomendación *f.* recommendation
recomendar (ie) to recommend (7)
reconocer (zc) to recognize
reconocido/a recognized, well-known
recopilado/a compiled
recordar (ue) to remember (8)
recorrer to travel through
recorte *m.* clipping (*newspaper*)
recreativo/a recreational
recreo recreation
recto/a straight
rector(a) university president
recubanizar (c) to become Cuban again
recuerdo souvenir; memory
recuperación *f.* recovery, recuperation
recurso resource; **recursos naturales** natural resources (14)
Red *f.* Net (12); Internet; **navegar (gu) la Red** to surf the Net (12)
redacción *f.* editorial staff
redecorado/a redecorated
redondo/a round
reducción *f.* reduction
reducir *irreg.* to reduce
reemplazar (c) to replace
reencarnación *f.* reincarnation
referencia reference
referente (a) referring, relating (to)
referirse (ie, i) (a) to refer (to)
refinado/a refined
reflejar to reflect
reflejo reflection
reflexivo/a reflexive
reformar to reform
refresco soft drink (6)
refrigerador *m.* refrigerator (9)
refugiarse to take refuge
refugio refuge
regalar to give (*as a gift*) (7)
regalo gift (2), present (2)
regatear to haggle (3), to bargain (3)
régimen *m.* regime
región *f.* region
registrar to search (18), to examine (18)
registro register; registration
regla rule
regresar to return (*to a place*) (1); **regresar a casa** to go home (1)
regulador (*m.*) **termómetro** thermostat
regular so-so (P), OK (P)
reina queen (17)
reino kingdom

reír(se) (i, i) (me río) to laugh (8); **reírse a carcajadas** to laugh one's head off
relación *f.* relation; *pl.* relationship
relacionarse con to be related to
relajante relaxing
relajarse to relax
relativo/a relative
religión *f.* religion
religioso/a religious
reloj *m.* clock; watch (3)
remar to row
remedio remedy
remodelado/a remodeled
remoto/a remote; **control** (*m.*) **remoto** remote control (12)
renovar (ue) to renovate
renunciar (a) to resign (from) (16)
reparar to fix, repair
repasar to review
repaso review
repente: de repente suddenly (10)
repertorio repertory
repetición *f.* repetition
repetir (i, i) to repeat
repetitivo/a repetitive
reportaje *m.* article; report
reportar to report
reportero/a reporter (17)
represa dam
representante *n. m., f.* representative
representar to represent (13)
república republic
requerir (ie, i) to require
requisito requirement
resaltar to emphasize
reserva reservation (18); **hacer** (*irreg.*)/**confirmar las reservas** to make/confirm reservations (18)
reservación *f.* reservation (18); **hacer** (*irreg.*)/**confirmar las reservaciones** to make/confirm reservations (18)
reservar to reserve
resfriado cold (*illness*) (10)
resfriarse (me resfrío) to get/catch a cold (10)
residencia dormitory (1)
residencial residential
residente *m., f.* resident
resolver (ue) (*p.p.* **resuelto**) to solve (14); to resolve (14)
respectivamente respectively
respecto: (con) respecto a with regard to, with respect to
respetar to respect
respeto respect

respiración *f.* breathing
respirar to breathe (10)
respiratorio/a respiratory
resplandor *m.* brilliance, radiance
responder to answer
responsabilidad *f.* responsibility (17)
responsabilizar (c) to make responsible
respuesta answer (5)
restaurante *m.* restaurant (6)
resto rest
restricción *f.* restriction
restringido/a restrained
resuelto/a (*p.p. of* **resolver**) solved, resolved
resultado result
resultar to turn out
resumen *m.* summary; **en resumen** in short
retener (*like* **tener**) to retain
reto challenge
retórico/a rhetorical
retrasado/a late
retratar to paint a portrait of
retrato portrait
reunión *f.* meeting; gathering
reunirse (me reúno) (con) to get together (with) (8)
revelar to reveal
revés: al revés backward
revisar (el aceite) to check (the oil) (14)
revista magazine (2)
revolución *f.* revolution
revolucionario/a revolutionary
revolver (ue) (*p.p.* **revuelto**) to scramble
revuelto/a (*p.p. of* **revolver**): **huevos** (*m. pl.*) **revueltos** scrambled eggs
rey *m.* king (17); **Día** (*m.*) **de los Reyes Magos** Day of the Magi (Three Kings)
rezar (c) to pray
Ricitos de Oro Goldilocks
rico/a rich (2)
ridículo/a ridiculous; **es ridículo que** it's ridiculous that (13)
riesgo risk
riesgoso/a risky
rígido/a rigid
rima rhyme
rincón *m.* corner
rinoceronte *m.* rhinoceros
riñón *m.* kidney
río river (14)
riqueza wealth
risa laughter; **muerto/a de risa** dying of laughter
ritmo rhythm (14), pace (14)

rito ritual
róbalo sea bass
robar to steal
robo robbery, theft
roca rock
rodaje *m.* shooting, filming
rodeado/a surrounded
rodilla knee
rojo/a red (3); **Caperucita Roja** Little Red
   Ridinghood
romance *m.* song
romano/a *n., adj.* Roman
romántico/a romantic
rompecabezas *m. inv.* puzzle
romper (*p.p.* **roto**) to break (11); **romper
   (con)** to break up (with) (15)
ron *m.* rum
ropa clothes (3), clothing (3); **cambiar de
   ropa** to change clothes (12); **lavar la
   ropa** to wash the clothes (9); **planchar
   la ropa** to iron clothing (9); **ropa
   interior** underwear (3)
rosa rose
rosado/a pink (3)
rostro face
roto/a (*p.p. of* **romper**) broken; torn
rubio/a blond(e) (2)
rueda de feria Ferris wheel; **rueda de
   andar** treadmill; **rueda de molino**
   treadmill (10)
ruido noise (4)
ruidoso/a noisy
ruinas *f. pl.* ruins (13)
ruiseñor *m.* nightingale
ruptura rupture, break
ruso *n.* Russian (*language*)
ruso/a *n., adj.* Russian; **montaña rusa**
   roller coaster
ruta route
rutina diaria daily routine (4)
rutinario/a *adj.* routine

S

sábado Saturday (4)
sábanas *f. pl.* sheets (*bed*) (18)
saber *irreg.* to know (6); **saber** + *inf.* to
   know how to (*do something*) (6)
sabiduría wisdom
sabor *m.* taste; flavor
sabroso/a tasty
sacar (qu) to extract (10); to take out,
   withdraw (*money*) (16); to get (*grades*)
   (11); **sacar el saldo** to balance a
   checkbook (16); **sacar fotos** to take
   photos (7); **sacar la basura** to take out

the trash (9); **sacar la lengua** to stick
   out one's tongue (10); **sacar una muela**
   to extract a tooth (10)
sacrificio sacrifice
sacudir los muebles to dust the
   furniture (9)
Sagitario Sagitarius
sagrado/a sacred
sal *f.* salt
sala room; living room (4); **sala de clase**
   classroom; **sala de emergencias/
   urgencia** emergency room; **sala de
   espera** waiting room (7); **sala de estar**
   living room; sitting room
salario salary (16)
salchicha sausage (6); hot dog (6)
saldo balance (*bank*); **sacar (qu) el saldo**
   to balance a checkbook (16)
salida departure (7)
saliente prominent
salir *irreg.* (**de**) to leave (from) (*a place*) (4);
   to go out (4); **salir (para)** to leave (*for/to
   a place*); **salir (con)** to go out (with) (4);
   salir bien/mal to turn/come out
   well/badly
salmón *m.* salmon (6)
salpicón *m. cold fish dish*
salsa sauce; salsa (*music*); **salsa de tomate**
   catsup; tomato sauce
saltar to jump
salteado/a sautéed
salto waterfall; jump
salud *f.* health (10)
saludable healthy
saludarse to greet each other (10)
saludo greeting
salvadoreño/a *n., adj.* Salvadoran
salvaje: animal (*m.*) **salvaje** wild
   animal (14)
salvo except
san, santo/a *n.* saint; **Día** (*m.*) **de San
   Patricio** St. Patrick's Day; **Día de
   Todos los Santos** All Saints' Day; **día
   del santo** saint's day; **santa patrona**
   patron saint
sancocho *stew prepared with meat or fish
   and other ingredients such as yucca, corn,
   and plaintains*
sandalia sandal (3)
sándwich *m.* sandwich (6)
sangre *f.* blood (10)
sanitario/a sanitary
sano/a healthy; **llevar una vida sana** to
   lead a healthy life (10)
santo/a *adj.* holy

santuario sanctuary
sardina sardine
sartén *f.* frying pan
satélite *m.* satellite
satirizar (c) to satirize
satisfacción *f.* satisfaction
satisfacer *irreg.* (*p.p.* **satisfecho**) to satisfy
satisfecho/a (*p.p. of* **satisfacer**) satisfied
se *refl. pron.* yourself (*form.*); himself,
   herself, itself, yourselves (*form.*);
   themselves; **se trata de** it's a question of
secadora clothes dryer (9)
sección *f.* section; **sección de (no) fumar**
   (non)smoking section (7)
seco/a dry; **fruto seco** nut
secretario/a secretary (1)
secreto *n.* secret
secuencia sequence
secundario/a secondary
sed *f.* thirst; **tener** (*irreg.*) **(mucha) sed** to
   be (very) thirsty (6)
seda silk (3); **es de seda** it's made of silk (3)
sede *f.* seat; headquarters
seguida: en seguida right away (10)
seguidor(a) follower
seguir (i, i) (g) to keep on going; to go; to
   continue (14); **seguir todo derecho** to
   go straight ahead (14)
según according to (2)
segundo *n.* second (*time*)
segundo/a second (13); **Segunda Guerra
   Mundial** World War II; **segundo piso**
   third floor (12)
seguridad *f.* security; **pasar por el
   control de la seguridad** to go/pass
   through security (7)
seguro *n.* insurance; **seguro social** social
   security
seguro/a *adj.* sure (5), certain (5); **es
   seguro que** it's a sure thing that (13); **no
   estar seguro/a (de)** to be (un)sure (of)
seis six (P)
seiscientos/as six hundred (3)
selección *f.* selection
seleccionar to choose
sellado/a sealed; stamped; closed
sello (postage) stamp (18)
selva jungle
semáforo traffic signal (14)
semana week; **día** (*m.*) **de la semana**
   weekday (4); **fin** (*m.*) **de semana**
   weekend (1); **semana que viene**
   next week (4); **una vez a la semana**
   once a week (2)
sembrar (ie) to plant

semejante similar
semejanza similarity
semestre *m.* semester
semiabierto/a partially open
semilla seed
senado senate
senador(a) senator
sencillo/a simple
senda path
sendero path
sensación *f.* sensation
sensible sensitive
sentarse (ie) to sit down (4)
sentencia judgment, verdict, sentence
sentido meaning; sense
sentimental sentimental
sentimiento feeling
sentir (ie, i) to regret (13); to feel sorry (13); **¡lo siento (mucho)!** I'm (very) sorry! (11); pardon me! (11); **sentirse** to feel (*an emotion*) (8)
señor (Sr.) *m.* man; Mr. (P); sir (P)
señora (Sra.) woman; Mrs. (P); ma'am (P)
señorita (Srta.) young woman; Miss (P)
separación *f.* separation (15)
separado/a separate
separar to separate; **separarse (de)** to separate (from) (15)
septiembre *m.* September (5)
séptimo/a seventh (13)
ser (*m.*) **humano** human being
ser *irreg.* to be (2); **llegar (gu) a ser** to become; **ser aburrido/a** to be boring (9); **ser aficionado/a (a)** to be a fan (of) (9); **ser alérgico/a (a)** to be allergic (to); **ser divertido/a** to be fun (9); **ser en** + *place* to take place at/in (*place*) (8); **ser flexible** to be flexible (11); **ser una lata** to be a pain, drag
serie *f. s.* series
serio/a serious
serpenteante winding
serpentino/a serpentine
serpiente *f.* snake
servicio service (14); **servicio de cuartos** room service (18); **servicio de habitación** *Sp.* room service; **servicio militar** military service (17); **servicios públicos** public services (14)
servido/a served
servilleta napkin
servir (i, i) to serve (4)
sesenta sixty (2)
sesión *f.* session

setecientos/as seven hundred (3)
setenta seventy (2)
severo/a severe
sevillano/a *n.* person from Seville; *adj.* of/from Seville
sexo sex
sexto/a sixth (13)
si if (2); **por si acaso** just in case (11); **si me hace el favor** if you would do me the favor
sí yes (P); **sí, me gusta...** yes, I like . . . (P)
siamés, siamesa *adj.* Siamese
sicoanálisis *m. inv.* psychoanalysis
sicología psychology (1)
sicólogo/a psychologist (16)
SIDA AIDS; **Fundación** (*f.*) **Alerta contra el SIDA** AIDS Awareness Foundation
siembra harvest
siempre always (2)
siento: ¡lo siento (mucho) I'm (very) sorry (11); pardon me! (11)
sierra mountain
siesta nap; **dormir (ue, u) la siesta** to take a nap (4)
siete seven (P)
siglo century
significado meaning
significar (qu) to mean
signo sign
siguiente *adj.* following (4)
sílaba syllable
silencio silence
silenciosamente silently
silla chair (1)
sillón *m.* armchair (4)
simbólico/a symbolic
simbolizar (c) to symbolize
símbolo symbol
simpatía affection; pleasantness
simpático/a nice (2); likeable (2)
simulador *m.* simulator
sin without (4); **fue sin querer** it was unintentional (11) **sin duda** without a doubt; **sin embargo** however (5); nevertheless; **sin fines de lucro** not-for-profit; **sin fines lucrativos** nonprofit
sinceridad *f.* sincerity
sincero/a sincere
sindical *adj.* pertaining to a labor union
sindicato *n.* (labor) union
sino but (rather); **sino que** *conj.* but (rather)
sinónimo synonym
sintético/a synthetic

síntoma *m.* symptom (10)
siquiatra *m., f.* psychiatrist (16)
siquiera: ni siquiera not even
sistema *m.* system; **analista** (*m., f.*) **de sistemas** systems analyst (16)
sitio place, location; room (*space*)
situación *f.* situation
situado/a situated
sobre *n. m.* envelope (18); *prep.* on; on top of; over; about; **sobre todo** especially; above all
sobredosis *f. inv.* overdose
sobrepasar to surpass
sobrepoblación *f.* overpopulation
sobrino/a nephew/niece (2)
social: seguro social social security; **trabajador(a) social** social worker (16)
socialista *adj. m., f.* socialist
socializar (c) to socialize
sociedad *f.* society
socioeconómico/a socioeconomic
sociología sociology (1)
socorro help, aid
sofá *m.* sofa (4)
sofisticado/a sophisticated
sofrito/a sautéed
sol *m.* sun; **hace (mucho) sol** it's (very) sunny (5); **tomar el sol** to sunbathe (7)
solar: energía solar solar energy (14)
soldado soldier (16); **mujer** (*f.*) **soldado** (female) soldier (16)
soleado/a sunny
soledad *f.* solitude
soler (ue) to be in the habit of, accustomed to
solicitante *m., f.* applicant
solicitar to request
solicitud *f.* application (form) (16); **llenar la solicitud** to fill out the application (16)
solista *m., f.* soloist
solitario/a solitary
sólo *adv.* only (1)
solo/a *adj.* alone (7); single
soltero/a single (2), unmarried
solución *f.* solution
solucionar to solve
sombra shadow
sombrero hat (3)
son *n.m. traditional music from Cuba*
son las... it's . . . (*hour*) (P)
sonar (ue) to ring (9); to sound (9)
sonido sound
sonreír(se) (*like* **reír**) to smile (8)
soñar (ue) (con) to dream (about)

sopa soup (6)

sorprendente surprising

sorprender to surprise; **me (te, le…) sorprende** it surprises me (you, him, . . .) (13)

sorpresa surprise (8); **fiesta de sorpresa** surprise party

soviético/a *adj.* Soviet

soy I am (P); **soy de…** I'm from . . . (P)

su(s) *poss. adj.* his, her, its, your *(form. s.)* (2); their, your *(form. pl.)* (2)

suaca *traditional music and dance from El Salvador*

suave soft

suavizar (c) to soften

subidor *m.* one of two **bomba** drums

subir (a) to climb; to go up (7); to get on *(a vehicle)* (7); to take, carry up

subjuntivo *gram.* subjunctive

submarino submarine

subordinado/a *gram.* subordinate

subrayar to underline

subsistir to survive

substituir (y) to substitute

subtítulo subtitle

sucio/a dirty (5)

sucre *m.* former monetary unit of Ecuador

sucursal *f.* branch (office) (16)

Sudáfrica South Africa

Sudamérica South America

sudamericano/a *n., adj.* South American

Suecia Sweden

suegro/a father-in-law / mother-in-law

sueldo salary (12); **aumento de sueldo** raise *(in salary)* (16)

suelo floor

suelto/a loose; free

sueño dream; **tener** *(irreg.)* **sueño** to be sleepy (3)

suerte *f.* luck; **¡qué mala suerte!** what bad luck! (11); **tener** *(irreg.)* **suerte** to be lucky

suéter *m.* sweater (3)

suficiente enough, sufficient; **dormir (ue, u) lo suficiente** to sleep enough (10)

sufijo *gram.* suffix

sufrir to suffer (11); **sufrir (muchas) presiones** to be under (a lot of) pressure (11)

sugerencia suggestion

sugerir (ie, i) to suggest (8)

Suiza Switzerland

sumamente extremely

superado/a exceeded

supercarretera superhighway

superlativo *n. gram.* superlative

supermercado supermarket

supervisar to supervise

supervisor(a) supervisor

supuesto/a *(p.p. of* **suponer***)*: **por supuesto** of course (11)

sur *m.* south (5)

surgir (j) to arise

suroeste southwest

surrealista *adj. m., f.* surrealistic

suspender to suspend

sustancialmente substantially

sustantivo *gram.* noun

sustituir (y) to substitute

sustituto substitute

suyo/a(s) *poss. adj.* your *(form.)*; his, her, its, their; *poss. pron.* (of) yours *(form.)*; (of) his, hers; (of) theirs

T

tabacalero/a *adj.* pertaining to tobacco

taberna tavern, open-air pub

tabla table, chart

tal such, such a; **con tal (de) que** *conj.* provided (that) (15); **¿qué tal?** how are you (doing)?; (P); **tal como** just as; **tal vez** perhaps

talento talent

talentoso/a talented

taller *m.* (repair) shop (14)

talonario de cheques *Sp.* checkbook

tamaño size

también too, also (P)

tambor *m.* drum

tamborileo drumming

tampoco neither (6), not either (6)

tan *adv.* so; as; **tan… como** as . . . as (5); **tan pronto como** as soon as (16)

tanque *m.* tank (14)

tanto *adv.* so much; **tanto como** as much as (5)

tanto/a *adj.* as much; so much; such a; *pl.* so many; as many; **tanto/a(s)… como** as much/many . . . as (5)

tapa *Sp.* appetizer

tarde *n. f.* afternoon; **buenas tardes** good afternoon (P); *(an hour)* **de la tarde** in the afternoon (P); **por la tarde** in the afternoon; *adv.* late (1)

tarea homework (4); chore

tarjeta card (7); **tarjeta de crédito** credit card (6); **tarjeta de identidad** identification card; **tarjeta de identificación** identification card (11);

tarjeta navideña Christmas card; **tarjeta postal** postcard (7)

tasa rate

tasca bar

Tauro Taurus

taxi *m.* taxi

taza cup

te *d.o. pron. s.* you *(fam.)*; *i.o. pron. s.* to/for you *(fam.)*; *refl. pron. s.* yourself *(fam.)*; **¿te gusta… ?** do you *(fam. s.)* like . . .? (P); **te molesta/sorprende que** it bothers/surprises you *(fam. s.)* that (13)

té *m.* tea (6)

teatral theatrical

teatro theater; **ir** *(irreg.)* **al teatro** to go to the theater (9)

techo roof

teclado keyboard

técnica technique

técnico/a *n.* technician (16); *adj.* technical

tecnología technology

tejano *traditional Mexican-American music*

tejer to weave (13)

tejidos *m. pl.* woven goods (13)

tele *f.* T.V.

telediario newscast

telefonear to call on the telephone

telefónico/a *adj.* telephone

teléfono (celular) (cellular) phone (12); **agenda de teléfonos** address/telephone book; **contestar el teléfono** to answer the phone (6); **hablar por teléfono** to talk on the phone (1)

telegrama *m.* telegram

telenovela soap opera

televidente *m., f.* (television) viewer

televisión *f.* television; **mirar la televisión** to watch television (2)

televisor *m.* television (set) (4)

tema *m.* subject, topic

temático/a: parque *(m.)* **temático** theme park

temblar to tremble

temer to fear (13)

temperatura temperature; **tomarle la temperatura** to take someone's temperature (10)

templado/a temperate

templo temple

temporada season

temporal seasonal; temporary

temprano *adv.* early (1)

temprano/a *adj.* early

tender (ie) a to tend to, be inclined to; **tender la cama** to make the bed

tener *irreg.* to have (3); **no tener buen aspecto** to not look right; **tener alergia a** to be allergic to; **tener... años** to be . . . years old (2); **tener (mucho) calor/frío** to be (very) warm, hot/cold (5); **tener cuidado** to be careful; **tener dolor de cabeza/estómago/muela** to have a headache/stomachache/toothache (10); **tener exceso de peso** to be overweight; **tener éxito** to be successful; **tener fiebre** to have a fever (10); **tener ganas de** + *inf.* to feel like (*doing something*) (3); **tener (mucha) hambre/sed** to be (very) hungry/thirsty (6); **tener la culpa** to be guilty; **tener lugar** to take place; **tener miedo (de)** to be afraid (of) (3); **tener prisa** to be in a hurry (3); **tener que** + *inf.* to have to (*do something*) (3); **(no) tener razón** to be right (wrong) (3); **tener sueño** to be sleepy (3); **tener suerte** to be lucky; **tener una entrevista** to have an interview (16)

tenis *m. inv.* tennis (9); **zapato de tenis** tennis shoe (3)

tensión *f.* tension

tenso/a tense

teoría theory

teorizar (c) theorize

tepui *m.* flat mountain top

tequila tequilla

terapia therapy

tercer, tercero/a *adj.* third (13); **tercer piso** second floor (12)

tercio *n.* third

terco/a stubborn

térmico/a thermal

terminación *f.* ending

terminar to end

término term

termómetro: **regulador** (*m.*) **termómetro** thermostat

termostato thermostat

terraza terrace

terremoto earthquake

terreno field (*sports*)

terrestre terrestrial

terrible: **es terrible que** it's terrible that (13)

territorio territory

terrorismo terrorism (17)

terrorista *n., adj. m., f.* terrorist (17); **ataque** (*m.*) **terrorista** terrorist attack (17)

tertulia *regular meeting of people for informal discussion of topics of interest*

testigo *m., f.* witness (17)

testimonio testimony

texto text; **libro de texto** textbook (1)

ti *obj.* (*of prep.*) you (*fam. s.*) (5)

tibio/a: **huevo tibio** poached egg

tiburón *m.* shark

tiempo time; *gram.* tense; weather (5); **a tiempo** on time (7); **de tiempo completo/parcial** full time / part time (11); **hace buen/mal tiempo** it's good / bad weather (5); **llegar (gu) a tiempo** to arrive on time; **pasar tiempo (con)** to spend time (with) (15); **¿qué tiempo hace hoy?** what's the weather like today? (5)

tienda shop (3), store (3); **tienda (de campaña)** tent (7)

tierra land; Earth (*planet*); soil

tigre *m.* tiger

tímido/a shy

tinta ink

tinto/a: **vino tinto** red wine (6)

tío/a uncle/aunt (2)

tiovivo merry-go-round

típico/a typical

tipo type

tipo/a *coll.* character, person

tira cómica comic strip

tirar to throw

titular to (en)title

título title

toalla towel (18)

tocar (qu) to touch; to play (*a musical instrument*) (1); **tocarle a uno** to be someone's turn (9)

todavía yet; still (5)

todo *adv.* entirely, completely

todo/a *n.* whole; all, everything; *adj.* all (2); every (2), each; *pl.* everybody, all; **a toda velocidad** at full speed; **ante todo** above all; first of all; **de todas formas** anyway; **de todas maneras** by all means; whatever happens; **de todo** everything (3); **de todos modos** anyway; **Día** (*m.*) **de Todos los Santos** All Saints' Day; **por todas partes** everywhere (11); **sobre todo** especially; above all; **todo derecho** straight ahead (14); **todos los días** every day (1); **venden de todo** they sell everything (3)

tolerante tolerant

tolteca *n., adj. m., f.* Toltec

tomar to take (1); to drink (1); **tomar el sol** to sunbathe (7); **tomar en cuenta** to take into account; **tomar una copa** to have a drink; **tomarle el pelo** to pull someone's leg; **tomarl(e) la temperatura** to take someone's temperature (10)

tomate *m.* tomato (6); **salsa de tomate** catsup; tomato sauce

tónico/a *gram.* stressed

tonto/a silly (2), foolish (2)

torcido/a twisted

toreo bullfighting

torero/a bullfighter, matador

torno: **en torno a** around

toro bull (14); **corrida de toros** bullfight; **plaza de toros** bullring

torpe clumsy (11); **¡qué torpe!** how clumsy! (11)

torre *f.* tower

tortilla potato omelet (*Sp.*); *thin unleavened cornmeal or flour pancake* (*Mex.*)

tos *f. s.* cough (10)

toser to cough (10)

tostado/a toasted; **pan** (*m.*) **tostado** toast (6)

tostadora toaster (9)

tóxico/a toxic

trabajador(a) *n.* worker (2); **Día** (*m.*) **Internacional de los Trabajadores** International Labor Day; **trabajador(a) agrícola** farm worker; **trabajador(a) social** social worker (16); *adj.* hard-working (2)

trabajar to work (1)

trabajo (piece of) work (11); job (11); report (11); **trabajo de tiempo completo/parcial** full time / part time job (11)

trabalenguas *m. inv.* tongue twister

tradición *f.* tradition

tradicional traditional

traducir *irreg.* to translate

traductor(a) translator (16)

traer *irreg.* to bring (4)

traficar (qu) **en drogas** to traffic in / deal drugs

tráfico traffic; **lío/embotellamiento de tráfico** traffic jam

tragedia tragedy

trágico/a tragic

tragicómico/a tragicomic

trago drink (*alcoholic*) (18)

traje *m.* suit (3); **traje de baño** swimsuit (3)

tranquilidad *f.* quiet, calm

tranquilizante calming, quieting

tranquilizar (c) to calm

tranquilo/a calm, quiet; **llevar una vida tranquila** to lead a calm life (10)

transbordador (*m.*) **espacial** space shuttle
transcurrir to take place
transferir (ie, i) to transfer
tránsito traffic (14)
transmisión *f.* transmission
transmitir to transmit
transportación *f.* transportation
transporte *m.* (means of) transportation (14); **modo de transporte** means of transportation (7); **transporte público** public transportation (14)
tras *prep.* after
trasladarse to move
tratamiento treatment
tratar to treat; to deal with (*a subject*); **se trata de** it's a question of; **tratar de +** *inf.* to try to (*do something*) (13)
trauma *m.* trauma
través: a través de across; through; throughout
travieso/a mischievous
trazado/a laid out
trece thirteen (P)
treinta thirty (P); **y treinta** half-past/30 minutes past (*the hour*) (P)
tremendo/a tremendous
tren *m.* train; **choque** (*m.*) **de trenes** train wreck; **estación** (*f.*) **del tren** train station (7); **ir** (*irreg.*) **en tren** to go by train (7)
tres *m. type of guitar*
tres three (P); **hotel** (*m.*) **de tres estrellas** three star hotel (18)
trescientos/as three hundred (3)
trimestre *m.* trimester
triste sad (5)
tristeza sadness
triunfar to triumph
trofeo trophy
trópicos tropics
tropiezo mishap
trozo piece
trucha trout
tú *sub. pron.* you (*fam. s.*) (1); **¿y tú?** and you? (P)
tu(s) *poss. adj.* your (*fam.*) (2)
tubería plumbing
turbulento/a turbulent
turismo tourism
turista *n. m., f.* tourist
turístico/a *adj.* tourist; **clase** (*f.*) **turística** tourist class (7)
turno turn
Turquía Turkey
tuyo/a(s) *poss. adj.* your (*fam. s.*); *poss. pron.* of yours (*fam. s.*)

U

u or (*used instead of* **o** *before words beginning with* **o** *or* **ho**)
ubicar (qu) to locate
último/a last; latest; **de los últimos años** in recent years; **¡es de última moda!** it's the latest style! (3); **por última vez** for the last time (11); **por último** finally
un, uno/a one (P); *ind. art.* a, an; **un millón** (*m.*) **(de)** one million (3); **una vez** once; **una vez a la semana** once a week (2)
único/a *adj.* only; unique
unidad *f.* unit
unido/a united; **Estados** (*m. pl.*) **Unidos** United States; **Naciones** (*f. pl.*) **Unidas** United Nations
unificación *f.* unification
unificarse (qu) to unify
unión *f.* union
unir to join (together); to unite
universidad *f.* university (1)
universitario/a university *adj.* (11), of the university (11)
unívoco/a univocal, of one voice; unambiguous
unos/as *ind. art.* some, a few
urbano/a urban
urgencia: caso de urgencia emergency; **sala de urgencia** emergency room
urgente: es urgente que it's urgent that (13)
uruguayo/a *n., adj.* Uruguayan
usar to use (3); to wear (3)
uso use
usted (Ud.) *sub. pron.* you (*form. s.*) (1); *obj.* (*of prep.*) you (*form. s.*); **¿cómo es usted?** what are you like? (P); **¿cómo se llama usted?** what is your name? (P); **¿de dónde es usted?** where are you from? (P); **¿y usted?** and you? (P)
ustedes (Uds.) *sub. pron.* you (*form. pl.*) (1); *obj.* (*of prep.*) you
usualmente usually
útil useful
utilización *f.* use, utilization
utilizar (c) to use, utilize
uva grape; **uva de mesa** table grape
¡uy! *interj.* oops!

V

vaca cow (14)
vacaciones *f. pl.* vacation; **de vacaciones** on vacation (7); **estar** (*irreg.*) **de vacaciones** to be on vacation (7); **ir**
(*irreg.*) **de vacaciones** to go on vacation (7); **vacaciones de primavera** spring break
vacilante hesitant
vacío *n.* emptiness; void
vacío/a *adj.* empty
vacuna vaccine
vahído blackout (fainting)
vainilla vanilla
valenciano/a of/from Valencia, Spain
valentía bravery
valer (*irreg.*) **la pena** to be worthwhile, worth the trouble
válido/a valid
valiente brave
valle *m.* valley
vallenato *traditional music from Colombia*
valor *m.* value; courage, bravery
vals *m. inv.* waltz
variación *f.* variation
variar (varío) to vary
variedad *f.* variety
varios/as several
vasco Basque (*language*)
vasco/a *n., adj.* Basque
vaso glass
vecindad *f.* neighborhood (12)
vecino/a *n.* neighbor (12); *adj.* neighboring
vegetal *adj.* vegetable
vegetariano/a vegetarian
vehículo vehicle (12)
veinte twenty (P)
veinticinco twenty-five
veinticuatro twenty-four
veintidós twenty-two
veintinueve twenty-nine
veintiocho twenty-eight
veintiséis twenty-six
veintisiete twenty-seven
veintitrés twenty-three
veintiún, veintiuno/a twenty-one
vejez *f.* old age (15)
vela candle
velludo/a hairy
velocidad *f.* speed; **a toda velocidad** at full speed; **límite** (*m.*) **de velocidad** speed limit (14)
vemos: nos vemos see you around (P)
vencido/a overcome
vendedor(a) salesperson (16)
vender to sell (2); **venden de todo** they sell everything (3)
venezolano/a *n., adj.* Venezuelan
venga *interj.* come on

venganza revenge

venir *irreg.* to come (3); **la semana que viene** next week (4); **venga** *interj.* come on

venta sale

ventaja advantage (10)

ventana window (1); **lavar las ventanas** to wash the windows (9)

ventilación *f.* ventilation

ver *irreg.* (*p.p.* **visto**) to see (4); **a ver** let's see; **ir** (*irreg.*) **a ver una película** to go to see a movie (9); **nos vemos** see you around (P)

veranear to spend summer vacation

verano summer (5)

verbo *gram.* verb

verdad *f.* truth; **¿verdad?** right?, don't they (you, *and so on*)? (3)

verdadero/a true; real

verde green (3)

verduras *f. pl.* vegetables (6)

verificar (qu) to verify

versión *f.* version

verso verse; line of a poem

verter (ie) to spill; to shed (*a tear*)

vestíbulo vestibule

vestido dress (3); **vestido de novia** wedding gown

vestir (i, i) to dress; **vestirse** to get dressed (4)

veterinario/a veterinarian (16)

vez *f.* (*pl.* **veces**) time; **a la vez** at the same time; **a veces** sometimes (2), at times (2); **alguna vez** once; ever; **cada vez más** increasingly; **de vez en cuando** once in a while; **dos veces** twice (10); **en vez de** instead of (16); **érase una vez** once upon a time; **otra vez** again; **por primera/última vez** for the first/last time (11); **tal vez** perhaps; **una vez** once; **una vez a la semana** once a week (2)

viajar to travel (7); **viajar al/en el extranjero** to travel abroad (18)

viaje *m.* trip (7); **agencia de viajes** travel agency (7); **agente** (*m., f.*) **de viajes** travel agent (7); **de viaje** on a trip (7); **hacer** (*irreg.*) **un viaje** to take a trip (4)

viajero/a traveler (18); **cheque** (*m.*) **de viajero** traveler's check (18)

vicepresidente/a vice president

víctima victim (17)

vida life; **esperanza de vida** life expectancy; **ganarse la vida** to earn a

living; **llevar una vida sana/tranquila** to lead a healthy/calm life (10)

vídeo video; **cámara de vídeo** video camera (12)

videocasetera videocassette recorder (VCR) (12)

videoclub *m.* video club

videoteca video library

vidrio glass

viejo/a *n.* old person; *adj.* old (2); **Noche** (*f.*) **Vieja** New Year's Eve (8)

viene: la semana que viene next week (4)

viento wind; **hace (mucho) viento** it's (very) windy (5)

viernes *m. inv.* Friday (4)

vietnamita *n., adj. m., f.* Vietnamese

villancico Christmas carol

vinícola *adj. m., f.* pertaining to wine

vino (blanco, tinto) (white, red) wine (6)

viñedo vineyard

violencia violence (14)

violento/a violent

violeta violet

violín *m.* violin

virgen *n. f.* virgin

visado visa

visigodo/a *n.* Visigoth

visión *f.* vision

visita visit; **hacer** (*irreg.*) **visitas** to visit

visitante *m., f.* visitor

visitar to visit; **visitar un museo** to visit a museum (9)

víspera eve

vista view (12); sight; **a primera vista** at first sight (15); **punto de vista** point of view

vistazo glimpse

visto/a (*p.p. of* **ver**) seen

vitamina vitamin

viudo/a widower/widow (15)

vivienda housing

vivir to live (2); **vivir en paz** to live in peace (17)

vivo/a lively

vocabulario vocabulary

vocación *f.* vocation

vocal *n. f.* vowel

volante: objeto volante no identificado (OVNI) unidentified flying object (UFO)

volcán *m.* volcano

volcánico/a volcanic

vólibol *m.* volleyball (9)

volumen *m.* volume

voluntad *f.* will; choice, decision

voluntario/a *n.* volunteer

volver (ue) (*p.p.* **vuelto**) to return (*to a place*) (4); **volver a** + *inf.* to (*do something*) again (4)

vos *sub. pron.* you (*fam. s. Arg., Uru., C.A.*); *obj.* (*of prep.*) you (*fam. s. Arg. Uru., C.A.*)

vosotros/as *sub. pron.* you (*fam. pl. Sp.*) (1); *obj.* (*of prep.*) you (*fam. pl. Sp.*)

votante *m., f.* voter

votar to vote (17)

vuelo flight (7); **asistente** (*m., f.*) **de vuelo** flight attendant (7); **vuelo sin escalas** nonstop flight

vuelta: billete (*m.*)/**boleto de ida y vuelta** round-trip ticket (7); **darse** (*irreg.*) **la vuelta** to turn oneself around; **de vuelta** returned

vuestro/a(s) *poss. adj.* your (*fam. pl. Sp.*) (2); *poss. pron.* yours, of yours (*fam. pl. Sp.*)

vulpeja vixen

W

walkman *m.* Walkman (12)

Y

y and (P); **y cuarto (quince)** a quarter (fifteen minutes) after (*the hour*) (P); **y media (treinta)** half-past/30 minutes past (*the hour*) (P); **¿y tú?** and you? (*fam. s.*) (P); **¿y usted?** and you? (*form. s.*) (P)

ya already (8); **ya no** no longer; **ya que** since

yacimiento deposit (*mineral*)

yerno son-in-law

yo *sub. pron.* I (1)

yogur *m.* yogurt (6)

Z

zampoña pan-flute (*Andean*)

zanahoria carrot (6)

zapatería shoe store

zapato shoe (3); **zapato de tenis** tennis shoe (3)

zona zone

English-Spanish Vocabulary

A

a lot **mucho** (1)
able: to be able **poder** (*irreg.*) (3)
abroad **extranjero** *n.* (18)
absent: to be absent (from) **faltar (a)** (8)
absentminded **distraído/a** (11)
accelerated **acelerado/a** (14)
according to **según** (2)
account **cuenta** (16); checking account **cuenta corriente** (16); savings account **cuenta de ahorros** (16)
accountant **contador(a)** (16)
ache *v.* **doler (ue)** (10); *n.* **dolor** *m.*
acquainted: to be acquainted with **conocer (zc)** (6)
actor **actor** *m.* (13)
actress **actriz** *f.* (*pl.* **actrices**) (13)
address **dirección** *f.* (9)
administration: business administration **administración** (*f.*) **de empresas** (1)
adolescence **adolescencia** (15)
advantage **ventaja** (10)
advice (piece of) **consejo** (6)
advisor **consejero/a** (1)
aerobic: to do aerobics **hacer** (*irreg.*) (*p.p.* **hecho**) **ejercicios aeróbicos** (10)
affectionate **cariñoso/a** (5)
afraid: to be afraid (of) **tener** (*irreg.*) **miedo (de)** (3)
after *prep.* **después de** (4); *conj.* **después (de) que** (16)
afternoon **tarde** *n. f.* (1); good afternoon **buenas tardes** (P); **(muy) buenas** (P); (*an hour*) in the afternoon **de la tarde** (P); in the afternoon **por la tarde** (1)
afterwards **luego** (4)
again: to do (*something*) again **volver (ue)** (*p.p.* **vuelto**) **a** + *inf.* (4)
age: middle age **madurez** *f.* (15) old age **vejez** *f.* (15)
agency: travel agency **agencia de viajes** (7)
agent: travel agent **agente** (*m., f.*) **de viajes** (7)
agree: I (don't) agree **(no) estoy de acuerdo** (2)
ahead of time **con anticipación** (18); straight ahead **todo derecho** (14)
air **aire** *m.* (14); air pollution **contaminación** (*f.*) **del aire** (14); clean air **aire puro** (14)
airplane **avión** *m.* (7)
airport **aeropuerto** (7)
alarm clock **despertador** *m.* (11)

all **todo/a(s)** *adj.* (2)
allow **permitir** (12)
almost **casi** (2); almost never **casi nunca** (2)
alone **solo/a** *adj.* (7)
along: to get along well/poorly (with) **llevarse bien/mal (con)** (15)
alongside of **al lado de** *prep.* (5)
already **ya** (8)
also **también** (P)
always **siempre** (2)
among **entre** *prep.* (5)
amusement **diversión** *f.* (9)
analyst: systems analyst **analista** (*m., f.*) **de sistemas** (16)
and **y** (P); and you? (*fam. s.*) **¿y tú?** (P); (*form. s.*) **¿y usted?** (P)
angry **furioso/a** (5); to get angry (at) **enojarse (con)** (8)
animal **animal** *m.* (14); domesticated animal **animal doméstico** (14); wild animal **animal salvaje** (14)
announce **anunciar** (7)
another **otro/a** (2)
answer *n.* **respuesta** (5); to answer the phone **contestar el teléfono** (16)
answering machine **contestador** (*m.*) **automático** (12)
antibiotic **antibiótico** (10)
any **algún, alguno/a** (6); not any **ningún ninguno/a** (6)
anybody **alguien** (6); not anybody **nadie** (6)
anything **algo** (3)
apartment **apartamento** (1); apartment building **bloque** (*m.*)**/casa de apartamentos** (12)
apologize **pedir (i, i) disculpas** (11)
apple **manzana** (6)
appliance: home appliance **aparato doméstico** (9)
applicant **aspirante** *m., f.* (16)
application (form) **solicitud** *f.* (16)
appreciate **apreciar** (13)
April **abril** *m.* (5)
architect **arquitecto/a** (13)
architecture **arquitectura** (13)
area **área** *f.* (*but* **el área**) (12)
argue (about) (with) **discutir (sobre) (con)** (8)
arm **brazo** (11)
armchair **sillón** *m.* (4)
army **ejército** (17)
around: see you around **nos vemos** (P)

arrival **llegada** (7)
arrive **llegar (gu)** (6)
art **arte** *f.* (*but* **el arte**) (1); work of art **obra de arte** (13)
artist **artista** *m., f.* (13)
arts and crafts **artesanía** *s.* (13)
as: as . . . as **tan… como** (5); as a child **de niño/a** (a) (9); as a youth **de joven** (9); as much as **tanto como** (5); as much/many as **tanto/a(s)… como** (5); as soon as **tan pronto como** *conj.* (16); **en cuanto** *conj.* (16)
ask: to ask a question **hacer** (*irreg.*) (*p.p.* **hecho**) **una pregunta** (4); **preguntas** (6); to ask for **pedir (i, i)** (4)
asleep: to fall asleep **dormirse (ue, u)** (4)
asparagus **espárragos** *m. pl.* (6)
assassination **asesinato** (17)
at **en** (P); **a** (*with time*) (P); at . . . (hour) **a la(s)…** (P); at first sight **a primera vista** (15); at home **en casa** (1); at least **por lo menos** (8); (*an hour*) at night **de la noche** (P); at night **por la noche** (1); at the beginning of **al principio de** (16); at times **a veces** (2); at what time? **¿a qué hora?** (P)
ATM **cajero automático** (16)
attack: terrorist attack **ataque** (*m.*) **terrorista** (17)
attend (*a class, function*) **asistir (a)** (2); to not attend **faltar (a)** (8)
attendant: flight attendant **asistente** (*m., f.*) **de vuelo** (7)
August **agosto** (5)
aunt **tía** (2)
automatic teller machine **cajero automático** (16)
autumn **otoño** (5)
avenue **avenida** (12)
avoid **evitar** (14)
away: right away **en seguida** (10)
awful: an awful lot **muchísimo** (7)

B

baby-sitter **niñero/a** (9)
backpack **mochila** (1)
bad **mal, malo/a** *adj.* (2); it's (very) bad weather **hace (muy) mal tiempo** (5); the bad thing, news **lo malo** (10); to have a bad time **pasarlo mal** (8); to make a bad impression on someone **caerle** (*irreg.*) **mal a alguien** (16); what bad luck! **¡qué mala suerte!** (11)

baked custard **flan** *m.* (6)

baggage **equipaje** *m.* (7)

balance: in a balanced way **equilibradamente** (10); to balance a checkbook **sacar (qu) el saldo** (16)

ballet **ballet** *m.* (13)

banana **banana** (6)

bank **banco** (16)

bar **bar** *m.* (9); to go to a bar **ir** (*irreg.*) **a un bar** (9)

bargain **ganga** (3)

baseball **béisbol** *m.* (9)

basketball **basquetbol** *m.* (9)

bath: room with(out) attached bath **habitación** (*f.*) **con/sin baño** (18) to take a bath **bañarse** (4)

bathroom **baño** (4); bathroom sink **lavabo** (4)

bathtub **bañera** (4)

battery **batería** (14)

be **estar** (*irreg.*) (1); **ser** (*irreg.*) (2); **encontrarse (ue)** (10); to be a fan (of) **ser aficionado/a (a)** (9); to be able **poder** (*irreg.*) (3); to be absent (from) **faltar (a)** (8); to be acquainted with **conocer (zc)** (6); to be afraid (of) **tener** (*irreg.*) **miedo de** (3); to be boring **ser aburrido/a** (9); to be born **nacer (zc)** (15); to be called **llamarse** (4); to be (very) cold **tener (mucho) frío** (5); to be comfortable (*temperature*) **estar bien** (5); to be flexible **ser flexible** (11); to be fun **ser divertido/a** (9); to be going to (*do something*) **ir** (*irreg.*) **a** + *inf.* (3); to be happy (about) **alegrarse (de)** (12); to be (very) hungry **tener (mucha) hambre** (6); to be in a hurry **tener prisa** (3); to be interesting **interesar** (7); to be late **estar atrasado/a** (7); to be left **quedar** (11); to be on a diet **estar a dieta** (6); to be on vacation **estar de vacaciones** (7); to be pleasing **gustar** (7); to be right **tener razón** (3); to be sleepy **tener sueño** (3); to be someone's turn **tocarle (qu) a uno** (9); to be (very) thirsty **tener (mucha) sed** (6); to be under (a lot of) pressure **sufrir (muchas) presiones** (11); to be (very) warm, hot **tener (mucho) calor** (5); to be wrong **no tener razón** (3); to be wrong (about) **equivocarse (qu) (de)** (11); to be . . . years old **tener… años** (2)

beach **playa** (5)

beans **frijoles** *m. pl.* (6)

beautiful **bello/a** (14)

because **porque** (2)

become + *adj.* **ponerse** (*irreg.*) (*p.p.* **puesto**) + *adj.* (8)

bed **cama** (4); to get up on the wrong side of the bed **levantarse con el pie izquierdo** (11); to go to bed **acostarse (ue)** (4); to make the bed **hacer** (*irreg.*) (*p.p.* **hecho**) **la cama** (9); to stay in bed **guardar cama** (10)

bedroom **alcoba** (4)

beer **cerveza** (1)

before *conj.* **antes (de) que** (15); *prep.* **antes de** (4)

begin **empezar (ie) (c)** (4); to begin to (*do something*) **empezar a** + *inf.* (4)

beginning: at the beginning of **al principio de** (16)

behave **portarse** (8)

behind **detrás de** *prep.* (5)

believe (in) **creer (y) (en)** (2)

bellhop **botones** *m. inv.* (18), **mozo** (18)

below **debajo de** *prep.* (5)

belt **cinturón** *m.* (3)

best **mejor** (5)

better **mejor** (5)

between **entre** *prep.* (5)

beverage **bebida** (6)

bicycle: to ride a bicycle **pasear en bicicleta** (9)

bicycling **ciclismo** (9)

big **gran, grande** (2)

bike **bicicleta** (12); mountain bike **bicicleta de montaña** (12)

bill (*for service*) **cuenta** (6); **factura** (16)

bird **pájaro** (2)

birth **nacimiento** (15)

birthday **cumpleaños** *m. inv.* (5); birthday cake **pastel** (*m.*) **de cumpleaños** (8); to have a birthday **cumplir años** (8)

black **negro/a** (3)

blanket **manta** (18)

blond(e) **rubio/a** *n., adj.* (2)

blood **sangre** *f.* (10)

blouse **blusa** (3)

blue **azul** (3)

board: room and full board **pensión** (*f.*) **completa** (18)

boardinghouse **pensión** *f.* (18)

boat **barco** (7); to go/travel by boat **ir** (*irreg.*) **en barco** (7)

body **cuerpo** (10)

bomb **bomba** (17)

book **libro** (1)

bookshelf **estante** *m.* (4)

bookstore **librería** (1)

boot **bota** (3)

border **frontera** (18)

bore **aburrir** (13)

bored **aburrido/a** (5); to get bored **aburrirse** (9)

boring **pesado** (9); to be boring **ser** (*irreg.*) **aburrido/a** (9)

born: to be born **nacer (zc)** (15)

borrow **pedir (i, i) prestado/a** (16)

boss **jefe/a** (12)

bother: it bothers me (you, him, . . .) that **me (te, le, …) molesta que** (13)

boy **muchacho** (4); **niño** (2)

boyfriend **novio** (5)

brain **cerebro** (10)

brakes **frenos** *m. pl.* (14)

branch (office) **sucursal** *f.* (16)

bread **pan** *m.* (6)

break **romper** (*p.p.* **roto**) (11); to break up (with) **romper (con)** (15)

breakfast **desayuno** (4); room with breakfast and one other meal **media pensión** *f.* (18); to have breakfast **desayunar** (6)

breathe **respirar** (10)

bride **novia** (15)

bring **traer** (*irreg.*) (4)

brother **hermano** (2)

brown **(de) color café** (3)

brunet(te) **moreno/a** *n., adj.* (2)

brush one's teeth **cepillarse los dientes** (4)

budget **presupuesto** (16)

build **construir (y)** (14)

building **edificio** *n.* (1); apartment building **bloque** (*m.*) / **casa de apartamentos** (12); building manager **portero/a** (12)

bull **toro** (14)

bump into **darse** (*irreg.*) **en/con/contra** (11); to bump against **pegarse (gu) en/con/contra** (11)

bureau (*furniture*) **cómoda** (4)

bus **autobús** *m.* (7); bus station **estación** (*f.*) **de autobuses** (7); bus stop **parada del autobús** (18); to go/travel by bus **ir** (*irreg.*) **en autobús** (7)

business **empresa** (16); business administration **administración** (*f.*) **de empresas** (1)

businessperson **hombre** (*m.*)/**mujer** (*f.*) **de negocios** (16)

busy **ocupado/a** (5)

but **pero** *conj.* (P)

butter **mantequilla** (6)

buy **comprar** (1)

by check **con cheque** (16)
bye **adiós** (P)

C

cabin **cabina** (*on a ship*) (7)
café **café** *m.* (18)
cafeteria **cafetería** (1)
cake **pastel** *m.* (6); birthday cake **pastel de cumpleaños** (8)
calculator **calculadora** (1)
calendar **calendario** (11)
call *v.* **llamar** (6); to be called **llamarse** (4)
calm: to lead a calm life **llevar una vida tranquila** (10)
campground **camping** *m.* (7)
camping: to go camping **hacer** (*irreg.*) (*p.p.* **hecho**) *camping* (7)
campus *campus* *m. inv.* (12); university campus *campus* (12)
can **poder** *v.* (*irreg.*) (3)
candidate **aspirante** *m., f.* (16)
candy **dulces** *m. pl.* (6)
cap **gorra** (3)
capital city **capital** *f.* (5)
car **coche** *m.* (2); **carro** (12); convertible car **carro/coche descapotable** (12)
card **tarjeta** (7); credit card **tarjeta de crédito** (6); identification card **tarjeta de identificación** (11); to play cards **jugar (ue) (gu) a las cartas** (9)
carrot **zanahoria** (6)
carry **llevar** (3)
case: in case **en caso de que** (15); just in case **por si acaso** (11)
cash **efectivo** (16); in cash **al contado/en efectivo** (16); to cash (*a check*) **cobrar** (16); to pay in cash **pagar (gu) al contado / en efectivo** (16)
cashier **cajero/a** (16); cashier window **caja** (16)
cat **gato/a** (2)
catch a cold **resfriarse (me resfrío)** (10)
CD **disco compacto, CD** *m.* (12)
CD-ROM **CD-ROM** *m.* (12)
celebrate **celebrar** (5)
cellular phone **teléfono cellular** (12)
ceramics **cerámica** *s.* (13)
ceremony: wedding ceremony **boda** (15)
cereal **cereal** *m.* (6)
certain **seguro/a** *adj.* (5); it's certain that **es cierto que** (13)
chair **silla** (1)
chalkboard **pizarra** (1)
change *v.* (channels, clothes, rooms) **cambiar (de canal, ropa, cuarto)** (12)

channel **canal** *m.* (12); to change channels **cambiar de canal** (12)
charge (*to an account*) **cargar (gu)** (16); (*someone for an item or service*) **cobrar** (16)
check (*bank*) **cheque** *m.* (16); (*for service*) **cuenta** (6); by check **con cheque** (16); traveler's check **cheque de viajero** (18); to check (the oil) **revisar (el aceite)** (14); to check into (*a hospital*) **internarse (en)** (10); to check (*baggage*) **facturar** (7); to go/pass through security check **pasar por el control de la seguridad** (7)
checkbook **chequera** (16); to balance a checkbook **sacar (qu) el saldo** (16)
checking account **cuenta corriente** (16)
checkup **chequeo** (10)
cheese **queso** (6)
chef **cocinero/a** (16)
chemistry **química** (1)
chess **ajedrez** *m.* (4)
chicken **pollo** (6); roast chicken **pollo asado** (6)
chief **jefe/a** (12)
child: as a child **de niño/a** (9); small child **niño/a** (2)
childhood **niñez** *f.* (*pl.* **niñeces**) (9)
children **hijos** *m. pl.* (2)
chop **chuleta** (6); pork chop **chuleta de cerdo** (6)
chore: household chore **quehacer** (*m.*) **doméstico**
Christmas **Navidad** *f.* (8); Christmas Eve **Nochebuena** (8)
citizen **ciudadano/a** (17)
city **ciudad** *f.* (2)
civic **cívico** (17)
class **clase** *f.* (1); first class **primera clase** (7); tourist class **clase turística** (7)
classroom **clase** *f.* (1)
classic **clasico/a** (13)
classical **clásico/a** (13)
classmate **compañero/a de clase** (1)
clean *adj.* **limpio/a** (5); **puro/a** (14); clean air **aire** (*m.*) **puro** (14); to clean the (whole) house **limpiar la casa (entera)** (9)
clear the table **quitar la mesa** (9)
clerk **dependiente/a** (1)
clever **listo/a** (2)
client **cliente** *m., f.* (1)
climate **clima** *m.* (5)
close *v.* **cerrar (ie)** (4)
close to *prep.* **cerca de** (5)
closed **cerrado/a** (5)
closet **armario** (4)

clothes **ropa** (3); clothes dryer **secadora** (9); to change clothes **cambiar de ropa** (12); to wash the clothes **lavar la ropa** (9)
clothing **ropa** (3)
cloudy: it's (very) cloudy **está (muy) nublado** (5)
clumsy **torpe** (11)
coat **abrigo** (3)
coffee **café** *m.* (1)
coffeemaker **cafetera** (9)
cold (*illness*) **resfriado** (10); it's (very) cold (*weather*) **hace (mucho) frío** (5); to be (very) cold **tener** (*irreg.*) **(mucho) frío** (5); to get/catch a cold **resfriarse (me resfrío)** (10); very cold **congelado/a** (5)
collect **recoger (j)** (11)
collide (with) **chocar (qu) (con)** (14)
collision **choque** *m.* (17)
color **color** *m.* (3)
comb one's hair **peinarse** (4)
come **venir** (*irreg.*) (3)
comfortable **cómodo/a** (4); to be comfortable (*temperature*) **estar** (*irreg.*) **bien** (5)
communicate (with) **comunicarse (qu) (con)** (17)
communication (*major*) **comunicación** *f.* (1); means of communication **medio de comunicación** (17)
community **comunidad** *f.* (12)
compact disc **disco compacto** (12); **CD** *m.* (12)
complain (about) **quejarse (de)** (8)
composer **compositor(a)** (13)
computer **computadora** (12); **ordenador** *m.* (*Sp.*) (12); computer disc **disco de computadora** (12); computer file **archivo** (12); computer science **computación** *f.* (1)
concert: to go to a concert **ir** (*irreg.*) **a un concierto** (9)
conductor **director(a)** (13)
confirm **confirmar** (18)
congested **congestionado/a** (10)
congratulations **felicitaciones** *f. pl.* (8)
conserve **conservar** (14)
contact lenses **lentes** (*m. pl.*) **de contacto** (10); to wear contact lenses **llevar lentes de contacto** (10)
content *adj.* **contento/a** (5)
continue **seguir (i, i) (g)** (14)
control: remote control **control** (*m.*) **remoto** (12)
convertible car **carro/coche** (*m.*) **descapotable** (12)

cook *v.* **cocinar** (6); *n.* **cocinero/a** (16)
cookie **galleta** (6)
cool: it's cool (*weather*) **hace fresco** (5)
copy *v.* **copiar** (12); **hacer** (*irreg.*) (*p.p.* **hecho**) **copia** (12)
corner (street) **esquina** (14)
corporation **empresa** (16)
cotton **algodón** *m.* (3); it's made of cotton **es de algodón** (3)
cough **tos** *f.* (10); to cough **toser** (10); cough syrup **jarabe** *m.* (10)
country **país** *m.* (2)
countryside **campo** (12); **paisaje** *m.* (12)
couple **pareja** (15); married couple **pareja** (15)
course (*of a meal*) **plato** (6)
cousin **primo/a** (2)
cover *v.* **cubrir** (*p.p.* **cubierto**) (14)
cow **vaca** (14)
crafts: arts and crafts **artesanía** *s.* (13)
"crash" (*of computers*) **fallar** (12)
crazy **loco/a** (5)
create **crear** (13)
credit card **tarjeta de crédito** (6)
crime **delito** (14)
cross **cruzar (c)** (18)
cry **llorar** (8)
custard, baked custard **flan** *m.* (6)
custom **costumbre** *f.* (9)
customs **aduana** *s.* (18)

D

dad **papá** *m.* (2)
daily routine **rutina diaria** (4)
dance **baile** *m.* (13); **danza** (13); to dance **bailar** (1)
dancer **bailarín, bailarina** (13)
date (*calendar*) **fecha** (5); (*social*) **cita** (15)
daughter **hija** (2)
day **día** *m.* (1); the day after tomorrow **pasado mañana** (4); the day before yesterday **anteayer** (10); every day **todos los días** (1)
deadline **fecha límite** (11)
dear **querido/a** *n., adj.* (5)
death **muerte** *f.* (15)
December **diciembre** *m.* (5)
delay *n.* **demora** (7)
dense **denso/a** (14)
dentist **dentista** *m., f.* (10)
deny **negar (ie) (gu)** (13)
department store **almacén** *m.* (3)
departure **salida** (7)
deposit **depositar** (16)
desk **escritorio** (1)

dessert **postre** *m.* (6)
destroy **destruir (y)** (14)
detail **detalle** *m.* (6)
develop **desarrollar** (14)
dictator **dictador(a)** (17)
dictatorship **dictadura** (17)
dictionary **diccionario** (1)
die **morirse (ue, u)** (*p.p.* **muerto**) (8)
diet: to be on a diet **estar** (*irreg.*) **a dieta** (6)
difficult **difícil** (5); **pesado/a** (9)
dining room **comedor** *m.* (4)
dinner **cena** (6); to have dinner **cenar** (6)
director **director(a)** (13); personnel director **director(a) de personal** (16)
dirty **sucio/a** (5)
disadvantage **desventaja** (10)
disaster **desastre** *m.* (17)
disc: compact disc **disco compacto, CD** *m.* (12); computer disc **disco de computadora** (12)
disco: to go to a disco **ir** (*irreg.*) **a una discoteca** (9)
discover **descubrir** (*p.p.* **descubierto**) (14)
discrimination **discriminación** *f.* (17)
dish (*course of a meal*) **plato** (6); dishes **platos** *m. pl.* (4); to wash dishes **lavar los platos** (9)
dishwasher **lavaplatos** *m. inv.* (9)
divorce **divorcio** (15)
divorced (from) **divorciado/a (de)** (15); to get divorced (from) **divorciarse (de)** (15)
dizzy **mareado/a** (10)
do **hacer** (*irreg.*) (*p.p.* **hecho**) (4); do you (*fam. s.*) like . . . ? **¿te gusta… ?** (P) do you (*form. s.*) like . . . ? **¿le gusta… ?** (P); to do aerobics **hacer ejercicios aeróbicos** (10)
doctor (*medical*) **médico/a** (2)
dog **perro/a** (2)
domesticated animal **animal** (*m.*) **doméstico** (14)
door **puerta** (1)
doorman **portero/a** (12)
dormitory **residencia** (1)
double (*hotel*) room (18) **habitación** (*f.*) **doble**
doubt **dudar** (12)
down: to fall down **caerse** (*irreg.*) (11)
downtown **centro** (3)
drama **drama** *m.* (13)
draw **dibujar** (13)
dress **vestido** (3)
dressed: to get dressed **vestirse (i, i)** (4)

dresser **cómoda** (4)
drink **bebida** (6); (*alcoholic*) **copa, trago** (18); *drink similar to a milkshake* **batido** (18); to drink **beber** (2); **tomar** (1)
drive **conducir** (*irreg.*) (14); **manejar** (12); hard drive **disco duro** (12)
driver **conductor(a)** (14); driver's license **licencia de manejar/conducir** (14)
during **durante** (4); **por** (4)
dust the furniture **sacudir los muebles** (9)
DVD **DVD** *m.* (12)
DVD player **lector** (*m.*) **de DVD** (12)

E

e–mail **correo electrónico** (12)
each **cada** *inv.* (4)
ear: inner ear **oído** (10); (outer) ear **oreja** (10)
early **temprano** *adv.* (1)
earn **ganar** (16)
earring **arete** *m.* (3)
east **este** *m.* (5)
Easter **Pascua (Florida)** (8)
easy **fácil** (5)
eat **comer** (2); eat breakfast **desayunar** (6); eat dinner, supper **cenar** (6)
economics **economía** *s.* (1)
economize **economizar (c)** (16)
egg **huevo** (6)
eight **ocho** (P)
eight hundred **ochocientos/as** (3)
eighteen **dieciocho** (P)
eighth **octavo/a** *adj.* (13)
eighty **ochenta** (2)
electric **eléctrico/a** (14); electric energy **energía eléctrica** (14)
electrician **electricista** *m., f.* (16)
electricity **luz** *f.* (*pl.* **luces**) (11)
elephant **elefante** *m.* (14)
eleven **once** (P)
embarrassed **avergonzado/a** (8)
emotion **emoción** *f.* (8)
employment office **dirección** (*f.*) **de personal** (16)
end table **mesita** (4)
endangered species **especie** (*f. s.*) **en peligro de extinción** (14)
energy **energía** (14); electric (nuclear, solar) energy **energía eléctrica (nuclear, solar)** (14)
engagement **noviazgo** (15)
engineer **ingeniero/a** (16)
English (*language*) **inglés** *m.* (1); *n., adj.* **inglés, inglesa** (2)

enjoy oneself **divertirse (ie, i)** (4)

enough **bastante** *adv.* (15); **lo suficiente** (10)

entertainment **diversión** *f.* (9)

envelope **sobre** *m.* (18)

environment (*nature*) **medio ambiente** (14)

equality **igualdad** *f.* (17)

equipment: photography equipment **equipo fotográfico** (12); stereo equipment **equipo estereofónico** (12)

era **época** (11)

eruption **erupción** *f.* (17)

evening **noche** *f.* (1); good evening **(muy) buenas** (P); **buenas noches** (P); (*an hour*) in the evening **de la noche** (P); in the evening **por la noche** (1)

event **acontecimiento** (17); **evento** (17); **hecho** (8)

every **cada** *inv.* (4); **todo/a(s)** *adj.* (2); every day **todos los días** (1)

everything **de todo**

everywhere **por todas partes** (11)

exactly (*time*) **en punto** (P)

exam **examen** *m.* (3)

examine **examinar** (10); **registrar** (18)

example: for example **por ejemplo** (11)

excuse me **con permiso** (P); **perdón** (P)

exercise **ejercicio** (3); to exercise **hacer** (*irreg.*) (*p.p.* **hecho**) **ejercicio** (4)

expect **esperar** (6)

expense **gasto** (12)

expensive **caro/a** (3)

explain **explicar (qu)** (7)

extract **sacar (qu)** (10); to extract a tooth **sacar una muela** (10)

eye **ojo** (10)

F

fact **hecho** *n.* (8)

factory **fábrica** (14)

faithful **fiel** (2)

fall (*season*) **otoño** (5); to fall **caer** (*irreg.*) (11); to fall asleep **dormirse (ue, u)** (4); to fall down **caerse** (11); to fall in love (with) **enamorarse (de)** (15)

family **familia** (2)

fan: to be a fan (of) **ser** (*irreg.*) **aficionado/a (a)** (9)

far from **lejos de** *prep.* (5)

farm **finca** (14); farm worker **campesino/a** (14)

farmer **agricultor(a)** (14)

fast *adj.* **rápido/a** (6); **acelerado/a** (14)

fat **gordo/a** (2)

father **padre** *m.* (2); **papá** *m.* (2)

fax **fax** *m.* (12)

fear: to fear **temer** (13)

February **febrero** (5)

feel **encontrarse (ue)** (10); to feel (*an emotion*) **sentirse (ie, i)** (8); to feel like (*doing something*) **tener** (*irreg.*) **ganas de** + *inf.* (3); to feel sorry **sentir (ie, i)** (13)

fever **fiebre** *f.* (10); to have a fever **tener** (*irreg.*) **fiebre** (10)

fiancé(e) **novio/a** (15)

field **campo** (14)

fifteen **quince** (P); fifteen minutes past (*the hour*) **y quince (cuarto)** (P); fifteen minutes to (*the hour*) **menos quince (cuarto)**

fifth **quinto/a** *adj.* (13)

fifty **cincuenta** (2)

fight **pelear** (9)

file **archivo** (12); computer file **archivo** (12)

fill (up) **llenar** (14); to fill out (*a form*) **llenar** (16)

finally **por fin** (4)

find **encontrar (ue)** (8); to find out (about) **enterarse (de)** (17)

fine **muy bien** (P)

finger **dedo (de la mano)** (11)

finish **acabar** (11)

first *adj.* **primer, primero/a** (13); *adv.* **primero** (4); at first site **a primera vista** (15); first class **primera clase** *f.* (7) first floor of a building **segundo piso** (12); the first of (*month*) **el primero de** (5)

fish (*cooked*) **pescado** (6); (*animal*) **pez** *m.* (*pl.* **peces**) (14)

five **cinco** (P)

five hundred **quinientos/as** (3)

fix **arreglar** (12)

fixed price **precio fijo** (3)

flat tire **llanta desinflada** (14)

flexibility **flexibilidad** *f.* (11); lack of flexibility **falta de flexibilidad** (11)

flexible **flexible** (11)

flight **vuelo** (7); flight attendant **asistente** (*m., f.*) **de vuelo** (7)

floor (*of a building*) **piso** (12); first floor **segundo piso** (12); ground floor **planta baja** (12); second floor **tercer piso** (12); to sweep the floor **barrer el piso** (9)

flower **flor** *f.* (7)

folkloric **folklórico/a** (13)

following *adj.* **siguiente** (4)

food **comida** (6)

foolish **tonto/a** (2)

foot **pie** *m.* (11)

football **fútbol** (*m.*) **americano** (9)

for **por** *prep.* (4); (intended) for **para** *prep.* (2); for example **por ejemplo** (11); for heaven's sake **por Dios** (11); for the first/last time **por primera/última vez** (11)

forbid **prohibir (prohíbo)** (12)

foreign languages **lenguas** (*f. pl.*) **extranjeras** (1)

foreigner **extranjero/a** (1)

forest **bosque** *m.* (14)

forget (about) **olvidarse (de)** (8)

form (*to fill out*) **formulario** (18)

forty **cuarenta** (2)

four **cuatro** (P)

four hundred **cuatrocientos/as** (3)

fourteen **catorce** (P)

fourth **cuarto/a** *adj.* (13)

free time **ratos** (*m. pl.*) **libres** (9)

freedom **libertad** *f.* (17)

freeway **autopista** (14)

freezer **congelador** *m.* (9)

French (*language*) **francés** *n. m.* (1); **francés, francesa** *n., adj.* (2); French fried potato **patata frita**

frequently **con frecuencia** (1)

fresh **fresco/a** (6)

Friday **viernes** *m. inv.* (4)

fried **frito/a** (6); **patata frita** French fried potato

friend **amigo/a** (1)

friendly **amistoso/a** (15)

friendship **amistad** *f.* (15)

from **de** (P); **desde** (7); from the **del** (*contraction of* **de** + **el**) (2)

front: front desk **recepción** *f.* (18); in front of **delante de** *prep.* (5)

frozen **congelado/a** (5)

fruit **fruta** (6); **jugo de fruta** fruit juice (6)

full **completo/a** (18); full time **de tiempo completo** (11); full time job **trabajo de tiempo completo** (11)

fun: fun activity **afición** *f.* (9); to be fun **ser** (*irreg.*) **divertido/a** (9)

function *v.* **funcionar** (12)

furious **furioso/a** (5)

furniture **muebles** *m. pl.* (4); to dust the furniture **sacudir los muebles** (9)

G

game **partido** (9)

garage **garaje** *m.* (4)

gas **gas** *m. s.* (12); gas station **estación** (*f.*) **de gasolina** (14); **gasolinera** (14)

gasoline **gasolina** (14)

generally **por lo general** (4)

German (*language*) **alemán** *m.* (1); **alemán, alemana** *n., adj.* (2)

get **conseguir** (*like* **seguir**) (8); **obtener** (*like* **tener**) (12); to get + *adj.* **ponerse** (*irreg.*) (*p.p.* **puesto**) (8); to get (*grades*) **sacar** (**qu**) (11); to get a cold **resfriarse (me resfrío)** (10); to get along well/poorly (with) **llevarse bien/mal (con)** (15); to get angry (at) **enojarse (con)** (8); to get bored **aburrirse** (9); to get divorced (from) **divorciarse (de)** (15); to get down (from) (*a vehicle*) **bajar (de)** (7); to get dressed **vestirse (i, i)** (4); to get off (of) (*a vehicle*) **bajar (de)** (7); to get on (*a vehicle*) **subir (a)** (7); to get sick **enfermarse** (8); to get together (with) **reunirse (me reúno) (con)** (8); to get up **levantarse** (4); to get up on the wrong side of the bed **levantarse con el pie izquierdo** (11)

gift **regalo** (2)

girl **muchacha** (4); **niña** (2)

girlfriend **novia** (5)

give **dar** (*irreg.*) (7); to give (*as a gift*) **regalar** (7); to give (someone) a shot, injection **poner(le)** (*irreg.*) (*p.p.* **puesto**) **una inyección** (10); give a party **dar** (*irreg.*)/ **hacer** (*irreg.*) (*p.p.* **hecho**) **una fiesta** (8)

glasses **gafas** *f. pl.* (10); to wear glasses **llevar gafas** (10)

go **ir** (*irreg.*) (3); **seguir (i, i) (g)** (14); to go to a bar / concert / disco **ir a un bar / un concierto / una discoteca** (9); to go by bus / plane / boat, ship / train **ir en autobús / avión / barco / tren** (7); to go camping **hacer** (*irreg.*) (*p.p.* **hecho**) *camping* (7); to go home **regresar a casa** (1); to go out (with) **salir** (*irreg.*) **(con)**; (4); to go shopping **ir de compras** (3); to go to (*a class, function*) **asistir (a)** (2); to go to bed **acostarse (ue)** (4); to go to see a movie **ir a ver una película** (9); to go to the movies / theater **ir al cine / teatro** (9); to go through security check **pasar por el control de la seguridad** (7); to go up **subir a** (7)

going: to be going (*to do something*) **ir** (*irreg.*) **a** + *inf.* (3)

golf **golf** *m.* (9)

good **buen, bueno/a** *adj.* (2); good afternoon **buenas tardes** (P); **(muy) buenas** (P); good evening **buenas tardes** (P); **(muy) buenas** (P); good morning **buenos días** (P); good night

buenas noches (P); it's (very) good weather **hace muy buen tiempo** (5); the good thing, news **lo bueno** (10); to have a good time **divertirse (ie, i)** (4); **pasarlo bien** (8); to make a good impression on someone **caerle** (*irreg.*) **bien a alguien** (16)

good-bye **adiós** (P); to say good-bye (to) **despedirse** (*like* **pedir**) **(de)** (8)

good-looking **guapo/a** (2)

gorilla **gorila** *m.* (14)

govern **gobernar (ie)** (17)

government **gobierno** (14)

grade **calificación** *f.* (11); **nota** (11); **grado** (9)

graduate (from) **graduarse (me gradúo) (en)** (16)

grandchildren **nietos** *m. pl.* (2)

granddaughter **nieta** (2)

grandfather **abuelo** (2)

grandmother **abuela** (2)

grandparents **abuelos** *m. pl.* (2)

grandson **nieto** (2)

gray **gris** (3)

great **gran, grande** (2)

green **verde** (3)

greet each other **saludarse** (10)

groom **novio** (15)

ground floor **planta baja** (12)

grow **crecer (zc)** (15)

guest **invitado/a** *n.* (8); **huésped(a)** (18)

guide **guía** *m., f.* (13)

H

habit **costumbre** *f.* (9)

haggle **regatear** (3)

hairstylist **peluquero/a** (16)

half-past (*the hour*) **y media** (P)

ham **jamón** *m.* (6)

hamburger **hamburguesa** (6)

hand **mano** *f.* (11); to hand in **entregar (gu)** (11)

handbag **cartera** (3)

handsome **guapo/a** (2)

happen **pasar** (5)

happening *n.* **acontecimiento** (17)

happy **alegre** (5); **contento/a** (5); **feliz** (*pl.* **felices**) (8); to be happy (about) **alegrarse (de)** (12)

hard **difícil** (5); hard drive **disco duro** (12)

hat **sombrero** (3)

hate **odiar** (7)

have **tener** (*irreg.*) (3); *auxiliary with past participle* **haber** (*inf. form of* **hay** there is, there are) (12); to have a birthday

cumplir años (8); to have a fever **tener fiebre** (10); to have a good time **divertirse (ie, i)** (4); to have a good/bad time **pasarlo bien/mal** (8); to have a headache / stomachache / toothache **tener dolor de cabeza / estómago / muela** (10); to have a pain in **tener dolor de** (10); to have a party **dar** (*irreg.*) / **hacer** (*irreg.*) (*p.p.* **hecho**) **una fiesta** (8); to have a picnic **hacer un** *picnic* (9); to have breakfast **desayunar** (6); to have dinner, supper **cenar** (6); to have just (*done something*) **acabar de** + *inf.* (6); to have lunch **almorzar (ue)** (4); to have to (*do something*) **tener que** + *inf.* (3)

he *subj. pron.* **él** (1); he is **es** (P)

head **cabeza** (10)

headache **dolor** (*m.*) **de cabeza** (10); to have a headache **tener** (*irreg.*) **dolor de cabeza** (10)

health **salud** *f.* (10)

healthy: to lead a healthy life **llevar una vida sana** (10)

hear **oír** (*irreg.*) (4)

heart **corazón** *m.* (10)

heat **gas** *m.* (12)

heaven: for heaven's sake **por Dios** (11)

heavy (*meal, food*) **fuerte** (6); not heavy **ligero/a** (6)

hello **hola** (P)

help **ayudar** (6)

her *poss. adj.* **su(s)** (2)

here **aquí** (1)

highway **carretera** (14)

his *poss. adj.* **su(s)** (2)

history **historia** (1)

hit **pegar (gu)** (9); to hit (*a part of one's body*) **pegarse (gu) en/con/contra** (11)

hobby **afición** *f.* (9); **pasatiempo** (9)

hockey **hockey** *m.* (9)

holiday **día** (*m.*) **festivo** (8)

home **casa** (2); at home **en casa** (1); home appliance **aparato doméstico** (9); to go home **regresar a casa** (1)

homework **tarea** (4)

honeymoon **luna de miel** (15)

hope **esperanza** (17); to hope **esperar** (12); I hope (that) **ojalá (que)** (13)

hors d'oeuvres **entremeses** *m. pl.* (8)

horse **caballo** (14); to ride a horse **montar a caballo** (9)

host **anfitrión** *m.* (8)

hostess **anfitriona** (8)

hot dog **salchicha** (6)

hot: to be (feel) (very) hot **tener** (*irreg.*) **(mucho) calor** (5); it's (very) hot **hace (mucho) calor** (5)

hotel **hotel** *m.* (18); hotel guest **huésped(a)** (18); luxury hotel **hotel de lujo** (18); two (three) star hotel **hotel de dos (tres) estrellas** (18)

house **casa** (2)

household chore **quehacer** (*m.*) **doméstico**

how? **¿cómo?** (P); how are you doing? **¿qué tal?** (P); how are you? **¿cómo está(s)?** (P); how many? **¿cuántos/as?** (1); how much? **¿cuánto/a?** (1); how much does it cost? **¿cuánto cuesta?** (3); how much is it **¿cuánto es?** (3)

how + *adj.*! **¡qué +** *adj.*! (11); how clumsy! **¡qué torpe!** (11); how strange that . . . ! **¡qué extraño que… !** (13); to know how to (*do something*) **saber +** *inf.* (6)

however **sin embargo** (5)

humanities **humanidades** *f. pl.* (1)

hundred **cien, ciento** (2)

hungry: to be (very) hungry **tener** (*irreg.*) **(mucha) hambre** (6)

hurry: to be in a hurry **tener** (*irreg.*) **prisa** (3)

hurt **doler (ue)** (10)

hurt oneself **hacerse** (*irreg.*) (*p.p.* **hecho**) **daño** (11)

husband **esposo** (2); **marido** (15)

I

I *subj. pron.* **yo** (1); I am **soy** (P); I (don't) agree **(no) estoy de acuerdo** (2); I hope, wish (that) **ojalá (que)** (13); I'm from . . . **soy de…** (P); I'm sorry **discúlpeme** (11); I'm (very) sorry! **¡lo siento (mucho)!** (11); I would (really) like **me gustaría** (7); yes, I (no, I don't) like . . . **sí, (no, no) me gusta…** (P)

ice cream **helado** (6)

ID **identificación** *f.* (16)

identification card **tarjeta de identificación** (11)

if **si** (2)

impossible: it's impossible that **es imposible que** (13)

improbable: it's improbable that **es improbable que** (13)

in **en** (P); in a balanced way **equilibradamente** (10); in advance **con anticipación** (18); in case **en caso de que** (15); in cash **al contado** (16); **en efectivo** (16); in front of **delante de** (5); in installments **a plazos** (16); in love

(with) **enamorado/a (de)** (15); in order to **para** (2); in the morning (afternoon, evening) **por la mañana (tarde, noche)** (1); (*an hour*) in the morning (afternoon, evening) **de la mañana (tarde, noche)** (P)

incredible: it's incredible that **es increíble que** (13)

inequality **desigualdad** *f.* (17)

inexpensive **barato/a** (3)

infancy **infancia** (15)

inform **informar** (17)

injection: to give (someone) an injection **ponerle** (*irreg.*) (*p.p.* **puesto**) **una inyección** *f.* (10)

injure oneself **lastimarse** (11)

inner ear **oído** (10)

insist (on) **insistir (en)** (12)

installment: to pay in installments **pagar (gu) a plazos** (16)

instead of **en vez de** (16)

intelligent **inteligente** (2)

intend **pensar (ie)** (4)

intended for **para** (2)

interest *n.* **interés** *m.* (16)

interesting: to be interesting **interesar** (7)

interview *n.* **entrevista** (16); *v.* **entrevistar** (16)

interviewer **entrevistador(a)** (16)

invite **invitar** (6)

iPod *iPod m.* (12)

iron clothing **planchar la ropa** (9)

island **isla** (5)

Italian (*language*) **italiano** *m.* (1)

its *poss. adj.* **su(s)** (2)

J

jacket **chaqueta** (3)

January **enero** (5)

jeans *jeans m. pl.* (3)

job **trabajo** (11); **puesto** (16); full time/part time job **trabajo de tiempo completo/parcial** (11)

jog **correr** (9)

joke **chiste** *m.* (8)

journalist **periodista** *m., f.* (16)

juice (6); fruit juice **jugo de fruta** (6)

July **julio** (5)

June **junio** (5)

just in case **por si acaso** (11)

K

keep **guardar** (12); to keep on going **seguir (i, i) (g)** (14); to keep peace **mantener** (*like* **tener**) **la paz** (17)

key *n.* **llave** *f.* (11); to key in **escribir** (*p.p.* **escrito**) **en la computadora** (16)

kind *adj.* **amable** (2)

king **rey** *m.* (17)

kiosk **quiosco** (118)

kitchen **cocina** (4)

know **conocer (zc)** (6); **saber** (*irreg.*) (6); to know how to (*do something*) **saber +** *inf.* (6)

L

laborer **obrero/a** (16)

lack **escasez** *f.* (*pl.* **escaseces**) (14); lack of flexibility **falta de flexibilidad** (11)

lake **lago** (14)

lamp **lámpara** (4)

landlady **dueña** (12)

landlord **dueño** (12)

language: foreign languages **lenguas** (*f. pl.*) **extranjeras** (1)

large **gran, grande** (2)

last *adj.* **pasado/a** (10); for the last time **por última vez** (11); last night **anoche** (10); to last **durar** (17)

late **tarde** *adv.* (1); to be late **estar** (*irreg.*) **atrasado/a** (7)

later: see you later **hasta luego** (P)

latest: the latest style **de última moda** (3)

laugh **reírse (i, i) (me río)** (8)

law **ley** *f.* (17)

lawyer **abogado/a** (16)

lazy **perezoso/a** (2)

lead a healthy/calm life **llevar una vida sana/tranquila** (10)

learn **aprender** (2); to learn (about) **enterarse (de)** (17)

least: at least **por lo menos** (8)

leave (*a place*) **salir** (*irreg.*) (4); to leave (behind) (in [*a place*]) **dejar (en)** (9); to leave (for, to) (*a place*) **salir (para)** (4); to leave (from) (*a place*) **salir (de)**

left: to be left **quedar(se)** (11); to the left (of) **a la izquierda (de)** (5)

leg **pierna** (11)

lend **prestar** (7)

lenses: contact lenses **lentes** (*m. pl.*) **de contacto** (10); to wear contact lenses **llevar lentes de contacto** (10)

less: less . . . than **menos… que** (5)

letter **carta** (2)

lettuce **lechuga** (6)

level **nivel** *m.* (14)

liberty **libertad** *f.* (17)

librarian **bibliotecario/a** (1)

library **biblioteca** (1)

license: driver's license **licencia de manejar/conducir** (14)

lie **mentira** (12)

life: to lead a healthy/calm life **llevar una vida sana/tranquila** (10)

light *adj.* **ligero/a** (6); *n.* **luz** *f.* (*pl.* **luces**) (11)

like: do you (*fam. s.*) like . . . ? **¿te gusta... ?** (9); do you (*form. s.*) like. . . ? **¿le gusta... ?** (9); I would (really) like . . . **me gustaría...** (7); to feel like (*doing something*) **tener** (*irreg.*) **ganas de** + *inf.* (3); to like very much **encantar** (7); yes, I (no, I don't) like . . . **sí, (no, no) me gusta...** (9); what are you like? **¿cómo es usted?** (9)

likeable **simpático/a** (2)

likely: it's likely that **es probable que** (13)

likewise **igualmente** (P)

limit: speed limit **límite** (*m.*) **de velocidad** (14)

line: to stand in line **hacer** (*irreg.*) (*p.p.* **hecho**) **cola** (7)

listen (to) **escuchar** (1)

literature **literatura** (1)

little *adj.* **poco/a** (3); *adv.* **poco** (1)

live **vivir** (2); to live in peace **vivir en paz** (17)

living room **sala** (4)

loan **préstamo** (16)

lobster **langosta** (6)

lodging **alojamiento** (18)

long **largo/a** (2)

look at **mirar** (2); to look for **buscar (qu)** (1)

lose **perder (ie)** (4)

lot: a lot (of) **mucho/a** (2); an awful lot **muchísimo** (7)

love **amar** (15); **encantar** (7); **querer** (*irreg.*) (15); *n.* **amor** *m.* (15); in love (with) **enamorado/a (de)** (15); to fall in love (with) **enamorarse (de)** (15)

luggage **equipaje** *m.* (7)

lunch **almuerzo** (6); to have lunch **almorzar (ue) (c)** (4)

lung **pulmón** *m.* (10)

luxury *n.* **lujo** (12); luxury hotel **hotel** (*m.*) **de lujo** (18)

–ly *adverbial suffix* **–mente** (11)

M

ma'am **señora (Sra.)** (P)

machine: answering machine **contestador** (*m.*) **automático** (12); automatic teller machine **cajero automático** (16)

magazine **revista** (2)

maid **criada** (18)

mail **correo** (18)

maintain **mantener** (*like* **tener**) (17); to maintain peace **mantener la paz** (17)

make **hacer** (*irreg.*) (*p.p.* **hecho**) (4); to make a good/bad impression on someone **caerle** (*irreg.*) **bien/mal a alguien** (16); to make a mistake (about) **equivocarse (qu) (de)** (11); to make plans to (*do something*) **hacer planes para** + *inf.* (9); to make stops **hacer escalas/paradas** (7); to make the bed **hacer la cama** (9)

mall: shopping mall **centro commercial** (3)

man **hombre** *m.* (1)

manager **gerente** *m., f.* (16)

many **muchos/as** (2); as many . . . as **tantos/as... como** (5); how many? **¿cuántos/as?** (1)

March **marzo** (5)

market(place) **mercado** (3)

marriage **matrimonio** (15)

married **casado/a** (2); married couple **matrimonio** (15); **pareja** (15)

marry **casarse (con)** (15)

masterpiece **obra maestra** (13)

match (*for lighting things*) **fósforo** (18); (*sport*) **partido** (9)

material **material** *n. m.* (3)

mathematics **matemáticas** *f. pl.* (1)

May **mayo** (5)

me *obj.* (*of prep.*) **mí** (5); with me **conmigo** (5)

meal **comida** (6)

means: means of communication **medio** (*s.*) **de comunicación** (17); means (of transportation) **modo** (*s.*) **(de transporte)** (7); **transporte** *m.* (14)

meat **carne** *f.* (6)

mechanic **mecánico/a** (14)

medical: medical doctor **médico/a** (2); medical office **consultorio** (10)

medicine **medicina** (10)

meet (*someone somewhere*) **encontrarse (ue) (con)** (10)

memory **memoria** (12)

menu **menú** *m.* (6)

merchant **comerciante** *m., f.* (16)

messy **desordenado/a** (5)

Mexican **mexicano/a** *n., adj.* (2)

microwave oven **horno de microondas** (9)

middle age **madurez** *f.* (15)

midnight **medianoche** *f.* (8)

military service **servicio militar** (17)

milk **leche** *f.* (6)

million **un millón** (*m.*) **de** (3)

mineral water **agua** *f.* (*but* **el agua**) **mineral** (6)

miss (*a function*) **perder (ie)** (4)

Miss **señorita (Srta.)** (P)

mistake: to make a mistake (about) **equivocarse (qu) (de)** (11)

modem **módem** *m.* (12)

modern **moderno/a** (13)

molar **muela** (10)

mom **mamá** (2)

Monday **lunes** *m. inv.* (4)

money **dinero** (1)

month **mes** *m.* (5)

moped **moto(cicleta)** *f.* (12)

more **más** *adv.* (1); more . . . than **más... que** (5)

morning: (*an hour*) in the morning **de la mañana** (P); in the morning **por la mañana** (1); good morning **buenos días** (P)

mother **mamá** *f.* (2); **madre** *f.* (2)

motorcycle **moto(cicleta)** *f.* (12)

mountain **montaña** (7)

mouse **ratón** *m.* (12)

mouth **boca** (10)

move (*residence*) **mudarse** (16)

movie **película** (4); movie theater **cine** *m.* (4); movies **cine** (4); to go to see a movie **ir** (*irreg.*) **a ver una película** (9); to go to the movies **ir al cine** (9)

Mr. **señor (Sr.)** *m.* (P)

Mrs. **señora (Sra.)** (P)

Ms. **señorita (Srta.)** (P)

much **mucho** *adv.* (1); as much as **tanto como** (5); as much . . . as **tanto... como** (5); how much **¿cuánto/a?** (1); how much does it cost? **¿cuánto cuesta?** (3); how much is it? **¿cuánto es?** (3); to like very much **encantar** (7); too much **demasiado** *adv.* (12)

museum: to visit a museum **visitar un museo** (9)

mushroom **champiñón** *m.* (6)

music **música** (13)

musician **músico/a** *n. m., f.* (13)

must (*do something*) **deber** (+ *inf.*) (2)

my *poss. adj.* **mi(s)** (2): my name is . . . **me llamo...** (P)

N

name: my name is . . . **me llamo...** (P); what's your (*fam. s.*) name **¿cómo te llamas?** (P); what's your (*form. s.*) name? **¿cómo se llama usted?** (P) nap: to take a nap **dormir (ue, u) la siesta** (4)

nationality **nacionalidad** *f.* (18)

natural resources **recursos** (*m. pl.*) **naturales** (14)

nature **naturaleza** (14)

nauseated **mareado/a** (10)

neat **ordenado/a** (5)

necessary **necesario/a** (2); it is necessary to (*do something*) **hay que** + *inf.* (13)

need *v.* **necesitar** (1)

neighbor **vecino/a** (12)

neighborhood **barrio** (12), **vecindad** *f.* (12)

neither **tampoco** (6)

nephew **sobrino** (2)

nervous **nervioso/a** (5)

Net **Red** *f.* (12); to surf the Net **navegar (gu) la Red** (12)

never **jamás** (6); **nunca** (2); almost never **casi nunca** (2)

new **nuevo/a** (2); New Year's Eve **Noche** (*f.*) **Vieja** (8)

newlywed (to) **recién casado/a (con)** (15)

news **noticias** *f. pl.* (17); news media **prensa** (17); piece of news **noticia** (8)

newscast **noticiero** (17)

newspaper **periódico** (2)

next **próximo/a** (4); next week **la semana que viene** (4)

nice **amable** (2), **simpático/a** (2); nice to meet you **encantado/a** (P)

niece **sobrina** (2)

night: at night **por la noche** (1); (*an hour*) at night **de la noche** (P); good night **buenas noches** (P); last night **anoche** (10)

nine **nueve** (P)

nine hundred **novecientos/as** (3)

nineteen **diecinueve** (P)

ninety **noventa** (2)

ninth **noveno/a** (13)

no **no** (P); **ningún, ninguno** (6); no one **nadie** (6); no vacancy **completo/a** (18)

nobody **nadie** (6)

noise **ruido** (4)

none **ningún, ninguno/a** (6)

nonsmoking section **sección** (*f.*) **de no fumar** (7)

north **norte** *m.* (5)

nose **nariz** (*pl.* **narices**) (10)

not any **ningún, ninguno/a** (6); not anybody **nadie** (6); not anything **nada** (6); not either **tampoco** (6); not heavy **ligero/a** (6); there is not / are not **no hay** (P); to not attend **faltar (a)** (8)

notebook **cuaderno** (1)

nothing **nada** (6)

November **noviembre** *m.* (5)

now **ahora** (1)

nuclear **nuclear** (14); nuclear energy **energía nuclear** (14)

number **número** (2)

nurse **enfermero/a** (10)

O

obey **obedecer (zc)** (14)

obligation **deber** *m.* (17)

obtain **conseguir** (*like* **seguir**) (8); **obtener** (*like* **tener**) (12)

ocean **océano** (7)

October **octubre** *m.* (5)

of *prep.* **de** (P); of course! **¡por supuesto!** (11); of the **del** (*contraction of* **de** + **el**) (2); of the university **universitario/a** (11)

off: to get off (of) (*a vehicle*) **bajar (de)** (7); to take off (*clothing*) **quitarse** (4); to turn off **apagar (gu)** (11)

offer *v.* **ofrecer (zc)** (7)

office **oficina** (1); employment office **direccion** (*f.*) **de personal** (16); (medical) office **consultorio** (10); personnel office **dirección** (*f.*) **de personal** (16)

oil **aceite** *m.* (14); to check the oil **revisar el aceite** (14)

OK **regular** *adj.* (P)

old **viejo/a** *adj.* (2); old age **vejez** *f.* (15); to be . . . years old **tener** (*irreg.*) . . . **años** (2)

older **mayor** (5)

on **en** (P); on a trip **de viaje** (7); on Mondays (Tuesdays, . . .) **los lunes (martes,…)** (4); on the dot (*time*) **en punto** (P); on time **a tiempo** (7); on top of **encima de** (5); to be on a diet **estar** (*irreg.*) **a dieta** (6); to be on vacation **estar de vacaciones** (7); to get on (*a vehicle*) **subir (a)** (7); to go on vacation **ir** (*irreg.*) **de vacaciones** (7); to put on (*clothing*) **ponerse** (*irreg.*) (*p.p.* **puesto**) (4); to talk on the phone **hablar por teléfono** (1); to turn on (*appliances*) **poner** (4)

once a week **una vez a la semana** (2)

one **un, uno/a** (P)

one hundred **cien, ciento** (2)

one-way (*ticket*) **de ida** (7)

oneself: to enjoy oneself **divertirse (ie, i)** (4); to hurt oneself **hacerse** (*irreg.*) (*p.p.* **hecho**) **daño** (11); to injure oneself **lastimarse** (11); to take care of oneself **cuidarse** (10)

only **sólo** *adv.* (1)

open **abierto/a** (5); to open **abrir** (*p.p.* **abierto**) (2)

opera **ópera** (13)

operate (*a machine*) **manejar** (12)

or **o** (P)

oral report **informe** (*m.*) **oral** (11)

orange (*color*) *adj.* **anaranjado/a** (3); orange (*fruit*) **naranja** (6)

order (*in a restaurant*) **pedir (i, i)** (4); (*someone to do something*) **mandar** (12); in order to **para** (2)

other **otro/a** (2); others **los/las demás** (12)

ought to (*do something*) **deber** (+ *inf.*) (2)

our *poss. adj.* **nuestro/a(s)** (2)

outdoors **afuera** *adv.* (5)

outskirts **afueras** *n. f. pl.* (12)

oven: microwave oven **horno de microondas** (9)

over there **allí** (3)

own *adj.* **propio/a** (15)

owner **dueño/a** (6)

P

pace **ritmo** (14)

pack one's suitcase(s) **hacer** (*irreg.*) (*p.p.* **hecho**) **la(s) maleta(s)** (7)

package **paquete** *m.* (18)

pain (in) **dolor** (*m.*) **(de)** (10); to have a pain in **tener** (*irreg.*) **dolor de** (10)

paint (the walls) **pintar (las paredes)** (9)

painter **pintor(a)** (13)

painting (*piece of art*) **cuadro,** (*general, art form, and piece of art*) **pintura** (13)

pair **par** *m.* (3)

pants **pantalones** *m. pl.* (3)

paper **papel** *m.* (1)

pardon me **con permiso** (P), **discúlpeme** (11); **lo siento** (11); **perdón** (P)

parents **padres** *m. pl.* (2)

park *n.* **parque** *m.* (5); to park *v.* **estacionar** (11)

part time **de tiempo parcial** (11); part time job **trabajo de tiempo parcial** (11)

participate (*in a sport*) **practicar (qu)** (9)

party **fiesta** (1); to give/have a party **dar** (*irreg.*)/**hacer** (*irreg.*) (*p.p.* **hecho**) **una fiesta** (8)

pass through security (check) **pasar por el control de la seguridad** (7)

passage **pasaje** *m.* (7)

passenger **pasajero/a** *n.* (7)

passport **pasaporte** *m.* (18)

past *adj.* **pasado/a** (10)

pastime **afición** *f.* (9); **pasatiempo** (9)

pastry (small) **pastelito** (18); pastry shop **pastelería** (18)

patient **paciente** *n., m., f.* (10)

patio **patio** (4)

pay (for) **pagar (gu)** (1); to pay cash **pagar al contado/en efectivo** (16); to pay in installments **pagar a plazos** (16)

peace **paz** *f. (pl.* **paces)** (17); to live in peace **vivir en paz** (17); to maintain, keep peace **mantener (***like*** tener) la paz** (17)

peas **arvejas** *f. pl.* (6)

peasant **campesino/a** (14)

pen **bolígrafo** (1)

pencil **lápiz** *m. (pl.* **lápices)** (1)

people **gente** *f. s.* (13)

perform (*a part*) **desempeñar** (13)

permit **permitir** (12)

person **persona** (1)

personnel director **director(a) de personal** (16); personnel office **dirección** *(f.)* **de personal** (16)

pet; animal *(m.)* **doméstico** (14); **mascota** (2)

pharmacist **farmacéutico/a** (10)

pharmacy **farmacia** (10)

philosophy **filosofía** (1)

phone: cellular phone **teléfono celular** (12) to talk on the phone **hablar por teléfono** (1)

photo(graph) **foto(grafía)** *f.* (7)

photographer **fotógrafo/a** (16)

photography **fotografía** (13); photography equipment **equipo fotográfico** (12)

photos: to take photos **sacar (qu) fotos** (7)

physics **física** *s.* (1)

pick up **recoger (j)** (11)

picnic: to have a picnic **hacer** *(irreg.) (p.p.* **hecho)** un *picnic* (9)

pie **pastel** *m.* (6)

piece: piece of advice **consejo** (6); piece of news **noticia** (8); piece of work **trabajo** (11)

pill **pastilla** (10)

pillow **almohada** (18)

pink **rosado/a** (3)

place **lugar** *m.* (1); *(in line)* **puesto** (7); to place **poner** *(irreg.) (p.p.* **puesto)** (4); to take place in/at *(place)* **ser** *(irreg.)* **en** + *place* (8)

plan to **pensar (ie)** (4); to make plans to (*do something*) **hacer** *(irreg.) (p.p.* **hecho) planes para** + *inf.* (9)

plane: to go/travel by plane **ir** *(irreg.)* **en avión** (7)

plates **platos** *m. pl.* (4)

play (*a game, sport*) **jugar (ue) (al)** (4); to play (*a musical instrument*) **tocar (qu)** (1); to play (*a part*) **desempeñar** (13); to play cards **jugar a las cartas** (9); to play chess **jugar ajedrez** (4); to play sports **practicar (qu) deportes** (10)

player **jugador(a)** (9); (tape) player **grabadora** (12)

playwright **dramaturgo/a** (13)

please **por favor** (P); to please **agradar** (13)

pleased to meet you **encantado/a, mucho gusto** (P)

pleasing: to be pleasing **gustar** (7)

plumber **plomero/a** (16)

poet **poeta** *m., f.* (13)

police officer **policía** *m., f.* (14)

politician **político/a** (17)

politics **política** *s.* (17)

pollute **contaminar** (14)

pollution: air pollution **contaminación** *(f.)* **del aire** (14) there's (lots of) pollution **hay (mucha) contaminación** *f.* (5)

poor **pobre** (2)

poorly **mal** *adv.* (1)

population **población** *f.* (14)

pork chop **chuleta de cerdo** (6)

port **puerto** (7)

porter **maletero** (7)

position **puesto** (16)

possible **posible** (2)

post office **correo; oficina de correos** (18)

postage stamp **sello** (18)

postcard **tarjeta postal** (7)

potato **papa** (6); **patata** *Sp.* (6); French fried potato **patata frita** (6)

pottery **cerámica** (13)

practice **entrenar** (9); **practicar (qu)** (1); to practice sports **practicar (qu) deportes** (10)

prefer **preferir (ie, i)** (3)

prepare **preparar** (6)

prescription **receta** (10)

present (*gift*) **regalo** *n.* (2)

press *n.* **prensa** (17)

pressure: to be under (a lot of) pressure **sufrir (muchas) presiones** (11)

pretty **bonito/a** (2)

price **precio** (3); fixed, set price **precio fijo** (3)

print **imprimir** (12)

printer **impresora** (12)

probable: it's probable that **es probable que** (13)

profession **profesión** *f.* (16)

professor **profesor(a)** (1)

programmer **programador(a)** (16)

prohibit **prohibir (prohíbo)** (12)

promise *v.* **prometer** (7)

protect **proteger (j)** (14)

provided (that) **con tal (de) que** (15)

psychiatrist **siquiatra** *m., f.* (16)

psychologist **sicólogo/a** (16)

psychology **sicología** (1)

public **público/a** *adj.* (14)

punish **castigar (gu)** (17)

pure **puro/a** (14)

purple **morado/a** (3)

purse **bolsa** (3)

put **poner** *(irreg.) (p.p.* **puesto)** (4); to put on (*clothing*) **ponerse** *(irreg.)* (4)

Q

quarter after/to (the *hour*) **y/menos cuarto** (P)

queen **reina** (17)

question: to ask (a question) **hacer** *(irreg.) (p.p.* **hecho) una pregunta** (4); **preguntar** (6)

quit **dejar** (16); (*doing something*) **dejar de** + *inf.* (10)

quiz **prueba** (11)

R

radio (*apparatus*) **radio** *m.* (12); (*medium*) **radio** *f.* (12); portable radio **radio portátil** (12)

rain **llover (ue)** (5); it's raining **llueve** (5)

raincoat **impermeable** *m.* (3)

raise **aumento** (12); (in salary) **aumento de sueldo** (16)

rather **bastante** *adv.* (15)

react **reaccionar** (8)

read **leer (y)** (2)

receive **recibir** (2)

recommend **recomendar (ie)** (7)

record **grabar** (12)

recorder (tape) **grabadora** (12)

recycle **reciclar** (14)

red **rojo/a** (3); red wine **vino tinto** (6)

reductions **rebajas** *f. pl.* (3)

refrigerator **refrigerador** *m.* (9)

regret **sentir (ie, i)** (13)

relative **pariente** *m., f.* (2)

remain **quedar** (11); to remain (*in a place*) **quedarse** (5)

remember **acordarse (ue) (de)** (11); **recordar (ue)** (8)

remote control **control** *(m.)* **remoto** (12)

rent *n.* **alquiler** *m.* (12); to rent *v.* **alquilar** (12) renter **inquilino/a** (12)

repair **arreglar** (12); repair shop **taller** *m.* (14)

report **informe** *m.* (11), **trabajo** (11), oral/written report **informe oral/escrito** (11)

reporter **reportero/a** (17)

represent **representar** (13)

reservations **reservaciones** *f. pl.* (18); **reservas** *f. pl.* (18)

resign (from) **renunciar (a)** (16)

resolve **resolver (ue)** (*p.p.* **resuelto**) (14)

resource **recurso**; natural resources **recursos** (*m. pl.*) **naturales** (14)

responsibility **deber** *m.* (17); **responsabilidad** *f.* (17)

rest *v.* **descansar** (4)

restaurant **restaurante** *m.* (6)

résumé **currículum** *m.* (*pl.* **currículos**) (16)

retire **jubilarse** (16)

return (*something*) **devolver** (*like* **volver**) (16); (*to a place*) **regresar** (1); **volver (ue)** (*p.p.* **vuelto**) (4)

rhythm **ritmo** (14)

rice **arroz** *m.* (*pl.* **arroces**) (6)

rich **rico/a** (2)

ride: to ride a bicycle **pasear en bicicleta** (9); to ride a horse **montar a caballo** (9)

ridiculous: it's ridiculous that **es ridículo que** (13)

right (*legal*) **derecho** *n.* (17); right? **¿no?**, (3), **¿verdad?** (3); right away **en seguida** (10); to be right **tener** (*irreg.*) **razón** (3); to the right of **a la derecha de** (5)

ring **sonar (ue)** (9)

river **río** (14)

road **camino** (14)

roast chicken **pollo asado** (6)

role (*in a play*) **papel** *m.* (13)

roller skates **patines** *m. pl.* (12)

rollerblade *v.* **patinar en línea** (9)

room **cuarto** (1); room (*in a hotel*) **habitación** *f.* (18); double room **habitación doble** (18); living room **sala** (4); room and full board (all meals) **pensión** (*f.*) **completa** (18); room service **servicio de cuartos** (18); room with(out) attached bath/shower **habitación con/sin baño/ducha** (18); room with breakfast and one other meal **media pensión** (18); single room **habitación individual** (18); to change rooms **cambiar de cuarto** (12); waiting room **sala de espera** (7)

roommate **compañero/a de cuarto** (1)

round-trip ticket **billete** (*m.*)/**boleto de ida y vuelta** (7)

routine: daily routine **rutina diaria** (4)

rug **alfombra** (4)

ruins *n.* **ruinas** *f. pl.* (13)

rule **gobernar (ie)** (17)

run **correr** (9); (*machines*) **funcionar** (12); to run (into) (*vehicles*) **chocar (gu) (con)** (14); to run into **darse** (*irreg.*) **en/con/contra** (11); **pegarse (gu) ·en/con/contra** (11); to run out (of) **acabar** (11)

S

sad **triste** (5)

salad **ensalada** (6)

salary **salario** (16); **sueldo** (12)

sales **rebajas** *f. pl.* (3)

salesperson **vendedor(a)** (16)

salmon **salmón** *m.* (6)

same **mismo/a** (10); same here **igualmente** (P)

sandal **sandalia** (3)

sandwich **sándwich** *m.* (6)

Saturday **sábado** (4)

sausage **salchicha** (6)

save (*a place*) **guardar** (7); (*documents*) **guardar** (12); (*energy*) **conservar** (14); (money) **ahorrar** (16)

savings account **cuenta de ahorros** (16)

say **decir** (*irreg.*) (*p.p.* **dicho**) (7); to say good-bye (to) **despedirse** (*like* **pedir**) **(de)** (8)

schedule **horario** (11)

school **escuela** (9); school subject **materia** (1)

schoolteacher **maestro/a** (16)

science **ciencias** *f. pl.* (*academic discipline*) (1); computer science **computación** *f.* (1)

script **guión** *m.* (13)

sculpt **esculpir** (13)

sculptor **escultor(a)** (13)

sculpture **escultura** (13)

sea **mar** *m.* (7)

search **registrar** (18)

season **estación** *f.* (5)

seat **asiento** (7)

second **segundo/a** *adj.* (13); second floor **primer piso** (12)

secretary **secretario/a** (1)

section: (non) smoking section **sección** *f.* **de (no) fumar** (7)

security: to go/pass through security check **pasar por el control de la seguridad** (7)

see **ver** (*irreg.*) (*p.p.* **visto**) (4); see you around **nos vemos** (P); see you later **hasta luego** (P); see you tomorrow **hasta mañana** (P)

seem **parecer (zc)** (13)

sell **vender** (2)

send **mandar** (7)

separate (from) *v.* **separarse (de)** (15)

separation **separación** *f.* (15)

September **septiembre** *m.* (5)

servant **criado/a** (16)

serve **servir (i, i)** (4)

service **servicio** (14); military service **servicio militar** (17); room service **servicio de cuartos** (18)

set: set price **precio fijo** (3); to set the table **poner** (*irreg.*) (*p.p.* **puesto**) **la mesa** (9)

seven **siete** (P)

seven hundred **setecientos/as** (3)

seventeen **diecisiete** (P)

seventh **séptimo/a** *adj.* (13)

seventy **setenta** (2)

shame: it's a shame that **es una lástima que** (13); what a shame that . . . ! **¡qué lástima que… !** (13)

shampoo **champú** *m.* (18)

shave oneself **afeitarse** (4)

sharp (*time*) **en punto** (P)

she *subj. pron.* **ella** (1); she is **es** (P)

sheets **sábanas** *f. pl.* (18)

shellfish **mariscos** *m. pl.* (6)

ship **barco** (7); to go/travel by ship **ir** (*irreg.*) **en barco** (7)

shirt **camisa** (3)

shoe **zapato** (3); tennis shoe **zapato de tenis** (3)

shop **tienda** (3); (repair) shop **taller** *m.* (14); tobacco shop **estanco** (18)

shopkeeper **comerciante** *m., f.* (16)

shopping **de compras** (3); shopping mall **centro comercial** (3); to go shopping **ir** (*irreg.*) **de compras** (3)

short (*in height*) **bajo/a** (2); (*in length*) **corto/a** (2)

shortage **escasez** *f.* (*pl.* **escaseces**) (14)

shot: to give (someone) a shot **ponerle** (*irreg.*) (*p.p.* **puesto**) **una inyección** *f.* (10)

should (*do something*) **deber** (+ *inf.*) (2)

show **mostrar (ue)** (7)

shower: room with attached shower **habitación** (*f.*) **con ducha** (18); to take a shower **ducharse** (4)

shrimp **camarones** *m. pl.* (6)

sick **enfermo/a** *adj.* (5); to get sick **enfermarse** (8) sight: at first sight **a primera vista** (15)

silk **seda** (3); it's made of silk **es de seda** (3)

silly **tonto/a** (2)

sing **cantar** (1)

singer **cantante** *m., f.* (13)

single (*not married*) **soltero/a** (2); single room **habitación** (*f.*) **individual** (18)

sink; bathroom sink **lavabo** (4)

sir **señor (Sr.)** *m.* (P)

sister **hermana** (2)

sit down **sentarse (ie)** (4)

six **seis** (P)

six hundred **seiscientos/as** (3)

sixteen **dieciséis** (P)

sixth **sexto/a** *adj.* (13)

sixty **sesenta** (2)

skate **patinar** (9)

skateboard **monopatín** *m.* (12)

ski **esquiar (esquío)** (9)

skirt **falda** (3)

skyscraper **rascacielos** *m. inv.* (14)

sleep **dormir (ue, u)** (4)

sleepy: to be sleepy **tener** (*irreg.*) **sueño** (3)

slender **delgado/a** (2)

small **pequeño/a** (2); small child **niño/a** (2); small pastry **pastelito** (18)

smart **listo/a** (2)

smile **sonreír(se)** (*like* **reír**) (8)

smoke **fumar** (7)

smoking section **sección** (*f.*) **de fumar** (7)

snow **nevar (ie)** (5); it's snowing **nieva** (5)

so: so-so **regular** (P); so that **para que** (15)

soap **jabón** *m.* (18)

soccer **fútbol** *m.* (9)

social worker **trabajador(a) social** (16)

sociology **sociología** (1)

sock **calcetín** *m.* (*pl.* **calcetines**) (3)

sofa **sofá** *m.* (4)

soft drink **refresco** (6)

solar **solar** *adj.* (14); solar energy **energía solar** (14)

soldier **soldado, mujer** (*f.*) **soldado** (16)

solve **resolver (ue)** (*p.p.* **resuelto**) (14)

some **algún, alguno/a/os/as** (6)

someone **alguien** (6)

something **algo** (3)

sometimes **a veces** (2)

son **hijo** (2)

song **canción** *f.* (13)

soon: as soon as *conj.* **en cuanto** (16); *conj.* **tan pronto como** (16)

sorry: I'm sorry **discúlpeme** (11); I'm (very) sorry! **¡lo siento (mucho)!** (11); to feel sorry **sentir (ie, i)** (13)

sound *v.* **sonar (ue)** (9)

soup **sopa** (6)

south **sur** *m.* (5)

Spanish (*language*) **español** *m.* (1); **español(a)** *n., adj.* (2)

spare time **ratos** (*m. pl.*) **libres** (9)

speak **hablar** (1)

species **especie** *f. s.* (14); endangered species **especie en peligro de extinción** (14)

speed limit **límite** (*m.*) **de velocidad** (14)

spend (*money*) **gastar** (8); (*time*) **pasar** (5); to spend time (with) **pasar tiempo (con)** (15)

sport **deporte** *m.* (9); to practice, play sports **practicar (qu) deportes** (10)

sporting *adj.* **deportivo/a** (9)

sports *adj.* **deportivo/a** (9)

sports-loving **deportivo/a** (9)

spring **primavera** (5)

stage **escenario** (13); (*period of time*) **etapa** (15)

stamp, postage stamp **sello** (18)

stand: stand in line **hacer** (*irreg.*) (*p.p.* **hecho**) **cola** (7); to stand up **levantarse** (4); tobacco stand **estanco** (18)

start up (*a car*) **arrancar (qu)** (14)

state **estado** (2)

station **estación** *f.* (7); bus station **estación de autobuses** (7); gas station **estación de gasolina** (14), **gasolinera** (14); station wagon **camioneta** (7); train station **estación del tren** (7)

stationery **papel** (*m.*) **para cartas** (18); stationery store **papelería** (18)

stay *n.* (*in a place*) **estancia** (18); to stay (*in a place*) **alojarse** (18); **quedar(se)** (5); to stay in bed **guardar cama** (10)

steak **bistec** *m.* (6)

stereo equipment **equipo estereofónico** (12)

stick out one's tongue **sacar (qu) la lengua** (10)

still **todavía** (5)

stockings **medias** *f. pl.* (3)

stomach **estómago** (10)

stomachache **dolor** (*m.*) **de estómago** (10); to have a stomachache **tener** (*irreg.*) **dolor de estómago** (10)

stop *v.* **parar** (14); (*doing something*) **dejar de** + *inf.* (10); bus stop **parada de autobús** (7); subway stop **estación** (*f.*) **de metro** (18); to make stops **hacer** (*irreg.*) (*p.p.* **hecho**) **escalas/paradas** (7)

store **tienda** (3)

stove **estufa** (9)

straight ahead **todo derecho** (14)

straighten (up) **arreglar** (12)

strange **raro/a** (8); how strange that . . . ! **¡qué extraño que... !** (13); it's strange that **es extraño que** (13)

street **calle** *f.* (12); **camino** (14)

stress **estrés** *m. inv.* (11); **tensión** *f.*

strike (*labor*) **huelga** (17)

strong **fuerte** (6)

student *n.* **estudiante** *m., f.* (1); *adj.* **estudiantil** (11); of students **estudiantil** (11)

study **estudiar** (1)

stuffed up **congestionado/a** (10)

style: it's latest style **es de última moda** (3)

subject (school) **materia** (1)

suburbs **afueras** *f. pl.* (12)

subway stop **estación** (*f.*) **de metro** (18)

succeed in (*doing something*) **conseguir** (*like* **seguir**) +*inf.* (8)

suddenly **de repente** (10)

suffer **sufrir** (11)

sufficiently **bastante** *adv.* (15)

suggest **sugerir (ie, i)** (8)

suit **traje** *m.* (3)

suitcase **maleta** (7); to pack one's suitcase(s) **hacer** (*irreg.*) (*p.p.* **hecho**) **las maleta(s)** (7)

summer **verano** (5)

sunbathe **tomar el sol** (7)

Sunday **domingo** (4)

sunny: it's (very) sunny **hace (mucho) sol** (5)

supper **cena** (6); to have/eat supper **cenar** (6)

support **apoyar** (17)

sure **seguro/a** *adj.* (5); it's a sure thing that **es seguro que** (13)

surf the Net **navegar (gu) la Red** (12)

surprise **sorpresa** (8); it surprises me (you, him, . . .) that **me (te, le, ...) sorprende que** (13)

sweater **suéter** *m.* (3)

sweep (the floor) **barrer (el piso)** (9)

sweets **dulces** *m. pl.* (6)

swim **nadar** (7)

swimming **natación** *f.* (9); swimming pool **piscina** (4)

swimsuit **traje** (*m.*) **de baño** (3)

symptom **síntoma** *m.* (10)

systems analyst **analista** (*m., f.*) **de sistemas** (16)

T

T-shirt **camiseta** (3)

table **mesa** (1); end table **mesita** (4); to clear the table **quitar la mesa** (9); to set the table **poner** (*irreg.*) (*p.p.* **puesto**) **la mesa** (9)

take **llevar** (3); to take **tomar** (1); to take (photos) **sacar (qu) (fotos)** (7); to take a bath **bañarse** (4); to take a nap **dormir (ue, u) la siesta** (4); to take a shower **ducharse** (4); to take a trip **hacer** (*irreg.*) (*p.p.* **hecho**) **un viaje** (4); to take a walk **dar** (*irreg.*) **un paseo** (9); to take care of oneself **cuidarse** (10); to take leave (of) **despedirse** (*like* **pedir**) **(de)** (8); to take off (*clothing*) **quitarse** (4); to take out (*money*) **sacar** (16); to take out the trash **sacar la basura** (9); to take place at/in (*place*) **ser** (*irreg.*) **en** + *place* (8); to take someone's temperature **tomar(le) la temperatura** (10)

talk **hablar** (1); to talk on the phone **hablar por teléfono** (1)

tall **alto/a** (2)

tank **tanque** *m.* (14)

tape **cinta** (3) tape recorder/player **grabadora** (12); to tape **grabar** (12)

tea **té** *m.* (6)

teach **enseñar** (1)

technician **técnico/a** *n.* (16)

teeth: to brush one's teeth **cepillarse los dientes** (4)

television set **televisor** *m.* (4); to watch television **mirar la televisión** (2)

tell **decir** (*irreg.*) (*p.p.* **dicho**) (7); **contar (ue)** (7)

teller **cajero/a** (16); automatic teller machine **cajero automático** (16)

temperature **temperatura** (10); to take someone's temperature **tomarle la temperatura** (10)

ten **diez** (P)

tenant **inquilino/a** (12)

tennis **tenis** *m. inv.* (9); tennis shoe **zapato de tenis** (3)

tent **tienda (de campaña)** (7)

tenth **décimo/a** (13)

terrible: it's terrible that **es terrible que** (13)

terrorism **terrorismo** (17)

terrorist **terrorista** *m., f.* (17); terrorist attack **ataque** (*m.*) **terrorista** (17)

test **examen** *m.* (3); **prueba** (11)

textbook **libro de texto** (1)

thank you **gracias** (P); thank you very much **muchas gracias** (P); thanks for **gracias por** (8)

that *dem. adj.* **ese/a** (3); that *dem. pron.* **eso** (3); that (*over there*) *dem. adj.* **aquel, aquello/a** (3); that (*over there*) *dem. pron.* **aquello** (3); that one *dem. adj.* **ese/a** (3); that one (*over there*) *dem. pron.* **aquel, aquello/a** (3); that *conj.* **que** (2); that means . . . **eso quiere decir...** (10)

theater: to go to the theater **ir** (*irreg.*) **al teatro** (9)

their *poss. adj.* **su(s)** (2)

then **luego** (4)

there is (not), there are (not) **(no) hay** (P); there's (lots of) pollution **hay (mucha) contaminación** (5)

there: (over) there **allí** (3)

therefore **por eso** (1)

these *dem. adj.* **estos/as** (2); *dem. pron.* these (ones) **estos/as** (2)

they *subj. pron.* **ellos/as** (1)

thin **delgado/a** (2)

thing **cosa** (1); it's a sure thing **es seguro que** (13); the bad thing **lo malo** (10); the good thing **lo bueno** (10)

think **creer (y) (en)** (2); to think (about) **pensar (ie) (en)** (4)

third **tercer, tercero/a** *adj.* (13); third floor **segundo piso** (12)

thirsty: to be (very) thirsty **tener** (*irreg.*) **(mucha) sed** (6)

thirteen **trece** (P)

thirty **treinta** (P); thirty past (*the hour*) **y media** (P), **y treinta** (P)

this *dem. adj.* **este/a** (2); *dem. pron.* **esto** (2); this one *dem. pron.* **este/a** (2)

those *dem. adj.* **esos/as** (3); those (ones) *dem. pron.* **esos/as** (3); those (over there) *dem. adj.* **aquellos/as** (3); those (ones) (*dem. pron.*) (*over there*) **aquellos/as** (3)

thousand **mil** *m.* (3)

three **tres** (P); three star hotel **hotel** (*m.*) **de tres estrellas** (18)

three hundred **trescientos/as** (3)

throat **garganta** (10)

Thursday **jueves** *m. inv.* (4)

ticket **billete** *m.* (7); **boleto** (7); **pasaje** *m.* (7); one-way ticket **billete/boleto de ida** (7); round-trip ticket **billete/boleto de ida y vuelta** (7)

tie **corbata** (3)

time (*period*) **época** (11); ahead of time **con anticipación** (18); at what time?

¿**a qué hora?** (P); for the first/last time **por primera / última vez** (11); free time **ratos** (*m. pl.*) **libres** (9); full time **de tiempo completo** (11); on time **a tiempo** (7); part time **de tiempo parcial** (11); to have a good time **divertirse (ie, i)** (4); to have a good/bad time **pasarlo bien/mal** (8); to spend time (with) **pasar tiempo (con)** (15); what time is it? ¿**qué hora es?** (P)

tip (*money given to an employee*) **propina** (18)

tire *n.* **llanta** (14)

tired **cansado/a** (5)

to **a** (P); according to **según** (2); close to *prep.* **cerca de** (5); in order to **para** (2); (*minutes*) to (*the hour*) **menos** (P); newlywed to **recién casado/a con** (15); to the **al** (*contraction of* **a** + **el**) (3); to the north / south / east / west **al norte / sur / este / oeste** (5); to the right/left of **a la derecha/izquierda de** (5)

toast **pan** (*m.*) **tostado** (6)

toaster **tostadora** (9)

tobacco stand/shop **estanco** (18)

today **hoy** (P); what's today's date? ¿**cuál es la fecha de hoy?** (5)

toe **dedo del pie** (11)

together **juntos/as** (15)

tomato **tomate** *m.* (6)

tomorrow **mañana** *adv.* (P); day after tomorrow **pasado mañana** (4); see you tomorrow **hasta mañana** (P)

tongue: to stick out one's tongue **sacar (qu) la lengua** (10)

tonight **esta noche** (5)

too much **demasiado** *adv.* (12)

tooth **diente** *m.* (10); **muela** (10); to extract a tooth **sacar (qu) una muela** (10)

toothache **dolor** (*m.*) **de muela** (10)

toothpaste **pasta dental** (18)

tourist: tourist class **clase** (*f.*) **turística** (7)

towel **toalla** (18)

trade **oficio** (16)

traffic **tránsito** (14), **circulación** *f.* (14); traffic signal **semáforo** (14)

train **tren** *m.* (7); train station **estación** (*f.*) **del tren** (7); to go/travel by train **ir** (*irreg.*) **en tren** (7); to train **entrenar** (9)

translator **traductor(a)** (16)

transportation **transporte** *m.* (14); means of transportation **modo de transporte** (7)

trash: to take out the trash **sacar (qu) la basura** (9)

travel **viajar** (7); travel agency **agencia de viajes** (7); travel agent **agente** (*m., f.*) **de viajes** (7); to travel by boat/ship **ir** (*irreg.*) **en barco** (7); to travel by bus/plane/train **ir en autobús/avión/tren** (7)

traveler **viajero/a** (18); traveler's check **cheque** (*m.*) **de viajero** (18)

treadmill **rueda de molino** (10)

treatment **tratamiento** (10)

tree **árbol** *m.* (14)

trip **viaje** *m.* (7); on a trip **de viaje** (7); round-trip ticket **billete** (*m.*)/**boleto de ida y vuelta** (7); to take a trip **hacer** (*irreg.*) (*p.p.* **hecho**) **un viaje** (4)

try to (*do something*) **tratar de** + *inf.* (13)

Tuesday **martes** *m. inv.* (4)

tuition **matrícula** (1)

tuna **atún** *m.* (6)

turkey **pavo** (6)

turn **doblar** (14); to turn in **entregar (gu)** (11); to turn off **apagar (gu)** (11); to turn on (*appliances*) **poner** (*irreg.*) (*p.p.* **puesto**) (4); to be someone's turn **tocarle (qu) a uno** (9)

twelve **doce** (P)

twenty **veinte** (P)

twice **dos veces** (10)

two **dos** (P); two star hotel **hotel** (*m.*) **de dos estrellas** (18)

two hundred **doscientos/as** (3)

type **escribir** (*p.p.* **escrito**) **en la computadora** (16)

U

U.S. *adj.* **estadounidense** *m., f.* (2)

ugly **feo/a** (2)

uncle **tío** (2)

understand **comprender** (2); **entender (ie)** (4)

underwear **ropa interior** (3)

unintentional: it was unintentional **fue sin querer** (11)

university **universidad** *f.* (1); *adj.,* of the university **universitario/a** (11); university campus *campus* *m. inv.* (12)

unless **a menos que** (15)

unlikely: it's unlikely that **es improbable que** (13)

unoccupied **desocupado/a** (18)

unpleasant **antipático/a** (2)

until *prep.* **hasta** (4); *conj.* **hasta que** (16)

urgent: it's urgent that **es urgente que** (13)

use **usar** (3); to use (*gas*) **gastar** (14); to use up completely **acabar** (14)

V

vacancy: no vacancy **completo/a** (18)

vacant **desocupado/a** (18)

vacation: to be on vacation **estar** (*irreg.*) **de vacaciones** (7); to go on vacation **ir** (*irreg.*) **de vacaciones** (7)

vacuum *v.* **pasar la aspiradora** (9); vacuum cleaner **aspiradora** (9)

VCR **videocasetera** (12)

vegetables **verduras** *f. pl.* (6)

vehicle **vehículo** (12)

very **muy** (1); very cold **congelado/a** (5); very well **muy bien** (P)

veterinarian **veterinario/a** (16)

victim **víctima** (17)

video camera **camara de vídeo** (12)

videocassette recorder (VCR) **videocasetera** (12)

view **vista** (12)

violence **violencia** (14)

visit a museum **visitar un museo** (9)

volleyball **vólibol** *m.* (9)

vote *v.* **votar** (17)

W

wait (for) **esperar** (6)

waiter **camarero** (6)

waiting room **sala de espera** (7)

waitress **camarera** (6)

wake up **despertarse (ie)** (*p.p.* **despierto**) (4)

walk **caminar** (10); to take a walk **dar** (*irreg.*) **un paseo** (9)

Walkman *walkman* *m.* (12)

wall **pared** *f.* (4); to paint the walls **pintar las paredes** (9)

wallet **cartera** (3)

want **desear** (1); **querer** (*irreg.*) (3)

war **guerra** (17)

warm: to be (very) warm, hot **tener (mucho)** (*irreg.*) **calor** (5)

wash *v.* wash (the clothes, the dishes, the windows) **lavar (la ropa, los platos, las ventanas)** (9)

washing machine **lavadora** (9)

watch **reloj** *m.* (3); to watch **mirar** (2); to watch television **mirar la televisión** (2)

water **agua** *f.* (*but* **el agua**) (6); mineral water **agua mineral** (6)

waterbed **cama de agua** (4)

we **nosotros/as** (1)

wear (*clothing*) **llevar** (3), **usar** (3); to wear contact lenses/glasses **llevar lentes de contacto/gafas** (10)

weather **tiempo** (5); it's (very) good/bad weather **hace (muy) buen/mal tiempo** (5); what's the weather like? **¿qué tiempo hace?** (5)

weave **tejer** (13)

wedding (ceremony) **boda** (15)

Wednesday **miércoles** *m. inv.* (4)

week: next week **la semana que viene** (4); once a week **una vez a la semana** (2)

weekday **día** (*m.*) **de la semana** (4)

weekend **fin** (*m.*) **de semana** (1)

welcome: you're welcome **de nada** (P), **no hay de qué** (P)

well **bien** *adv.* (P); well . . . *interj.* **bueno...** (2)

well-being **bienestar** *m.* (10)

west **oeste** *m.* (5)

whale **ballena** (14)

what **lo que** (4); what a shame that . . . ! **¡qué lástima que... !** (13); what bad luck! **¡qué mala suerte!** (11)

what? **¿qué?** (P); what? **¿cuál(es)?** (1); at what time? **¿a qué hora?** (P); what are you (*form. s.*) like? **¿cómo es usted?** (P); what time is it? **¿qué hora es?** (P); what's the weather like? **¿qué tiempo hace?** (5); what's today's date? **¿cuál es la fecha de hoy?** (5); what's your (*form. s.*) name? **¿cómo se llama usted?** (P); what's your (*fam. s.*) name? **¿cómo te llamas?** (P)

when? **¿cuándo?** (1)

where? **¿dónde?** (P); where (to)? **¿adónde?** (3); where are you (*fam. s.*) from? **¿de dónde eres?** (P); where are you (*form. s.*) from? **¿de dónde es usted?** (P)

which? **¿cuál(es)?** (1)

while **mientras** *conj.* (9)

white **blanco/a** (3); white wine **vino blanco** (6)

who **que** (2)

who? **¿quién(es)?** (1)

whole: to clean the whole house **limpiar la casa entera** (9)

whom? **¿quién(es)?** (1)

whose? **¿de quién?** (2)

why? **¿por qué?** (2)

widow **viuda** (15)

widower **viudo** (15)

wife **esposa** (2); **mujer** *f.* (15)

wild animal **animal** (*m.*) **salvaje** (14)

win **ganar** (9)

window **ventana** (1); to wash the windows **lavar las ventanas** (9)

windshield **parabrisas** *m. inv.* (14)

windy: it's (very) windy **hace (mucho) viento** (5)

wine (white, red) **vino (blanco, tinto)** (6)

winter **invierno** (5)

wish **deseo** (8); **esperanza** (17); I wish (that) **ojalá (que)** (13)

with **con** (1); with me **conmigo** (5); with you *fam. s.* **contigo** (5)

withdraw (*money*) **sacar (qu)** (16)

without **sin** (4)

witness **testigo** *m., f.* (17)

woman **mujer** *f.* (1)

wool **lana** (3); it's made of wool **es de lana** (3)

word **palabra** (P)

work *n.* **trabajo** (11); (of art) **obra (de arte)** (13); piece of work **trabajo** (11); to work **trabajar** (1); (*machine*) **funcionar** (12)

worker **obrero/a** (16); **trabajador(a)** (2); social worker **trabajador(a) social** (16)

world **mundo** (7)

worried **preocupado/a** (5)

worse **peor** (5)

would: I would (really) like . . . **me gustaría...** (7)

woven goods **tejidos** *m. pl.* (13)

write **escribir** (*p.p.* **escrito**) (2)

writer **escritor(a)** (13)

written **escrito/a** (*p.p. of* **escribir**) (11); written report **informe** (*m.*) **escrito** (11)

wrong: to be wrong **no tener** (*irreg.*) **razón** (3); to be wrong (about) **equivocarse (qu) (de)** (11) to get up on the wrong side of the bed **levantarse con el pie izquierdo** (11)

Y

yard **jardín** *m.* (4); **patio** (4)

year **año** (5); (*in school*) **grado** (9); to be . . . years old **tener** (*irreg.*)**... años** (2)

yellow **amarillo/a** (3)

yes **sí** (P); yes, I like . . . **sí, me gusta...** (P)

yesterday **ayer** (4); the day before yesterday **anteayer** (10)

yogurt **yogur** *m.* (6)

you *sub. pron.* **tú** *fam. s.* (1); **usted (Ud.)** *form. s.* (1); **ustedes (Uds.)** *form. pl.* (1); **vosotos/as** *fam. pl.* (1); *obj. of prep.* **ti** *fam. s.* (5); and you? *fam.s.* **¿y tú?** (P); *form. s.* **¿y usted?** (P); you (*fam. s.*) are **eres** (P); you (*form. s.*) are **es** (P)

you're welcome **de nada** (P), **no hay de qué** (P)

young **joven** *m., f.* (2)

younger **menor** (5)

your *poss. adj.* **tú(s)** *fam.* (2); **su(s)** *form.* (2); **vuestro/a(s)** *fam. pl. Sp.* (2)

youth **juventud** *f.* (15); as a youth **de joven** (9)

Z

zero **cero** (P)

Photos

Page 1 left: © Ulrike Welsch; p. 1 right: © Ulrike Welsch; p. 10: © Stuart Cohen; p. 13: SuperStock; p. 17 bottom: SuperStock; p. 17 top: PICTOR/ImageState; p. 18 bottom: © Peter Menzel; p. 18 top left: Antonio Mendoza/Stock Boston; p. 18 top right: © Ulrike Welsch; p. 21: PhotoDisc; p. 24: © Ken Welsh/age fotostock; p. 33 bottom: © Tim Mosenfelder/Getty Images; p. 33 middle: AP Wide World Photos; p. 33 top: AP Wide World Photos; p. 40: AP Wide World Photos; p. 41: Photography by Marsha Miller, Courtesy of University of Texas at Austin; p. 43: US Postal Service; p. 44: © Ulrike Welsch; p. 49: © Jimmy Dorantes/LatinFocus.com; p. 56: PICTOR/ImageState; p. 65 bottom: Vince Bucci/AFP/Getty Images; p. 65 top: © Mike Ramirez/LatinFocus.com; p. 66: Museo del Prado, Madrid, Spain/Giraudon, Paris/SuperStock; p. 73 bottom: © Fernando Botero, courtesy, Marlborough Gallery, New York; p. 73 top: © Trapper Frank/Corbis Sygma; p. 75: Commissioned by the Trustees of Dartmouth College, © Clemente Orozco Valladares; p. 76: © 1987 Carmen Lomas Garza Photo credit: Wolfgang Dietze; Collection of Leonila Ramirez, Don Ramon's Restaurant, San Francisco, California; p. 79: © Tomas Stargardter/Latin Focus.com; p. 82: © Reuters NewMedia Inc./Corbis; p. 83: © Gonzalo Endara Crow; p. 94 bottom: German Miranda/LA PRENSA; p. 94 middle: AP/Wide World Photos; p. 94 top: HO/AFP/Getty Images; p. 97: Topham/The Image Works; p. 98: © Robert Frerck, Odyssey Productions, Chicago; p. 100: John Mitchell/DDB Stock Photography; p. 105: © Beryl Goldberg; p. 108: © Ric Ergenbright; p. 116 bottom: John Dominis/Time Life Pictures/Getty Images; p. 116 middle: © Dave G. Houser/Corbis; p. 116 top: Ardis L. Nelson; p. 120: © Robert Holmes/Corbis; p. 121: © Victor Englebert; p. 123: © Bill Gentile/Corbis; p. 127: © Moises Castillo/LatinFocus.com; p. 131: AP Wide World Photos; p. 142 top & bottom: "A logo for America" by Alfredo Jaar; p. 143 bottom: AP Wide World Photos; p. 143 top: Pierre Boulat/Time Life Pictures/Getty Images; p. 144 bottom: © Ulrike Welsch; p. 144 top: PICTOR/ImageState; p. 148 © J.J. Halber/DDB Stock Photo; p. 150: © Rob Crandall/The Image Works; p. 151: Frans Lanting; p. 152: PhotoDisc/Getty Images; p. 155: © John Neubauer; p. 158 left: © FoodPix; p. 158 right: © Peter Guttman/Corbis; p. 168 middle: © Don Tremain/Alamy; p. 168 right: Rosario de Mou; p. 168 top: Courtesy of Prof. Carlos "Cubena" Guillermo Wilson, Ph.D.; p. 174: © Jimmy Dorantes/LatinFocus.com; p. 176: Courtesy of Oswaldo & Alice Arana; p. 181: © Chris Sharp/DDB Stock: p. 185 bottom: Michael J. Doolittle/The Image Works; p. 185 top: © Stuart Cohen; p. 194 middle: Yolocamba I Ta; p. 194 top: Clementina c. 1940; p. 200 bottom: © PhotoDisc/Getty Images; p. 200 top: © Corbis; p. 202: © Stephen and Donna O'Meara/Photo Researchers, Inc.; p. 203: © Alfredo Maiquez/Lonely Planet Images; p. 207: © A. Garcia/LatinFocus.com; p. 210: © Jack Kurtz/The Image Works; p. 219 middle left: © Peter Turnley/Corbis; p. 219 middle right: J. J. Orts/Courtesy of Nebenegra; p. 219 top: Bettman/Corbis; p. 222: Bob Riha Jr./Getty Images; p. 223: © Lorenzo Armendariz/LatinFocus.com; p. 225: Prensa Latina/Getty Images; p. 229: EPA/Miguel Mendez V./Landov Ê; p. 231: Reuters/Bettmann/Corbis; p. 239 left: Stephane Cardinale/Corbis Sygma; p. 239 middle: © Reuters NewMedia/Inc./Corbis; p. 239 right: AP Wide World Photos; p. 241: © Michael Kim/Corbis; p. 242 bottom: The Grosby Group; p. 242 middle: © Jeremy Horner/Corbis; p. 242 top: AP Wide World

C

Marty Knorre was formerly Associate Professor of Romance Languages and Coordinator of basic Spanish courses at the University of Cincinnati, where she taught undergraduate and graduate courses in language, linguistics, and methodology. She received her Ph.D. in foreign language education from The Ohio State University in 1975. Dr. Knorre is coauthor of *Cara a cara* and *Reflejos* and has taught at several NEH Institutes for Language Instructors. She received a Master of Divinity at McCormick Theological Seminary in 1991.

Thalia Dorwick recently retired as McGraw-Hill's Editor-in-Chief for Humanities, Social Sciences, and Languages. For many years she was also in charge of McGraw-Hill's World Languages college list in Spanish, French, Italian, German, Japanese, and Russian. She has taught at Allegheny College, California State University (Sacramento), and Case Western Reserve University, where she received her Ph.D. in Spanish in 1973. She was recognized as an Outstanding Foreign Language Teacher by the California Foreign Language Teachers Association in 1978. Dr. Dorwick is the coauthor of several textbooks and the author of several articles on language teaching issues. She is a frequent guest speaker on topics related to language learning, and she was also an invited speaker at the *II Congreso Internacional de la Lengua Española,* in Valladolid, Spain, in October 2001. In retirement, she consults for McGraw-Hill, especially in the area of world languages, which are of personal interest to her. She also serves on the Board of Trustees of Case Western Reserve University and on the Board of Directors of the Berkeley Repertory Theater.

Ana María Pérez-Gironés is an Adjunct Associate Professor of Spanish at Wesleyan University, Middletown, Connecticut, where she teaches and coordinates Spanish language courses. She received a *Licenciatura en Filología Anglogermánica* from the *Universidad de Sevilla* in 1985, and her M.A. in General Linguistics from Cornell University in 1988. Professor Pérez-Gironés' professional interests include second language acquisition and the use of technology in language learning. She is a coauthor of the *Student Manuals for Intermediate Grammar Review* and *Intensive and High Beginner Courses* that accompany *Nuevos Destinos.*

William R. Glass is the Publisher for World Languages and Health and Human Performance at McGraw-Hill Higher Education. He received his Ph.D. from the University of Illinois at Urbana-Champaign in Spanish Applied Linguistics with a concentration in Second Language Acquisition and Teacher Education (SLATE). He was previously Assistant Professor of Spanish at The Pennsylvania State University where he was also Director of the Language Program in Spanish. He has published numerous articles and edited books on issues related to second language instruction and acquisition.

Hildebrando Villarreal is Professor of Spanish at California State University, Los Angeles, where he teaches undergraduate and graduate courses in language and linguistics. He received his Ph.D. in Spanish with an emphasis in Applied Linguistics from UCLA in 1976. Professor Villarreal is the author of several reviews and articles on language, language teaching, and

Spanish for Native Speakers of Spanish. He is the author of *¡A leer! Un paso más*, an intermediate textbook that focuses on reading skills.

A. Raymond Elliott is Associate Professor of Spanish and Chair of the Department of Modern Languages at the University of Texas, Arlington. He received his Ph.D. from Indiana University-Bloomington in 1993. His areas of specialization are Spanish applied linguistics, second language acquisition, the acquisition of second language phonological skills, and the historical development of Spanish. Dr. Elliott has published several articles, book chapters, reviews in *The Modern Language Journal, Hispania,* and with Georgetown University Press. He served as a panelist in the McGraw-Hill Annual Teleconference on Authentic Materials, and as a member of the Academic Advisory Board for the package to accompany *Nuevos Destinos*. He is the author of *Nuevos Destinos: Español para hispanohablantes*.

In this index, communication strategies, cultural topics, reading strategies, and vocabulary topic groups are listed by individual topic as well as under those headings. References to pages A-1 through A-17 are references to the appendixes that appear after chapter 18.

Datos[a] esenciales

La Argentina (Capítulo 14)

- Nombre oficial: República Argentina
- Capital: Buenos Aires
- Población: 39.144.753 habitantes
- Moneda:[b] el peso
- Idioma[c] oficial: el español

Bolivia (Capítulo 13)

- Nombre oficial: República de Bolivia
- Capitales: La Paz (sede[d] del gobierno), Sucre (capital constitucional)
- Población: 8.724.156 habitantes
- Moneda: el (peso) boliviano
- Idiomas: el español (oficial), el quechua, el aimara

Chile (Capítulo 15)

- Nombre oficial: República de Chile
- Capital: Santiago
- Población: 15.823.957 habitantes
- Moneda: el peso
- Idiomas: el español (oficial), el mapuche, el quechua

Colombia (Capítulo 9)

- Nombre oficial: República de Colombia
- Capital: Santafé de Bogotá (Bogotá)
- Población: 42.310.775 habitantes
- Moneda: el peso
- Idioma oficial: el español

Costa Rica (Capítulo 4)

- Nombre oficial: República de Costa Rica
- Capital: San José
- Población: 3.956.507 habitantes
- Moneda: el colón
- Idioma oficial: el español

Cuba (Capítulo 8)

- Nombre oficial: República de Cuba
- Capital: La Habana
- Población: 11.308.764 habitantes
- Moneda: el peso cubano
- Idioma oficial: el español

El Ecuador (Capítulo 13)

- Nombre oficial: República del Ecuador
- Capital: Quito
- Población: 13.212.742 habitantes
- Moneda: el dólar (el sucre)
- Idiomas: el español (oficial), el quechua

El Salvador (Capítulo 7)

- Nombre oficial: República de El Salvador
- Capital: San Salvador
- Población: 6.587.541 habitantes
- Moneda: el dólar*
- Idioma oficial: el español

España (Capítulo 18)

- Nombre oficial: Reino de España
- Capital: Madrid
- Población: 40.280.780 habitantes
- Moneda: el euro (la peseta)
- Idiomas: el español, el catalán, el gallego y el vasco[†]

Los Estados Unidos (Capítulo 1)

- La población hispánica total de los Estados Unidos: casi 40 millones en el año 2003.
- Orígenes de la población hispánica en los Estados Unidos:
  México: 67%
  Centroamérica y Sudamérica: 14%
  Puerto Rico: 9%
  Cuba: 4%
  Otros países:[e] 7%

Guatemala (Capítulo 5)

- Nombre oficial: República de Guatemala
- Capital: la Ciudad de Guatemala
- Población: 14.280.596 habitantes
- Moneda: el quetzal
- Idiomas: el español (oficial), 23 lenguas indígenas (que incluyen el quiché, el cakchiquel y el kekchi)

[a]*Facts*   [b]*Currency*   [c]*Language*   [d]*seat*   [e]*Otros… Other countries*

---

*The **colón** was replaced by the dollar on January 1, 2001.*

[†]*El español es el lenguaje oficial de todo el país; el catalán, el gallego y el vasco también son lenguas oficiales en Cataluña, Galicia y el País Vasco, respectivamente.*